T0323382

On Inequality and Freedom

On Inequality and Freedom

Edited by

LAWRENCE M. EPPARD AND HENRY A. GIROUX

OXFORD

UNIVERSITY PRESS

OXFORD
UNIVERSITY PRESS

Oxford University Press is a department of the University of Oxford. It furthers
the University's objective of excellence in research, scholarship, and education
by publishing worldwide. Oxford is a registered trade mark of Oxford University
Press in the UK and certain other countries.

Published in the United States of America by Oxford University Press
198 Madison Avenue, New York, NY 10016, United States of America.

CIP data is on file at the Library of Congress
ISBN 978–0–19–758302–9

DOI: 10.1093/oso/9780197583029.001.0001

1 3 5 7 9 8 6 4 2

Printed by Sheridan Books, Inc., United States of America

Contents

PART III RACE, GENDER, SEXUALITIES, AND FREEDOM

PART IV FREEDOM IN OTHER DOMAINS

PART V   PARTING THOUGHTS

Contributors

Jonathan Bradshaw
Emeritus Professor of Social Policy
Social Policy Research Unit
University of York
York, UK

David Brady
Professor
School of Public Policy
University of California, Riverside
Riverside, CA, USA

K. L. Broad
Associate Professor
Center for Gender, Sexualities, and
Women's Studies Research
University of Florida
Gainesville, FL, USA

Peter Callero
Professor Emeritus
Department of Sociology
Western Oregon University
Monmouth, OR, USA

Allison C. Carey
Professor
Department of Sociology and
Anthropology
Shippensburg University
Shippensburg, PA, USA

Robert Cavazos
Assistant Professor of Environmental
Sociology
Department of History, Sociology,
Geography, and GIS
Tarleton State Univesity
Stephenville, TX, USA

Carla Corroto
Associate Professor and Chair
Department of Environmental Science,
Policy & Management
University of California
Berkeley, CA, USA

Alison Dagnes
Professor
Political Science
Shippensburg University
Shippensburg, PA, USA

Martin Daly
Professor Emeritus
Department of Psychology, Neuroscience
& Behaviour
McMaster University
Hamilton, ON, Canada

Nancy DiTomaso
Distinguished Professor
Management and Global Business
Rutgers Business School—Newark and
New Brunswick
Newark, NJ, USA

Emine Ecem Ece
Graduate Teaching Assistant
Department of Sociology
University of Florida
Gainesville, FL, USA

Lawrence M. Eppard
Assistant Professor of Sociology
Shippensburg University
Shippensburg, PA, USA

Joe Feagin
Professor
Department of Sociology
Texas A&M University
College Station, TX, USA

Luke Ferretter
Professor
Department of English
Baylor University
Waco, TX, USA

Henry A. Giroux
McMaster University Professor for
Scholarship in the Public Interest and The
Paulo Freire Distinguished Scholar in
Critical Pedagogy
English and Cultural Studies
McMaster University
Hamilton, ON, Canada

Bandy Lee
Forensic Psychiatrist
Yale University
New Haven, CT, USA

Arelys Madero-Hernandez
Assistant Professor
Criminal Justice
Shippensburg University of Pennsylvania
Shippensburg, PA, USA

Raoul Martinez
Independent writer
London, GB

Michael Mascarenhas
Associate Professor
Department of Society & Environment
Division
University of California, Berkeley, CA,
United States

David Monaghan
Assistant Professor
Department of Sociology/Anthropology
Shippensburg University of PA
Shippensburg, PA, USA

Hilarie Burton Morgan
Writer
NY, USA

Alex Nowrasteh
Director
Cato Institute
Washington, DC, USA

Mark Rank
Herbert S. Hadley Professor of Social
Welfare
School of Social Work
Washington University
St. Louis, Missouri, USA

Carlos E. Rojas-Gaona
Assistant Professor
Criminal Justice
Shippensburg University of Pennsylvania
Shippensburg, PA, USA

Deondra Rose
Associate Professor of Public Policy,
Political Science, and History
Sanford School of Public Policy
Duke University
Durham, NC, USA

Dan Schubert
Associate Professor
Department of Sociology
Dickinson College
Carlisle, PA, USA

James A. White
Professor of Political Science
Department of Social Sciences
Concord University
Athens, WV, USA

Michael D. Yates
Professor Emeritus
Department of Economics
University of Pittsburgh-Johnstown
Johnstown, PA, USA

INTRODUCTION

1

Expanding the Meaning of Freedom

Lawrence M. Eppard and Henry A. Giroux

Freedom[1] is a central part of the American identity, "one of America's most cherished values."[2] When it comes to what freedom entails, most Americans would agree that there are political, social, and economic dimensions. Most agree that in a free society there is a need for order, justice, security, opportunity, and fairness. There is a shared sense that freedom requires the absence of harm and undue interference. Most believe that freedom requires a variety of rights, including those related to speech, property, voting, religion, fair legal treatment, assembly, the press, and so on.[3]

But while Americans may agree on these things in broad, abstract terms, they are often divided over their precise meanings. What does true opportunity entail? What types of security are needed in order to be free? Similar questions could continue. Americans also disagree about which freedoms the government should guarantee and which ones should be left to markets and individuals.

So while many Americans may prize freedom in general terms, it is not always clear that they are talking about the same thing.

Most Americans, for instance, agree that there should be equality of educational opportunity. But a problem arises when one attempts to establish a shared sense of what equality of educational opportunity actually means in practice. Does it simply mean access to a public school? If that is the case, we have achieved such equality in the United States. For many, however, this is inadequate if the schools that different children attend are not of the same quality. Many would go even further and argue that when some children face unequal challenges outside of the schoolhouse (e.g., a lack of important economic/cultural/social resources or living in a dangerous neighborhood), they cannot be said to have an equal opportunity to succeed in school. Indeed, we have made such arguments elsewhere:

> As society is always inside of us, we are always inside of society. By virtue of our existence, we constantly impact and are impacted by the people and contexts around us. What goes on beneath the skin is important, as are the forces outside of ourselves that constantly impact our life's path. From the families we belong to, to the neighborhoods we live in and schools we attend, to the peer networks we are a part of, and beyond, our opportunities and direction in life are

Lawrence M. Eppard and Henry A. Giroux, *Expanding the Meaning of Freedom* In: *On Inequality and Freedom.*
Edited by: Lawrence M. Eppard and Henry A. Giroux, Oxford University Press. © Oxford University Press 2022.
DOI: 10.1093/oso/9780197583029.003.0001

constantly impacted by people, environments, institutions, and forces outside of our control. . . . In order to be truly free, individuals need agency, or the ability to freely decide on the life that they want to lead, and be able to think and act autonomously in pursuit of that life. We define true agency as the combination of (a) the full development of one's abilities and (b) having access (unrestricted by unjust barriers) to resources and opportunity pathways. . . . Opportunity pathways cannot be fully utilized with few resources and compromised abilities, and abilities and resources are of little use without opportunities. . . . How will individuals become the best version of themselves if their home, neighborhood, and school environments stunt the development of their abilities? Or if they are lucky enough to have those abilities developed, how far will they go in life if good schools and well-paying jobs are not accessible to them? Because individuals and societies are not separate and distinct entities, but inextricably intertwined, one cannot understand the life of an individual without understanding how their society has profoundly shaped their abilities, resources, and opportunity pathways. If we are not in full control of our abilities, resources, or opportunities, we are not in full control of our destiny.[4]

From this perspective, equality of educational opportunity then becomes about much more than access to a seat in a school classroom. As Amartya Sen asserted, "Without the substantive freedom and capability to do something, a person cannot be responsible for doing it."[5] Equality includes not only having access to a school but also accessing one that is well supported and provides a quality learning environment. It means growing up in a safe and loving household. It includes not being stuck in a neighborhood besieged by crime, drug abuse, hopelessness, or pollution.

Household, neighborhood, and community factors—not to mention state- and national-level forces—are inextricably associated with unequal educational outcomes. Equality of educational opportunity thus includes access to a quality school *and* a variety of other necessary conditions.

We use educational opportunity as but one example of the disagreements and various perspectives involved in debates about freedom.

Why should we think so deeply about what freedom truly entails? Because it is an important value for so many Americans, and to understand both the limits of our current freedom and potential for future expansions of freedom, we need to understand the complicated ways in which social arrangements and policy decisions constrain our freedom. In coming to a better understanding of these constraints, we can make better demands of our elected representatives, pressing them to work tirelessly to help provide the conditions that enact freedom for the largest number of people.

We need to think deeply about the nuances of true freedom beyond just freedom from government (a notion of freedom that far too many Americans fall back on) to include freedom to live the lives we desire for ourselves: not only "freedom *from*," but also "freedom *to*."

As George Lakoff noted, we need to "know our own minds" and develop a deep understanding of how we define core concepts and values, because such definitions are the unconscious basis for many of our moral and political choices:

> Your deep frames and metaphors define the range within which your "free will" operates. You can't will something that is outside your capacity to imagine. Free will can operate only on ideas in your brain; it cannot operate on ideas you do not have. Free will is thus not totally free. It is radically constrained by the frames and metaphors shaping your brain and limiting how you see the world.[6]

Lakoff continued to explain that our deeply held frames and metaphors establish our norms of behavior, help us to understand right and wrong, help us to interpret both the past and the present, and shape what we think is possible and desirable for the future. These conceptual frames contain certain structures and assumptions while excluding others. They tap into some of our deepest emotions. Once internalized, conceptual frames can impact your thoughts and behavior in an unconscious and automatic manner (he argued that most thought is unconscious) without requiring you to examine where those ideas came from and their moral and political implications. According to Lakoff, when it comes to how we define freedom, "Ownership of the word means ownership of the idea that goes with the word, and with it, domination of the culture defined by the idea."[7]

* * *

In this book, a variety of authors have contributed essays arguing that a number of issues facing American society today are issues of freedom. While many Americans may agree, far too many fail to make a strong connection between these issues and liberty. We believe it is important to highlight some of these issues and their relationships to freedom as we all collectively chart the future of our nation. If we do not address these problems in an effective manner, we ensure less freedom not only for millions of Americans today, but also for many more *in future generations to come.*

You would likely not choose to live in a society that allowed slavery. You would probably reject a caste system. It is highly likely you would choose to live in a democratic society, a system that Winston Churchill famously described as "the worst form of Government except for all those other forms that have been tried from time to time."[8]

You would probably reject societal designs that unfairly distributed abilities, resources, and opportunities based on one's social class, race/ethnicity, gender, sexual orientation, or other group membership. You would reject all of these designs out of fear that it is you who would end up in a subordinate position. Most people would still likely design a society that, to the greatest extent possible, rewarded hard work and smart choices—but they would demand institutions and practices that prevented one's inherited social position from dictating her/his life.

Behind a veil of ignorance,[9] you would not allow racism or sexism or concentrated disadvantage or violence or child poverty.[10] You'd likely reject inequalities that limited your ability to succeed based on your inherited social class, race/ethnicity, or other social status. It is doubtful that you would allow climate change, given that you do not know whether you will be born in 1950, 2050, or 2150 or whether you will be born in Denver or Malé, Maldives. You would probably want good healthcare, no matter to whom or where you were born. You would not allow those with more money than you to distort the political system to their advantage. You would likely support a high-quality free press and access to the findings of experts, so that society functioned well and so that you personally had the highest quality and quantity of information possible, regardless of your station in life.

Our elected officials should always be in pursuit of solutions to our most pressing social problems. They should always be committed to the long-term American project of securing the highest degree of freedom for the most people. They should always design social policies from behind a veil of ignorance, never allowing people's life chances to be determined by forces outside of their control.[11]

What to do about the constraints on freedom discussed in this book is of course subjective and a matter of the preferences of voters. The answer is not always major government interventions or significant increases in public spending. But these problems place demonstrable limits on our freedom, and we should not stand for them to be left unaddressed.

America was founded on lofty ideals centered on notions of freedom. These were clearly aspirational, as they were not realized at the founding, but our history has been one of gradual (although uneven) progress toward that aspirational society. Our elected leaders will be obligated to continue this pursuit only if they are held accountable for their failures. We should all therefore examine the constraints on freedom in America and reward politicians truly dedicated to unlocking freedom for all Americans.

If you hear and/or use a conceptual frame enough times, you internalize it and think and behave in automatic, unconscious ways based on these frames.[12] We need to think deeply about our own assumptions about what true freedom requires. We need to analyze the ideological content of the messages we receive daily (perhaps especially ones that make us feel good). We need to talk about freedom in its actual complexity and demand that others do the same.

And we need to hold our elected leaders accountable for bringing such freedom to fruition.

Notes

1. Eppard and Giroux adapted this introduction from the 2020 article, "Obligations to the Future," from the *Journal of Working-Class Studies*. Permission to adapt and re-print was granted by the journal's editors. For the original article, please visit their website: https://workingclassstudiesjournal.files.wordpress.com/2020/10/jwcs-vol-5-issue-2-october-2020-eppard-nelson-cox-bonilla-silva.pdf.

2. Orlando Patterson and Ethan Fosse, "Stability and Change in Americans' Perception of Freedom," *Contexts* 18, no. 3 (2019): 26.

3. George Lakoff, *Whose Freedom? The Battle Over America's Most Important Idea* (New York: Farrar, Strauss, and Giroux, 2006).

4. Lawrence M. Eppard, Mark Robert Rank, and Heather E. Bullock, *Rugged Individualism and the Misunderstanding of American Inequality* (Bethlehem, PA: Lehigh University Press, copublished by Rowman & Littlefield, 2020), 18–19. Further in this passage we added, "An extensive literature demonstrates the importance of environmental factors and forces beyond individual control in shaping an individual's behavior, well-being, and circumstances. Our individual characteristics—such as our individual identities, beliefs, inclinations, abilities, resources, behaviors, and so on—as well as our opportunities, are all shaped from birth (and in fact earlier in the womb) by a variety of forces beyond our control. A number of interlocking environments not of our choosing, from our family, neighborhood, peer network, school, and community to the country and historical period into which we are born, shape who we become as individuals and the opportunities available to us. The social groups we belong to and how those groups are either privileged or disadvantaged by the larger society shape who we become and how we will fit into society. Large-scale economic and political forces impact us at the individual level, profoundly shaping our development and path through the world. Social environments, relations, institutions, and forces significantly impact how our lives develop across time. Every major outcome in life—from educational attainment, to employment status, to earnings and wealth, to health and life expectancy, to risk of criminal involvement or victimization, just to name a few—is deeply impacted by forces beyond the individual" (p. 19).

5. Amartya Sen, *Development as Freedom* (New York: Anchor Books, 1999), 284.

6. Lakoff, *Whose Freedom?*, 15–16.

7. Lakoff, *Whose Freedom?*, 17.

8. Winston Churchill, "The Worst Form of Government," International Churchill Society, https://winstonchurchill.org/resources/quotes/the-worst-form-of-government/.

9. John Rawls, *A Theory of Justice* (Cambridge, MA: Belknap Press of Harvard University Press, 1971/1999).

10. The costs of childhood poverty in the United States—in terms of impacts on future economic productivity, healthcare costs, criminal justice costs, and other costs—have been estimated to be over one trillion dollars per year, which is over a quarter (28 percent) of the federal budget. For every dollar spent on reducing childhood poverty, the United States would save at least seven dollars due to the corresponding reduction in the societal costs of poverty. Mark Rank, one of the study's authors, noted that, "It is not a question of paying or not paying. Rather, it is a question of how we pay, which then affects the amount we end up spending. In making an investment up front to alleviate poverty, the evidence suggests, we will be repaid many times over by lowering the enormous costs associated with a host of interrelated problems." See Michael McLaughlin and Mark R. Rank, "Estimating the Economic Cost of Childhood Poverty in the United States," *Social Work Research* 42, no. 2 (2018): 73–83. See also Mark R. Rank, "The Cost of Keeping Children Poor," *New York Times*, April 15, 2018.

11. As Raoul Martinez noted, "We do not choose to exist. We do not choose the environment we will grow up in. We do not choose to be born Hindu, Christian or Muslim, into a war-zone or peaceful middle-class suburb, into starvation or luxury. We do not choose our parents, nor whether they'll be happy or miserable, knowledgeable or ignorant, healthy or sickly, attentive or neglectful. The knowledge we possess, the beliefs we hold, the tastes we develop, the traditions we adopt, the opportunities we enjoy, the work we do—the very lives we lead. . . . This is the lottery of birth." He later noted that, "Whether we inherit a lot of money or property, are free from oppression and prejudice, are well educated, bright, strong, healthy, resourceful or beautiful, is ultimately down to luck." See Raoul Martinez, *Creating Freedom: The Lottery of Birth, the Illusion of Consent, and the Fight for Our Future* (New York: Pantheon Books, 2016), 3, 68. In the words of Norbert Elias, people take on the "stamp" of their experiences and relationships "from the history of the whole human network within which [she or he] grows up and lives." People carry their history and their whole human network with them at all times, according to Elias, whether they are "actively working in a big city or shipwrecked on an island a thousand miles from [their] society." See Norbert Elias, *The Society of Individuals* (New York: Continuum International, 1991), 27. And as we have written elsewhere, "Rather than thinking of the individual and of society as separate and distinct entities, as many do, it is useful to think of both as constituting each other. Individuals and society exist in a reciprocal relationship where both are inextricably linked together. Just as individuals shape society, society profoundly shapes individuals. One cannot step into or out of society. We are always inside of society, and society is always inside of us. The person you become in life is deeply impacted by your lifetime of experiences and relationships. We might even think of ourselves at any given moment as the accumulation of these experiences and relationships. . . . Society exists inside of us, beneath the skin, so that extricating ourselves from this accumulation of experiences and relationships is impossible. An astronaut who blasts off into space on a solitary mission does not shed this lifetime of experiences and relationships that have defined

her or his identity, perceptions, beliefs, inclinations, abilities, behaviors, and so on" (Eppard, Rank, and Bullock, *Rugged Individualism*, 17–18). Philosopher Slavoj Žižek argued that, "What Americans don't want to admit is that not only is there not a contradiction between state regulation and freedom, but in order for us to actually be free in our social interactions, there must be an extremely elaborated network of health, law, institutions, moral rules and so on. . . . Ideology today is unfreedom which you sincerely personally experience as freedom." See Luke Massey, "Slavoj Žižek: 'Most of the Idiots I Know Are Academics,'" *New Statesman*, October 8, 2013.

12. Lakoff, *Whose Freedom?*

2

Freedom Has Been Weaponized

Raoul Martinez

Freedom is an ideal embraced by people across the political spectrum. The world's dominant systems—capitalism and democracy—are routinely defended in terms of their capacity to protect and promote this inspiring concept. Just think of the central institutions of modern society: free markets, free trade, free elections, free speech, free media. Yet, for all the consensus surrounding the value of this ideal, there is huge disagreement over what it means, or rather what it *should* mean. Many of the most contentious political battles of our time are rooted in competing conceptions of this seven-letter word. We all want to be on the side of freedom. The question is, what and whose freedom are we talking about?

Different conceptions serve different interests. This fact becomes all the more apparent when we start thinking about inequalities of power and wealth. Depending on your definitions, inequality can be presented as either a consequence of freedom or an obstacle to it. For decades, the dominant view has endorsed the former definition, claiming that inequality is the price we must pay if we want a free society. Is this true? To challenge extreme inequality, are we obliged to place ourselves in opposition to freedom? Or has the idea of freedom been distorted to justify its opposite, weaponized to empower the powerful?

The answers we give matter. The meaning we attribute to this hallowed ideal will form a lens through which we view the inequality in our world, shaping our positions and informing our actions. However, before outlining an answer, let's first try to understand the extent of this inequality.

The Great Divide

Global inequality is falling and has been for a while. At least, that's what you may have heard. According to the World Bank, inequality has been declining consistently since 1990.[1] Bill Gates claims that "The speed of reduction in global inequality is faster than ever in history. It's mind-blowing."[2] Over the last few years, a stream of articles has led with such breathless headlines as, "Global Inequality Is Falling No Matter What Anyone Says" (*Forbes*), "Income Inequality Is Not Rising

Raoul Martinez, *Freedom Has Been Weaponized* In: *On Inequality and Freedom*. Edited by: Lawrence M. Eppard and Henry A. Giroux, Oxford University Press. © Oxford University Press 2022. DOI: 10.1093/oso/9780197583029.003.0002

Globally. It's Falling" (*New York Times*), and "Believe It or Not, Global Inequality Is Falling" (Institute of Economic Affairs).[3] Are they right? To answer the question, let's examine two forms of inequality: first income, then wealth.

Statistics do not fall from heaven. They are subject to human judgment. Every statistic, every graph is the result of human decisions about what to measure, how to measure, what thresholds to use, and how to present the information. These decisions make a huge difference to the story we tell. Those who decide the metric decide the narrative. The good-news headlines about global income inequality focus on a *relative* measure. To appreciate the difference between relative inequality and absolute inequality, imagine that a year ago you earned $100 a day, whereas I earned only $1 a day—a daily income difference of $99. Now suppose this year you earn $200 a day and I earn $3 a day. Has our inequality gone up or down? In absolute terms the inequality gap has ballooned to $197, but in relative terms it has decreased, because your income has only doubled whereas mine has tripled. To maintain the good-news story of falling global inequality, it is necessary to focus on relative inequality and ignore the absolute numbers.

Since the mid-1970s, absolute global inequality—as measured by the "absolute Gini coefficient"—has been rising; over the same period, relative global inequality—measured by the "relative Gini coefficient"—has been steadily falling.[4] This is shown in Figure 2.1.

Here's another example. Changes in global earnings are often analyzed by dividing the world's population into income groups ranging from the poorest to

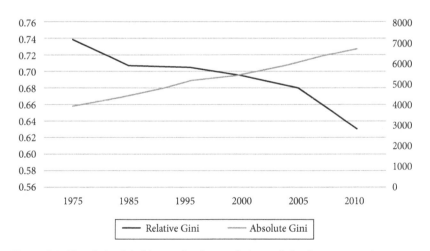

Figure 2.1 Trends in global inequality from relative and absolute perspectives.

Note: This figure is reproduced here by permission of UNU-WIDER, Helsinki.

Source: Miguel Niño-Zarazúa, Laurence Roope, and Finn Tarp, "Income Inequality in A Globalising World," Vox CEPR Policy Portal, September 20, 2016. https://voxeu.org/article/income-inequality-globalising-world

the richest and plotting the income gains made by each group over a given time period. Gains can be expressed in relative or absolute terms. By presenting income gains in relative terms, the standard approach, it becomes easy to claim that a person whose daily earnings increase from $2 to $3 has gained as much as someone whose earnings increase from $2 million to $3 million because the relative gain in each case is 50 percent. Clearly, the danger of focusing solely on relative gains is that it obscures the true beneficiaries of our economic system. On the other hand, if we plot absolute gains, as in Figure 2.2, there is no question whose interests are primarily being served.[5]

The richest 10 percent of the world's population—especially the top 1 percent of global earners—have been the undisputed winners of globalization over the last four decades. The poorest 60 percent of humanity have experienced a small boost in annual income, averaging $1,200, but this figure is 14 thousand times less than the average person in the top 0.001 percent. (Even with a relative measure, the top 0.001 percent come out with the highest gains.)

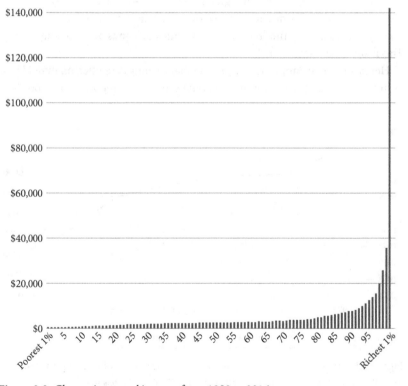

Figure 2.2 Change in annual income from 1980 to 2016.
Note: This figure is reproduced here by permission of Jason Hickel.
Source: Jason Hickel, *Less Is More* (London: William Heinemann, 2020), 205.

How does income inequality look within nations? The popular website, Our World in Data, claims that "It's a mistake to think that inequality is rising everywhere. Over the last 25 years, inequality has gone up in many countries and has fallen in many others."[6] If you focus exclusively on a relative measure, you can convince yourself this is true. Once again, though, a different picture emerges if we measure absolute inequality. Looking at the data in different regions, and focusing on the share of income that goes to the top 10 percent of earners, the World Inequality Report finds "rising inequality almost everywhere."[7]

Among rich nations, income inequality in the United States is extreme. The top 1 percent of adults in 2014 took over 20 percent of total income, almost double the share taken by the bottom 50 percent of earners, who acquired only 12.5 percent. The gap has not always been so large. Since 1980, the growth in pretax income for the bottom 50 percent has stagnated, whereas the top 1 percent of earners have experienced an increase in their share of 204 percent.[8] Globally, exceptions to the trend of rising inequality are to be found in the Middle East, parts of Latin America, and sub-Saharan Africa, where it has stabilized at some of the highest levels in the world.[9]

As for inequality of wealth, the figures are mind-boggling. According to the World Inequality Report, "Available data show that global wealth inequality is extreme and on the rise."[10] It found that the wealthiest 1 percent have seen their share of global wealth increase from 28 percent in 1980 to 33 percent in 2017. Compare this to the trajectory of the poorest 75 percent of humanity, who have seen their share of wealth stagnate for almost four decades, oscillating around 10 percent. In fact, things are far worse than these figures suggest because they are based on a data set that includes only China, Europe, and the United States. The report states that, "Wealth concentration levels would probably be even higher if Latin America, Africa, and the rest of Asia were included in the analysis, as most people in these regions would be in the poorer parts of the distribution."[11] According to Oxfam, if we include the whole world, the richest 1 percent now possess more wealth than the other 99 percent combined.[12]

Within nations, wealth inequality is far worse than income inequality. In the United States, wealth inequality has risen rapidly and consistently since the mid-1980s. The top 10 percent now own 77 percent of all wealth; the top 0.1 percent own about as much wealth as the bottom 90 percent of the population combined.[13] There have also been large rises in the wealth shares of the richest people in China and Russia, following the transition towards capitalist economies. In fact, whether we talk about the United States, the United Kingdom, Russia, China, or France, the top 10 percent have seen their share of wealth trend upward since 1990.

Research shows that people vastly underestimate the extent of inequality that exists in their home nation and the world at large. However, as we have seen, wealth and income inequality, within and between nations, is extreme. What's more, high levels of inequality are correlated with a laundry list of damaging social effects: more violence, worse mental and physical health, lower life expectancy, higher prison populations, lower educational outcomes, more obesity, and less social mobility.[14] Inequality, as recognized by the World Inequality Report, is also an obstacle to tackling poverty, which remains a shameful scar on humanity. According to World Bank's data, and using a modest poverty threshold of $7.40 a day—the minimum amount needed to attain average life expectancy, meet basic nutritional needs, and provide children with a decent chance of surviving their first 5 years of life—we find that most of humanity, 58 percent, currently live in extreme poverty. That's 4.2 billion people.

The current distribution of the world's resources sacrifices human potential, health, and well-being on an unimaginable scale. Challenging this distribution is a matter of moral urgency. One means of doing this is to confront the ideological justifications that shield this inequality from public understanding, outrage, and action. In the modern world, many of the most influential justifications revolve around the concept of freedom.

Voluntary, Mutually Beneficial Transactions

Milton Friedman, one of the most influential economists of the twentieth century, claimed that even if capitalism was less efficient than some other system, he would still favor it due to its unique capacity to deliver the "freedom to choose." In his writings, he presents the market, as many still see it today, as a bastion of freedom—an institution characterized by voluntary, mutually beneficial transactions.[15] Over time, these "free" transactions may yield significant material inequalities but, he would say, that is the price of freedom.

If I'd met Mr. Friedman, I would have asked him to imagine the following scenario. You're walking down the street and someone points a gun to your head, threatening to kill you unless you hand over your wallet. What do you do? Well, if you hand over your cash, that's a mutually beneficial transaction. You get to keep your life; your assailant gets to keep your money. Of course, it's not a voluntary transaction—you were compelled by circumstance to accept it. But the reality is that in the market, every single day, people are compelled by circumstances to accept all kinds of things: to do difficult, dangerous, demeaning, poorly paid work. They are compelled by need: the need to feed their children, to heat their homes, to pay their rent, to care for sick relatives. In a market society, poverty makes a mockery of the idea of voluntary transactions. Poverty is coercive. For a contract to be voluntary, its participants must have attractive alternative options. The desperation of workers may be profitable—allowing employers to drive down wages—but it is incompatible with any meaningful notion of voluntary participation. The prospect of starvation, serious illness, or homelessness is as coercive as any gun to the head.

Freedom in the market expands and contracts with spending power. You might think this is uncontroversial, but it has long been denied by supporters of the free market, be they conservative, liberal, neoliberal, or libertarian. Much effort has been expended to make the world safe for inequality. Central to these efforts is the attempt to define and defend a concept of freedom that excludes poverty as one of its constraints. In practice, this has meant conflating the defense of individual liberty with the defense of free markets and ownership rights. Once this conflation is accepted, any interference in the market—such as taxing the rich to feed the poor—can be framed as a violation of individual freedom by a coercive state. Critics of this view point out that market outcomes, free from state interference, deprive many people of the resources necessary to meet their basic needs. Free marketeers might respond that a homeless person is as free as anyone else to buy a mansion; they just lack the capability to do so. The claim is that the poor have the same formal freedoms as the rich, they just lack the resources to exercise them.

If you find this argument persuasive, imagine a society in which people are only allowed to express an opinion if they have the money to pay for the privilege. It costs $500, say, to share one's thoughts. Do the majority of citizens who are too poor to express themselves have as much freedom as their wealthier counterparts airing every view that pops into their head? After all, according to free marketeers, the silenced majority have the same formal freedom to share their views; they just lack the resources to exercise it. I would suggest that, unless we are to mangle the meaning of the term *freedom*, distorting it beyond recognition, the answer is clearly in the negative. This is not a new claim. Thinkers from the revolutionary thinker Karl Marx to Nobel Prize–winner Amartya Sen have pointed out that poverty reduces freedom in fundamentally important ways. Nevertheless, resistance to this conclusion has been fierce and influential, so let us scrutinize its various formulations more closely.

State Intervention and Negative Liberty

We make our choices against a backdrop of external constraints. Laws of nature limit what is physically possible. Laws of government prohibit certain actions and prescribe punishments for noncompliance. There is also a rich array of social incentives that attach penalties and privileges to different modes of behavior. Depart from acceptable ways of being—as defined by family, friends, or community—and you may find yourself deprived of affection, respect, community, or employment. The question is: Which external limits count as constraints on our freedom? Does gravity count? What about taxation? Or poverty?

In his famous 1958 essay, *Two Concepts of Liberty*, the liberal thinker Isaiah Berlin articulated two distinct forms of freedom.[16] They were not new, but Berlin's explorations, conclusions and terminology proved influential. He called his two concepts "positive liberty" and "negative liberty."[17] We possess negative liberty to the extent that no external force is preventing us from doing what we want to do. Berlin chose the name negative liberty because to possess it appears to depend on the absence of external interference, such as barriers, threats, or coercion. On the other hand, we have positive liberty in the sense that we are able to choose rationally, according to our deepest values, in a way that enables us to take control of our lives. This freedom is positive because it depends on the presence of internal resources, such as self-discipline, reason, and knowledge.

Berlin argued that, although both forms of freedom are valuable, the state should focus on protecting negative liberty. Allowing the state to promote positive liberty would risk opening the door to totalitarian tendencies, whereby governments are granted the power to decide what is in our best interest. For present purposes, what's significant is how negative freedom—the absence of external constraints—has come to be understood. On the crucial question of whether or not poverty should count as an obstacle to negative liberty, Berlin is generally interpreted as believing it should not.[18] Another renowned liberal thinker, John Rawls, arrived at the same conclusion. In his seminal work, *A Theory of Justice*, he thought of poverty not as a constraint on freedom but as something that reduced its worth.[19] Whatever the motivation, this amounted to an ideological gift from leading twentieth century liberals to leading neoliberals. It enabled thinkers such as Milton Friedman, Friedrich Hayek, and Robert Nozick to claim, with greater plausibility, not only that their primary concern was individual liberty but also that market interventions eroded freedom.

In arguing that poverty imposes no constraint on freedom, the libertarian philosopher Robert Nozick claimed that: "Other people's actions may place limits on one's available opportunities. Whether this makes one's resulting action non-voluntary depends upon whether these others had the right to act as they did."[20] So, we cannot judge the freedom of an individual until we know whose actions have impacted their life and whether or not those actions were "legitimate." Pioneer of neoliberalism Friedrich Hayek argued that freedom meant "freedom from coercion, freedom from the arbitrary power of other men, release from the ties which left the individual no choice but obedience to the orders of a superior." In his view, it did not mean "freedom from necessity, release from compulsion of circumstances."[21] In other words, to count as a restriction on our freedom, a constraint caused by the actions of others had to be brought about *intentionally* (Berlin said something very similar).

Nozick and Hayek's conceptions of freedom have much in common. Both go beyond a person's capabilities—what they can actually do—to the legitimacy or motivation of other people's actions. Both interpretations make it possible to conclude that if the rules of the market are not violated, everyone's freedom has been preserved, whatever the outcomes may be (even if millions are too poor to meet their basic needs). Both conceptions also face the same damning objection. To detach a person's freedom from what they are able to do is to hollow out the ideal, obliterating that which makes it appealing and precious. If you are convicted of murder and imprisoned for the rest of your life, your freedom is constrained *whether or not* the conviction is legitimate. If someone infects you with a debilitating virus, your freedom is constrained whether or not you were infected intentionally. Equally, if poverty leads you to homelessness or hunger, your freedom has been constrained whether or not other market participants followed the rules or acted with malice.

In public discourse, arguments against market intervention do not typically draw on the careful, if unconvincing, distinctions made by the likes of Friedman, Hayek, and Nozick. They take a simpler form, exploiting a generalized suspicion of "big government." Strategically, this makes a lot of sense. The dangers of concentrated state power were made abundantly clear throughout the twentieth century, from Mussolini to Hitler, Stalin to Mao. This dark history gives us good reason to constrain the coercive force of those who rule. Framing intervention in the market as an abuse of state power, therefore, connects with a well-founded fear, paving the way for a now familiar binary between "lovers of liberty" on the right, who believe in free markets, and "egalitarians for equality" on the left, who believe in state intervention.

When egalitarians accept this framing, they lose the argument before it begins, for the terms of debate being presented are neither neutral nor coherent. The opposition proposed by free marketeers between interventionists on the left and noninterventionists on the right is entirely spurious. It only holds if we view state intervention from the vantage point of the wealthy and accept as a given the existing distribution of property rights. As we will see, there is no reason to make these concessions. The question of who should own what, and the form this ownership should take, is precisely what is being disputed by opposing camps on the ideological spectrum.

From the perspective of those at the bottom of society, the right-wing state is anything but small. It blocks, constrains, and punishes at every turn. To see this, think of money as a permission slip that allows those who have it to access goods and services that otherwise would be denied to them by state power.[22] Try to eat a meal, board a train, sleep in a house, or obtain medicine without being able to pay for the privilege, and the state will be waiting in the wings to stop you. Without sufficient money in your pocket, your basic right to sustenance, movement, shelter, and health will be trampled on by a coercive authority. Is this not state intervention by big government? Does this not deprive citizens of their negative liberty?

If you are affluent, you will not encounter this form of state intervention. You will not experience the real constraints of an indebted, underpaid worker struggling to make ends meet. For the wealthy, money functions much like a VIP pass, allowing them to access all areas. If your bank account holds enough currency, be it dollars, pounds, euros, or yen, almost no location, good, or service will be off limits. With few exceptions, the state recedes into the shadows, becomes invisible, leaving you to get on with whatever it is you want to do. The most noticeable forms of state intervention are likely to be taxation of your income and regulation of the means by which you acquire it. From the perspective of the rich, it is not hard to see how these unwelcome intrusions become emblematic of big government and the curbing of individual liberty. But theirs is only one perspective, and a minority one at that.

To protect the human rights of the poor, it has always been necessary to infringe on the property rights of the rich. On balance, such infringement constitutes a defense of freedom rather than its curtailment. Deployed wisely, taxes can enhance the basic capabilities of millions of people, and with them their freedom. A rise in the top rate of tax, even a large rise, won't sacrifice the health of a single person but, through the provision of universal healthcare, say, could save many thousands of lives. Compare this to a society without universal healthcare, in which the state is empowered to forcibly prevent some of its poorer citizens accessing life-saving medicine, treatment, and care. Of the two cases, surely the more serious infringement of individual liberty is the one that condemns to death those being coerced. Similarly, regulations that protect workers, consumers, and the environment may be a nuisance to chief executive officers (CEOs) concerned with maximizing profit but a matter of life and death, sickness and health, to everyone else.

The notion of a "free market" has always been a convenient fantasy. Markets are necessarily governed by state-enforced rules and regulations. What matters is the nature of these rules and the interests they serve. Confusion arises when the legal constraints on market processes become so internalized that most people fail to notice them. In 1819, laws were introduced banning children younger than 9 from working in cotton factories. At the time, many people railed against these laws, claiming they were a subversion of the free market. They were right. They *were* a subversion of the market. But, we might ask, who cares? Today we barely notice such regulations because they chime with our moral intuitions, which have been shaped by struggles fought and won long before we were born. The lesson is clear: Deciding where to draw the boundaries of the market is not a technical question, but a moral one. The positions we take reflect our values, concerns, and priorities.

The state is *always* interventionist. The important question is: Whose interests will it intervene to protect?

Wealth Has a History

The boundaries and barriers within which our lives play out create paths of permitted behavior, channeling us in particular directions. Different arrangements of these boundaries and barriers—some of them visible, many unseen—privilege the freedoms of some over those of others. As we change legal and cultural incentives, the balance of rights and liberties also changes. One of the central questions of our time is how to determine this balance. By what mechanism should we decide whose freedoms prevail when conflicts occur? For over a century, an epic struggle has taken place between two very different answers to this question. One answer has been that conflicting freedoms should be settled through democratic processes; the other answer has been that they should be settled by market logic. Modern societies have long been home to a tense compromise between these two approaches, one grounded in citizenship, the other ownership.

Since the 1980s, and the rise of neoliberalism championed by Ronald Reagan and Margaret Thatcher, this struggle has brought about a decisive shift toward the market. This shift has manifested in two ways. First, it changed how states intervene in the dynamics and outcomes of the economy. We have seen, for instance, enormous reductions in the top rates of taxation, the slashing of regulations, and the wholesale privatization of public services. Second, it expanded the scope of the market through the increased commodification of our lives. What can be owned, priced, bought, and sold is never a given. It only seems that way when we have internalized the norms of our society. Should we treat genes, seeds, sex, ideas, land, fuel, food, water, data, animals, education, healthcare, and housing as commodities? These are contentious questions that have triggered bitter struggles. Over the last 40 years, however, the answer of governments to such questions has increasingly been a resounding "yes."

As the boundaries of the market expand, the clash of freedoms between different groups is increasingly settled by the property rights system. Naturally, this benefits those with the most property, those in possession of great wealth. Rampant inequality means that property rights are concentrated in a small minority of the world's population. What's more, ownership tends to be exclusive. Once I own something, say a piece of land, the rest of the world requires my permission to use it.

If we are to leave many of the most crucial decisions in society to the property rights system, it is natural to ask if the existing distribution of property rights can be justified. Has it been arrived at "legitimately," without "intentionally" constraining freedoms? Milton Friedman felt that it was difficult to favor one distribution over another on moral grounds. He advised that, instead of worrying about the distribution of property rights, we should concern ourselves with making them clear-cut to avoid ambiguity.[23] According to this influential view, the current wealth distribution should be taken as a given.

This is a remarkable position. It ignores the common-sense observation that an additional $100 means nothing to the billionaire but could mean the difference between life and death to the person sleeping on the street. Though mainstream economic theory obfuscates the point, money does not have the same value in all hands. If an additional million dollars accidently found its way into the bank account of Bill Gates, would he even notice? If our goal is to efficiently convert resources into well-being, or indeed freedom, it is extremely wasteful to allow vast fortunes to accrue in the hands of a few. The data suggest that beyond a certain level, increases in a person's income do not correlate with greater happiness. In fact, beyond a certain threshold, which varies from place to place (roughly $100,000 in the United States, but much lower in some other countries), greater income has been linked with a slight drop in happiness.[24] Redistributing wealth creates value; hoarding wealth destroys it. If we accept the assumption that everyone's happiness matters, then there are strong moral grounds for greater equality.

Contrary to the claims of many neoliberal thinkers, high taxes on top earners *are* compatible with a thriving economy. To illustrate the point, progressives often recall the "golden era of capitalism" when the United States taxed its highest earners at a top rate of over 90 percent (the top rate is now 37 percent). But we can draw on more recent data. For instance, economists have compared different tax policies across rich countries over recent decades to see what impact they had on that dubious yet influential indicator of economic performance: gross domestic product (GDP). In 2011, Thomas Piketty and his colleagues found that "rich countries have all grown at roughly the same rate over the past 30 years—in spite of huge variations in tax policies."[25] Informed by their research, they argued that the top rate of tax should be at least 80 percent.

Friedman once wrote: "I find it hard . . . to see any justification for graduated taxation solely to redistribute income. . . . This seems a clear case of using coercion to take from some in order to give to others and thus to conflict head-on with individual freedom."[26] As we have seen, there are many problems with this position. Among them, it ignores the path by which today's wealth distribution was reached. If we are going to defer to the property rights system as a means of settling conflicting claims to freedom, we are entitled to investigate its origins.

Why, for instance, is the Global North so much richer than the Global South? Why, in many nations, are some ethnic groups far wealthier, on average, than others? Stating that it should be taken as a given invites us to ignore histories of enclosure, slavery, genocide, patriarchy, colonialism, exploitation, and debt bondage that have enriched a few at the expense of many through systematic oppression, violence, and theft.

The scale of this coercively obtained wealth is staggering. To give one example, recent research focusing on two centuries of colonialism in India arrived at an estimate for the total value of the wealth that was extracted. Assuming a modest rate of interest and excluding the onerous debt imposed by Britain, economist Utsa Patnaik calculated that a staggering $45 trillion was drained from India over this period.[27] The value of the entire UK economy today is a fraction of this, standing at $2.85 trillion. The flow of wealth from the Global South to the Global North continues apace. A report written by Dr. Dev Kar based at Global Financial Integrity added up the net outflows from poor nations to rich nations since 1980. He and his colleagues found that the developing world had, on balance, lost $16.3 trillion over 26 years.[28] In effect, then, poor countries are the ones helping to develop rich countries, not the other way around as is commonly claimed.

All wealth has a history. Much of it is an ugly, bloody, shameful history—both illegitimate and intentionally coercive. Why, then, should we defend a grossly unequal wealth distribution brought about by centuries of violence and, to make matters worse, do so in the name of freedom?

Responsibility and Reward

There is an unspoken assumption, a powerful moral intuition, that colors the whole subject of inequality and freedom. It is the belief that people tend to get what they deserve. This leads to the conclusion that, in general, the poor are responsible for their poverty while the rich are responsible for their wealth. If true, why should those who have worked hard and achieved success be forced to subsidize those who have not? Does this not encourage freeloading, laziness, dependency? Is it not simply unfair?

I suspect that, for many people, this line of argument provides a compelling explanation and justification for inequality. It implies there is some natural justice to be found in the disparities we see in the world. Psychologists have discovered that many of us need, or at least want, to believe that the world is ultimately fair. This is known as just world theory. The impulse is not difficult to understand. The idea that good things happen to good people and bad things happen to bad people is reassuring. It can reduce feelings of helplessness and insecurity and quiet the anxious soul. Unfortunately, it is false. Every day, good people—men, women, and children—are raped and killed, starved and imprisoned, exploited and persecuted, while some of the worst among us grow rich and powerful. Justice is an ideal to be pursued, not a feature of existence.

Even if we ignore the histories of violence and oppression that yielded today's wealth distribution, the idea that people get what they deserve remains a form of magical thinking that rests on at least two false beliefs. The first—that people can be held truly responsible for their life outcomes—ignores the all-pervasive role of luck in our lives. The lottery of birth has far more influence on our journeys through life than most of us appreciate.

We don't choose our genes or the environment we grow up in, yet, together, these factors determine who we are, who we want to be, and the options available to us. The fateful role of luck exerts its influence from the moment of conception, determining the nutrients available to our growing fetus; the health, safety, and stress levels of our mother that—along with many other factors—dictate our chances of survival in the first months of life. Prospects vary wildly. A child born in Mali is 16 times more likely to die in its first year than a child born in the United Kingdom.

Luck determines whether our home is rich or poor, peaceful or violent, healthy or polluted. It determines key aspects of our identity—from our gender, skin color and appearance, to our religion, class, and sexuality—that will have profound impacts on the treatment we receive. Luck determines our intellectual, physical, and emotional potential as well as the opportunities available for realizing them. Luck determines the wealth, priorities, and status of our parents and how much love, care, and attention we will receive. It determines whether we are abused or neglected, encouraged or undermined. The list goes on and on. As we grow and mature, we acquire not only a language but also a belief system, a culture, a set of values, and an outlook, all of which set us on a particular trajectory through life.

When you take all of these factors into account, it becomes clear that the machinery with which we make decisions has been constructed by a process far beyond our control. This process determines the architecture of our neural circuitry, how our brains are wired. Our capacity for love, hate, patience, and joy and our ability to concentrate, to persevere, to be self-controlled, they are all products of this construction process. We make choices with a brain—or mind—we didn't choose.

By the time we decide to question our inherited identity, we are already very much in possession of one. We can certainly decide to change aspects of our character and behavior, but the way in which we want to change, and our degree of success in doing so, will be determined by how we already are as a result of genes and experience. This makes it very difficult to maintain the idea that a person "gets what they deserve" or that the world is inherently just.

Having made this argument in a variety of contexts, I've learned that although people are willing to accept that talent and opportunity may be the product of forces beyond our control, many struggle to view effort in the same way. It's not hard to believe that a beautiful face or a talent for physics is a matter of luck, but the willingness to persevere, to sacrifice, to be self-disciplined—*this*, it seems, is the stuff of character, where notions of responsibility come into their own. The trouble is, we don't create our character either. Just like beliefs, dietary preferences, and fashion sense, character emerges from the interaction between biological inheritance and experience. With different genes and different environmental influences, we would have a different character.

Research has shown that the capacity for effort is influenced by our prenatal environment, whether we suffered childhood abuse, the amount of glucose in our blood, how much sleep we're getting, whether we live in a collective or individualist culture, and a number of other factors. Perhaps the most compelling piece of research on character formation came from the Adverse Childhood Experiences study, which tracked the long-term effects of childhood trauma on health and behavior.[29] The largest study of its kind, its findings showed that early trauma significantly increases a person's chances of suffering social, emotional, and cognitive impairment. The more traumatic episodes a person has experienced, the more severe the impairment is likely to be. Over a lifetime, this impairment greatly increases the risk of illness, disease, addiction, disability, violence, and early death.

Of course, some individuals manage to subvert every expectation, achieving remarkable things from humble beginnings. It's tempting to interpret these inspiring examples as evidence that we are, after all, responsible for our destinies—but that would be a mistake. A life journey is influenced by a wide range of unpredictable factors. Variations in genes and experience do not need to be large to have an impact on the paths we take. With a slight tweak in starting conditions, the woman who died at 25 from a drug overdose might have lived to hug her grandchildren or even win a Nobel Prize. Small variations can have significant repercussions, setting in motion events that result in dramatically different outcomes. What's more, whenever we encounter a crucial fork in the road, apparently trivial conditions can make all the difference, nudging us one way or another: the weather that day, when we last ate, how stressful the prior 48 hours have been, and so on.

Though we often have little control over it, the context in which we make our choices can be decisive. As the philosopher Thomas Nagel put it: "Someone who was an officer in a concentration camp might have led a quiet and harmless life if the Nazis had never come to power in Germany. And someone who led a quiet and harmless life in Argentina might have become an officer in a concentration camp if he'd not left Germany for business reasons in 1930."[30]

Forces beyond our control determine the emotional, psychological, and material resources we have at our disposal to carve out a path in life. These resources may enable some people to achieve remarkable things, but no one can take ultimate credit for the resources at their disposal. And for each miracle story, there are endless counterexamples of people—with the same potential, the same determination—who were crushed by the forces of poverty, oppression, and injustice. The reassuring notion of people "getting what they give" is refuted, time and again, by history, logic, and common sense. It overlooks the fact that what people can give depends on what they first receive from their biological and social inheritance. Of course, that doesn't stop people peddling the myth of rugged individualism. In the words of former Republican Party presidential candidate Herman Cain: "If you don't have a job and are not rich, blame yourself."[31] It will always be convenient for the guardians of inequality to divert attention from structural factors onto the lone individual stripped of context.

A second false belief lurks behind the fairy tale that "people get what they deserve." It holds that we are rewarded according to how hard we work and how valuable our work is. Most economists would say that, in a free market, people are rewarded according to the value of their contribution. Marginal productivity theory tells us that if a worker produces $100 worth of value per hour, then that is what the worker will be paid. We have already seen that what we are able to give is ultimately decided by forces beyond our control. What are we to make of this separate claim that people are rewarded according to the nature of their contribution?

During the coronavirus pandemic that swept the world in 2020, it quickly became obvious which workers contributed the most to society. While much of the economy was shut down and millions of people were told to stay at home, essential workers—those without whom society would collapse—had to continue doing their jobs, often risking their health in the process. They included nurses, farmers, teachers, cleaners, carers, garbage collectors, shelf stackers, truck drivers, and postal workers—by no means the highest paid professions in our society. Top CEOs can receive financial rewards hundreds of times greater than these essential workers. Narrowing our focus to the effort involved in these jobs, we might ask how many CEOs work harder than a cleaner in a hotel, a carer looking after the elderly, a nurse in an underfunded hospital, or an unpaid mother of infants? Even if we found such a CEO, we might ask, how much harder? Twice as hard? Three times as hard?

At the turn of the millennium, CEOs earned 368 times the salary of the average worker in the United States. What's more, CEO compensation in the United States has grown 940 percent since 1978, while, over the same period, the typical worker has experienced a pay rise of only 12 percent.[32] Economist Robert Reich noted that: "Anyone who believes CEOs deserve this astronomical pay hasn't been paying attention. The entire stock market has risen to record highs. Most CEOs have done little more than ride the wave."[33] Even when CEOs oversee dramatic company losses, they often walk away with extortionate pay packets.

Clearly, something other than hard and valuable work determines how people are rewarded. Perhaps it is some rare, extraordinary ability? This explanation doesn't work either. Just think of the immense talents of the great scientists and mathematicians on whose discoveries modern society rests, the likes of Newton, Einstein, and Turing. They are never the ones to whom the world's riches flow. The same applies to the artistic and humanitarian giants of our civilization, all of whom make incalculable contributions to humanity.

To make sense of how people are rewarded, it helps to note that almost all work is done in teams. A company like Amazon makes billions of dollars a year in profits as a result of tasks carried out over many territories by hundreds of thousands of workers doing very different jobs. It is extremely difficult, often impossible, to identify the value of each person's contribution, from the ware-house to the boardroom. As the economist Thomas Piketty has argued: "The very notion of individual marginal productivity becomes hard to define. In fact, it becomes something close to a pure ideological construct on the basis of which justification for higher status can be elaborated."[34] The way that a company's revenue is divided among those who produce it depends on various factors. Ultimately, though, the decisive factor is power.

Contracts formalize how people will be rewarded for their work. The terms depend on the bargaining power of those who negotiate it, and bargaining power boils down to the resources we control relative to others. For many of us, the resources we bring to the negotiating table are personal: knowledge, phys-ical ability, skill—what is sometimes called "human capital." However, a small number of people bring something else entirely: property, "traditional capital." In our society, these people tend to wield the greatest bargaining power.

Suppose you have been walking for days in the desert, lips parched, desperate for a drink. Suddenly I appear in front of you, holding in one hand a bottle of water and in the other a contract that would legally commit you to working as my butler for $1 a day for the next year. If you want the water, I say, you must sign the contract. Clearly, this is an exploitative deal, reflecting our relative bargaining power, but it's also mutually beneficial, capturing the motivating logic of most economic contracts. Given your unattractive options, the rational course of ac-tion—as for poorly paid workers the world over—is to sign away your freedom.

When economists claim that people are remunerated according to the value of their contribution, they mean value *as determined by the market*. But the market is a social construct that functions within the larger power structures of society. These structures determine how much power is possessed by different market participants. If, for instance, workers got to vote on the wages of their bosses—as they do in the world's largest cooperative, the Mondragon corporation—the world would be a far more equal place. Were power more fairly distributed, Amazon's workforce would enjoy far higher wages, far more rights, and its CEO, Jeff Bezos, would not be a billionaire.

Historically, the rewards distributed to different groups in society have changed according to shifts in the balance of power. This goes a long way to explaining why wealth concentration has been inversely correlated with union membership (see Figure 2.3). As union membership rose throughout the twentieth century and the bargaining power of workers increased, the share of income going to the top 10 percent of the population declined. When union membership fell, the share of income going to the top 10 percent crept back up.

Since their formation in the mid-nineteenth century, unions have been on the front line in a bitter class war, repeatedly attacked, often outlawed. Today's distribution of income and wealth is, in large part, an outcome of this ferocious war. In 2017, the global top 1 percent took possession of 82 percent of all the new wealth that was created by the workers of the world.[35] As the billionaire Warren Buffet put it: "There's class warfare, all right, but it's my class, the rich class, that's making war, and we're winning." Under the existing economic order, people do not get

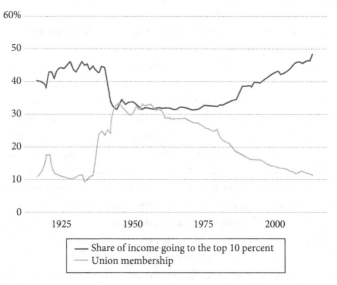

Figure 2.3 Union membership and share of income going to the top 10 percent in the United States.

Note: This figure is reproduced here by permission of Colin Gordon.

Source: Colin Gordon, "Union Membership and the Income Share of the Top Ten Percent," Economic Policy Institute. https://www.epi.org/blog/union-membership-income-share-top-ten-percent/

what they deserve, but what they are able to take. What counts is not effort, contribution, or genius, but power.

Imbalances of power echo through the ages due to intergenerational transfers of wealth. It may be a well-kept secret, but the majority of wealth in existence has been inherited, not earned. This fact is another nail in the coffin of the idea that people get what they deserve. If the lottery of birth gifts you wealthy relatives, you can live a life of affluence no matter who you are or what you do. What's more, without lifting a finger, your wealth can generate more wealth forevermore. If you inherit, say, $100 million from a grandparent, you need only hire some savvy investors to ensure that your fortune grows, year on year into the future. As Thomas Piketty pointed out, over the long term, the rate of return on investments is greater than the rate of economic growth. This means that, left to its own logic, capitalism concentrates wealth over time. And not only does wealth generate wealth, the more wealth you own, the quicker it will grow.

These facts reveal a fundamental feature of our economic system: People get rich—really rich—because of what they own, not what they do. Some people end up with very high annual incomes but that is rarely the source of immense wealth. The fortunes that flow to billionaires derive from ownership rights: of shares, of patents, of land, of buildings, of resources. Property rights are not facts of nature but collective fictions. The socially sanctioned paths to ownership—as well as the scope, form, and timescale that ownership takes—are profoundly political constructs, whose perceived legitimacy changes dramatically over time and place, bound up as they are with beliefs about justice, morality, and freedom.

Cheats, Exploiters, and Free-Riders

The idea that people get what they deserve has many flaws. But it does connect to something important: For a community of any kind to endure and prosper it needs to be wary of those who would exploit it, those who would free-ride. From a sports team to a nation, all groups develop ways to prevent members reaping the benefits of cooperation without bearing any of the costs. If too many people choose to free-ride on the contributions of others, the viability of the community itself will be jeopardized, and the immense benefits of cooperation will evaporate for all. People across the political spectrum—socialists, liberals, conservatives—agree that this is a danger. However, they disagree on where the real exploiters are to be found. Are they at the bottom of society or the top? Rich or poor? Which groups are getting something for nothing?

Much ink and many speeches have been deployed to persuade us that society's free-riders live in the poorest regions and possess the fewest rights. This view portrays the unemployed, the disabled, and migrants as threats to the national interest. If correct, the solution is clear: make welfare and social security harder to access while tightening up immigration controls. Indeed, this has been the manifesto of right-wing political parties for decades (along with hefty tax cuts for the rich). The alternative view holds that the real exploiters are to be found not at the bottom of society but the top. And these exploiters cheat us out of so much more than a welfare check, although they do that, too.

In the United States, someone who qualifies for unemployment benefits might, if they are lucky, get around $400 a week. By contrast, the fossil fuel industry, imperiling the future of humanity, receives over $12 billion a week in state subsidies.[36] In 2008, thousands of ordinary Americans who had nothing to do with causing the financial crisis were thrown out of their homes. The banks that brought about the crisis, however, were bailed out to the tune of hundreds of billions of public dollars, with no strings attached. If a typical American worker repeatedly fails to pay their income tax, they can be sent to prison. In 2018, Amazon reported profits of $11 billion in the United States yet paid no tax[37]—not a single dollar. On the contrary, Amazon, one of the world's most profitable companies, received a handout of $129 million from the federal government.[38] The ideological divide is often framed as a struggle between socialists and capitalists, between welfare queens who want free handouts and rugged individualists who believe we should all earn our way. In reality, most developed nations already have socialism; it just happens to be limited to the wealthy.

Financial support of the rich is not the exception but the rule. Of America's richest corporations, 91 paid no taxes on collective profits worth over $100 billion.[39] Instead of funding schools, hospitals, or urgent climate solutions, these corporate profits are tucked away in tax havens. In 2017, American Fortune 500 companies held an *estimated $2.6 trillion* offshore. And globally, the richest individuals have hidden away an estimated $8.7 trillion.[40] That is free-riding on an industrial scale. After all, no company gets rich on its own. All businesses benefit enormously from the legal, physical, and educational infrastructure of the nations in which they operate. Without this infrastructure, they could not function. Corporate taxes are therefore a way of repaying this debt. To claim society is fleecing corporations through taxation is to get things upside down. Taxation is how we prevent profit-maximizing corporations fleecing society.

Jeff Bezos, CEO of Amazon, is now the richest person in the world, with a fortune valued at around $140 billion. According to one estimate, he makes over $8 million an hour.[41] It would take an average Amazon employee—on the minimum wage, working 12 hours a day, every day—over 136 years to pocket 1 hour's worth of Bezos's income. Let's be clear, the $8 million an hour is not for what Jeff Bezos does. What could anyone possibly do to create that much value in an hour? It is for what he owns. Believe it or not, his annual salary as CEO is $81,840.[42] Almost all his wealth comes from ownership of Amazon's shares.

He could stay in bed all day while his workers exhaust themselves generating Amazon's profits and still make millions of dollars a minute. On the other hand, if Amazon's workers stayed in bed, while Mr. Bezos busied himself at the office, Amazon's profits would evaporate, and the company would soon collapse. Like all billionaires, Bezos has perfected the art not of creating wealth, but taking wealth. He happens to live in a society that lets him get away with it.

Capitalism, Democracy, and the Future

Marking a ballot takes a second and, with that act, a typical voter's democratic participation ends until the next election. The influence of wealth, however, is continuous. The richest individuals and industries devote hundreds of millions of dollars a year to shaping political outcomes. Concentrated wealth in the United States and elsewhere routinely renders electoral systems dysfunctional by means of party funding, lobbyists, think tanks, media ownership, and delayed bribery via the revolving door that links big business to government. It's a reinforcing system. The more the rich spend on politics, the more influence they attain, and the more they can rig the system in their favor so that next time around they can spend even more. With each cycle, the inequalities of society deepen.

Research spanning decades has exposed the immense influence of concentrated wealth on electoral politics. This influence was consolidated with the Supreme Court's 2010 *Citizens United* decision, which abolished election-spending regulations on the basis that they restricted the right of corporations to free speech (the ruling itself was opposed by 77 percent of voters).[43] Corporations are not people, despite what the law may suggest, and spending money on politics is not a way of exercising free speech. It is best understood as a business investment. The reason for spending today is to get more tomorrow. Numerous studies and reports confirmed this. I'll mention just two.

The first, a report in 2018 by the *Guardian* newspaper, looked at which policies were supported by American billionaires.[44] They found a strong consensus existed among this elite group. It consisted of cutting taxes, especially estate taxes, which impact only the wealthiest of Americans; cutting funding for government programs aimed at helping people with jobs, incomes, healthcare, or retirement pensions; cutting or privatizing social security benefits; and opposing banking regulation and legislation to protect the environment. One thing unites these policies. They are all geared to expanding the domain and protecting the outcomes of market logic.

The second piece of research comes from Princeton University and was published in 2014. It found that, when the will of voters conflicts with the interests of the wealthy, voters have extremely limited influence on policy. According to its authors: "Strong support among high-income Americans roughly doubles the probability that a policy will be adopted," whereas "strong support among the middle class has essentially no effect."[45] They also found that "when the affluent strongly oppose a policy, it's associated with a 25 to 30 percentage point decline in the likelihood that it will be adopted; but when the middle class strongly oppose a policy, that's associated with a small *increase* in the likelihood it will be adopted."[46] The authors concluded that the United States is better described as an oligarchy than democracy. This conclusion gives us yet another reason to support substantial taxation of the rich for, even if it is poorly spent, a high top rate of tax fulfills a vital social function by reducing the power of the affluent to subvert democracy.

Studies like this necessarily underestimate the influence of money in politics because they take the preferences of voters as a given. Yet concentrated wealth exerts its influence long before a ballot is cast. The all-encompassing perceptual environment that media create is constructed by a small number of people who decide what story, with what angle, using which words, will appear on tomorrow's front pages and digital screens. They and the algorithms they design decide who and what will be celebrated, condemned, and ignored. Change the people in control of these decisions and you change the perceptual environment, and with it the "common sense" of the age.

As things stand, from the United States and United Kingdom to Mexico and India, most media are owned by a small number of billionaires—and, as we have seen, most billionaires have a predictable political agenda. In contemporary democracies, the media are largely free from one form of concentrated power—the state—but firmly in the grip of another, the corporate elite. If a central purpose of media is to facilitate democracy, this is a major design flaw: a structural bias in favor of the 0.001 percent. We might all share the freedom to speak, but we do not all share the freedom to be heard. Consistent access to that freedom comes with a hefty price tag that only the likes of Rupert Murdoch, Jeff Bezos, and Lord Rothermere can afford. The unfortunate results have been meticulously documented by media scholars for decades.

Almost a century ago, the influential U.S. intellectual Walter Lippmann wrote about the need to "manufacture consent" as a solution to the threat of democracy. Since then, techniques for controlling the flow of ideas, facts, and perspectives through society have increased in their reach and sophistication. The latest developments draw on big data. You may have heard about Cambridge Analytica, a company whose principal investor was U.S. billionaire Robert Mercer, a patron of right-wing outlets like Breitbart News. By exploiting the growing field of psychometrics, which draws on vast stores of personal data, this small company is reported to have influenced electoral outcomes across the globe, including in the

United Kingdom and United States, contributing to the success of both Brexit and Trump.

I started this short essay noting that the two dominant systems of our age—capitalism and democracy—are both justified in terms of their capacity to protect and promote freedom. But these systems are built on incompatible conceptions of this cherished ideal. One privileges citizenship, the other ownership. Ultimately, then, there is a profound contradiction between the logics of capitalism and democracy. The concentrated wealth produced by capitalism subverts popular governance in ways that concentrate wealth even further. Under capitalism, the principle of one person, one vote is overwhelmed by the principle of one dollar, one vote.

Those who question the wisdom of capitalism are often misunderstood. To be clear, neither capitalism nor communism has succeeded in respecting, cultivating, or defending a robust conception of freedom. Soviet Russia and Maoist China were totalitarian societies that crushed liberty and those who craved it. To free ourselves, we must unshackle our imaginations from the crude binary of these failed systems. Human society has always been rich with possibility. There are many ways to organize ourselves on this planet: many ways to distribute resources, share power, and live with nature. Thankfully, the systems we call capitalism and communism do not exhaust our available options. What they share is a failure to tolerate and nurture that most radical of ideas, without which freedom withers: democracy.

Humanity's experiment with large-scale democracy is in its infancy—an unfinished revolution. Never has it been more important to deepen, extend, and reimagine what democracy means in the economy, the workplace, finance, education, politics, and media, both nationally and internationally. The point of reducing great disparities of wealth is not to achieve perfect equality—whatever that may mean—but to expand freedom by eradicating the constraints of poverty and rejuvenating the idea of popular control over society's central institutions. To borrow a formulation from Amartya Sen, we expand people's freedom when we expand their capabilities.

Extreme inequality is not a consequence of freedom but an obstacle to it. At this fateful moment in history, it is also an obstacle to our collective survival. In the years ahead, humanity faces its greatest ever challenge: the threat of civilizational breakdown as a result of ecological collapse. Research has shown that the global economy has overstepped several planetary boundaries. Scientists warn that we must bring the scale of economic activity—our extraction, production, consumption, and waste—back within nature's limits. The only way to do this without causing unprecedented human suffering and triggering devastating global conflict is to share more equitably the limited resources that can safely be used. The people of the world face a stark choice: cooperate and survive or compete and perish. If we are to make the right choice, the democracy-destroying force of extreme inequality will need to be overcome. It appears, then, that to reduce inequality we need to reduce inequality. As ever, the only way beyond this circular solution is to educate, agitate, and organize.

Notes

1. "Tackling Inequality Vital to Ending Extreme Poverty by 2030," World Bank, October 2, 2016, https://www.worldbank.org/en/news/press-release/2016/10/02/tackling-ine quality-vital-to-end-extreme-poverty-by-2030.

2. Paul Muggeridge, "Bill Gates: Global Inequality Is Falling Faster Than Ever," World Economic Forum, April 19, 2016, https://www.weforum.org/agenda/2016/04/bill-gates-global-inequality-is-falling-faster-than-ever/.

3. Tim Worstall, "Global Inequality Is Falling No Matter What Anyone Says," Forbes, August 30, 2014; Tyler Cowen, "Income Inequality Is Not Rising Globally. It's Falling," New York Times, July 19, 2014; Philip Booth, "Believe It or Not, Global Inequality Is Falling," Institute of Economic Affairs, November 13, 2017.

4. Miguel Niño-Zarazúa, Laurence Roope, and Finn Tarp, "Income Inequality in a Globalising World," Vox CEPR Policy Portal, September 20, 2016, https://voxeu.org/article/income-inequality-globalising-world.

5. Jason Hickel, Less Is More (London: William Heinemann, 2020).

6. Quoted by Chris Johns, "Reasons to Be Cheerful Amid Globalisation and Rising Inequality," Irish Times, December 30, 2019, https://www.irishtimes.com/busin ess/economy/reasons-to-be-cheerful-amid-globalisation-and-rising-inequality-1.3744436.

7. Facundo Alvaredo et al., "World Inequality Report 2018: Executive Summary," 6, https://wir2018.wid.world/files/download/wir2018-summary-english.pdf.

8. Alvaredo et al., "World Inequality Report 2018," Part II, 2.4, 80.

9. Alvaredo et al., "World Inequality Report 2018," Part II, 2.1, 40.

10. Alvaredo et al., "World Inequality Report 2018, Part IV, 4.1," 200.

11. Alvaredo et al., "World Inequality Report 2018, Part IV, 4.1," 200.

12. "Oxfam Says Wealth of Richest 1% Equal to Other 99%," BBC News, January 18, 2016, https://www.bbc.co.uk/news/business-35339475.

13. Alvaredo et al., "World Inequality Report 2018, Part IV, 4.3," 213.

14. Richard Wilkinson and Kate Pickett, The Spirit Level (London: Penguin Books, 2010).

15. Milton Friedman, Capitalism and Freedom (London: University of Chicago Press, 2002), 13.

16. Isaiah Berlin, Four Essays on Liberty (Oxford: Oxford University Press, 1969), 118–172.

17. I use the term liberty as a synonym for "freedom."

18. George Crowder, Isaiah Berlin: Liberty and Pluralism (Cambridge, UK: Polity Press, 2004), 82.

19. John Rawls, *A Theory of Justice* (Cambridge, MA: Harvard University Press, 1971), 204.
20. Robert Nozick, *Anarchy, State, and Utopia* (Oxford, UK: Blackwell, 1972), 262.
21. Friedrich Hayek, *The Road to Serfdom* (New York: Routledge, 2009), 26.
22. For this framing, I'm indebted to Gerald Cohen, *Self-Ownership and Equality* (New York: Cambridge University Press, 1995), 58.
23. For a useful discussion of this topic, see Robin Hahnel, *The ABCs of Political Economy* (New York: Pluto Press, 2002), Chapter 10.
24. Andrew T. Jebb et al., "Happiness, Income Satiation and Turning Points Around the World," *Nature Human Behaviour* 2, no. 1 (January 2018): 33–38, https://doi.org/10.1038/s41562-017-0277-0.
25. Thomas Piketty, Emmanuel Saez, and Stefanie Stantcheva, "Taxing the 1%: Why the Top Tax Rate Could Be Over 80%," Vox CEPR Policy Portal, December 8, 2011, https://voxeu.org/article/taxing-1-why-top-tax-rate-could-be-over-80.
26. Milton Friedman, *Capitalism and Freedom* (London: University of Chicago Press, 2002), 174.
27. Jason Hickel, "How Britain Stole $45 Trillion From India," *Al Jazeera*, December 19, 2018, https://www.aljazeera.com/indepth/opinion/britain-stole-45-trillion-india-181206124830851.html.
28. Dev Kar, "Financial Flows and Tax Havens: Combining to Limit the Lives of Billions of People," Global Financial Integrity, December 5, 2016, https://gfintegrity.org/report/financial-flows-and-tax-havens-combining-to-limit-the-lives-of-billions-of-people/.
29. Vincent J. Felitti et al., "Relationship of Childhood Abuse and Household Dysfunction to Many of the Leading Causes of Death in Adults. The Adverse Childhood Experiences (ACE) Study," *American Journal of Preventive Medicine* 14, no. 4 (May 1, 1998): 245–258, https://doi.org/10.1016/S0749-3797(98)00017-8.
30. Thomas Nagel, *Mortal Questions* (Cambridge: Cambridge University Press, 1979), 26.
31. Steven Pearlstein, "*Hermanomics: Let Them Eat Pizza,*" *Washington Post*, October 15, 2011, https://www.washingtonpost.com/business/economy/hermanomics-let-them-eat-pizza/2011/10/11/gIQAgTOmmL_story.html.
32. Lawrence Mishel and Julia Wolfe, "CEO Compensation Has Grown 940% Since 1978," Economic Policy Institute, August 14, 2019, https://www.epi.org/publication/ceo-compensation-2018/.
33. Robert Reich, "How to Fix Sky High CEO Pay in Companies That Pay Workers Like Serfs," *Alternet*, April 22, 2014, https://www.alternet.org/2014/04/robert-reich-how-fix-sky-high-ceo-pay-companies-pay-workers-serfs/.
34. Thomas Piketty, *Capital in the 21st Century* (Cambridge, MA: Harvard University Press, 2014), 331.
35. Katie Hope, "'World's Richest 1% Get 82% of the Wealth,' Says Oxfam," *BBC News*, January 22, 2018, https://www.bbc.co.uk/news/business-42745853.
36. James Ellsmoor, "United States Spend Ten Times More on Fossil Fuel Subsidies Than Education," *Forbes*, June 15, 2019, https://www.forbes.com/sites/jamesellsmoor/2019/06/15/united-states-spend-ten-times-more-on-fossil-fuel-subsidies-than-education/#1c941f454473.

37. Christopher Ingraham, "Amazon Paid No Federal Taxes on $11.2 Billion in Profits Last Year," *Washington Post*, February 16, 2019, https://www.washingtonpost.com/us-policy/2019/02/16/amazon-paid-no-federal-taxes-billion-profits-last-year/.

38. Andrew Davis, "Why Amazon Paid No 2018 US Federal Income Tax," *CNBC*, April 4, 2019, https://www.cnbc.com/2019/04/03/why-amazon-paid-no-federal-income-tax.html.

39. Jesse Pound, "These 91 Companies Paid No Federal Taxes in 2018," *CNBC*, December 17, 2019, https://www.cnbc.com/2019/12/16/these-91-fortune-500-companies-didnt-pay-federal-taxes-in-2018.html.

40. Nicholas Shaxson, "Tackling Tax Havens," International Monetary Fund, September 2019, https://www.imf.org/external/pubs/ft/fandd/2019/09/tackling-global-tax-havens-shaxon.htm.

41. Hillary Hoffower, "We Did the Math to Calculate How Much Money Jeff Bezos Makes in a Year, Month, Week, Day, Hour, Minute, and Second," *Business Insider*, January 9, 2019, https://www.businessinsider.com/what-amazon-ceo-jeff-bezos-makes-every-day-hour-minute-2018-10?r=US&IR=T.

42. Tomi Kilgore, "Amazon CEO Jeff Bezos Has Had the Same 'Low Salary' for Decades, a Little More Than Double the Median U.S. Employee's Pay," *Market Watch*, April 17, 2020, https://www.marketwatch.com/story/amazon-ceo-jeff-bezos-has-made-the-same-salary-for-decades-a-little-more-than-double-the-median-us-employees-pay-2020-04-16.

43. Katrina vanden Heuvel, "Reversing 'Citizens United,'" *Washington Post*, January 18, 2011, https://www.washingtonpost.com/opinions/reversing-citizens-united/2011/01/18/ABa6aRR_story.html.

44. Benjamin I. Page, Jason Seawright, and Matthew J. Lacombe, "What Billionaires Want: The Secret Influence of America's 100 Richest," *Guardian*, October 31, 2018, https://www.theguardian.com/us-news/2018/oct/30/billionaire-stealth-politics-america-100-richest-what-they-want.

45. Martin Gilens and Benjamin Page, "Critics Argued With Our Analysis of U.S. Political Inequality. Here Are 5 Ways They're Wrong," *Washington Post*, May 23, 2016, https://www.washingtonpost.com/news/monkey-cage/wp/2016/05/23/critics-challenge-our-portrait-of-americas-political-inequality-heres-5-ways-they-are-wrong/.

46. Gilens and Page, "Critics Argued."

3

Structural Violence and Structural Awareness

Bandy X. Lee

Structural violence may be as old as civilization, even if the phrase is relatively new. For the phrase, we need only go back to a semtiinal essay by the Norwegian sociologist Johan Galtung, who defined structural violence as "the cause of the difference between the potential and the actual."[1] It refers to a form of violence wherein social structures harm people by preventing them from meeting their basic needs. Although less visible, it is by far the most lethal form of violence through causing excess deaths—deaths that would not need to occur in more equal societies. This chapter examines (a) the history and concept of structural violence; (b) how it is the deadliest form of violence; (c) how it stunts human development, as we can see in the case study of U.S. society; and (d) how the healing of this violence is fundamental to human freedom, growth, and democracy.

The concept of structural violence developed in part in the 1950s and 1960s through liberation theologians in the Catholic Church in Latin America, principally as a moral reaction to the poverty and social injustices in the region.[2] Galtung credited his inspiration to Mohandas Gandhi, the leader of the Indian independence movement who called poverty "the worst form of violence."[3]

Canadian peace researchers Gernot Köhler and Norman Alcock devised ways to quantify it.[4] They used Sweden as the model of a society that had come closest to eliminating structural violence, with the most equal standards of living and the highest life expectancy of all nations. As a first measure, they asked how many deaths could be avoided if all countries enjoyed the same living conditions as Sweden. A second measure they used was the "egalitarian model," for which they calculated a complete and equal redistribution of the available global wealth. They then asked how many deaths could be avoided if this kind of equitable sharing could ever be achieved. The results were stark. When the authors compared life expectancies elsewhere in the world with those in Sweden, they calculated that some 18 million deaths each year could be attributed to structural violence, or the social, political, and economic inequalities that exist globally.

They worked from the assumption that life expectancy is a function of relative socioeconomic position.[5] Then, plotting gross national product (GNP) per

Bandy X. Lee, *Structural Violence and Structural Awareness* In: *On Inequality and Freedom*. Edited by: Lawrence M. Eppard and Henry A. Giroux, Oxford University Press. © Oxford University Press 2022.
DOI: 10.1093/oso/9780197583029.003.0003

capita for each nation on Earth, they were able to show that life expectancy in nations with a GNP per capita equal to the world average was 68.3 years in the year 1965. A remarkable finding from this model of life expectancy is its magnitude. Spreading wealth and resources equally raised the average life expectancy by approximately 40 years for the country with the lowest life expectancy, which in 1965 was 27 years in Guinea. Meanwhile, it lowered life expectancy by only 6 years for the country with the highest life expectancy, which was 74.7 years in Sweden. In other words, achieving conditions of complete global equality would produce only a marginal loss in life expectancy in richer countries while creating a tremendous number of extra years of life in poorer nations.

Today, the differences are starker: A child born in a Glasgow, Scotland, suburb can expect a life 28 years shorter than another living only 13 kilometers away. A girl in Lesotho is likely to live 42 years less than another in Japan. In Sweden, the risk of a woman dying during pregnancy and childbirth is 1 in 17,400; in Afghanistan, the odds are 1 in 8. The Commission on Social Determinants of Health of the World Health Organization has declared that structural violence is killing people on a grand scale.[6] It is a violence that is built into the structure of the society and constitutes differences in life chances while manifesting in infant mortality, slow starvation, disease, despair, and humiliation that destroys almost every aspect of life. In this manner, social and economic policies that create and augment the differences between—and within—countries are crucial factors in whether a child will grow and develop to full potential and live a flourishing life or whether its life will be blighted. Additionally, not only is structural violence the most lethal form of violence, but also it is the most powerful cause of other forms of violence, such as behavioral violence.[7] British social epidemiologists Richard Wilkinson and Kate Pickett concluded that egalitarian societies would do enormously better overall with only minor compromises from the wealthy.[8]

One of the greatest problems in describing structural violence is the fact that this type of violence is barely perceptible when compared to behavioral violence. The tolls of street violence or war seem at first glance much higher, but in reality the "tranquil" waters of structural violence are much more harmful. It is indeed a rule of thumb for violence that the least damaging forms are the most overt, while the most destructive ones are hidden. American violence scholar James Gilligan compared structural violence to the most deadly military conflicts in history.[9] Estimating a total of 49 million military and civilian fatalities from World War II, or about 8 million deaths per year from 1939 to 1945, and also considering the death toll from a hypothetical nuclear exchange between the United States and the former Soviet Union to be 232 million, Gilligan concluded that these numbers could not even begin to compare with the harm of structural violence. The structural violence continues year after year, during times of peace as well as of war, and roughly every 15 years, on average, as many people have died because of relative poverty as would die in a nuclear war that caused 232 million deaths. This means that we are currently enduring the equivalent of a slow-moving, not only ongoing, but also accelerating thermonuclear war or genocide every year of every decade, throughout the world.

Gilligan also described structural violence in terms of increased rates of disabilities and deaths among people who occupy the bottom class. The suffering of people from the lower rungs of society is a function of the more privileged classes having collective bargaining power to determine how and where to allocate resources. Unlike behavioral violence, the lethal effects of structural violence operate continuously rather than sporadically. They can occur independently of any intention to kill anyone; for example, they can be a byproduct of wishing to maximize one's own wealth and power. Structural violence is usually invisible, in the sense that deaths from structural violence may appear to have other causes, be they natural or violent. Gilligan emphasized that feelings of shame, humiliation, and inferiority, which become pronounced as the disparity between classes increases, are the most potent cause of behavioral violence,[10] such as suicide, homicide, warfare, and capital punishment.[11]

More recently, American anthropologist Paul Farmer defined structure as a pattern of collective social actions that occur within institutional practices, laws, economic policies, and other elements of everyday life.[12] These structures are not just collective thoughts and beliefs but are manifest materially in roads, server systems, hospitals, and schools. From Farmer's perspective, violence is suffering that results from social arrangements that put individuals in harm's way. Since the exertion of structural violence is systematic—that is to say, indirectly applied by all members of a societal order—no particular individual is fully at fault, while at the same time everyone in that order is partly at fault. Cumulative historical forces and processes work together to constrain individuals and to deny them the benefits of social progress.

Why do we call this structural *violence,* instead of simply social injustice or oppression? Structural violence may at first seem a misnomer for it concerns stable structures and contrasts sharply with the vehemence of behavioral violence. Nevertheless, it is a product of human decisions.[13] We decide to divide our society into rich and poor, powerful and weak, and superior and inferior—and these are therefore correctable and preventable and not natural occurrences.[14] Indian economist Amartya Sen won the Nobel Prize in Economics in part for demonstrating that the mass deaths that occur during famines are not the result of food shortage, but rather of the poor's shortage of purchasing power: They cannot afford to buy the food that is already available in their countries.[15] Nevertheless, a key aspect of structural violence is that it is often subtle, invisible, and accepted as a matter of course. Even more difficult than detecting it is assigning culpability for it since the actors are often impossible to identify, hidden as they are behind anonymous institutions or long disappeared while the violence continues. There are no concrete operators directly attacking others, as when one person kills another. Yet, from the victim's perspective, structural violence has similar effects as behavioral violence, including death.[16] If someone dies of tuberculosis, autoimmune deficiency syndrome (AIDS), or another curable disease in the modern world, where advanced medications exist but are not accessible to them, then one has died all the same.[17] Market globalization and the more rapid changes in existing and new structures further lessen the gap between structural and behavioral violence.

The purpose of naming is to highlight theoretically important dimensions that can lead thinking, research, and it is hoped action that bring about meaningful improvement. It is illogical to name smaller, episodic, and incidental acts of violence as such but leave out the deadliest form that causes the greatest injury and death. For example, the last few decades saw an alarming rise in structural violence between high-income and low- or middle-income countries, as well as within most countries. The injuries of structural violence also run deeper. Unlike more visible and obvious forms of violence, which may be explosive but have a chance to heal over time, structural violence is economically, politically, and culturally pervasive, working together in such a way as to limit victims from ever achieving a full quality of life.[18] Embedded within very stable social structures where there is little overt disruption, persistent and insidious damage results. The effects of unequal control over the distribution of resources worsen if those low in income are also low in education, in health, and in power—as is frequently the case, as these dimensions interlink within the societal structure. Not only does structural violence cause the greatest rate of excess, premature deaths and damage, but also, under the conditions it creates, the rise of other forms of violence is only a matter of time.[19]

On the other hand, the desire for psychic numbing grows with the scale of a problem.[20] When the scope and pervasiveness of a problem seem too much for the mind to handle, there is a desire to understate if not to deny it. In line with this has been the recent investment in the belief that violence is less and less of a problem because its most overt forms are declining: namely, homicides and interstate wars. Popular "scholars" of violence have seized the opportunity to indulge the public's desire for reassurance[21] in ways that have arguably contributed to the problem through the lessening of consciousness.[22] Consciousness is the critical first step to recognizing a problem and solving it. Furthermore, suicides account for more deaths around the world than all the homicides, mass violence, and war casualties combined,[23] and in countries like the United States, suicides have been escalating even as homicides have declined.[24] This is still without addressing the even greater violence of destroying our common natural habitat or maintaining the technology to wipe out the entire human species many times over.[25]

Because of the human tendency to wish to minimize or to deny a problem when it seems too great, it is especially important to apply critical consciousness. As the most important causal relations are the least self-evident ones, consciousness allows for the application of preventive measures further upstream, where it is more manageable. Recognizing the abyss for what it is,[26] and hence not diverting from a better understanding, allows for the tools to tackle it and to develop a vision beyond it. Confrontation of the truth can cause distress; the whole truth, however, reveals the greater human capacity for transformation. Self-deception, on the other hand, might initially comfort but requires ever greater energy to maintain and misses the chance for self-realization. It is the same for human societies.

The United States is an excellent case study of structural violence and its consequences. Its similarity until the 1980s and then divergence from other large economies makes it a particularly compelling historical study of the effects of income and wealth inequality. In 1975, for example, the top 1 percent earned a similar share of the income in the United States as in countries such as Canada, France, Germany, Italy, Japan, and the United Kingdom. But since 1987, the share of income going to the top 1 percent in the United States exceeded all these countries, year after year. Its income share for the top 1 percent income kept rising, on average, at twice the rate of the United Kingdom and exceeding other advanced economies even more throughout the 1990s and the 2000s. By 2014, the top 1 percent had captured 18 percent of income, up from the 1975 figure of 8 percent.[27]

By 2018, the top 20 percent of the population earned 52 percent of all U.S. income,[28] and the bottom 20 percent earned only 3.1 percent of the nation's income. Most low-wage workers cannot save, which creates wealth inequality. They also receive no health insurance, sick days, or pension plans from their employers. They cannot get ill and have no hope of retiring. That creates healthcare inequality. Since the rich got richer faster, their piece of the pie grew larger. The wealthiest 1 percent of people increased their share of total income by 10 percent. Everyone else saw their piece of the pie shrink by 1 to 2 percent. This also decreased economic mobility. Average wages remained flat despite an increase in worker productivity of 15 percent, while corporate profits increased by 13 percent per year.[29]

What kind of effect has this had on average Americans and on the culture? Since human beings are symbolic creatures, income, wealth, and health inequality matters for not only the economic well-being but also the psychological well-being of a society. It has influences in many ways. American sociologists Richard Sennett and Jonathan Cobb, in their groundbreaking study of the psychology of social class through the experience of manual laborers and their families, discovered: "The terrible thing about class in our society is that it sets up a contest for dignity,"[30] a contest that those on the bottom rung of society by definition lose. Psychologically, the hardest part of being poor is not the material deprivation but the sense of "injured dignity," or the loss of self-respect and pride when measured against others. A hierarchical system of respect thus creates an endless game of shaming and self-doubt.

Barbara Ehrenreich described in *Nickel and Dimed* her first-hand experience of how even in times of relative prosperity, many Americans were living demeaning lives on minimum wage, surviving in run-down motels, unable to afford good food as they approached payday, and on occasion sleeping in their cars.[31] People in the lowliest occupations could only get by with exceptional mental and muscular effort, sometimes working two or three jobs. A different story emerges in *Hillbilly Elegy* more than a decade later. J. D. Vance described a dysfunctional culture of substance abuse, knockdowns, fights, and a feeling that people just could not get ahead no matter what they did, which he called "learned helplessness."[32] An entire region of the country gives up without trying, and a common feeling of victimhood and a desire to blame others binds them. Excessive class differences demoralize and depress as a psychological consequence of structural violence. In 2018, Philip Alston, United Nations special rapporteur on extreme poverty and human rights, published a report saying about 40 million live in poverty, 18.5 million in extreme poverty, and 5.3 million live in Third World conditions of absolute poverty.[33]

Rather than address the sources of structural violence, the economic and social characteristics of the United States synergistically work to maximize feelings of individual responsibility and hence shame and humiliation. First, there is the Horatio Alger myth, named after a nineteenth-century American novelist of "rags to riches" stories, which says that anyone can get rich if you are smart and work hard—which also means, if you are not rich, you must be stupid, lazy, or both. Second, a whole economic system of mass production is set up to stimulate people to want to get rich; this is done through advertisements, marketing, and a flood of ever newer consumer goods. Third, a defining feature of the American Dream is that children will have better opportunities and a better life than their parents. As Chetty and colleagues showed, however, that while this dream came true for about 90 percent of children born in 1940, it held true only for half of children born in 1984.[34]

The socioeconomic reality in the United States is actually the opposite of the Horatio Alger myth. Several large studies in recent years have found, contrary to historic perceptions, that the United States is less mobile than the United Kingdom or much of Europe. In 2006, to answer the question, "Do Poor Children Become Poor Adults?" Corak reviewed more than 50 studies of nine countries and ranked Canada, Norway, Finland, and Denmark as the most mobile, with the United States and Britain roughly tied at the other extreme.[35] Jantti and colleagues found that just 8 percent of American men at the bottom rose to the top fifth, compared with 12 percent of British men and 14 percent of Danes.[36] According to the Economic Mobility Project of the Pew Charitable Trusts, about 62 percent of Americans raised in the top fifth of incomes stay in the top two fifths, while 65 percent born in the bottom fifth stay in the bottom two fifths.[37] In 2012, an Economic Report to Congress found that growing income inequality was inexorably leading to lower economic mobility—so that inequality begets inequality.[38]

The psychological effect of these features of U.S. society is that the gap between aspiration and attainment will produce far greater opportunity and intensity of feelings of inferiority and humiliation. American economists Anne Case and Angus Deaton wrote in *Deaths of Despair and the Future of Capitalism* that deaths from suicide, drug overdoses, and alcoholic liver disease are ravaging, overwhelmingly, less-educated Americans following a loss of jobs, community, and dignity. They blamed the policies and politics transforming the U.S. economy into an engine of inequality and suffering: "The American economy has shifted away from serving ordinary people and toward serving businesses, their managers, and their owners."[39]

The association between income distribution and population health is remarkable, as in the example of the United States. Despite being the richest nation on Earth, it has wider income disparities that create the conditions for a lower average life expectancy than other developed countries.[40] Trends show that, while life expectancy in the United States was similar to comparable countries in 1980, since then, the United States has gained just 4.9 years of life expectancy, while comparable countries have gained an average of 7.8 years.[41]

A society of large levels of structural violence divides the population into those who are "inferior" and those who are "superior." As this paradigm seeps into the larger culture, it works synergistically with other forms of structural violence. One reason poor Whites have not been quick to revolt against their oppression is because Black Americans have always been there to occupy a lower rung on the social ladder than even the poorest Whites. As long as there was a group to look down on from one's inferior position, one's inferior position could be tolerated and even pretended to be beneficial.[42] In this manner, economic inequality exacerbates racial inequality and White supremacist ideology. Political scientist Hannah Arendt noted that worse than humiliation is to be ignored, vis-à-vis all White, rich and poor: "The institution of slavery carries an obscurity even blacker than the obscurity of poverty; the slave, not the poor man, was 'wholly overlooked.' "[43] Many Black American authors have said this about the experience of being Black in America, notably W. E. B. DuBois, in *Dusk of Dawn*,[44] and Ralph Ellison, the title of whose novel, *The Invisible Man*,[45] expresses the same point. The 2016 election of Donald Trump to the

U.S. presidency reflects an acceleration of psychological pull, as expressed in contemporaneous publications, *White Fragility*[46] and Carol Anderson's *White Rage*,[47] which describe the White ambivalence and backlash against challenges to these assumptions.

The hidden aspects of racism are more destructive than overt ones. Racism is a system of advantage and hierarchy based on race, not merely prejudicial sentiments or beliefs.[48] Psychologists Steven Roberts and Michael Rizzo outlined the structural factors that contribute to American racism: (a) categories, which organize people into distinct groups; (b) factions, which trigger in-group loyalty and intergroup competition and threat; (c) segregation, which hardens racist perceptions, preferences, and beliefs through restrictions of intergroup contact; (d) hierarchy, which emboldens people to think, feel, and behave in racist ways; (e) power, which legislates racism on both micro and macro levels; (f) media, which legitimize overrepresented and idealized representations of White Americans while marginalizing and minimizing people of color; and (g) passivism, such that overlooking or denying the existence of racism obscures this reality, allowing racism to fester and persist.[49]

The criminal justice system exacerbates and strengthens these structures. Racial profiling refers in law enforcement to suspecting individuals of wrongdoing based on stereotypes about their race rather than on their behavior. As a result, ethnic minorities are far more likely to be arrested than White Americans. Once arrested, they are more likely to be convicted. Once convicted, they are more likely to face stiff sentences for the same crimes. Black men account for an annual rate of incarceration of Black men 3.8 to 10.5 times greater than that of White men across all age groups.[50] Black Americans are stereotyped drug addicts—despite similar prevalence of illicit drug use among White Americans—and disproportionately targeted for incarceration.[51] Even though Black Americans and White Americans are homicide victims in nearly equal numbers, four out of five executions since the reinstatement of the death penalty have involved White victims.[52] Michelle Alexander, in *The New Jim Crow*, points out that mass incarceration functions as a system of racialized social control: bringing in entire segments of minority communities and branding them as criminals relegates them to a permanent second-class status upon release, stripping them of the right to vote, to serve on juries, to be free of legal and employment discrimination, and to access education and other public benefits.[53] Furthermore, the practice of leasing out mostly Black American convicts for negligible or no income into abysmal working conditions has been called "slavery by another name."[54] The race-based murders by law enforcement personnel and the resurgence of possible lynching of Black and Brown bodies[55] go hand in hand with structural racism. Racism generates prejudice, or negative attitudes and beliefs that promote differential treatment of members of these groups by both individuals and social institutions.[56] It becomes a vehicle that systematically and institutionally injures individuals while tearing communities apart. The large, interconnected system of racism encompasses not only the criminal justice system but also housing, education, employment, healthcare, and the media. These systems and patterns of practices in turn reinforce discriminatory beliefs, values, and distribution of resources. Structural violence refers to the ease with which humans reduce the socially vulnerable to expendable "nonpersons." This implicitly gives them the license—even duty—to kill them.[57]

Although the exact mechanisms are difficult to identify, racism and racial discrimination contribute to a wide range of health inequities and negative outcomes for population health. As of 2017, Black Americans had an average life expectancy of 74.9 years at birth, compared to White Americans, who had 78.8 years.[58] Increasingly, research is linking interpersonal racism to various biomarkers of disease and well-being, such as allostatic load ("wear and tear" from chronic stress), inflammation, and hormonal imbalance.[59] Mental health effects are also considerable: Self-reported racism was associated with increased depression, anxiety, distress, psychological stress, negative affect, and post-traumatic stress, and decreased self-esteem, life satisfaction, control and mastery, and well-being.[60] Although adult physical and psychological problems would naturally have an effect on children and their development, a thorough understanding is still lagging. Stressors from prejudicial treatment, systemic barriers, and internalized oppression can operate through physiological pathways[61] and pervasively threaten well-being.[62] The concept of "linked lives"[63] and the ecological nature of human development[64] show how indirect caregivers' and general communal experiences of discrimination may influence those of children.[65] Vicarious experiences of racism can start as early as in the womb, with small-for-gestational-age births,[66] to a child's diminished sense of the world as fair, just, and safe.[67] Maternal mortality in Black women is 3.2 times as high as that of White women,[68] and infant mortality in non-Hispanic Black women is about 2.3 times that of non-Hispanic White women.[69] Caregiver experiences of racial discrimination are associated with depressive symptoms in their children[70] and lower psychological well-being in adolescents.[71] We are only beginning to come to grips with the enduring ways in which poor attachment, toxic stress, and other adverse conditions have consequences throughout the life span, with ramifications throughout society.

In this manner, structural violence forms an undercurrent in society that harms deeply. While we examined here the instance of the United States, where the trends are extreme, it is also a growing global problem. At a time when areas such as healthcare, education, and communications are advancing rapidly, the majority of humankind is increasingly left behind, with consequences that amount to life and death. There is increasing recognition that adverse environments that affect parents' ability to rear their children and have negative consequences for social harmony and health, contributing to societal and political upheavals.[72] Structural violence is the most lethal form of violence, but, being embedded within social structures, it is less perceptible and seems as merely ordinary difficulties of life. As long as unjust socioeconomic structures go unaddressed, behavioral violence, whatever the form—suicides, homicides, terrorism, or ever-evolving forms of mass violence—will find fertile ground for expression. Reliance of weapons, military, and the police only exacerbate the problem by creating new and more serious conflicts, even if they are not employed explicitly to protect the arrangements of structural violence (which they often are).[73]

We have noted that, in addition to being the deadliest form of violence, structural violence is the most potent stimulant of behavioral violence. American civil rights activist Martin Luther King Junior called the crimes of Black Americans to be "derivative crimes"—born of the greater crimes of White society.[74] We can see how this is true from the recent rises in mass shootings and of domestic terrorism among White nationalists not only in the United States but also around the world as one expression of the ravages of inequality.[75] Gilligan has drawn a relationship between structural violence—which divides society into superiority and inferiority—and the feelings of shame, stress, and humiliation that become the seed for murders, suicides, mass shootings, and wars.[76] Violent societies vary greatly, but a common characteristic is inequality. Strict hierarchies such as Japan before World War I, the Kwakiutl Native Americans, the Yanomami of South America, and the American South in the nineteenth century were all highly stratified societies, with privileged classes. This means there were always groups that belonged less and shared less in the resources and the prestige. In these societies, violence became a great source of honor and pride, while nonviolence was a source of shame. Social codes that often emphasized honor to the death led to high rates of war and violence. The same dynamic occurs in male violence: In patriarchies, strict gender roles and cultural norms cause men to establish masculinity and especially violent masculinity to set themselves apart from women as well as from other men.[77] The symbolic nature of violence makes it more about identity, recognition, and approval—and rarely survival. Violence is thus a seismograph for growing social and economic inequalities and is "individualized" insofar as it exposes the loss of social bonding forces on the one hand, and on the other, the variation in extent of individual ways of coping with social problems.[78]

As such, inequality becomes the greatest predictor of all forms of violence. A World Bank–sponsored study proved that in 39 nations around the world, homicide rates increased with inequality.[79] For 26 European nations, from

1970 to 2007, every 1 percent increase in unemployment, which is a measure of inequality,[80] indicated a 0.79 percent rise in suicides and a 0.79 percent rise in homicides.[81] Another cross-sectional study of 165 countries showed that economic development, inequality, and poverty are significant predictors of homicide, although there are many variations in homicide for lower income countries.[82] In the United States, presidencies of the Republican party, which traditionally supported more unequal social arrangements, were consistently associated with increasing rates of violent deaths, compared to Democratic presidencies, which were consistently associated with decreasing rates of violent deaths, with only two exceptions over 110 years.[83]

There are other manifestations of political decay in relation to relative deprivation or a perception of injustice arising from a growing discrepancy between expectations and economic and social realities. The structural violence of domination, exploitation, and humiliation needs to draw on physical violence in order to coerce its victims to submit. Threatened power structures are inclined to employ police brutality, and the lesser their legitimacy or authority, the greater this inclination.[84] Well-established democracies also make less war,[85] while inequality among nations is associated with interstate wars.[86]

Yet, the advantaged groups in societies of high structural violence do not always do better. In settings of high economic inequality, suicide among the poor rises drastically, but so does suicide among the rich, to a lesser degree.[87] Recent decades have witnessed, in spite of the technical and material achievements, there has been a drastic loss of social connectedness and sense of well-being. Residents of countries with higher income inequality have worse health,[88] not just of the poor[89] but of the rich.[90] Greater income inequality is also associated with higher levels of mental illness[91]; depression[92]; obesity and obesity-related death[93]; murder and assault[94]; as well as drug abuse, teenage pregnancy, racism, incarceration, and a number of other societal problems.[95] These countries also have more sociopolitical instability in the form of riots, assassinations, and coups[96]; worse institutions, including less efficient governments, higher regulatory burdens, and weaker rule of law[97]; and more corruption.[98] The wealthy have stronger motivations to keep institutions weak in order to minimize redistribution, at the same time as their having more power to influence institutions, given the relative abundance of their resources.[99] Eventually, even the rich will not be able to protect themselves exclusively in a society of rising tensions, discontent, and evolving forms of violence that increasingly threaten the entire planet through nuclear war or climate devastation.[100]

Here it is important to note the role of the global economy. While our outwardly prosperous era has great potential, any deeper examination reveals that it is not placid by any measure. Many countries have been struggling with rising food costs, growing income and wealth inequality, and the global financial

crisis and recession that generated widespread unemployment and impoverishment, all of which the recent global pandemic has worsened.[101] The spread of
democracy had an enormous effect in generating peace,[102] but only because it
came with the reduction of structural violence and of the behavioral violence it
generates.[103] As global capitalism and a system of privileges shortly followed, it
became capable of offsetting the gains of democracy.[104] As the exploitation, intimidation, and greed inherent in structural violence corrode the general health
of society, we need to be mindful of an economic structure that reproduces oligarchies or authoritarian regimes even as it squanders the democratic principles
it claims to espouse.

Nurturing awareness of structural violence is critical for avoiding being
caught in psychological exploitation. Capitalism markets to people the lure of
becoming rich as it leaves large populations poorer and more defenseless. In an
advanced economy such as the United States, the "consent" of the majority itself is manufactured[105] with increasing psychological sophistication and social
manipulation. And while material oppression is severe, none is more oppressive
than the hijacking of the mind. When human development and actualization are
stunted to the point where citizens become willing pawns for those in power,
then ever-greater structural violence is possible. Maintaining this system may
sometimes require mentally unsound leaders capable of tapping into the mal-
adaptive defenses of the population, including White supremacy—one form of
defense against feelings of inferiority. And the greater the need of the population to distract itself from reality, the more attractive it will find a leader with
delusions about himself as omnipotent savior or with paranoid tendencies that
offer easy scapegoats for one's miseries.[106]

Enduring peace, therefore, is unachievable through the mere pacification of
those who are suffering. American political scientist Quincy Wright rejected a
simplistic, negative definition of peace as the mere absence of war in favor of a
more positive definition that views peace as international justice and a spirit of
cooperation.[107] Galtung expanded this idea of a positive peace to include the social integration of human community through a more just distribution of power
and resources.[108] We can equate this notion of peace with concepts of nonviolence, whereby nonviolence is a state that is more than just the absence of violence.[109] In structural violence, perpetuation of the status quo itself becomes a
perpetration, but at the same time we are all capable of instituting change for the
better, and the suffering can arouse the power of the people.

There are hopeful signs in the midst of rising structural violence. While
vulnerable groups are often the first to succumb to the kinds of behavioral violence that prevent personal, local, and national development, with critical consciousness, these weaknesses can be transformed into knowledge and power.[110]
Greater awareness of the need to defend vulnerable populations led to the 1993

World Conference on Human Rights, which animated the 50th anniversary celebrations of the 1948 Universal Declaration of Human Rights and ultimately influenced the 2030 Agenda for Sustainable Development. It has become possible to envision:

> a world of . . . equal opportunity permitting the full realization of human potential and contributing to shared prosperity. . . . One in which democracy, good governance and the rule of law as well as an enabling environment at national and international levels, are essential for sustainable development.[111]

Indeed, this vision has become mandatory if humanity is to survive beyond the immediate future.

Structural violence is human-made, and the positive aspect of this is that it can be human-corrected. As daunting as the deeper structures of human violence may seem, a more profound understanding is possible and, with it, more enduring solutions. The common roots of our problems reveal how early, preventive measures can lead to widespread results that allow for global human thriving. Hence, recognizing the abyss and fully understanding it gives us a greater capacity for solutions. Awareness helps us to decide on policies that reduce all forms of violence at the structural level, with vast reductions of suffering at a very small cost. What we gain psychologically should not be underestimated: Social solidarity, or a feeling of participation, connection, and belonging would resolve many problems, including the divisions we create over cohesion and meaning. As American Reformed theologian Reinhold Niebuhr noted, and as American philosopher Cornell West echoed, justice is how love takes expression in public.[112] When we can locate the source of our collective suffering in ourselves and learn to recognize and refuse the violence before it takes root everywhere in all forms, we can then begin to transform our world.

Notes

1. Johan Galtung, "Violence, Peace, and Peace Research," *Journal of Peace Research* 6, no. 3 (1969): 167–191.
2. Gustavo Gutiérrez, *A Theology of Liberation: History, Politics, and Salvation* (Maryknoll, NY: Orbis Books, 1973).
3. Johan Galtung, "Twenty-Five Years of Peace Research: Ten Challenges and Some Responses," *Journal of Peace Research* 22, no. 2 (1985): 141–158.
4. Gernot Köhler and Norman Alcock, "An Empirical Table of Structural Violence," *Journal of Peace Research* 13, no. 4 (1976): 343–356.
5. Johan Galtung and Tord Høivik, "Structural and Direct Violence: A Note on Operationalization," *Journal of Peace Research* 8, no. 1 (1971): 73–76.

6. World Health Organization, *Health Equity Through Action on the Social Determinants of Health* (Geneva: World Health Organization, 2008) http://apps.who.int/iris/bitstream/handle/10665/43943/9789241563703_eng.pdf?sequence=1

7. Alexander Butchart and Karin Engström, "Sex-and Age-Specific Relations Between Economic Development, Economic Inequality and Homicide Rates in People Aged 0–24 Years: A Cross-Sectional Analysis," *Bulletin of the World Health Organization* 80 (2002): 797–805.

8. Richard G. Wilkinson and Kate E. Pickett, "Income Inequality and Socioeconomic Gradients in Mortality," *American Journal of Public Health* 98, no. 4 (2008): 699–704.

9. James Gilligan, "Structural Violence," in *Violence in the United States: An Encyclopedia*, ed. Ronald Gottesman (New York: Scribners and Sons, 1999), 229–233.

10. James Gilligan, *Preventing Violence* (London: Thames and Hudson, 2001).

11. Sandra L. Bloom, *Violence: A Public Health Menace and a Public Health Approach* (London: Karnac Books, 2001).

12. Paul Farmer, *Pathologies of Power: Health, Human Rights, and the New War on the Poor* (Berkeley: University of California Press, 2001).

13. Barak Morgan et al., "Genes, Brains, Safety, and Justice," in *Pathways to Peace: The Transformative Power of Children and Families*, ed. James F. Leckman, Catherine Panter-Brick, and Rima Salah (Cambridge, MA: M.I.T. Press, 2014), 15:95–128.

14. Deborah DuNann Winter and Dorothea Cross Leighton, "Structural Violence," in *Peace, Conflict, and Violence*, ed. Daniel J. Christie, Richard V. Wagner, and Deborah DuNann (New York: Prentice Hall, 2001), 585–599.

15. Amartya K. Sen, *Choice, Welfare, and Measurement* (Cambridge, MA: MIT Press, 1982).

16. Morgan et al., "Genes, Brains, Safety, and Justice."

17. Kathleen Ho, "Structural Violence as A Human Rights Violation," *Essex Human Rights Review* 4, no. 2 (2007): 1–17.

18. Akhil Gupta, *Red Tape: Bureaucracy, Structural Violence, and Poverty in India* (Durham, NC: Duke University Press, 2012).

19. Butchart and Engström, "Sex- and Age-Specific Relations."

20. Robert Jay Lifton, *The Broken Connection: On Death and the Continuity of Life* (New York: Touchstone, 1979).

21. Steven Pinker, *The Better Angels of Our Nature: Why Violence Has Declined* (New York: Viking, 2011).

22. Jennifer Mitzen, "The Irony of Pinkerism," *Perspectives on Politics* 11, no. 2 (2013): 525–528.

23. Etienne G. Krug et al., *World Report on Violence and Health* (Geneva: World Health Organization, 2002), http://apps.who.int/iris/bitstream/10665/42495/1/9241545 615_eng.pdf.

24. Centers for Disease Control and Prevention (CDC), *Compressed Mortality File* (Washington, DC: Centers for Disease Control and Prevention), https://wonder.cdc.gov/mortsql.html.

25. Bandy X. Lee, *Violence: An Interdisciplinary Approach to Causes, Consequences, and Cures* (New York: Wiley-Blackwell, 2019).

26. Robert Jay Lifton, *The Future of Immortality and Other Essays for a Nuclear Age* (New York: Basic Books, 1987).

27. Facundo Alvaredo et al., "The World Wealth and Income Database, 2015," 2015, http://www.wid.world/.

28. Jessica Semega et al., "Income and Poverty in the United States: 2018," in *Current Population Reports* (Washington, DC: U.S. Census Bureau, 2019), 60–266.

29. Steven Greenhouse, *The Big Squeeze: Tough Times for the American Worker* (New York: Anchor, 2009).

30. Richard Sennett and Jonathan Cobb, *The Hidden Injuries of Class* (New York: Vintage, 1972).

31. Barbara Ehrenreich, *Nickel and Dimed* (New York: Henry Holt, 2001).

32. J. D. Vance, *Hillbilly Elegy: A Memoir of a Family and Culture in Crisis* (New York: HarperCollins Books, 2016).

33. United Nations, "Report of the Special Rapporteur on Extreme Poverty and Human Rights on His Mission to the United States of America," 2018, https://undocs.org/A/HRC/38/33/ADD.1.

34. Raj Chetty et al., "The Fading American Dream: Trends in Absolute Income Mobility Since 1940," *Science* 356, no. 6336 (2017): 398–406.

35. Miles Corak, "Do Poor Children Become Poor Adults? Lessons From a Cross-Country Comparison of Generational Earnings Mobility," *Research on Economic Inequality* 13, no. 1 (2006): 143–188.

36. Markus Jantti et al., "American Exceptionalism in a New Light: A Comparison of Intergenerational Earnings Mobility in the Nordic Countries, the United Kingdom and the United States," 2006, http://ftp.iza.org/dp1938.pdf.

37. Jason DeParle, "Harder for Americans to Rise From Lower Rungs," *New York Times*, January 4, 2012.

38. Robert Lenzner, "Income Inequality From Generation to Generation," *Forbes*, May 26, 2012.

39. Anne Case and Angus Deaton, *Deaths of Despair and the Future of Capitalism* (Princeton, NJ: Princeton University Press, 2020).

40. Sandeep C. Kulkarni et al., "Falling Behind: Life Expectancy in US Counties From 2000 to 2007 in an International Context," *Population Health Metrics* 9, no. 1 (2011): 16.

41. Organization for Economic Cooperation and Development, "Life Expectancy at Birth," 2020, https://doi.org/10.1787/27e0fc9d-en.

42. James Gilligan, *Violence: Our Deadly Epidemic and Its Causes* (New York: G. P. Putnam, 1996).

43. Hannah Arendt, *On Revolution* (New York: Viking, 1963).

44. W. E. B. DuBois, *Dusk of Dawn* (New York: Harcourt, Brace, 1940).

45. Ralph Ellison, *The Invisible Man* (New York: Random House, 1952).

46. Robin DiAngelo, *White Fragility* (Boston: Beacon Press, 2018).

47. Carol Anderson, *White Rage: The Unspoken Truth of Our Racial Divide* (London: Bloomsbury, 2016).

48. David T. Wellman, *Portraits of White Racism* (Cambridge: Cambridge University Press, 1993).

49. Steven Roberts and Michael Rizzo, "The Psychology of American Racism," *OSF Preprints*, June 1, 2020, https://doi.org/10.31219/osf.io/w2h73.
50. E. Ann Carson, *Prisoners in 2014 (NCJ 248955)* (Washington, DC: Bureau of Justice Statistics, 2015).
51. Elizabeth K. Hinton, *From the War on Poverty to the War on Crime: The Making of Mass Incarceration in America* (Cambridge, MA: Harvard University Press, 2016).
52. David C. Baldus, George Woodworth, and Charles A. Pulaski, *Equal Justice and the Death Penalty: A Legal and Empirical Analysis* (Boston: Northeastern University Press, 1990).
53. Michelle Alexander, *The New Jim Crow: Mass Incarceration in the Age of Colorblindness* (New York: New Press, 2010).
54. Douglas A. Blackmon, *Slavery by Another Name: The Re-Enslavement of Black Americans From the Civil War to World War II* (New York: Anchor, 2008).
55. Stacey Patton, "Police Say Deaths of Black People by Hanging Are Suicides. Many Black People Aren't So Sure," *Washington Post*, June 22, 2020.
56. David R. Williams and Selina A. Mohammed, "Discrimination and Racial Disparities in Health: Evidence and Needed Research," *Journal of Behavioral Medicine* 32, no. 1 (2009): 20–47.
57. Nancy Scheper-Hughes, "Small Wars and Invisible Genocides," *Social Science and Medicine* 43, no. 5 (1996): 889–900.
58. Elizabeth Arias, and Jiaquan Xu, "United States Life Tables, 2017" *National Vital Statistics Reports* 68, no. 7 (June 24, 2019).
59. Yin Paradies et al., "Racism as a Determinant of Health: A Systematic Review and Meta-Analysis," *PloS One* 10, no. 9 (2015): e0138511.
60. Paradies et al., "Racism."
61. Bruce S. McEwen, "Stressed or Stressed Out: What Is the Difference?" *Journal of Psychiatry and Neuroscience* 30, no. 5 (2005): 315–318.
62. Hector F. Myers, Tene T. Lewis, and Tyan Parker-Dominguez, "Stress, Coping and Minority Health," in *Handbook of Racial and Ethnic Minority Psychology*, ed. Guillermo Bernal (Thousand Oaks, CA: Sage, 2003), 4:377–400.
63. Gilbert C. Gee, Katrina M. Walsemann, and Elizabeth Brondolo, "A Life Course Perspective on How Racism May Be Related to Health Inequities," *American Journal of Public Health* 102, no. 5 (2012): 967–974.
64. Urie Bronfenbrenner, *The Ecology of Human Development* (Cambridge, MA: Harvard University Press, 1979).
65. Nancy Krieger, "Discrimination and Health," *Social Epidemiology* 1 (2000): 36–75.
66. Maeve E. Wallace et al., "Joint Effects of Structural Racism and Income Inequality on Small-for-Gestational-Age Birth," *American Journal of Public Health* 105, no. 8 (2015): 1681–1688.
67. Tyan Parker Dominguez et al., "Racial Differences in Birth Outcomes: The Role of General, Pregnancy, and Racism Stress," *Health Psychology* 27, no. 2 (2008): 194.
68. Emily E. Petersen et al., "Racial/Ethnic Disparities in Pregnancy-Related Deaths— United States, 2007–2016," *Morbidity and Mortality Weekly Report* 68, no. 35 (2019): 762–765.

69. Sherry L. Murphy et al., *Mortality in the United States, 2017. N.C.H.S. Data Brief 328* (Washington, DC: U.S. Centers for Disease Control and Prevention, 2018).

70. Ronald L. Simons et al., "Discrimination, Crime, Ethnic Identity, and Parenting as Correlates of Depressive Symptoms Among African American Children: A Multilevel Analysis," *Development and Psychopathology* 14, no. 2 (2002): 371–393.

71. Kahlil R. Ford et al., "Caregiver Experiences of Discrimination and African American Adolescents' Psychological Health Over Time," *Child Development* 84, no. 2 (2013): 485–499.

72. James F. Leckman, Catherine Panter-Brick, and Rima Salah, eds., *Pathways to Peace: The Transformative Power of Children and Families*, vol. 15 (Cambridge, MA: M.I.T. Press, 2014).

73. Nick Buxton and Ben Hayes, eds. *The Secure and the Dispossessed: How the Military and Corporations Are Shaping a Climate-Changed World* (London: Pluto Press, 2016).

74. Martin Luther King Jr., "Nobel Peace Prize Lecture: The Quest for Peace and Justice. Stockholm: Nobel Foundation," 1964, http://www.nobelprize.org/nobel_prizes/peace/laureates/1964/king-lecture.html.

75. Barry Sheppard, "Mass Shootings Reveal Danger of White Supremacist Terror," *Green Left Weekly* 1233 (2019): 12.

76. James Gilligan, *Violence: Our Deadly Epidemic and Its Causes* (New York: Putnam, 1996).

77. Michael Meuser, "Doing Masculinity: Zur Geschlechtslogik männlichen Gewalthandelns," in *Gewalt-Verhältnisse: feministische Perspektiven auf Geschlecht und Gewalt*, ed. Regina-Maria Dackweiler and Reinhild Schäfer (Frankfurt, Germany: Campus Verlag, 2002), 19:53–78.

78. Wilhelm Heitmeyer and John Hagan, *International Handbook on Violence Research*, (Dordrecht, Netherlands: Kluwer, 2003).

79. Pablo Fajnzylber, Daniel Lederman, and Norman Loayza, "Inequality and Violent Crime," *Journal of Law and Economics* 45, no. 1 (2002): 1–40.

80. James K. Galbraith, *Created Unequal: The Crisis in American Pay* (New York: Free Press, 1998).

81. David Stuckler et al., "The Public Health Effect of Economic Crises and Alternative Policy Responses in Europe: An Empirical Analysis," *Lancet* 374, no. 9686 (2009): 315–323.

82. Marc Ouimet, "A World of Homicides: The Effect of Economic Development, Income Inequality, and Excess Infant Mortality on the Homicide Rate for 165 Countries in 2010," *Homicide Studies* 16, no. 3 (2012): 238–258.

83. Bandy X. Lee, Bruce E. Wexler, and James Gilligan, "Political Correlates of Violent Death Rates in the U.S., 1900–2010: Longitudinal and Cross-Sectional Analyses," *Aggression and Violent Behavior* 19, no. 6 (2014): 721–728.

84. Hannah Arendt, *On Violence* (New York: Harcourt Brace Jovanovich, 1970).

85. R. J. Rummel, *Power Kills: Democracy as a Method of Nonviolence* (Piscataway, NJ: Transaction Books, 2003).

86. Stephen Van Evera, *Causes of War: Power and the Roots of Conflict* (Ithaca, NY: Cornell University Press, 20130.

87. Mary C. Daly, Daniel J. Wilson, and Norman J. Johnson, "Relative Status and Well-Being: Evidence From US Suicide Deaths," *Review of Economics and Statistics* 95, no. 5 (2013): 1480–1500.

88. Jason Beckfield, "Does Income Inequality Harm Health? New Cross-National Evidence," *Journal of Health and Social Behavior* 45, no. 3 (2004): 231–248.

89. Richard G. Wilkinson, "Income Distribution and Life Expectancy," *British Medical Journal* 304, no. 6820 (1992): 165–168.

90. Subu V. Subramanian and Ichiro Kawachi, "Income Inequality and Health: What Have We Learned So Far?" *Epidemiologic Reviews* 26, no. 1 (2004): 78–91.

91. Jonathan K. Burns, Andrew Tomita, and Amy S. Kapadia, "Income Inequality and Schizophrenia: Increased Schizophrenia Incidence in Countries With High Levels of Income Inequality," *International Journal of Social Psychiatry* 60, no. 2 (2014): 185–196.

92. Erick Messias, William W. Eaton, and Amy N. Grooms, "Economic Grand Rounds: Income Inequality and Depression Prevalence Across the United States: An Ecological Study," *Psychiatric Services* 62, no. 7 (2011): 710–712.

93. Kate E. Pickett et al., "Wider Income Gaps, Wider Waistbands? An Ecological Study of Obesity and Income Inequality," *Journal of Epidemiology and Community Health* 59, no. 8 (2005): 670–674.

94. Ching-Chi Hsieh and Meredith D. Pugh, "Poverty, Income Inequality, and Violent Crime: A Meta-Analysis of Recent Aggregate Data Studies," *Criminal Justice Review* 18, no. 2 (1993): 182–202.

95. Richard G. Wilkinson and Kate Pickett, *The Spirit Level: Why More Equal Societies Almost Always Do Better* (London: Allen Lane, 2009).

96. Alberto Alesina and Roberto Perotti, "Income Distribution, Political Instability, and Investment," *European Economic Review* 40, no. 6 (1996): 1203–1228.

97. William Easterly, "Inequality Does Cause Underdevelopment: Insights From a New Instrument," *Journal of Development Economics* 84, no. 2 (2007): 755–776.

98. Jong-Sung You and Sanjeev Khagram, "A Comparative Study of Inequality and Corruption," *American Sociological Review* 70, no. 3 (2005): 136–157.

99. Nicholas R. Buttrick and Shigehiro Oishi, "The Psychological Consequences of Income Inequality," *Social and Personality Psychology Compass* 11, no. 3 (2017): e12304.

100. Bandy X. Lee, *Violence*.

101. World Bank Group, *Global Economic Prospects* (Washington, DC: World Bank, 2020), https://www.worldbank.org/en/publication/global-economic-prospects.

102. Michael W. Doyle, "Kant, Liberal Legacies, and Foreign Affairs," *Philosophy and Public Affairs* 2, no. 3 (1983): 205–235.

103. Phillip Marotta et al., "Government Political Structure and Violent Death Rates: A Longitudinal Analysis of Forty-Three Countries, 1960–2008," *Aggression and Violent Behavior* 47, no. 1 (2019): 262–267.

104. Noreena Hertz, *The Silent Takeover: Global Capitalism and the Death of Democracy* (New York: Simon and Schuster, 2002).

105. Noam Chomsky and Edward S. Herman, *Manufacturing Consent: The Political Economy of the Mass Media* (New York: Pantheon Books, 1988).

106. Jerrold M. Post, *Leaders and Their Followers in a Dangerous World: The Psychology of Political Behavior* (Ithaca, NY: Cornell University Press, 2004).
107. Quincy Wright, *A Study of War* (Chicago: University of Chicago Press, 1942).
108. Johan Galtung, "A Structural Theory of Integration," *Journal of Peace Research* 5, no. 4 (1968): 375–395.
109. Richard Bartlett Gregg, *The Power of Non-Violence* (London: Routledge, 1936).
110. Paulo Freire, *Pedagogy of the Oppressed* (New York: Seabury Press, 1968).
111. United Nations, *Transforming Our World: The 2030 Agenda for Sustainable Development* (New York: United Nations, 2015), https://sustainabledevelopment. un.org/content/documents/21252030%20Agenda%20for%20Sustainable%20Deve lopment%20web.pdf.
112. J. Sharlet, "The Supreme Love and Revolutionary Funk of Dr. Cornel West, Philosopher of the Blues," *Rolling Stone*, May 28, 2009, 54–61.

PART I
COVID-19, INEQUALITY, AND FREEDOM

4

Normalizing Inequality in the Age
of COVID-19

Henry A. Giroux

Inequality under neoliberal capitalism is a cancer that functions as a form of slow violence that attacks the social fabric, the welfare state, and the body politic. It is all the more visible as a result of the current pandemic crisis. It relentlessly subjects workers, the disabled, the homeless, the poor, children, people of color, and more recently front-line hospital and emergency workers and all those others considered at risk to lives of despair, precarity, and in some cases death.[1] Many others are just one hospital bill or failed harvest away from slipping into extreme poverty. In some cases, people who cannot afford healthcare are being put in jail over medical bills.[2] The statistics on inequality globally are scandalous. Oxfam International 2019 reported the following:

> The world's richest 1% have more than twice as much wealth as 6.9 billion people who make up 60 percent of the planet's population. Meanwhile, around 735 million people are still living in extreme poverty. [In addition] the super-rich are paying the lowest levels of taxes in decades while 10,000 people die each day because they lack access to affordable health care. In addition, over 100 million people are pushed into extreme poverty due to healthcare costs."[3]

Another stark statistic reveals that in 2018, the world's 26 richest men had as much wealth as the poorest half of the world's population, some 3.8 billion people. Nearly 3 billion people, half of the world's population, live on less than $2.50 a day, and "more than 1.3 billion live in extreme poverty—less than $1.25 a day."[4] In the United States, the wealthiest three billionaires—Jeff Bezos, Bill Gates, and Warren Buffett—have as much wealth as the bottom half of the U.S. population combined.[5] Yet, inequality historically under neoliberal capitalism has been either largely ignored by the mainstream press or treated as part of the natural order.[6] Prior to the pandemic, the gap between the rich and the poor widened to dangerous levels without being seen as a major societal and political problem. In an age of increasing inequality, punishing class divisions, extreme poverty, and the collapse of democratic institutions and civic culture, neoliberal capitalism

Henry A. Giroux, *Normalizing Inequality in the Age of COVID-19* In: *On Inequality and Freedom*. Edited by: Lawrence M. Eppard and Henry A. Giroux, Oxford University Press. © Oxford University Press 2022. DOI: 10.1093/oso/9780197583029.003.0004 is a presence that needs to be more fully understood and challenged. In the current historical moment, rapidly escalating levels of inequality cannot be divorced from the political formation in which it is legitimated and reproduced. At the very least, neoliberalism and inequality with their historical and contemporary roots and antidemocratic and authoritarian tendencies need to be denaturalized, removed from the calculus of commonsense, and challenged as a political, economic, and ideological regime of management and control.

Since the election of President Ronald Reagan in 1980, the financial elite and right-wing populists have gained increasing control of a range of cultural apparatuses and pedagogical platforms. One effect has been that the categories of class, class divisions, and extreme iniquitous relations of power have largely disappeared from the vocabulary of neoliberal political culture and the mainstream media.[7] For the last few decades, the prescient comment attributed to both Fredric Jameson and Slavoj Zizek "that it is easier to imagine the end of the world than to imagine the end of capitalism" has been deeply ingrained as a widely held and commonsense belief in American politics.[8]

Viewed as part of the natural order, it was assumed that capitalism and democracy were the same thing. Furthermore, neoliberalism was not only viewed as a template for shaping a market-driven economy but also elevated to the status of a worldview designed to govern all aspects of social life. Neoliberalism as an ideological and pedagogical system conflated freedom with an unchecked individualism, argued for citizens as consumers, and created modes of identification that celebrated harsh competition, commercial relations, and the elevation of self-interest to a national ideal. In addition, the political sovereignty of the state morphed into a form of corporate sovereignty as political and class power were consolidated in the hands of the financial elite. The state was now remade on the model of finance and used to dismantle an array of social institutions while promoting policies that rescued, benefitted, privileged, and protected the economy. At the same time, ideology was weaponized in its defense of neoliberal capital and grotesque forms of inequality. The structural and ideological forces that laid the foundation for neoliberalism were considered beyond the pale of the dreams, imagination, and hopes for a future. Neoliberalism as both a politics and ideology was taken for granted, free from the ruthless forms of class divisions, racism, culture of self-absorption, survival-of-the-fittest ethic, unrestrained individualism, and market-driven modes of agency at the heart of what it meant to be human in a society where the very notion of the social was viewed with disdain.

Since the 1970s, in particular, inequities in wealth and power paved the way for a neoliberal project intent on deregulating restrictions on corporate power, cutting taxes for the rich, expanding the military, privatizing public education, suppressing civil liberties, waging a war against dissent, treating Black communities as war zones, and dismantling all public goods. The war on the social sphere, the social safety net, and notions of compassion, mutual dependencies, community, and democratic values gave way to an erosion of civic culture and shared notions of citizenship. Education was increasingly instrumentalized and defined through market metrics. Every American president from Reagan on argued for utterly instrumental and technocratic educational reforms based on a corporate and market-driven rationality.[9] Training now passes as the dominant form of education, while ignorance, especially under the Trump regime, has become an organizing principle for a spectacularized mode of politics and governance. Neoliberal rationality has also intensified and accelerated a culture of selfishness and cruelty in a social order defined increasingly through the Hobbesian categories of winners and losers, terms endemic to the reality TV programming that paved the way for Trumpism. In addition, those who benefitted from deep inequities in society were recast as heroes, flat-earth-level ignorance became a cultural standard, and the level of social atomization and alienation "reached such a state that it seem(ed) as if the world [was] in danger of ending."[10]

Thresholds of Disappearance

Mark Jenkins, writing in *The Point*, observed, "Absence creates a space where presence can be sought. And, just maybe, where presence can be discovered."[11] Taken further, it can be said that every society has an imaginary zone of willful barbarism that it wishes to hide accompanied by a threshold of disappearance in which matters of power, class, exclusion, violence, and poverty are rendered invisible. How else to explain the apathy and moral indifference to obscene levels of poverty and inequality on the part of the U.S. public in light of the fact that "nearly 23 percent of households said they lacked money to get enough food, compared with about 16 percent during the worst of the Great Recession [and] among households with children, the share without enough food was nearly 35 percent, up from about 21 percent in the previous downturn."[12]

Neoliberalism's threshold of disappearance is buttressed by a rampant and depoliticizing language and culture of consumerism and the heavy hand of systemic violence administered through incapacitating social and economic structures. For those considered disposable, life is either defined by the exhaustive and debilitating efforts to just survive amid widespread precarity, inequality, and the collapse of the welfare state. For those rendered invisible or in fear by virtue of their ethnicity, color, or class, survival takes on a more desperate register with the threat of incarceration, police violence, and incarceration or deportation. Under such circumstances, the space for meaningful collective action disappears as the social sphere collapses into a market-driven space of solitary individuals, the collapse of the social contract, "mounting egoization," and social atomization.[13] Or one is rendered mute under the heavy hand of the punishing state and the militarization of everyday life. The latter points to the fact that neoliberalism is not only about economic structures and policies, but also about a pandemic pedagogy that legitimates a depoliticizing form of individualism, a brand of economic Darwinism that promotes ruthless competitiveness that degrades collaboration, a punitive militarized value system based on a survival-of-the-fittest ethos, an attack against equality, and a war against dissent. The endpoint here is not only the intensification of economic and social inequality, but also the emergence of what I have called neoliberal fascism.[14]

This worldview gains its power through its ability to both normalize itself and to make its power invisible by hiding the ideological narratives that define it. John and Jean Comaroff rightly capture the ongoing nature of this process with the following observation:

> There is a strong argument to be made that neoliberal capitalism in its millennial moment, portends the death of politics by hiding its own ideological underpinnings in the dictates of economic efficiency: in the fetishism of the free market, in the inexorable, expanding needs of business, in the imperatives of science and technology. Or, if it does not conduce to the death of politics, it tends to reduce them to the pursuit of pure interest, individual or collective."[15]

Isolation, accentuated by the COVID-19 pandemic, is normalized through what feels like "living in a continuous present."[16] Under Trump, the effects of this shattering of the social revealed a politics without a conscience, a permanent lockdown in an imposed culture of Trumpian ignorance, lies, and corruption—all of "which threaten[s] to normalize the outrageous, and numb people to the very real threats posed to our democracy."[17] Clearly, this form of ideological hegemony individualizes the social and further argues, in the words of Margaret Thatcher: "There is no such thing as society. . . . There are only individuals and families."[18] Thatcher echoed here one of neoliberalism's central beliefs that structural issues such as economic inequality, the abuse of corporate power, and the concentration of wealth and power in a few hands do not count as serious political categories while further legitimating stripping government of its civic functions and social responsibilities. Central to neoliberal ideology is the notion that economic activity and human action can be removed from social costs. There is no room in this overcharged notion of self-referentiality for the concerns, needs, and suffering of others. Moral impulses, empathy, and compassion now dissolve into a dystopian era of nihilist passions and apocalyptic prophecies. This is an era marked by the proliferation of disimagination workstations and a depoliticizing politics that wages war on historical memory, moral witnessing, and critical thought. Pandemic pedagogy gains its strength at a moment in history when the relationship between cultural institutions, political power, and everyday life emerge as powerful new historical configurations of power and repression.

The Burden of Freedom

Neoliberalism is a politics written in the language of market fundamentalism and ideological deceit. This is a language in which freedom is reduced to consuming, and responsibility is recast as a responsibility limited to oneself. This is what Erich Fromm termed "freedom from" in his monumental *Escape from Freedom*. Freedom in this view is hollowed out and reduced to freedom from outside interference, which in neoliberal ideology translates into the notion that politics and government are the enemy of freedom when they attempt to regulate corporations, markets, and workings of the financial elite. As Wendy Brown succinctly put it, under neoliberalism rationality has an "antipathy to power sharing" and narrows the role of freedom to the autonomy of the economic sphere and the deregulation of markets. According to Brown:

> [Neoliberalism] . . . treats politics and democracy as at best ruining markets and at worst leading toward tyrannical social justice programs and totalitarianism. It solicits in the place of politics and democracy a form of statism based on business principles and the support of markets a statism that includes law and policing, and a strong measure of authority."[19]

At work here is the assumption that, on the one hand, corporations should not be regulated, and on the other, it legitimates the notion that individuals should be free to do anything they wish irrespective of larger social consequences. This regressive notion of freedom signals not only the fragility and erasure of human bonds, but also an assault on the foundations of democracy itself.

This regressive definition of freedom in the parlance of the market is tied to a notion of choice absent any understanding of the larger constraints that limit the choices individuals make. In this discourse, freedom and choice become synonymous, collapsing into a politics that is utterly personal and market driven, suggesting that the choices we make are mostly the result of individual character, will power, and resilience. The emphasis on freedom of choice is a core assumption of neoliberalism that is "granted in theory but unattainable in practice" without, what Zygmunt Bauman has termed, the collective support of the social state.[20] This view is nothing more than an apology for inequality and functions to largely blame the victims for the circumstances that limit both their access to power and their capacity for being full-fledged active agents who learn how to govern rather than be governed.

Michael D. Yates, the renowned economist, has argued that in this fantasy world of neoliberalism, low wages, unemployment, poverty, and other social problems are the direct result of choices made by individuals.[21] Unequal power disappears to suggest that, for instance, children born into extreme poverty have the same chances in life as individuals born into rich families. Zygmunt Bauman has argued rightly that freedom in the neoliberal playbook is localized in the sphere of consumption and self-advancement and loses "any connection with the most important thing: believing that you can change something in the world."[22] Crucial here is the implied notion that individual freedom is not possible without communal freedom exercised in conjunction with a fully functioning social state that guarantees not only political and personal freedom but also economic rights.[23]

The more amplified notion of freedom, what Fromm called "freedom to," does not suggest a withdrawal into a privatized universe but a full-fledged critical engagement with society in all of its political, economic, and social registers. In this sense, freedom becomes the crucial foundation for agency. In certain circumstances, the freedom to can be onerous for a critical mass of people and too difficult to bear and they "take the opportunity to cede their agency—whether it's to Martin Luther, Adolf Hitler, or Donald Trump." Coupled with the notion that there is no alternative to neoliberal capitalism, both the fear of freedom and its collapse into the private sphere aids in the shrinking of the horizons of the political. It also undercuts meaningful notions of solidarity, the social sphere, and public goods and must be analyzed and critically engaged for both the immense injustices it perpetuates and the ruling interest it serves. In a time of plagues when the false promises of capitalism lose their force, new opportunities emerge to examine the failures of neoliberalism, especially its ideologically bankrupt notion of freedom, which can be exposed along with its fog of ideological mystification.

Learning From History

In the midst of disasters such as the 2008 financial crisis, capitalism's threshold of disappearance was ruptured, making visible the destruction and hardship wrought by the austerity policies of hypercapitalism. Attempts to challenge neoliberal capitalism in the aftermath of the financial crisis were evident in the rise of both left and right populist movements, which "eroded the political and intellectual hegemony of the all-encompassing [neoliberal] worldview."[24] This was particularly true with the rise of the Occupy movement, which mounted an impressive but short-lived protest against economic inequality while attempting to further social and economic justice in the name of a radical democracy. Yet, in the end, it did not provide sufficient resistance to challenge and delegitimize neoliberal capitalism. In part, this was evident not only in the failure to create a sustainable mass movement against the modern plague of inequality, but also in its inability to bring together a range of siloed left movements in order to challenge with a mass political formation the rise of the neoliberal punishing state and its draconian austerity measures and its shameful bailing out of the banks, hedge funds, and other criminal enterprises. In the end, the financial crisis further ruptured social bonds and accelerated class divisions by creating a red-hot anger, especially among elements of the White working class who would later give their allegiance and votes to the alleged antiestablishment, hate-mongering, ultranationalist Donald Trump.

What we can learn from this history is the need to engage what I have called the violence of organized forgetting.[25] To paraphrase Antonio Gramsci, periods of social and historical amnesia often emerge out of a crisis in which the old is dying and the new is emerging. In such historical moments, or what might be called an interregnum, language and its relationship to power, politics, and everyday life become vivid and take on a measure of urgency. Jason Frank rightly argued that in periods of crisis new political forms emerge that "challenge 'politics as usual' as well as the concepts we use to navigate that familiar terrain."[26] Such formations can be either liberatory or oppressive, giving rise to either right-wing or left-wing forms of populism or a mix of both. The current COVID-19 pandemic offers the possibility of learning how the financial crisis of 2008, which exposed the intellectual project of neoliberalism, failed to give rise to a sustained form of collective resistance. In this case, a mass resistance capable of overthrowing the neoliberal machinery of death that canceled out the future by making inequality, mass poverty, and weak civic institutions a blueprint for the social order.

This pedagogical project of learning from history would have analyzed how the workings of the Trump administration accelerated the worse dimensions of neoliberalism as both an economic movement and as a form of pandemic pedagogy. The challenge here would be to analyze Trump's rise to power as both symptomatic and the endpoint of a politics characterized by a failed state, a broken and cruel economy, and a culture that celebrated unchecked individualism, scoleric notions of personal responsibility, and a regressive view of character as the sole determinant of agency and the choices made by individuals. This would be an initial step in a crucial but incomplete strategy to begin to energize the collective imagination and the call to mass resistance to break through the arc of deceit and denial at the heart of neoliberal capitalism with its mix of fear, uncertainty, precarity, misery, and extreme inequality. If one takes at face value Marx's misrepresented statement to not merely interpret the world, but to change it, the assertion can be interpreted as a call for blind activism. A more insightful reading points to Marx suggesting that one has to understand history and the world before a change can take place in a meaningful way. Rather than a call for blind activism, Marx wanted to situate how we thought "about social problems within history rather than outside it."[27] This is precisely why historical memory and education are central to politics and the bedrock of critical agency and individual and collective resistance.

With Trump's elevation to the presidency, the punishing state was put, without apology, into high gear, and modes of neoliberal governance took a more expansive and dangerous turn. Not only was the carceral state expanded, especially with regard to the incarceration of undocumented immigrants and poor people of color, but also it accelerated its increasing efforts to criminalize social problems rather than dealing with their systemic causes.[28] Hence, matters of poverty, homelessness, dissent, social rights, and civil disobedience are treated as crimes. The irony, if not the moral barbarism, at work here is hard to miss. In a society in which massive inequalities in wealth and power have reached obscene levels, it is the powerless, and vulnerable who suffer from draconian and punitive state policies the most.

Furthermore, as wealth and power become more concentrated in fewer hands, politics becomes more corrupt, colonized by a financial elite intent on destroying any of the democratic institutions designed to limit the power and wealth of the financial players that now dominate the economy. Pandemic pedagogy functions to induce a type of sleepwalking, turning people into the walking dead unwilling or unable to think critically and act responsibly, especially in the midst of the COVID-19 crisis. As politics is emptied of any substantive meaning, Trump's pedagogical apparatuses go into overtime to ensure that people become blind to the plague in all of its forms.

The ongoing dynamic of state and ideological repression has accelerated in the last decade out of the realization on the part of the ruling elite that as soon as people recognize that market relations are social categories, shaped by relations of power, the ideological force of neoliberalism might break down, opening the door to new political arrangements and modes of resistance. Put differently, when the political, economic, and social damages produced through extreme inequality become impossible to ignore, capitalism faces both a structural crisis and a legitimation crisis and will do everything possible to downplay the systemic roots of such a crisis while increasing the heavy hand of state repression. This may be premature, but the COVID-19 crisis has exposed in stark relief the draconian nature of the pandemic of inequality and neoliberal capitalism, especially for "the bottom rung of the working class" and those deemed essential workers."[29] Joan Benach insightfully analyzes the elements of neoliberal economics at work behind the current pandemic, stating that the existing global medical crisis cannot be seen as part of the natural order of things. She wrote:

> And what's behind it all? A systemic process of accumulation, exponential growth and inequality, inherent to an unbridled economic system, that is, capitalism, which, as many scientific studies show, crashes against the planetary biophysical limits. It is not just that there is an eco-social or climatic crisis, but there is a political-economic project that generates the conditions for these crises to occur. What lies behind the phenomena we are experiencing is an economy that makes us sick when it grows and that also makes us sick when we go into crisis.[30]

Pandemic Madness

As the COVID-19 crisis rages out of control in the United States, it becomes clearer that iniquitous relations of power and wealth correlate with the loss of public goods, the disinvestment in essential institutions to protect public health, and the concentration of wealth in the hands of a financial elite. Under neoliberalism, economic justice not only is detached from economic prosperity, but also is viewed with disdain, as is the role of the state in using its power to invest in social goods such as public and higher education, public health systems, hospitals, and an economic model that moves more toward equality and sustainability.[31] One unfortunate consequence of concentrating wealth and power in the hands of the rich has been a devaluation of those scientific institutions, research programs, and medical experts that were necessary in addressing and containing the pandemic in the first place.

As Tim Dickinson remarked in *Rolling Stone,* "The White House's inability to track the disease as it spread across the nation crippled the government's response and led to the worst disaster this country has faced in nearly a century."[32] Moreover, as the plague accelerated it made visible profound class and racial difference, mediated by a mix of despair for the most vulnerable and shameless opportunism by the ruling elite. For instance, as Professor Ronald Aronson observed: "the African American death rate doubles and triples the death rate among white Americans, as workers go on wildcat strikes demanding safety, as the stress of unemployment and poverty hits those least able to afford it . . . the government creates slush funds for the largest corporations."[33]

The pandemic has crippled economic institutions and laid bare the ideological swindle of neoliberalism. Global capitalism has been brought to a halt, at least temporarily. The neoliberal state failed in the face of the pandemic, exposing its fault lines, revealing its inability to protect the poor, essential workers, and the most vulnerable from disproportionate levels of risk and death. The pandemic made evident the wreckage of structural, social, and economic inequality, revealing it in all of its cruelty and effects, less as timeless conditions than as predictable expressions of a society in which wealth and power are concentrated in relatively few hands. As the poor, homeless, incarcerated, and unemployed are viewed as a general threat to society as possible carriers of the virus, their status becomes more visible, though this happens less through the language of human rights than through the discourse of fear and preventive health measures. In some cases, the pandemic has brought to the surface underlying currents of cruelty and a collapse of moral values pervasive in the ideology of extreme individualism and the retreat back into the privatized space of the self. This is obvious in the growing demand on the part of many protesters to reopen the economy, against the advice of medical experts. The narratives informing these demands often take an ugly turn at many protests across the country. For instance, one Tennessee protester's sign asserted: "Sacrifice the Weak/Re-open TN."[34] In a Chicago protest, a woman displayed a sign with a Nazi slogan.[35] Armed far-right protesters rallying against social distancing in Michigan displayed swastikas and other Nazi insignia. President Trump referred to them as "very good people." This is similar to the same language Trump used to defend neo-Nazis and white nationalists in Charlottesville, whom he also referred to as "very fine people."[36]

What the pandemic reveals is that the neoliberal narrative pushed for decades by both political parties, which argued "that illness, homelessness, poverty, and inequality are minor aberrations in an otherwise healthy society" now appears transparently false.[37] In addition, the pandemic has drawn unprecedented attention to how interdependent we are on each other. It has also resurrected, if not highlighted, a notion of the social that leaves little room for tolerating a society where "over 31 million are without health insurance . . . more than 38 million people live below the poverty line [and] 140 million are poor or just a $400 emergency from that state."[38] The pandemic has made visible the borders and walls that blocked out large parts of the working class, especially poor Blacks and Latinos, who support the daily life workings of the entire population. It also revealed the shocking cruelty and machinery of inequality that decides which lives are worth living and which lives are designated as precarious and thus dispensable.[39] In this instance, structural inequality and corporate power were uncovered not only as an injustice, but also as a threat to human life, to the planet, and a major source of democratic decline.

In spite of the bankruptcy of neoliberalism with its attack on public goods and social safety nets, the issue of economic inequality is still pushed to the back burner for media coverage among the mainstream press. In addition, this takes place regardless of the fact that the Trump administration in the midst of a raging pandemic could no longer cover up its failure. These failures include, and this is the short list, the inability to provide adequate testing, ventilators, and protective equipment for front-line and emergency workers, largely due to its unwillingness to support a federal plan that would provide robust investments in an equitable healthcare system, a strong welfare system, and crucial social provisions. Instead, the Trump administration has expanded and deepened those structural forces and policies that privilege the rich while supporting the amassing of huge profits in the hands of the few over social needs.

Pandemic Pedagogy and the Politics of the Spectacle

The COVID-19 pandemic has revealed the social costs of dizzying increases in inequality over the last 40 years as it stripped government of its civic functions and produced steep wages in human suffering and death. This is especially true regarding its approach to healthcare, which it treats as a commodity that imposes a crippling financial burden on millions of Americans who don't have health insurance or for those whose policies are threadbare and vastly inadequate.[40] One consequence has been the unmasking of a neoliberal ethos rooted in massive inequalities that is incapable of explaining away mass unemployment, the loss of record numbers of jobs, and a health crisis that is unprecedented in American history. Not only has inequality become comparable to gasoline being thrown on a burning fire in the midst of the current pandemic, its unethical tactics have been used in the midst of the COVID-19 crisis to lavish privileges on the rich by transferring monumental amounts of "wealth from the bottom of the economic ladder to the top" furthering the gap between the financial elite and the poor.[41] Neoliberalism never runs away from a crisis because it relentlessly appropriates it for its own use and gives new energy to what has been called by Joseph Schumpeter "creative destruction."[42] David Harvey captures the violent dynamic at the heart of creative destruction in the following comments:

> The effect of continuous innovation . . . is to devalue, if not destroy, past investments and labour skills. Creative destruction is embedded within the circulation of capital itself. Innovation exacerbates instability, insecurity, and in the end, becomes the prime force pushing capitalism into periodic paroxysms of crisis. . . . The struggle to maintain profitability sends capitalists racing off to explore all kinds of other possibilities.[43]

In this scenario, capitalism uses a crisis not to address reasons for its underlying causes and destructive effects but to think how capitalism can invent new ways of using the crisis to its own advantage while "indifferent to the moral consequences of unbridled capitalism," whether they be the polluting of the atmosphere, defunding of public goods, or the furthering of income inequality.[44] For example, in the age of the COVID-19 pandemic, the financial and political elite use the radioactive fog of mass anxiety and fears produced by the crisis in order to legislate reforms that in actuality reward themselves and further deepen the gap between the rich and the poor. This shift in policy is done not only through legislation but also through a pandemic pedagogy that convinces the general public through a barrage of corporate and mainstream propaganda disseminated through a range of media platforms.

Parading as commonsense, pandemic pedagogy attempts to persuade the general public that it is in their best interest rather than in the interest of the ruling financial elite, big corporations, investment houses, and the mammoth banks to reorganize society around gaping class divisions. This death-dealing policy reveals the cruelty and greed at the heart of neoliberal capitalism. Given its greed for profits and profiteering from people suffering or dying because they are poor or considered economically unproductive, neoliberalism is an utterly destructive socioeconomic system and bears the marks of a monstrous social order. Inequality sharpens the social divide and in doing so worsens class, racial, and gendered divisions.[45]

As Max Fisher, writing in the *New York Times*, observed, inequality and poverty in the midst of the COVID-19 pandemic exacerbates the possibility of transmission and death for everyone, but especially for those populations that traditionally have been considered disposable by virtue of their class and racial marginalization. He wrotes

> As the coronavirus spreads across the globe, it appears to be setting off a devastating feedback loop with another of the gravest forces of our time: economic inequality. In societies where the virus hits, it is deepening the consequences of inequality, pushing many of the burdens onto the losers of today's polarized economies and labor markets. Research suggests that those in lower economic strata are likelier to catch the disease. They are also likelier to die from it. And, even for those who remain healthy, they are likelier to suffer loss of income or health care as a result of quarantines and other measures, potentially on a sweeping scale."[46]

It gets worse. Even as Trump's Twitter storms and incessant lying fall flat in an attempt to divert the underlying failure of the government to address the pandemic crisis, the mainstream press has focused very little on the issue of deepening inequality and more on surging unemployment metrics. Surprisingly, inequality and societal class divisions have been downplayed in the press in spite of the fact that inequality is crucial in analyzing both "the weakness in our health care infrastructure and social safety nets—institutions that Trump has willfully undermined," and how diverse individuals and groups both experience the pandemic and suffer the risks and consequences differently.[47] Anthony DiMaggio addressed this issue in his comment:

> We face a rapid rise in jobless claims, with various estimates suggesting unemployment reached between 16 to 20 percent by late April. But it is not clear why it unemployment should be seen as a more important economic metric than inequality, at a time when COVID-19 is disproportionately ravaging neighborhoods populated by poor people of color, and low-pay service workers on the frontlines of the crisis. . . . Inequality is also highly significant when considering that lower income Americans are more likely to work in jobs that require extensive contacts between individuals, whereas higher-income white-collar workers have been able to escape regular contacts with others by retreating into remote work tele-jobs that radically reduce their potential contacts with Covid-19-positive individuals."[48]

Under such circumstances, what emerges in the midst of the current pandemic crisis is not only an economic crisis but also a crisis of ideas, language, morality, and the inability of capitalist societies to solve practical, if not essential, social and economic problems. Human rights have no place in this discourse. In the age of pandemics, Jürgen Habermas's concept of the legitimation crisis with its emphasis on blockages, dysfunctions, economic downturns, and the emptying out of the language of normalization offers new possibilities for analyzing inequality as not only an economic issue, but also pedagogical and ideological concerns.

In the midst of the COVID-19 pandemic, the face of inequality becomes more visible as the American public is bombarded by shocking images of long food lines, the stacking of dead bodies, long lines of refrigerated trucks symbolizing the plague of death, desperate individuals and families applying for unemployment benefits, hospital workers putting their lives on the line and in some cases dying, and warnings to stay away from others for fear of catching the virus. What this pandemic reveals in all its ugliness is the death-producing mechanisms of systemic inequality, deregulation, the dismantling of the welfare state, and the increasingly dangerous assault on the environment. Beneath the massive failure of leadership from the Trump administration lies the sordid history of concentrated power in the hands of the 1 percent, shameless corporate welfare, political corruption, and the merging of money and politics to deny those most vulnerable access to healthcare, a living wage, worker protection, and strong labor movements capable of challenging corporate power and the cruelty of austerity and right-wing policies that maim, cripple, and kill hundreds of thousands, as is evident in the current pandemic.

The brutality of neoliberal capitalism and its reproduction of iniquitous relations of wealth and power is openly defended in the call to reopen the economy by restricting or eliminating protective measures that would slow the pace of the virus. Once again, most at risk are those populations who have been considered disposable such as Blacks, undocumented immigrants, the poor, the elderly, and the working class. Inequality makes a mockery of social distancing, especially for healthcare workers who lack adequate protective gear, and even more so for migrants, the elderly, the poor, and those mostly minorities of color incarcerated in prisons, jails, and detention centers, which lack any form of protection and adequate medical services.

Vulnerable populations are now held hostage to policies that fail to protect them; simultaneously, they are told to sacrifice their lives in the interest of filling the financial coffers and ideological waste bins of the corporate elite and the political zombies that rule the United States. Each day, the grim numbers indexing infections and deaths worldwide are accompanied by the call to wash hands, wear masks, and practice social distancing. These are crucial medical practices, but they collapse matters of power, politics, and class differences into an individualized and personalized script, one that mimics a neoliberal ethos. What is also forgotten in this largely Western medical narrative is how the pandemic of inequality demands a much more comprehensive view of global politics and its relationship to the current COVID-19 crisis. Crucial here is what it suggests about prioritizing both public health and social justice for everyone and not just those in the West caught in the eye of the viral storm. For instance, "UNICEF notes one in three people in the world do not have access to clean water and that more than 300 million Africans do not have running water. The pandemic is devastating the world's poor, even before the coronavirus has fully affected them."[49]

Individualizing the Social

What has become clear is that the raging coronavirus pandemic has pulled the curtain away from the barbarism and horror of neoliberalism's individualizing of the social. The pandemic crisis has shattered the myth that each of us are defined exclusively by our self-interest and as individuals are solely responsible for the problems we face. Both myths have completely collapsed under the Trump regime as it becomes obvious that as the pandemic unfolds shortages in crucial medical equipment, lack of testing, lack of public investments, and failed public health services are largely due to right-wing neoliberal measures and regressive tax policies that have drained resources from healthcare systems, public goods, and other vital social institutions. The pandemic has torn away the cover of a neoliberal economic system marked by what Thomas Piketty called "the violence of social inequality."[50] Neoliberalism "no longer offers any hope to segments of the population facing increasing inequality and a downward spiral of social and economic mobility." The suffering of those considered disposable is no longer invisible. Inequality is on full display as a toxin that destroys lives, democratic institutions, and civic culture and is normalized through a pandemic pedagogy produced by a right-wing media culture that has become a toxic sounding board for the rich and powerful.

Neoliberal pedagogy reproduces the myth that economic prosperity has nothing to do with economic justice, and that increasing levels of inequality and the concentration of wealth in few hands will produce prosperity and increased levels of social mobility. In the midst of the COVID-19 crisis, this narrative appears not only false, but also shockingly cruel and heartless. As the social is individualized, it becomes more difficult to translate private issues into systemic considerations. One consequence is that inequality becomes normalized, and the pandemic crisis is isolated from the political, economic, social, and cultural conditions that fuel it. The coronavirus pandemic has made clear the false and dangerous neoliberal notion that all problems are reduced to matters of individual responsibility and that cost-benefit schemes should be prioritized over addressing human needs and saving lives. In this instance, individual responsibility is turned against society, frozen in the mutually informing registers of self-absorption and selfishness. Rather than fulfilling its democratic capacities when combined with feelings of compassion and solidarity, it is marooned in the suffocating logic of self-interest. The underlying barbarism of this ideology plays out in the magnitude of the disparity of effects produced by the pandemic and how they bear down on vulnerable groups. As Judith Butler observed:

> For those who are homeless or unemployed, the economic forecast could not look bleaker. Without a working and equitable health care system, the affirmation of health care as a public good and a mandate of government, the unemployed are left to scramble for alternatives to avoid falling ill and dying for lack of care. This is the stunning cruelty of the U.S. that shocks large portions of the world. Many workers are not just temporarily out of work, but are registering the collapse of their work worlds, the prospect of no paycheck, homelessness, a pervasive sense of being abandoned by the society to which they should rightly belong.[51]

The pedagogical and ethical challenge here is to view inequality as part of a broader and more comprehensive politics that can only be understood both historically and relationally in terms of its connections to the central ethos and dynamics of neoliberal capitalism. This would include connecting inequality to the attack on the welfare state, unions, workers, climate change denial, deregulation, runaway privatization, crass selfishness, and the defunding of public goods. It would also point to the rise of right-wing populism and fascist politics as part of the same political process of the working of finance capital and its ongoing machineries of exploitation, exclusion, class divisions, social death, and racial cleansing. In the midst of the pandemic crisis, the health of the nation was replaced by a discourse that focused on the health of the economy. Trump attempts to empty politics with this type of discourse, which functions to cover up and erase his bumbling and incompetent response to the COVID-19 crisis.

Of course, there is more at stake here than a lack of leadership. There is also the needless loss of lives due to the lack of a national policy capable of providing hospital beds, funding health facilities, expanding rather than disbanding a pandemic task force, and taking the advice of scientific experts rather than firing those who did not bend to Trump's disregard for evidence and demand for sycophantic loyalty. What the pandemic reveals in brutally savage and cruel terms is a racially and ageist rationale on the part of the Trump administration for prioritizing untenable levels of inequality while advancing the assumption that lives be measured and valued only in terms economic output. One egregious example is evident in Texas Lieutenant Governor Dan Patrick's suggestion that "grandparents' or old people who are more at risk should volunteer to die in order to save the economy, or as one of Trump's chief economic advisors put it 'we're gonna have to make some difficult trade-offs,' or as *Vanity Fair* writer Bess Levin interprets the remark 'we're going to have to let some people die so the stock market can live.' "[52] In this heartless equation and present in the concept of herd immunity, the elderly, immigrants, the poor, and Blacks and others viewed as disposable are considered unproductive and unworthy of the protections against the virus that the ruling elite have at their disposable. Judith Butler illuminated this point, though more cautiously than I would. She wrote:

> Because "the vulnerable" are not deemed productive in the new quasi-Aryan community, they are not valued lives, and if they die, that is apparently acceptable, since they are not imagined as productive workers, but "drains" on the economy. Although the herd immunity argument may not make this claim explicitly, it is there."[53]

Depoliticizing the discourse of economic inequality and its ruthless effects is a central project of neoliberalism—a project bolstered by forms of social and historical amnesia, the collapse of social conscience, and a struggle to narrow and control the stories that define a nation's past and present. Under the Trump administration, record levels of inequality and rising volumes of poverty, misery, and suffering were the price the administration was willing to endure in order to reward the ultrarich and big corporations. In the age of the pandemic crisis, inequality is a plague normalized through the discourses of fear, unchecked individualism, the demonization of others, and the relentless investment in greed and self-interest. The furtherance of social and economic inequality and the expanding discourses of precarity, anxiety, and fear have become central organizing principles of governance. This is a model of neoliberal governance that mimics totalitarian regimes of the past and looks to align itself with the leadership and racist and repressive ideologies of a number of current hardline authoritarian governments that include Brazil, Hungary, and Turkey to more moderate antidemocratic societies such as the United Kingdom under Boris Johnson's bumbling leadership.[54]

In this global neoliberal discourse, inequality becomes a central tool of oppression and authoritarianism. Hope collapses into narrow market-driven schemes and is renounced for its fidelity and obligation to justice and to what Jacques Derrida has called "the ghosts of those who are not yet born or who are already dead."[55] Draping itself in the language of common sense, society is defined as a market removed from any notion of justice and social responsibility. As Jacque Ranciere has noted, what passes for democracy today "comprises traits that until quite recently were attributed to totalitarianism."[56] In the age defined by the rule of finance capital, the productive economy is replaced by the financialization of the market, public goods are privatized, efforts at voter suppression are increased, police violence is legitimated at the highest levels of government, a frontal assault is waged on undocumented immigrants, and there is a widening inequality in wealth, income, and power.[57] In addition, globally there is a pandemic of inequality that receives too little attention even though the cost of such inequality is staggering in terms of the massive suffering, misery, and death it produces. COVID-19 has created a crisis that accelerates the urgency for saving lives in a time of mounting deaths globally.

As Kehinde Andrews reminded us, the mounting death toll "should stand as a reminder to the scale of the task at hand if we are serious about addressing global inequality. Poverty is a pandemic claiming millions of lives each year, and the only way to address this is to take truly radical action."[58] Such action is particularly urgent at a time when nearly 1.3 billion people live in extreme poverty and "approximately 3.1 million children die from undernutrition each year."[59] In addition, in the richest country in the world in 2020 it is estimated that "11.9 million American kids—16.2% of the total—live below the official poverty line."[60] Moreover, race plays a crucial role in accentuating poverty for black and brown kids. The poverty rate for black children is 17.8%; for Hispanic kids, 21.7%; for their white counterparts, 7.9%."

As educators, it is crucial for us to examine how we talk, teach, and write about inequality as an object of critique in an age of precarity, uncertainty, and the current pandemic crisis. How do we situate our analysis of education as part of a broader discourse and mode of analysis that interrogates the promises, ideals, and claims of a substantive democracy? How do we fight against iniquitous relations of power and wealth that empty power of its emancipatory possibilities and, as Hannah Arendt has argued, "makes most people superfluous as human beings"?[61] How might we understand how neoliberal ideology with its appropriation of market-based values, regressive notions of freedom, and agency use of language to infiltrate daily life? How does a pandemic pedagogy in the service of neoliberalism produce identities defined by market values and normalize a notion of responsibility and individuality that convinces people that whatever problem they face they have no one to blame but themselves?

Depoliticization and the Authoritarian Turn

Neoliberalism is not only an economic system, but also an ideological apparatus that relentlessly attempts to structure consciousness, values, desires, and modes of identification in ways that align individuals with its governing structures. Central to this pedagogical project is the attempt to prevent individuals from translating private issues and troubles into broader systemic considerations. As the bridges between private and public life are dismantled, it becomes difficult to lift ideas into the public realm in order develop a comprehensive understanding of the connection between discreet private troubles and larger systemic forces. By doing this, it becomes difficult for individuals to grasp the historical, social, economic, and political forces at work in shaping a social order as a human activity deeply immersed in specific relations of power. Neoliberalism's attempt to erase or rewrite historical and social forces makes it difficult for individuals to both imagine alternative notions of society, themselves as collective actors, and view their problems as more than the limitations of faulty character, moral failure, or a problem of personal responsibility. Reducing individuals to isolated, discrete, hermetically sealed human beings whose lives are shaped only by notions of self-reliance and self-sufficiency is a pedagogical strategy that utterly depoliticizes people, leading them to believe that however a society is shaped, it is part of a natural order. President Trump echoed this no-alternative narrative when asked about celebrities and rich people having special access to being tested for the coronavirus while few others had access. He replied: "Perhaps that's been the story of life."[62]

This individualization of the social with its mounting privatization, gated communities, and social atomization undermines collective action, any viable notion of solidarity, and weakens the notion of global connectivity. The philosopher Byung-Chul Han has rightly argued that contemporary neoliberal society is shaped by a dysfunctional notion of solitude and hermetically sealed notions of agency, all of which undermine the values and social connections vital to a democracy. He wrotes

> Those subject to the neoliberal economy do not constitute a we that is capable of collective action. The mounting egoization and atomization of society is making the space for collective action shrink. ... The general collapse of the collective and the communal has engulfed it. Solidarity is vanishing. Privatization now reaches into the depths of the soul itself. The erosion of the communal is making all collective efforts more and more unlikely."[63]

This panoptical nature of hyperindividualism is more aligned to shared fears than shared responsibilities. Under such circumstances, trust and the notion that all life is related become difficult to grasp as the myopic language of private self-interest inures individuals to wider social problems, such as extreme inequality. There is no understanding in this discourse of the damage fanatical entrepreneurialism does to our embodied collectivity. And there is not any value attributed to the important responsibilities, social values, and notion of the common good that exceeds who we are as individuals or how we have been shaped by diverse social forces in particular ways.

It should be clear that questions of economic and social justice cannot be addressed by a neoliberal pedagogy that enshrines self-interest and privatization while converting every social problem into individualized market solutions or regressive natters of personal responsibility. Under neoliberalism's disimagination machine, individual responsibility is coupled with an ethos of greed, avarice, and personal gain. One consequence is the tearing up of social solidarities, public values, and an almost pathological disdain for democracy. Slavoj Žižek is partly right in arguing that "the ruling ideology of today is not patriarchy, racism, or even consumerism. It is an all-encompassing narcissism, a radical form of privatization that eliminates the public sphere for the endless registering of self-consuming narrations and individual interests."[64] What he misses is that this radical form of privatization is also a powerful force for the rise of fascist politics because it depoliticizes individuals, immerses them in the logic of social Darwinism, and makes them susceptible to the dehumanization of those considered a threat or disposable.

Just as the spread of the pandemic virus in the United States was not an innocent act of nature, neither is the rise and pervasive grip of inequality. What is clear is that neoliberal support for unbridled individualism has weakened democratic pressures and eroded democracy and equality as governing principles. Individualism is defined under neoliberalism as a central feature in the legitimacy of "capitalism's dominant ethic of primitive accumulation and individual gratification."[65] Moreover, as a mode of public pedagogy it has undercut social provisions, the social contract and support for public goods such as education, public health, essential infrastructure, public transportation, and the most basic elements of the welfare state. As a form of pedagogical practice, neoliberalism has morphed into a form of pandemic pedagogy that sacrifices social needs and human life in the name of an economic rationality that places reviving economic growth over human rights. As a lived system of meaning, affects, and values, self-reliance and rugged individualism are the only categories available for shaping how individuals view themselves and their relationship to others and to the planet. The individualization of everyone and the reduction of social problems to private troubles is paralleled by sanctioning a world marked by borders, walls, racism, hate, and a rejection of government intervention in the interest of the common good. Most importantly, neoliberal individualization personalizes power, creating a depoliticized subject whose only obligation as a citizen is defined by consuming and living in a world free from ethical and social responsibilities. In many ways, it not only empties politics of any substance, but also destroys its emancipatory possibilities.

The neoliberal strategists not only use education to mask their abuses and the effects of their criminogenic policies, but also in a time of crisis, when mass dissatisfaction of the masses might lead to chaos, revolts, and dangerous levels of resistance, move dangerously close to creating the conditions for a fascist politics. The noted theologian Frei Betto is right in stating that under such conditions:

> They cover up the causes of social ills and cover up their effects with ideologies that, by obscuring causes, fuel mood in the face of the effects. That's why neoliberalism is now showing its authoritarian face—building walls that divide countries and ethnic groups, executive power over legislature and judiciary, disinformation about digital networks, the cult of the homeland, the brazen offensive against human rights."[66]

Neoliberalism and its regressive notion of individualism and individual responsibility has undermined the belief that human beings both make the world and can change it. The pandemic has ushered in a crisis that undermines that belief and opens the door for rethinking what kind of society and notion of politics will be faithful to the creation of a socialist democracy that speaks to the core values of justice, equality, and solidarity. Under such circumstances, private resistance must give way to collective resistance and personal and political rights must include economic rights. If inequality is to be defeated, the social state must replace the corporate state, and social rights must be guaranteed for all. There can be no adequate struggle for economic justice and social equality unless economic inequality on a global level is addressed along with a movement for climate justice, the elimination of systemic racism, and a halt to the spiraling militarism that has resulted in endless wars. This can only take place if the antidemocratic ideology of neoliberalism, with its collapse of the public into the private and its institutional structures of domination are fully addressed and discredited. Etienne Balibar was right in stating that the triumph of neoliberalism has resulted in the "death zones of humanity."[67] Following Balibar, what must be made clear is that neoliberal capitalism is itself a pandemic and a dangerous harbinger of a updated fascist politics.

Conclusion

What kind of societies will emerge after the pandemic crisis is up for grabs? In some cases, the pandemic crisis will give way to or reinforce authoritarian regimes such as Chile, China, Hungary, and Turkey, all of whom have used the urgency of the crisis as an excuse to impose more state control and surveillance, squelch dissent, eliminate civil liberties, and concentrate power in the hands of an authoritarian political class. As is well documented, history in a time of crisis also has the potential to change dominant ideologies, rethink the meaning of governance, and enlarge the sphere of justice and equality through a vision that fights for a more generous and inclusive politics. It is crucial to rethink the project of politics in order to imagine forms of resistance that are collective, inclusive and global, and capable of producing new democratic arrangements for social life, more radical values, and a "global economy which will no longer be at the mercy of market mechanisms?"[68] This is a politics that must move beyond siloed identities and fractured political factions in order to build transnational solidarities in the service of an alternative radically democratic society.

Central to such a vision is development of a language that refuses to look away and be commodified. Such a language should be able to break through the continuity and consensus of common sense and appeals to the natural order of things. This is a language connected to the acquisition of civic literacy and demands a different regime of desires and identifications, and enables us to move from "shock and stunned silence toward a coherent visceral speech, one as strong as the force that is charging at us."[69] The COVID-19 pandemic amplifies matters of loss, existential anxiety, and the ever-present fear of death. Such sentiments invoke not only a new understanding of how we are all connected but also what it means to acknowledge public health as a public good and in its absence the terrible cost it inflicts on individuals reduced to simply trying to survive. The integrated notions of social justice and equality need to be rethought through a broader understanding of the commons, what we share as essential services and resources in a substantive democracy. The language of neoliberalism has been exhausted and should be considered the enemy of democracy and economic justice.

Developing a critical vocabulary is difficult in not only a time of overcharged crisis, but also when leaders such as Trump "emit a daily list of lies, racist comments, misogynist ramblings, and outrageous self-dealing."[70] Of course, there is more at stake here than a struggle over meaning; there is also the struggle over power, over the need to create a formative culture that will produce informed critical agents who will fight for and contribute to a broad social movement that will translate meaning into a fierce struggle for economic, political, and social justice. Agency in this sense must be connected to a notion of possibility and education in the service of radical change. Reimagining the future only becomes meaningful when it is rooted in a fierce struggle against the horrors and totalitarian practices of a pandemic pedagogy that falsely claims that it exists outside history. The plague has amplified the horrors produced by inequality, a politics driven by money, and the production of modes of agency fit for a zombie film. The plague is a form of zombie politics, which is an avatar for death and cruelty and the production of the walking dead among the financial elite who suck the life out of the common good, public values, and democracy itself.

Vaclav Havel, the late Czech political dissident turned politician, once argued that politics follows culture, by which he meant that changing consciousness is the first step toward building mass movements of resistance.[71] What is crucial here in the age of the pandemic is a thorough grasp of the notion that critical and engaged forms of agency are a product of emancipatory education. Moreover, at the heart of any viable notion of politics is the recognition that politics begins with attempts to change the way people think, act, and feel with respect to how they view both themselves and their relations to others. There is more to agency than the neoliberal emphasis on the "empire of the self" with its unbridled narcissism and unchecked belief in the virtues of a form of self-interest that despises the bonds of sociality, solidarity, and community. If education is central to politics, it is crucial to place morality and responsibility at the forefront of not only agency but also politics itself. In this scenario, truth and politics themselves erupt in a pedagogical awakening at the moment when the rules are broken, taking risks becomes a necessity, self-reflection narrates its capacity for critically engaged agency, and thinking the impossible is not an option but a necessity.

Notes

1. The critical literature on inequality is enormous; I have learned a great deal from this small selection: Thomas Piketty, *Capital and Ideology* (Cambridge, U.K.: Belknap, 2020); Keith Payne, *The Broken Ladder: How Inequality Affects the Way We Think, Live, and Die* (New York: Penguin, 2017); (Michael D. Yates, *The Great Inequality* (New York: Routledge, 2016); Anthony B. Atkins, *Inequality: What Can Be Done?*

(Cambridge, MA: Harvard University Press, 2015); Joseph E. Stiglitz, *The Price of Inequality* (New York: Norton, 2012); Richard Wilkinson and Kate Pickett, *The Spirit Level: Why Equality Is Better for Everyone* (New York: Penguin, 2010).

2. "'You Wouldn't Think You'd Go to Jail Over Medical Bills': County in Rural Kansas Is Jailing People Over Unpaid Medical Debt," *CBS News*, February 13, 2020, https://www.cbsnews.com/news/coffeyville-kansas-medical-debt-county-in-rural-kansas-is-jailing-people-over-unpaid-medical-debt/.

3. Oxfam International, "5 Shocking Facts About Extreme Global Inequality and How to Even It Up," 2019, https://www.oxfam.org/en/5-shocking-facts-about-extreme-global-inequality-and-how-even-it.

4. Sandra Clark, "Help End World Poverty," RallyCall, October 16, 2019, https://rallyc all.io/campaign-details/Help_End_World_Poverty_1571272330.

5. Chuck Collins, "Bernie's Right: Three Billionaires Really Do Have More Wealth Than Half of America," Inequality.Org, June 28, 2019, https://inequality.org/great-divide/bernie-3-billionaires-more-wealth-half-america/.

6. Anthony DiMaggio, "The Censorship of Inequality in the Covid-19 Era: How Corporate and Market-Based Metrics Rule the News, and Why It Matters," Project Censored, May 12, 2020, https://www.projectcensored.org/the-censorship-of-ine quality-in-the-covid-19-era-how-corporate-and-market-based-metrics-rule-the-news-and-why-it-matters/?doing_wp_cron=1589310856.0858778953552246093 750&fbclid=IwAR16thSCoz94c33Voiq11sr-ovOuCN2zJJCa7HIGRIJiofljJN38 AIJHGqY.

7. DiMaggio, "The Censorship."

8. Fredric Jameson, "Future City," *New Left Review*, May–June 21, 2003, http://newlef treview.org/II/21/fredric-jameson-future-city.

9. Henry A. Giroux, *Neoliberalism's War on Higher Education*, 2nd ed. (Chicago: Haymarket Books, 2019); Kenneth J. Saltman and Alexander J. Means, eds., *The Wiley Handbook of Global Educational Reform* (New York: Wiley Blackwell, 2018).

10. Chris Wright, "Capitalism, Socialism, and Existential Despair," *Socialist Project*, January 31, 2020, https://socialistproject.ca/2020/01/capitalism-socialism-and-exis tential-despair/.

11. Mark Jenkins, "Absence," *The Point*, May 7, 2020, https://thepointmag.com/quarant ine-journal/.

12. Jason DeParle, "As Hunger Swells, Food Stamps Become a Partisan Flash Point," *New York Times*, May 6, 2020, https://www.nytimes.com/2020/05/06/us/politics/coro navirus-hunger-food-stamps.html?campaign_id=56&emc=edit_cn_20200507&inst ance_id=18282&nl=on-politics-with-lisa-lerer&regi_id=51563793&segment_id= 26782&te=1&user_id=ac16f3c28b64af0b86707bb1a8f1b07c.

13. Byung-Chul Han, *In the Swarm: Digital Prospects*, trans. Erik Butler (Cambridge, MA: MIT Press, 2017), 13–14.

14. See Henry A. Giroux, *Neoliberalism's War on Higher Education*, 2nd ed. (Chicago: Haymarket Books, 2019).

15. Jean Comaroff and John L. Comaroff, "A Millennial Capitalism: First Thoughts on a Second Coming," *Public Culture* 12, no. 2 (2000), 322.

16. Michiko Kakutani, "Coronavirus Notebook: Finding Solace, and Connection, in Classic Books," *New York Times Book Review*, May 5, 2020, https://www.nytimes.com/2020/05/05/books/review/coronavirus-new-york-life-michiko-kakutani.html?te=1&nl=books&emc=edit_bk_20200515.

17. Kakuani, "Coronavirus Notebook."

18. Cited in Zygmunt Bauman, "Has the Future a Left," *Soundings*, no. 35 (Spring 2007), 8.

19. Wendy Brown, "Apocalyptic Populism," *Eurozine*, September 5, 2017. http://www.eurozine.com/apocalyptic-populism/.

20. Bauman, "Has the Future a Left," p. 24.

21. Michael D. Yates, *The Great Inequality* (New York: Routledge, 2016).

22. Zygmunt Bauman and Leonidas Donskis. *Liquid Evil* (Cambridge, U.K.: Polity Press, 2016), 8.

23. Zygmunt Bauman, "Freedom From, In and Through the State: T.H. Marshall's Trinity of Rights Revised," *Theoria*, December, 2005, 18–19.

24. Conor Lynch, "Neoliberalism Has Radicalized a Whole Generation," *Truthdig*, February 26, 2020, https://www.truthdig.com/articles/neoliberalism-has-radicalized-a-whole-generation/.

25. Henry A. Giroux, *The Violence of Organized Forgetting* (San Francisco: City Lights Books, 2014).

26. Jason Frank, "Populism Isn't the Problem," *Boston Review*, August 15, 2018, http://bostonreview.net/politics/jason-frank-populism-not-the-problem.

27. Mark Murphy, "What Did Marx Mean by Thesis Eleven?" *Social Theory Applied*, August 10, 2013, https://socialtheoryapplied.com/2013/08/10/what-did-marx-mean-by-thesis-eleven/.

28. On the rise of the racial incarceration state and war on poverty, see Elizabeth Hinton, *From the War on Poverty to the War on Crime: The Making of Mass Incarceration in America* (Cambridge, MA: Harvard University Press, 2016); Michelle Alexander, *The New Jim Crow* (New York: New Press, 2010).

29. Sonali Kolhatkar, "Is There Any Better Time Than Now for a General Strike?" *Counterpunch*, April 21. 2020, https://www.counterpunch.org/2020/04/21/is-there-any-better-time-than-now-for-a-general-strike/.

30. Joan Benach, "The Pandemic Kills the Poor: Inequality Will Kill Them Even More," *Socialist Project*, May 6, 2020, https://socialistproject.ca/2020/05/pandemic-kills-the-poor-inequality-will-kill-more/.

31. Amy Goodman, "Economist Thomas Piketty: Coronavirus Pandemic Has Exposed the 'Violence of Social Inequality,'" *Democracy Now!* April 30, 2020, https://www.democracynow.org/2020/4/30/thomas_piketty.

32. Tim Dickinson, "The Four Men Responsible for America's COVID-19 Test Disaster," *Rolling Stone*, May 10, 2020, https://www.rollingstone.com/politics/politics-features/covid-19-test-trump-admin-failed-disaster-995930/.

33. Ronald Aronson, "Camus' Plague Is Not Ours," *Tikkun*, April 14, 2020, https://www.tikkun.org/camus-plague-is-not-ours.

34. Chacour Koop, "'Sacrifice the Weak' and 'Give Me Liberty': Signs at Coronavirus Protests Across US," *Miami Herald*, April 21, 2020, https://www.miamiherald.com/news/coronavirus/article242182796.html.

35. Bill Hutchinson, "Nazi Slogan Sign Displayed at 'Re-open Illinois' Rally Ripped by Auschwitz Memorial, Gov. J.B. Pritzker," *ABC News*, May 3, 2020, https://abcn ews.go.com/US/nazi-slogan-sign-displayed-open-illinois-rally-ripped/story?id= 70480524.

36. Eric Cortellessa, "Jewish Dems Leader Calls Trump 'Depraved' for Backing Armed Far-Right Protesters," *Times of Israel*, May 2, 2020, https://www.timesofisrael.com/us-jewish-leader-calls-trump-depraved-for-backing-armed-far-right-protesters/.

37. Liz Theoharis, "Inequality and the Coronavirus: Or How to Destroy American Society From the Top Down," *Tom Dispatch*.com, April 21, 2020, http://www.tomd ispatch.com/post/176691/tomgram%3A_liz_theoharis%2C_circling_the_ruins/.

38. Theoharis, Inequality and the Coronavirus."

39. George Yancy, "Judith Butler: Mourning Is a Political Act Amid the Pandemic and Its Disparities," *Truthout*, April 30, 2020, https://truthout.org/articles/judith-butler-mourning-is-a-political-act-amid-the-pandemic-and-its-disparities/.

40. David Sirota, "Health Insurance Companies Are Pissing on You and Saying It's Raining," *Jacobin*, April 2020, https://jacobinmag.com/2020/05/health-insurance-coronavirus-cobra-medicare-for-all.

41. Miles Kampf-Lassin, "The U.S. Response to Covid-19 Has Lavished Wealth on the Rich," *In These Times*, May 6, 2020, http://inthesetimes.com/article/22514/covid-19-coronavirus-wealthy-corporate-welfare.

42. Joseph A. Schumpeter, *Capitalism, Socialism and Democracy* (London: Routledge, 1942, 1994) 82–83.

43. David Harvey, *The Condition of Postmodernity* (Hoboken, NJ: Wiley-Blackwell, 1991), 147.

44. Thomas M. Magstadt, "Capitalism in America: The Coming Crisis," *Counterpunch*, January 30, 2020. https://www.counterpunch.org/2020/01/30/capitalism-in-amer ica-the-coming-crisis/.

45. David Harvey, "Anti-Capitalist Politics in an Age of Covid-19," *Tribune Magazine*, March 23, 2020, https://tribunemag.co.uk/2020/03/david-harvey-anti-capitalist-politics-in-an-age-of-covid-19.

46. Max Fisher, "As Coronavirus Deepens Inequality, Inequality Worsens Its Spread," *New York Times*, [March 15, 2020]. https://www.nytimes.com/2020/03/15/world/eur ope/coronavirus-inequality.html.

47. Kakutani, "Coronavirus Notebook.

48. DiMaggio, "The Censorship."

49. Benach, "The Pandemic Kills the Poor."

50. Thomas Piketty, *Capital and Ideology* (Cambridge, MA: Belknap, 2020).

51. Yancy, "Judith Butler."

52. Bess Levin, "Texas Lt. Governor: Old People Should Volunteer to Die to Save the Economy," *Vanity Fair*, March 24, 2020, https://www.vanityfair.com/news/2020/03/ dan-patrick-coronavirus-grandparents.

53. Yancy, "Judith Butler."

54. Timothy Snyder, "How Did the Nazis Gain Power in Germany?" *New York Times*, June 14, 2018, https://www.nytimes.com/2018/06/14/books/review/benjamin-car ter-hett-death-of-democracy.html.

55. Jacques Derrida interview with Jean Birnbaum, *Learning to Live Finally: The Last Interview* (Brooklyn, NY: Melville House, 2007), 12–13.

56. Jacque Ranciere, *Hatred of Democracy* (London: Verso, 2014), 55.

57. I take up these issues in detail in *The Terror of the Unforeseen* (Los Angeles: Los Angeles Review of Books, 2019) and in Henry A. Giroux, *American Nightmare: Facing the Challenge of Fascism* (San Francisco: City Lights Books, 2018).

58. Kehinde Andrews, "The Other Pandemic," in *The Quarantine Files*, Brad Evans, ed. (Los Angeles: Los Angeles Review of Books, 2020), https://lareviewofbooks.org/article/qua rantine-files-thinkers-self-isolation/?fbclid=IwAR3VDovJfePU7AaIW6o0BQ5jZvL FoqdbQ7tS4jGXLY6CdmU4VmHbHz-Km-o.

59. UNICEF, "Malnutrition Rates Remain Alarming: Stunting Is Declining Too Slowly While Wasting Still Impacts the Lives of Far Too Many Young Children," 2018a, http://data.unicef.org/topic/nutrition/malnutrition/#.

60. Rajan Menon, "The Shame of Child Poverty in the Age of Trump," *Counterpunch*, February 5, 2020, https://www.counterpunch.org/2020/02/05/the-shame-of-child-poverty-in-the-age-of-trump/.

61. Cited in Elisabeth Young-Bruehl, *Why Arendt Matters* (Victoria, Australia: Integrated Publishing Solutions, 2006), 38–39.

62. Abigail Weinberg, " "That's Been the Story of Life': Trump on Why Rich People Are Getting Tests First," *Mother Jones*, March 18, 2020, https://www.motherjones.com/coronavirus-updates/2020/03/thats-been-the-story-of-life-trump-on-why-rich-peo ple-are-getting-tests-first/.

63. Han, *In the Swarm*.

64. Slavoj Žižek, *Demanding the Impossible* (London: Polity, 2013), 79.

65. Pankaj Mishra, "The New World Disorder: The Western Model Is Broken," *Guardian*, October 14, 2014, https://www.theguardian.com/world/2014/oct/14/-sp-western-model-broken-pankaj-mishra.

66. Frei Betto, "Neoliberalism: From the Market Economy to the Subjectivity of Persons," *Granma*, October 7, 2019, de.granma.cu/mundo/2019-10-07/ neoliberalismus-von-der-marktwirtschaft-zur-subjektivitat-der-personen.

67. Etienne Balibar, "Outline of a Topography of Cruelty: Citizenship and Civility in the Era of Global Violence," in *We, The People of Europe? Reflections on Transnational Citizenship* (Princeton, NJ: Princeton University Press, 2004), p. 128.

68. Slavoj Zizek, "Slavoj Zizek, 'Coronavirus is 'Kill Bill'-esque blow to capitalism and could lead to reinvention of communism," *RT*, February 27, 2020, https://www. rt.com/op-ed/481831-coronavirus-kill-bill-capitalism-communism/.

69. Maaza Mengiste, "Unheard-of Things," *Massachusetts Review* 57, no. 1 (2016):128.

70. Fred Nagel, "The Unspoken Spread of Fascism," *La Progressive*, May 11, 2020, https://www.laprogressive.com/spread-of-fascism/.

71. See, for instance, "Czech Republic: Vaclav Havel's 1997 Makes State of the Nation Speech," cited in Radio Free Europe, December 9, 1997. https://www.rferl.org/a/1087 560.html.

5

A Tale of Two Pandemics

Freedom and Environmental Justice in a Time of COVID-19

Michael Mascarenhas

The scope of environmental injustice for the poor and for non-Whites in the United States has become remarkably clear during the novel coronavirus pandemic. For example, as of April 9, 2020, *Newsweek* reported that all COVID-19 deaths in St. Louis, Missouri, were African American.[1] The *New York Times* reported that in Illinois, 43 percent of people who have died from the disease and 28 percent of those who have tested positive are African Americans, a group that makes up just 15 percent of the state's population. African Americans, who account for a third of positive tests in Michigan, represent 40 percent of deaths in that state even though they make up 14 percent of the population. In Louisiana, about 70 percent of the people who have died are Black, yet African Americans only comprise a third of that state's population.[2] In California, Black people had almost two times the rate in deaths than the population at large. Latinos in California make up 39 percent of the state's population but account for almost half of all reported virus cases. In Iowa, Latinos account for more than 20 percent of coronavirus cases though they are only 6 percent of the population. Latinos in Washington State make up 13 percent of the population but 31 percent of cases. In Florida, they are just over a quarter of the population but account for 40 percent of the virus cases where ethnicity is known.[3] *US News* reported that the governor of New Mexico, Michelle Lujan Grisham, in a phone call to President Trump warned that coronavirus "could wipe out tribal nations" in the United States.[4] The Navajo Nation has more coronavirus cases per capita than any state in the United States according to data released by the Navajo Nation.[5] Some of the largest Filipino enclaves in the New York City borough of Queens and northern New Jersey are also the very places now being ravaged by COVID-19. Meanwhile, millions of low-wage service workers, farm employees, contingent workers, the un- and underemployed, the homeless, and other uninsureds have neither the means nor the safety net to safeguard them and their loved one's health.[6] In no other place in the world has race and ethnicity been such a factor in determining one's experience with an otherwise colorblind threat than in the

Michael Mascarenhas, *A Tale of Two Pandemics* In: *On Inequality and Freedom*. Edited by: Lawrence M. Eppard and Henry A. Giroux, Oxford University Press. © Oxford University Press 2022. DOI: 10.1093/oso/9780197583029.003.0005

United States. Now, perhaps, it is more obvious than ever that to be Black and Brown in the United States also means to be the wrong complexion for protection. But this form of environmental injustice is neither the result of hostile and intentional acts of racism nor the consequence of unequal environmental protection. Rather, the environmental injustice of COVID-19 in the United States is a function of the way in which White privilege has been collapsed into American society, embodied in pervasive institutions of life and liberty, and realized in multiple forms of injustice from the continued and normalized violence against racialized groups to the illusion of freedom to prosper; dreams differed, hidden behind the colorblind veil of White supremacy.[7]

The human consequences of the coronavirus pandemic are hidden from most urban and suburban White Americans as they continue to have no idea what it means to be a person of color in this country. Moreover, as millions of people of color suffer from premature death and ill health or have to endure the personal loss of loved ones, others, mostly Whites, have taken to their cars, streets, and state capital buildings to protest what they see as overreaching government restrictions that limit their freedom and civil liberties. For example, thousands of demonstrators, many armed, convened in Lansing Michigan on April 15 to protest against the governor's stay-at-home order. Later demonstrators took part in an "American Patriot Rally," organized by Michigan United for Liberty, demanding the reopening of businesses. The state of Michigan eventually closed down its capitol building and canceled its legislative session after online death threats were made against Governor Gretchen Whitmer.[8]

Facilitated through private invitation-only Facebook[9] groups and sponsored by a well-funded, dark monied, and antigovernment right-wing infrastructure, similar protests are being strategically organized all across the country. "Indiana Citizens Against Excessive Quarantine," "Operation Gridlock Tennessee," "Pennsylvanians Against Excessive Quarantine," and "Minnesotans Against Excessive Quarantine" are just four of a handful of the many groups organizing protests across the United States. Egged on by President Trump calling for the liberation of states, three Democrat states in particular—Michigan, Minnesota, and Virginia—protesters have claimed that statewide shutdown orders are a violation of their constitutional rights and freedoms. Folks have taken to the usual symbols of White supremacy. Dozens of protesters have called for Whitmer to be hanged, lynched, shot, beaten, or beheaded. In Kentucky, another right-wing group opposed Governor Andy Beshear's coronavirus restrictions by hanging an effigy of the governor on a tree at his residence.

Moreover, as the disproportionate impact of the epidemic has become increasingly apparent, many White folk have begun to regard the rising death toll less as a national emergency and more of a personal inconvenience. Their push to reopen is in part motivated by the fact that they feel their Whiteness, in particular, as well as their youth and class, is their immunity, knowing full well that the personal costs and risks of reopening the country will not be borne by them but by the disproportionate deaths of Black and Brown folks and the elderly, a consequence they have always been willing to rationalize. In March 2020, Goldman Sachs reassured their anxious global investors that while the morality rate would increase by 2%, it would not mean an additional 3 million deaths but rather elder people dying sooner due to respiratory issues associated with COVID-19. This may stress the healthcare system they noted, but there would be no systemic risk to the world's financial system.[10] Conversely, explanations regarding disparate and disproportionate environmental impact from COVID-19 in communities of color have taken a remarkably different tone, largely focusing on the preexisting or underlying health conditions of these subpopulations. Lost in this dominant discursive response is any discussion of how the colored dialectics of American capitalism have enabled White people to develop their abilities to their fullest, and in a time of COVID have access to resources like healthcare, running water, safe shelter, and work-from-home options, while unjustly blocking those resources and opportunities from others.

To this slow violence of environmental racism we must add the fast violence of the police killings and neighborhood vigilantes. The death of George Floyd in Minneapolis on May 25, 2020, underscores what can only be described as White rage toward Black and Brown people in this country.[11] Cell phone footage captured when one of the officers, Derek Chauvin, forced his knee on Floyd's neck while on top of him on the ground for nearly 9 minutes, while three other officers stood by and spectated. Floyd's desperate struggle and gasps to breathe stood in stark contrast to the calmness of the White man who took his life. With one hand casually in his pocket, it appeared that Chauvin might even pull out his cell phone to take a selfie to celebrate his latest trophy. It was not fear of the Black body that Chauvin projected through his calm stance but rather disregard. Equally disturbing is the murder of Breonna Taylor in the evening of March 13, 2020, shot at least eight times after three officers entered her apartment in Louisville to serve her partner a search warrant.

Environments of Injustice and Freedom

For those who are unfamiliar with the topic, environmental justice activists and scholars present a broad concept of the environment in which we live, work, learn, play, and pray, including the places where we are hospitalized, housed, and imprisoned. The environment from this perspective is not a people-free biophysical system but rather the ambient and immediate surroundings of everyday life activities and relationships linking people with their immediate environs. These include, but are not limited to, residential environments, working environments, and recreational environments.[12] Originally forged from a synthesis of the civil rights movements, antitoxic campaigns, and environmentalism in the 1960s, environmental justice has focused on the class and racial inequalities of pollution. Beginning in the early 1970s, a substantial body of literature began to emerge in the United States documenting the existence of environmental inequalities among particular social groups, specifically minority, Aboriginal, and poor communities. In 1983, the U.S. General Accounting Office conducted a study of several southern states and found that a disproportionate amount of landfills (about three out of every four) were located near predominantly minority communities.[13] In 1987, a national study, "Toxic Wastes and Race in the United States," commissioned by the United Church of Christ Commission on Racial Justice found that race was the most significant factor in determining where waste facilities were located in the United States.[14] Among other findings, the study revealed that three out of five African Americans and Hispanic Americans lived in communities with one or more uncontrolled toxic waste sites, and 50% of Asian/ Pacific Islander Americans and Native Americans lived in such communities.

Twenty years later, the national study was repeated using 2000 census data, an updated database of commercial hazardous waste facilities, and newer methods and concluded that significant racial and socioeconomic disparities persisted and in some cases had worsened.[15] These findings were a tremendous setback for the national grassroots environmental justice movement. It also spoke volumes to both the efficacy and legitimacy of government intention to remedy environmental inequality and injustice brought about by its unequal laws, regulations, and policies. Today, hundreds of studies have substantiated the degree to which people of color, the poor, Indigenous and immigrant populations, and other marginalized communities are disproportionately prejudiced by unequal laws and policies.[16] Yet in this chapter I argue that the framework of environmental justice as generally employed is still incomplete. I believe that the degree of measurable or observable difference of environmental disproportionality says little about the network of relations in which these inequalities arise and are used. In effect, I argue that we need to draw attention to how an environmentally racialized social existence is reasoned, produced, and normalized.

To do this, I suggest we also need to highlight the role of White supremacy in producing and normalizing environmental racism and other forms of environmental injustice outcomes. White supremacy is reproduced every day in this country through not only acts of hate and aggression as carefully documented by historian Carol Anderson in her brilliant book *White Rage: The Unspoken Truth of Our Racial Divide* but also structurally and institutionally by policies and politics as usual that free White people of all sorts of environmental burdens. In the United States White lives are made better and easier every day simply by the way in which society is organized. Whites live longer, have better access to health-care, have better education, own more, and enjoy superior social status than non-Whites. The doctrine of White supremacy, Dr. Martin Luther King Jr. wrote, was nothing more than a form of rationalization that gave legitimacy and moral sanction to a profitable but deeply immoral system.[17] White supremacy is rooted in the multiple ways in which White people have access to resources, spaces, and places—environments—that are simply off limits to people of color. Access to home ownership, investment in White suburbs, subsidized water rates, exclusive schools, clean parks, and opportunities for recreation are just a few examples of these exclusively "White-first" environments.

For example, a year after President Franklin Roosevelt's New Deal created the Home Owners' Loan Corporation (HOLC), Congress passed the National Housing Act (1994), which created the Federal Housing Administration (FHA). The FHA provided mortgage insurance on long-term mortgage loans by banks and other private lenders for home construction and sale, effectively providing loan guarantees to financial institutions and shifting the risk of mortgage default to the federal government. The FHA's mortgage insurance policy also adopted existing assumptions and appraisal methods of HOLC. The consequences proved effective in the production and sedimentation of a racialized environment of White supremacy. Between 1934 and 1962, George Lipsitz wrote the FHA and (later) the Veterans Administration financed more than $120 billion worth of new housing.[18] Almost all of this investment went to new home construction in the suburbs. Less than 2 percent of this real estate was available to African Americans and other non-Whites, with the overwhelming majority, 98%, going to Whites. FHA appraisers flatly denied federally supported loans to the majority African American (Negro: 95%) "slums and fire hazards" neighborhoods of Lafayette Park, Eastern Market, and Forest Park. Similarly, prospective buyers in the racially mixed neighborhoods of Detroit were also denied mortgage insurance. But 7 miles away in the 100% White and deed-restricted, residential zoned neighborhood of Grosse Pointe, federal loans would be guaranteed in spades.

At the time, FHA loans required that all of its new mortgage-backed developments included federal and state assistance for sidewalks, paved roads, highway projects, water and sewer lines, and other utilities. So while Whites were being heavily subsidized by FHA housing development, and White suburbs were enjoying massive public and private investment, majority Black and mixed neighborhoods in cities like Detroit were being systematically aban-doned. Together, these massive and systemic investments have made American whiteness one of the most systematically subsidized identities in the world.[19] In addition to increased real estate values, subsidized White homeowners enjoyed neighborhood stability, a better quality of life, and superior educa-tion, funded mostly through local property taxes and growing employment opportunities—safe White spaces for capital to invest in.[20] Black and Brown families migrating to the region for work were forced into highly segregated and crowded urban neighborhoods. Those Black professionals who wanted to leave the rapidly forming urban ghettos and also take advantage of Michigan's possessive investment in White suburbs, quickly found out the degree to which White supremacy would be defended as banks, insurance companies, field surveyors, and real estate agencies implemented a "system of popular, legal, and administrative Jim Crow."[21] The combination of rising population, massive evictions, rising real estate prices, and the rigidity of the residential color line, historian Andrew Highsmith wrote, played an important role in forging Jim Crow, making Michigan cities like Flint and Detroit among the most segregated cities in the country.[22]

These forms of White supremacy are the consequences of years of structural adjustments that are maintained and reinforced by what George Lipsitz has coined the "possessive investment in whiteness."[23] The majority of White people in the United States don't profit only from White identity politics, but also from the beneficial way in which environmental racism and other forms of environmental injustice have been *structured* into supposedly colorblind government policy. In effect, I argue that we are in need of a different framing for what is happening in majority Black and Brown spaces in this country, a critical environmental justice perspective that roots freedom and injustice dialectically in the environmental relations of Black and White social existence.[24]

Freedom and Environmental Justice in a Time of COVID-19

Two very different observations are becoming increasingly apparent with regard to freedom and environmental justice. First, an increasing militarized, antigovernment, and White supremacy movement has taken to the street to protest what they see as overreaching government restrictions that limit their freedom. This commonly held perspective focuses on the idea of negative freedom, or on governments' imposed constraints on daily activities, such as shopping, driving, playing, and working. Protesters have claimed that their constitutional rights were being trampled by the public health stay-at-home orders to "flatten the curve" of cases of COVID-19. For example, protest signs in Southern California read: "Pandemics does [sic] NOT cancel our Constitutional rights!! Freedom over fear," and "No Liberty, No Life, Reopen California." For people of color, the relationship between environmental justices and freedom is very different from their White counterparts. In particular, the pandemic exposes the stark racial divide in access to largely privatized healthcare services, the Affordable Care Act being the exception to these unjust policies. But even President Obama was unable to bring about a truly equitable single-payer, universal healthcare system in this country: The United States is the only so-called core country not to have this important social program. And Trump continued to try to take health insurance away from poor and working-class families in an effort prevent access to resources that would otherwise alleviate the burden that so many people of color carry from living without reliable quality healthcare. As the data slowly accumulate, it is becoming increasingly apparent even to the most willfully colorblind that race is the most important determining factor in who lives and dies in the United States in the age of COVID-19. And as I explain below, these gross inequities are spread over many different environments.

I Can't Work (Safely)

The pandemic has highlighted the deep inequities in how people of different races work in this country. For many Americans, COVID-19 and the government strictures to prevent its spread are limiting their ability to earn a living. These mostly White working-class Americans want to get back to work. Other Americans, more privileged and mostly White, have the option to work from home. Major tech firms like Google, Facebook, and Microsoft have given their employees the option to work from home at least until next year. However, for other Americans, working has meant disproportionate exposure to COVID-19. For example, thousands of meatpacking workers across the country were recently ordered back to work in plants that have seen massive outbreaks of COVID-19. A quarter of the employees—570 workers—at one Tyson poultry-processing facility in Wilkesboro, North Carolina, have tested positive for the coronavirus.[25] According to data collected by the nonprofit Food & Environment Reporting Network, as of June 3, at least 271 meatpacking and food-processing plants and 36 farms and production facilities have confirmed cases of COVID-19. At least 24,273 workers (21,230 meatpacking workers, 1,596 food-processing workers, and 1,447 farmworkers) have tested positive for COVID-19, and sadly at least 85 workers (77 meatpacking workers, 6 food-processing workers, and 2 farmworkers) have died.[26] Four out of every five workers deemed essential in the United States are Latino. Their employment is heavily concentrated in construction, food processing, retail, and farming. They don't have the privilege of being able to work from home, commented Domingo Garcia, national president of the League of United Latin American Citizens (Lulac), and therefore they're being exposed to COVID-19 in ways that many American workers are not.[27]

The *Guardian* newspaper reported that Latino workers have been particularly hard hit in some areas by their reliance on jobs in meat-processing plants or large warehouses that have been kept open during the pandemic, despite reports of poor health and safety standards and a lack of personal protective equipment (PPE).[28] It is a wasted opportunity that this moment is not used to reflect on the harmful social and environmental consequences of industrial meat production, where a few multinational corporations own outright or exert contract control over most of the industry, or on the lack of safety conditions at meatpacking plants from years of deregulation, or on simply the lack of PPE for essential employees during a pandemic. Government officials, like Health and Human Services (HHS) Secretary Alex Azar suggested that the spike in COVID-19 outbreaks at processing facilities was due to the social habits and living conditions of workers at meatpacking plants. This sentiment that the virus was being spread in the homes of Latino workers was echoed by South Dakota Governor Kristi Noem and a Smithfield spokeswoman.[29] The belief that people of color are somehow responsible for their own misfortune is a key strategy in the doctrine of White supremacy and serves to normalize this and other forms of environmental racism while giving legitimacy to decades of policies in which elites weaponized White racism and Black pathology to further their political and economic influence over the country and its citizens. We see a similar version of White supremacy employed in the barbaric murder of George Floyd.

I Can't Breathe

On May 25, George Floyd was murdered by four Minneapolis police officers. For 8 minutes and 46 seconds Derek Chauvin kneeled on George Floyd's neck—a move banned by most police departments—until Floyd could no longer breathe. While laying on the street face down, George Floyd repeated at least 16 times in less than five minutes that he couldn't breathe as the four officers looked on in what appeared as casual amusement, with Chauvin had one hand in his pocket. To his list of his palmaries, which included 17 previous complaints, including 3 police shootings, 1 of them fatal, Derek Chauvin could now add the public lynching of George Floyd. Two autopsies, one by the state, the other by the Floyd family, both ruled his death a homicide. However, the county autopsy reported that Floyd died of "cardiopulmonary arrest complicating law enforcement subdual, restraint and neck compression." The report also noted that Floyd had "other significant conditions," including "arteriosclerotic and hypertensive heart disease; fentanyl intoxication; [and] recent methamphetamine use." Suggesting, once again, that there was something else to explain this Black man's violent demise, in this case chronic medical conditions and possible intoxicants. This report underscores the power of an emboldened White supremacy ready to explain away yet another Black man's death even against the stark reality for all to see that if it wasn't for the sustained force of a White police officer's knee on his neck for almost 9 minutes, George Floyd would alive today.[30]

The language of I can't breathe has defined this particular conjunction of environmental racism in the United States. The fatal encounters of George Floyd, Ahmaud Arbery, and Trevyon Martin, to mention only three of the thousands of deaths of people of color at the hands of White people each year is a form of environmental racism. Their crime was being in the wrong place at the wrong time. The death of Treyvon Martin was in part normalized because a Black teenage boy was walking in a White gated neighborhood. Before fatally shooting the Black teenager, White neighborhood watch captain George Zimmerman called 911 and reported a suspicious person in the neighborhood. Similarly, Eric Garner was simply standing in front of a beauty supply store on Bay Street in Tompkinsville, Staten Island, when he was approached by New York Police Department police officers and strangled to death. Similarly, the deaths of Michael Brown in Ferguson, Missouri; Walter Scott in North Charleston, South Carolina; Freddie Gray in Baltimore, Maryland; and Philando Castile in Falcon Heights, Minnesota, represent just a few more tragic examples of over policing in Black and Brown communities. When found in White spaces,[31] the color of one's skin is a key determinant of their experience. The Amy Cooper incident, where a White woman who called the police on Christian Cooper, a Black man, in Central Park, New York, after he asked her to leash her dog is one of the most recent striking examples of this form of environmental racism. Moreover, in most of these fatal cases—the coroner ruled Eric Garner's death a homicide—predominantly White juries failed to bring charges against the White offenders. In fact, one of the potential jurors in the Treyvon Martin case said: "This could have been prevented had he not been up here," had this Black youth not been in this White neighborhood.

The disproportionate infection rates and premature deaths of people of color from COVID-19 also underscore the unequal environs in which people of color in this country work, live, and play. People of color are exposed to greater environmental hazards than Whites in their homes, neighborhoods, workplace, schools, and playgrounds. For example, longitudinal research shows that race is a significant predictor of where hazardous waste sites are located in this country.[32] People of color make up most of those living in neighborhoods within 2 miles of commercial hazardous waste facilities, and that trend has worsened with the increasing rollback of environmental regulation by federal and state governments.[33] In effect, where you live—your zip code—affects your health and chances of leading flourishing lives. The devastating health impacts of the coronavirus pandemic on Black and Brown people are not the result of preexisting conditions but rather negative environmental conditions brought on by unequal laws, regulations, and policies that disproportionately expose communities and people of color to harmful environs. Whether it's the streets we walk down, the location of our neighborhoods, or the places we work, learn, pray, or play, racism permeates every aspect of American society and culture.

Conclusion

COVID-19 and the recent murders of unarmed Black people by White police officers lay bare the multiple and interconnected ways in which the color of one's skin determines the fate of their lives. For many White Americans, COVID-19 and the government strictures to prevent its spread are limiting their freedom. Other White Americans have the privilege to work from home, even home school their children. The demand for real estate is unexpectedly rocketing in wealthy regions outside San Francisco, as major tech firms have given their employees the option to work from home and the prospect of relocating to affluent California areas around the Bay Area such as Napa, Marin, and even Lake Tahoe, Nevada. Conversely, people of color—many of them deemed essential workers—are forced to work in conditions that disproportionately expose them and their families to COVID-19. What this particular conjunction underscores—and what every person of color protesting on the streets has repeated—is that White society is deeply implicated in Black and Brown dispossession. White institutions created this racial contract, and White society continues to condone it.

Notes

1. Jeffrey Martin, "All Coronavirus Deaths in St. Louis, Missouri Have Been African Americans," *Newsweek*, April 9, 2020.
2. John Eligon et al., "Black Americans Face Alarming Rates of Coronavirus Infection in Some States," *New York Times*, April 7, 2020.
3. Miriam Jordan and Richard A. Oppel Jr., "For Latinos and COVID-19, Doctors Are Seeing an 'Alarming' Disparity," *New York Times*, May 7, 2020.
4. Katherine Faulders and Olivia Rubin, "New Mexico's Governor Warns Tribal Nations Could Be 'Wiped Out' by Coronavirus," *ABC News*, March 20, 2020, https://abcn ews.go.com/Politics/mexicos-governor-warns-tribal-nations-wiped-coronavirus/ story?id=69884997.
5. Rebecca Klar, "Navajo Nation Reports More Coronavirus Cases Per Capita Than Any US State," *The Hill*, May 11, 2020, https://thehill.com/policy/healthcare/497091-nav ajo-nation-has-more-coronavirus-cases-per-capita-than-any-us-state.
6. Mike Davis, "Mike Davis on COVID-19: The Monster Is at the Door," Haymarket Books, https://www.haymarketbooks.org/blogs/110-mike-davis-on-covid-19-the-monster-is-at-the-door.

7. See João H. Costa Vargas, *Never Meant to Survive. Genocide and Utopias in Black Diaspora Communities* (Lantham, MD: Rowman and Littlefield, 2008). See also Henry Louis Gates Jr. and Terri Hume Oliver, eds., *The Souls of Black Folk: Norton Critical Editions* (W. W. Norton, 1999).

8. Daniel Villarreal, "Michigan Closes Down Capitol in Face of Death Threats From Armed Protesters Against Gov. Whitmer," *Newsweek*, May 14, 2020, https://www.newsweek.com/michigan-closes-down-capitol-face-death-threats-armed-protesters-against-gov-whitmer-1504241.

9. ZZZ It is worth noting that Mark Zuckerberg net worth has increased by $30 billion since California went under lockdown on March 17th, 2020. Making him the 3rd-richest person in the world. Despite the economic fallout from the pandemic, not to mention the loss of life and personal suffering, for Facebook, facilitating this sort of right-wing, neo-conservative, racialized violence has proven highly profitable.

10. Abram Brown, "The Private Goldman Sachs Coronavirus Meeting That's Setting The Internet On Fire," *Forbes*, March 16, 2020, https://www.forbes.com/sites/abrambrown/2020/03/16/the-private-goldman-sachs-coronavirus-meeting-thats-setting-the-internet-on-fire/?sh=5e8e4dc950dd.

11. Carol Anderson, *White Rage. The Unspoken Truth of Our Racial Divide* (New York, NY: Bloomsbury, 2016).

12. Michael Mascarenhas, "Environmental Inequality and Environmental Justice," pp. 161–178 n *Twenty Lessons in Environmental Sociology. Second Edition*, edited by Kenneth Gould and Tammy Lewis, (New York, NY: Oxford University Press, 2015).

13. United States General Accountability Office, "Siting of Hazardous Waste Landfills and Their Correlation with Racial and Economic Status of Surrounding Communities," https://www.gao.gov/products/RCED-83-168.

14. Commission for Racial Justice, "Toxic Wastes and Race in the United States: A National Report on the Racial and Socio-Economic Characteristics of Communities with Hazardous Waste Sites," United Church of Christ, https://www.nrc.gov/docs/ML1310/ML13109A339.pdf.

15. See Bullard et al., "Toxic Wastes and Race at Twenty 1987–2007." See also Robert D. Bullard et al., "Toxic Wastes and Race at Twenty: Why Race Still Matters After All of These Years," *Environmental Law* 38 (2008): 371–411.

16. See David Naguib Pellow, "Toward a Critical Environmental Justice Studies. Black Lives Matter as an Environmental Justice Challenge," *Du Bois Review: Social Science Research on Race* (2016): 1–16. See also David Naguib Pellow, *What Is Critical Environmental Justice?* (Medford, MA: Polity Press, 2018). See also Evan Ringquist, "Assessing Evidence of Environmental Inequalities: A Meta-Analysis," *Journal of Policy Analysis and Management* 24, no. 2 (2005): 223–247.

17. Martin Luther King Jr., *Where Do We Go from Here: Chaos or Community?* (Boston, MA: Beacon Press, 1968).

18. George Lipsitz, *The Possessive Investment in Whiteness: How White People Profit From Identity Politics* (Philadelphia, PA: Temple University Press, 2006).

19. Lipsitz, *The Possessive Investment*.

20. See Andrew R. Highsmith, *Demolition Means Progress: Flint, Michigan, and the Fate of the American Metropolis* (Chicago: University of Chicago Press, 2015). See also George Lipsitz, *How Racism Takes Place* (Philadelphia, PA: Temple University Press, 2011).

21. Highsmith, *Demolition*, 34.

22. Highsmith, *Demolition*.

23. Lipsitz, *The Possessive Investment*.

24. See Pellow, "Toward a Critical Environmental Justice Studies." See also Pellow, *What Is Critical Environmental Justice?*

25. Kerri Brown, "570 Workers Test Positive for Coronavirus at North Carolina Poultry Plant," *NPR*, May 21, 2020, https://www.npr.org/sections/coronavirus-live-updates/2020/05/21/860545442/570-workers-have-coronavirus-at-north-carolina-poultry-plant?utm_medium=RSS&utm_campaign=nprblogscoronavirusliveupdates.

26. Leah Douglas, "Mapping Covid-19 Outbreaks in the Food System," *Food & Environment Reporting Network*, https://thefern.org/2020/04/mapping-covid-19-in-meat-and-food-processing-plants/.

27. Adam Gabbatt, "Latino Workers Face Discrimination Over Spread of Coronavirus in Meat Plants," *Guardian*, May 25, 2020.

28. Gabbatt, "Latino Workers Face Discrimination."

29. Rafael Bernal, "HHS Chief Suggests Workers Are to Blame for COVID Outbreaks at Meatpacking Plants," *The Hill*, May 7, 2020, https://thehill.com/latino/496589-hhs-chief-suggests-workers-are-to-blame-for-covid-outbreaks-at-meatpacking-plants.

30. Before he was killed by a White police officer in Minneapolis, George Floyd lost his job because of the coronavirus pandemic. George Floyd also tested positive for COVID-19 in April.

31. Amy Cooper, the White woman who called the police on a Christian Cooper, a Black man, in Central Park, New York, after he asked her to leash her dog is one of the most recent striking examples.

32. Commission for Racial Justice, "Toxic Wastes and Race."

33. See Bullard et al., "Toxic Wastes and Race at Twenty." See also Paul Mohai and Robin Saha, "Which Came First, People or Pollution? A Review of Theory and Evidence From Longitudinal Environmental Justice Studies," *Environmental Research Letters* 10, no. 12 (2015): 1–9.

6

We Can See Clearly Now

Inequality and the COVID-19 Pandemic

Michael D. Yates

Capitalist economies are crisis prone. There are many reasons for this, which is to say that a severe economic downturn can be triggered by a multitude of events. At the time of this writing, in May 2020, we are experiencing the most precipitous collapse, in nearly every country, in the history of capitalism. The immediate cause has been a global pandemic, the worst since the great flu pandemic of 1918–1919. COVID-19 has already killed at least a quarter-million people globally and more than 90,000 in the United States. As businesses and public entities such as schools have been forced to close, output has steeply and rapidly declined, and unemployment has skyrocketed. Between March and May, more than 30,000,000 U.S. workers applied for unemployment compensation, and in April 2020 the official (Bureau of Labor Statistics or BLS) unemployment rate was 14.7 percent (however, if we correct for an error made by the BLS, it was 19.3 percent). The International Labor Organization (ILO) warns: "The continued sharp decline in working hours globally due to the COVID-19 outbreak means that 1.6 billion workers in the informal economy—that is nearly half of the global workforce—stand in immediate danger of having their livelihoods destroyed."[1]

Crisis helps to lay bare the naked reality of a social system. What was once hidden and taken for granted now comes to the surface. This catastrophe is no exception. To understand this, consider the following three-paragraph description of capitalism.

The Nature of Capitalism

Capitalism is a system founded and reproducing itself through exploitation and expropriation. Wherever there is capitalism, most people will be compelled to sell their capacity to work, their labor power, to survive. This implies that they do not own the land, raw materials, tools, and machinery necessary, in

Michael D. Yates, *We Can See Clearly Now* In: *On Inequality and Freedom.* Edited by: Lawrence M. Eppard and Henry A. Giroux, Oxford University Press. © Oxford University Press 2022. DOI: 10.1093/oso/9780197583029.003.0006 combination with labor, to produce life's necessities. In turn, this requires that these "means of production" are owned by a small minority of any society's persons, those we call capitalists. The monopoly of possession of the few allows them to compel the many to work long and hard enough to bring forward a mass of goods and services that, when sold, will provide at least subsistence wages to their employees and a surplus of profits for the owners. This surplus represents the exploitation of labor. It accrues only to capital and solely because they own what workers need.

For exploitation to have been possible in the first place, multiple expropriations—a taking without compensation—were and are necessary. Peasant lands were confiscated, and the traditional rights of those who worked the land were abolished. The air and water were appropriated as if they were private property. When peasant labor proved insufficient for new capitalist enterprises, slave labor, the direct expropriation of human bodies, ran rampant as capital began its march across the globe. The United States provides one of the best examples of this. First the lands of the Indigenous people were stolen. Second, this and directly genocidal policies exterminated large numbers of them. When they could not be enslaved—because they were too few in number or able to successfully resist or flee—Black men, women, and children from Africa were forced into slavery. The bodies of women were expropriated as well, in a process of removing them from direct production in the precapitalist household economy. All forms of expropriation enhanced the exploitation of wage labor. And they continue to do so.

One immediate consequence of exploitation and expropriation is the great and growing inequality in the distribution of both society's wealth and the yearly product of goods and services. These can be attenuated if there is strong resistance by the working class and peasants, organized in labor unions and political parties and organizations. But if these are absent, capitalism reverts to its default position, which is unrestricted exploitation and expropriation. Workers and peasants without power will become relatively poorer as their employers and landlords tighten the screws, increasing the intensity of work, introducing machinery that deskills work, extending the length of the working day, forcing more and more peasants off their land, swelling the reserve army of labor, and so forth. Money flows in a flood toward the rich, enhancing their political power so that they get still richer and everyone else becomes still poorer.

These three preceding paragraphs may be reasonably clear, if lacking necessary detail, but to fully understand them requires a good deal of study and reflection.[2] They are not so crystal clear that they immediately resonate. In a severe crisis, however, we begin to see and to feel exactly what the system does, to us and all of those like us. Let us consider inequality in light of the pandemic and the resultant economic collapse.

Inequality in Income and Wealth

We know a great deal about both the rise in inequality and the impacts of it. There are many kinds of inequality, and for the most part these are interconnected. Let's look at several of these and then consider some of the effects. First, we know that the distributions of income and wealth[3] have become more and more unequal, reaching levels not seen in the United States, for example, since the age of the great robber barons. Any number of statistics tell the story. During the first 3 years of recovery from the Great Recession (2009 to 2012), 90 percent of income recipients in the United States captured 91 percent of the total increase in income during this period.[4] Globally, for wealth, "Since the turn of the century [2000], the poorest half of the world's population has received just 1% of the total increase in global wealth, while half of that increase has gone to the top 1%."[5]

These numbers are remarkable, but what do they mean concretely? Today, however, we can give particularly appalling examples by observing what is happening every day. Since January 1, 2020, the wealth of Jeff Bezos, owner of Amazon and Whole Foods, has risen by at least $25 billion, an unprecedented increase. It would take a worker earning $30,000 per year 833,333 years to make this much money, and $25 billion is less than one-quarter of Bezos's wealth. Many other billionaires have seen enormous windfall gains.[6] In Jackson, Wyoming, a favorite haunt of the rich—two decades ago, a joke had it that in Jackson, the billionaires were chasing out the millionaires—wealthy families have decamped from private jets to their second (I use this word knowing that the house might be one of many) homes to ride out the pandemic. One man brought his own ventilator and tried, unsuccessfully to get a local doctor to see that it worked properly.[7] Meanwhile, hundreds of millions of people everywhere in the world are without work, often desperate for food. Ten thousand cars lined up near a food bank in San Antonio, Texas.[8]

Adding insult to injury, those whose financial resources are considerable, even growing, declaim so-called essential workers as "heroes," even as the companies they own or manage have failed to provide their employees with adequate protective equipment and safe workplaces. They and their political allies have actually blamed those who labor in meat-processing plants for getting sick and dying, saying that "these people" have lifestyles conducive to the spread of the virus.

South Dakota Governor Kristi Noem said in an interview with Fox News in April that Smithfield employees at a Sioux Falls meat-processing plant were not getting sick at work but at home, "because a lot of these folks who work at this plant live in the same community, the same buildings, sometimes in the same apartments."

At least 783 workers from the Smithfield plant have been diagnosed with COVID-19, and two have died.

In late April, a Smithfield representative echoed Noem's comments, telling BuzzFeed News that the plant's "large immigrant population" in which "living circumstances in certain cultures are different than they are with your traditional American family" contributed to the hundreds of COVID-19 cases.[9]

Consider that these are people doing extraordinarily dangerous jobs, for little pay, and forced not by culture but by harsh economic and political realities to live in conditions most of us would consider unfit for human habitation. Think, too, that another billionaire, Donald Trump, in league with Tyson Foods, compelled the reopening of the processing plants by using the Defense Production Act. How can we call this anything but an intentional infliction of harm, amounting to homicide for every dead worker?

We have all heard, ad nauseam, that capitalism is a system of opportunity, one in which we all have a decent chance to greatly improve our life circumstances. The land of opportunity. The American dream. A true meritocracy. We all know of rags-to-riches stories; they are emblems of capitalist mythology. The data do not bear these myths out. Economists have shown that during the era or rising inequality, economic mobility has diminished markedly. If we divide incomes into fifths (called quintiles), such that the first quintile represents the poorest 20 percent of individuals and the fifth the richest 20 percent, if your parents are in the first quintile, then you are likely to end up there as well, perhaps moving into the second quintile but very unlikely to get to the fifth. If the situation is reversed, you will not likely fall below the fifth quintile and you will almost surely not end up in the first. Also, the state of the economy when a person enters the labor market has a decisive impact on career earnings (and wealth as well, given that a person can convert some income into wealth). Those who begin in a period of growth and overall prosperity will fare considerably better than those who start out in a time of economic recession or depression.[10]

COVID-19 is widening inequality as those with money are suffering much less than those without. This means that mobility will be further dampened. We know that low-income households are bearing the brunt of the economic collapse. Their suffering will be transferred in the future to their children. Think about a teenager from a poor household who has managed to get into college. Her parents have limited resources, and now they have lost most of these. The colleges are shut down now, offering only online instruction. A person from a poor family will be less likely to be able to keep up with her studies; it may be the case that there is not even a decent Internet connection in her home. Imagine that she is a senior and graduates. Going on to a job market in the face of an official unemployment rate of 27.4 percent, in April 2020, for those between the ages of 16 and 24. At least 20 million jobs were lost in April. How is she going to find any job, much less a good one. Each year will thereafter see many more young persons entering the labor market, again facing depressed conditions. During the Great Recession, the income loss suffered by new labor market entrants was more than 20 percent compared to entering during a boom, such as that of the years before the housing market fell apart. Today, however, the loss is bound to be much worse, given that the United States has never faced such an immediate and vertical decline in jobs and production. At the same time, those whose parents are wealthy, who went to prestigious schools, who have connections, will fare much better, even if they too face some difficulties.

A Hierarchy of Jobs: Employment

Second, let us look at jobs. Before the pandemic, there had been considerable job growth in the United States. However, much of this was in low-wage and insecure work.[11] A November 2019 *Forbes* article pointed out that, despite 100 consecutive months of steady employment increase and remarkably low unemployment rate:

> The reality for most people is inconsistent with the employment figures. Stories of job seekers spending an exceedingly long period of time searching for a suitable job, lackluster salary offers, relatively small wage increases for employees and the rapid growth of gig-economy jobs—such as Uber and Lyft drivers, Instacart shoppers and DoorDashers—repudiate the "best job market ever" narrative.[12]

In the United States and in the rest of the world, there is a hierarchy of jobs that matches the inequality in income and wealth. If there is a large and growing gap in income and wealth, there must be similar disparities in jobs, given that most of us get our incomes and wealth from our wages.

Imagine a work triangle. At the base are the worst jobs. Globally, the International Labor Organization estimates a global labor force (those employed plus those unemployed) of about 3.5 billion persons. Child labor (the labor force includes only those at least 15 years of age), which is widespread and exists even in rich countries, is excluded from this total. The vast majority of these jobs are at or close to the base of the jobs triangle. There are more than 800 million farm laborers in the world; 33 million child laborers; 11 million persons in prison, most of whom engage in forced labor; 180 million construction workers, most in the informal sector (without formal employment contracts) working for low pay under deplorable conditions (e.g., removing asbestos without protective clothing); at least 60 million garment workers; 18 million electronics workers; and tens of millions of transit, warehouse, and logistic employees. In India alone, there are 5 million bidi workers, almost all women, hand rolling cheap cigarettes and cigars called bidis.

In the United States, over 40 percent of the workforce comprises "automobile workers; secretaries, administrative assistants, and office support personnel; clerks; restaurant workers; security employees; custodians; and medical workers."[13] Most of these jobs are poorly paid, nonunion, and low social status. The BLS projections for the occupations that will have the largest employment growth between 2018 and 2028 predict: "The fastest growing groups include healthcare support occupations (18.2 percent), personal care and service occupations (17.4 percent), computer and mathematical occupations (12.7 percent), healthcare practitioners and technical occupations (11.9 percent), and community and social service occupations (11.2 percent)."[14] Except for computer and mathematical occupations, these are all near the bottom of the jobs triangle.

What has been the impact of the pandemic on jobs? For those who have continued to work, other than certain health professionals, the less they are paid, the higher the risk of infection.[15] Those with higher incomes are much more likely to be able to work from home. Only 9.2 percent of those in the bottom 25 percent of income recipients can work from home, while 61.5 percent of those in the top quartile can do so.[16] If we use education as a proxy for good versus bad jobs, "Those with college degrees were more likely to telecommute. Some 63% of workers with at least a bachelor's degree worked entirely from home, but only 20% of those with high school education or less did so."[17]

For workers on the front line of risk for infection, the stories are heart rending. A passenger coughs near a bus driver in Detroit, Michigan, and the driver is dead 11 days later. His coworkers have to strike to get the transit company to provide minimal protection.[18] It is difficult not to cry when reading about those who toil in meat-processing plants. A worker took Tylenol to lower her temperature so she could continue to work and not lose a small bonus the company had offered. She later died.[19] These workers know they are in imminent danger of death, but living with no income is not an option. Many are immigrants and undocumented, and they will never receive government assistance.[20] A pastor in New York City has lost 44 parishioners to COVID-19. Why? " 'We are dying at a higher rate because we have no other choice,' Frankie Miranda, president of the Hispanic Federation, told CNN. 'These are the delivery food people, the people that are the day workers, the farm workers, these are people that are working in restaurants. They are essential services, and now they are not enjoying the protections that maybe in other industries people can have.' "[21]

A Hierarchy of Jobs: Unemployment

There is always unemployment in capitalist economies; it rises and falls as production falls and rises. Countries determine the amount and percentage of unemployment in different, sometimes complicated, ways. An entire book could be written about this alone, and many pages could provide all manner of unemployment data. However, the pandemic has made unemployment palpable, and it has shown with great clarity the inequality in its incidence and impact.

Those who have lost their jobs were much less likely to be at the top of our work triangle. Of the 20 million workers shed by businesses (if we count independent contractors and the self-employed, job losses were 22 million), 7.7 million were in leisure and hospitality, mainly restaurant and drinking establishment workers. Retail trade employment fell by 2.1 million. Professional and business services dropped by 2.2 million, half in temporary help services and in services to buildings and dwellings. Employment in the other services industries declined by 1.3 million, with nearly 800,000 in personal and laundry services. These losses are mainly for low-wage workers. And in healthcare, manufacturing, transportation and warehousing, and construction, many of the more than 4 million losses were for those closer to the bottom of the jobs triangle.[22]

Those out of work are, given their prior employment, singularly unable to maintain their normal spending without help. Stories abound of those unable to pay rent, of people fearful of going to hospitals because they fear incurring large bills. In the United States, the federal government has offered some monetary assistance, and the states have supplied some as well. However, while 36 million have applied for unemployment compensation, by no means have all of them gotten it. For more than 40 years, it has become increasingly difficult to qualify for this benefit, as states have succumbed to corporate pressure to limit tax burdens and as neoliberal ideologues have demonized the unemployed as lazy. If we give people benefits when not working, they will not want to work at all. In states like Florida and North Carolina, it has proved nearly impossible to receive compensation, not only because requirements are so stringent but also because the computerized systems applicants must use have been set up not to function efficiently. Some unemployed workers have tried and failed even to get through on these systems more than 1,000 times! Now that states are opening their economies, with little concern for employee safety, workers are being forced to return to their jobs, often at reduced pay and fewer hours, on pain of losing benefits or being accused of fraud. From a *New York Times* report: "Jason Cooper, 43, went back to his serving job at the Savour restaurant in Tallahassee, Fla., in early May without ever receiving the jobless benefits he spent weeks trying to track down." Mr. Cooper hopes to track down the unpaid benefits after he gets back to work.[23]

If we extend our view to the world, especially that part in the Global South, those who have been thrown out of work, overwhelmingly desperately poor, have faced much more dire consequences. It is worth quoting Indian writer Arundhati Roy at length to see the horror story that has been unfolding in her country:

Finally, on March 19, the Indian prime minister addressed the nation. He hadn't done much homework. He borrowed the playbook from France and Italy. He told us of the need for "social distancing" (easy to understand for a society so steeped in the practice of caste) and called for a day of "people's curfew" on March 22. He said nothing about what his government was going to do in the crisis, but he asked people to come out on their balconies, and ring bells and bang their pots and pans to salute health workers.

He didn't mention that, until that very moment, India had been exporting protective gear and respiratory equipment, instead of keeping it for Indian health workers and hospitals.

Not surprisingly, Narendra Modi's request was met with great enthusiasm. There were pot-banging marches, community dances and processions. Not much social distancing. In the days that followed, men jumped into barrels of sacred cow dung, and BJP supporters threw cow-urine drinking parties. Not to be outdone, many Muslim organisations declared that the Almighty was the answer to the virus and called for the faithful to gather in mosques in numbers.

On March 24, at 8pm, Modi appeared on TV again to announce that, from midnight onwards, all of India would be under lockdown. Markets would be closed. All transport, public as well as private, would be disallowed.

He said he was taking this decision not just as a prime minister, but as our family elder. Who else can decide, without consulting the state governments that would have to deal with the fallout of this decision, that a nation of 1.38bn people should be locked down with zero preparation and with four hours' notice? His methods definitely give the impression that India's prime minister thinks of citizens as a hostile force that needs to be ambushed, taken by surprise, but never trusted.

Locked down we were. Many health professionals and epidemiologists have applauded this move. Perhaps they are right in theory. But surely none of them can support the calamitous lack of planning or preparedness that turned the world's biggest, most punitive lockdown into the exact opposite of what it was meant to achieve.

The man who loves spectacles created the mother of all spectacles.

The lockdown worked like a chemical experiment that suddenly illuminated hidden things. As shops, restaurants, factories and the construction industry shut down, as the wealthy and the middle classes enclosed themselves in gated colonies, our towns and megacities began to extrude their working-class citizens—their migrant workers—like so much unwanted accrual.

Many driven out by their employers and landlords, millions of impoverished, hungry, thirsty people, young and old, men, women, children, sick people, blind people, disabled people, with nowhere else to go, with no public transport in sight, began a long march home to their villages. They walked for days, towards Badaun, Agra, Azamgarh, Aligarh, Lucknow, Gorakhpur—hundreds of kilometres away. Some died on the way.

Our towns and megacities began to extrude their working-class citizens like so much unwanted accrual.

They knew they were going home potentially to slow starvation. Perhaps they even knew they could be carrying the virus with them, and would infect their families, their parents and grandparents back home, but they desperately needed a shred of familiarity, shelter and dignity, as well as food, if not love.

As they walked, some were beaten brutally and humiliated by the police, who were charged with strictly enforcing the curfew. Young men were made to crouch and frog jump down the highway. Outside the town of Bareilly, one group was herded together and hosed down with chemical spray.

A few days later, worried that the fleeing population would spread the virus to villages, the government sealed state borders even for walkers. People who had been walking for days were stopped and forced to return to camps in the cities they had just been forced to leave.

. . . Even still, these were not India's poorest people. These were people who had (at least until now) work in the city and homes to return to. The jobless, the homeless and the despairing remained where they were, in the cities as well as the countryside, where deep distress was growing long before this tragedy occurred. . . .

When the walking began in Delhi, I used a press pass from a magazine I frequently write for to drive to Ghazipur, on the border between Delhi and Uttar Pradesh.

The scene was biblical. Or perhaps not. The Bible could not have known numbers such as these. The lockdown to enforce physical distancing had resulted in the opposite—physical compression on an unthinkable scale. This is true even within India's towns and cities. The main roads might be empty, but the poor are sealed into cramped quarters in slums and shanties.

Every one of the walking people I spoke to was worried about the virus. But it was less real, less present in their lives than looming unemployment, starvation and the violence of the police. Of all the people I spoke to that day, including a group of Muslim tailors who had only weeks ago survived the anti-Muslim attacks, one man's words especially troubled me. He was a carpenter called Ramjeet, who planned to walk all the way to Gorakhpur near the Nepal border.

"Maybe when Modiji decided to do this, nobody told him about us. Maybe he doesn't know about us", he said.

"Us" means approximately 460m people.[24]

Inequality and Health

Third, inequality has marked impacts on health. As income and wealth have flowed from bottom to top, political power has become more skewed. The wealthy use their money to influence governments at all levels, and the state gradually utilizes them and their lackeys to fill public posts. People with hundreds of millions or billions of dollars (or the equivalent in other currencies) finance campaigns to get politicians who will do their bidding elected; they even run for office themselves. What they want are minimal taxes and the privatization of as much public property as possible. Public healthcare, for example, has suffered throughout the Global North as austerity budgets have been the rule. The same has been true as well for the international health institutions like the World Health Organization.[25] Those with the cash get the best healthcare; there are even "concierge" doctors who travel with the global elite to give them the best care available.[26]

The consequences of extreme disparities in healthcare have become apparent. Rich people live longer than the poor, and the gap is widening:

> One of the most disquieting facts about life in the United States today is that the richest American men live 15 years longer than the poorest men, while for women it's 10 years. Put a different way, the life expectancy gap between rich and poor in the U.S. is wider than the gap between the average American and the average Yemeni or Ethiopian.
>
> This gap is only getting wider. According to a report by the Health Inequality Project, from 2001–2014, the richest Americans gained approximately three years in life expectancy while the poorest Americans experienced no gains. A three-year difference in life expectancy may seem trivial, but, as the report's authors note, this gain in lifespan is the equivalent of curing cancer for only the rich. Going back further, the numbers only get worse: The richest American males gained six years in life expectancy from 1980 to 2010, while outcomes for the poorest men remained stagnant.[27]

What is more, there is mounting evidence that inequality in and of itself, that is, other things equal, worsens the health of those at the lower ends of the income and wealth distributions. If, for example, we compare two states in the United States, or two countries, one of which has greater income equality than the other but both have similar average incomes, differences in health outcomes—life expectancy, infant mortality, various diseases—will be apparent. In the places with greater inequality, we will notice similar disparities in these outcomes, meaning that the poor will be relatively less healthy the greater is the inequality where they live. The reason for this seems to be that poorer people have greater anxiety, stress, and feelings of hopelessness. Researchers have coined the term "deaths of despair" to describe the decline in life expectancies, especially among poor White persons in the United States. The response to a loss of hope can be alcohol and drug abuse and other behaviors that increase the likelihood of disease and death. A *New Republic* article put it succinctly:

> A life of poverty can mean a life of constant stress. The poor have little control over their work schedules or wages. (In the Whitehall studies, one's level of control in the workplace, even for workers within the same organization, accounted for one-half of health disparities.) They fear suddenly losing their job and being unable to pay the bills. They despair over their own future, and how to give their children a better life. They are exhausted and socially isolated by second or third jobs, long commutes, and weekend shifts. They lack the means to take much-needed time off or pay for relaxing hobbies. And often their social support systems are decimated by incarceration, addiction, and depression.
>
> It's no wonder that the poor have consistently worse health outcomes. Their brains are working overtime all the time.[28]

Given everything said so far, it was inevitable that the pandemic would create still starker differences between those at the pinnacle of the income/wealth distributions and those at their base. Imagine the care the hundreds of millions of Indians Arudhati Roy described in the essay quoted above and compare this meted out to India's many billionaires. In the United States, New York City was one of the worst-hit places in the country, with nearly 200,000 cases and 16,000 deaths as of mid-May 2020. The poorest parts of the city were the hardest hit. Central Queens is a case in point. The understaffed and underequipped public hospital had people jamming the halls waiting for beds. Heartbreaking is too weak a word to describe what has happened. Deaths, sicknesses, mind-boggling unemployment, poverty, crowded and inadequate housing, no health insurance, no physician. All the good people who do society's hardest, dangerous, and poorest paid jobs: invisible men, women, and children to most of us, visible only to themselves.[29]

There is also an ongoing mental health crisis. The stress, depression, and hopelessness that the least well-off suffer compared to their economic betters has worsened with the pandemic. The economic collapse and its attendant lack of resources will certainly lead to more suicides and drug overdoses, along with ongoing mental illnesses. Mental health practitioners have already noted the following:

Nearly half of Americans report the coronavirus crisis is harming their mental health, according to a Kaiser Family Foundation poll. A federal emergency hotline for people in emotional distress registered a more than 1,000 percent increase in April compared with the same time last year. Last month, roughly 20,000 people texted that hotline, run by the Substance Abuse and Mental Health Services Administration.

Online therapy company Talkspace reported a 65 percent jump in clients since mid-February. Text messages and transcribed therapy sessions collected anonymously by the company show coronavirus-related anxiety dominating patients' concerns.[30]

Yet governments have done little to address what is and will be happening.

The Ubiquity of Racism and Patriarchy

Many scholars have argued persuasively that capitalism has been racialized and patriarchal from its inception, so that we cannot speak of capitalism without an understanding that race and gender are built into its DNA.[31] Space does not permit a full explication of this, but the data provide evidence that these two forces are alive and well. Here, we confine our statistics to the United States, where the legacy of Native American land theft and murder of so many Native people, slavery, and oppression of women is alive and well. No matter what metric we use—income, wealth, poverty, life expectancy, infant mortality, pregnancy-related mortality, unemployment, jobs, housing, schooling, and people in prison or on parole—Blacks fare much worse than Whites. For example, the ratio of median Black family income to that for Whites was not much higher in 2017 than it was in 1947, and the 2017 ratio of 59.1 percent was lower than that for 1969 when it was 61.3. Median wealth for Black households in 1916 was 9 percent that of White households. Black workers earn less than Whites irrespective of occupation. For jobs, a report from the Economic Policy Institute found that, astonishingly, "A $10,000 increase in the average annual wage of an occupation is associated with a seven percentage point decrease in the proportion of black men in that occupation." Black prisoners comprise a fraction of all prisoners nearly three times greater than the Black share of the U.S. population. Poverty rates between Blacks and Whites diverge markedly; for children less than 18 years old, the rate in 2018 for Black children was 32 percent, while for Whites it was 11 percent.[32] Were we to use Hispanics or Native Americans, we would find similar inequalities.[33]

Inequality between men and women is also palpable in the United States. A United Nations report lays out the basics for all nations: "Once in the paid labor force, women everywhere find themselves earning less than men for the same types of work; engaging more frequently in unskilled, low-wage labor; or spending less time in income-generating work and more time in unpaid care-giving work at home."[34] Specific data abound. Women would benefit much more than men if the minimum wage were raised to $15, meaning that women are overrepresented in low-wage jobs. For single parents, who are mainly women, this increase would be even more beneficial, with 44.6 percent of all working single mothers getting a raise.[35] For wages in general, with education level constant:

> Women in the workforce have increased their educational attainment, yet women's pay lags men's at every level of education. Women with a high school degree are paid around 80 percent of what men are paid and women with a college or advanced degree are paid just 73 percent. Furthermore, women who hold advanced degrees are paid even less than men with bachelor's degrees."[36]

Poverty rates are more than 20 percent higher for women than for men; for women heads of households, it is more than 25 percent higher.[37] In 2016, women in the United States made up 47 percent of the overall workforce, but they encompassed 58 percent of the low-wage and 69 percent of the lowest wage workforces. And this overrepresentation is true at every education level.[38] Let us note here that race, ethnicity, and gender intersect, and this means that women of color typically face more adverse circumstances than do White men and men of color. Also, we need hardly show statistics to know that women perform much more household work than do men. More than ever, given the increase in women's labor force participation, they face a double day, working for wages and laboring at home. In the United States, women do 60 percent more reproductive labor than men.[39]

The COVID-19 pandemic has served to expose racism and patriarchy. It has had a significant, lopsided impact on women and persons of color, widening the multiple gaps between them and White males. Black persons have died at a much higher rate than any racial or ethnic group. Some states have astonishingly higher rates for Black persons: seven times higher in Kansas; six in Missouri, Wisconsin, and Washington, D.C.; and five in Michigan. In one of the first-hit states, Louisiana, 70 percent of fatalities were of Black persons. Enough was known by early May to state: "If all Americans had died of COVID-19 at the same rate as White Americans, 10,500 Black Americans, 1,400 Latino Americans and 300 Asian Americans would still be alive." This quotation shows as well that Latinx and Asian American deaths were disproportionate to those of White persons.[40]

Native Americans have been especially devastated. In the Navajo Nation, which stretches across parts of Arizona and New Mexico, there were 3,100 cases and 100 deaths as of early May 2020, a rate of 18 cases per 1,000 people, higher than in any U.S. state. The Nation has always been starved of health-care funds and many other things most of us take for granted, such as running water (Native peoples "are 19 times likelier than white Americans to lack in-door plumbing"). The isolation of the Navajo makes it impossible to effectively order goods online, and social distancing is difficult in the few stores and re-tail outlets available to them. Now, the virus had overwhelmed what healthcare treatments and facilities are available, and even outside help from groups like Doctors Without Borders has not been enough to stop the spread of the disease. Given how poor Native peoples are, how many have preexisting conditions, how crowded limited housing is, how few have Internet access, it is no wonder that the pandemic has wreaked such havoc on them. And the federal govern-ment has done very little to help.[41]

With respect to employment, those working in essential occupations are often people of color. We have already alluded to this for beef-, pork-, and chicken-processing plants, where numerous employees are also immigrants, substantial numbers without documents. The same is true for farm laborers, warehouse workers, and many others. Overall, 41.2 percent of front-line workers are people of color. They are overrepresented in building cleaning services, childcare and social services, bus drivers, transit workers, warehouse laborers, and "most of the top 10 occupations in Trucking, Warehouse, and Postal Service; most of the top 10 occupations in Building Cleaning Services; all of the top 10 occupations in Health Care, except registered nurses, physicians, managers, and secretaries and administrative; four of the top 10 occupations in Child Care and Social Services (childcare workers, personal care aides, social workers, and nursing assistants)." There are large numbers of immigrants in these jobs, as well as in groceries, home health care, janitorial services, and in domestic labor (maids and housekeepers, e.g.). Most of these workers earn low wages with no or limited benefits, and many have childcare responsibilities.[42]

For the unemployed, the data above for the sectors hardest hit by job losses in April 2020 tell us that those who lost their jobs were disproportionately per-sons of color. In terms of the unemployment rates of that month, 14.2 percent for Whites, 16.7 percent for Blacks, 14.5, and 18.9 percent for Hispanics. If we were able to account for the error made by the BLS, as well as for a broader measure of labor market slack, one that included involuntary part-time workers and those who have dropped out of the labor force for economic reasons, these numbers, especially the last two, would be much higher.[43]

The deep recession now underway in the United States is being called a "shecession," because women, more so than men, are its victims. In April 2020, female unemployment hit double digits for the first time since 1948, with an official rate of 15 percent, compared to 13 percent for men. For Black women,

it was 16.4 percent, and for Hispanic women it was 20.2 percent. Fifty-five percent of all job losses were of women. A million single mothers have lost employment since February.[44]

Conclusion

It would be remiss of an author not to offer some ideas about what might be done
to address the problems described in an essay such as this. The German revolutionary Rosa Luxemburg famously said Socialism or Barbarism. This pandemic
and those surely to follow are the result of capitalism's long assault on the environment, as scholars have shown.[45] The COVID-19 crisis has, in multiple ways,
shown us that today the rallying cry should be socialism or exterminism. Our
current social system simply cannot cope with pandemics and the damage they
do to human bodies and spirits. Perhaps more than at any time before, we have
a chance to alter course. Do we really want to return to life as it was before the
virus struck? To the same rotten jobs, with endless and deadening labor and constant surveillance by the boss? To dirty air, polluted water, constant noise, dying
species, and ruined land? To the same needless consumption? To continued exploitation and harassment by employers, landlords, bill collectors, and police? To
alienation, fear, and despair? To watch as an unconscionable inequality goes on
and on? As governments cater to those at the top and ignore and vilify those at
the bottom? To endure such intense hatred of women and people of color?

   If it is true, as Roy said, that the pandemic is a portal revealing the ugly truth,
so often hidden, about capitalist society, it can also be an opening to something
beautiful, revealing a true light at the end of the tunnel. We are seeing large
numbers of protests around the world, of workers demanding safety, of renters
and debtors demanding relief, of the hungry demanding food. Perhaps, and it
is hoped, out of these there will arise, in every country, a desire for something
better, more communal, healthier, loving. And out of these desires will come a
global movement for the creation of a new society.[46]

Notes

1. "ILO: As Job Losses Escalate, Nearly Half of Global Workforce at Risk of Losing
   Livelihoods," April 29, 2020, https://www.ilo.org/global/about-the-ilo/newsroom/
   news/WCMS_743036/lang--en/index.htm.
2. See Michael D. Yates, *Can the Working Class Change the World?* (New York: Monthly
   Review Press, 2018) and sources cited therein for a more thorough discussion of exploitation and expropriation.

3. Income represents a flow of money over some time period, usually a year, to individuals, households, or families. Wages, rents, interest, and dividends are examples. In most data, capital gains, money received when an asset such as a stock share is sold at a price higher than that at which it was purchased, are excluded from income. Wealth is a stock, measured at a point in time, and measures the current money value of everything owned by an individual, household, or family. Homes, stocks, bonds, unincorporated businesses, cash, and real estate are examples.

4. Emmauel Saez, "Striking It Richer: The Evolution of Top Incomes in the United States" (updated with 2012 preliminary estimates), http://eml.berkeley.edu/~saez/saez-UStopincomes-2012.pdf.

5. "An Economy for the 1%," oxfam.com, January 18, 2016, https://www-cdn.oxfam.org/s3fs-public/file_attachments/bp210-economy-one-percent-tax-havens-180116-en_0.pdf.

6. Chuck Collins, Omar Campo, and Sophia Paslaski, "Billionaire Bonanza 2020," Institute for Policy Studies, April 21, 2020, https://mronline.org/wp-content/uploads/2020/04/Billionaire-Bonanza-2020-April-21.pdf. This paper contains research done by the Institute for Policy Studies.

7. Justin Farrell, "Where the Very Rich Go to Hide," April 2015, 2020, https://www.nytimes.com/2020/04/15/opinion/jackson-hole-coronavirus.html?action=click&module=Opinion&pgtype=Homepage.

8. John Burnett, "Thousands of Cars Line Up at One Texas Food Bank as Job Losses Hit Hard," April 17, 2020, https://www.npr.org/2020/04/17/837141457/thousands-of-cars-line-up-at-one-texas-food-bank-as-job-losses-hit-hard.

9. Kate Taylor, "At Least 4,500 Tyson Workers Have Caught COVID-19, With 18 deaths. The Meat Giant Still Doesn't Offer Paid Sick Leave, as the Industry Blames Workers for Outbreaks," May 11, 2020, https://www.businessinsider.com/tyson-4500-covid-19-cases-as-meat-industry-blames-workers-2020-5.

10. See Lawrence Mishel et al., "Mobility," in The State of Working America, 12th ed. (Ithaca, NY: Cornell University Press, 2012), Chap. 3; Hilary Wething, "Why Young People Should Care About a Lame Labor Market," August 28, 2014, https://www.epi.org/blog/young-people-care-lame-labor-market/, and sources linked therein.

11. Data on job growth can be found every month in the BLS's summary of its household and business employment surveys. For the October 28, 2021, report, see see U.S. Bureau of Labor Statistics, "Employment Situation Summary," September 8, 2021, https://www.bls.gov/news.release/empsit.nr0.htm. For a summary of the rise of what can fairly be called "bad" jobs, see Jack Kelly, "The Frightening Rise In Low-Quality, Low-Paying Jobs: Is This Really A Strong Job Market?" Forbes, November 25, 2019, https://www.forbes.com/sites/jackkelly/2019/11/25/the-frightening-rise-in-low-quality-low-paying-jobs-is-this-really-a-strong-job-market/#230ee5f04fd1.

12. Kelly, "The Frightening Rise,"

13. Yates, "Can the Working Class," 30.

14. See U.S. Bureau of Labor Statistics, "Employment Projection: 2020–2030 Summary," September 8, 2021, https://www.bls.gov/news.release/ecopro.nr0.htm.

15. Marcus Lu, "The Front Line: Visualizing the Occupants With the Highest COVID-19 Risk," *Visual Capitalist*, April 15, 2020, https://www.visualcapitalist.com/the-front-line-visualizing-the-occupations-with-the-highest-covid-19-risk/?fbclid=IwAR0g muyElQq79TpwCCXEC0lzkhq-5ZuW8Hnu8DYLC4lUS4T3nn81ZjARHIk.

16. Lu, "The Front Line."

17. Tami Luhby, "Nearly 40% of Low-Income Workers Lost Their Jobs in March," *CNN*, May 15, 2020, https://www.cnn.com/2020/05/14/economy/low-income-layoffs-coro navirus/index.html.

18. Michael Levenson, "11 Days After Fuming About a Coughing Passenger, a Bus Driver Died From the Coronavirus," *New York Times*, April 4, 2020, https://www.nytimes. com/2020/04/04/us/detroit-bus-driver-coronavirus.html.

19. Ana Swanson, David Yaffe-Bellany, and Michael Corkery, "Pork Chops vs. People: Battling Coronavirus in an Iowa Meat Plant," *New York Times*, May 10, 2020, https://www.nytimes.com/2020/05/10/business/economy/coronavirus-tyson-plant-iowa.html.

20. See Jessica Lussenhop, "Coronavirus at Smithfield Pork Plant: The Untold Story of America's Biggest Outbreak," *BBC News*, April 17, 2020, https://www.bbc.com/news/world-us-canada-52311877.

21. Catherine E. Shoichet and Daniel Burke, "This New York Pastor Says His Parish Lost 44 People to Coronavirus," *CNN*, May 2020, https://www.cnn.com/interactive/2020/05/us/new-york-church-coronavirus-deaths-cnnphotos/index.html.

22. These data are taken from U.S. Bureau of Labor Statistics, "Employment Situation Summary.".

23. See Patricia Cohen and Tiffany Hsu, "'Rolling Shock' as Job Losses Mount Even With Reopenings," *New York Times*, May 14, 2020, https://www.nytimes.com/2020/04/30/upshot/unemployment-state-restrictions-pandemic.html?fbclid=IwAR3-HtpLMjxn8P_3ZXMddFnPbc5W5s8DZ2ebFXuDbR-c1fu223CmNAhxptA.

24. Arundhati Roy, "The Pandemic Is a Portal," April 3, 2020, https://forhuma nliberation.blogspot.com/2020/04/3341-pandemic-is-portal.html?fbclid= IwAR1azZlbrVDT1KOiKmkqE7iBiqSoRf4yHrBdnglmSYzm5-Km8EZYQY0Kweo.

25. For an excellent essay covering these issues and many more, see Mike Davis, "C'est La Lutte Finale," *Progressive International*, April 30, https://progressive.international/blueprint/34da398a-af05-43bb-9778-c27023932630-la-lutte-finale/en2020.

26. Rex Weiner, "Keeping the Wealthy Healthy—and Everyone Else Waiting," Inequality. org, July 11, 2017, https://inequality.org/research/keeping-wealthy-healthy-every one-else-waiting/.

27. Roge Karma, "The Gross Inequality of Death in America," *New Republic*, May 10, 2019, https://newrepublic.com/article/153870/inequality-death-america-life-exp ectancy-gap.

28. Karma, "The Gross Inequality." See also Sam Pizzigati, "Inequality Is Literally Killing Us," *Common Dreams*, October 9, 2019, https://www.commondreams.org/views/2019/10/09/inequality-literally-killing-us?cd-origin=rss&utm_term=AO&utm_c ampaign=Daily%20Newsletter&utm_content=email&utm_source=Daily%20New

sletter&utm_medium=Email; R. G. Wilkinson and K. E. Pickett, "Income Inequality and Social Dysfunction," *Annual Review of Sociology*, 35 (2009): 493–511; Nico Pitney, "Scientists Find Alarming Deterioration in DNA of the Urban Poor," *Huffington Post*, May 5, 2015, http://huffingtonpost.com/2015/05/08/poverty-race-ethnicity-dna-telo meres_n_7228530.html (suggesting that inequality can negatively affect the DNA of the poorest people).

29. Annie Correal and Andrew Jacobs, "'A Tragedy Is Unfolding: Inside New York's Virus Epicenter," *New York Times*, April 9, 2020, updated May 6, 2020, https://www.nyti mes.com/2020/04/09/nyregion/coronavirus-queens-corona-jackson-heights-elmhu rst.html?fbclid=IwAR2Sf-SuXglg7gjqtEQM5PNof4XmDDWz9Ldxf4n9vBQU qDUH51bMlMDiJ04.

30. William Wan, "The Coronavirus Pandemic Is Pushing America Into a Mental Health Crisis," *Washington Post*, May 4, 2020, https://www.washingtonpost.com/health/ 2020/05/04/mental-health-coronavirus/?fbclid=IwAR3mscgUfjhAP2tsRa3Y-cv5QOu5JwIfebS6TRdiQZWh6AgGJhxbWI5ircw.

31. For a summary, see Yates, "Can the Working Class," Chap. 2, "Some Theoretical Considerations," and sources cited therein.

32. The data in this paragraph are taken from Michael D. Yates, "It's Still Slavery by Another Name," *Monthly Review*, 72, no. 1 (May 2020): 42–45; and http://bls.gov/ news.release/wkyeng.t03.htm; http://epi.org/page/-/BriefingPaper288.pdf.

33. On child poverty rates, for example, see Janelle Jones, "One-Third of Native American and African American Children Are (Still) in Poverty," Economic Policy Institute, September 20, 2017, https://www.epi.org/publication/one-third-of-native-ameri can-and-african-american-children-are-still-in-poverty/. For data on Native Americans, see Roxanne Dunbar-Ortiz, *An Indigenous Peoples' History of the United States* (Boston: Beacon Press, Reprint ed., 2015).

34. United Nations Population Fund (UNFPA), "Worlds Apart: Reproductive Health and Rights in an Age of Inequality," 2017, 46, https://www.unfpa.org/swop.

35. "How Raising the Minimum Wage to $15 by 2024 Will Benefit Women," Economic Policy Institute, May 25, 2017, https://www.epi.org/publication/how-raising-the-minimum-wage-to-15-by-2024-will-benefit-women/.

36. Elise Gould and Teresa Kroeger, "Women Can't Educate Their Way Out of the Gender Wage Gap," Economic Policy Institute, March 6, 2017, https://www.epi.org/publicat ion/women-cant-educate-their-way-out-of-the-gender-wage-gap/.

37. Jessica Semega, "Pay Is Up. Poverty Is Down. How Women Are Making Strides," United States Census Bureau, September 10, 2019, https://www.census.gov/libr ary/stories/2019/09/payday-poverty-and-women.html. These numbers were improvements over the year before, but this was before the pandemic.

38. Jasmine Tucker and Kayla Patrick, "Low-Wage Jobs Are Women's Jobs: The Overrepresentation of Women in Low-Wage Work," National Women's Law Center, August 2017, https://nwlc.org/wp-content/uploads/2017/08/Low-Wage-Jobs-are-Womens-Jobs.pdf.

39. Gus Wezerek and Kristen R. Ghodsee, "Women's Unpaid Labor is Worth $10,900,000,000,000," *New York Times*, March 5, 2020, https://www.nytimes.com/ interactive/2020/03/04/opinion/women-unpaid-labor.html.

40. Data in this paragraph are taken from "The Color of Coronavirus: Covid-19 Deaths by Race and Ethnicity in the U.S.," APM Research Lab, May 12, 2020, https://www.apm researchlab.org/covid/deaths-by-race; Gordon Russell and Sam Karlin, "Coronavirus Disparity in Louisiana: About 70% of the Victims Are Black, But Why?" NOLA.com, April 6, 2020, https://www.nola.com/news/coronavirus/article_d804d410-7852-11ea-ac6d-470ebb61c694.html?fbclid=IwAR3oIAH_O-F1Xw6fPQTflube5idE2E8h yybrQPPhLYhVC7FzfUgyrpfKl2M.

41. Max Ufberg, "The Navajo Nation Is Being Decimated by This Virus," *Monthly Review*, May 12, 2020, https://mronline.org/2020/05/20/the-navajo-nation-is-being-decima ted-by-this-virus/.

42. Hye Jin Rho, Hayley Brown, and Shawn Fremstad, "A Basic Demographic Profile of Workers in Frontline Industries," Center for Economic and Policy Research, April 2020, https://cepr.net/wp-content/uploads/2020/04/2020-04-Frontline-Workers.pdf.

43. U.S. Bureau of Labor Statistics, "Employment Situation Summary."

44. Alisha Haridasani Gupta, "Why Some Women Call This Recession a 'Shecession,'" *New York Times*, May 13, 2020, https://www.nytimes.com/2020/05/09/us/unemp loyment-coronavirus-women.html.

45. See the many works of John Bellamy Foster, Brett Clark, and others, both their books published by Monthly Review Press and their essays in *Monthly Review*. See John Bellamy Foster and Brett Clark, *The Robbery of Nature: Capitalism and the Ecological Rift* (New York: Monthly Review Press, 2020).

46. For examples of pandemic protests, see https://paydayreport.com/; https://viacampes ina.org/en/what-are-we-fighting-for/international-solidarity/; https://www.npr.org/ 2020/04/27/843849435/hometown-heroes-or-whatever-low-wage-workers-want-more-than-praise; https://www.scmp.com/news/world/europe/article/3082551/amid-coronavirus-pandemic-workers-worldwide-stage-labour-day.

PART II

POVERTY, ECONOMIC INEQUALITY, AND FREEDOM

7

Inequality, Violence, and Freedom

Martin Daly and D. B. Krupp

Is inequality a source of violence? A considerable body of evidence suggests that the answer is "yes." Over the past 50 years, for example, researchers have consistently found strong associations between income inequality and homicide rates[1] in comparisons at spatial scales ranging from neighborhoods within a large city[2] to entire countries.[3]

Figure 7.1 illustrates the inequality-homicide relationship in the year 2015, in a cross-national sample of 107 countries selected on no criterion other than availability of the requisite data.[4] The measure of income inequality is the Gini index, which varies, in principle, from 0.0 if everyone gets an identical slice of the pie to 1.0 if a single individual gets every penny and everyone else gets nothing. The "individuals" in this case are households, and the incomes that are being compared are "disposable" household incomes after taxes and government transfers. Many additional variables—policing, emergency medicine, gun availability, cultural norms, and local history, among others—surely have effects on homicide rates, and the data cannot be assumed to be of uniformly high quality for either measure. Nevertheless, the correlation between the two measures is impressively large ($r = .605, p < .001$).

According to Figure 7.1, the United States is a "normal," middle-of-the-pack country, albeit one that is above the world median with respect to both income inequality and lethal violence. For a rich country, however, the United States is exceptional. Figure 7.2 zooms in on the developed world: The data are a subset of those in Figure 7.1, limited to the countries that the United Nations classifies as having "developed economies."[5] Here, the United States stands first in inequality and second in homicide, surpassed only by Lithuania, which ranks second in inequality. Latvia ranks third in both measures.

Japan is a conspicuous outlier in Figure 7.2, combining the lowest homicide rate of any developed country with a higher than average Gini. It may be relevant that a generation ago Japan was one of the least unequal countries in the world. According to the Standardized World Income Inequality Database, Japan's disposable income Gini index has risen more or less steadily from 0.248 in 1975 to 0.321 in 2015. Norway's, by comparison, started a little higher, at 0.259 in 1975, but has remained stable thanks to social welfare policies designed to ensure that

Martin Daly and D. B. Krupp, *Inequality, Violence, and Freedom* In: *On Inequality and Freedom*. Edited by: Lawrence M. Eppard and Henry A. Giroux, Oxford University Press. © Oxford University Press 2022. DOI: 10.1093/oso/9780197583029.003.0007

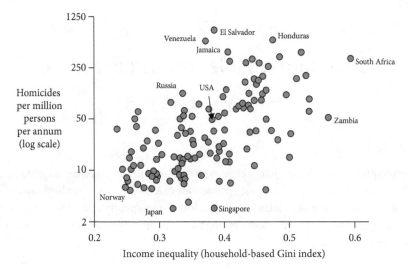

Figure 7.1. National homicide rates as a function of income inequality.

Source: The homicide measure is the average of the annual rates for 2014, 2015, and 2016, as estimated by the UNODC (United Nations Office on Drugs and Crime). Income inequality is the average estimate of the Gini index for disposable household incomes in 2015 or the closest available prior year, according to the SWIID (Standardized World Income Inequality Database).*

*Frederick Solt, "Measuring Income Inequality Across Countries and Over Time: The Standardized World Income Inequality Database," *SocArXiv Papers* (July 2019).

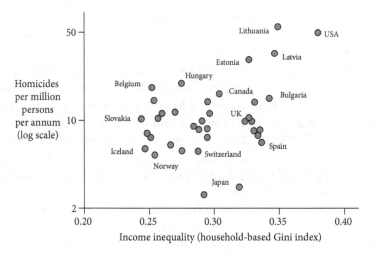

Figure 7.2 Homicide rates as a function of income inequality in developed countries.

Source: See Figure 7.1 source.

the North Sea oil windfall would enrich the many, not just a few,[6] and by 2015, it was 0.255.

This historical trajectory of the Gini index is of potential relevance because the effects that a society's level of inequality has on its frequency of violence must be mediated largely, if not entirely, through the cumulative effects of the ways in which past inequality has affected the psychology and behavior of its citizens. In the jargon of statistics, the effects of inequality include "lagged" effects. So, might a Gini index from the past be a better predictor of the current homicide rate (and of other social ills) than the current Gini? There is some evidence in the datasets analyzed here that this may indeed be the case. For 80 of the 120 countries in Figure 7.1, the Standardized World Income Inequality Database (UNODC) reported a 2015 homicide rate, and the Standardized World Income Inequality Database (SWIID) provided Gini estimates for both 2005 and 2015. The correlation between the log of the 2015 homicide rate and the concurrent Gini in those 80 countries is 0.634, whereas that between the log of the 2015 homicide rate and the Gini 10 years previously is 0.703. We have not (yet) systematically explored this issue, and as far as we know, neither has anyone else,[7] but research aimed at elucidating the lagged effects of past inequality is clearly needed. The delays and magnitudes of the lags will provide important hints about how the experience of inequality worms its way into the physiology, emotions, and decision processes of individual human beings.

Why does inequality predict violence? With the partial exception of a few "rational choice theorists," criminologists have shed little light on this question, largely because many seem to believe that resorting to violence is inherently pathological. Granted, a minority of murderers have damaged brains, but violence is *not*, in general, pathological. It is instead a complex, organized capability of human beings, especially in contexts of social competition for limited resources, and such contexts are precisely the ones within which the great majority of homicides occur.[8] People are relatively willing to adopt extreme tactics of competition in situations in which outcome distributions are relatively inequitable, and anyone who will not compete fiercely is a likely loser. And because monetary outcomes provide a means to the end of satisfying many wants, the magnitude of inequality in economic payoffs is a crucial aspect and indicator of the intensity of social competition. It follows that perfectly sane, self-interested people will be relatively inclined to resort to violence when economic inequality is relatively high.

Apologists for privilege are many, and their voices are disproportionately loud. It is therefore no surprise that the proposition that inequality promotes lethal violence has come under attack. One line of argument maintains that associations between inequality and homicide such as those portrayed in our figures must be incidental rather than causal since the two quantities are sometimes seen to be moving in opposite directions, as for example when homicide rates were falling in the United States during the 1990s even as inequality was on the rise. This argument loses whatever force it may have had as soon as one realizes that effects of inequality include lagged effects, and hence that there was never any reason to expect that inequality and the things that it affects should rise and fall in lock step.

A second argument that has been forcefully advanced is that economic inequality ("relative poverty") is just an innocent bystander that happens to be statistically associated with a genuine cause of criminal violence, "absolute poverty." The primary advocate of this argument has been University of Indiana criminologist William Alex Pridemore, who makes two strong claims: (a) that research comparing jurisdictions within the United States is consistent in showing that the number of persons living in poverty is what really matters; and (b) that in comparisons among countries, his own novel introduction of a statistical control for poverty makes the apparent effects of inequality shrink or vanish.[9] Even researchers whose own results contradict Pridemore's commonly cite his work respectfully.[10] This is unfortunate because both of his claims are false.

Let's consider Pridemore's second claim first. It is true that researchers have not incorporated controls for "absolute" (as distinct from "relative") poverty in cross-national studies, but there is a simple, compelling reason why they have not: The experience of poverty is in large part a matter of the relative deprivation that inequality can cause. Being impoverished entails an imminent risk of starvation in the poorest countries and "mere" exclusion and humiliation in others. According to British sociologist Peter Townsend's influential definition, people "can be said to be in poverty when they lack the resources to obtain the types of diet, participate in the activities and have the living conditions and amenities which are customary, or are at least widely encouraged or approved, in the societies to which they belong."[11] But if one wishes to push on with the intuitive distinction between absolute and relative poverty anyway, the problem is what to use as a measure of the former. Pridemore chose an odd proxy: the infant mortality rate. What he seems not to have known is that infant mortality is more strongly associated with measures of inequality such as the Gini index than with absolute material well-being![12] Adding infant mortality to a set of homicide predictors that already includes the Gini therefore muddies estimation of the impact of inequality and demonstrates nothing.

As regards Pridemore's other claim that absolute poverty outperforms inequality as a predictor of homicide rates within the United States, a number of studies, including many of the best, have found precisely the opposite.[13] Figure 7.3 presents state-level homicide rates in 2015 as a function of income inequality. The relationship is clear and statistically significant ($r = .654$, $p < .001$). However, in this particular case, inequality is "confounded" (highly correlated)

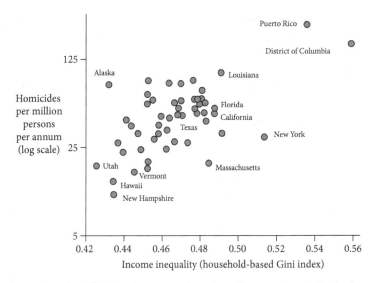

Figure 7.3 State-level homicide rates as a function of income inequality in the United States.

Source: Homicide rates are from the U.S. Federal Bureau of Investigation's Uniform Crime Reports. Gini values are based on gross household income distributions in 2015 according to the American Community Surveys conducted by the U.S. Bureau of the Census.

with absolute poverty (the percentage of the population below the federal poverty line), and this poverty measure predicts homicide ($r = .578, p < .001$) almost as well as the Gini index. The question thus becomes which of these two confounded economic indicators continues to be a meaningful predictor of homicide rates when the other is statistically controlled, and the answer is that only the Gini index survives. The partial correlation between Gini and homicide with the effect of poverty "held constant" is .429 ($p < .002$). The partial correlation between poverty and the homicide rate with the effect of Gini held constant is .226 ($p > .1$).

This is not an idiosyncratic result. Exactly the same conclusion was arrived at in an earlier analysis using 2010 data,[14] and the basic pattern is unchanged if one or both of Puerto Rico and the District of Columbia are removed from the analysis: In all cases, income inequality remains a statistically significant predictor of the homicide rate when percentage below the poverty line is controlled, whereas poverty ceases to be a significant predictor when inequality is controlled.

Recent studies suggested that the inequality-violence relationship is complicated by a different variable altogether: the highly local geography of most competitive interactions. Inequality may cause all sorts of trouble in general, but it seems particularly dangerous when it arises between rivals competing for the same resources, status, or romantic partners. Under these circumstances, competition acts like an amplifier, boosting the effects of inequality dramatically.[15] There are several implications of this.

First, the majority of studies that predict homicide rates from indices of income inequality do so at the level of whole cities, regions, or countries, but none of these is likely to be the most appropriate scale. Killers and their victims are people in close physical proximity to one another, whereas Gini coefficients usually reflect income distributions over spans of hundreds or thousands of square kilometers. If violence is a strategic response to inequality, it ought to reduce (or, even better, reverse) that inequality on average. Just as men in Honduras don't kill one another "in order to" narrow the income gap with Americans, men in the Bronx don't kill one another to narrow the income gap with Manhattanites. Rivalry and homicide are *local* phenomena, and measuring inequality at highly local scales would almost certainly improve the quality of prediction.

Second, and relatedly, differences between economic inequality's trajectories on different spatial scales may provide a further reason why changes in homicide rates don't always track changes in income inequality over the same period. It is well known that income inequality at the national and state levels was increasing in the United States in the second half of the twentieth century, but it is less well known that economic segregation was also increasing.[16] The simultaneity of these trends makes it unclear how the social experiences that create feelings of relative deprivation may have been changing. In principle, inequality increasing at one level of aggregation can even cause it to decrease at another level. For example, individuals who strike it rich may move from a less prosperous neighborhood to a more prosperous one in the same city. As a consequence, additional inflows of money can increase inequality at the city level but decrease it at the neighborhood level, as wealthier individuals segregate themselves from their poorer counterparts.[17] These considerations reinforce the need for future research that investigates whether measuring income inequality at finer spatial scales will yield a more accurate picture of its effects on violence.

Finally, taking competition into account can explain collective forms of violence: When groups compete with each other, the magnitude of between-group inequality in resources, and the particular resources that are up for grabs, both affect the likelihood and extent of violence that the groups will engage in. Early research found no effect of countrywide income inequality on the onset of civil war,[18] but more recent research that measures inequality between the competing groups does,[19] and the story is much the same for variation in rates of ethnic and interstate conflict.[20] Whether perpetrated by individuals or by groups, violence is a scourge, but it is nonetheless a logical and predictable outcome of circumstances that breed conflict. To reduce inequality among competitors for limited resources is to shape a safer world.

What does all this have to do with freedom? Nobody is free to pursue basic needs and pleasures during major civil strife, of course, and violent crime deprives both its victims and its perpetrators of their freedoms. But the individual-level violence that is represented by homicide rates further constrains human freedom in ways that extend far beyond the protagonists. According to various surveys, about 60% of all Americans report that fear of becoming a victim of violent crime constrains their routine social activities and keeps them away from places where they might otherwise go.[21] The causal pathways between fear and isolation apparently run both ways, but the link is mainly a matter of fear constraining behavioral choices.[22]

Researchers studying the fear of crime have dwelt inordinately on the question of whether it is "unrealistic" and "irrational," mainly because women and the elderly are victimized less often than men and younger adults, respectively, and yet express more fear.[23] It should be obvious that equating "rationality" with quantitative accuracy in this way is a mistake,[24] but these contrasts oblige us to ask whether fear is really associated with crime rates at all. This question has received surprisingly little attention, but the available evidence indicates that the fear of crime is indeed associated with crime rates and, more specifically, with those at the very local level of one's immediate neighborhood.[25] In cross-national analyses, fear of crime is yet another variable that is significantly correlated with income inequality, and perhaps surprisingly, actual crime rates neither mediate this association nor account for additional variability in fear[26]; this should be taken with a grain of salt, however, since only gross rates of reported crime have been examined, and it remains plausible that homicide rates or other measures of violent crime would produce different results.

For some of us, the most "ordinary" pleasures—a midday picnic in the park, a lively night at the bar, a moonlit stroll through city streets—are freedoms that we sometimes take for granted. But they are denied to many others by levels of societal disorder, incivility, and violence that are the fruits of extreme inequality.

Notes

1. Martin Daly, *Killing the Competition. Economic Inequality and Homicide* (Piscataway, NJ: Transaction, 2016).
2. Margo Wilson and Martin Daly, "Life Expectancy, Economic Inequality, Homicide, and Reproductive Timing in Chicago Neighbourhoods," *British Medical Journal* 314, no. 7089 (April 26, 1997): 1271–1274.
3. Marc Ouimet, "A World of Homicides. The Effect of Economic Development, Income Inequality, and Excess Infant Mortality on the Homicide Rate for 165 Countries, 2010," *Homicide Studies* 16, no. 3 (August 2012): 238–258.

4. Figure 7.1 includes all countries for which (1) homicide rate estimates were available from the UNODC for at least 2 of the 3 years 2014–2016 and (2) disposable income Gini estimates were available from the SWIID for 2015 or for a prior year after 2010.

5. United Nations, "Country Classification Data Sources, Country Classifications and Aggregation Methodology," in *World Economic Situation and Prospects*, 2014, https://www.un.org/en/development/desa/policy/wesp/wesp_current/2014wesp_country_classification.pdf.

6. Erling Holmøy, "Mineral Rents and Social Policy: The Case of the Norwegian Government Oil Fund," in *Financing Social Policy*, ed. Katja Hufo and Shea McClanahan (London: Palgrave Macmillan, 2009), 183–212.

7. But see Hui Zheng, "Do People Die From Inequality of a Decade Ago?" *Social Science and Medicine* 75, no. 1 (July 2012): 36–45.

8. See Martin Daly and Margo Wilson, *Homicide* (Hawthorne, NY: Aldine de Gruyter, 1988). See also Daly, *Killing the Competition*.

9. See William Alex Pridemore, "A Methodological Addition to the Cross-National Empirical Literature on Social Structure and Homicide: A First Test of the Poverty-Homicide Thesis," *Criminology* 46, no. 1 (February 2008): 133–153. See also William Alex Pridemore, "Poverty Matters. A Reassessment of the Inequality-Homicide Relationship in Cross-National Studies," *British Journal of Criminology* 51, no. 5 (September 2011): 739–772.

10. Daly, *Killing the Competition*, 72–73.

11. Peter Townsend, *Poverty in the United Kingdom* (London: Penguin, 1979).

12. Anthony T. Flegg, "Inequality of Income, Illiteracy, and Medical Care as Determinants of Infant Mortality in Developing Countries," *Population Studies* 36, no. 3 (April 1982): 441–458. See also Robert J. Waldmann, "Income Distribution and Infant Mortality," *Quarterly Journal of Economics* 107, no. 4 (November 1992): 1283–1302. See also Steven F. Messner, Lawrence E. Raffalovich, and Gretchen M. Sutton, "Poverty, Infant Mortality, and Homicide Rates in Cross-National Perspective: Assessments of Criterion and Construct Validity," *Criminology* 48, no. 2 (May 2010): 509–537.

13. Daly, *Killing the Competition*, 70–73.

14. Daly, *Killing the Competition*, 69, footnote 9.

15. D. B. Krupp and Thomas R. Cook, "Local Competition Amplifies the Corrosive Effects of Inequality," *Psychological Science* 29, no. 5 (May 2018): 824–833.

16. Paul A. Jagorsky, "Take the Money and Run: Economic Segregation in U.S. Metropolitan Areas," *American Sociological Review* 61, no. 6 (December 1996): 984–998.

17. Sean F. Reardon and Kendra Bischoff, "Income Inequality and Income Segregation," *American Journal of Sociology* 116, no. 4 (January 2011): 1092–1153.

18. James D. Fearon and David D. Laitin, "Ethnicity, Insurgency, and Civil War," *American Political Science Review* 97, no. 1 (February 2003): 75–90.

19. See Lars-Erik Cederman, Kristian Skrede Gleditsch, and Halvard Buhaug, *Inequality, Grievances, and Civil War* (New York: Cambridge University Press, 2013). See also Gudrun Østby, "Polarization, Horizontal Inequalities and Violent Civil Conflict," *Journal of Peace Research* 45, no. 1 (January 2008): 143–162.

20. See Susan Olzak, *The Dynamics of Ethnic Competition and Conflict* (Stanford, CA: Stanford University Press, 1992). See also Paul R. Hensel, Sara McLaughlin Mitchell, and Thomas E. Sowers II, "Conflict Management of Riparian Disputes," *Political Geography* 25, no. 4 (May 2006): 383–411. See also Toby J. Rider and Andrew P. Owsiak, "Border Settlement, Commitment Problems, and the Causes of Contiguous Rivalry," *Journal of Peace Research* 52, no. 4 (July 2015): 508–521.

21. Yaw Ackah, "Fear of Crime Among an Immigrant Population in the Washington, DC Metropolitan Area," *Journal of Black Studies* 30, no. 4 (March 2000): 553–573.

22. Allen E. Liska, Andrew Sanchirico, and Mark D. Reed, "Fear of Crime and Constrained Behavior. Specifying and Estimating a Reciprocal Effects Model," *Social Forces* 66, no. 3 (March 1988): 827–837.

23. C. Hale, "Fear of Crime: A Review of the Literature," *International Review of Victimology* 4, no. 2 (January 1996): 79–150.

24. Peter M. Todd and Gerd Gigerenzer, eds., *Ecological Rationality: Intelligence in the World* (Oxford: Oxford University Press, 2012).

25. Gregory D. Breetzke and Amber L. Pearson, "The Fear Factor: Examining the Spatial Variability of Recorded Crime on the Fear of Crime," *Applied Geography* 46, no. 1 (January 2014): 45–52.

26. See Christin-Melanie Vauclair and Boyka Bratanova, "Income Inequality and Fear of Crime Across the European Region," *European Journal of Criminology* 14, no. 2 (March 2017): 221–241. See also Dina Hummelsheim et al., "Social Insecurities and Fear of Crime: A Cross-National Study on the Impact of Welfare State Policies on Crime-Related Anxieties," *European Sociological Review* 27, no. 3 (March 2011): 327–345.

8

A Structural Vulnerability Understanding of American Poverty

Mark R. Rank

Few conditions undermine positive freedom and agency more than that of poverty. Poverty acts to truncate an individual's ability to partake in the American ideals of life, liberty, and the pursuit of happiness. Those in poverty suffer from worse health, social and political isolation, stigma and discrimination, and a wide range of conditions that reduce the overall quality of life.[1] The result is that impoverished Americans experience considerably less freedom than their more well-to-do counterparts.

Furthermore, as I argue throughout this chapter, such poverty is not by choice. Rather, it is the structural result of a lack of opportunities in society. This makes the constraints on freedom and agency that much more troublesome. In a society that highly values the ideal of freedom, the fact that so many Americans are structurally blocked from being able to fully partake in such freedom should be disturbing. As is apparent throughout this book, it is one thing to theoretically and legally grant various liberties; it is quite another to ensure that all are able to actually enjoy such freedoms.

In considering the relationship between poverty and freedom, it is particularly important to understand why poverty exists. This chapter develops what I have referred to in previous work as a structural vulnerability explanation of poverty. The perspective has developed out of my prior work examining the lives of welfare recipients,[2] those in poverty,[3] and the pursuit of the American dream.[4] It is designed to provide a new framework for understanding who loses out at the economic game, while emphasizing that the game itself is structured in a way that ultimately produces economic losers.

There are three basic premises underlying the structural vulnerability perspective. The first is that specific characteristics such as the lack of human capital (e.g., education, skills, training, etc.) tend to place individuals in a vulnerable position when detrimental events and crises occur. The incidence of these events (e.g., the loss of a job, family breakup, ill health) often result in poverty. In addition, the lack of human capital also increases the likelihood of such events occurring (particularly those related to the labor market). In this sense, human

Mark R. Rank, *A Structural Vulnerability Understanding of American Poverty* In: *On Inequality and Freedom.*
Edited by: Lawrence M. Eppard and Henry A. Giroux, Oxford University Press. © Oxford University Press 2022.
DOI: 10.1093/oso/9780197583029.003.0008

capital characteristics help to explain who in the population is likely to encounter poverty more frequently and for longer periods of time.

Second, the acquisition of such human capital is strongly influenced by the impact that social class has on this process. Those who find themselves growing up in a working class or lower income home will face greater odds against acquiring marketable education and skills during their lifetime. Moreover, the process of cumulative inequality serves to accentuate these earlier disadvantages across the life course. Additional background characteristics also play a role in the acquisition of human capital, including race, gender, and particular innate abilities.

Finally, while individual characteristics help to explain who loses out at the economic game, structural forces ensure that there will be losers in the first place. In this sense the dynamic of poverty can be described as a game of musical chairs in which those with the least advantageous characteristics are likely to find themselves without a chair and left standing with a heightened risk of economic vulnerability. Each of these components is discussed throughout this chapter.

Economic Vulnerability and Human Capital

Essential to an initial understanding of poverty are the concepts of economic vulnerability and the importance of the lack of human capital in accentuating such vulnerability. Individuals more likely to experience poverty tend to have attributes that put them at a disadvantage vis-à-vis their earnings ability within the labor market.

These attributes can be thought of largely in terms of human capital, or that basket of skills, attributes, education, and qualifications that individuals bring with them into the economy.[5] Those who do well in the labor market often do so as a result of the human capital they have acquired (in particular, they possess marketable skills and training). As a result, they are in greater demand by employers, and consequently will enjoy brighter job and earnings prospects.[6]

On the other hand, those facing an elevated risk of poverty tend to have acquired less valuable human capital. For example, education may be truncated or of an inferior quality, while job experience and skills may be less marketable. This results in individuals being less attractive in the job market. Additional attributes can also limit the ability to effectively compete in the labor market. Households residing in inner cities or remote rural areas often face diminished job prospects. Single mothers with young children experience reduced flexibility in their ability to take a job as a result of having to arrange child care. Likewise, those with a physical or mental disability may be more limited in terms of the type of jobs and number of hours they may work. In addition, factors such as race and gender can result in employers using such characteristics to screen and/or limit the promotion of potential employees. In short, those who experience poverty are more likely to have attributes that place them at a disadvantage in terms of competing in the labor market.

However, these factors alone do not directly cause poverty. If they were solely responsible, how might we explain the fluid movements of people in and out of poverty as indicated by the research into the longitudinal dynamics of poverty?[7] The typical pattern is that individuals may be poor for 1 or 2 years and then get themselves above the poverty line, perhaps experiencing an additional spell of poverty in the future. Furthermore, the life course patterns of poverty also indicate the commonality of short but recurring periods of impoverishment.[8] For many people, their personal characteristics have remained constant while their poverty status has not. An explanation that focuses solely on human capital cannot in and of itself account for such transitions.

What is argued here is that the lack of human capital results in certain life crises occurring more often and with greater intensity. This would appear particularly the case for labor market difficulties. Those with less human capital are more likely to experience job instability, longer periods of unemployment, lower wages, and part-time work. Each of these, in turn, is associated with an elevated risk of poverty.[9]

In addition, the lack of human capital places the individual in a more economically vulnerable position when faced with the loss of employment, changes in family status, illness and incapacitation, and so on. Individuals and families who are marginalized in terms of their ability to participate in the free market system will have a more difficult time weathering such storms. It will take them longer to find a job or to earn enough to tide them over the breakup of a family. When such events take place, they often throw individuals into poverty for a period of time until they are able to get back on their feet.[10]

Thus, a lack of human capital increases the likelihood that particular detrimental economic events will occur, such as not having a job that can sustain a family, as well as making it more difficult to weather such events when they do occur. As a result, those who are lacking in human capital might be thought of as walking a very fine line. If nothing out of the ordinary happens, many of these families are able to just get by. However, should a crisis occur such as the loss of a job, an unanticipated medical problem, or a costly but needed repair of an automobile, it generally places the household into an economic tailspin.

Many of the families that I interviewed for my book *Living on the Edge* were households straddling the borderline between self-sufficiency and dependence. One wrong step and they were likely to land back in poverty and on welfare. They simply did not have the resources and assets necessary to tide them over for more than several weeks. For example, I asked Cindy and Jeff Franklin, a married couple with two children, to describe these types of situations:

CINDY: Well, I think it's running out of money. [Sighs] If something comes up—a car repair or [pause] our refrigerator's on the fritz. . . . We have enough money for a nice, adequate, simple lifestyle as long as nothing happens. If something happens, then we really get thrown in a tizzy. And I'd say that's the worst—that's the worst.

JEFF: Yeah, 'cause just recently, in the last month, the car that we had was about to rust apart. Sort of literally. And so we had to switch cars. And my parents had this car that we've got now, sitting around. They gave it to us for free, but we had to put about two hundred dollars into it just to get it in safe enough condition so that we don't have to constantly be wondering if something's gonna break on it.

CINDY: I think that sense of having to choose—the car is a real good example of it—having to choose between letting things go—in a situation that's unsafe, or destituting ourselves in order to fix it. Having to make that kind of choice is really hard.[11]

The phrase "one paycheck away from poverty" is particularly apt in describing the situations for many of these households.

Other work has revealed parallel findings. Studies examining blue-collar or working-class families have found a similar dynamic.[12] As a result of less marketable skills and education, these households experience a heightened vulnerability to economic deprivation and poverty. For example, the title of Lillian Rubin's book *Families on the Faultline* exemplifies this notion with regard to working class families. As Rubin wrote:

> These are the men and women, by far the largest part of the American work force, who work at the lower levels of the manufacturing and service sectors of the economy; workers whose education is limited, whose mobility options are severely restricted, and who usually work for an hourly rather than a weekly wage. . . . They go to work every day to provide for their families, often at jobs they hate. But they live on the edge. Any unexpected event—a child's illness, an accident on the job, a brief layoff—threatens to throw them into the abyss.[13]

The first factor therefore in understanding the occurrence of poverty is the concept of economic vulnerability and the role that the lack of human capital plays in accentuating such vulnerability. People who have fewer skills and education, or who possess other attributes putting them at a disadvantage in terms of competing in the labor market (e.g., single parenthood or having a disability) are more likely to experience detrimental economic events, at the same time being more adversely affected when they occur. These episodes often result in pushing individuals and families below the poverty line.

The Impact of Social Class and Cumulative Inequality on Human Capital Acquisition

Given that skills and education bear on poverty (by causing varying degrees of vulnerability), why are individuals lacking these in the first place? A major reason often neglected in such discussions is the importance of social class and cumulative inequality. This is the second component of the structural vulnerability framework.

Analyses of the American system of stratification have shown that while some amount of social mobility does occur, social class as a whole tends to reproduce itself.[14] Those with working or lower class parents are likely to remain working or lower class themselves.[15] Similarly, those whose parents are affluent are likely to remain affluent.[16] Why? The reason is that parental class differences result in significant differences in the resources and opportunities available to their children. These differences, in turn, affect children's future life chances and outcomes, including the accumulation of skills and education. This process of cumulative advantage or disadvantage results in widening inequalities over time.[17]

While it is certainly possible for someone to rise from rags to riches, that tends to be much more the exception than the rule. Again turning to Lillian Rubin's analysis:

> Our denial notwithstanding, then, class inequalities not only exist in our society, they're handed down from parents to children in the same way that wealth is passed along in the upper class. True, American society has always had a less rigid and clearly defined class structure than many other nations. Poor people climb up; wealthy ones fall. These often well-publicized figures help to fuel the myth about equality of opportunity. But they're not the norm. Nor is the perpetuation of our class structure accidental. The economy, the polity, and the educational system all play their part in ensuring the continuity and stability of our social classes.[18]

The impact of differences in income and social class from one generation to the next is therefore a critical factor in understanding the human capital and skill differences that exist in today's society.

A game analogy helps to illustrate this process. Imagine three players beginning a game of Monopoly. Normally, each player would be given $1,500 at the start of the game. The playing field is in effect level, with the outcome of each determined by the roll of the dice as well as their own skills and judgments.

Now let us imagine a modified game of Monopoly, in which the players start out with quite different advantages and disadvantages, much as they do in life.

Player 1 begins with $5,000 and several Monopoly properties on which some houses have already been built. Player 2 starts out with the standard $1,500 and no properties. Finally, Player 3 begins the game with only $250.

Who will be the winners and losers in this modified game of Monopoly? Both luck and skill are still involved and the rules of the game have remained the same, but given the differing sets of resources and assets that each player begins with, they become much less important in predicting the game's outcome. Certainly, it is possible for Player 1 (with $5,000) to lose and for Player 3 (with $250) to win, but that is unlikely given the unequal allocation of money at the start of the game. Moreover, while Player 3 may win in any individual game, over the course of hundreds of games, the odds are that Player 1 will win exceedingly more often, even if Player 3 is much luckier and more skilled.

In addition, the way each of the three individuals is able to play the game will vary considerably. Player 1 is able to take greater chances and risks. If he or she makes several tactical mistakes, they probably will not matter much in the larger scheme of things. If Player 3 makes one such mistake, it may very well result in disaster. In addition, Player 1 will easily be able to purchase assets in the form of properties and houses that Player 3 is largely locked out of. These assets, in turn, will generate further income later in the game for Player 1 and in all likelihood result in the bankrupting of Player 3.

This analogy illustrates the concept that Americans are not beginning their lives at the same starting point. Parental differences in income and resources exert a major influence over their children's ability to acquire valuable skills and education. These differences in human capital will, in turn, strongly influence how well such children are able to compete in the labor market and therefore determine the extent of their economic vulnerability during the course of their lives.

This process is what is known as cumulative inequality. The argument is that as a result of the position one starts in life, particular advantages or disadvantages may be present.[19] These initial advantages or disadvantages can then result in further advantages or disadvantages, producing a cumulative process in which inequalities are widened across the life course.[20]

The assertion that the economic race is run as an altered game of Monopoly has been confirmed in an array of empirical work. For example, if a father has a level of income that falls in the bottom 20 percent of the income distribution, 42.2 percent of the sons from such a father will wind up in the bottom quintile of the income distribution when they grow up, while only 7.9 percent will reach the top quintile in terms of the income distribution. On the other hand, if a father has an income in the top 20 percent of the income distribution, 36 percent of his sons will be earning an income in the top quintile of the income distribution, while only 9.5 percent will fall into the bottom quintile.[21]

Another way of conceptualizing this association is that research over the past 25 years has revealed a sizable correlation between father's and son's incomes, averaging around .5.[22] A correlation of .5 is approximately the correlation between father's and son's heights. Thus, "if people's incomes were represented by their heights, the similarity in income between generations would resemble the similarity observed in the heights of fathers and sons."[23] More recent studies have found even higher correlations. For example, using Social Security records and longitudinal survey data for fathers' and sons' earnings, Bhashkar Mazumder[24] reported an intergenerational correlation between .6 and .7. This results in an even greater narrowing within our visual image of father's and son's heights.

Research focusing on the transmission of occupational status has also found a strong connection between parents and children.[25] For example, Daniel McMurrer and Isabel Sawhill reported that children of professionals are "significantly more likely to become professionals as adults, and children of blue collar workers significantly more likely to work in blue collar occupations.... Men with white collar origins are almost twice as likely as those with blue collar origins to end up in upper white collar jobs."[26]

Or, if one looks at the transmission of wealth, a similar pattern emerges.[27] William Gale and John Scholz estimated that intended family transfers and bequests account for 51 percent of current U.S. wealth, while an additional 12 percent is acquired through the payment of college expenses by parents. Consequently, nearly two thirds of the net worth that individuals have acquired is through family transfers.[28] Parents with considerable wealth are able to pass on these assets and advantages to their children. As a result, it is estimated that "children of the very rich have roughly 40 times better odds of being very rich than do the children of the poor."[29]

Additional work has focused on the impact that growing up in poverty has on one's later economic well-being.[30] In our Monopoly example, this might represent the player beginning the game with 250 dollars. Joan Rodgers has found that of those who experienced poverty as an adult, 50 percent had experienced poverty as a child, while an additional 38 percent had grown up in homes that were defined as near poor (below 2.00 of the poverty line).[31] Once again, we see that the social class a child is reared in has a profound impact on their later economic well-being and outcomes.

This is not to say that economic movement is nonexistent. Individuals do move up and down the economic ladder across adulthood.[32] However, when such movement does happen, it usually transpires over relatively short distances from their economic origins. In fact, contrary to popular myth, the United States tends to have less intergenerational mobility than a number of other industrialized countries[33] and that such mobility has been declining over time.[34] The empirical evidence clearly points to the fact that children from a lower class background will be much more at risk of economic vulnerability in their adult lives than children from wealthier families.

The reasons for this are primarily that children from a working or lower class background simply do not have the range and depth of opportunities as children from a middle or upper class background. This then affects the quantity and quality of human capital they are able to acquire. Likewise, the vast differences in educational quality by residence and income quickly illuminate the magnitude of these opportunity differences.[35]

For example, the work of Thomas Shapiro illustrates the manner in which wealthier families are able to utilize their assets (a significant portion of which have been received through inheritance and/or gifts from parents) in order to acquire a high-quality primary and secondary education for their children.[36] This is accomplished through either purchasing a home in an affluent school district or sending their children to private schools. In-depth interviews conducted with scores of parents in Boston, St. Louis, and Los Angeles made this point abundantly clear. As Shapiro and Johnson noted: "By accessing quality school systems parents ensure specific kinds of schooling for their children and in this way help to pass their own social position along to the next generation."[37]

And of course this process continues with higher education. Children from wealthier families are often able to attend elite private universities, children from middle-class backgrounds might enroll at state public universities, while children from lower class backgrounds will probably not continue on to college, and if they do, will likely attend a community or 2-year college. As McMurrer and Sawhill noted:

> Family background has a significant and increasing effect on who goes to college, where, and for how long. With the rewards for going to college greater than ever, and family background now a stronger influence over who reaps those rewards, the United States is at risk of becoming more class stratified in coming decades.[38]

Beyond social class there are several other factors that clearly play a role in the acquisition of human capital. A sizable amount of research over the years has established that race exerts a powerful effect on the life chances of children above and beyond social class.[39] For example, patterns of racial residential segregation further ensure that Black children with similar social class backgrounds to White children find themselves in more heavily segregated schools with inferior resources.[40] These patterns apply to Latino children as well.[41]

Gender has also been shown to impact the acquisition of human capital.[42] For example, throughout their schooling, girls have been more likely to be steered into less lucrative career paths. In addition, differences in innate abilities such as cognitive reasoning can play a role in the acquisition of human capital. All of these factors will influence the ability of children to acquire human capital and compete effectively in the labor market.

Consequently, where one begins one's life exerts a powerful effect throughout the life course. This process was succinctly described by Howard Wachtel:

> If you are black, female, have parents with low socioeconomic status, and [are] dependent upon labor income, there is a high probability that you will have relatively low levels of human capital which will slot you into low-paying jobs, in low wage industries, in low wage markets. With this initial placement, the individual is placed in a high risk category, destined to end up poor some-time during her working and nonworking years. She may earn her poverty by working fulltime. Or she may suffer either sporadic or long periods of unem-ployment. Or she may become disabled, thereby reducing her earning power even further. Or when she retires, social security payments will place her in poverty even if she escaped this fate throughout her working years. With little savings, wealth, or private pension income, the retiree will be poor.[43]

Thus, in order to understand why people are lacking in skills and education in the first place, one important place to look is the impact that a child growing up in a lower income family versus a child growing up in a well-to-do family has on that child's acquisition of human capital, which then impacts their eco-nomic outcomes. This process of cumulative inequality is often neglected in po-litical and policy discussions, but unfortunately the class you are born into has wide-ranging implications on your life course. As Billie Holiday sang 80 years ago: "Them that's got shall get, them that's not shall lose. So the Bible says, and it still is news."

Two Levels of Understanding Poverty

A third element of the structural vulnerability perspective is that there are two levels to understanding impoverishment. On one hand, we can understand who is more likely to experience poverty through the previously discussed impact that human capital exerts on creating individual economic vulnerability. On the other hand, why poverty occurs in the first place can largely be ascertained through structural failings. To illustrate these two levels, another analogy is used—that of musical chairs. The key is whether one chooses to analyze the losers of the game or the game itself.

Let us imagine eight chairs and ten players. The players begin to circle around the chairs until the music stops. Who fails to find a chair? If we focus on the winners and losers of the game, some combination of luck and skill will be involved. In all likelihood, the losers will be those in an unfavorable position when the music stops, somewhat slower, less agile, and so on. In one sense, these are appropriately cited as the reasons for losing the game.

However, if we focus on the game itself, then it is quite clear that given only eight chairs, two players are bound to lose. Even if every player were suddenly to double his or her speed and agility, there would still be two losers. From this broader context, it really does not matter what the loser's characteristics are, given that two are destined to lose.

I would argue that this musical chairs analogy can be applied to what has occurred in America economically, socially, and politically. Given that there is unemployment, which translates into a shortage of jobs; given that we are producing more and more low-paying jobs lacking benefits; given that countless inner-city and rural communities have been devastated by economic restructuring; given the weak safety net in place to provide economic protection to the vulnerable; given that there is a scarcity of decent quality, affordable child care; given that there are few provisions to care for those who can no longer participate in the economy because of an illness—someone is going to lose at this game.

The losers will generally be those who are lacking in skills, education, and training and therefore cannot compete as effectively and are more vulnerable than their counterparts who have acquired greater skills and education. In one sense, we can focus on these deficits, such as a lack of education, as the reasons for why individuals are at a greater risk of becoming poor.

Yet if we focus on the game itself, then the causes of poverty move from the individual's lack of skills or education to the fact that the economy produces unemployment, creates low-paying jobs, bypasses low-income communities, offers little social supports and protection, lacks affordable child care, or does not provide for those who can no longer participate economically due to an illness. These then become the more fundamental reasons for why people are poor in this country.

Certainly the degree and intensity of these structural failings may vary over time. In our musical chairs analogy, there may be nine chairs for every ten players or only six or seven. Likewise, the circumstances surrounding the economic game can and do change, which in turn affects the overall number of losers. Such changes result from a variety of factors, including economic upturns and downturns, public policy initiatives and changes, and demographic shifts in the population. The number of losers produced by the economic, social, and political systems in this country are therefore not written in stone.

For example, during the 1930s, the Great Depression resulted in a dramatic reduction in the number of economic opportunities, creating widespread unemployment and poverty. Within this window of time the number of available chairs versus participants in the game was significantly reduced. More recently, the coronavirus pandemic has resulted in a severe economic downturn, again resulting in millions facing unemployment.

However, the 1960s saw a booming economy coupled with federal initiatives to address poverty. The result was a dramatic increase in the number of chairs available, resulting in a significant drop in the overall rates of poverty during the decade. While the ratio of opportunities to participants fluctuates over time, nevertheless at any given point there tends to be a significant number of losers produced by the overall game.

What this means is that when we focus solely on personal characteristics, such as education, we can shuffle individual people up or down in terms of their being more likely to find a job, but we are still going to have somebody lose out if there are not enough decent-paying jobs to go around.

What greater education and skills allows an individual to do is to move further up in the overall queue of people looking to find a good-paying and rewarding job. However, because of the limited number of such jobs, only a set amount of people will be able to land such jobs. Consequently, one's position in the queue can change as a result of human capital, but the same amount of people will still be stuck at the end of the line if the overall opportunities remain the same. In short, we are playing a game of musical chairs in this country with ten players but only eight chairs.

Many examples of this mismatch exist in today's society. Perhaps the most important is the previously mentioned imbalance between the number of jobs that can support a family in the current economy versus the number of families in need of such jobs. In his study of long-term unemployment, Thomas Cottle talked with one man who had worked for 25 years with the same company only to be downsized. After two and half years of searching, he eventually found a job at a much lower pay scale, but felt fortunate to have such a job nonetheless. He referred to his job search using the musical chairs analogy discussed above:

> The musical chairs of work still have me in the game. The music plays, we run around, the music stops and I dive for a chair. Took me two and half years to find this last one, I don't want the music to stop again. I'm only fifty-two, but pretty soon they'll take all the chairs away. Then what? That's the part I don't want to think about.[44]

Or, take the spatial mismatch between the number of people in economically depressed geographical areas versus the number of opportunities in such areas. This is particularly apparent for those residing in urban inner cities or remote rural regions. Such areas are not hard to find: the rural Mississippi delta; inner-city Cleveland, Chicago, or St. Louis; American Indian reservations across the southwest; the Appalachian Mountain region. In these regions, economic opportunities have largely moved away (or were never there in the first place), leaving behind many scrambling for the few chairs that are left.

William Julius Wilson documented this process in his study of inner-city Chicago residents, aptly titled *When Work Disappears*. Wilson stated: "The increasing suburbanization of employment has accompanied industrial restructuring and has further exacerbated the problems of inner-city joblessness and restricted access to jobs."[45] Illustrative of this is Katherine Newman's ethnography of jobs and economic conditions in central Harlem during the mid-1990s, in which she found that there were as many as 14 applicants for each fast food job offered.[46]

Similarly, Cynthia Duncan described the process of diminishing jobs and opportunities in rural Appalachia, leaving behind thousands who must compete with one another for the dwindling number of viable economic opportunities. As she noted:

> Work is hard to find. Only half the working-age men are employed, only a quarter of working-age women. *These days you can't even buy a job*, complains one young man recently laid off from a mine. *Even men have hard time getting work around here*, a young single mother from Michigan explains. She was told to go on welfare when she went looking for work through the Department of Employment.[47]

In the above cases, it is relatively easy to visualize the mismatch between the number of players versus the number of chairs. Yet such a mismatch is operating on an overall national level as well. This mismatch illustrates the third point of the structural vulnerability explanation of poverty: Given the structural failures, a certain percentage of the American population will experience economic vulnerability regardless of what their characteristics are. As in the musical chairs analogy, the game is structured such that some of the players are bound to lose. Cindy Franklin (who previously discussed her problems with unanticipated expenses) put it succinctly:

> There are only so many good-paying jobs that exist in this society, and there are tons and tons of minimum wage jobs. And as long as we expect people to work them, there are gonna be people who can't make it without help. There's only so many people can rise to the top, and then no more can.[48]

Increasing everyone's human capital will do little to alter the fact that there are only a limited number of decent-paying jobs available. In such a case, employers will simply raise the bar in terms of their employee qualifications, leaving behind

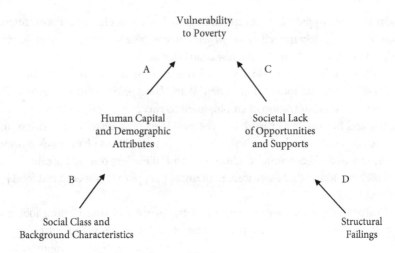

Figure 8.1   Structural vulnerability model of poverty.

a more qualified percentage of the population at risk of economic deprivation. Consequently, although a lack of human capital and its accompanying vulnerability leads to an understanding of who the losers of the economic game are likely to be, the structural components of our economic, social, and political systems explain why there are losers in the first place.

Visualization

As I have noted, researchers and social commentators investigating poverty have largely focused on individual deficiencies and demographic attributes in order to explain the occurrence of poverty in America. In doing so, they have reinforced the mainstream American ethos of interpreting social problems as primarily the result of individual failings and pathology.[49] In contrast, this chapter has argued that the dynamic of poverty can be better grasped through a perspective of structural vulnerability.

This framework is illustrated in Figure 8.1. It suggests that there are two ways of understanding individual vulnerability to poverty. Paths A and B deal with the question of who is at risk of poverty in America, while paths C and D focus on the question of why poverty exists in America.

The bulk of the empirical research pertaining to American poverty has focused on Path A. Economists, sociologists, and demographers have concerned themselves with understanding the individual attributes that are associated with a greater risk of impoverishment. As we have discussed previously, these attributes can largely be understood in terms of limiting an individual's ability to compete in the labor market. Consequently, those with less education, fewer job skills, or health problems; who are single mothers, minorities living in inner cities, and so on will face a heightened vulnerability to poverty.

Path B suggests that several background characteristics largely determine which Americans are more likely to be lacking in such human capital. The most important of these is social class: Those growing up in lower or working class families are more likely to have their acquisition of human capital assets truncated. In addition, race, gender, and differences in innate abilities can also play a role in influencing the acquisition of human capital.

Paths A and B therefore explain who in America is at a greater risk of experiencing poverty during their lives. The critical mistake has been the following: Poverty analysts have confused the question of who is at risk of poverty, with the question of why poverty exists. They have stopped at Path A in their explanation of poverty. According to mainstream research, the question of why poverty exists is typically answered by noting that the poor are lacking in education, skills, and so on, and that these are the reasons for impoverishment. We can see in Figure 8.1 that this is an incomplete and misleading account.

The right-hand side of the structural vulnerability model includes Paths C and D. These explain why so many Americans are at an elevated risk of poverty. Path C suggests that the lack of opportunities and social supports is a critical reason for this risk. As discussed, there is a mismatch between the number of jobs that will adequately support a family versus the number of families in need of such jobs. Likewise, American society has failed to provide the necessary supports for those in need: The United States has been marked by a minimal safety net, inadequate child care assistance, lack of healthcare coverage, a dearth of affordable low-cost housing, and so on. This lack of economic opportunities and social supports has significantly raised the number of Americans vulnerable to the risk of poverty.

The shortage of opportunities and adequate supports has been produced by structural failings at the economic and political levels (Path D). The tendency of our free market economy has been to produce a growing number of jobs that will no longer support a family. In addition, the basic nature of capitalism ensures that unemployment exists at modest levels.[50] Both of these directly result in a shortage of economic opportunities in American society. In addition, the absence of social supports stems from failings at the political and policy levels. The United States has traditionally lacked the political desire to put in place effective policies and programs that would support the economically vulnerable.[51] Structural failings at the economic and political levels have therefore produced a lack of opportunities and supports, resulting in high rates of American poverty. To return to our previous analogy, Paths A and B are designed to explain who is more likely to lose out at the game, while Paths C and D are intended to explain why the game produces losers in the first place.

Consequently, we can think of the dynamic of poverty as a large-scale game of musical chairs. For every ten American households, there are good jobs and opportunities at any point in time to adequately support roughly eight of those ten. The remaining two households will be shut out of such opportunities, often resulting in poverty or near poverty. Individuals experiencing such economic deprivation are likely to have characteristics putting them at a disadvantage in terms of competing in the economy (lower education, fewer skills, single-parent families, illness or incapacitation, minorities residing in inner cities, etc.). These characteristics help to explain why particular individuals and households are at a greater risk of poverty.

Yet given the previously discussed structural failures, a certain percentage of the American population will experience economic vulnerability regardless of what their characteristics are. The structure of the American economy, in consort with its weak social safety net and public policies directed to the economically vulnerable, ensure that millions of Americans will experience impoverishment at any point in time, and that a much larger number will experience poverty over the course of a lifetime. The fact that three quarters of Americans will experience poverty or near poverty during their adulthoods is emblematic of these structural-level failings.[52]

Concluding Thoughts

In summary, the approach taken in this chapter has been to provide a new framework for understanding the dynamics of American poverty. Previous work has often placed this dynamic within the framework of individual deficiencies. I have argued here that such a perspective is misdirected. Whereas individual attributes (e.g., human capital) help to explain who faces a greater risk of experiencing poverty at any point in time, the fact that substantial poverty exists on a national level can only be understood through an analysis of the structural dynamics of American society.

Understanding the reasons behind poverty is essential not only for appreciating the nature of poverty, but also in terms of building our individual and societal responses to the condition of American poverty. If poverty is viewed as affecting a small proportion of the population who are plagued by moral failings and individual inadequacies, our individual and societal response will likely follow the familiar course we have taken in the past. That direction has been to assume relatively little collective responsibility toward the problem of poverty, while continually focusing on welfare reform initiatives that attempt to strengthen the work and family incentives for the poor. This approach has accomplished very little in terms of rectifying the problem of poverty. On the other hand, if poverty is viewed as a failing at the structural level, this would suggest a much different approach for building an effective response to the issue.

Such an understanding should also raise concerns regarding the importance placed on particular core values in American society. Americans strongly believe in the principle of equality of opportunity. Yet as we have seen, the dynamic producing poverty clearly undermines the existence of equality of opportunities for many Americans. Children raised in poverty have far fewer opportunities available to them than their nonpoor counterparts. This inequality of opportunity only becomes magnified across the life course.

In addition, the process of structural vulnerability makes it clear that those in poverty experience a dramatic reduction in their ability to enjoy various freedoms and liberties. Indeed, the economist Amartya Sen has defined the essence of poverty as "a lack of freedom."[53] For a nation that places such a high premium on the importance of freedom, this should be extremely troubling.

Notes

1. Mark Robert Rank, *Confronting Poverty in the United States* (Thousand Oaks, CA: Sage, 2021).
2. Mark Robert Rank, *Living on the Edge: The Realities of Welfare in America* (New York: Columbia University Press, 1994).
3. Mark Robert Rank, *One Nation, Underprivileged: Why American Poverty Affects Us All* (New York: Oxford University Press, 2004).
4. Mark Robert Rank, Thomas A. Hirschl, and Kirk A. Foster, *Chasing the American Dream: Understanding What Shapes Our Fortunes* (New York: Oxford University Press, 2014).
5. Gary S. Becker, *A Treatise on the Family* (Cambridge, MA: Harvard University Press, 1981); Gary S. Becker, *Human Capital: A Theoretical and Empirical Analysis With Special Reference to Education* (Chicago: University of Chicago Press, 1993); Lynn Karoly, "Investing in the Future: Reducing Poverty Through Human Capital Investments," in *Understanding Poverty*, ed. Sheldon H. Danziger and Robert H. Haveman (New York: Russell Sage Foundation, 2001), 314–356; Teresa Sommer et. al., "A Two-Generation Human Capital Approach to Antipoverty Policy," *Russell Sage Foundation Journal of the Social Sciences* 4 (2018): 118–143.
6. David B. Bills, Valentina Di Stasio, and Klarita Gerxhani, "The Demand Side of Hiring: Employers in the Labor Market," *Annual Review of Sociology* 43 (2017): 291–310.
7. Ann Huff Stevens, "Transitions Into and Out of Poverty in United States" (Policy Brief) (Davis: Center for Poverty Research, University of California–Davis, 2012), vol. 1, no. 1.

8. Mark Robert Rank, *One Nation.*

9. Mark Robert Rank, *Confronting Poverty.*

10. Mark Robert Rank, *Confronting Poverty.*

11. Mark Robert Rank, *Living on the Edge*, 57.

12. Amy Goldstein, *Janesville: An American Story* (New York: Simon and Schuster, 2017); Jonathan Morduch and Rachel Schneider, *The Financial Diaries: How American Families Cope in a World of Uncertainty* (Princeton, NJ: Princeton University Press, 2017); Lawrence M. Eppard, Mark Robert Rank, and Heather E. Bullock, *Rugged Individualism and the Misunderstanding of American Inequality* (Bethleham, PA: Lehigh University Press, 2020).

13. Lillian B. Rubin, *Families on the Faultline: America's Working Class Speaks About the Family, the Economy, Race, and Ethnicity* (New York: HarperCollins, 1994), 30–31.

14. Samuel Bowles, Herbert Gintis, and Melissa Osborne Groves, *Unequal Chances: Family Background and Economic Success* (New York: Russell Sage Foundation, 2005); John Ermisch, Markus Jaantti, and Timothy Smeeding, *From Parents to Children: The Intergenerational Transmission of Advantage* (New York: Russell Sage Foundation, 2012).

15. Bhashkar Mazumder, "Intergenerational Mobility in the United States: What We Have Learned From the PSID," *Annals of the American Academy of Political and Social Science* 680 (2018): 213–234.

16. Fabian T. Pfeffer and Alexandria Killewald, "Generations of Advantage: Multigenerational Correlations in Family Wealth," *Social Forces* 96 (2018): 1411–1442.

17. Mark R. Rank, "Reducing Cumulative Inequality," in *Toward a Livable Life: A 21st Century Agenda for Social Work*, ed. Mark Robert Rank (New York: Oxford University Press, 2020), 94–113.

18. Rubin, *Families on the Faultline*, 36.

19. Robert K. Merton, *Social Theory and Social Structure* (New York: Free Press, 1949); Robert K. Merton, "The Matthew Effect in Science: The Reward and Communication System of Science," *Science* 199 (1968): 55–63.

20. Mark R. Rank, "Reducing Cumulative Inequality."

21. Markus Jantti et al., "American Exceptionalism in a New Light: A Comparison of Intergenerational Earnings Mobility in the Nordic Countries, the United Kingdom and the United States," (Discussion Paper 1938) (Bonn, Germany: Institute for the Study of Labor, 2006).

22. Marie Connolly, Miles Corak, and Catherine Haeck, "Intergenerational Mobility Between and Within Canada and the United States," *Journal of Labor Economics* 52 (2019): 595–641.

23. Alan B. Krueger, "Economic Scene; The Apple Falls Close to the Tree, Even in the Land of Opportunity," *New York Times*, November 14, 2002.

24. Mazumder, "Intergenerational Mobility."

25. Michael Hout, "Americans Occupational Status Reflects Both of Their Parents," *Proceedings of the National Academy of Sciences of the United States of America* 115 (2018): 9527–9532.

26. Daniel P. McMurrer and Isabel V. Sawhill, *Getting Ahead: Economic and Social Mobility in America* (Washington, DC: Urban Institute Press, 1998), 2.

27. Richard A. Bentron and Lisa A. Keister, "The Lasting Effect of Intergenerational Wealth Transfers: Human Capital, Family Formation, and Wealth," *Social Science Research* 68 (2017): 1–14; Alexandra Killewald, Fabian T. Pfeffer, and Jared N. Schachner, "Wealth Inequality and Accumulation," *Annual Review of Sociology* 43 (2017): 379–404.

28. William G. Gale and John Karl Scholz, "Intergenerational Transfers and the Accumulation of Wealth," *Journal of Economic Perspectives* 8 (1994): 145–160.

29. Jagdeesh Gokhale and Larence J. Kotlikoff, "Simulating the Transmission of Wealth Inequality," *American Economic Review* 92 (2002): 268.

30. Greg J. Duncan and Richard J. Murnane, "Rising Inequality in Family Incomes and Children's Educational Outcomes," *Russell Sage Foundation Journal of the Social Sciences* 2 (2016): 142–158; Kyle Crowder and Scott J. South, "Neighborhood Distress and School Dropout: The Variable Significance of Community Context," *Social Science Research* 32 (2003): 659–698.

31. Joan R. Rodgers, "An Empirical Study of Intergenerational Transmission of Poverty in the United States," *Social Science Quarterly* 76 (1995): 178–194.

32. Mark R. Rank and Thomas A. Hirschl, "The Likelihood of Experiencing Relative Poverty Across the Life Course," PLoS One 10 (2015): e01333513.

33. Miles Corak, "Chasing the Same Dream, Climbing Different Ladders: Economic Mobility in the United States and Canada," Economic Mobility Project (Pew Charitable Trusts, 2010); Liana Fox, Florencia Torche, and Jane Waldfogel, "Intergenerational Mobility," in *The Oxford Handbook of the Social Science of Poverty*, ed. David Brady and Linda M. Burton (New York: Oxford University Press, 2016), 528–554; Mark Robert Rank, Lawrence M. Eppard, and Heather E. Bullock, *Poorly Understood: What America Gets Wrong About Poverty* (New York: Oxford University Press, forthcoming 2021).

34. Jonathan David and Bhashkar Mazumber, "The Decline in Intergenerational Mobility After 1980" (FRB of Chicago Working Paper No. WP-2017-5, 2020); Song et al., "Long-Term Decline in Intergenerational Mobility in the United States Since the 1850s," *Proceedings of the National Academy of Sciences of the United States of America* 117 (2020): 251–258.

35. Florian Rolf Hertel and Fabian T. Pfeffer, "The Land of Opportunity? Trends in Social Mobility and Education in the United States," in *Social Mobility in Europe and the United States*, ed. Richard Breen and Walter Muller (Stanford, CA: Stanford University Press, 2020), 29–68.

36. Thomas M. Shapiro, *The Hidden Cost of Being African American: How Wealth Perpetuates Inequality* (New York: Oxford University Press, 2004); Thomas M. Shapiro, *Toxic Inequality: How America's Wealth Gap Destroys Mobility, Deepens the Racial Divide, and Threatens Our Future* (New York: Basic Books, 2017); Thomas M. Shapiro, Tatjana Meschede, and Sam Ossoro, "The Roots of the Widening Racial Wealth Gap: Explaining the Black-White Economic Divide" (Research and Policy Brief, February 2013), Institute on Assets and Social Policy, Brandeis University.

37. Thomas M. Shapiro and Heather Beth Johnson, "Assets, Race, and Educational Choices" (Center for Social Development Working Paper, No. 00-7) (St. Louis, MO, Washington University, 2000), 2.

38. McMurrer and Sawhill, *Getting Ahead,* 69.

39. Deirdre Bloome, "Racial Inequality Trends and the Intergenerational Persistence of Income and Family Structure," *American Sociological Review* 79 (2014): 1196–1225; Raj Chetty et al., "Race and Economic Opportunity in the United States: An Intergenerational Perspective," *Quarterly Journal of Economics* 135 (2020): 711–783; Dalton Conley, *Being Black, Living in the Red: Race, Wealth, and Social Policy in America* (Berkeley: University of California Press, 1999); Joe R. Feagin, *Racist America: Roots, Current Realities, and Future Reparations* (New York: Routledge, 2010); Mark R. Rank and Thomas A. Hirschl, "Estimating the Risk of Food Stamp Use and Impoverishment During Childhood," *Archives of Pediatrics and Adolescent Medicine* 163 (2009): 994–999.

40. Douglas A. Massey, *Categorically Unequal: The American Stratification System* (New York: Russell Sage Foundation, 2007); Ann Owens, "Income Segregation Between School Districts and Inequality in Students Achievements," *Sociology of Education* 91 (2018): 1–27; Gary Orfield and Chungmei Lee, "Why Segregation Matters: Poverty and Educational Inequality" (The Civil Rights Project) (Cambridge, MA: Harvard University, 2005).

41. Erica Frankenberg et al., "Harming Our Common Future: America's Segregated Schools 65 Years After *Brown*" (The Civil Rights Project) (Cambridge, MA: Harvard University, May 10, 2019).

42. Matthew Wiswall and Basit Zafar, "Preference for the Workplace, Investment in Human Capital, and Gender," *Quarterly Journal of Economics* 133 (2018): 457–507.

43. Howard M. Wachtel, "Looking at Poverty From a Radical Perspective," *Review of Radical Political Economics* 3 (1971): 1–19.

44. Thomas J. Cottle, *Hardest Times: The Trauma of Long Term Unemployment* (Westport, CT: Praeger, 2001), 216.

45. William Julius Wilson, *When Work Disappears: The World of the New Urban Poor* (New York: Knopf, 1996), 37.

46. Katherine Newman, *No Shame in My Game: The Working Poor in the Inner City* (New York: Knopf, 1999).

47. Cynthia M. Duncan, *Worlds Apart: Poverty and Politics in Rural America* (New Haven, CT: Yale University Press, 2014), 6.

48. Mark Robert Rank, *Living on the Edge,* 127.

49. Alice O'Conner, *Poverty Knowledge: Social Science, Social Policy, and the Poor in Twentieth-Century U.S. History* (Princeton, NJ: Princeton University Press, 2001); Alice O'Conner, "Poverty Knowledge and the History of Poverty Research," in *The Oxford Handbook of the Social Science of Poverty,* ed. David Brady and Linda M. Burton (New York: Oxford University Press, 2016), 169–192.

50. Erik O. Wright, *Interrogating Inequality: Essays on Class Analysis, Socialism, and Marxism* (London: Verso, 1994).

51. Alberto Alesina and Edward L. Glaeser, *Fighting Poverty in the US and Europe: A World of Difference* (New York: Oxford University Press, 2004).
52. Mark Robert Rank, *One Nation*.
53. Amartya Sen, *Inequality Reexamined* (New York: Russell Sage Foundation, 1992).

9

Child Poverty

Europe Versus the United States

Jonathan Bradshaw

Children who live in families in poverty have much diminished lives. They tend to suffer from worse diets, poorer physical and mental health, worse quality housing with more overcrowding, and poorer neighborhoods with more pollution. They do less well at school and are more likely to be bullied and excluded; not surprisingly, they have lower subjective well-being (they are less happy). These experiences in childhood have knock-on effects in adulthood: They are less likely to work, to get a decent job. They tend to partner earlier, have children earlier, and suffer family breakdown more. They die earlier. The costs of child poverty are breathtaking for the individual, the state, and society.[1]

There is much debate about the causes of child poverty. Broadly, this is a debate about the respective contributions of individual behavior and social structures. Behavior is of course important. Adults have children and particularly if they have more than they can afford or are or become lone parents their behavior is likely to have generated poverty. But this is not inevitable. As we shall see, different nations vary in the proportion of their children who are poor, and that variation is not completely related to their general wealth. It depends on the structure of their economy and society and particularly the efforts their governments make to reduce child poverty directly by policies. No doubt these efforts are influenced by "ideologies of welfare" that determine the balance of responsibility for tackling child poverty between the family, the market, and the state.

Regardless of the balance between the behavioral and structural causes of poverty, child poverty remains a particular injustice.[2] Children don't have a choice about their poverty. They are blinded to their prospects. They lack the understanding to realize their circumstances, at least in early childhood, and even later they are not well placed to do anything about their injustice. They are innocent, even if they do not entirely lack agency. They cannot choose their parents, family, community, or country. It might have been expected from this that they would be the particular focus of discussions of social justice, but as Gordon[3] has argued:

Jonathan Bradshaw, *Child Poverty* In: *On Inequality and Freedom*. Edited by: Lawrence M. Eppard and Henry A. Giroux, Oxford University Press. © Oxford University Press 2022. DOI: 10.1093/oso/9780197583029.003.0009

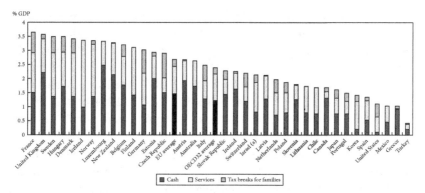

Figure 9.1   Public expenditure on family benefits by type of expenditure.
Note: In percentage of GDP. Data are 2015 or latest available.
Source: OECD Family database Table PF1.1A.

A space alien visiting earth and reading the economic theory and political philosophy literature on distributional justice for children would be unlikely to
discern that children are citizens with human rights that are independent and
coequal with adults with whom they live. The space alien might also conclude
that these academic authors had never seen children were unlikely to have children of their own, or at least if they did have children they were completely un-
concerned with the distributional justice or the economic goods their children
received.

Analysis

States assist families in the burdens of childrearing through interventions in the
market economy to ensure adequate wages, gender-equal pay, and managing the
economy to maximize employment. They also provide free or subsidized services—education, care, health, housing, and sometimes commodities like water,
energy, or food subsidies. But by far the most important element of state intervention are transfers of direct cash and tax benefits that increase the incomes
of families with children or reduce their tax liabilities.[4] The Organization for
Economic Cooperation and Development (OECD) provides analysis of the
varying efforts that rich countries make.

It can be seen in Figure 9.1 that the highest spenders all tend to be European
countries, while the United States is a comparatively low spender—just ahead
of Mexico, Greece, and Turkey. The highest spenders tend to make more use of
cash benefits, while the United States makes almost no use of cash benefits and

relies on services and tax breaks. In the last 20 years, the United States has cut its spending on cash spending from 0.29% of the gross domestic product (GDP) in 1995 to 0.07% in 2015. It increased its spending on services from 0.30% to 0.57% of GDP and on tax breaks from zero[5] to 0.48% of GDP over the same period. The picture for other countries varies, but to take the United Kingdom for an example, it increased cash spending from 1.59% of GDP to 2.25% of GDP, services spending from 0.42% to 1.32%, and tax spending from zero to 0.13% over the same period.

In order to understand the impact of this spending effort on child poverty, we need to relate it to child poverty rates.[6] This is easiest for European Union countries because Eurostat, the European Union statistical service, runs a survey that produces data that enable us to compare child poverty before and after transfers. Before transfers means the level child poverty would be if families only had to rely on their net earnings from the marketplace. After transfers is the poverty rate that exists after the income from benefits is taken into account. Ideally, it would be desirable to separate the impact of cash benefits and tax benefits, and that would be possible if we had access to the raw data,[7] but it is not possible using the published data. Figure 9.2 shows the child poverty rates for the latest year available before and after transfers. The countries are ranked by the percentage reduction in child poverty achieved by transfers (highest on the right). The at-risk-of-poverty rate is equivalent income before housing costs less than 60% of the national median.

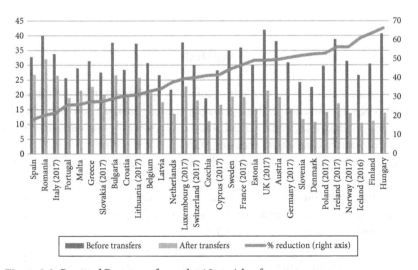

Figure 9.2 Pre- and Post-transfer under 18 at-risk-of-poverty rates.
Note: Data from 2018 unless stated. Countries ranked by percentage reduction (right axis).
Source: Eurostat database extracted May 2020.

The first thing to note in this figure is how variable both the pretransfer and post-transfer poverty rates are. The pretransfer child poverty rate is over 40% in the United Kingdom and less than 20% in Czechia. The post-transfer child poverty rate is over 30% in Romania and less than 10% in Iceland. But the real purpose of the figure is to demonstrate the impact of transfers. Child poverty rates fell by more than 60% in Hungary, Finland, and Iceland entirely due to state effort. But there are countries at the other end of the distribution that achieved much less reduction in their child poverty rates; Spain, Romania, and Italy had reductions of less than 15%. These countries tend to be those spending least in Figure 9.1.

How does the United States compare? Unfortunately, there are no comparative data available on pre- and post-transfer child poverty rates. We can however make some comparisons of poverty rates from three sources: the Luxembourg Income Study (LIS), the UNICEF Innocenti Research Center in Florence Report Card, and OECD.

First LIS. They publish child poverty rates for countries included in their study. Not many have very up-to-date data, but Table 9.1 extracts child poverty rates for a selection of countries that have fairly recent data (circa 2016). It shows that the United States had the highest child poverty rates on all three thresholds, except for Estonia at the less than 40% and 50% median threshold. The United States is higher than Australia, Canada, and all the other European countries included on all other measures.

Second, the UNICEF Office for Research in Florence has published a series of Innocenti Report Cards on child well-being in rich countries based on a range of indicators, including child poverty. Innocenti Report Card 16 is the latest and provides the child poverty rates based on the threshold of net income less than 60% of the median. The data for EU countries is derived from EU SILC, but for the other countries comes from analysis of national sources on a common basis. Figure 9.3 presents the results and shows the United States had the 42nd highest child poverty rate out of 46 countries, only exceeded by Israel, Turkey, Romania, and Mexico.

The third source is the OECD, which publishes child poverty rates using a threshold of 50% of the median. Table 9.2 shows that the United States had a child poverty rate of 20.9%, much higher than the OECD average and higher than any EU country except Spain. The OECD data also allow us to compare the poverty rates of various types of households with children. The United States has higher poverty rates of lone-parent and couple households than most European countries and higher poverty rates than most European countries for working households. Only its poverty rates for nonworking households are not exceptional in the European context; they are quite similar to Sweden's, for example.

Table 9.1 Child Poverty Rates for Selected Countries at Three Net Equivalent Income Thresholds

	<40%	<50%	<60
Australia 2014	5.8	11.4	18.9
Austria 2016	7.3	11.4	17.7
Belgium 2016	5.1	12.2	18.7
Canada 2017	6.3	11.9	20.7
Czechia 2016	4.9	9.3	14.2
Denmark 2016	1.8	4.3	11
Finland 2016	1.2	3.4	8.9
Germany 2016	5.9	11.4	18.7
Hungary 2015	4.3	9.3	17.6
Italy 2016	11.2	20.4	28.9
Poland 2016	4.6	8.4	14.8
Estonia 2016	16	22	28.3
United Kingdom 2016	5.2	10.9	21.5
United States 2016	12.8	21.3	30.5

Note: Circa 2016.

Source: Luxembourg Income Study key figures: https://www.lisdatacenter.org/lis-ikf-webapp/app/search-ikf-figures

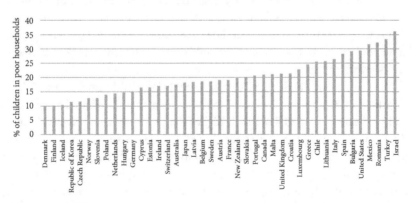

Figure 9.3 Child poverty rate.

Note: Net income less than 60% median.

Source: UNICEF Innocenti Report Card 16. Forthcoming 2020.

Discussion

There is pretty clear and consistent evidence here that for a rich country the United States has unusually high child poverty rates, whichever poverty threshold is used. Why is this? There are a variety of national characteristics that could explain this finding—demographic, labor market, the earnings structure, and social policies. We can rule out quite a number of these factors. Labor demand has been quite buoyant in the United States in recent years (and before the COVID-19 global pandemic), with high levels of male and female employment and low unemployment. Hours worked in the United States are much higher than in European countries, and the minimum wage is at least comparable. Single-parent families are more common in the United States, but not as high or very different from some European countries; anyway, the poverty rates for couples are higher, as we have observed in the previous table.[8] Fertility is comparatively high but not exceptionally different from some European countries, and it is very unlikely that these differences in child poverty could be driven by family size or structure.

What is clearly to blame is social policy. What makes the difference is the lack of family benefits—cash transfers that in other countries contribute to reducing the child poverty rates that would exist if families just relied on market income. We have already seen some evidence to support this conclusion in Figure 9.1: The United States has very low spending as a proportion of its GDP on family benefits. Further evidence comes from comparative analysis of the value and structure of family benefits. The United States has never had the universal tax funded child benefit that exists in most European countries. It did have a means-tested child benefit in the form of Aid to Families With Dependent Children (AFDC), but it was replaced by Temporary Assistance for Needy Families (TANF), which has time limits and is not an entitlement. The only other help that poor families can get is from the food stamps program (SNAP, Supplemental Nutrition Assistance Program). One innovation that has been of great help to working families with children was the introduction of Earned Income Tax Credits, but the problem is that they only benefit those with some earned income who file tax returns.

One way that the impact of these policies can be observed is by modeling them using standard cases.[9] The OECD tax/benefit model enables this to be done, and in Figure 9.4 we present the results for the United States compared to European countries for a couple with two children with one parent working full time on 65% of the average wage. It shows the level of the benefits they would receive and the taxes they would pay as a proportion of average earnings. In the United States (actually, the model is based on Wisconsin rules), net wages would be increased by $3,505 or 6.5% of average earnings. This is entirely due to the Earned Income Tax Credit; this family case is not eligible for SNAP or a housing

Table 9.2 Child Poverty Rate and Poverty Rates by Various Characteristics of Households with Children

	Children (0–17)	All working-age households with at least one child	Single adult household with at least one child	Two or more adult household with at least one child	Jobless households with at least one child	Working households with at least one child
Australia	12.5	10.9	36.7	8.4	65.0	5.3
Austria	11.5	10.9	24.1	10.0	71.7	8.0
Belgium	12.3	10.9	32.2	8.6	71.8	5.3
Brazil	30.1	25.6	54.8	23.3	83.1	20.2
Canada	14.2	12.5	46.9	10.3	81.2	9.7
Chile	21.5	18.9	42.6	16.7	73.9	16.3
China	33.1	28.5	42.3	27.1	48.1	27.4
Costa Rica	27.5	23.4	49.7	20.9	76.7	19.8
Czech Republic	8.5	7.0	32.8	5.0	74.1	4.5
Denmark	3.7	3.0	8.2	2.7	31.7	1.9
Estonia	9.6	8.8	21.6	7.6	67.6	7.8
Finland	3.3	2.8	14.9	1.5	35.5	1.4
France	11.5	9.4	25.9	6.0	43.2	6.9
Germany	12.3	10.6	29.6	7.7	43.3	4.0
Greece	17.6	17.2	27.7	16.9	63.5	14.0
Hungary	7.7	6.1	23.5	4.8	59.5	3.7
Iceland	5.8	5.0	23.0	2.8	16.5	4.7
Ireland	10.0	8.6	34.5	5.4	50.8	3.3
Israel (a)	23.2	20.1	31.8	19.7	81.6	17.1
Italy	17.3	16.5	37.0	15.0	81.4	14.1

Japan	13.9	12.8	50.8	10.7	36.3	12.5
Korea	15.2	14.0	56.6	12.9	57.8	13.3
Latvia	13.2	10.7	34.5	8.3	95.9	8.5
Lithuania	17.7	14.9	45.8	10.7	86.6	12.1
Luxembourg	13.0	12.2	41.1	10.7	67.3	10.8
Mexico	19.8	17.4	34.7	16.3	49.4	16.8
Netherlands	10.9	8.9	29.5	6.3	65.3	5.4
New Zealand	14.1	11.3	46.1	7.3	75.3	7.0
Norway	7.7	6.3	21.8	4.2	59.0	4.3
Poland	9.3	8.6	16.4	8.4	60.1	7.6
Portugal	15.5	13.9	30.2	12.8	80.5	10.8
Russian Fed.	19.6	16.5	35.0	15.6	61.2	15.2
Slovak Republic	14.0	11.0	37.3	10.2	88.9	6.6
Slovenia	7.1	6.3	31.6	5.0	73.4	5.3
South Africa	32.0	26.7	49.8	23.2	77.8	11.9
Spain	22.0	20.1	40.2	19.0	86.8	17.6
Sweden	8.9	7.4	25.8	4.9	77.0	5.0
Turkey	25.3	21.4	31.4	21.3	51.6	19.1
United Kingdom	11.8	10.5	23.2	8.6	39.2	7.0
United States	20.9	18.2	46.3	14.6	74.5	14.2
OECD average	13.1	11.6	32.5	9.8	63.9	8.9

Note: Net equivalent income less than 50% median. Circa 2016.

Source: OECD Family database Charts CO2.2.A, C and D.

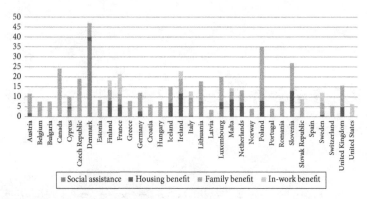

Figure 9.4 Child benefit package.

Note: As percentage of average earnings. Couple plus two children; one adult employed for 65% of the average wage, other adult not working. 2018.

Source: Author's calculations using http://www.oecd.org/els/soc/tax-benefit-web-calculator/.

benefit. Other countries tend to use a combination of elements. The package in the United States is not actually the lowest among these countries, but it is considerably below the level of most.

It is beyond the scope of this chapter to explain why the U.S. social policies for families with children are so much less generous than most European countries. Family benefits do not follow the normal path of the political economy of the welfare state theories.[10] There the U.S. welfare state is classified as liberal, but the same is true for the United Kingdom and Ireland, with much more generous family benefits. Nevertheless, the absence of an adequate safety net for children in the United States drives the much higher child poverty rates, which has long-term consequences for American society as well as enormous extra costs. It also makes families with children much more vulnerable in a crisis—in a recession[11] or now at the time of writing a dreadful global pandemic. Most national responses to the epidemic seemed to have involved attempts to maintain employment and in some places short-term increases in sickness and unemployment benefits—but for families with children, they only have limited impact when there are no or inadequate child benefits.

Notes

1. There is a huge and international literature. But see, for example, Julia Griggs with Robert Walker, *The Costs of Child Poverty for Individuals and Society: A Literature Review* (York, U.K.: Joseph Rowntree Foundation, 2008), (chrome-extension://efaid nbmnnnibpcajpcglclefindmkaj/viewer.html?pdfurl=https%3A%2F%2Fwww.jrf.org. uk%2Fsites%2Fdefault%2Ffiles%2Fjrf%2Fmigrated%2Ffiles%2F2301-child-pove

rty-costs.pdf&clen=298117&chunk=true); and Donald. Hirsch, "An Estimate of the Cost of Child Poverty in 2013," 2013, http://www.cpag.org.uk/sites/default/files/Cost%20of%20child%20poverty%20research%20update%20(2013).pdf.

2. J. Bradshaw, "Social Justice for Children," in *A Handbook on Global Social Justice*, ed. G. Craig (Edward Elgar, 2018).

3. D. Gordon, "Children, Policy and Social Justice," in *Social Justice and Public Policy: Seeking Fairness in Diverse Societies*, ed. G. Craig, T. Burchardt, and D. Gordon (Policy Press, 2008), 157–180.

4. N. Van Mechelen and J. Bradshaw, "Child Benefit Packages for Working Families, 1992–2009," in Minimum Income Protection in Flux, Houndmills, ed. I. Marx and K. Nelson (Basingstoke, U.K.: Palgrave Macmillan, 2013), 81–107.

5. However, there was actually a child dependent exemption in the tax code for those who paid tax.

6. There are a variety of ways of measuring poverty. Here, we use the standard relative methods, which are different from the U.S. government's measures.

7. As has been recently demonstrated in an assessment of transfers on inequality J. Bradshaw and O. Movshuk, "Inequality in the UK in Comparative Perspective," in *Inequalities in the United Kingdom: New Discourses, Evolutions and Actions*, ed. D. Fee and A. Kober-Smith (Paris: Emerald, 2018),.

8. R. Nieuwenhuis and L. Maldonado, eds., *The Triple Bind of Single-Parent Families: Resources, Employment, and Policies to Improve Wellbeing* (Bristol, U.K.: Policy Press, 2018).

9. J. Bradshaw, "Family Benefit Systems," in *Handbook of Child and Family Policy*, ed. G. Bjork Eydal and T. Rostgaard (Edward Elgar, 2018).

10. G. Esping Anderson, *The Three Worlds of Welfare Capitalism* (Princeton University Press, 1990).

11. B. Cantillon et al., eds., *Children of Austerity: Impact of the Great Recession on Child Poverty in Rich Countries* (Oxford: Oxford University Press, 2017); S. Hämäläinen, Y. Chzhen, and J. Vargas, *Significant Changes to Family-Related Benefits in Rich Countries* During *the Great Recession* (UNICEF Office of Research Working Paper WP-2014-13) (Florence, Italy: UNICEF, 2014).

10

Power Resources, Institutionalized Power Relations, and Poverty

David Brady

Poverty is one of the greatest threats to freedom. This is because a lack of sufficient economic resources to meet one's needs undermines one's capacity to realize and actualize freedom. This view has long been prominent in scholarship about both poverty and freedom. For instance, Sen argued that poverty should be defined as a lack of substantive freedom and what he called "capabilities."[1] Capability implies having the freedoms to participate fully and equally with the mainstream of society, the opportunities to purchase well-being, and the capacity to achieve valuable "functionings."[2] This conception is also closely linked to Rawls, who argued that basic liberties should be prioritized in a just society. Rawls argued that a society can be judged according to how it treats the "least advantaged" or "least fortunate group in society."[3] Rawls was concerned with these people "being drawn into the public world and seeing themselves as full members of it."[4] Rawls contended that poverty deeply threatened basic liberties. Indeed, Rawls suggested the least advantaged group could be defined with standard poverty measures, like those with less than half of the median income.

Building on these literatures framing poverty as a lack of freedom, this chapter focuses exclusively on how politics shape poverty. Thinking of poverty as a threat to freedom, the big question is what causes poverty. For most of the history of the field, poverty research has focused predominantly on the individual characteristics of the poor as the "cause" of poverty.[5] Poverty scholarship has argued that people are poor because of certain demographic behaviors and risks, such as single motherhood, unemployment, young headship, and low education.[6] This emphasis on individual behaviors is informed by explanations of poverty focused on culture, incentives, and the individual traits of the poor.[7] As Katz explained, "The idea that poverty is a problem of persons—that it results from moral, cultural, or biological inadequacies—has dominated discussions of poverty for well over two hundred years and given us the enduring idea of the undeserving poor."[8]

In recent decades, however, there has been growing interest in political explanations of poverty.[9] Political theories contend that power and institutions

David Brady, *Power Resources, Institutionalized Power Relations, and Poverty* In: *On Inequality and Freedom.* Edited by: Lawrence M. Eppard and Henry A. Giroux, Oxford University Press. © Oxford University Press 2022. DOI: 10.1093/oso/9780197583029.003.0010 cause policy, which causes poverty and moderates the relationship between be-havior and poverty. Directly challenging behavioral theories, political theories question why particular individual risks are associated with poverty and argue instead that policy can usually moderate those risks. In contrast to some "struc-tural" theories—focused on demographic and economic contexts—political the-ories conjecture that governments can steer and moderate the effects of structural changes like deindustrialization. Even though macro- and meso-level structural contexts matter to poverty—and certainly more than behavioral factors—polit-ical theories propose that states can accomplish low poverty almost regardless of structural contexts.

This chapter reviews the most well-developed theoretical tradition among the political theories of poverty: power resources theory. It summarizes the broader power resources theory and then articulates a more specific version of that theory called institutionalized power relations theory. It then reviews recent empirical evidence for these theories. The chapter demonstrates that political explanations of poverty have become increasingly convincing in part because the field has revealed a number of significant limitations of the dominant indi-vidualistic behavioral explanations of poverty. At this point, political accounts of poverty present a host of arguments and evidence that fundamentally challenges this aforementioned paradigm.

Power Resources and Institutionalized Power Relations Theory

Growing out of the welfare state literature, the most influential political expla-nation of poverty has been power resources theory.[10] Power resources theory contends that collective actors bond together and mobilize less advantaged classes of citizens around shared interests.[11] Such groups form unions and help Left parties win elections, and when in political power, these parties expand the welfare state.[12] Power resources theory claims that the mobilization of such groups of less advantaged citizens is pivotal because the default distribution of political power in a capitalist democracy favors elites and business. This default leads to a default unequal distribution of income. Hence, the working class, poor, and others must bond together and attract some of the middle class to gain any real political power.

Although power resources theory was often presented as a theory of the variation in welfare state generosity, it actually offered a more comprehensive theory of income distribution, and the welfare state's variation was one part of that broader model.[13] In a nutshell, the basic idea is the distribution of political power determines the distribution of economic resources. In addition to poverty, considerable research applies power resources theory to income inequality.[14] The key transition that occurred in the 2000s was to apply power resources directly to poverty and inequality, treating the welfare state as a mediating (albeit crucial) variable.

While classical power resources theory has been extremely useful, it does have some limitations, and scholars have sought to modify and revise it. Still within the family of power resources theory, there have been a few variants that explicitly stand on the shoulders of the giant of power resources theory. For instance, Huber and Stephens called their version a "power constellations approach."[15] Institutionalized power relations theory was one attempt to address at least five shortcomings of power resources theory: (a) an overemphasis on the rational self-interest of the poor and working class; (b) an underemphasis on ideology as a micro-level mechanism in the politics of social policy; (c) a neglect of the support of groups besides the working class and poor because of either rational interest (e.g., as constituencies of beneficiaries of social policies) or ideology; (d) an underappreciation of other social hierarchies like race, gender, and nativity; and (e) an overemphasis on political militancy over institutionalization. Institutionalized power relations theory aimed to embrace the foundations and core arguments of power resources, while updating it to address these concerns.[16]

Institutionalized power relations theory is called "institutionalized" because it intends to prioritize and emphasize the distinctive centrality of formal political power. I have argued that the Left has been too romantic about what can be accomplished outside and against the state and has harbored an exaggerated skepticism of states and social policies. Of course, civil society and protests do matter in helping form interests and ideologies and even pressuring leftist policymakers. However, institutionalized power relations makes clear that the real political action on poverty happens because of bureaucratic formal political organizations operating within the state. Only the state has the economic resources to substantially reduce poverty and inequality, and this is because no nongovernmental or charitable organization has the power to tax. Moreover, the politics of poverty is institutionalized because it is path dependent. Rather than the novel outcome of recent negotiations and struggles over transformational elections or legislation—sometimes the imagery in classic power resources accounts—the politics of poverty is more due to the confluence of interest and ideology that evolves slowly from cumulative negotiations and incremental expansions of social policies. Rather than dissensus politics that disrupts and attacks the status quo from the outside, poverty is driven by the balance of political power on the inside of the governing status quo.

Institutionalized power relations features four factors that cumulatively and interactively cause poverty: (a) ideologies and interests; (b) latent coalitions for egalitarianism; (c) leftist politics; and (d) welfare generosity. All of this is represented by Figure 1.2 in Brady's *Rich Democracies, Poor People.*[17] The causal chain starts with ideologies and interests, although the theory expects even ideologies and interests are endogenous to prior levels of welfare generosity and poverty (i.e., there is a feedback effect). Ideologies and interest drive latent coalitions for egalitarianism.

These latent coalitions are the diffuse groups of political actors who come together to support generous welfare states and social equality. These latent coalitions often hold ideological beliefs about poverty and social equality. Because many members of these latent coalitions are not personally vulnerable to poverty; normative expectations drive the mobilization of these actors. I call these coalitions "latent" because what brings them into partnerships supporting egalitarianism is not always anticipated or intended and is sometimes accidental. Central to these latent coalitions are the constituencies of beneficiaries who receive public assistance, pensions, and services. For example, although pensioners might seem to have little in common with groups particularly vulnerable to poverty like single mothers, the partnership with pensioners makes these coalitions more politically powerful. That power then results in generous social policies, which end up (almost inadvertently) reducing the poverty of single mothers.

Driven by both interests/ideologies and latent coalitions, leftist collective political actors play a crucial mediating role. Leftist politics include the traditional organizations and institutions committed to a more equal distribution of a society's resources. Among the most prominent are labor unions and leftist parties. Simply put, where leftist politics have historically been strong, the welfare state is more generous and less poverty results. The theory also emphasizes that it is collective, not individual, political actors that matter most to poverty.

Leftist collective political actors can directly reduce poverty. Regardless of welfare generosity, labor unions can shape poverty by raising wages and reducing labor market inequality (e.g., VanHeuvelen, 2020).[18] Nevertheless, the most important reason that leftist politics matter is because they drive welfare generosity. Welfare generosity is the dominant and central cause of poverty in institutionalized power relations theory. As discussed below, there is debate about how to measure the welfare state. However measured, both power resources and institutionalized power relations theory present the welfare state as the paramount factor explaining variation in poverty. To a certain extent, this means that countries politically choose their levels of poverty. To a certain extent, this also means that the accident of birth and simply where one resides exerts tremendous influence on whether one will be poor.[19]

Welfare generosity is the dominant determinant of poverty largely because of the many ways states control the distribution of economic resources. Brady and colleagues catalogued a generic list of several mechanisms for how states can shape poverty.[20] First, states organize the distribution of resources.[21] Typically, this mechanism is presented as redistribution. Through taxation, transfers, and services, states take resources from one part of the population and distribute them to others. However, states also influence how resources are distributed in the market "before" redistribution.[22] States also tax many transfers, opt to eschew taxes as an indirect way to subsidize certain market activities, and occasionally even disproportionately tax the poor.

Second, states insure against risks. Many social policies are public insurance programs against unexpected (e.g., illness and accidents), somewhat unexpected (e.g., unemployment) events, and relatively expected events (e.g., having a child or growing old). States often also are actively involved in preventing risks through regulation. Thus, states both reduce the likelihood of poverty-inducing events and mitigate the consequences when such events occur.

Third, states invest in capabilities. States feed and house their residents, though it is mostly through education, training, care, and healthcare that states improve peoples' well-being and development. Fourth, and closely related, states allocate opportunities. In addition to educating and training for jobs and caring for people when they cannot work, states actually create jobs. States are often the largest employers in their countries, and public employment is especially relevant to poverty. Putting all of these mechanisms together—and other potential mechanisms not listed here—states have tremendous influence on the poverty rates in their societies and whether an individual in their domains will or will not be poor.

Mounting Empirical Research

In the past 20 years, there has been a growing wave of research demonstrating how power resources shape poverty. Starting in the late 1990s and early 2000s, a series of studies began to examine why poverty varied across rich democracies.[23] These studies were prompted by the then-novel availability of high-quality "post-fisc" income (i.e., incorporating taxes and transfers) data on many different countries and over time.[24] Because of the Luxembourg Income Study (LIS), and for the first time, scholars were able to use individual-level data to estimate comparable and standardized poverty rates and inequality indices across countries and over time.[25] Among others, Brady (2003) and Moller and colleagues (2003) analyses both showed that poverty and poverty reduction were principally driven by politics and welfare states.[26] Brady argued that leftist power resources combine with and channel through generous social policies to produce lower poverty in some rich democracies. Moller and colleagues demonstrated that the size and generosity of welfare states largely explain the variation in how countries reduce poverty through taxes and transfers. Subsequently, Brady demonstrated that welfare generosity is the dominant factor that accounts for cross-national and historical variation in poverty among rich democracies.[27] While power resources[28] are the dominant cause of and combine with welfare state generosity,[29] the paramount and pivotal factor is welfare generosity. As well, Brady showed that welfare generosity has much larger effects on poverty than well-studied factors like demographic composition, economic growth, and deindustrialization.[30]

The initial research directly linking power resources to poverty relied on macro-level regression analyses of poverty across countries and years (see Brady et al., 2016).[31] On some level, this macro-level approach remains essential as the orienting questions are partly about why poverty varies so tremendously across places and time. Moreover, the macro-level is the level at which Leftist politics and welfare generosity operate. In this sense, power resources explanations inherently emphasize the macro- or at least meso-level context that determines an individual's chances of being poor. Indeed, some recent research makes a contribution by dramatically expanding the number of countries or timepoints to estimate more comprehensive regression models (or to apply the theory to new settings like Latin America; see Huber and Stephens, 2012).[32] For instance, Alper and colleagues[33] nearly tripled the sample size of Moller and colleagues[34] by including more countries and including 10–15 additional years. This is particularly valuable because, for example, Alper and colleagues were able to provide novel evidence of the declining effectiveness of the welfare state for poverty reduction.

Beyond these macro-level analyses, the field has shifted in the past 5–10 years as more studies used multilevel analyses nesting individuals in contexts.[35] For example, Brady and colleagues provided one of the first multilevel analyses of LIS of individual working-age adults nested in 18 rich democracies.[36] This allowed them to control for all the standard individual-level characteristics, behaviors, and risks that predict individual poverty. Even net of those individual-level variables, they demonstrated the odds of poverty in the United States (the least generous welfare state) were greater by a factor of 16.6 than a person with identical characteristics in Denmark (the most generous welfare state).

Moreover, Brady and colleagues' multilevel approach enabled them to show that welfare generosity moderates the effects of salient individual risks. For instance, they showed that welfare generosity moderates how much poverty is predicted by low education, single motherhood, young households, and the number of children in the household. This theme of the moderating effect of welfare states on individual-level risks was taken up in several subsequent papers. For instance, Brady and Burroway showed that single-mother households— probably the most well-studied risk group—were much less likely to be poor in generous welfare states.[37] Indeed, along with Brady and colleagues,[38] they showed that single mothers are unusually and extraordinarily disadvantaged in the United States. Brady and colleagues demonstrated that single motherhood is not even statistically significantly related to poverty in the majority of rich democracies. The United States is actually an outlier, and that single motherhood causes poverty in the United States is an exception, not the rule. Similarly, Baker showed that the association between single motherhood and child poverty declined substantially over time within the United States (while the association with employment increased).[39] This means that what individualistic behavioral research had presumed was a "cause" of poverty is actually something that most countries have politically chosen to be unrelated to poverty. This reveals quite starkly how the behavioral risks of poverty are almost always going to be politically manipulable.

Brady and colleagues[40] generalized this conclusion to all four of the major individual-level risks of poverty: unemployment, low education, young headship, and single motherhood. They developed a framework for decomposing the risks of poverty into prevalences and penalties. Prevalences are the share of the population with a risk, and penalties are the increased probability of poverty associated with a risk. They demonstrated there is far more cross-national variation in penalties than prevalences. Indeed, every country has a share of its population making bad choices and engaging in poverty-increasing behavior. The United States surprisingly has below average prevalences, so prevalences cannot explain why the United States has high poverty or whether reducing prevalences would substantially reduce poverty. By contrast, the United States has the highest penalties, and reducing penalties would reduce poverty more substantially. There is not actually not much cross-national variation in prevalences, but there is considerable cross-national variation in penalties. This means countries can choose how much to penalize risks. Consistent with institutionalized power relations theory, high American penalties are a political choice, and risks need not be automatically or naturally associated with poverty. More recently, others applied the prevalences and penalties framework to analyze poverty across the U.S. states, child income poverty before and after the Great Recession in liberal welfare states, and asset child poverty across rich democracies.[41] All these studies suggested that the prevalence of risks cannot explain much of the variation in poverty.[42]

One of the more promising developments in this literature has been the increased application of power resources approaches to poverty within the United States. Reflecting American ideology about what causes poverty,[43] American poverty researchers are far more likely to subscribe to individualistic behavioral explanations of poverty.[44] The entry of power resources scholars into the analysis of American poverty challenges these behavioralists on their own turf. While still emerging, recent research convincingly showed that variations in poverty even within the United States are greatly shaped by power resources.[45] A few studies highlighted the particularly important impact of labor unions.[46]

For example, Brady and colleagues use multilevel and panel models to show that state-level union density influences working poverty even net of individual-level characteristics.[47] Moreover, they showed that state-level unionization is much more important than state-level economic development or business cycles. Extending beyond this unionization research, Baker used power resources theory to explain why the American South has more poverty than other regions in the United States.[48] She showed that state-level unionization and leftist politics combine with social policy generosity to explain a substantial share of the South's disproportionate poverty.

One final emerging theme in the recent empirical literature is an old theme. Because welfare generosity sits at the center of power resources explanations of poverty, the measurement of welfare generosity is crucial.[49] The field has a fairly standard definition of the welfare state. Welfare states include progressive taxes, cash and near-cash assistance, publicly funded services such as healthcare, public programs that guarantee economic security, and government activities to ensure social inclusion and economic capability.[50] The welfare state relieves citizens from being forced to exclusively depend on the market for economic resources.[51] Also, welfare states define whether citizens are entitled to the "social right" of economic security.[52]

The first wave of empirical research mainly used classic measures of welfare effort like social welfare expenditures as a percentage of gross domestic product.[53] This departed from the prevailing approach of the time. Since at least the early 1990s, welfare state scholars had moved away from such cruder total measures of welfare effort. The reasoning was that welfare effort conflated generosity and the composition of the population and prevalence of households with recognized needs.[54]

However, the reason welfare effort turned out to be so relevant to poverty is precisely because it captures the size of government in the society and people's lives.[55] Because the "public share" of the economy is typically more equally distributed than the private share, poverty will mechanically decline as the public share grows. Even though welfare effort conflates needs and generosity, this criticism obscures the political choices about which needs receive public support. Welfare states politically choose to automatically spend money on the unemployed or elderly and not to spend money automatically on other risk groups. Thus, by choosing to recognize certain needs, welfare states choose to publicly address those particular risks. If countries choose to publicly address more risks, greater welfare effort and lower poverty should result. For instance, Brady showed that government size, measured very simply as government revenue as a percentage of the gross domestic product, is a remarkably strong predictor of child poverty in rich democracies.[56] In fact, no country in the world has ever had a low rate of child poverty without having an above-average government size.

In recent years, scholars have explored this 1990s debate about the measurement of the welfare state. This is partly because of innovations improving the measurement of concepts like social rights and related data sets supplying those measures.[57] On one hand, Alper and colleagues (2020) were able to improve on Moller and colleagues (2003) and measure welfare state generosity with an index of social rights.[58] Alper and colleagues argued that social rights better capture the generosity dimension without the conflating of need. Their results do make a convincing case that such measures can improve our understanding of how welfare states shape poverty. On the other hand, scholars have largely debunked the 1990s impression that countries fell into a typology of welfare state regimes.[59] The welfare state literature has relied very heavily on typologies of say, socialist, conservative, and liberal regimes or typologies of liberal and coordinated market economies.[60] However, the poverty literature has provided a great deal of evidence that these typologies are not very useful. Countries change over time in ways that increasingly depart from these static typologies. There do not appear to be qualitative regime differences that cannot be explained by quantitative measures of welfare generosity. Moreover, the effects of welfare generosity on poverty do not differ by regime types. In short, recent research showed that countries vary along a continuum—not by type—in fighting poverty.

Partly informed by these debates, several scholars have investigated the "dimensions" of welfare states.[61] By dimensions, I mean the strategies for equality and underlying distributional properties of the total package of social policies.[62] The three most important dimensions are transfer share, low-income targeting, and universalism. Transfer share is the size or extent of the welfare state within the average household's income or the share of household income that is socialized or publicly provided. Low-income targeting is defined as the disproportionate concentration of welfare transfers in low-income households. Universalism is defined as homogeneity across the population in benefits, coverage, and eligibility. Low-income targeting and universalism are not simply opposites. While targeting involves heterogeneous benefits across the income distribution, there can be heterogeneity by sex, age, or other categories. These categories are never perfectly associated with the income distribution. Therefore, universalism captures a wider variety of sources of heterogeneity and distinctively involves homogeneity of benefits in general and across any and all categories (not just the income distribution). Brady and Burroway showed that universal benefits better reduce poverty among single mothers than targeted benefits.[63] Brady and Bostic showed that poverty is negatively associated with transfer share and universalism, and universalism and transfer share are positively associated with each other.[64] In contrast to the purported efficiencies of low-income targeting, transfer share and universalism are far more effective than low-income targeting for fighting poverty. In contrast to the purported trade-offs between low-income targeting and welfare generosity, low-income targeting is not negatively associated with transfer share and low-income targeting is not positively associated with poverty and inequality.

Conclusion

This chapter began with the orientation that poverty is a threat to freedom. It then asks what causes poverty and contends that politics is the fundamental cause of poverty. Theories and research on the political causes of poverty have grown into a prolific literature in the past 20 years. Whereas poverty research in the United States has long been dominated by an individualistic focus on culture, incentives, behavior, and risks, the recent wave of theory and research on how politics drive poverty has fundamentally challenged this prevailing paradigm. The most influential theoretical tradition in this political literature is power resources theory. This chapter reviews power resources theory and devotes particular attention to institutionalized power relations theory as one version of power resources theory. In addition to providing a coherent theoretical perspective on the politics of poverty, there has been a wave of empirical research supporting many of its key arguments. Any serious investigation of poverty needs to incorporate political factors, and poverty research that remains solely focused on individualistic behaviors is likely to be an incomplete and potentially incorrect approach. More generally, attempts to understand the threats to freedom should aim to understand poverty. This essay argues that understanding poverty requires an understanding of its political causes.

Notes

1. Amartya Sen, *Development as Freedom* (New York: Anchor Books, 1999).
2. Rod Hick and Tania Burchardt, "Capability Deprivation," in *The Oxford Handbook of the Social Science of Poverty*, ed. D. Brady and L.M. Burton (Oxford University Press, 2016), 75–92.
3. John Rawls, *Justice as Fairness: A Restatement* (Cambridge, MA: Harvard University Press, 2001).
4. Rawls, *Justice as Fairness*, 130.
5. See Lawrence M. Eppard, Mark Robert Rank, and Heather E. Bullock, *Rugged Individualism and the Misunderstanding of American Inequality* (Bethlehem, PA: Lehigh University Press, 2020). See also Alice O'Connor, *Poverty Knowledge* (Princeton, NJ: Princeton University Press, 2001). See also Mark Robert Rank, *One Nation, Underprivileged* (New York: Oxford University Press, 2005).

6. See David Brady, Ryan Finnigan, and Sabine Huebgen, "Rethinking the Risks of Poverty: A Framework for Analyzing Prevalences and Penalties," *American Journal of Sociology* 123 (2017): 740–786. See also Jeff Madrick, *Invisible Americans* (New York: Knopf, 2020).

7. See David Brady, "Theories of the Causes of Poverty," *Annual Review of Sociology* 45 (2019): 155–175. See also Eppard et al., *Rugged Individualism*.

8. Michael B. Katz, *The Undeserving Poor*, 2nd ed. (New York: Oxford University Press, 2013), 269.

9. See Brady, "Theories of the Causes," and Madrick, *Invisible Americans*.

10. David Brady, Agnes Blome, and Hanna Kleider, "How Politics and Institutions Shape Poverty and Inequality," in *The Oxford Handbook of the Social Science of Poverty*, ed. David Brady and Linda M. Burton (New York: Oxford University Press, 2016), 117–140.

11. See Walter Korpi, *The Democratic Class Struggle* (Boston: Routledge, 1983). See also Walter Korpi and Joakim Palme, "The Paradox of Redistribution and Strategies of Equality: Welfare State Institutions, Inequality, and Poverty in the Western Countries" *American Sociological Review* 63, no. 5 (October 1998): 661–687.

12. See David Brady, *Rich Democracies, Poor People* (New York: Oxford University Press, 2009). See also Evelyne Huber and John D. Stephens, *Development and Crisis of the Welfare State* (Chicago: University of Chicago Press, 2001). See also Evelyne Huber and John D. Stephens, *Democracy and the Left* (Chicago: University of Chicago Press, 2012). See also Tom VanHeuvelen, "The Right to Work, Power Resources, and Economic Inequality," *American Journal of Sociology* 125 (2020): 1255–1302. See also Korpi, *Democratic Class Struggle*.

13. See Brady, *Rich Democracies*. See also Korpi, *Democratic Class Struggle*.

14. See David Jacobs and Jonathan C. Dirlam, "Politics and Economic Stratification: Power Resources and Income Inequality in the United States," *American Journal of Sociology* 122 (2016): 469–500. See also Thomas W. Volscho and Nathan J. Kelly, "The Rise of the Super-Rich: Power Resources, Taxes, Financial Markets, and the Dynamics of the Top 1 Percent, 1949 to 2008," *American Sociological Review* 77 (2012): 679–699. See also Korpi and Palme, "The Paradox of Redistribution."

15. See Huber and Stephens, *Development and Crisis*.

16. Brady, *Rich Democracies*.

17. Brady, *Rich Democracies*.

18. VanHeuvelen, "The Right to Work."

19. See Brady et al., "Rethinking the Risks." See also Brady, *Rich Democracies*.

20. Brady et al., "How Politics and Institutions."

21. See Janet C. Gornick and Timothy M. Smeeding, "Redistributional Policy in Rich Countries: Institutions and Impacts in Nonelderly Households," *Annual Review of Sociology* 44 (2018): 441–468. See also Stephanie Moller et al., "Determinants of Relative Poverty in Advanced Capitalist Democracies," *American Sociological Review* 68 (2003): 22–51.

22. Kaitlin Alper, Evelyne Huber, and John D Stephens, "Poverty and Social Rights Among the Working Age Population in Post-Industrial Democracies," *Social Forces* 99, no. 4 (2021): 1710–1744.

23. See Gornick and Smeeding, "Redistributional Policy." See also Korpi and Palme, "The Paradox of Redistribution."

24. See Kenneth Nelson, "Counteracting Material Deprivation: The Role of Social Assistance in Europe," *Journal of European Social Policy* 22 (2012): 148–163. See also Lyle Scruggs and James Allan, "Welfare State Decommodification in 18 OECD Countries: A Replication and Revision," *Journal of European Social Policy* 16 (2006): 55–72.

25. See Arthur S. Alderson, Jason Beckfield, and Francois Nielsen, "Exactly How Has Income Inequality Changed? Patterns of Distributional Change in Core Societies," *International Journal of Comparative Sociology* 46 (2006): 405–423. See also Gornick and Smeeding, "Redistributional Policy."

26. See David Brady, "The Politics of Poverty: Left Political Institutions, the Welfare State and Poverty," *Social Forces* 82 (2003): 557–88. See also Moller et al., "Determinants of Relative Poverty."

27. Brady, *Rich Democracies*.

28. See Huber and Stephens, *Development and Crisis*. See also Huber and Stephens, *Democracy and the Left*.

29. Brady, "The Politics of Poverty."

30. Brady, *Rich Democracies*.

31. Brady et al., "How Politics and Institutions."

32. See Huber and Stephens, *Democracy and the Left*.

33. Alper et al., "Poverty and Social Rights."

34. Moller et al., "Determinants of Relative Poverty."

35. Brady et al., "How Politics and Institutions."

36. David Brady, Andrew S. Fullerton, and Jennifer Moren Cross, "Putting Poverty in Political Context: A Multi-Level Analysis of Adult Poverty Across 18 Affluent Democracies," *Social Forces* 88, no. 1 (September 2009): 271–299.

37. David Brady and Rebekah Burroway, "Targeting, Universalism, and Single-Mother Poverty: A Multilevel Analysis Across 18 Affluent Democracies," *Demography* 49 (2012): 719–46.

38. Brady et al., "Rethinking the Risks."

39. Regina S. Baker, "The Changing Association Among Marriage, Work, and Child Poverty in the United States, 1974–2010," *Journal of Marriage & Family* 77 (2015): 1166–1178.

40. Brady et al., "Rethinking the Risks."

41. See David W. Rothwell and Annie McEwen, "Comparing Child Poverty Risk by Family Structure During the 2008 Recession," *Journal of Marriage and Family* 79 (2017): 1224–1240. See also David W. Rothwell, Timothy Ottusch, and Jennifer K. Finders, "Asset Poverty Among Children: A Cross-National Study of Poverty Risk," *Children and Youth Services Review* 96 (2019): 409–419. See also Jennifer Laird et al., "Poor State, Rich State: Understanding the Variability of Poverty Rates Across U.S. States," *Sociological Science* 5 (October 2018): 628–652.

42. Madrick, *Invisible Americans*.

43. Matthew O. Hunt and Heather E. Bullock, "Ideologies and Beliefs About Poverty," in *The Oxford Handbook of the Social Science of Poverty*, ed. David Brady and Linda M. Burton (New York: Oxford University Press, 2016), 93–116.

44. See Eppard et al., *Rugged Individualism*. See also Madrick, *Invisible Americans*. See also Rank, *One Nation*. See also O'Connor, *Poverty Knowledge*.

45. See Laird et al., "Poor State." See also Zachary Parolin, "Temporary Assistance for Needy Families and the Black-White Child Poverty Gap in the United States," *Socio-Economic Review* 19 (2021): 1005–1035. See also Zachary Parolin and David Brady, "Extreme Child Poverty and the Role of Social Policy in the United States," *Journal of Poverty & Social Justice* 27 (2019): 3–22.

46. See Jake Rosenfeld and Jennifer Laird, "Unions and Poverty," in *The Oxford Handbook of the Social Science of Poverty*, ed. David Brady and Linda M. Burton (New York: Oxford University Press, 2016), 800–819. See also VanHeuvelen, "The Right to Work."

47. See David Brady, Regina S. Baker, and Ryan Finnigan, "When Unionization Disappears: State-Level Unionization and Working Poverty in the United States," *American Sociological Review* 78 (2013): 872–896.

48. Regina S. Baker, "Why Is the American South Poorer?" *Social Forces* 99 (2020): 126–154.

49. See Jason Beckfield, *Political Sociology and the People's Health* (New York: Oxford University Press, 2018). See also Huber and Stephens, *Development and Crisis*.

50. Brady, *Rich Democracies*.

51. Scruggs and Allan, "Welfare State Decommodification."

52. Alper et al., "Poverty and Social Rights."

53. See Brady, *Rich Democracies*. See also Brady et al., "Putting Poverty in Political Context." See also Moller et al., "Determinants of Relative Poverty."

54. Scruggs and Allan, "Welfare State Decommodification."

55. David Brady and Amie Bostic, "Paradoxes of Social Policy: Welfare Transfers, Relative Poverty, and Redistribution Preferences," *American Sociological Review* 80 (2015): 268–298.

56. David Brady, "Bernie Sanders Wants the U.S. to Stop Having the Highest Child Poverty Rate Among Rich Countries. Here's How You Can Do It," *Washington Post*, April 13, 2016.

57. See Nelson, "Counteracting Material Deprivation." See also Scruggs and Allan, "Welfare State Decommodification."

58. See Alper et al., "Poverty and Social Rights." See also Moller et al., "Determinants of Relative Poverty."

59. See Brady, *Rich Democracies*. See also Scruggs and Allan, "Welfare State Decommodification."

60. See Beckfield, *Political Sociology*. See also Huber and Stephens, *Development and Crisis*.

61. See Brady and Burroway, "Targeting." See also Brady and Bostic, "Paradoxes of Social Policy."

62. See Korpi and Palme, "The Paradox of Redistribution."

63. Brady and Burroway, "Targeting."

64. Brady and Bostic, "Paradoxes of Social Policy."

11

Poverty, Politics, and Perspective

A View of Political Failure from Appalachia[*]

James A. White

America's most disadvantaged group is those poor persons who also happen to live in areas—that is, states and counties and localities within states—that fail to undertake effective action to remediate poverty. Inherent political flaws, which can be overcome but must first be recognized, have hampered efforts to combat poverty in Appalachia and elsewhere.

Brandeis asserted that federalism allows state and local governments to serve as laboratories of democracy. Regrettably, many Americans stuck in dysfunctional, ineffective laboratories bear disparate costs. Moreover, history shows that competing towns, villages, cities, counties, and states can race to the bottom as easily as to the top; that is, poverty, discrimination, disenfranchisement, gerrymandering, and environmental degradation can and have persisted, incidentally and purposively.

We have too many fellow Americans who are afflicted with poverty because of not only poor decisions they may have made but also who their parents are; where they were born; where they currently live; and decisions made by elected and appointed officials where they live, including governors, state legislators, university administrators, school superintendents, school board members, and high school principals. Federal elected, appointed, and permanent officials aren't always on the side of progress, either.

Kristoff and WuDunn explain America's ongoing collective failure to reduce poverty: "It may seem odd that, at a time of rising inequality, there aren't more vigorous efforts to help those who are struggling. But political scientists have found that even in a democracy, inequality awards the wealthy not only with more wealth but also with more political power. The rich then use this power to

[*] This paper benefitted from research done by colleagues at the West Virginia Center on Budget and Policy, including Rick Wilson, Sean O'Leary, and Ted Boettner, as well as Concord University students, including Jenna Arthur, Gavin Brandenburg, Seth Cardwell, Dustin Carter, Taylor Carter, Noah Clark, Maggie-Jean Cook, Lanie Craig, Ben Evans, Jack Garwood, Carley Graves, Simun Kovac, Edith Martinez, Alexandria Miller, Trevor Mullins, Lucas Pettus, Colten Ramsey, Allie Sears, Donna Smith, Jacob Snuffer, and Perri Williams.

James A. White, *Poverty, Politics, and Perspective* In: *On Inequality and Freedom*. Edited by: Lawrence M. Eppard and Henry A. Giroux, Oxford University Press. © Oxford University Press 2022.
DOI: 10.1093/oso/9780197583029.003.0011

consolidate their own wealth. The upshot is that the more urgent economic justice becomes, the less likely it is to be pursued." Additionally, federalism hinders universal implementation of effective strategies. Britain, which has a unitary rather than federal system, "made a concerted effort to cut child poverty, and in just five years it cut the rate almost in half—so it can be done. . . . Talent is universal, opportunity is not."[1]

The public choice model explains the observed shortcomings of American democracy, including inequality. This model, developed by economists James Buchanan and Gordon Tullock with political applications advanced by, among others, Anthony Downs and Mancur Olson, has been ascendant in political and social sciences since the mid-twentieth century. Many disdain the public choice model, assuming that it is biased against collective action.[2] Description and prescription must not be conflated, however, and a useful model should not be dismissed for association with laissez-faire capitalism and neoliberalism. The model, while imperfect, is not inherently biased.

We can acknowledge the benefits of private property and unfettered markets while also realizing that the free market will both underproduce desired goods and overproduce undesired ones. National defense, infrastructure, public education, labor and environmental regulations, Social Security, Medicare, and Medicaid are testaments to the practice of government interventions undertaken to optimize outcomes. Just like these public interventions have been funded since the founding, the inherent flaws in democracy were evident to the framers and were discussed in the *Federalist Papers*.

Even the most ardent believers in American exceptionalism must acknowledge the country's glaring suboptimal results. Contemporary heirs of the founders undertaking to establish a more perfect union, to promote the general welfare, and to secure the blessings of liberty to ourselves and our posterity would not seek to produce low levels of political participation, high and persistent federal budget deficits, and mass incarceration. The public choice model explains that those outcomes and others—poverty, inequality, disenfranchisement, gerrymandering, a political system awash with money and characterized by toxic and pervasive negative advertising, and massive incumbency advantage, to name just a few—result from the rational actions of self-interested individuals seeking to maximize their own net benefits.

The principal agent problem contributes to poor outcomes. Our agents, elected officials, and other policymakers might and often do rationally prefer outcomes that are different from the ones preferred by us principals, whose policy preferences the agents are supposed to implement. Many agents have a stake in keeping a flawed system the way it is, in spite, or perhaps because, of those flaws.

Those of us who not only study but also teach American government to typical undergraduates receive daily lessons that help us understand the current state of American democracy. Most Americans don't have college degrees, and just a bit more than half of contemporary high school students pursue further higher education. Having or pursuing a college degree, however, does not require or correlate with great knowledge of American government.

This paucity of basic familiarity with facts about American government is no surprise to any of us who ever watched Leno's "Jaywalking" segment on the *Tonight Show* or to any of us who have had political discussions at a bar, reunion, or holiday gathering. It is easy to observe that lack of information is uncorrelated with the strength of our fellow Americans' political opinions. In our democracy, widespread adherence to strong, illogical, and counterfactual opinions—for example, it's become demonstrably clear that we can't balance the federal budget by cutting taxes and foreign aid, no matter how fervently many of us believe and assert that we can—clearly makes solving public policy problems more difficult.[3]

Unfortunately, rampant, outcome-diminishing policy ignorance persists because it is rational to pay little heed to political news. Individuals can receive the collective benefit of living in a democracy even if they do not vote or even pay attention to politics, freeriding on the efforts of those who do participate. The rationality of political ignorance explains rampant and unequal political disengagement, including low turnout and its disproportionate prevalence among those with lower incomes and less education.[4]

Self-interested behavior by individuals and groups, outside of government and within, allows inequality to persist. As Madison observed in *Federalist Paper 10*, different individuals and groups of individuals have different preferences. Factions composed of a few, many, or even most might advocate policies contrary to the public good. Moreover, because of both uncertainty and the principal agent problem, reelection-seeking incumbent politicians may rationally fail to advance policies that might ameliorate inequality; personal, immediate benefits might prevail over collective, contingent ones.

In our federal system of separate branches sharing power, all legislative achievements are difficult to attain, and successfully enacting, funding, implementing, and sustaining redistributive programs is especially difficult. Moreover, in many/most constituencies, efforts to provide additional services to the disadvantaged would not provide net reelection benefits—campaign funding and votes—to incumbents. It may be immoral to fail to advocate, vote for, and implement policies that are shown to be effective at reducing inequality, but for many policymakers such dithering, or worse, is not irrational. Acknowledging the rationality of inaction is not the same as advocating or excusing it.

It is tempting to make a case that Appalachians in general and a subset of young Appalachians in particular are the most disadvantaged. It is, however, misleading to lump Appalachians together as distinctively disadvantaged. Poverty afflicts too many Appalachians, but it also afflicts too many Americans who live outside Appalachia.

American poverty persists even though we know how and have the resources to reduce its incidence. Understanding is a necessary but insufficient element of diminishing poverty, the causes of which are complex. The question of who is responsible for any individual's or family's poverty is one of agency, and the obvious and empirically supported answer is that the responsibility is shared by all who could, but choose to not, diminish the affliction.

We know that individual choices about school, work, and starting a family matter when it comes to poverty. Haskins and Sawhill quoted Moynihan regarding political approaches to addressing poverty: "The core conservative truth is that culture matters . . . and the core liberal truth is that government can reshape culture."[5] Haskins and Sawhill stressed the importance of following the "success sequence" of graduating from high school, obtaining employment, and getting married before having children as a practice to "virtually eliminate . . . the possibility of living below the poverty line. By contrast, 76 percent of those living in families that do not adhere to any of these norms are poor."[6] They also acknowledge, however, that meeting the norms of high school graduation, obtaining and keeping a job, and delaying childbirth is easier said than done, particularly in some parts of our country, concluding, "Circumstances that make education, work, and marriage difficult will not be resolved anytime soon."[7]

Some popular authors denigrate those who fail to follow the "success sequence," calling them "underclass," "welfare queens," "loafers," and "hillbillies." Vance wrote that hillbillies

> spend our way into the poorhouse. We buy giant TVs and iPads. Our children wear nice clothes thanks to high-interest credit cards and payday loans. We purchase homes we don't need, refinancing them for more spending money, and declare bankruptcy, often leaving them full of garbage in our wake. Thrift is inimical to our being. . . . Our homes are a chaotic mess. . . . At least one member of the family uses drugs. . . . We don't study as children, and we don't make our kids study when we're parents. . . . We choose not to work when we should be looking for jobs. Sometimes we'll get a job, but it won't last. We'll get fired for tardiness, or for stealing merchandise . . . or for having a customer complain about the smell of alcohol on our breath.[8]

Of course people in all geographic and demographic groups fail to follow the success sequence. Prejudicial attacks inflame rather than inform, ignoring the truth that many of us "got where we got largely by dumb luck and by what Warren Buffet calls winning the ovarian lottery."[9] Moreover, the more likely connection between the disproportionately non-White urban poor and the disproportionately White rural poor is not their presumed shared shiftlessness but rather the failure of Americans to provide all, urban, suburban, and rural alike, with equal access to good jobs and high-quality child care, education, and healthcare.

We might have more success reducing inequality if we practiced antiracism and anticlassism, as Ibram Kendi noted:

> Class racism is as ripe among White Americans—who castigate poor Whites. . . . as it is in Black America. . . . Constructs of 'ghetto Blacks' (and 'White trash') are the most obvious ideological form of class racism. . . . To be antiracist is to say the political and economic conditions, not the people, in poor Black neighborhoods are pathological. Pathological conditions are making the residents sicker and poorer while they strive to survive and thrive, while they invent and reinvent cultures and behaviors that may be different but never inferior to those of residents in richer neighborhoods.[10]

Othering is just one of the problems facing America's poor, whose political difficulties include insufficient political clout. The public choice model tells us that rational politicians respond to those who vote, and turnout rates among the poor and children run the range from extremely low to nonexistent. Those with no political voice are, unsurprisingly, unheard and grossly underserved: "Let's be blunt: America as a nation is guilty of child neglect. We have punished children, mainly because they don't vote. Meanwhile, other countries offer home visitation, paid family leaves and monthly cash allowances for families with children to reduce disadvantage."[11]

Nationwide underinvestment is exacerbated by local issues in our federalist system. "Education should theoretically provide an escape route for at-risk children, but in reality, across the country, mostly it doesn't: poor children generally go to weak schools. . . . and often can't afford either community college or a four-year college."[12]

As the success sequence demonstrates, choices matter: Individuals and their families will do better if they stay in school, learn, and graduate, ideally both high school and postsecondary school. Moreover, individuals should work, not take on unaffordable debt, avoid illegal activity, delay childbearing, and parent lovingly. Communities, however, make collective choices, too, and we must acknowledge the reality that community as well as individual action can facilitate better outcomes. We have chosen to tolerate high levels of "poverty . . . homelessness, overdose deaths, crime and inequality—and now it's time to make a different choice."[13]

Putnam wrote:

> We Americans like to think of ourselves as "rugged individualists"—in the image of the lone cowboy riding toward the setting sun, opening the frontier. But at least as accurate a symbol of our national story is the wagon train, with its mutual aid among a community of pioneers. . . . In the past half century, we have witnessed, for better or worse, a giant swing toward the individualist (or libertarian) pole in our culture, society, and politics. At the same time, researchers have steadily piled up evidence of how important social context, social institutions, and social networks—in short, our communities—remain for our well-being and our kids' opportunities.[14]

The Constitution prescribes both collective and individual action to "promote the general welfare" and "secure the blessings of liberty to ourselves and our posterity." For most of the last half century, the ascendant ideology has proscribed collective action, ignoring both the founding command and centuries of effective policy:

> Yet the pioneer spirit triumphed not only because of rugged individualism, but also because of government policy. The pioneers didn't buy covered wagons and roll toward Oregon purely as actions of individual initiative. . . . The Homestead Act was later supplemented with public education, land-grant universities, rural electrification, and subsidies for home buyers and university students in the G.I. Bill of Rights. Time after time government provided escalators, citizens jumped on board, and America benefitted. . . . Now it's time for America to get back in the escalator business.[15]

We know what causes poverty to persist disproportionately in a geographic area: lack of employment and educational opportunity; poor healthcare; unequal policing; and inadequate child care, transportation, and quality, affordable housing. Exhorting individuals to supply these services for themselves through individual initiative makes as much sense as advising them to create their own food safety, air traffic control, interstate highway, and space exploration systems.

Decades of evidence have demonstrated what policies work to diminish individual poverty: qualified, well-compensated teachers in every classroom; access to extracurricular activities; high levels of social capital, including active engagement in politics; access to affordable higher education; and the ability to start college ready to succeed and, ideally, with some already-earned course credit.

In general, Appalachia is disproportionately afflicted with both maladies and generally insufficient remedial efforts. We must, however, note that Appalachia is not monolithic with regard to impoverishment and insufficient opportunity.

Contiguous areas of disproportionate distress in Appalachia cause legitimate concern, but they must be viewed in context. Poverty afflicts people and not the land and water where those people reside, although the physical environment can also suffer as the result of human poverty. While it is true that people living in certain parts of Appalachia are disproportionately poor, it is also clear that other parts of Appalachia are prosperous. Moreover, economic diversity exists within both distressed and thriving jurisdictions.

Appalachian Maryland, for example, is not poor. In fact, there are Appalachian and Appalachian-adjacent towns and counties in many states that are some of the most desirable places in the country in which to live. Those places are experiencing population growth, fueled in part by fellow Appalachians who are out-migrating from the most distressed parts of the region. Economic rationality fuels migratory patterns between and within jurisdictions, in Appalachia and elsewhere. Author Monica Potts wrote about her hometown in rural Arkansas: "Many . . . who want to live in a place with better schools, better roads and bigger public libraries have . . . moved to places that can afford to offer them. This includes many of my peers from high school who left for college or jobs and permanently settled in bigger, wealthier cities and towns around the region."[16]

The Appalachian Regional Commission (ARC) index divides the more than 3,000 American counties/county equivalents into five groups based on economic outcomes.[17] The middle 50 percent of counties (i.e., those ranking from the 26th through 75th percentiles, or, statistically, the "midspread" or "interquartile range") are called "transitional." Fifty-one percent of Appalachia's 420 counties (213) fall into this category. ARC labels the most prosperous 10 percent of counties "attainment" (only three of Appalachian counties fall into this category), and the bottom 10 percent "distressed" (80, or 19 percent of, Appalachian counties are in this category). The remaining 30 percent of counties (i.e., from the 11th through 25th percentile and from the 76th through 90th percentiles) are called, respectively, "competitive" (Appalachia has 10 counties, 2 percent of all Appalachian counties, in this category) and "at risk" (Appalachia has 110, or 26 percent, in this category). As summarized in Table 11.1, Appalachia has significantly fewer counties that are doing comparatively well and significantly more that are doing poorly.

Again, however, we must not conflate areas and people. Appalachia's poorest counties are losing population, relative to both the rest of the country and the rest of Appalachia. From 2000 to 2010, the U.S. population grew 9.7 percent, about 40 percent more than the 6.8 percent growth in Appalachia during the same period. Appalachia's growth was not uniform, however: The growth rate in the 80 distressed counties was less than 1 percent (the median distressed county actually experienced population decline during the first decade of the century), whereas the growth in the remaining 340 counties was 7.3 percent.[18]

Just as it is important to realize that Appalachia is not monolithic when it comes to poverty or population changes, it is important to understand that areas with disproportionate poverty are not monolithically poor. Within poor areas there exist elites who do not suffer from poverty. Poor places have private, non-profit, and public-sector elites who are wealthy and/or have high-paying jobs.

For many of us with sufficient resources, Appalachia is a great place to live. Housing prices are low, and our children have access to quality educational opportunities in and out of state. Moreover, our friends and family members have access to jobs with little outside competition.[19] In fact, the perceived back-wardness of the region helps contribute to the creation of a scissors effect, where the fortunes of the well-off and the dispossessed diverge rather than converge. As Elazar cautioned half a century ago, some may benefit and some may suffer from a dearth of well-qualified competitors drawn to particular regions: "Without a first rate elite to draw upon traditionalistic culture political systems degenerate into oligarchies."[20]

Importantly, those of us working in positions of authority are generally not held accountable for the outcomes experienced by our most disadvantaged fellow Appalachians. Our fellow citizens, like many other Americans and with and without elite assistance, blame the poor themselves for their own poverty. Isenberg documented that we have had centuries of experience perfecting this practice and denigrating efforts to assist the unworthy:

> Poverty . . . is an essential part of American history. So too is the backlash that occurs when attempts are made to improve the conditions of the poor. Whether it is New Deal policies or LBJ's welfare programs or Obama-era health care re-form, along with any effort to address inequality and poverty comes a harsh and seemingly inevitable reaction. Angry citizens lash out: they perceive govern-ment bending over backward to help the poor (implied or stated: undeserving) and they accuse bureaucrats of wasteful spending that steals from hardworking men and women. . . . In the larger scheme of things, the modern complaint against state intervention echoes the old English fear of social leveling, which is said to encourage the unproductive. . . . Through a process of rationaliza-tion, people have long tended to blame failure on the personal flaws of individ-uals. . . . They are depicted as slothful, rootless vagrants, physically scarred by their poverty. They are often renamed, but they do not disappear.[21]

Again, federalism exacerbates the intransigent problems of poverty and ine-quality, and malfeasant local elites are rarely the sole problem. The sources of suf-fering are more mundane and harder to eradicate: scarce resources, complexity, confusion, and rational self-interest, including rational ignorance. Few doubt the good intentions of the vast majority of the people who serve Appalachians, including state legislators and other elected and appointed officials, including state and local bureaucrats, school superintendents, school board members, college administrators, teachers, professors, and staff. Regrettably, good intentions are not sufficient to produce good outcomes.

A state judicial decision several decades ago intended to equalize educational opportunity throughout the state of West Virginia.[22] A recent review of research found ongoing absolute and relative disadvantage in the state, however:

> West Virginia continues to rank at the bottom with regard to many educational and economic issues. The state's college-going rate is among the lowest in the United States and lower than any state bordering West Virginia. Median household income is also among the lowest . . . in the country. . . . Only three states saw a bigger decline in [college] student enrollment than West Virginia since the Great Recession; in the same period, only three states cut higher education more than West Virginia. The state's ability to keep college graduates is also concerning. . . . A third of in-state students leave following graduation . . . [and] 90 percent of out-of-state students leave following graduation.

The study also found great variation in the availability of Advance Placement (AP) classes, with some high schools offering more than 20 different AP opportunities and about 10 percent offering zero.[23]

We know more about poverty solutions than is generally acknowledged. A century ago, older Americans were more likely than any other age group to live in poverty; now, children under 18 have that dubious distinction. How did that happen, and why does disproportionate poverty persist among the young?

If the question involves poverty, the answer involves money. Social Security accounts for about a quarter of annual federal expenditures, and those intergenerational transfers have had a profound impact. "A careful analysis of the impact of Social Security on poverty rates among those born between 1885 and 1930 shows that Social Security can explain the entire decline in the official rate of poverty." Moreover, Social Security "grew rapidly in the 1960s and 1970s, covering more people and paying bigger benefits, and the poverty rate among the elderly fell sharply—from 35 percent in 1959 to 10 percent in 2007."[24]

It's problematic to provide money directly to children, and biases about the moral character of their guardians have rendered such cash transfers politically toxic, particularly when rational ignorance renders most Americans unaware of the empirical poverty-reducing effects of cash transfers. Still, there are less direct methods that we know would help diminish poverty, in the short, medium, and long terms. Ironically, these indirect methods are more expensive but have more political support: Rational ignorance inhibits attainment of rational outcomes. Expanding educational and support activities from pre-K through college, including extracurricular activities, would help. Former Obama Education Secretary Arne Duncan recommended "access to free, high-quality pre-K for every four-year-old. . . . After-school and enrichment programs should be provided to all students . . . [ensuring that] every school [has] a great principal and every classroom a great teacher. . . . Every high school student should graduate with some college credit, an industry certification, or both."[25]

Putnam emphasized the vital role of extracurricular activities, equal access to which has declined as geographic and economic differences between rich and poor have increased and rural schools have been consolidated. These extracurriculars, which require access to facilities, coaching, and equipment, build

> soft skills—strong work habits, self-discipline, teamwork, leadership, and a sense of civic engagement. . . . Extracurricular participation matters for upward mobility. It is thus distressing to learn that every study confirms a substantial class gap in extracurricular participation. . . . What can explain these growing class gaps in extracurricular involvement? . . . Lack of transportation might be a factor. . . . Fifty years ago, offering opportunities for all kids to take part in extracurricular activities was recognized as an important part of a public school's responsibilities to students, their parents, and the wider community. . . . in our new era of budget belt-tightening, high-stakes testing, and academic "core competencies," however, school boards everywhere have decided that extracurricular activities and soft skills are "frills."[26]

Equalizing educational opportunities is vital to reducing unequal outcomes. "Disparities in educational attainment lead to greater inequalities of all kinds, which in turn have long term effects. . . . High inequality reverberates through societies on multiple levels, correlating with, if not causing, more crime, less happiness, poorer mental and physical health, less racial harmony, and less civic and political participation."[27] Additionally:

> The overall level of educational attainment in the United States today is too low and stagnant. . . . And it is finishing programs of study—earning degrees, not just starting in college—that is the metric to be emphasized. . . . Second, the U.S. educational system harbors huge disparities in outcomes . . . that are systematically related to race/ethnicity and gender, as well as to socio-economic status. . . . Third, these two problems are linked: the only way to substantially improve overall levels of educational attainment is by improving graduation rates for . . . students from low-SES backgrounds. . . . Public universities have to be the principal agents of progress in addressing these challenges.[28]

Bowen et al. provided a road map for achieving these goals: emphasizing grades over standardized test scores, "making college less expensive for students from modest backgrounds . . . and [f]inding more resources for need-based student aid," setting high expectations, and paying attention to campus life.[29]

Our collective response has not been promising, particularly in those parts of the country where robust efforts are needed. To the extent that we are making progress in helping the poor, we are making it slowly in the comparatively few and well-resourced areas that are undertaking efforts, and we are making it extremely slowly as the result of individual efforts of policy entrepreneurs and individuals who are trying to accomplish the unmanageable task of lifting themselves up by their own bootstraps.

Read social media posts and you will find business owners, college professors and administrators, teachers, principals, doctors, police officers, lawyers, politicians, ministers, and other folks complaining about the out-of-touch elites who are ruining the lives of real Americans who live in places like Appalachia. The sort of "out-of-touch" policies that despised coastal elites support include things like gun regulations, reductions in carbon emissions, prohibition on school prayer and other religious activities in schools, and rights for women and minority groups, including reproductive rights and protections against discrimination toward the LGBTQ (lesbian, gay, bisexual, transitioning, queer/questioning) community. Often these posts, echoing comments on talk radio and elsewhere, will cite election results in places like Appalachia as evidence of working class opposition to elite recommendations made by former education secretaries, Harvard and other college professors, *New York Times* editorialists, and other self-important, ivory-towered elites.

It does not matter that empirical evidence refutes the myth of working class support for candidates opposing redistributive policies.[30] We Americans have inalienable rights to hold and disseminate our opinions, whether or not they have factual support,[31] and passionate disagreement is to be expected in a healthy democracy. Moreover, there is nothing new about complaints about geographically and socially distant elites, who have been derided as eggheads; pointy-headed intellectuals; effete, impudent snobs; nattering nabobs of negativism; and the intelligentsia.[32]

Frank challenges the hoary bogeyman of the all-powerful, distant elite:

Consider, for example, the stereotype of liberals that comes up so often . . . arrogant, rich, tasteful, fashionable, and all-powerful. In my real-world experience liberals are nothing of the kind. They are an assortment of complainers—for the most part impoverished complainers—who wield about as much influence over American politics as the cashier at Home Depot does over the company's business strategy. This is not a secret, either; read any issue of The Nation or In These Times . . . and you figure out pretty quickly that liberals don't speak for the powerful or wealthy.[33]

Moreover, the truly harmful elites are the proximate ones who are responsible for local government actions and inactions. To quote Pogo: "We have met the enemy and he is us."[34] Similarly, Putnam wrote: "The absence of personal villains in our stories does not mean that no one is at fault. Many constraints on equal opportunity in America today . . . are attributable to social policies that reflect collective decisions. Insofar as we have some responsibility for those collective decisions, we are implicated by our failure to address removable barriers to others' success."[35]

Self-interested lying is to be expected, but endemic credulity exacerbates the lies. Duncan started his book with the statement "Education runs on lies," adding "in America, there's no reason that a kid born in one place should not have the same chances and opportunities as a kid born in another." Lies perpetuate our unequal system, and these lies "more often than not . . . existed to protect resources or to safeguard jobs. . . . Nearly all the lies had to do with money and where power was concentrated, not education."[36]

Bigotry exacerbates our truth problems. Our continuing tolerance of the denigration of the poor for their poverty excuses the lack of action to remediate the problem, and that "cruelty to those left behind . . . speaks to a skewed moral compass . . . emerges from a growing empathy gap in America, one consequence of which is scorn for those left behind."[37]

Ironically, malign neglect reduces absolute poverty, albeit slowly, painfully, and to the further detriment of those left behind. Those who can leave the most afflicted areas do leave, and new people do not move in to an area plagued with poor public services disproportionately populated by the impoverished. People die younger, and hospitals, schools, and colleges close. It's a bummer all around, excepting, perhaps, for the few at the very top of the local pyramid—and even these folks may, like colonizers, maintain residences outside of the distressed areas.

Poverty and inequality are not the only problems we Americans have allowed to fester. We have responded to epidemic gun violence, suicides, and school shootings by terrifying young children with regular active shooter drills and calls for firearm proliferation in public schools and on college campuses, all in the name of liberty, empirical research, and safety be damned. Duncan lamented the confounding hypocrisy:

At the time of writing, and since 2009, there have been 288 school shootings in the United States. The country with the second most is Mexico—with

eight.... The students in ... other countries don't have to do active shooter drills
at school.... After Newtown, our lack of empathy and our inability to do what
was right was [*sic*] completely exposed. These were babies who'd been executed
in their classroom. When the dust was settled, we chose to protect our guns, not
our kids. We chose metal over flesh. This should have been a massive source of
civic shame, but somehow it wasn't.... The lives of black and brown Americans
are absolutely and systematically less valued than those of white Americans, but
Newtown showed that, in truth, we don't value the lives of our young people at
all. It exposed so much hypocrisy, so much mendacity.[38]

Analogously, we have responded to rampant substance abuse and addiction
with criminalization and mass incarceration in the name of safety, empirical research, liberty, and ideological consistency be damned. Appalachians may suffer
disproportionately from opioid addiction, but the denizens of hills and hollers
did not prescribe opiates to themselves, did not ship millions of pills to rural
pharmacies, did not ignore laws requiring tracking of excessive sales, did not disseminate addictive drugs like Doritos,[39] and did not make fortunes off the crisis.
Multinational pharmaceutical companies and retailers, with too much complicit
local elite participation, tolerance, and indifference, addicted and killed tens of
thousands, breaking up families and overwhelming government justice, health,
and child welfare systems. "Some 80 percent of Americans addicted to opioids
began with prescription pain killers.... Essentially, pharmaceutical executives
acted like ... drug lords, with legal approval.... The biggest drug dealers wear
white lab coats or pinstripe suits."[40]

Likewise, we have responded to growing inequality perversely, with policies that limit access to higher education. A study by a think tank in West
Virginia found:

> West Virginia is one of 14 states that cut funding for higher education by more
> than 24% per student between 2008 and 2018, despite improvements in the
> state economy.... These cuts have helped drive up the cost of public colleges
> and universities, imposing the greatest cost burden on families of color and
> those with low incomes. Average published tuition at public four-year univer-
> sities in West Virginia grew by 52.8% between 2008 and 2018 after adjusting
> for inflation. Meanwhile, median household income for West Virginians has
> remained stagnant for nearly two decades. West Virginia was one of 12 states
> where tuition has increased by more than 50%.[41]

We underpay teachers,[42] tolerate grossly unequal opportunities, and blame
the underpaid and the underserved for underachievement. We mortgage the future of young people by making college more expensive, adding private debt to

their federal public debt, and this public debt has burgeoned mostly in order to cut the taxes of those who already have copious resources and based on demonstrably fallacious arguments that the cuts will pay for themselves.[43] The richest country in the history of the world provides meager benefits to the poor and threatens to take even those away unless recipients take and pass drug tests, pay exploitative fines and fees, and demonstrate the ability to find nonexistent jobs.[44] In the name of thrift, we squander resources on work requirements, fine collection, and drug tests, arguing that those who are desperately struggling to sustain themselves need threats to motivate their lazy selves.[45] Our policies regarding the poor are analogous in their gratuitous cruelty and illogic to throwing weights rather than life preservers to the drowning.

Our challenges in Appalachia generally and West Virginia particularly are many and dire. West Virginia has the lowest workforce participation rate,[46] suffers from population loss,[47] has low voter turnout,[48] and has experienced the highest death rate from opioid overdoses.[49] Nevertheless, our state policy debates remain largely focused on issues like campus carry, reproductive rights, charter schools, tax cuts, right-to-work legislation, same-sex marriage, and school prayer.[50] The state government reporter at the *Charleston Gazette-Mail*, the flagship newspaper in the only state that is entirely Appalachian, editorialized about the State of the State address preceding the 2020 session of the State Legislature:

A brutally honest State of State would have gone like this: "Folks, you'll hear a lot of numbers in tonight's speech, but only one matters: 1.7. Since the last time I addressed a joint session of the Legislature, the state's population has fallen below the 1.8 million mark, dropping to its lowest point since the early 1930s.

"Our best and brightest young people are fleeing the state for better opportunities elsewhere. Those remaining are older and are aging out. Our communities are devastated by the opioid epidemic, and despite our best efforts, our public schools continue to underachieve, failing to prepare many of our students for college or career.

"We've clung too long to extractive industries that have exploited our people and our state for generations, at the detriment of building a diversified 21st-century economy. We have 20th-century infrastructure that is crumbling, and lack much of the 21st-century infrastructure needed to compete in a modern economy.

"Folks, 1.7 million is a flashing warning light. Our rocket-ship of a state is in a spiral dive, and we don't have long to figure out how to pull ourselves out of it. We need to figure out why people and businesses don't want to come to West Virginia, and why those that are here are leaving the state, and we must take corrective measures immediately.

"Fortunately, we have small pockets of prosperity in the state, in north-central West Virginia and the Eastern Panhandle, and we need to ascertain what those areas are doing right and how we can translate those successes into other parts of our state.

"We've only got 60 days to start pulling out of this death spiral, and we can't waste time on bills that perpetuate our image nationally as being backward, closed-minded, anti-intellectual and anti-progress. Any issues that divide us, that pit faction against faction, that would make us look like laughingstocks in the national media, or would attempt to deny full rights of citizenship to any of us must be set aside to address the core issue of why the state of our state is in peril."[51]

That's not the state of the state address West Virginians got in January 2020, and it is not one that we could have reasonably expected given what we know about self-interest, incumbency advantage, rational ignorance, and abstention. Gun manufacturers want to sell more guns, employers want to pay lower wages, ministers want to increase their flocks, and incumbents want to be reelected.

Still, we know from experience that we can get much better results in our most challenged places because we know other places, some very nearby, do get much better results. And that is why we publish yet one more article arguing for the implementation of policies that will reduce poverty and diminish inequality.

Efforts highlighting our agency and lamenting our failures do make sense. Information, widely and freely disseminated, is a therapy for better government results, including more equality. Poverty persists in our democracy because of forces malign and mundane: inertia, ignorance, cynicism, self-interest, and complexity. For half a century, faux-populists have spent billions thwarting progress against inequality, spreading half-truths[52] and degrading opponents as socialist disseminators of fake news.

In fact, researchers, educators, and journalists have professional, personal, civic, and moral obligations to search for, discuss, and publish truths. The material and purposive rewards associated with honest research and debate have value, real and intrinsic. Democratic progress is slow and uncertain, but victories over tyranny and injustice have been and continue to be won, setbacks notwithstanding. The framers knew and expected self-interested citizens to protect the public interest, too, for themselves and their posterity. Experience shows that poverty-reducing successes are replicated, as Brandeis has suggested they will be. The free-rider and principal agent problems can be overcome by individuals acting to reduce the costs borne by others. Therapeutic action includes simple and common acts of good, engaged citizenship: becoming informed independently; being active in civil society, including by voting; tolerating dissent; and caring about others.[53] Progress toward eradicating poverty may be too slow, but we're making more than we would by surrendering to demagogues, no matter how well-funded and persuasive they may be.

Notes

1. Nicolas Kristoff and Sheryl WuDunn, *Tightrope* (New York: Alfred A. Knopf, 2020), 259–261.
2. Sessions wrote: "In the work of thinkers like Friedrich Hayek, Milton Friedman, and James Buchanan, neoliberalism was always a response to calls for democratization and redistribution from below. . . . The jargon of 'incentives,' 'choice,' 'special interests,' and 'unintended consequences' were vehicles by which universal public services with egalitarian intent were attacked as the root of the decade's economic woes. . . . Public funding of higher education remains dramatically lower than it was a half-century ago." See David Sessions, "How College Became a Commodity," *Chronicle of Higher Education*, January 14, 2020, https://www.chronicle.com/interactives/how-coll ege-became-a-commodity?utm_source=at&utm_medium=en&cid=at&source= ams&sourceId=410215.
3. As Bertrand Russell has observed, "Fools and fanatics are always so sure." The fact that certain fools are unaware of their own foolishness and are likely to fancy themselves experts is called the Dunning-Kruger effect.
4. Anthony Downs, *An Economic Theory of Democracy* (New York: HarperCollins, 1957), 244–246, 274.
5. Ron Haskins and Isabel Sawhill, *Creating an Opportunity Society* (Washington, DC: Brookings, 2009), 85.
6. Haskins and Sawhill, *Creating*, 70.
7. Haskins and Sawhill, *Creating*, 75.
8. J. D. Vance, *Hillbilly Elegy* (New York: HarperCollins, 2016), 146–147.
9. Kristoff and WuDunn, *Tightrope*, 212–213.
10. Ibram X. Kendi, *How to Be an Antiracist* (New York: One World, 2019), 153.
11. Kristoff and WuDunn, *Tightrope*, 220.
12. Kristoff and WuDunn, *Tightrope*, 239.
13. Kristoff and WuDunn, *Tightrope*, 253.
14. Robert Putnam, *Our Kids: The American Dream in Crisis* (New York: Simon and Schuster, 2015), 206.
15. Kristoff and WuDunn, *Tightrope*, 250.
16. Monica Potts, "In the Land of Self-Defeat," *New York Times*, October 4, 2019.
17. Appalachian Regional Commission, "County Economic Status in Appalachia," 2020, https://www.arc.gov/research/MapsofAppalachia.asp?MAP_ID=149.
18. Appalachian Regional Commission, "County Economic Status in Appalachia."
19. Ryan Quinn, "New Meeting, Same Result: Kanawha School Board again Appoints Williams as Superintendent," *Charleston Gazette-Mail*, February 5, 2020.

20. Daniel Elazar, *American Federalism, A View From the States* (Binghamton, NY: Thomas Y. Crowell, 1966), 109.

21. Nancy Isenberg, *White Trash* (New York: Penguin Books, 2016), 311–320.

22. *Pauley v. Bailey.* 1984. 162 W.Va. 672, 255 S.E.2d 859 (1979) (West Virgnia Supreme Court of Appeals, December 12). The decision cited the West Virginia State Constitutional mandate for the provision of a "thorough and efficient system of free schools."

23. Ben Evans et al., "Examining Advanced Placement Course Offerings at West Virginia Public High Schools" (poster session, Concord University Undergraduate Research Day, Athens, WV, 2018).

24. Haskins and Sawhill, *Creating*, 46.

25. Arne Duncan, *How Schools Work* (New York: Simon and Schuster, 2018), 212–215.

26. Putnam, *Our Kids*, 174–180.

27. William Bowen, Matthew Chingos, and Michael McPherson, *Crossing the Finish Line* (Princeton, NJ: Princeton University Press, 2009), 9.

28. Bowen et al. *Crossing*, 223–224.

29. Bowen et al., *Crossing*, 226–236.

30. Nicholas Carnes and Noam Lupu, "It's Time to Bust the Myth: Most Trump Voters Were Not Working Class," *Washington Post*, June 5, 2017. Osnos wrote that Trump supporters in his hometown of Greenwich, Connecticut, "don't have much in common with the clichéd image of his admirers: anxious about losing status to minorities, resentful of imperious élites, and marooned in places where life expectancy has fallen. But the full picture has never been that simple. As early as May, 2016, exit polls and other data showed that Trump supporters earned an average of seventy-two thousand dollars a year, while supporters of Hillary Clinton earned eleven thousand dollars less. Two-thirds of Trump's supporters had incomes higher than the national median—sometimes, as in Greenwich, much higher." See Evan Osnos, "How Greenwich Republicans Learned to Love Trump," *The Atlantic*, May 3, 2020.

31. As Madison wrote in *Federalist 10*: "As long as the reason of man continues fallible, and he is at liberty to exercise it, different opinions will be formed. As long as the connection subsists between his reason and his self-love, his opinions and his passions will have a reciprocal influence on each other; and the former will be objects to which the latter will attach themselves. The diversity in the faculties of men, from which the rights of property originate, is not less an insuperable obstacle to a uniformity of interests. The protection of these faculties is the first object of government."

32. Charles Murray, *Losing Ground* (New York: Basic Books, 1984), 42, building on a foundation provided by George Wallace, William Safire, Pat Buchanan, and Spiro Agnew, among others.

33. Thomas Frank, *What's the Matter With Kansas* (New York: Henry Holt, 2004), 240.

34. Gale also used Walt Kelly's cartoon character to describe our ongoing national debt issues. See William Gale, *Fiscal Therapy* (New York: Oxford University Press, 2019), 104.

35. Putnam, *Our Kids*, 230.

36. Duncan, *How Schools Work*, 1, 13.

37. Kristoff and WuDunn, *Tightrope*, 102–103.

38. Duncan, *How Schools Work*, 189–191.

39. See Scott Higham, Sari Horwitz, and Steven Rich, "76 Billion Opioid Pills: Newly Released Federal Data Unmasks the Epidemic," *Washington Post*, July 16, 2019. See also Scott Higham, Sari Horwitz, and Steven Rich, "Internal Drug Company Emails Show Indifference to Opioid Epidemic," *Washington Post*, July 19, 2019.

40. See Kristoff and WuDunn, *Tightrope*, 82–83. See also Higham et al., "76 Billion Opioid Pills." See also Scott Higham, Sari Horwitz, and Steven Rich, "Internal Drug Company Emails Show Indifference to Opioid Epidemic," *Washington Post*, July 19, 2019.

41. Sean O'Leary, "Higher Education Funding Cuts Have Hurt Students and the State's Future," West Virginia Center on Budget & Policy, 2019, https://wvpolicy.org/higher-education-funding-cuts-have-hurt-students-and-the-states-future/.

42. Duncan wrote: "The lie underneath all of this is one that says America values its teachers. But the truth is that we don't. If we really valued the women and men dedicated to educating our children, then our teachers would be more respected, better paid, and have tons of support from all levels of society. They could count on us. But as it is, they can't count on us, and we should be ashamed because of it. But the root lie on which all of the lies in this book is built is far, far worse, and should be the ultimate source of our shame. The truth is that we not only don't value our teachers. It's that we don't value our kids." See Duncan, *How Schools Work*, 177–178.

43. Gale, *Fiscal Therapy*, 2019.

44. Campbell Robertson, "What Happened When a State Made Food Stamps Harder to Get," *New York Times*, January 13, 2020.

45. See Rick Wilson, "Corporate Tax Cuts Get WV Nowhere," *Charleston Gazette-Mail*, January 29, 2020. See also Rick Wilson, "Here We Go Again," *Charleston Gazette-Mail*, December 12, 2019. See also Rick Wilson, "Improve Rural Health Care, Don't Cut Medicaid," *Charleston Gazette-Mail*, February 11, 2020.

46. Erica Anderson and Molly DeCarli, "Does West Virginia Have the Nation's Lowest Workforce Participation Rate?" PolitiFact, 2019, https://www.politifact.com/factchecks/2019/feb/27/e-gordon-gee/does-west-virginia-have-nations-lowest-workforce-p/.

47. Sean O'Leary, "The Where and the How of West Virginia's Population Decline," West Virginia Center on Budget & Policy, 2019, https://wvpolicy.org/the-where-and-the-how-of-west-virginias-population-decline/.

48. Voting is correlated with education and income, and, not surprisingly, West Virginia has among the lowest voter turnout in the nation. See West Virginia Secretary of State, "WV Secretary of State," https://sos.wv.gov. See also Michael McDonald, "United States Elections Project," http://www.electproject.org/. Putnam wrote: "The inheritance of political involvement presents a double whammy. Educated parents are more likely to be politically engaged. . . . But in addition, kids from educated homes are much more likely to grow up to be educated adults themselves, and their greater education also favors their political engagement as adults." He noted that: "This yawning

class gap . . . has expanded in recent decades—yet another scissors gap." See Putnam, *Our Kids*, 237–238.

49. National Institute on Drug Abuse, "West Virginia: Opioid-Involved Deaths and Related Harms," 2020, https://www.drugabuse.gov/opioid-summaries-by-state/west-virginia-opioid-involved-deaths-related-harms.

50. An editorialist wrote about international stories referencing the Mountain State: "The worst are those days when West Virginia makes the national news over some act of bigotry and/or craven groveling to exploitative corporations. The last year or so has been . . . a bigotry/groveling boom." See Wilson, "Here We Go."

51. See Phil Kabler, "Justice's Altered State of the State," *Charleston Gazette-Mail*, January 12, 2020. See also Wilson, "Corporate Tax."

52. See Jane Mayer, *Dark Money* (New York: Doubleday, 2016). See also Thomas Mann and Norman Ornstein, *It's Even Worse Than It Was* (New York: Basic Books, 2012).

53. Russell Dalton, *The Good Citizen* (Washington, DC: CQ Press, 2008).

12

Identity, Meritocracy, and the Unique Challenges of Human Freedom

Peter Callero

When the Declaration of Independence was drafted in 1776, the 56 signers famously asserted that "all men" have a natural, God-given right to liberty. This was not an inconsequential philosophical claim. The American colonies had already entered into a war of independence, and the Declaration served to formalize their separation from British rule. Less intentionally, the provocative statement also established "freedom" and "liberty" as the watchwords of a new nation. To this day, the concept of *freedom* continues to exemplify American culture and the particular value systems of its citizens. We see evidence of this in both comparative social science research[1] and the rhetoric of our contemporary political leaders. President George W. Bush, for example, used the word *freedom* 49 times in his second inaugural address. President Obama, in his first inaugural, acknowledged America's commitment to securing freedom as a national priority: "That is our generation's task—to make these words, these rights, these values of life and liberty and the pursuit of happiness real for every American." And more recently, President Donald Trump boasted to the United Nations General Assembly that: "In America, we believe in the majesty of freedom and the dignity of the individual."[2]

In a nation noticeably divided by political ideology, there appears to be an enduring consensus among partisans on both the left and right that freedom is positive and that the struggle for liberty is a worthy cause. No political party, elected official, or political activist today is arguing against freedom and liberty. But the question remains: Is this truly evidence of common ground, or might our collective support for freedom be merely a façade of rhetorical harmony? Linguist George Lakoff thinks it is the latter. In fact, Lakoff believes that "there are two very different views of freedom in America today, arising from very different moral and political worldviews dividing the country."[3] —One is decidedly conservative and the other distinctly liberal. Similarly, historian Eric Foner has shown that freedom in America has always been a contested concept, and that different ideas of freedom have been conceived and implemented in different periods of American history. This is because "freedom embodies not a single idea

Peter Callero, *Identity, Meritocracy, and the Unique Challenges of Human Freedom* In: *On Inequality and Freedom.* Edited by: Lawrence M. Eppard and Henry A. Giroux, Oxford University Press. © Oxford University Press 2022. DOI: 10.1093/oso/9780197583029.003.0012

but a complex of values, [and] the struggle to define its meaning is simultaneously an intellectual, social, economic, and political contest."[4]

In this chapter, I do not attempt to engage the varied political uses of liberty
and freedom; instead, I explore the idea of freedom from a sociological perspective. More specifically, I develop four arguments: (a) that freedom is properly understood as a social process, (b) that certain qualities unique to human persons
complicate our experience of freedom, (c) that our socially constructed identity
categories are especially unique and complicating, and (d) that the American
cultural narrative of meritocracy is a barrier to the realization of freedom.

Freedom Is a Social Process

A popular misconception often propagated in primary school history lessons is
that the Emancipation Proclamation issued by President Lincoln in 1863 "freed
the slaves" and liberated them from the oppressive conditions of the southern
plantation. More sophisticated historical accounts, however, acknowledge that
the vast majority of slaves had to wait until the end of the war in 1865 for their
liberation from bondage. But even then, the de jure end of slavery did not translate into immediate freedom from servitude and repression. Once emancipated
from the physical and legal bondage of the plantation, most former slaves simply
traded one form of repression for another.

Consider, for example, the experience of Joseph Miller; his wife, Isabella; and
their four children. Like many slave families who escaped their masters' control
during the chaos of the war, the Millers surreptitiously headed north on foot in
search of freedom. It was the fall of 1864, and without shelter, food, or clothing,
their journey was perilous, and as "fugitive slaves" they were at risk of being captured or murdered. The Millers, however, were fortunate in that they made it
safely to Camp Nelson, a Union fortress near Lexington, Kentucky, where they
slept in a tent alongside another 500 emancipated slaves. Joseph then enlisted
in the Union army under the assumption that his family would be cared for and
protected—they were not.

On the morning of November 22, 1864, a Union general ordered his soldiers
to evacuate the families of the former slaves who were encamped outside of Fort
Nelson. When a mounted guard demanded that the Miller family leave the camp,
Joseph protested, but to no avail: "I told the man in charge of the guard that it
would be the death of my boy. I told him that my wife and children had no place
to go. I told him that I was a soldier of the United States."[5] Isabella and the four
children were forced into a military wagon and driven into the Kentucky wilderness. The Miller's 7-year-old son, who was sick at the time, died while being evac-
uated from the camp. Three weeks later, Isabella and Joseph Jr. died. Shortly after

that, Joseph's daughter, Maria passed, and a few weeks later, Joseph's son Calvin also died. In less than 6 weeks, Joseph Miller lost his entire family. Then, tragically, 1 week after the death of Calvin, Joseph also died. In the words of historian Jim Dowd: "The Miller family did not experience liberation from chattel slavery as a jubilee, but rather as a continuous process of displacement, deprivation, and ultimately death."[6]

Unfortunately, the experience of the Miller family is not unique. While it is difficult to estimate the mortality rate of former slaves during this period (no officials attempted to maintain a count, and most who perished during the war were buried in unmarked graves), historians believe the number to be in excess of 500,000, and perhaps as high as 1 million. Most were not casualties of combat but were instead victims of unsanitary conditions, untreated disease, injury, malnutrition, and exposure to the elements. After the war ended, survival continued to be challenging, and the failure of free slaves to thrive off the plantation served to buttress the arguments of proslavery Southerners, who claimed that Blacks were incapable of sustaining independent lives. Similar arguments persisted during the period of Reconstruction when former slave families and their descendants who lacked formal education, land, or access to capital were at a structural disadvantage in a wage-based economy.

The disconnection between being released from captivity and actually achieving freedom is a real-world illustration of the philosophical distinction between positive and negative liberty that was famously articulated by Isaiah Berlin.[7] Negative liberty is defined by *removal and absence*, as in the removal of barriers and the absence of constraint. Positive liberty, on the other hand, is defined by *achievement* and the realization of meaningful, egalitarian relationships in a just community. When the Miller family escaped from the plantation, they left behind the physical constraints imposed by their overseer and the legal barriers enforced by the Southern Confederacy, but this negative liberty was not enough. The entire family died because they were denied the resources necessary to achieve a positive liberty. Northern politicians and military officials did not want to assist the former slaves because they were afraid that doing so would perpetuate a dependency relationship. "The fear of dependency ran like a cancer throughout the rhetoric of Union officials in the Civil War South. Both federal leaders in Washington and local military leaders in camps feared that any gesture of help or support would encourage former bondspeople to become dependent on federal aid and assistance."[8] But without aid and assistance, former slaves struggled to achieve freedom and were blocked in their attempts to realize a meaningful life.

The tribulations of the Millers and other former slaves serves as a gruesome illustration of the complex social forces that both enable and constrain the experience of freedom. There is no doubt that the Emancipation Proclamation and the disruptions of the Civil War enabled Joseph Miller and his family to escape the bondage of servitude, but they soon learned that their freedom was conditional. If you could find work, if you had land, if you could secure a loan, if you were literate, if your relatives were free, or if you possessed wealth, you stood a chance of survival. Otherwise, freedom remained a utopian ideal realized only in one's imagination. Without access to enabling resources, the experience of freedom was nearly impossible. And we should not forget that the enslavement of the Millers was also enabled by the construction of racial categories, the devaluation of Black people, the profitability of a slave-based economy, as well as the establishment of elaborate cultural and political systems that sustained and legitimated the institution of slavery.

Clearly, the achievement of freedom is a complicated social process that involves more than the breaking of chains, the escape from bondage, or the removal of barriers. The realization of freedom also requires access to resources and the cooperation of a supportive community. In the following section, I take a closer look at the social forces that both enable and constrain the attainment of human freedom, but first we need to ask: What makes human freedom unique?

What Makes Human Freedom Unique?

Humans persons are by nature social animals. We are born into a network of social relationships, depend on our relationships for survival, and require a network of social relationships if we are going to fully develop and thrive. Most animals are social, and like other animals, human lives are diminished under conditions of captivity. If we are to flourish, we need to be able to freely interact with other people. In this way, we have much in common with other species (especially those that have not been domesticated by humans). Consider for example the life of a typical African lion—an apex predator living in the savannahs of sub-Saharan Africa. If this lion were to be captured as a cub and raised in a cage or enclosure of some kind, it would lose its capacity to survive in its natural habitat. It would not know how to effectively hunt, its ability to communicate with other lions would be diminished, and it would have little fear of humans. As a result, some of the qualities that make a lion a lion would not develop. When a lion is truly free, it is capable of making natural choices about its future. We see this in the wild when it chooses to accept a mate, decides to pursue its prey, or flees a predator. It is also true that a lion appears to relish its freedom in the wild when it communicates with its pride, socializes its cubs, or grooms a companion. These forms of purposive activity are examples of what philosopher Martin Hägglund calls *natural freedom*, which is to say there is a freedom of movement and freedom to realize one's nature.[9] Here we have much in common with lions.

Humans also require natural freedom to thrive. If a person were to be held in a cage for most of their life or be prevented from interacting with other humans, our physical, social, and psychological development would be stunted.

But, there is also another dimension to the experience of human freedom that sets us apart from lions and other nonhuman animals. Because our species has a highly evolved capacity for symbolic communication and self-reflection, we are able to critically evaluate the conditions of our lived experience; we are able to question and critique social norms and challenge ascribed identities. Indeed, one of the most important distinguishing features of the human animal is our capacity to create and employ symbolic categories of meaning. For example, for human persons, sex differences are not simply matters of anatomy and physiology associated with procreation, childbirth, and child care. Instead, we embroider the plain cloth of biology with elaborate and colorful meanings, social practices, religious traditions, normative rules, and political values. Like other animals, our species has evolved in a physical world with a natural environment and an ecological niche. But unlike nonhuman animals, we have also evolved to live within a symbolic environment of our own construction. And this has a tremendous impact on our prospects for understanding and experiencing freedom.

Since lions (and other nonhuman species) have a very limited capacity for symbol use and self-consciousness, their experience of freedom is not contested. Unlike human persons, the goal or ends of the lion's free movement are never challenged or questioned by another lion. Because the lion lacks self-consciousness, the lion does not experience regret over decisions, and most importantly, lions do not consider the question of what they "ought" to do. We implicitly recognize this distinction in our actions toward animals given that we do not hold them accountable for moral failures, acts of injustice, or unethical behavior. The choices that animals make are never constrained by self-judgment.

In contrast, human behavior is unique in our "ability to ask which imperatives to follow in light of our ends, as well as the ability to call into question, challenge, and transform our ends themselves."[10] It is here that we engage the question: "What should I do?" and by implication: "Who should I be?" Because our actions define our identity, we in effect possess the capacity to transform our understanding of what it means to be a human person. This is a capacity not shared by other species. It is a type of freedom that sets us apart. This feature of human freedom is in addition to our experience of natural freedom. For our species, freedom does not mean doing whatever one wants, but rather demands that we consider what is right. Human freedom is unique in that it presupposes a moral question that directs us to ponder the challenge of doing good. It is in this moment of ethical judgment that freedom for the human animal is distinctive. We are, in the words of sociologist Christian Smith, "moral believing animals" in search of "a larger moral order by which to know who one is and how one ought to live."[11]

Of course, knowing what is good and right is not a given, and answering the question of what we ought to do is not always obvious. For this reason, the realization of human freedom is contested and often accompanied by controversy, discord, and debate. This is why Thomas Jefferson could own more than 500 slaves and at the same time famously assert that "all men are created equal." And James Madison, also a slave holder, could argue without a sense of hypocrisy that racial discrimination created "the most oppressive dominion ever exercised by man over man."[12] Indeed, 12 U.S. presidents owned slaves while at the same time publicly advocating for the foundational value of freedom in America. No doubt, the complexity of our socially constructed world contributes to these contradictions in the advocacy of freedom, and for this reason, much of American history can be seen as a series of skirmishes over differing interpretations of who we are and what we ought to do. These battles have been part of larger culture wars, political conflicts, and at times actual combat between forces seeking to either enhance or limit different interpretations of freedom. Both sides have drawn on a cache of resources in the fight. Some of the resources have been physical objects intended to kill our opponents (e.g., swords, guns, ammunition), but most resources have been socially constructed assets in the form of normative rules, cultural narratives, and identity categories. The battle over slavery, for example, was at its core an economic dispute, but it was also a cultural and moral clash over the personhood of Africans. So, too, the political and economic subjugation of women has been a long conflict over the meaning of gender categories and the legitimacy of male superiority. In the next section, I examine these cultural resources in more depth and pay particular attention to the power of socially constructed identity categories that serve to enable and constrain freedom.

Identity Categories and Freedom

Contrary to some optimistic assumptions of American individualism, it is not possible to live in a society where we are recognized as a unique, independent person with exceptional qualities unassociated with the stereotypes of a larger group. Rather, when we interact with each other, we do so as representatives of various social categories—whether we like it or not. When we encounter another person for the first time, we are implicitly identified in terms of our gender, race, class position, age, family, nationality, and the like—and we do the same thing to others. These symbolic labels are our *identities*, and they serve as the initial markers of who we are in the eyes of another person.

Moreover, because every identity has cultural meanings associated with various amounts of value, power, and status, opportunities for realizing positive freedom are unequally distributed. This is most obviously evident when it comes to identities linked to one's economic class. With more wealth comes more freedom—a point widely recognized by most Americans. In a recent nationally representative survey of U.S. adults, respondents were asked: "How much freedom do you have today?" Not surprisingly, the researchers found that those individuals with the highest level of perceived freedom were those with the most money. The data show that with every additional dollar of income, there was an increase in the probability of having a high level of perceived freedom.[13]

Although less obvious, our other identities have a similar influence on our opportunities for freedom (independent of social class). Holding income, wealth, and occupation constant, being Black or Brown, or Asian, or female, or queer, or foreign born, or disabled will negatively impact the experience of freedom. This is because these identity resources are culturally devalued and have associated with them relatively less power than White, male, straight, able-bodied, and native-born identities. Consider for example the identity of "woman." For most of American history, women have been viewed as second-class citizens, an injustice that has been legitimated using negative identity meanings. Women's participation in politics, and civil society more generally, has been prohibited because they have been perceived to be less rational, more emotional, and not aggressive enough for public life. Moreover, these qualities have often been viewed as natural and God given and therefore immutable. Historically, most major religious traditions have assumed female inferiority, a position that has been reinforced by religious leaders for thousands of years. "Woman is naturally subject to man," argued St. Thomas Aquinas, "because in man the discretion of reason predominates."[14] Two centuries later, Martin Luther took a similar position: "For woman seems to be a creature somewhat different from man, in that she has dissimilar members, a varied form and a mind weaker than man."[15] And today the prohibition of women from leadership roles in most churches, synagogues, and temples is evidence that sexism in religious traditions persists. Of course, other institutions have a similar history of sexism, including schools, the family, business, and government. Somewhat surprisingly, scientific theory has also been used to legitimate the devalued identity of woman. Charles Darwin himself argued that natural selection had produced in men "a higher eminence, in whatever he takes up, than can women—whether requiring deep thought, reason, or imagination, or merely the use of the senses and hands."[16] And shockingly, a version of Darwin's interpretation continues to this day among some evolutionary psychologists.[17]

The point here is that identities such as race and gender are socially constructed categories that often serve as cultural resources for limiting freedom. But despite the fact that identity categories are often experienced as natural, they are in fact malleable and impermanent creations of a community and are therefore open to change. While it is not possible to simply eliminate the use of identity categories (they are part of what makes us human), the cultural meanings of devalued identities may be collectively transformed in a way that enhances freedom. To be sure, this does not mean that material conditions of exploitation are irrelevant. Walls, chains, weapons, law enforcement practices, and other institutional barriers remain obvious impediments to freedom, but social movements have had success in disrupting cultural stereotypes associated with devalued identities. Social movement activists recognize that identity categories are powerful cultural resources that may be used for both exploitation *and* emancipation, and the most effective strategy for deploying identity as a resource for freedom relies on the creation of a "collective identity."

A collective identity develops when experiences of deprivation move from a "me" orientation (I am deprived) to a "we" orientation (all of us are deprived). But more importantly, collective identities go beyond traditional forms of group solidarity and mutual trust to include new identity meanings defined by protest, collective action, and social change. When this happens, a collective identity becomes a powerful resource for freedom. The achievement of gay rights in the United States is a particularly striking example. In a period of less than 50 years, gay men and lesbians were able to achieve historic advances toward liberation, including the repeal of sodomy laws, the removal of homosexuality from the list of mental disorders, legal protections in the workplace, as well as the right to marry and adopt children. Along the way, the public's attitude toward gay people has undergone a correspondingly dramatic shift such that the gay identity is now more positively valued, and same-sex sexual behavior is considered less morally offensive in American society. For example, in 1973 when a representative sample of U.S. adults was asked whether "sexual relations between two adults of the same sex is always wrong, almost always wrong, wrong only sometimes, or not wrong at all," a large majority of respondents (70%) said "always wrong," and only 11% stated "not wrong at all." However, by the year 2018, only 31% believed that it was always wrong for same-sex adults to have sexual relations, while a majority (57%) held the view that it was "not wrong at all."[18] This striking swing in social policy and public beliefs about sexual relations is the result of a powerful social movement built around a collective identity that has successfully altered the cultural meanings of identities associated with sexual behavior and same-sex relationships.

This example highlights the paradox of identity. Socially constructed identities are important resources for both building a free society and legitimating control and domination. On one side are traditional institutions, entrenched cultural norms, and exploitive economic systems that operate to limit freedom and opportunity by stabilizing devalued identities. On the other side are authentic social relationships that enhance community support and provide the freedom-enhancing resources that enable the defining question of our humanity: What *ought* we do with our time?

Freedom and the American Discourse on Meritocracy

When considering what ought to be done, humans do not share a common moral vision. The diversity of our socially constructed environment guarantees different interpretations and understandings of what is right, who is good, and how best to behave. As we saw above, one impediment to freedom is associated with the devaluation of socially constructed identities. In this section, I examine another barrier that is also the product of our symbol-using capacity: the social construction of cultural narratives.

We can think of a *cultural narrative* as a commonly accepted storyline with a familiar plot that is recognizable to a wide audience. Some stories are harmless and may even enhance the quest for freedom. Others, however, work to legitimate oppressive social norms, fortify negative identity meanings, and limit the realization of freedom. Consider for example the cultural narrative associated with success in America. In American literature, the rags-to-riches stories written by Horatio Alger in the nineteenth century are representative of a dominant cultural narrative of American meritocracy. Sold to young adults, Alger's fiction described the struggles of teenage boys who worked their way from poverty to middle-class respectability through honesty, hard work, and perseverance. This *meritocracy narrative* is built on a corresponding narrative of individualism in that success is assumed to be a personal achievement largely independent of social support, family advantage, or luck.

The danger of the meritocracy narrative is that it reinforces the belief that the unequal distribution of wealth, power, and status in a society is simply a reflection of individual differences in knowledge, skill, honesty, and effort. Under this familiar storyline, persons who work the hardest, sacrifice the most, display the most grit, and act morally are successful and deserve what they have earned. But the dangerous corollary to the narrative is that those who are poor and powerless are unsuccessful because they are weak, lazy, and unscrupulous. In this view, the poor also get what they deserve. The American meritocracy narrative has a long history and can be traced back to the early colonial era when the first Puritan settlers arrived with their theological interpretation of work as a calling from God. This *Protestant work ethic* soon established a cultural link among diligence, personal discipline, and Christian morality.

Our cultural commitment to the meritocracy narrative persists to this day in stories of personal success that are widely shared and well known. From Oprah Winfrey, who escaped poverty to become an entertainment billionaire, to the fictional Rocky Balboa, who went from small-time gangster to become a world boxing champion, a belief in the rewards of individual effort and personal integrity is reinforced. The meritocracy narrative is also embedded in the so-called American dream and reflected in the conviction that individuals must "pull oneself up by their bootstraps" lest they become dependent on charity or welfare. As was noted previously, the fear of dependency has been a particularly effective emotion in the suppression of African Americans in the United States. It was used during the Civil War to justify the withholding of housing and medical assistance from fugitive slaves, and again during Reconstruction by politicians who opposed federal relief efforts. More recently, it was deployed by Whites who resisted the goals of civil rights activists in the 1960s. In fact, in a television interview conducted in 1967, the Reverend Martin Luther King Jr. was confronted with this cultural narrative when asked to explain the higher rates of poverty for Blacks when compared to White immigrant groups. His response displays both an understanding of positive liberty and a rejection of the meritocracy narrative.

White America must see that no other ethnic group has been a slave on American soil. That is one thing that other immigrant groups haven't had to face. The other thing is that the color becomes a stigma. American society made the negros' color a stigma. America freed the slaves in 1863 through the Emancipation Proclamation of Abraham Lincoln but gave the slaves no land or nothing in reality to get started on. At the same time, America was giving away millions of acres of land in the West and Midwest, which meant there was a willingness to give the white peasants of Europe an economic base and yet refused to give its black peasants from Africa, who came here involuntarily in chains, and had worked free for 244 years any kind of economic base. And so emancipation for the negro was really freedom to hunger. It was freedom to the winds and rains of heaven. It was freedom without food to eat or land to cultivate and therefore it was freedom and famine at the same time. And when white Americans tell the negro to lift himself by his own bootstraps they don't look over the legacy of slavery and segregation. I believe we ought to do all we can and seek to lift ourselves by our own bootstraps, but it is a cruel jest to say to a bootless man that he ought to lift himself by his own bootstraps. And many negroes by the thousands and millions have been left bootless as a result of all of these years of oppression and as a result of a society that deliberately made his color a stigma and something worthless and degrading.[19]

The strength of Dr. King's eloquent response is that he provides important historical context, reminding the television viewers that African families did not arrive
voluntarily and were held as slaves for centuries. He then emphasized significant differences in access to material resources, noting that White immigrants
had opportunities and governmental assistance that were denied to families of
former slaves. Finally, Reverend King pointed to the power of cultural barriers,
emphasizing that a cultural narrative of individualism and self-sufficiency is
nothing more than a "cruel jest" when the larger historical and sociological context is ignored.

The pernicious influence of a meritocracy narrative is also evident in crucial
court decisions that have shaped public policy in the United States. This was particularly evident in 1978 with the Supreme Court's landmark decision in *Regents
of the University of California v. Bakke*. In this case, Allan Bakke, a White, male,
Viet Nam veteran, applied to medical school at the University of California,
Davis, and was not accepted. He blamed the school's affirmative action policy
for his rejection, arguing that the practice of reserving 16 out of 100 seats for
qualified minority students was discriminatory. The court ruled in favor of Mr.
Bakke and agreed that the racial quota system was a violation of the Civil Rights
Act of 1964.

This court case is of historical significance because it altered the way in which
affirmative action policies are implemented and in the process reinforced barriers
to higher education for minority students. For our purposes it is also significant
for the reasoning employed by the court in their decision, a reasoning that relied
on the presumptive value of meritocracy. This has been demonstrated by legal
scholar Robin West, who has analyzed how the justices came to the conclusion
that affirmative action violates the principle of fairness when it considers factors
unrelated to merit. "The Court's arguments against affirmative action plans,"
Professor West maintained, "rely heavily on stories about individual merit which
typically purport to be historical, but which almost invariably are to some degree
fictionalized"[20] In other words, the court was influenced by a cultural narrative
of meritocracy that was not based on fact.

In Justice Powell's opinion, Bakke would have been admitted to medical school
given his test scores and grade point average, but the racial quota policy blocked
his entry. Powell believed that "objective" measures demonstrated that Baake was
more meritorious than those admitted on the basis of affirmative action. Put another way, Baake played by the rules, outperformed other candidates, and was
not admitted—a clear violation of the meritocracy narrative. To agree with this
reasoning, however, one must accept the argument that Bakke and the other
candidates were competing on a level playing field. If not, then the entire process
is unfair. As noted already, the meritocracy narrative asks us to be color blind,
gender blind, and blind to the social forces that establish inequalities of identity.

But in fact, Bakke earned his "objective" advantage as a White man, raised in a White family, living in a White neighborhood, and attending a White school system. He was, in other words, advantaged by all of the privileges afforded his racial identity. When compared to Black students, Baake had an antimeritocratic benefit, an advantage that is invisible to most White people, including Justice Powell. Social capital in the form of family, friends, neighbors, teachers, and other influential personal connections, is affirmative action of a different kind. It is an affirmative action that speaks to the privilege of whiteness in a voice too soft for White people to hear. By using the story of merit, the justices strengthened the power of a damaging cultural narrative and bolstered an invisible barrier to freedom.

Conclusion

The achievement of freedom typically conjures up images of an isolated individual who is liberated from the bars of a prison cell, resigns from the demands of a grinding job, or escapes the smothering social expectations of a controlling family, church, or small town. In other words, freedom is widely understood to be a state independent of other individuals or groups of people—guards, bosses, parents, neighbors. There is obviously an element of truth to this view of freedom. No one would say that the inmate is free, or that socially imposed limits on one's thoughts, words, or actions is liberating. But this is only one aspect of freedom. What advocates of this "negative liberty" fail to appreciate is that human persons are by nature social animals.

We cannot realize a free self in isolation; it is only experienced in our connections and commitments to a community of others. Human freedom is therefore social. Freedom cannot be fully achieved in the escape from exploitive or oppressive relationships; it also requires social resources, community commitments, and a social environment that supports human flourishing. In meaningful relations with others, we are more likely to live a dignified and humane life—one in which we may explore the fundamental question of freedom: What *ought* we do with our time?

If we are spending our time struggling to meet our most basic biological needs for food and shelter, we are not in a position to ask ourselves this question. Thus, one prerequisite of freedom is access to resources necessary for survival. But even when we have access to material resources for survival, we may not be free if cultural resources are deployed as barriers to our liberation. When socially constructed identity categories are devalued and cultural narratives are used to justify inequality for certain groups, we are blocked from the experience of freedom. Think in terms of a "freedom ladder" in which the first rung provides for the basic biological needs for survival, the second rung provides for the time and resources that allow for the pursuit of the question: "What *ought* we do with our time?" The third rung is where we collectively engage in the reordering of our shared, collective resources for the benefit of all persons. Ultimately, freedom is not a means to an end, but an end in itself, and it is an end that cannot be achieved alone. In the pursuit of personal freedom, we are compelled to consider how one person's action will enhance freedom for all of humanity.

Notes

1. Christian Welzel, *Freedom Rising: Human Empowerment and the Quest for Emancipation* (New York: Cambridge, 2013).
2. Remarks by President Trump to the 73rd Session of the United Nations General Assembly on September 25, 2018, New York, NY.
3. George Lakoff, *Whose Freedom: The Battle Over America's Most Important Idea* (New York: Picador, 2006), 3.
4. Eric Foner, *The Story of American Freedom* (New York: W. W. Norton, 1998), xv.
5. Jim Downs, *Sick From Freedom: African-American Illness and Suffering During the Civil War and Reconstruction* (New York: Oxford, 2012), 19
6. Downs, *Sick From Freedom*, 21.
7. Isaiah Berlin, *Two Concepts of Liberty: An Inaugural Lecture Delivered Before the University of Oxford on 31 October 1958* (Oxford, U.K.: Clarendon Press, 1958).
8. Downs, *Sick From Freedom*, 55–56.
9. Martin Hägglund, *This Life: Secular Faith and Spiritual Freedom* (New York: Pantheon Books, 2019).
10. Hägglund, *This Life*, 175.
11. Christian Smith, *Moral Believing Animals: Human Personhood and Culture* (New York: Oxford University Press, 2003), 118.
12. Foner, 1998, *The Story of American Freedom*, 35.
13. Orlando Patterson and Ethan Fosse, "Stability and Change in Americans' Perception of Freedom," *Contexts*, 18, no. 3 (2019): 26–31.
14. Thomas Aquinas, *Summa Theologica*, trans. Fathers of the English Dominican Province (New York: Bezinger Brothers, 1911–1925), I, q. 92, a.1.
15. Martin Luther, *Commentary on Genesis*, Chapter 2, Part V, 27b.
16. Charles Darwin, *The Descent of Man, and Selection in Relation to Sex* (D. Appleton, 1896), 564.
17. Angela Saini, *Inferior: How Science Got Women Wrong—and the New Research That's Rewriting the Story* (Boston: Beacon, 2018).
18. General Social Survey Data Explorer, "Is It Wrong for Same-Sex Adults to Have Sexual Relations? https://gssdataexplorer.norc.org/trends/Gender%20&%20Marri age?measure=homosex.

19. "Martin Luther King Jr. "Speaks With NBC News Eleven Months Before Assassination: May 8, 1967, Interview at the Ebenezer Baptist Church in Atlanta With NBC News' Sander Vanocur" https://www.nbcnews.com/video/martin-luther-king-jr-speaks-with-nbc-news-11-months-before-assassination-1202163779741

20. Robin West, "Constitutional Fictions and Meritocratic Success Stories," *Washington and Lee Law Review* 53, no. 3(1997): 18.

PART III
RACE, GENDER, SEXUALITIES, AND FREEDOM

13

White Privileges and Black Burdens[*]

Joe R. Feagin and Kimberley Ducey

In an interview project that the senior author conducted, a distinguished Black professor who taught for many years at a major historically White university explained well the cost of dealing with racism:

> If you can think of the mind as having one hundred ergs of energy, and the av-
> erage man uses 50 percent of his energy dealing with the everyday problems
> of the world . . . then he has 50 percent more to do creative kinds of things that
> he wants to do. Now that's a white person. Now a black person also has one
> hundred ergs; he uses 50 percent the same way a white man does, dealing with
> what the white man has [to deal with], so he has 50 percent left. But he uses
> 25 percent fighting being black, [with] all the problems being black and what
> it means.[1]

By virtue of an accident of birth, African Americans must typically expend an enormous amount of energy defending themselves and their families from the recurring assaults of White racism. In contrast, over lifetimes, White Americans on average have a major life energy advantage, for very few have to waste large amounts of time dealing with anti-White discrimination from people of color.

More generally, *White privilege* includes the large set of advantages and benefits inherited by each generation of those routinely defined as "white" in the social structure and processes of U.S. society. White privileges, and the sense that one is entitled to them, are inseparable parts of a greater whole. These advantages are *material*, *symbolic*, and *psychological*. Let us briefly review some of these advantages.

Privileging White Experiences and Interpretations

Much research indicates that a substantial majority of Whites still have an un-critical habit of mind that accepts the existing racial order with little questioning.

[*] This chapter was originally published in Joe Feagin and Kimberley Ducey's *Racist America* from Routledge. It has been reprinted here with permission.

Joe R. Feagin and Kimberley Ducey, *White Privileges and Black Burdens* In: *On Inequality and Freedom.* Edited by: Lawrence M. Eppard and Henry A. Giroux, Oxford University Press. © Oxford University Press 2022. DOI: 10.1093/oso/9780197583029.003.0013

In this research, most Whites, including White youth, tend to explain persisting racial inequalities without connecting them to the larger historical system of White power and privilege. A majority even deny that they as a group have benefited greatly from past or present racial discrimination.[2]

Karyn McKinney is one of several sociologists who have collected racial autobiographies from White college students. Her autobiographies reveal that most of these Whites do not understand their White racial privileges, largely because they do not face everyday discrimination and do not have significant equal-status contacts with people of color. Still, this and similar research has revealed that some Whites, albeit a modest number, have come to better understand racial privilege. At a certain turning point, Whites who have had significant and sustained contacts with people of color may come to understand more about how everyday racism operates and about their privileged racial place. Today, as in the past, a central difficulty in bringing more racial change lies in the fact that a majority of Whites do *not* have truly close and strong equal-status relationships with Black Americans, or indeed other Americans of color. Most Whites have the option to stay relatively isolated in socioracial terms and to avoid regularly encountering the critical views and painful experiences of Americans of color.[3]

White privilege also includes an entitlement to decipher and name a person of color's everyday reality. For example, the mother of one newborn reported a White nurse's comment on seeing her infant: "Oh, this one's a militant, a little Black Panther!"[4] The newborn was immediately constructed as "black" (in this case, the mother was White, the father Black) and downgraded, humorously, in White eyes as an alien racial other. Whites often take it for granted that they are entitled to their interpretation of the realities and conditions of people of color without consulting them.

In addition, a majority of Whites are very defensive when reminded of their White privilege and position in society's racial hierarchy. In one study, researchers asked groups of White college students to write an essay about the ways in which they had been privileged or had been disadvantaged because they were White. Those Whites who wrote about their racial privileges later scored higher on a modern racism scale with anti-Black items (e.g., "Blacks are getting too demanding in their push for equal rights") than did those students who did not write about their racial privileges. When these Whites had to consider racial privilege and inequality, most "justified their privileged status by denying the existence of discrimination" and accenting the White frame's anti-Black stereotypes. Like other research, this study suggests Whites' racial understandings typically involve a strong sense of their advantaged position on the racial ladder, and a need to defend that unjustly derived position.[5]

Social Transmission of White Privilege

From the beginning, the North American system of racial oppression was designed to bring many benefits for Whites. Slavery, Jim Crow segregation, and contemporary discrimination have all provided Whites with a great many social, economic, and political advantages. For that reason Whites, as individuals and as a group, have a vested interest in actively maintaining this system. Systemic racism ensures Whites "greater resources, a wider range of personal choice, more power, and more self-esteem than they would have if they were . . . forced to share the above with people of color."[6]

Today, most Whites underestimate not only the level of their racial privileges but the degree to which these privileges exist because for most they have, to a substantial degree, been passed down from generations of White ancestors. Consider the legal principle of unjust enrichment. The coercive taking of one's personal possessions by an individual criminal, unjust enrichment under U.S. law, has some similarities to the coercive taking of one's labor or earned assets by a White slaveholder or, later, by an array of White discriminators.[7] Such unjustly gained advantages often have a strong societal inertia. When large groups of Whites gained jobs, income, property, status, or wealth unjustly under slavery and Jim Crow segregation and then passed these advantages and wealth to numerous later generations, that did *not* make the advantages and wealth inherited (and enhanced today) by their White descendants to be justly held.

Each White generation benefits from societal transmission processes that pass earlier unjustly gained economic and cultural capital to later White generations. And each White generation's discriminatory actions create new opportunities for unjust enrichment. For centuries, the system of oppression has created extensive inequalities in life chances between Whites and Blacks (as well as between Whites and many other Americans of color), and the cross-generational transmission of these great inequalities remains critical to the continuing reproduction of that racial oppression.

Racial Consciousness: Elite and Ordinary Whites

Over the course of our history, elite Whites have intentionally tried to divide ordinary White and Black Americans in order to reduce or eliminate the possibility of joint protests over difficult working conditions and other inegalitarian economic or political conditions. However, while there have been historical periods when some White farmers and workers have joined with their Black counterparts, for most of our history the overwhelming majority of White farmers and workers have been active players in maintaining systemic racism.[8]

Over the last century, a majority of White workers have usually rejected social class solidarity with Black workers, accepting the "public and psychological wage of whiteness" previously discussed. By doing that, they have regularly weakened their own consciousness of social class and of themselves as exploited workers under an inegalitarian capitalistic system.

Indeed, today most nonelite Whites still strongly accept a racially framed society and elite-dominated country. The majority also seem to accept the White elite's capitalistic ("neoliberal") framing that accents many government cutbacks and much privatization as being good for Whites generally. Researcher Randolph Hohle has shown that since the 1960s civil rights movement elite Whites have joined a traditional White racial framing of Black Americans with a reinvigorated capitalistic framing that emphasizes privatization and the language of free-market fundamentalism. Expanding their economic operations in formerly Jim Crow areas in southern and border states, since the 1970s the White capitalistic elite has networked with formerly segregationist White government officials there to reduce government regulations and increase privatization, which is profitable to large corporations. Mostly White regional and national corporate capitalists thereby have secured major reductions in taxes and government regulations and also secured aggressive privatization of numerous government services. Moreover, these powerful Whites have conned much of the White population, in the South and elsewhere, into often thinking and speaking of "public schools" and "public spending" as "bad" for Whites and privatization or elimination of numerous government programs as "good" for Whites. That is, the meanings of low taxes and weaker public programs were intentionally racialized and accepted by a great many Whites.[9] Here we observe variations on the old pro-White subframe (a positive evaluation of White low-tax and privatization efforts) and the antiothers subframes (negative evaluations of discriminated-against Black people and other people of color who need traditional public services and facilities).

Today, as in the past, White workers living in modest circumstances often do not feel privileged, especially relative to elite Whites. They sense the need for significant economic improvements in their own lives. However, because most accept major versions of the old White racial frame, with its many racial myths and misconceptions, they seem unable to see deeply into the real sources of their class oppression under modern oligopoly capitalism. That is, despite overwhelming evidence that major tax cuts very disproportionately benefit elite Whites, and usually do not generate much job growth and other economic benefit for ordinary workers, the majorities of the White working and middle classes have continued to mostly support oligopoly capitalists and their political candidates. Their own White racial framing makes it hard for most of them to understand well not only the situation of the racially oppressed, but also their own situation of persisting class oppression.

Still, this lack of understanding does not mean that class oppression is not still a major part of this country's social fabric. In the United States today, as in the past, racial structure and class structure constantly coexist, overlap, and interrelate. Being White includes not only a higher racial status in society no matter what one's social class is, but also *on average* having a higher social class position and greater income and resources than if one were Black. More often than not, a somewhat higher or much higher position in the class system comes with birth into the top "white" rank in the system of racial categorization.

Benefits of Whiteness: A Brief Overview

Privileged Access to Societal Resources

From the mid-1600s to the 1960s, this country's economy was openly run as a racist system, often using Black labor and Native American lands to create resources and prosperity for Whites. Historically, Whites have also been the direct beneficiaries of much government assistance intended to create more White prosperity and upward mobility. These programs of unjust favoritism for Whites have long provided a substantial basis for that prosperity and mobility. For example, in the 1600s several colonies provided significant land grants to White colonists, land unavailable to those enslaved. From the 1860s to the 1930s, the federal government, operating under the Homestead Acts, gave away millions of acres of government land for little or no cost to White families homesteading midwestern and western areas. African Americans were generally excluded from access to this land because they were then enslaved (in the 1860s) or, later during the Jim Crow era, because they were locked into the near-slavery of debt peonage in southern agriculture. Overt violence was also used by Klan-type groups to drive out Black families that did manage to gain some land. The federal homestead program created many billions of dollars of wealth for White homesteaders and their descendants, with the latter often benefiting to the present day.[10]

Numerous large-scale preferential programs for Whites have been implemented for centuries. Later, White entrants into the United States, such as millions of immigrants from southern and eastern Europe, benefited greatly from anti-Black discrimination during the late nineteenth and early twentieth centuries. These White immigrant groups generally had huge advantages over the African Americans who were already in the cities into which these immigrants settled. The European newcomers were able to move up the economic ladder because most arrived when the economy was expanding greatly and jobs were relatively abundant; because many had some skills or money resources; because most faced much less discrimination than Black urbanites; because they were not excluded from residential areas near workplaces as Black urbanites often were; and because cities were then increasingly under control of White political machines oriented to the White immigrant voters. As a result, these immigrants and their descendants were generally able to do much better economically, politically, and residentially than the still-segregated Black Americans who had already resided in the country for generations before these White immigrants arrived.[11]

Moreover, until the 1960s most unions discriminated openly against Black workers, reinforcing racial segregation in the labor market and increasing White workers' incomes relative to those of Black workers.[12] Not surprisingly, this long history of White workers' racial privilege is the backdrop for present-day racial privilege. In recent years many Black workers have still confronted informal job tracking favoring White workers within their workplaces. Much of this tracking is done by White employers and managers, but some job tracking involves mostly segregated social networks outside workplaces. White workers are often racially privileged by access to entirely or overwhelmingly White networks in terms of getting leads on where the good jobs are. Because of past legal segregation in housing and employment, most Whites have long held better paying jobs, and current White employees are more likely to pass along information on jobs to White workers in their segregated White networks than to workers of color.[13] In addition, Black workers often face informal discrimination in workplaces that is created by or collaborated in by White workers. In examining such workplaces, numerous researchers have found that these discriminatory practices range from subtle to blatant harassment—such as putting racist effigies at Black workers' job positions—and that White managers often ignore these actions. By means of everyday discrimination, White workers maintain their dominance of certain desirable jobs in many settings. As a result, Black workers and other workers of color are frequently kept in a state of stress that may keep them from performing as well as they might otherwise, or that forces them to quit—responses that mean more job opportunities, promotions, or other benefits for White workers.[14]

More Government "Handouts" for Whites

In the first decades of the twentieth century yet other major government-controlled resources were given away, or made available on reasonable terms, almost exclusively to White Americans. For example, the Air Commerce Act gave U.S. air routes to new companies, mainly those started by aviators trained during World War I. African Americans were not allowed into the Army Air Corps and had no opportunity to participate in this giveaway of major resources that over time generated significant wealth. Numerous other economic resources and opportunities, such as access to government-controlled mineral resources and the radio and television airwaves, were kept from African Americans, especially in the early twentieth century, by means of overt discrimination.[15]

Similarly, during the 1930s and 1940s, numerous federal New Deal programs provided very discriminatory access to yet more important resources. Key government programs heavily favored Whites. One of the most important subsidy programs was the Federal Housing Administration's loan insurance and related programs, later buttressed by veterans' housing programs. These enabled millions of Whites to buy their first homes. Many Whites accumulated enough home equity to use later on for startup capital for businesses or funding education for children and grandchildren. Other 1930s New Deal programs provided much important aid to White farmers, bankers, and business executives, enabling them to survive the Great Depression and to thrive during World War II and the postwar years. Their descendants have benefited, to the present, from long-term effects of these discriminatory programs.[16]

While many relief programs of the Great Depression and most postwar housing and veterans' programs looked nondiscriminatory on their face, and to varying degrees African Americans did benefit from them, their routine administration was usually left in the hands of local White officials. These White officials generally privileged White individuals and families in need, and, overall, Black individuals and families received *far less* government assistance than they deserved. Some major programs such as Social Security intentionally excluded lower paid categories of workers, such as household workers and farmworkers, categories where many Black Americans and other Americans of color worked. As Katznelson has put it, the era of aggressive public assistance programs from the 1930s to the 1960s was one when government "affirmative action was white."[17]

In the decades just before and after World War II, many government programs helped White builders, contractors, and other businesspeople to get a start and often to thrive. Over the decades since, these and other multibillion-dollar federal aid programs have helped to build up prosperity for many White businesses.[18] The histories of contemporary White families reveal five times more access to an array of these various government-assisted assets than the histories of contemporary families of color do.

Cultural, Legal, and Political Advantages for Whites

Whites have profited not only economically but also educationally, politically, legally, and aesthetically from centuries of systemic racism. Whites have, on the whole, had much greater access to good educational programs than have Black Americans. Until the 1960s, most colleges and universities—except historically

Black colleges—were all White or nearly so. Today, White students' access to first-rate college programs is still significantly greater than for Black students—and unencumbered by the racist barriers Black students currently face. For most of the years since public elementary and secondary schools were first created on a significant scale in the nineteenth century, they have been overtly or informally segregated along racial lines. The period of active school desegregation was brief, and resegregation is increasingly the trend. Typically, all-White or mostly White public schools have better educational resources and facilities than schools composed predominantly of students of color. Once a family's children have access to good educational resources, they are more likely to be successful in securing good jobs and housing and thus to pass along substantial economic and cultural benefits to their descendants.

Generally speaking, much contemporary U.S. culture is still substantially shaped by the White population's European heritage. White views and values, especially those of Anglo-Protestant groups, have been determinative in U.S. political-economic and legal development. From the 1600s forward, European-origin whiteness has been the normative standard for much of what is valued in society. The dominant language has long been English, with the most privileged variant and accent being that of middle-class Whites. In addition, the core U.S. legal system is rooted substantially in the English legal system, and the capitalistic economy is heavily European in its shape and values. The U.S. political system was also crafted mainly using European political ideas. Today this political system often does little to implement full-fledged democracy in its operations at state, local, and federal levels. Indeed, from the beginning the U.S. political system has allowed those with substantial money, usually well-off Whites, to shape and substantially control the major political institutions.[19]

In recent analyses of U.S. society, there is a tendency to play down this White European dominance in favor of a "melting pot" perspective that sees the central U.S. culture as a grand mixture with substantial input from many and diverse immigrant groups over several centuries, including Africans and other immigrants of color. However, apart from a few matters, such as popular entertainment, music, certain foods and sports, and, to some degree, religion, most of the U.S. culture and political economy is still heavily shaped by White European values, practices, and arrangements.

Controlling Institutions: The Dominant Role of White Men

Whites not only have dominated the economic, political, legal, and educational values of this society, but also have been in firm control of most of the key roles and top positions in all the powerful institutions for centuries. In previous chapters we have seen how this dominance was established and then transmitted over generations. Today, major large-scale institutions remain mostly White normed and White framed in their internal sociocultural structures, and White individuals are mostly in command at and near the top.

Even after decades of moderate affirmative action efforts for Americans of color and White women, the overwhelming majority of those who run most of the more powerful political, economic, and legal organizations in society are not only White, but also still White men. One exception was President Barack Obama, the first American president of color. Yet, much research shows that there is still a concrete ceiling that generally blocks Black Americans, many other Americans of color, and White women from many of the highest level institutional positions.[20]

For example, most higher level executives in major firms in various business sectors are White men. Clear evidence of the corporate world's failure to promote meritorious Black employees is the fact that so few Fortune 500 companies have *ever* had a Black executive at the very top. In the most recent count, there are only four Black chief executive officers (CEOs) (all men), with one reportedly departing soon from his position. There are only six Latino and nine Asian CEOs. Thus, Whites make up 96 percent of CEOs, and 92 percent are White men. Whites, mostly elite White men, are also substantially overrepresented on corporate boards and boards of major nonprofit organizations. They make up 96 percent of Fortune 500 corporations' board chairs and 86 percent of board members. In contrast, the U.S. workforce is about 64 percent White and just under one-third White male.[21]

This elite White, especially White male, dominance is not likely to change much in the near future. Recent research analyses that examined senior managerial ranks from which corporate CEOs are usually selected showed that there are relatively few people of color in those ranks. Citing new research by sociologists Richard Zweigenhaft and Bill Domhof, one journalist has summarized their data:

> More than two-thirds of potential future CEOs were white men, followed by white women . . . around 20 percent. Asian men accounted for just under 8 percent of this group, and black and Hispanic candidates of both genders combined to make up less than 7 percent of the pool. . . . In the most elite professional circles, mentees are often chosen based on how comfortable an existing team of executives or board members might feel with them.[22]

That is, powerful White men generally prefer White men over people of color and then, if necessary, White women. Candidates of color are often rejected directly or covertly as not "fitting in," which means into the elite White male ways of doing things.

In recent years numerous, mostly White, commentators have dramatized the unfounded notion that many Whites label "reverse discrimination" or "anti-White bias," especially in areas such as education and employment. Recall that recent surveys indicated that many Whites believe that discrimination against people of color has declined dramatically and that Whites, especially men, are now major victims of discrimination.[23] However, empirical research shows that this is a *fiction* that Whites commonly use to deflect discussions from their racially privileged reality. Drawing on interviews with many Whites, researcher Nancy DiTomaso has found that the persisting opposition by most Whites to affirmative action for people of color is not so much about fear of "reverse discrimination," but much more about the way in which the most effective affirmative action programs have sought to weaken old patterns of institutionalized *favoritism* for Whites. A really good antidiscrimination action program attempts to reduce the institutionalized racial bias favoring Whites in competition for most of society's better paying jobs. In the nearly 1,500 job situations that DiTomaso's White respondents talked about in detailed interviews, she found only *two* situations where a White person might have lost a job because of an affirmative action effort on behalf of Black Americans. There is no concrete evidence of significant anti-White discrimination in U.S. employment.[24]

While a few White men in historically White institutions have occasionally lost one opportunity for hiring or advancement because of a modest affirmative action program—usually to well-qualified White women or people of color—societal statistics also contradict the notion of widespread discrimination affecting White men. We have examined numerous data on White male dominance previously, such as their overwhelming dominance at the top of hundreds of major corporations. Indeed, the most successful racial "quota" program in U.S. history appears to be the one that sees to it that well-off White men dominate exclusively or very disproportionately most major U.S. institutions.

Note, too, that White men still dominate among those Americans with the greatest amounts of wealth. The latest *Forbes* study of the wealthiest 400 Americans found that almost all (94 percent) are White. Only 2 are Black, 5 are Latino, and 16 are South or East Asian. There are relatively few women, so the overwhelming majority of the wealthiest Americans are White men. Most have inherited substantial money capital and/or significant cultural capital—such as access to a very good education and exclusive social networks—that have enabled them to move up economically over their lifetimes. Contrary to much public discussion, the majority of these are *not* "self-made men."[25]

White Women: Second-Class Citizens and Racial Acolytes

What scholars call *intersectionality* is again important here—the reality of being White and female. White women are significantly underrepresented at the top of major corporations and other powerful organizations, as we see in the recent figure of just 22 White women serving as Fortune 500 CEOs. Women are a majority of U.S. workers. Yet these 22 women, plus 2 women of color (one Latina, one Asian Indian), make up less than 5 percent of these top CEOs.[26] The modest numbers of White women at the top in major business sectors and numerous other major organizational sectors make it clear that White women have not penetrated these decision-making heights in anything akin to proportionate numbers. Gender discrimination remains central, and changes have come slowly. White women have historically played a less central and less powerful role than White men in creating and maintaining the ongoing system of racial oppression. While White women were not explicitly singled out for gender oppression in the new U.S. Constitution, they were seen by the White male founders as unequal by nature and in need of patriarchal control. State and federal laws made them second-class citizens. However, in the early United States and subsequently, White women did have certain legal rights, in great contrast to the situations of Black women and men. Constitutionally, they were "free persons" with limited rights, but only those rights allowed by powerful White men who made the laws. In major contrast, as the *Dred Scott* case (1857) made clear, Black Americans "had *no rights* that the White man was bound to respect."[27]

In addition, most White feminist leaders of the nineteenth and early twentieth centuries adopted a White-racist framing, generally supporting the country's dominant racial hierarchy with Whites at the top. Most did not hold egalitarian views. Almost all supported White male leaders' imperialism across the globe, which developed dramatically in the late nineteenth century. Historian Louise Newman summarized this reality of White women, highlighting their racial superiority over women and men of color: White racism "was center stage: an integral element in feminism's overall understanding of citizenship, democracy, political self-expression, and equality."[28]

From the 1600s to the 1860s White women in middle- and upper-income groups sometimes inherited socioeconomic resources, including enslaved African Americans. In subsequent decades, many White women at these class levels have greatly benefited from the labor of exploited Black servants working in their homes. Over generations, many have benefited to a significant degree from undeserved enrichment of their families through the discriminatory arrangements of slavery, legal segregation, and contemporary racial discrimination. For centuries, White women's access to economic and cultural resources and socioeconomic opportunities has on the average been *much* greater than that of Black women or men.[29]

Indeed, since the 1980s modest numbers of White women have played an increasingly significant role, in or near the top decision-making positions, in perpetuating U.S. society's racially inegalitarian institutions—including those economic and political institutions originally established and still run mostly by dominant White men. The few top corporate managers who are White women mostly share the same higher social class, family status, and educational backgrounds as the White men, so it is not surprising that they mostly share a similar racial framing of society. Many elements of this dominant frame are embraced by these more powerful women, and in their important positions in major institutions they also regularly reinforce contemporary patterns of systemic racism.[30]

A good example of this supportive role can be seen in presidential elections since the 1950s. A majority of White female voters have supported the less progressive political (Republican) party and candidate in all but 2 of these 17 elections. This was exemplified in the 2016 election, when a little over half voted for the White-nationalist sympathizer Donald Trump over the much more racially progressive and gender-progressive candidate, Hillary Clinton. The majority appear to have accented their racial-group interest over their gender-group interest in reducing institutional sexism—that is, they voted against a White female candidate committed strongly to women's rights, but one that most of them likely considered to be in a party too linked to voters of color. As the scholar Jane Junn put it, political analysts should "consider the positionality of White women as second in sex to men, but first in race to minorities, and the invocation of White womanhood in political rhetoric and practice as a potential explanation of the Trump majority."[31]

The Many Costs of Racial Oppression

Unjust impoverishment and the struggle against racism for Americans of color are the other side of the unjust enrichment and enhanced opportunities for Whites. In previous discussions we examined many burdens and barriers that constitute racial oppression, including discriminatory barriers in employment, housing, education, law, politics, and public accommodations. For African Americans and other Americans of color, this recurring and widespread discrimination has many costs and consequences—not only economic costs but also psychological, physical, family, and community costs.

Substantial Economic Costs

Recently, the National Urban League issued a *State of Black America* report that summarized the general state of contemporary Black America across several institutional areas. The economic area showed the most relative inequality for African Americans with respect to White Americans—an economic index of 56.5 percent. (Equality with Whites would be 100 percent.) This index means that that "African Americans are missing *close to half* of the economics mini-pie."[32] Indeed, in recent decades U.S. Census data have revealed the median family income of Black families to be consistently in the range of 55 to 62 percent of the median family income of White families. During the late 1980s and into the 1990s, this percentage declined, and today it is only 60.7 percent. Current Pew Research Center data based on the U.S. Census indicated that Black households still have a much lower median (adjusted) household income ($42,300) than White households ($71,300). Consider also the cumulative impact of such household inequality. Examining data for the generation of Americans now entering retirement years, researchers have estimated that the average White baby boom family will have earned $450,000 *more* than the average Black baby boom family over their respective lifetimes of work. Unmistakably, anti-Black discrimination has created huge and lasting economic costs for African Americans.[33]

An even more dramatic indicator of generations of accumulating and privileged White access to socioeconomic resources is seen in measures of household wealth. According to a 2016 Pew report, the median net worth of White households is many times greater than that of Black households—with Black households at only $11,200 and White households at $144,200. (The picture for Latino households is similar to that of Black households.) This wealth inequality has stayed very high for centuries. Over the life cycle—that is, as the adults in families age—these racial inequalities in wealth tend to increase. A major reason why the median wealth of White families is much higher than that of Black (and Latino) families is because of the housing equities that a majority of Whites have built up over generations of discrimination limiting Black and Latino access to buying houses, as well as to other important resources.[34] White families are far more likely than Black and Latino families to have significant wealth in the form of interest-bearing bank accounts and stock in companies. Wealth is more than just money for it provides "insurance against tough times, tuition to get a better education and a better job, savings to retire on, and a springboard into the middle class. In short, wealth translates into opportunity."[35]

Sociologist Thomas Shapiro concluded that most African Americans have been prevented from producing and sustaining much wealth due to enduring and systemic racism, including unjust public policies that have protected the existing wealth of better off White Americans. Racial inequality is intergenerational, and Shapiro labeled it "toxic inequality." He added:

Wealth and race map together to consolidate historic injustices, which now weave through neighborhoods and housing markets, educational institutions, and labor markets, creating an increasingly divided opportunity structure. So long as we have entrenched wealth inequality intertwined with racial inequality, we cannot even begin to bend the arc toward equity. . . . The rich and powerful will continue to write rules that protect and expand their vast advantages at the expense of those struggling to keep pace, especially younger adults and families and communities of color.[36]

Economic inequality data do sometimes appear in the mainstream media, but there is usually no sustained attempt to understand the role of *systemic* racism in generating that racial inequality. Instead, many White mainstream analysts repeatedly suggest that Black workers and their families are mostly to blame, and they rarely bring up the continuing impacts of extreme past discrimination, such as slavery and Jim Crow segregation or the still-substantial contemporary discrimination. Most White Americans share the view that past discrimination is not relevant to current conditions. In a 2017 national survey, only 29 percent of White respondents agreed that past racial discrimination is a major factor in Blacks' current lower average wealth level. In contrast, 62 percent of Black respondents felt that it is.[37]

This White framing of Black workers and families has major political implications, including in recent elections. Over the last few years, numerous political commentators—including those trying to explain Donald Trump's victory in the 2016 election—have made the argument that many working-class Whites are angry because they lost economic ground due to government programs that allegedly improved the economic conditions of workers of color at the expense of White workers. Yet, the available economic data do not come close to supporting this fictional contention. Since the 1960s civil rights programs, Whites have *not* lost economic ground compared to Blacks. Researcher Paul Campos has explained that the "income gap between black and white working-class Americans, like the gap between black and white Americans at *every* income level, remains every bit as extreme *as it was five decades ago*."[38] Once again, the country's huge and persisting racial inequalities are not what common White racial framing contends that they are.

To these economic inequalities one must add other, often related, social inequalities. The previously mentioned National Urban League's *State of Black America* report summarized an array of inegalitarian conditions faced by contemporary Black Americans. These contemporary data showed a little decline over the previous decade in the overall societal position of Black Americans relative to Whites—from a summary equality statistic of 72.6 percent in 2007 to a summary equality statistic of 72.3 percent in 2017. (Recall that equality with Whites would be 100 percent.) In addition to finding a little decrease in Black–White economic equality from 2007 to 2017, this report also found that educational equality also declined over this period. In regard to health issues, the report found continuing racial inequality, but some improvement due to the Affordable Care Act. The Urban League data also showed much relative inequality and a significant decline over this period on a composite social-criminal justice measure, due in part to an increase in imprisonment rates for Black Americans.[39]

The Value of Stolen Black Labor

Gaining an adequate explanation for these large racial inequalities requires much deeper probing. Undeserved impoverishment for Blacks and undeserved advantages for Whites began at a very early point in this country's history. Much of the economic advantage and prosperity of Whites in earlier centuries came directly or indirectly from the labor of enslaved Africans and African Americans or from the country's economic development spurred by profits from slave farms, slave plantations, and the slave trade.

The scholar Thomas Craemer has calculated the hours worked by enslaved Black men, women, and children from 1776 (the Declaration of Independence) to 1865 (the official end to slavery). He estimated that the cost of reparations for this largely uncompensated labor would be in the range of $5.9 trillion to $14.2 trillion. The $5.9 trillion estimate supposes a typical 12-hour workday, 7 days a week, and is based on wages paid to White laborers in the era. Because those enslaved were allowed to sleep only so they could provide forced labor, Craemer calculated a second compensation estimate for all 24 hours of the day—$14.2 trillion in current dollars.[40] Extending his calculation from the beginning of enslavement in the early 1600s to its end in 1865 would increase the dollar value of this lost wealth to a yet higher trillion-dollar figure.

Moreover, for scholars like economist William Darity, reparations to African Americans should address additional racial injustices: "I would be inclined to argue that the basis for reparations is slavery, Jim Crow, and ongoing discrimination and racism in the United States."[41] After the Civil War, newly freed African Americans faced continuing racial oppression. There were proposals in Congress to give them some federal land to begin new lives. However, relatively few gained access to the land promised, and inequality in agricultural land was a major cause of persisting racial inequalities after the war. Using anti-Black violence, as well as segregation laws, Whites in southern and border states denied Blacks access to good farmland, fair credit arrangements, political power, and educational capital. (Note, too, that much of this federal land had been stolen by Whites from Native Americans.) The costs of Jim Crow for Black workers included little access to economic capital over the next several generations—even in the form of small businesses or farms—and lower wages stemming from widespread discrimination. Again, economic losses were high. Researchers have estimated the costs of the labor market discrimination against Black Americans from 1929 to 1969 (in

1983 dollars) at about $1.6 trillion.[42] Calculating the cost of labor discrimination for a longer period, from the end of slavery in 1865 to 1969, the official end of legal segregation, and putting it into current-year dollars would increase that cost of the Jim Crow estimate to far more. Moreover, since the end of official segregation, Black Americans have suffered additional major economic losses from discrimination. The Urban Institute has estimated that over some years Black workers lost more than $120 billion annually because of persisting employment discrimination.[43]

A simple total of just the current economic worth of all Black labor stolen by Whites through the means of slavery, segregation, and contemporary discrimination is huge—perhaps 10–20 trillion dollars. This last figure is exceedingly high, about the size of the estimated gross domestic product (GDP) generated in the United States in 2017.

In addition, these monetary figures do not include other major costs—the great pain and suffering inflicted, the physical abuse, or the many untimely deaths. Consideration of this massive noneconomic damage needs to be figured into the ultimate social cost accounting for this country's White oppression targeting African Americans. For example, scholars Desmond King and Jennifer Page contended that the abolition of the current, often unjust, large-scale mass incarceration of Black Americans would likely require the payment of additional reparations because "there is common ground between the aims of domestic reparations movements and transitional justice."[44] Adding in the economic and noneconomic costs inflicted on other Americans of color would raise the total social cost of systemic racism to a staggeringly high figure.

Over recent decades, this country has seen several serious discussions of substantial reparations to African Americans for these centuries of heavy imposed costs. For example, a recent United Nations panel recommended wide-ranging U.S. Black reparations for "the legacy of colonial history, enslavement, racial subordination and segregation, racial terrorism and racial inequality." In spite of post–Jim Crow progress, "a systemic ideology of racism ensuring the domination of one group over another continues to impact negatively on the civil, political, economic, social and cultural rights of African Americans today."[45] Thus, scholars King and Page underscored the point that because "a group housed at the United Nations chose to spend time and political capital on the subject, suggests that reparations to African Americans are not a fringe idea."[46] In addition, beyond U.S. borders the Black reparations movement has endured for decades. For instance, Caribbean heads of governments created the Caricom Reparations Commission (CRC), whose directive has been to formulate a case for reparatory justice for that region's Indigenous and African descendants.[47]

Economic Consequences of Generations of Racial Barriers

In order to build up successful families and provide for children, parents obviously need access to significant economic, educational, and other social resources. Exclusion from even one major opportunity to secure resources can have immediate and long-term consequences for families. Stephen DeCanio has developed an economic model that suggests that African Americans who had no significant material property because of slavery and who were emancipated without the promised arable land were as a group fated to endure major long-term economic inequality compared to Whites even if they had experienced favorable employment conditions, which they did not. The initial gap in land access "would have produced by itself most of the gap in income between blacks and white Americans throughout the late nineteenth and early twentieth centuries."[48] This huge racial disparity has passed along to subsequent generations, to the present. The long-term impact of initial inequality in agricultural resources would "prevent attainment of racial equality even if current discrimination ended and blacks and whites had identical tastes and preferences."[49] Not only were Black families substantially excluded from wealth-generating homestead lands by law or violence, they were forced into racially segregated schools, workplaces, and residential areas. Legal segregation in the South and de facto segregation in the North generally kept Black families from generating the socioeconomic resources necessary to compete effectively with Whites over many generations.

The impact continues into the present. Consider a Black person and a White person trying to set up a new business. Often such entrepreneurs must draw on family savings, such as a house equity, or borrow from relatives and banks. The Black entrepreneur is much less likely than a White entrepreneur to have significant personal or family resources to draw on because his or her family has been unable to build up economic resources over generations of systemic racism. A Black entrepreneur is more likely to face discrimination today in getting bank loans. Once White families garner economic resources, they may invest those assets and profit from what might be called the "money value of time." Having significant economic and other family resources, often unjustly gained because of systemic racism, over some period of time allows for the further enhancement of family resources. In the past, however, the Black businessperson's parents and grandparents likely faced extreme racial segregation, which cut down sharply on what they could earn, save, and pass on to later generations. The removal of legal segregation in the 1960s did not get rid of its substantial and lasting impact in the current economy.[50]

As noted previously, over the last several generations there has been significantly less monetary inheritance for Black families as compared with White families. The majority of those securely in the Black middle class today have not had the time to accumulate substantial assets for several generations like the majority of White middle-class families. Historically, a great many Whites have gotten some advantages in terms of the transmission of material assets in the form of homes, home equities, savings, land, securities, or small businesses. Many have gotten other significant advantages, such as access to quality education, that translate into material advantages.[51] Thus, social science research has shown that the current White–Black differential in wealth is *not* the result of differences in savings rates, but exists because Black individuals typically inherit much less than Whites from their families. Oliver and Shapiro summarized the impact of various government programs aggressively favoring Whites:

> There is a long and rich history that includes the homestead act of 1862 and the land-grant colleges of the 19th century, Federal Housing Administration loans, Social Security, and the GI Bill, as well as the continuous benefits of tax codes that subsidize homeownership, property, and wealth. America's broad middle class accumulates two-thirds of its wealth through homeownership enabled more by federal actions than private thrift, savings, and investments. The reach of these social-investment actions, however, by both intent and omission, has not been extended to low and moderate-income families, and only barely to Hispanics and African Americans.[52]

Interestingly, in recent opinion polls substantial numbers of Whites say that Black Americans are now at least roughly equal with them, responding as though they do not see the many barriers and costs of racism faced today by Black Americans. However, at some level, most Whites seem aware that being Black in America involves major personal, family, and economic costs. Social scientist Andrew Hacker has reported on asking White college students how much they would seek in compensation if they were suddenly changed from White to Black. Most indicated that "it would not be out of place to ask for $50 million, or $1 million for each coming Black year."[53]

Persisting racial inequality is evident in the dramatic differences between White poverty rates and those of Blacks and Latinos. In the latest Census Bureau data, the White poverty rate was 8.8 percent, as compared with a much higher Black rate of 22 percent and Latino rate of 19.4 percent. Recently, a United Nations special rapporteur, a human rights researcher and legal scholar, conducted an information-gathering mission to California, Georgia, Puerto Rico, West Virginia, and Washington, D.C. His assigned U.N. task was to examine government attempts to eliminate poverty, including that inflicted on millions of impoverished Americans of color. Reviewing the U.S. government's compliance with international human rights law, he underscored the striking disparity between the way that the bottom fifth of the population lives as compared with the more affluent part of the country. In effect, his analysis condemned the mostly White decision makers substantially responsible for continuing U.S. poverty and associated political disenfranchisement, especially that faced by Americans of color:

> There is a prevalence of caricatured, racist narratives about the poor, particularly the notion that welfare recipients are scammers. While funding for the IRS to audit wealthy taxpayers has been reduced, efforts to identify welfare fraud are being greatly intensified. The undermining of democracy, assisted by overt disenfranchisement of felons, gerrymandering, and the imposition of unnecessary voter ID requirements, results in the deprivation of the poor, minorities, and other disfavored groups of their voting rights.

He added that in a country as prosperous as the United States, the "persistence of extreme poverty is a political choice made by those in power."[54]

Additional Cultural and Health Costs

From the colonial period to the present, African Americans have taken much strength from their social and cultural heritage, one rooted in extended families and friendship networks. The knowledge carried in these networks includes positive values and perspectives on life, as well as portraits of role models that buttress identity and self-respect. Black Americans have had to be like experienced anthropologists and know White society well in order to survive or thrive; they have had to be experts on how to respond to hostile White actions. Black American culture has not arisen freely but under conditions of oppressive slavery, segregation, and contemporary discrimination. It thus incorporates important elements of cultural resistance and counterframing to White racism. While this Black culture has many strengths and draws on its African heritage, it also reflects the past and present exclusion of Black Americans from the many privileges and resources available to Whites, as well as the *forced assimilation* into Anglo-American ways pressed on Black Americans. Reflecting on earlier centuries, legal scholar Patricia Williams has concluded that Black enslavement "was that of lost languages, cultures, tribal ties, kinship bonds, and even of the power to procreate in the image of oneself and not that of an alien master."[55]

In recent years some analysts have tried to counter arguments that racism is still systemic with the contention that the United States now has a "rainbow culture." The suggestion is that many Whites accept much music (e.g., jazz and rap) and other entertainment that has emerged from African American communities.

However, Whites in decision-making positions, such as heads of powerful media corporations, generally control the way in which much Black music and other entertainment elements move into the White-dominated culture. In its early stages after the 1960s civil rights movement rap (hip-hop) emerged substantially as protest music and commentary, as resistance against a racist society. However, since it came under the control of these large media corporations, much of this assertiveness against White racism has been significantly channeled or watered down. As Ellis Cashmore has put it, Whites have frequently converted certain Black culture "into a commodity, usually in the interests of white-owned corporations," and Blacks have generally "been permitted to excel in entertainment only on the condition that they conform to whites' images of blacks."[56]

This apparently respectful acknowledgment of Black cultural achievements often conceals, just below the surface, old White-framed stereotypes of Black Americans as entertaining, hypersexualized, thug-like, or marginal to the White-dominated culture. In addition, much of what was once a protest music form, rap (hip-hop), is substantially altered, and no longer has the power of anti-racist resistance it once had. The absorption of a few elements of a subordinated culture into the dominant culture does not mean much if there is little change in the fundamental aspects of the dominant culture and society, such as in its prevailing legal practices, discriminatory ways of employment, and discriminatory political and business practices.[57]

The Broad Psychological Impact

Writing at a time when efforts at racial desegregation were starting to be reduced in the 1960s, Dr. Martin Luther King Jr. contended that, if racism is to be eradicated, then Whites "must begin to walk in the pathways of [their] black brothers and feel some of the pain and hurt that throb without letup in their daily lives."[58] In much recent research many Black Americans have indicated that they still feel like "outsiders" in the United States. The omnipresent reality of White hostility and discrimination generates this common distressed feeling. Racism is constructed in not only racist framing in White minds, but also the many concrete ways that Whites interact with Black men, women, and children. Thus, when a Black person enters an organization that is predominantly White or walks down a street where Whites are numerous, "race" is seen and created in those specific places by recurring White framing, animosities, and actions. In important interactions with Whites, Blacks are often excluded from full human recognition, important social positions, and significant societal rewards.[59]

Recurring discrimination can bring a significant psychological toll on Black men, women, and children. For example, in her autobiography, the great scholar-activist Angela Y. Davis captures well the authentic and painful under-standing of everyday racism that comes to Black children:

> My childhood friends and I were bound to develop ambivalent attitudes to-ward the white world. On the one hand, there was our instinctive aversion to those who prevented us from realizing our grandest as well as our most trivial wishes. On the other hand, there was the equally instinctive jealously which came from knowing that they had access to all the pleasurable things we wanted. . . . I have a very vivid recollection of deciding very early, that I would never—and I was categorical about this—never harbor or express a desire to be white. . . . I constructed a fantasy in which I would slip on a white face and go unceremoniously in the [racially segregated] theatre or amusement park of wherever I wanted to go. After thoroughly enjoying the activity, I would make a dramatic, grandstand appearance before the white racists and with a sweeping gesture, rip off the white face, laugh widely and call them all fools.[60]

White discrimination has long had a very negative impact on children of color, yet as here they frequently develop a countering response, especially in their own minds, to preserve their personal sense of self-worth.

Black adults face many similar dilemmas. Today, when a Black man is near, White women will sometimes tightly clutch their purses and White women and men will take such defensive actions as getting out of elevators, crossing the street, or locking car doors. If such actions come to Whites' attention, they tend to view them at most as just "minimal slights." Yet, these actions can have a neg-ative and lasting impact, for the targeted Black man will probably feel like an outcast or alien. At a minimum, every Black person has to develop strategies to counter this psychological warfare by Whites. Contemporary social science has documented the severe negative effects that such dehumanization has on phys-ical and emotional health. In addition, several recent surveys have shown that the substantial majority of African Americans have become more pessimistic about the racial future of the United States, especially since the recent increase in more overt White-nationalist organization and activity.[61]

Recurring Challenges to Self-Confidence and Identity

The impact of everyday racism includes a range of psychological reactions—from anxiety and worry to depression, anger, and rage. In interviews with many African Americans, we have found that they speak poignantly about the recur-ring impact of blatant and subtle discrimination on the self-esteem and self-con-fidence of themselves and of friends and relatives. In recent research, we have found that a great many African Americans, especially older women and men who had significant experience with Jim Crow, today suffer from something like the post-traumatic stress syndrome—with its pain, depression, and anxiety—that has been documented for military veterans of U.S. wars overseas.[62]

Many African Americans are especially concerned about the negative impact of White racism on the youth. For example, psychologists have extensively examined the impact of racist stereotypes on Black student performance. In numerous studies, Claude Steele and his colleagues have given Black and White students some skills tests similar to the Graduate Record Examination (GRE). In his analysis of the test results, Steele emphasized a form of personal identity contingency termed *stereotype threat*, which is a significant element in the underperformance of students of color in higher education.[63] When skills tests were presented to Black students as tests of their "intellectual ability," they did less well than White students of otherwise comparable ability. In contrast, when skills tests were presented to the Black students without the suggestion that it was a type of intelligence testing, they performed at a level similar to that of Whites. In the first case the stereotype threat—commonplace anti-Black stereotyping—was brought to the front of Black students' minds and created anxiety or self-consciousness that hurt test performance. The racial stereotype threat in research settings has a short-run impact. Yet, in the longer term the many recurring stereotype threats from Whites in the larger society can seriously undermine the self-esteem and confidence of those thereby threatened.[64]

Ours is still a society where the lack-of-intelligence stereotype is regularly pressed on Black Americans and some other Americans of color in schools, other institutions, and the mainstream media. Discussion of White–Black "IQ" differentials reappears every few years, resurrected by hostile or uninformed Whites. Such spoken and written stereotypes, especially when repeated, have negative impacts, perhaps reducing many people's efforts to achieve important personal or family goals. From cradle to grave, Whites force Black Americans to live out their lives under a constant bombardment of such White-racist threats and, as a result, to create an important repertoire of psyche-saving and community-saving frames and other measures to counter them.

Rage and Energy Loss

Some time ago, psychiatrists William Grier and Price Cobbs examined the extent to which anger and rage among Black Americans are created by the pervasiveness and complexities of everyday discrimination. Drawing on clinical interviews, they concluded that successful psychological counseling with Black Americans must deal directly with this omnipresent discrimination. They concluded that

Black Americans "have been asked to shoulder too much. They have had all they can stand. They will be harried no more. Turning from their tormentors, they are filled with rage."[65] Today, anger and rage over White racism are still common-place. Overtly expressed or silent, this rage can lead to personal turmoil, emotional withdrawal, or physical problems.

The seriousness of Black anger over discrimination is made clear in the following comments from an interview with the distinguished Black professor whose quotation opened this chapter. Replying to a question about the level of his anger (on a scale from 1 to 10) toward White racism, he answered: "Ten! I think that there are many Blacks whose anger is at that level. Mine has had time to grow over the years more and more and more until now I feel that my grasp on handling myself is tenuous. . . . Like many Blacks you get tired, and you don't know which straw would break the camel's back."[66] In his interview he made it clear that he gets most angry from observing the discrimination that Whites constantly inflict on Black Americans, especially on youth. Recent studies regularly confirmed this anger over White racism among African Americans.[67] Indeed, it is one major motivation for joining in antidiscrimination efforts and organizations.

Dealing with this racism regularly entails an array of other psychological costs. For example, a rather vigilant, cautious, and/or defensive approach to life is usually necessary. For decades, social scientists have pointed out that to survive everyday racism a Black person has to view every White person as "a potential enemy unless he [or she] personally finds out differently."[68] Recall again the opening quotation from the distinguished Black professor that noted the huge energy loss imposed on African Americans. These African Americans must expend an enormous amount of energy defending themselves and their families from the assaults of White racism on a recurring basis and over lifetimes. In contrast, over lifetimes White Americans on average have a major life-energy advantage for they do not waste large amounts of energy dealing with anti-White discrimination.

Negative Impacts on Physical Health

The stress, anger, and rage created by everyday racism can generate serious physical health consequences. Sociologist William Smith has described a key aspect of this reality that he terms *racial battle fatigue*, which is "caused by the constant redirection of energy needed for emergency situations, mainly for psychosocial reasons, to deal with race-related stress."[69] When asked in interview studies about the costs of the discrimination they face, African American respondents frequently cite a broad range of stress-related health problems—from hypertension and stress diabetes to stress-related heart and stomach conditions.

One qualitative field study by the senior author and his colleagues in-volved focus group interviews with middle-class African Americans. Several participants gave details on how high blood pressure and other health problems seemed to be linked, at least in part, to everyday discrimination. One nurse in the Midwest commented on her body's reactions to a workplace with a hostile racial climate:

> That's when I got high blood pressure. And my doctor . . . I told him what my reaction, my body's reaction would be when I would go to this place of em-ployment . . . which was a nursing home. When I turned into the drive-way I got a major headache. I had this headache eight hours until I walked out that door leaving there. I went to the doctor because the headaches had been so continuously . . . . going through what I was going through wasn't really worth it because I was breaking my own self down. . . . It was constant intimidation. Constant racism, but in a subtle way. You know, but enough whereas you were never comfortable. . . . And then I finally ended up on high blood pressure pills because for the longest, I tried to keep low. . . . It didn't work. *I hurt me.*[70]

Like other research studies using in-depth interviews with Black Americans, we found that they reasonably associate the everyday discrimination they en-counter over a lifetime with such physical problems as hypertension, back pain, insomnia, stomach problems, and serious headaches.

Numerous research studies document the likely significant impact of everyday racism on various diseases faced by African Americans. For example, one study of a large sample of Black women found modest statistical associations between breast cancer incidence and level of reported experience with discrimination. This relationship between cancer incidence and discrimination experience held true when other factors affecting cancer risk were controlled for.[71] Demographic data on longevity and mortality indicate the physical harshness of cumulative racism in cold statistical terms. African Americans average significantly shorter lives than White Americans, which has been true for centuries. Historical studies indicate that most enslaved Black Americans died by the age of 40, while on av-erage White slaveholders lived more than 40 years. By 1900 the life expectancy for an average Black person was only 32–35 years, about 16 years less than that for the average White person.[72] Today, this Black–White gap has closed signifi-cantly but is still significant. In recent government data, the average Black person has a life expectancy 3 and 5 years (female and male, respectively) less than the average White person. In addition, studies showed that Blacks aged 18–64 years are more likely to die an early death than Whites; that those aged 35–64 years are much more likely to endure high blood pressure than Whites; and that those aged 18–49 years are far more likely to die of heart disease than Whites.

Blacks are more likely to die from all major cancers than Whites.[73] Public health researchers have, for decades now, documented these major racial inequalities in disease, mortality, and longevity.

Persuasive research evidence suggests that systemic racism plays a major role in these health inequalities. Black Americans, for example, face high levels of residential segregation, which often reduces access to healthcare resources and often exposes them to environmental contaminants or substandard housing quality.[74] In our recent review of current healthcare research, we found numerous studies that documented the reality and negative health impacts of the discrimination that African Americans (and other Americans of color) frequently face in dealing with White medical personnel.[75] As we have seen throughout this book, individual and institutionalized discrimination in various other societal sectors likely plays a significant part in generating these racial inequalities. Indeed, for many deceased African Americans, everyday racism could be listed on their death certificates as a major contributing cause of death.

A Complex and Accumulating Burden

Thinking in terms of the complex and cumulative impacts, sociologist Rodney Coates described everyday racism as a cage:

> To the casual observer, each wire does not appear to be sufficient in and of itself to retain the bird. But when viewed from either within or as a whole we see a finely constructed cage. The problem, from a pedagogical, policy, research, or activist perspective, is that we tend to concentrate on only one wire or phenomenon, removal of which leads to great anticipation that the war has been won. Unfortunately, while even more insidious wires are being constructed, the others are left intact.[76]

Repeated encounters with White-racist framing and racial mistreatment accumulate across many institutional arenas and over long periods of time. The lifetime number of such encounters for the average Black adult is undoubtedly in the thousands. Moreover, the impact on an individual is usually much greater than what a simple summing of her or his experiences might suggest. The cumulative impact of psychological and physical problems directly or indirectly linked to everyday racism can likely be seen in the significant differentials in health and in life expectancy noted previously.

For many White commentators, what they view as the little discrimination remaining in society is only a problem of individual bigots and temporary impacts. This view is way off the mark. Today, as in the past, the recurring assaults of blatant, covert, and subtle racism have strong effects not only on individual African Americans and other Americans of color, but also on their larger social circles, for the reality and pain of repeated discriminatory acts are usually shared with relatives and friends as a way of coping with such inhumanity. Over time the long-term pain and memory of one individual becomes part of the pain and collective memories of larger networks, extended families, and communities. This negative impact requires the expenditure of much individual, family, and community energy to endure the oppression and to develop important counterframing and active strategies for fighting back.[77]

The Price Whites Pay for Racism

In the major 1968 Supreme Court case *Jones et ux. v. Alfred H. Mayer Co.*, the famous progressive White Justice William O. Douglas argued that the

> true curse of slavery is not what it did to the black man, but what it has done to the white man. For the existence of the institution produced the notion that the white man was of superior character, intelligence, and morality.[78]

Such White-racist framing of society has been commonplace from slavery days to the present, but it is still very unhealthy and entails *living a lie*, for Whites are not in fact superior in character, intelligence, or morality.

Moreover, according to surveys cited previously, a majority of Whites do not have much empathy for the suffering of Black Americans and others who face contemporary racial discrimination. For a great many, participation in racial discrimination, or winking at its practice by other Whites, feeds a desired distancing of the racialized others. This social distancing feeds further discrimination, social alexithymia, or insensitivity. Not surprisingly, to take one important example, analyses of corporate workplaces have concluded that discrimination by White male executives and managers often lies in their inability to deal well with any group—be it Black or female—that is quite different socially from themselves. As a result of this difference, there is an often unconscious failure to extend to the racialized others the same recognition of humanity they enjoy themselves.[79]

Living a Rhetorical and Hypocritical Ethic

Traditionally optimistic approaches to U.S. racial matters have accented the egalitarian values supposedly held by the majority of White Americans. Some decades back, Gunnar Myrdal, a Swedish social scientist, and his U.S. colleagues conducted a major study of Jim Crow segregation, reported in the influential 1944 book *An American Dilemma*. Representing the small liberal wing of the U.S. elite, these researchers argued that Whites were under the spell of the American creed. This creed encompassed the "ideals of the essential dignity of the individual human being, of the fundamental equality of all men, and of certain inalienable rights to freedom, justice, and a fair opportunity."[80] As the book emphasized, this abstract equality ethic, as stated prominently in U.S. law and public rhetoric, was in great tension with the society's legal segregation—thus the phrase "an American dilemma."

However, Myrdal failed to fully understand that the problem of U.S. racism is not at base a problem of failed grand ideals, but rather of the social, economic, and political interests of Whites as a racially privileged group. The vested interests of Whites orient them to keeping in place an extensive system of racial privilege and hierarchy that works greatly to their advantage; for most, this certainly outweighs their mostly *rhetorical* commitments to equality and justice values.[81]

Suffering for the Racist System

Part of the generally unrecognized price that systemic racism has demanded from Whites can be calculated in lives. For example, the slavery system not only cost millions of African and African American lives over the course of its bloody existence, but also took numerous White lives. Being a White sailor on slave ships or a White slaveholder or overseer on slave plantations was often dangerous because those enslaved sometimes lashed out at or killed their immediate oppressors. Additionally, the 1860s Civil War took 620,000 lives on both the Union and Confederate sides. African American soldiers died in significant numbers fighting against slavery and for the Union, but most of those soldiers killed and maimed in the carnage were ordinary White farmers and workers.[82]

In the past and the present, ordinary White farmers and workers who accepted the psychological wage of White superiority have been much less likely to organize effectively with farmers and workers of color. For centuries, this lack of united organization has meant less desirable working and living conditions for ordinary Americans, including White Americans. Today, the impact of historical Jim Crow segregation can still be seen in continuing divisions between many White workers and workers of color. When White workers have refused to organize effectively with workers of color against very exploitative employers, they have often received less in the way of wage and workplace improvements than they might well have collectively secured.

Before and after the Civil War, ordinary Whites paid a heavy political price for systemic racism. In creating an undemocratic society where barbaric violence against African Americans was enshrined in many laws, such as fugitive slave laws, or legitimated by informal practice, such as thousands of brutal lynchings, Whites lost some liberty as well. This was especially true for southern and border states with large numbers of enslaved Black Americans where the system of social control for enslaved Blacks spilled over into greater political inequality for less powerful Whites there than in the North. The dominant political arrangements, for Whites as well as Blacks, were authoritarian—with elite-dominated, one-party political systems the general rule. Autocratic White leaders dominating local and state governments were typically uninterested in providing adequate public health programs, schools, and colleges for ordinary Whites or for Blacks.[83]

Today, southern states still reflect this heritage. As a group, these still mostly White-run states have larger proportions of poverty-stricken citizens and generally weaker public schools and universities, public health programs, and other programs providing for the general welfare of citizens than do the northern states as a group. Inferiority in public services affects the White, Black, and other citizens of these states in very significant ways. In addition, the intense political conservatism of the substantial majority of southern White voters today is in significant part a lingering consequence of the South's extraordinarily racist past. This White political conservatism is a constant drag on attempts at improving an array of public services from which ordinary Whites would benefit greatly—and thereby facilitates the neoliberal deregulation and privatization mentioned previously, which mainly benefit the interests of large corporations and well-off Whites.[84]

Some Costs of Social Isolation

Today White and Black Americans are substantially segregated in terms of residence and neighborhood. As we have seen numerous times in this book, such segregation has had severe consequences for Black Americans, regularly limiting access to jobs and services. It has also had some negative consequences for Whites, who have fled the central cities and moved to distant suburbs, directly or indirectly for racist reasons. In the process White families have often paid a price in terms of higher housing costs, long-distance commuting, pollution from automobiles, and problems associated with central city decline. This suburban expansion is costly in terms of infrastructural costs—for transportation, water, flood control, and sewage systems—that usually increase greatly with sprawling suburban and exurban development. Residential segregation and residence/job mismatch have also been shown in some cases to negatively affect overall metropolitan economic growth.[85]

Whites also pay for continuing racism in elevated levels of racial fear and ignorance. Several studies have shown that Whites who live mostly segregated lives are often fearful of Blacks and other people of color with whom they have few or no equal status contacts. Such isolation is serious because it means that Whites with greater privileges and power do not have the experience necessary to view other Americans with accuracy and sensitivity. Most do not understand the oppressive reality faced by Americans of color. Thus, as the prominent social scientist Gary Orfield suggested, Whites growing up in heavily White suburban enclaves typically have "no skills in relating to or communicating with minorities."[86] In the near future, as the United States becomes much more diverse, this White orientation will become a more serious individual and group disadvantage. In addition, such White isolation will be more of a liability as the United States becomes yet more involved in international trade, politics, and diplomacy in a world where the political and economic leadership is also becoming more diverse and where non-European countries are becoming ever more powerful politically and economically.

Conclusion

Systemic racism has had, and currently has, profound human consequences. This is regularly recognized by international agencies. Periodically, United Nations' reports calculate a major Human Development Index (HDI). The HDI is an evaluation of quality of life and incorporates data on income, health, and education indicators for various countries and for subgroups within these countries. For the 188 countries examined in the recent (2017) index, the United States ranked *an astonishing 10th* in terms of its overall quality of life.[87] In addition, a similar index, the American Human Development Index, rated quality-of-life statistics for Black Americans, Latinos, Native Americans, Asian Americans, and Whites. White Americans and Asian Americans ranked at the top on this composite quality-of-life index, while African Americans, Native Americans, and Latinos ranked significantly lower.[88] These figures for African, Native, and Latino Americans underscore some of the serious long-term human costs of systemic racism.

To these statistics should be added yet other human costs of the centuries of uncounted suffering, health damage, loss of resources, and rage over injustice. Only by adding all these important human factors together can one assess accurately the true long-term impacts of slavery, segregation, and continuing White racism. The total cost of four centuries of systemic racism has been extraordinarily high. While Whites as a group do pay some price for the centuries-old system of U.S. racism, that group price pales when put up against that paid by African Americans and other Americans of color.

Notes

1. Joe R. Feagin and Melvin P. Sikes, *Living With Racism: The Black Middle-Class Experience* (Boston: Beacon Press, 1994), 295–296; Joe R. Feagin and Karyn D. McKinney, *The Many Costs of Racism* (Lanham, MD: Rowman & Littlefield, 2003), 39–64.

2. Karyn D. McKinney, "'I Really Felt White': Turning Points in Whiteness Through Interracial Contact," *Social Identities* 12 (2006): 183; Joe R. Feagin and Eileen O'Brien, *White Men on Race: Power, Privilege and the Shaping of Cultural Consciousness* (Boston: Beacon Press, 2003); Joyce E. King, "Dysconscious Racism: Ideology, Identity, and the Miseducation of Teachers," *Journal of Negro Education* 60 (1991): 135.

3. McKinney, "'I Really Felt White,'" 183 and passim; Joe R. Feagin, *The White Racial Frame: Centuries of Racial Framing and Counter-Framing*, 2nd ed. (New York: Routledge, 2013), 222–224.

4. Jane Lazarre, *Beyond the Whiteness of Whiteness* (Durham, NC: Duke University Press, 1996), 41.

5. Nyla R. Branscombe, Michael T. Schmitt, and Kristin Schiffhauer, "Racial Attitudes in Response to Thoughts of White Privilege," *European Journal of Social Psychology* 37 (2007): 203–215. The quotation is on p. 213.

6. Frances Lee Ansley, "Stirring the Ashes: Race, Class and the Future of Civil Rights Scholarship," *Cornell Law Review* 74 (September 1989): 1035.

7. See Theodore Cross, *The Black Power Imperative: Racial Inequality and the Politics of Nonviolence* (New York: Faulkner, 1984), 510.

8. David R. Roediger, *The Wages of Whiteness: Race and the Making of the American Working Class* (London: Verso, 1991), 12; see also Joe R. Feagin, Clairece B. Feagin, and David Baker, *Social Problems*, 6th ed. (Upper Saddle River, NJ: Prentice Hall, 2005), 462–463, 500.

9. Randolph Hohle, *Race and the Origins of American Neoliberalism* (New York: Routledge, 2015), 4. See also Randolph Hohle, *Racism in the Neoliberal Era* (New York: Routledge, 2018), passim.

10. Trina Williams, "The Homestead Act—Our Earliest National Asset Policy" (paper presented at the Center for Social Development's symposium, Inclusion in Asset Building, St. Louis, Missouri, September 21–23, 2000); Kenneth W. Smallwood, "The Folklore of Preferential Treatment," unpublished manuscript, Southfield, Michigan, 1985; Cross, *The Black Power Imperative*, 515–518.

11. Theodore Hershberg et al., "A Tale of Three Cities: Blacks, Immigrants, and Opportunity in Philadelphia, 1850–1880, 1930, 1970," in *Philadelphia: Work, Space, Family and Group Experience in the Nineteenth Century*, ed. T. Hershberg (New York: Oxford University Press, 1981), 462–464.

12. Herbert Hill, "The Racial Practices of Organized Labor—The Age of Gompers and After," in *Employment, Race and Poverty*, ed. Arthur M. Ross and Herbert Hill (New York: Harcourt, Brace & World, 1967), 365; Stanley B. Greenberg, *Race and State in Capitalist Development* (New Haven, CT: Yale University Press, 1980), 349.

13. Amy McCaig, "Racial Makeup of Labor Markets Affects Who Gets Job Leads," Rice University News Media, January 13, 2016, http://news.rice.edu/2016/01/13/racial-makeup-of-labor-markets-affects-who-gets-job-leads-2.

14. Sophia Hong, "New Noose Incident in Hempstead Town Building," Newsday, January 11, 2008, A22; Joe R. Feagin, Systemic Racism: A Theory of Oppression (New York: Routledge, 2006), 199–207; Southern Poverty Law Center, "Update: More Than 400 Incidents of Hateful Harassment and Intimidation Since the Election," November 15, 2016, https://www.splcenter.org/hatewatch/2016/11/15/update-more-400-incidents-hateful-harassment-and-intimidation-election. On the costs, see Joe R. Feagin, Kevin Early, and Karyn D. McKinney, "The Many Costs of Discrimination: The Case of Middle-Class African Americans," Indiana Law Review 34 (2001): 1313–1360.

15. See Cross, The Black Power Imperative, 515–518; Melvin L. Oliver and Thomas M. Shapiro, Black Wealth/White Wealth: A New Perspective on Racial Inequality (New York: Routledge, 1995), 36–45.

16. Ira Katznelson, When Affirmative Action Was White: An Untold History of Racial Inequality in Twentieth-Century America (New York: W. W. Norton, 2005), 38ff.

17. Katznelsn, When Affirmative Action Was White, 38–39; David Roediger, Working Toward Whiteness (New York: Basic Books, 2005).

18. Harvard Sitkoff, A New Deal for Blacks (New York: Oxford University Press, 1978); Joe R. Feagin, "Slavery Unwilling to Die: The Background of Black Oppression in the 1980s," Journal of Black Studies 17 (December 1986): 173–200; Cross, The Black Power Imperative, 515.

19. See Joe R. Feagin, White Party, White Government: Race, Class, and U.S. Politics (New York: Routledge, 2012), passim.

20. Crosby Burns, Kimberly Barton, and Sophia Kerby, The State of Diversity in Today's Workforce (Washington, D.C.: Center for American Progress, 2012), 4.

21. Gillian B. White, "There Are Currently 4 Black CEOs in the Fortune 500," The Atlantic, October 26, 2017, www.theatlantic.com/business/archive/2017/10/black-ceos-fortune-500/543960; Burns et al., The State of Diversity in Today's Workforce, 4.

22. White, "There Are Currently 4 Black CEOs."

23. See Paul Waldman, "Why White People Think They're the Real Victims of Racism," The Week, October 25, 2017, http://theweek.com/articles/732849/why-white-peo ple-think-theyre-real-victims-racism; Ipsos Public Affairs, "Reuters/Ipsos/UVA Center for Politics Race Poll," September 11, 2017, https://www.centerforpolitics. org/crystalball/wp-content/uploads/2017/09/2017-Reuters-UVA-Ipsos-Race-Poll-9-11-2017.pdf; on White voters' views of "reverse discrimination," see Christopher Ingraham, "White Trump Voters Think They Face More Discrimination Than Blacks," Washington Post, August 2, 2017, https://www.washingtonpost.com/news/ wonk/wp/2017/08/02/white-trump-voters-think-they-face-more-discrimination-than-blacks-the-trump-administration-is-listening.

24. Nancy DiTomaso, "How Social Networks Drive Black Unemployment," New York Times blog, May 5, 2013, http://opinionator.blogs.nytimes.com/2013/05/05/how-soc ial-networks-drive-black-unemployment.

25. huck Collins and Josh Hoxie, "Billionaire Bonanza: The Forbes 400 and the Rest of Us," Institute for Policy Studies, December 1, 2015, https://www.ips-dc.org/billiona ire-bonanza. We draw on our biographical checks of those on Forbes list. See also United for a Fair Economy Staff, *Born on Third Base: What the Forbes 400 Really Says About Economic Equality and Opportunity in America* (Boston, MA: United for a Fair Economy, 2012), 14–15.

26. Fortune Editors, "These Are the Women CEOs Leading Fortune 500 Companies," *Fortune*, June 7, 2017, https://fortune.com/2017/06/07/fortune-500-women-ceos; Valentina Zarya, "The 2017 Fortune 500 Includes a Record Number of Women CEOs," *Fortune*, June 7, 2017, https://fortune.com/2017/06/07/fort une-women-ceos.

27. *Dred Scott v. John F. A. Sandford*, 60 U.S. 393, 407 (1857); emphasis added. On women in Fortune 500, see Burns et al., *The State of Diversity in Today's Workforce*, 4–5.

28. Louise M. Newman, *White Women's Rights: The Racial Origins of Feminism in the United States* (New York: Oxford University Press, 1999), 183.

29. Mary Beth Norton, *Liberty's Daughters* (Boston: Little, Brown, 1980); Edmund S. Morgan, *American Slavery, American Freedom: The Ordeal of Virginia* (New York: W. W. Norton, 1975), 165.

30. Joe R. Feagin and Kimberley Ducey, *Elite White Men Ruling: Who, What, When, Where, and How* (New York: Routledge, 2017).

31. Jane Junn, "The Trump Majority: White Womanhood and the Making of Female Voters in the U.S.," *Politics, Groups, and Identities* 5 (2017): 343.

32. National Urban League, *2017 State of Black America: Protect Our Progress* (New York: National Urban League, 2017), 5, italics added.

33. Pew Research Center, "On Views of Race and Inequality, Blacks and Whites Are Worlds Apart," June 27, 2016, https://www.pewsocialtrends.org/2016/06/27/1-demo graphic-trends-and-economic-well-being; Carmen DeNavas-Walt, Bernadette D. Proctor, and Jessica C. Smith, "Income, Poverty and Health Insurance Coverage in the United States: 2011," U.S. Census Bureau, September 2012, https://www.cen sus.gov/newsroom/releases/archives/income_wealth/cb12-172.html; Graduate Minority Student Project, University of California (Berkeley), "Statistics of Racism in the United States: Income, Health, and Rights," http://struggle4reparations.com/star key/rep_sta.html.

34. Pew Research Center, "On Views of Race and Inequality"; Signe-Mary McKernan et al., *Less Than Equal: Racial Disparities in Wealth Accumulation* (Washington, DC: Urban Institute, 2013), 5. See Thomas Shapiro, Tatjana Meschede, and Sam Osoro, *The Roots of the Widening Racial Wealth Gap: Explaining the Black–White Economic Divide* (Waltham, MA: Brandeis Institute on Assets and Social Policy, 2013).

35. McKernan et al., *Less than Equal*, 1. We also draw on Thomas M. Shapiro, *The Hidden Cost of Being African American: How Wealth Perpetuates Inequality* (New York: Oxford University Press, 2004), 31.

36. Thomas M. Shapiro, "How Did America's Wealth Inequality Reach This Level of Toxic?" *Alternet*, April 11, 2017, www.alternet.org/books/toxic-inequality-book-race-income-and-wealth.

37. The link to the YouGov survey is in Theodore R. Johnson, "Africans Have Apologized for Slavery, So Why Won't the US?" *The Root*, https://www.theroot.com/africans-have-apologized-for-slavery-so-why-won-t-the-1790876029.

38. Paul F. Campos, "White Economic Privilege Is Alive and Well," *New York Times*, July 30, 2017, 3.

39. National Urban League, *2017 State of Black America: Protect Our Progress* (New York: National Urban League, 2017).

40. Thomas Craemer, "Estimating Slavery Reparations: Present Value Comparisons of Historical Multigenerational Reparations Policies," *Social Science Quarterly* 96 (June 2015): 639–655.

41. Adam Simpson and Carla Skandier, "For Reparations: A Conversation With William A. Darity, Jr.," The Next System Project, March 10, 2017, https://thenextsystem.org/for-reparations.

42. Roger L. Ransom and Richard Sutch, "Growth and Welfare in the American South in the Nineteenth Century," in *Market Institutions and Economic Progress in the New South 1865–1900*, eds. Gary Walton and James Shepherd (New York: Academic Press, 1981), 150–151; David H. Swinton, "Racial Inequality and Reparations," in *The Wealth of Races: The Present Value of Benefits From Past Injustices*, ed. Richard F. America (New York: Greenwood Press, 1990), 156.

43. See Kevin Merida, "Did Freedom Alone Pay a Nation's Debt?" *Washington Post*, November 23, 1999, C1.

44. Desmond S. King and Jennifer M. Page, "Towards Transitional Justice? Black Reparations and the End of Mass Incarceration," *Ethnic and Racial Studies* 41 (2017): 749.

45. Quoted in Max Ehrenfreund, "The Cost of Slavery Reparations Is Now Within the Boundaries of the Politically Acceptable," *Washington Post*, September 29, 2016, https://www.washingtonpost.com/news/wonk/wp/2016/09/29/the-cost-of-slavery-reparations-is-now-within-the-boundaries-of-the-politically-acceptable.

46. King and Page, "Towards Transitional Justice?" 754.

47. Jamal Eric Watson, "Experts Discuss Global Case for Reparations for Slavery," *Diverse Issues in Higher Education*, November 5, 2015, http://diverseeducation.com/article/78769.

48. Stephen J. DeCanio, "Accumulation and Discrimination in the Postbellum South," in *Market Institutions and Economic Progress in the New South 1865–1900*, eds. Gary Walton and James Shepherd (New York: Academic Press, 1981),105, see also 103–125.

49. Swinton, "Racial Inequality and Reparations," 157.

50. Martin J. Katz, "The Economics of Discrimination: The Three Fallacies of *Croson*," *Yale Law Journal* 100 (January 1991): 1041–1045.

51. Shapiro, *The Hidden Cost of Being African American*, 30–51; Oliver and Shapiro, *Black Wealth/White Wealth*, 36–50.

52. Melvin L. Oliver and Thomas M. Shapiro, "Creating an Opportunity Society," *American Prospect* 18 (May 2007), A27. See Shapiro, *The Hidden Cost of Being African American*, 70–72; Benjamin P. Bowser, *The Black Middle Class: Social Mobility—And Vulnerability* (Boulder, CO: Lynne Rienner, 2007), 87.

53. Andrew Hacker, *Two Nations: Black and White, Separate, Hostile, Unequal* (New York: Scribner's, 1992), 31–32.

54. "US Is Becoming a Champion of Inequality, Human Rights Expert Finds," New York University, December 20, 2017, http://www.nyu.edu/about/news-publications/news/2017/december/us-is-becoming-a-champion-of-inequality--human-rights-expert-fin.html, italics added.

55. Patricia J. Williams, "Alchemical Notes: Reconstructing Ideals From Deconstructed Rights," *Harvard Civil Rights and Civil Liberties Review* 22 (1987): 415.

56. Ellis Cashmore, *The Black Culture Industry* (New York: Routledge, 1997), 1, 3.

57. We are indebted here to discussions with Charity Clay.

58. Martin Luther King Jr., *Where Do We Go from Here? Chaos or Community?* (New York: Bantam Books, 1967), 122.

59. Joe R. Feagin, *The White Racial Frame: Centuries of Racial Framing and Counter-Framing*, 2nd ed. (New York: Routledge, 2013), Chap. 6 and 7; Feagin and Sikes, *Living With Racism: The Black Middle Class Experience*.

60. Angela Y. Davis, *Angela Davis: An Autobiography* (New York: Random House, 1974), 85.

61. Joe R. Feagin and Zinobia Bennefield, "Systemic Racism and U.S. Health and Health Care," *Social Science and Medicine* 103 (2014) 7–14; Judith Lichtenberg, "Racism in the Head, Racism in the World," *Philosophy and Public Policy* 12 (Spring/Summer 1992): 4; Tara Bahrampour, "African-Americans Deeply Pessimistic About Where Country Is Heading, Poll Finds," *Mercury News*, September 26, 2017, https://www.mercurynews.com/2017/09/26/african-americans-deeply-pessimistic-about-where-country-is-heading-poll-finds-2.

62. Ruth Thompson-Miller, Joe R. Feagin, and Leslie H. Picca, *Jim Crow's Legacy: The Segregation Stress Syndrome* (Lanham, MD: Rowman & Littlefield, 2015); Ruth Thompson-Miller and Joe R. Feagin, "Continuing Injuries of Racism: Counseling in a Racist Context," *The Counseling Psychologist* 35 (2007): 106–115. See also Feagin and McKinney, *The Many Costs of Racism*, 46–120.

63. Claude M. Steele, *Whistling Vivaldi: And Other Clues to How Stereotypes Affect Us* (New York: W. W. Norton, 2010); Phillip Atiba Goff, Claude M. Steele, and Paul G. Davies, "The Space Between Us: Stereotype Threat and Distance in Interracial Contexts," *Journal of Personality and Social Psychology*, 94 (January 2008): 91–107.

64. Claude M. Steele and Joshua Aronson, "Stereotype Threat and the Intellectual Test Performance of African Americans," *Journal of Personality and Social Psychology* 69 (1995): 797–811. See also Feagin and McKinney, *The Many Costs of Racism*, 39–64; Claude M. Steele, "A Threat in the Air: How Stereotypes Shape Intellectual Identity and Performance," *American Psychologist* (June 1997): 627.

65. William H. Grier and Price M. Cobbs, *Black Rage* (New York: Basic Books, 1968), 4. See also Feagin and McKinney, *The Many Costs of Racism*.

66. Feagin and Sikes, *Living with Racism*, 294. See also Feagin and McKinney, *The Many Costs of Racism*, 39–52, 142–145.

67. See, for example, Thompson-Miller et al., *Jim Crow's Legacy*.

68. Alexander Thomas and Samuel Sillen, *The Theory and Application of Symbolic Interactionism* (Boston: Houghton Mifflin, 1977), 54. For current data, see Thompson-Miller et al., *Jim Crow's Legacy.*

69. William A. Smith, "Understanding the Corollaries of Offensive Racial Mechanisms, Gendered Racism, and Racial Battle Fatigue" (Research Brief), UCLA Center for Critical Race Studies, June 2016, 2.

70. Feagin and McKinney, *The Many Costs of Racism*, 78. See also Thompson-Miller and Feagin, "Continuing Injuries of Racism," 106–115, italics added.

71. Teletia R. Taylor et al.,,, "Racial Discrimination and Breast Cancer Incidence in US Black Women," *American Journal of Epidemiology* 1 (2007): 46–54; Thompson-Miller et al., *Jim Crow's Legacy.*

72. James Oakes, *The Ruling Race: A History of American Slaveholders* (New York: Vintage Books, 1983); Kenneth M. Stampp, *The Peculiar Institution: Slavery in the Ante-Bellum South* (New York: Vintage Books, 1956), 318–321; Thomas F. Pettigrew, *A Profile of the Negro American* (Princeton, NJ: Van Nostrand, 1964), 99.

73. CDC Newsroom, "African-American Death Rate Drops 25 Percent: Progress Reducing Leading Causes of Death, Still More Are Likely to Die at a Younger Age," Centers for Disease Control and Prevention, May 2, 2017, https://www.cdc.gov/media/releases/2017/p0502-aa-health.html. See also Amadu Jacky Kaba, "Life Expectancy, Death Rates, Geography, and Black People: A Statistical World Overview," *Journal of Black Studies* 39 (2009): 337–347.

74. Tené T. Lewis, Courtney D. Cogburn, and David R. Williams, "Self-Reported Experiences of Discrimination and Health: Scientific Advances, Ongoing Controversies, and Emerging Issues," *Annual Review of Clinical Psychology* 11 (March 2015): 407–440.

75. Feagin and Bennefield, "Systemic Racism and U.S. Health and Health Care," 7–14; and Shaida Kalbasi, "Health Care Discrimination Experiences of Middle Eastern Women," *Women's Health & Urban Life* 13 (2017): 5–19.

76. Rodney Coates, personal communication, November 9, 1995. See also Marilyn Frye, *The Politics of Reality* (Trumansburg, NY: Crossing Press, 1983), 4.

77. See Feagin, *The White Racial Frame*, passim.

78. "Concurring Opinion" in *Jones et ux. v. Alfred H. Mayer Co.*, 392 U.S. 409, 445 (1968).

79. Stevie Watson, Osei Appiah, and Corliss G. Thornton, "The Effect of Name on Pre-Interview Impressions and Occupational Stereotypes: The Case of Black Sales Job Applicants," *Journal of Applied Social Psychology* 41 (2011): 2405–2420; Marc Bendick Jr., Mary Lou Egan, and Louis Lanier, "The 'Business Case for Diversity' and the Pernicious Practice of Matching Employees to Customers" (paper presented at Tenth International Human Resource Management Conference, Santa Fe, NM, June 2009).

80. Gunnar Myrdal, *An American Dilemma* (New York: McGraw-Hill, 1964 [1944]), 1:4.

81. See Oliver C. Cox, *Caste, Class, and Race: A Study in Social Dynamics* (New York: Doubleday, 1948), 531; Feagin and O'Brien, *White Men on Race.*

82. William Lee Miller, *Arguing About Slavery: The Great Battle in the United States Congress* (New York: Knopf, 1996), 10.

83. Joe R. Feagin, *White Party, White Government: Race, Class, and U.S. Politics* (New York: Routledge, 2012).
84. Randolph Hohle, *Racism in the Neoliberal Era* (New York: Routledge, 2018), passim.
85. Huiping Li, Harrison Campbell, and Steven Fernandez, "Residential Segregation, Spatial Mismatch and Economic Growth across U.S. Metropolitan Areas," *Urban Studies* (May 2013): 1–19.
86. Quoted in George J. Church, "The Boom Towns," *Time*, June 15, 1987, 17. This section draws on discussions with Gregory D. Squires.
87. Human Development Report Office, "United States Country Profile: Human Development Indicators," http://hdrstats.undp.org/en/countries/profiles/USA.html.
88. Social Science Research Council, "The Measure of America 2013–2014," June 19, 2013, https://www.measureofamerica.org/measure_of_america2013-2014.

14

The Paradox, Contradictions, Interdependencies, and Stark Realities of Inequality and Freedom

Nancy DiTomaso

The United States celebrates July 4 as a national holiday because this is the day on which the original 13 colonies in 1776 announced in one of the critical founding documents, the Declaration of Independence, that the colonies would no long be subject to the authority of Great Britain. The colonists claimed the right to be free and independent. When Americans think about freedom, they think in terms of their independence from legal authorities that would try to oppress them, take advantage of them, or subject them to taxation without their consent (i.e., "taxation without representation"). They also think in terms of the freedom to follow their own religion without other religious groups imposing their own beliefs or regulations. The Declaration of Independence stated as part of its preamble that "all men are created equal" and hence closely tied their claims to freedom and independence to the notion of equality. But American independence was never this simple, and it was also certainly not equal in terms of the economic, social, or political circumstances for those who shared the continent. The Declaration of Independence actually shows the interdependence among the signers by their final claim to "mutually pledge to each other our Lives, our Fortunes and our sacred Honor."[1] Thus, even in the founding of the country, freedom did not mean individual liberty, but rather embeddedness in a community among people who shared mutual obligations for each other's welfare, including the collective challenge to the authority of the government at the time. Freedom in this conception was about binding together a community of people to throw off the bonds of an oppressive government and to claim the right to self-government through elected leaders. At the time of the Revolutionary War and the signing of the Declaration of Independence, however, only some people were part of the bonds that were forged, in both the colonies and beyond them, and equality of circumstance except for a limited few was never part of the experience of the country.

Nancy DiTomaso, *The Paradox, Contradictions, Interdependencies, and Stark Realities of Inequality and Freedom*
In: *On Inequality and Freedom.* Edited by: Lawrence M. Eppard and Henry A. Giroux, Oxford University Press. © Oxford
University Press 2022. DOI: 10.1093/oso/9780197583029.003.0014

Freedom and Slavery in Ancient Greece

From the outset, therefore, independence actually meant interdependence, and equality had a very narrow intent, which even in that regard, applied only to some men and not to women at all. In a monumental work endeavoring to trace the historical evolution of the concept of freedom, Patterson argued that there are three interrelated ideas of freedom that need to be understood in their relationship to each other: personal, sovereignal, and civic.[2] In Patterson's definitions, personal freedom is the ability to do what you want subject to others wishing to do the same; sovereignal freedom is the ability to do what you want despite what others want; and civic freedom is the ability of adults in a community to participate in its life and governance. According to Patterson, these have been uneven in their importance and in tension with each other at different historical periods and places, but these three types of freedom, in his view, constitute necessary and interrelated components of what we mean when we talk about freedom as a value to be defended.

Patterson argued that the concept of freedom as a central value emerged only in the West, and importantly, he also argued that the value placed on freedom was made possible only because of the existence of slavery under the conditions that were taking place between the sixth and fifth centuries B.C. in Greece, specifically in Athens.[3] In other words, he argued that freedom for some existed only because of the lack of freedom for others. Although slavery existed in all parts of the world, as Patterson has documented in other work,[4] it was only under the conditions that arose at that time in the West that slavery contributed to the value claimed for freedom. In his analysis, two interrelated conditions were needed for freedom to emerge as a central value in the context of chattel slavery, one interpersonal and one social. First, the interpersonal condition is that slaves had to serve a productive role for their masters, which was not a given in many places in the world. Slavery was a spoils of war that was considered as an option only when there was a sufficient social surplus within hunter and gatherer communities to sustain the population, including the slaves. Until that time, the victors in wars often killed the losers so that they could not regroup and fight again.[5] High-status captives might be enslaved to demonstrate the honor and superiority of the victors, although they were often subsequently killed in ritual sacrifices. In some periods, the men were killed, but the women were enslaved to provide household labor or sexual services or to work in the fields (considered women's work at the time).

Once cities became settled and trade became more prevalent as a basis for the economy, male slaves became valued for their work as tradesmen or in agriculture. The evolution of slavery into a productive asset for the slave owners, however, created a problem of how to motivate slaves to work hard enough. Patterson argues that holding out the prospect of manumission was one solution to the problem of motivation. Manumission was not a meaningful incentive, however, if there was no possibility for a freedman to have a life in the community he or she had left or in the new one after having been a slave. Patterson argued that slavery was a form of "social death," meaning that the slave was someone who should have died, but who was allowed to live for a time.[6] Patterson also claimed in his analysis that slaves were natally alienated, meaning that they were considered to have neither a past nor a future. Being enslaved was a dishonor that could not be removed in that those who were socially dead could not socially live again. In this regard, although the slave may have wanted freedom in the sense of not wanting to be a slave, he or she did not want to be free in the sense of being disconnected from a community because there was no viable role for a person without social ties. Life in a community was based on interdependence, especially to ancestors and kin, not on independence.

Second, the social condition for the emergence of freedom as a core value according to Patterson required that there was some benefit to the community as well as to the slave owners. Although each slave had a master, slavery was a practice that was possible only because it was supported by the community, often in hunter and gatherer societies because it symbolically defined the boundaries of the community and provided ritualistic ways to reinforce the meaning of being a community member. As societies became more complex, however, so did the internal divisions within the community, with slaves in a class of their own as socially dead and natally alienated, dishonored persons.[7] Some members of the community benefited more from slavery than did others, contributing to growing tensions between large landowners, small farmers, and others with regard to slavery.[8] An important dimension of those tensions in Greek city states such as Athens, according to Patterson, was that slavery was increasingly an outcome, of not only war, but also debt bondage that included the sale of Greek slaves to foreigners. Further, a combination of factors contributed to enslaving more males than had been the case previously because of the labor they could provide.

As the population grew, the productivity of grain harvests declined, making it difficult for many in the population to feed themselves. The elite landowners also began to shift their production from grain to olives and fruit, which could earn more when traded abroad but also required more labor and did not provide the needed food for the local population. All of these factors led to an increase in the proportion of slaves in the community. Contrary to seeing slavery as benefiting them, freeborn Greek small farmers saw slaves as competition and also as a threat to their way of life. The labor needs of large landowners could not be resolved with freeborn persons because, Patterson argued, as slavery grew as a dishonored state and played a greater role in economic production, freeborn small farmers were increasingly disdainful toward manual labor, especially in the form of working as hired laborers for others. That made slavery both more necessary to maintain productivity for the landed elite but also more scandalous for the freeborn population. It is in this context that Patterson argued that slavery was a foundation for the emergence of freedom as a core value.

Patterson argued, for example, that the existence of slavery contributed to a more explicit conception of personal freedom, both as a yearning of the slave and as an honor in contrast for the freeborn. The growing presence of slavery as a source of labor and its dishonor contributed to both a sense of superiority for the freeborn and a sense of threat about what was at stake if wars were lost or debt became more burdensome. As a consequence, conflict intensified among the landed elite, the small farmers, an emerging commercial class, and a growing number of slaves freed by manumission, all in the context of the increasingly large number of slaves created both out of war and debt bondage. These tensions created unrest that over time led to efforts to reduce or forgive debts and, importantly, to an extension of civic freedom to freeborn small farmers in exchange for their loyalty to the political system. A shift as well from representation in governance structures by clans or kinship to representation based on residence, which was part of the reforms that were introduced in Greece during this period, has also been seen as a precursor to the birth of democracy (i.e., to civic freedom). Patterson argued that the expansion of representation in the government, albeit quite limited for small farmers and others, reduced the tensions between the lower classes and the landed elite, but it also contributed to antagonism between the freeborn and slaves and freedmen in ways that helped control the slaves on behalf of the landed elite who were the slave owners. The newfound civic freedom for small farmers, however, only applied to men, not to women or slaves. As in the birth of the United States, freedom for "all" actually meant freedom for those who met limited criteria of both wealth and gender, and only for those who were freeborn.

Slavery and Freedom in the Development of the United States

This particular story about the birth of "freedom" in ancient Greece turns out not to be isolated historically, although only two examples are addressed in this analysis. Especially in the West, at different times and places the needs of the landed elite for labor and the limitations in their ability to subordinate, exploit, and subjugate their own countrymen contributed to ongoing political conflicts among different class and status groups. This conflict led, on the one hand, to slavery or at later times other slave-like conditions, and on the other hand, to an exchange of freedom for loyalty to and reduced conflict with the dominant class among freeborn status groups. Across history, conflicts frequently centered on the need by dominant groups for labor to support their economic privileges. In some parts of the world, these labor needs were resolved by enslavement, while in other parts of the world, labor was provided by slave-like conditions from those who were technically not slaves.[9] Especially in the West, freedom and equality were values that were promoted for the freeborn in a given society but at the expense of the enslavement or subjugation of others.

In addition to his accounts of the connection between freedom and slavery in ancient Greece, Patterson also discussed freedom and slavery in the Roman Republic, the Roman Empire, and through the Middle Ages.[10] Morgan provided a similar account of freedom and slavery in colonial Virginia.[11] That is, consistent with the argument that Patterson developed more generally in his recounting of how slavery provided a foundation for the emergence of freedom in the ancient and medieval West, Morgan argued that slavery and freedom were inherently interlinked in the development of the United States as well.[12] There are similar themes to the arguments offered by Patterson and Morgan, although they were writing about very distant historical cases separated by about 2000 years. Morgan (whose book was published about a decade earlier than Patterson's) calls it the "central paradox of American history" that the "rise of liberty and equality in this country was accompanied by the rise of slavery."[13] Morgan noted that for many years historians considered slavery in a country that claimed the ideals of freedom and democracy as an aberration or "an exception" to the values such as those articulated in the Declaration of Independence.[14] But Morgan discovered in his own analysis that slavery was not an exception or an aberration. Rather, he argued that it was fundamental to and necessary for the development of the freedom demanded by large landholders, who were delegates to the Continental Congress that declared themselves free of the authority of Great Britain and who had claimed that "all men are created equal." Morgan argued that slavery solved the "problem" of having a large group of landless poor who might organize and threaten the landed elite. Large landowners solved this problem, as described by Morgan, by completely subjugating the newly enslaved, keeping them from any possibility of organizing, and creating laws that made slavery of mutual benefit to both large landowners and small farmers. Morgan explained that the confluence of slavery and freedom in colonial Virginia was integral to the development of the United States as a whole[15]:

> There it was. Aristocrats could more safely preach equality in a slave society than in a free one. Slaves did not become leveling mobs, because their owners would see to it that they had no chance to. The apostrophes to equality were not addressed to them. And because Virginia's labor force was composed mainly of

slaves, who had been isolated by race and removed from the political equation, the remaining free laborers and tenant farmers were too few in number to constitute a serious threat to the superiority of the men who assured them of their equality. Moreover, the small farmers had been given a reason to see themselves as already the equals of the large. . . .

In the republican way of thinking as Americans inherited it from England, slavery occupied a critical, if ambiguous, position: it was the primary evil that men sought to avoid for society as a whole by curbing monarchs and establishing republics. But it was also the solution to one of society's most serious problems, the problem of the poor. Virginians could outdo English republicans as well as New England ones, partly because they had solved the problem: they had achieved a society in which most of the poor were enslaved.

The need for labor was central to the viability of the colonies, but especially for the wealth accumulation of those granted large parcels of land. All of the industries that were fundamental to the development of the "new world"—tobacco, sugar, and ultimately cotton—were labor intensive and required hard and dangerous work. The initial solution was the use of indentured laborers, sent to the colonies both voluntarily and through the system of "transportation" (as punishment for those accused of crimes) that England used to rid itself of an excess population of the landless poor. Various accounts suggest that the lives of indentured servants in colonial America were not measurably better than those of slaves who substituted for them.[16] Indentured servants were mistreated, poorly fed, severely punished, and could even be bought and sold to others. Further, small infractions could lead to extending the period of indenture, whether real or fabricated. Morgan also argued that a large proportion of those who came as indentured servants died from the harsh conditions or disease, so many did not make it to the end of their indentured period. At the end of their term of service, indentured servants were supposed to be provided with land and a payment that would enable them to establish themselves, but for many these were false promises.[17] Because of the monopolization of land by the aristocrats, even when indentured servants were able to obtain land, it was often on the outskirts of the colonies, where there were more threats from conflicts with Native Americans. Although the colonists, especially the large landholders, were desperate for workers, the use of indentured servants soon became problematic because they resisted the subjugation, were unable to support themselves as independent farmers if they lived to the end of their service, and were a source of disorder and threat to the large landowners who employed them. In a sense, according to Morgan, England exported the problems of their landless poor to the colonies. The large tracts of land granted to the elite required substantial labor to make them profitable, and as large landowners extended their holdings, they pushed those who finished their indentured periods further into the wilderness and closer to conflict with Native Americans. As a consequence, former indentured servants were also dangerous because they needed to have guns to protect from Indian attacks, but they could also organize and use those guns to challenge the authority of the landed elite.

In this context, according to Morgan, slavery became an attractive alternative to meet the labor needs of large landowners and to resolve the growing conflict created by the large number of indentured servants who came to the end of their contracts but were not able to succeed on their own. Although slaves were initially more expensive than indentured servants, slaves had the advantage of not having an end date to their service. Slaves could also be more thoroughly subjugated in ways that were increasingly restricted toward indentured servants. In response to growing rowdiness and disorder among former indentured servants, the landed elite who controlled the governmental bodies in Virginia began to pass legislation that increasingly differentiated the treatment of slaves from that of servants as a means to appease the growing unrest of the indentured servants. In the ensuing legislation, slaves were no longer able to own property of their own or to have representation in courts, and intermarriage, which had been prevalent until that point, was outlawed. Even free blacks were stripped of rights that they had previously held. Large landholders had been harsh with indentured servants, but they became especially so with slaves. As new legislation removed slaves from any rights that had ostensibly restrained their behavior toward indentured servants, slave owners addressed the challenge of trying to motivate slaves to work hard primarily through a punishment system based on the threat of pain. Unlike in ancient Greece and Rome, there were no incentives for eventual freedom offered through manumission.

Morgan argued that these measures had the result of drawing large and small landowners together in a sense of common fate that differentiated Whites and Christians from those who were neither. In a sense, the landowners were able through these measures to pay off the former indentured servants and small landowners with the "wages of whiteness."[18] Although slavery had existed in most places in the world, it was not for most of that history based on skin color, in part because slaves were often captives in wars with those who were in proximate territories. Once technologies such as shipbuilding, navigation, and new types of weaponry made it possible to sail across oceans, the African slave trade became feasible and increasingly replaced indentured servitude as a source of needed labor. Smedley argued that the need to resolve the disorder in the colonies was thought increasingly urgent,[19] especially after Bacon's Rebellion in 1676, which involved not only former indentured servants but also African slaves in challenging the authority of Governor William Berkeley.[20] Wealthy landowners were so alarmed by this coalition of former indentured servants and slaves and by the violence of their attacks that they felt it necessary to pass laws that differentiated the treatment of slaves from servants to try to undermine any future coalition building among them. By 1691, the colonists began to refer specifically to being White in association with being Christian, which contributed to the confluence of Black skin color with slavery and racism going forward.[21] The 1705 Slave Codes set apart "negros, mulattos, or Indians, although Christians, or Jews, Moors, Mahometans, and other infidels" from Christian Europeans for greater restrictions, stripping them of rights to which they had previously been entitled and undermining both their independence and their ability to develop resources.[22] Note that although these statutes preserved rights for Christians that were denied to those who were not, if African slaves adopted Christianity, they were not able thereby to gain any of the rights that were otherwise reserved for "White" Christians.[23]

There was some effort among colonists to enslave Native Americans as well as Africans, but those efforts were not as successful. Native Americans both resisted enslavement and posed a threat of violence from surrounding tribes. If captured and enslaved, Native Americans had the prospect of running away to rejoin their tribes and therefore also to join again in fighting the colonists. Native Americans were also decimated by diseases that the Europeans had brought with them and to which they were not immune. The strategies toward Native Americans, therefore, often were to kill them or, in some cases, to capture them and sell them into slavery in the Caribbean. In fact, Bacon's Rebellion involved efforts to gain rights to kill Native Americans to protect the frontier areas. The inability to count on subjugating Native Americans to serve as a labor force for the colonists contributed to the enthusiasm for importing African slaves, who could not run away to rejoin their communities of origin and who were more vulnerable because the color of their skin made them more easily identifiable as slaves.[24]

The enslavement of Africans and the attempted enslavement of Native Americans were not seen as contradictory to the promotion of freedom and equality for Whites and Christians. Morgan suggested that shifting labor primarily to slaves both reduced the tensions between large and small landowners and provided an everyday demonstration of what the loss of liberty could mean. He argued that the colonists who feared the tyranny of monarchs and who wanted to declare their freedom from tyranny for themselves at the same time supported and participated in the enslavement of those they considered as unlike themselves. African slaves were described as property just like animals or "real estate." Over the course of the seventeenth century, whatever rights slaves may have had previously were removed, including by the early eighteenth century any possibility of manumission. Thus, the problem posed by the "poor," as described by Morgan, was resolved by slavery.

Prior to the large-scale development of slavery in Virginia and elsewhere in the colonies, Morgan described the disdain for the landless poor in both Great Britain and in the colonies.[25] The same men who were organizing themselves to resist the potential tyranny of monarchs by claiming the rights of freedom and equality for themselves were at the same time fearful of poor people who had no means to support themselves except by working for others as hired labor or through public charity. The freedom promised by a republican form of government was intended only for landowners, large or small, while the landless poor were expected to serve others until they could purchase land for themselves or be given it as part of the indentured contract. Morgan described the commentary prominent in England among those advocating a republican government prior to the American Revolution about the need to enslave the poor or at least to force them into labor in workhouses, indenture, or being impressed into the military. There was fear among scholars of republican government and by the Founding Fathers of the United States of those who were dependent on others for their survival. They feared that the landless poor could be bought off by tyrants or scoundrels by bread or bribes and, therefore, denied them the right to vote. Hence, the initial requirement that enfranchisement was available only to property owners. According to Morgan, the large number of indentured servants from Europe brought the problems of poverty from England to the colonies, while the substitution of indentured servants by African slaves resolved the immediate problem of disruption and dissent, although not subsequent fear of slave revolts.[26] As the numbers of slaves grew, there was less need for indentured servants, and as the colonists extended further west into the lands of Native Americans, it was more possible to provide land or to absorb the former indentured servants into the economy. Slavery, therefore, made it unnecessary further to hold indentured servants in slave-like conditions. Slavery also both spurred concern for freedom from the tyranny of Great Britain and reminded the colonists of the fate they were trying to avoid.

Freedom, Slavery, and Slave-like Alternatives

Patterson and Morgan told similar stories about the emergence of freedom and its relationship to slavery in very different contexts. They outlined the need of large landowners for labor that could not be addressed by hiring their own countrymen without creating a population of landless poor and thereby, in the view of the landed elite, contribute to growing unrest that might threaten their power and control. In that context, slave labor filled labor needs, but created additional fissures within the society, especially when small farmers could not compete with slave labor or became themselves indebted to the landed elite and at risk of debt bondage. Both small farmers and the landless poor posed a threat to large land-owners. When unrest mounted, and especially the threat of armed conflict to-ward the landed elite, demands for redress contributed to reforms that extended freedom for the freeborn but the enslavement of others. That is, the creation of slave societies contributed to the birth of freedom for the slave owners and their fellow countrymen at the expense of those enslaved.

While these two cases are two millennia apart, they underline the complex-ities of domination. Slavery existed all over the world even before the period of ancient Greece, usually as a consequence of war or conquest. And slavery con-tinued into the nineteenth century and in various forms to the present. Both slavery and its alternatives, however, invoked resistance and the threat of revolt, and its contradictions contributed to unrest among those in lower estates. Slavery also has several distinct disadvantages. Perhaps most notable is that slaves have no incentive to work hard. Two alternative solutions were used to motivate slave labor, either the eventual promise of manumission after many years of service or the use of extreme violence and its threat. Neither of these solutions, however, re-solved the contradictions that were created by the juxtaposition of freedom with slavery. Patterson argued that in ancient Greece and later in the Roman Empire manumission after a long term of service was offered as a means to motivate slaves to work harder, but the growing proportion of both slaves and freedmen created tensions with small farmers that eventually led to an expansion of civic freedom for the small farmers. In colonial Virginia, the inability to fulfill the promises to indentured servants to provide them with land and enough support so they could establish themselves as independent farmers led to unrest and the threat-ening prospect that servants and slaves might band together to overthrow the rule of the large landowners. In this circumstance, the landed elite took actions to try to divide servants and slaves, hoping to solve the problem of having a po-tentially unruly group of landless poor. Unlike in Greece and Rome, however, the Virginia Assembly, which was made up of large landowners, outlawed man-umission, leaving slave owners only the pathway of extreme and often capricious violence as a means to induce the slaves to work harder.[27] Desmond argued that to maximize the return on their investments, slave owners developed accounting methods that kept close track of how much work each slave contributed, and he argues that unpredictable violence was part of this system.[28]

The effort to solve the labor needs of large landowners created the conditions in both of these cases, as well as in others, for the birth of freedom on a foundation of slavery, but also created contradictions, stresses, and interdependencies. The two solutions to the inefficiencies of slavery, the promise of manumission or the threat of violence, both created problems for slave owners. Offering inducements to indentured servants or manumission to freed slaves created a set of obligations that the landowners either could not or did not want to fulfill, and both invoked opposition from small landowners. The use of violence invoked the possibility of resistance and even the threat of revolt, which the large landowners feared. The solution in both of these cases was to reduce the need for hired labor by the adoption of slavery and then to buy the acquiescence of small landowners by expanding their civic freedom while using more extreme forms of subjugation for slaves. Gaining the support of small farmers for the expansion of slavery required that they both gain civic freedom and see a benefit for themselves of a slave system, which was the hope of large landowners but not always the outcome. Further, the promotion of a doctrine of freedom and equality as a means to buy off the loyalty of small famers, although intended only for the freeborn, contributed in both ancient Greece and colonial Virginia, as in other historical cases, to inherent contradictions for the rulers who had to disperse power in order to keep it.

The ideology of freedom as a central value required not only a slave system built on extreme violence, but also an ideology that demarcated slaves from others and endeavored to justify the distinction. The more the ideology of freedom came to be accepted as a fundamental value, however, the more it contributed at various times to countermovements of both abolition and resistance. The contradictions of slavery and freedom created both administrative challenges and ideological ones, both overlaid on a structure of inequality that frequently led to unrest if not to revolt. These conditions created demands for redistribution that often undermined the ability for elites to hold on to power.

Bendix[29] argued, for example, that for empires to grow they required an administrative structure that forced sharing of responsibility across people and regions. This distribution of power to others required accommodations from emperors or kings to local rulers, who then became an alternative base of power. Bendix further argued that the need to share responsibility for oversight of conquered territory and people contributed substantially to the transition, albeit slowly and often with violent conflicts, in many places in the world from the authority of "kings" to the authority of "people," that is, from absolutism to democracy. As Bendix explained[30]:

> In theory the ruler owned the whole realm, but in practice the territorial possessions of the royal house were the main source of revenue and of favors in peace and war. These possessions were scattered, and the realm as a whole was governed through various forms of delegation. Rulers were typically torn between the need to delegate authority and the desire not to lose it.

Bendix noted that tyrants were better able to hold on to control when their positions were overlaid with religious justifications such as the divine right of kings or claims to be descendants of the gods. But these ideological or religious claims eroded with the dispersal of power to others.

As Bendix described it, administering an empire often required forming alliances, risking trust in others, as well as appealing to higher principles. Bendix cited Rousseau to explain the challenges: "The strongest are still never sufficiently strong to ensure them continual mastership, unless they find means of transforming force into right, and obedience into duty."[31] While "kings" everywhere endeavored to claim their legitimacy through their relationship to gods, that did not protect them from constant challengers to the throne and from palace intrigues. Bendix gave the example of the century between 180 and 285 C.E. in the Roman Empire in which he explained that "thirty different emperors were put on the throne and few of them died a natural death."[32] The existence of a landed elite itself (i.e., an aristocracy) reflects the need for the division of authority and the multiple bases of power that arose in the efforts to administer empires or kingdoms. In the process of expanding governance structures in ways that endeavored to secure the authority of kings, they faced constant resistance, which required that they often granted rights to members of the aristocracy and eventually to lower classes. Tilly[33] explained the widespread resistance that was prevalent throughout European state-making:

> Most of the European population resisted each phase of the creation of strong states. Our analyses of taxation, of food supply, and (less directly) of policing show that the resistance was often concerted, determined, violent, and threatening to the holders of power. The prevalence of tax rebellions, food riots, movements against conscription, and related forms of protest during the great periods of state-making help gauge the amount of coercion it took to bring people under the state's effective control.

Bendix argued that it was increasingly hard for monarchs to hold on to unquestioned power in the West, especially after 1500 C.E. in the context of wars for religious freedom and after the Reformation weakened the central power of the Catholic Church in its interrelations with monarchies across the European continent.[34] Bendix noted that in addition to the Reformation and the fight for religious freedom that undermined the authority of the Catholic Church hierarchy, the rise of humanism in intellectual thought, the invention of the printing press, and the growth of modern science all contributed to avenues for questioning the authority of monarchies.[35] Those who challenged the authority of kings did so on the growing claims about the "rights of man."

Thus, the administrative problems of empires were overlaid with ideological problems in justifying or legitimating the rule of monarchs.[36] The need to share power to administer empires led to ideological solutions to expand freedom that also created social movements for democracy. Claims about the "rights of man," as exemplified in what is called the "social contract," even when limited to freeborn, adult, White, Christian, landowning men, created fuel for social movements that unsettled the landed elite and led others to expect greater freedom. The limitations and inconsistencies of claims about natural rights and universal freedom, however, were, indeed, ideologies, not descriptions of historical facts. Mills[37] argued that the social contract that supported the opposition to the presumed tyranny of European monarchies and in the name of universal rights demanded freedom in the form of self-government was actually a "racial contract" that enabled some men to enjoy rights only through the exploitation of others.

In this regard, Mills's argument is consistent with those of both Patterson and Morgan about the interrelationship of slavery and freedom. The social contract as outlined by the major scholars of the Enlightenment contributed to the justification for both the American and French Revolutions on the claims that all men were endowed with natural rights and that they gave up those rights to a government in order to protect themselves from wrongdoing by others and, importantly, to restrain the exploitation—or tyranny—by government itself. According to social contract theory, when government fails to protect those rights or abuses them, then those with natural rights have justification to rebel and to reform the government or to change it.

Mills argued, however, that social contract theory was always based on false premises and, importantly, that it was based on what he claimed was an "epistemology of ignorance" that produces "the ironic outcome that whites will in general be unable to understand the world they themselves have made."[38] According to Mills, the racial contract is a contract of White supremacy that takes for granted that Whites, with whatever boundaries were drawn around groups to define them as White versus non-White, are superior and thus entitled to freedom and equality, while non-Whites are considered subhuman or "other" and hence appropriate targets for exploitation. As Mills described it: "The general purpose of the [racial] Contract is always the differential privileging of the whites as a group with respect to nonwhites as a group, the exploitation of their bodies, land, and resources, and the denial of equal socioeconomic opportunities to them."[39]

The attitudes toward the enslavement of Africans coincided at this time with similar attitudes toward the poor. Morgan described Enlightenment thinking in Great Britain as justifying the enslavement of the landless poor, suggesting that they could only be redeemed by work.[40] As an example, Morgan explained[41]:

John Locke, who wrote the classic defense of the right of revolution, does not seem to have thought of extending that right to the poor. His proposals for working schools where the children of the poor would learn labor—and nothing but labor—from the age of three stopped a little short of enslavement, though it may require a certain refinement of mind to discern the difference.

The development of the African slave trade to provide labor for large land-owners in colonial Virginia and elsewhere, however, enabled a more generous view of the English poor, eventually even the Catholic Irish, but a solidification of the attitudes toward non-Whites as barbarians who did not make good use of their land and the resources around them. The racial contract included the assumption that Whites brought civilization to people who did not exhibit it, that White settlers and colonizers made productive use of resources that the non-White barbarians squandered, and that the profits derived from the work of non-Whites, as slaves in colonial America or as subjects of colonial regimes around the world were rightfully for the benefit of Whites. Mills noted that, iron-ically, while social contract theory is based on a hypothetical state of nature that occurred in some mythical time in the far distant past, the racial contract is based on real historical events that are easily documented, even if not a conscious part of the understanding of Whites of their own history.[42]

Thus, those who point with pride to the claims of the Declaration of Independence about inalienable rights and freedom for all ignore the real his-tory of the founding of the United States and much of its history since. As Mills noted,[43] what had been domination based on geography, religion, or culture all were subordinated into racial domination through which Whites believed them-selves to be superior to all non-Whites and that they were entitled to rule over them, exploit them, and even enslave, kill, or exterminate them. The competition among European powers to colonize during this period led to their domination over about 85% of the world, and the legacies of this history still affect the social, political, and economic conditions of the present.[44] In telling this history, Whites tout the special qualities of Europeans in terms of their motivation, technology, and moral superiority to explain why White-led countries are currently more developed, richer, and indeed more democratic than the rest of the world. Mills reminded us that from the perspective of the racial contract there is a different reality, not just a different interpretation. As he noted[45]:

> The basic theme is that the exploitation of the empire (the bullion from the great gold and silver mines in Mexico and Peru, the profits from planation slavery, the fortune made by the colonial companies, the general social and economic stimulus provided by the opening up of the "New World") was to a greater or lesser extent crucial in enabling and then consolidating the takeoff of what had previously been an economic backwater. . . . Overall, then, colonialism "lies at the heart" of the rise of Europe.

Of course, the history of colonialism and imperialism did not eliminate dissen-sion and unrest among Whites. Although the invention of a racial hierarchy and the formulation of the concept of "White people" created a new form of domination,[46] from the outset and continuing for centuries after, there has been fluidity in terms of who is counted as White and allowed to be included within the category of superior people.

The U.S. "Founding Father" Thomas Jefferson was a slaveholder who was rumored to have had a long-term sexual relationship with one of his slaves, Sally Hemings. Jefferson was steeped in the writings of the Enlightenment and drew from the ideas about the social contract as the principal author of the Declaration of Independence in 1776. Further, before being elected the third president of the United States, Jefferson was appointed as an envoy to France for the 5 years just before the French Revolution in 1789. While in France, Jefferson helped with the drafting of the French Declaration of the Rights of Man and of the Citizen, and then he returned to the United States just after the beginning of the French Revolution. The U.S. Declaration of Independence focused on the rights to "life, liberty, and the pursuit of happiness," whereas in the French Declaration, natural rights were defined as "liberty, property, safety and resistance against oppression," and it even included a separate article stating that property is "an inviolable and sacred right."[47] In the expression of the "social contract" in the U.S. declaration, the allusions to freedom and equality were intended only for men, for Whites, and for those who held property.

Although Jefferson discussed in some of his writings the possibility of freeing slaves, he did not support doing so, and he assumed that if slaves were ever to be freed, then they would have to leave the United States and presumably return to Africa. According to Morgan, Jefferson was concerned with the threats of having a large group of landless poor, whether freed slaves or indentured servants.[48] Jefferson, along with others of the Founding Fathers, believed that both the landless poor and freed slaves posed a threat to the republic that they were trying to create. They feared that those who could not support themselves by working their own land would have to rely on charity or on crime. Most importantly, they feared that the lack of independence for those without land to work to support themselves also meant, in the views of Jefferson and the other Founding Fathers, that those who were landless could be bought by tyrants and that they would undermine the freedom for which the Revolution was fought. According to Morgan, this fear created a direct link between the creation of African slavery and their own fight for freedom. As he noted[49]: "Racism became an essential, if unacknowledged, ingredient of the republican ideology that enabled Virginians to lead the nation."

It is especially ironic, therefore, that already by the time of the American Revolution, the Industrial Revolution and the creation of an industrial working class that was both landless and poor was well under way in both England and the American colonies. And as predicted, their poverty, hunger, and overall desperation did lead to efforts to both organize and challenge the authority of not only large landowners, but also company owners and governmental authorities. The situation of newly created factory workers and miners was often characterized as "wage slavery." Indeed, as the largest industry to develop in the early period of the Industrial Revolution was textiles, there was a close link between the lives of landless workers in factories and slaves on plantations.[50] The growing of cotton became an even more lucrative business for slave owners than had been tobacco, and the productivity from cotton plantations fed the mills that produced textiles for both the American and the British markets.

The growth of the cotton industry was intimately tied to slavery; to industrial production and landless factory workers; to colonialism and imperialism, notably in India, as well as in the Americas; to the westward expansion of the United States further into Indian territory; and ultimately to the Civil War as the fight over whether slavery would be expanded into these new territories became a central point of conflict between the southern and northern states. Jefferson's ties to France perhaps contributed once he became the U.S. president to his overseeing of the Louisiana Purchase in 1803. Jefferson envisioned the new land as a means to expand the population of small farmers as landowners to further secure his notion of what a "free" republic required. The purchase of Louisiana, as a side note, was related to the inability of France to defeat the slave revolt in Saint-Domingue (now Haiti), where slaves ultimately obtained their freedom in 1804. Rather than preserving the United States as a country of small farmers, the growth of the cotton industry strengthened the commitment in the South to slavery, accelerated the Industrial Revolution, and tied the United States to the colonial and imperialist expansion around the world. As Beckert noted in his study of cotton and world capitalism[51]: "The empire of cotton was, from the beginning, a site of constant global struggle between slaves and planters, merchants and statesmen, farmers and merchants, workers and factory owners. In this as in so many other ways, the empire of cotton ushered in the modern world."

It is worth noting that although slavery was outlawed in Great Britain in 1807, it continued in other parts of the British Empire (notably in the Caribbean) until 1833, and throughout the time of slavery in the United States, British investors continued to benefit greatly from the growth of "King Cotton." The United States similarly banned the importation of slaves in 1808, but it did not end slavery. Thus, even when the slave trade was outlawed, it continued for many years. Further, the end of slavery did not end the need of large landowners and subsequently large factory owners or mine operators for cheap and subservient labor. The contradictions of slavery and freedom continued in other forms once slavery itself ended. As suggested by Mills's articulation of the racial contract,[52] those involved in the slave trade and the slave owners themselves believed that they were justified in their actions because they were the exemplars of civilization.[53] Slave owners believed that they were enslaving barbarians or savages who did not deserve to rule themselves. But Davis argued that ironically those who supported and promoted the abolition of slavery did so under a theory of progress that at the same time justified the expansion of colonialism and the domination of European powers as a means of bringing salvation and civilization to the world. As Davis noted[54]: "But if religious mission could originally justify the enslavement of millions of Africans for the good of their souls, it could later justify the subjection of 'backward' peoples to colonial rule for the good of their civilization." Davis made the rather startling claim[55]: "It was not the enslavers who colonized and subjugated Africa, but the European liberators."

As Davis described it, there were just as many contradictions in the history of emancipation as in the history of slavery itself, and in many places and circumstances, slave-like conditions prevailed when slavery could not. This was true in the United States, as Blackmon explained in his book *Slavery by Another Name*.[56] In colonial America, indentured servants were treated much like slaves until their unrest extended some modicum of civic freedom in exchange for their support of African slavery. The system of transportation, in which England rid itself of its poor by arresting them for vagrancy and petty crimes and then sending them to the colonies in the United States, Brazil, and Australia to serve out their sentences in hard labor, was certainly slave-like. The use of poorhouses or workhouses, debtor's prisons and other forms of debt bondage, and the extension of this concept into a system of convict labor existed in the United States and in many other places in the world, both before and after the Civil War. Company towns also facilitated a type of forced labor by progressively indebting workers to mine owners so that they could not leave. Systems of contract labor around the world, often with false promises of good jobs and wages, have ended up in extremely exploitative conditions, even today, for example, in the Middle East. Serfdom continues even now in some places in the world. Further, the practice of selling children to pay debts or "selling daughters as wives, servants, or prostitutes" has been widespread as well.[57] As Davis noted, the effort to emancipate slaves around the world often encountered the broader problem of human rights "in a world plagued by destitution, growing inequality, and political tyranny."[58] Some might add to this list of exploitative labor the circumstances for undocumented immigrants in both the United States and other parts of the world, where they exist without protection and often without rights.

Conclusions

The promise of freedom has always depended on to whom the promises are relevant. The social movements that claimed that freedom was a fundamental right that was natural and inalienable was at the time intended only for men, for property owners, for (some) Whites, and for citizens. At the outset, such claims left out women, non-Whites, and foreigners. It took centuries of struggle by groups who were excluded to gain the promises of freedom, and that struggle continues all over the world. The efforts to make such promises real, however, have often been undermined because of the failure to actually link freedom to equality. The extent of inequality threatens the ability of people who are poor and desperate to protect themselves from exploitation and from being subjected to conditions that leave them little room for the kind of human growth and prosperity expected and promised, for example, by the Declaration of Independence.

Even the efforts to extend the concept of freedom and equality, for example, in the 1948 Universal Declaration of Human Rights, which arose from a committee of the United Nations chaired by Eleanor Roosevelt, faltered as with other efforts because of concerns that rights would be granted in some countries and under some political or religious systems to those who were not thought of as entitled to such rights. Although adopted by 48 of the 58 members of the United Nations at the time, the declaration was not considered binding and, indeed, has often been violated by countries around the world. The promise of freedom, combined with meaningful equality, are still works in progress that will continue, undoubtedly, through the political struggle of those who have not been able to claim such rights. The struggle for freedom and equality for all is not likely to ever be a settled issue, but most likely each new generation will need to fight for and defend their "natural" rights on behalf of themselves and others in the country and around the world.

Notes

1. U.S. Declaration of Independence.
2. Orlando Patterson. *Freedom Volume 1: Freedom in the Making of Western Culture* (New York, NY: Basic Books, 1991).
3. Patterson, *Freedom Volume 1*.
4. Orlando Patterson, *Slavery and Social Death: A Comparative Study* (Cambridge, MA: Harvard University Press, 1982).
5. Reinhard Bendix, *Kings or People: Power and the Mandate to Rule* (Berkeley, CA: University of California Press, 1978).
6. Patterson, *Slavery and Social Death*.
7. Patterson, *Freedom Volume 1*.
8. Patterson, *Freedom Volume 1*.
9. David Brion Davis, *Slavery and Human Progress* (New York,: Oxford University Press, 1984).
10. Patterson, *Freedom Volume 1*.

11. Edmund S. Morgan, "Slavery and Freedom: The American Paradox," *Journal of American History* 59, no. 1 (1972): 5–29; Edmund S. Morgan, *American Slavery, American Freedom* (New York: W. W. Norton, 1975).

12. Morgan, *American Slavery, American Freedom*.

13. Morgan, "Slavery and Freedom," 5–6.

14. Morgan, "Slavery and Freedom," 5.

15. Morgan, *American Slavery, American Freedom*, 380–381.

16. Audrey Smedley, *Race in North America: Origin and Evolution of a Worldview* (Boulder, CO: Westview Press, 2007).

17. Morgan, "Slavery and Freedom."

18. W. E. Burghardt Du Bois, *Black Reconstruction in America, 1860–1880* (New York: Atheneum, 1992 [1935, 1962]); David R. Roediger, *The Wages of Whiteness: Race and the Making of the American Working Class* (London: Verso Press, 1991).

19. Smedley, *Race in North America*.

20. Morgan, *American Slavery, American Freedom*.

21. Smedley, *Race in North America*.

22. General Assembly, "An Act Concerning Servants and Slaves," 1705, https://www.encyclopediavirginia.org/_An_act_concerning_Servants_and_Slaves_1705.

23. Nell Irvin Painter, *The History of White People* (New York, NY: W. W. Norton, 2011).

24. Morgan, *American Slavery, American Freedom*.

25. Morgan, *American Slavery, American Freedom*.

26. Morgan, "Slavery and Freedom."

27. Morgan, *American Slavery, American Freedom*, 337.

28. Matthew Desmond, "In Order to Understand the Brutality of American Capitalism, You Have to Start on the Plantation," New York Times Magazine, the 1619 Project (2019).

29. Reinhard Bendix, *Kings or People: Power and the Mandate to Rule* (Berkeley: University of California Press, 1978).

30. Bendix, *Kings or People*, 7.

31. Bendix, *Kings or People*, 8, citing Jean Jacques Rousseau, The Social Contract (New York: Hafner, 1957), 8–9.

32. Bendix, *Kings or People*, 23.

33. Charles Tilly, ed., *The Formation of Nation States in Western Europe* (Princeton, NJ: Princeton University Press, 1975), 72.

34. Bendix, *Kings or People*.

35. Bendix, *Kings or People*, 10.

36. Thomas Piketty, *Capital and Ideology*, trans. Arthur Goldhammer (Cambridge, MA: The Belknap Press of Harvard University Press, 2020).

37. Charles W. Mills, *The Racial Contract* (Ithaca, NY: Cornell University Press, 1997); Thomas Hobbes, *Leviathan*, ed. Richard Tucker (Cambridge: Cambridge University Press, 1991); John Locke, *Two Treatises of Government*, ed. Peter Laslett (Cambridge: Cambridge University Press, 1960); Jean-Jacques Rousseau, *Discourse on the Origins and Foundations of Inequality Among* Men, trans. Maurice Cranston

(London: Penguin, 1984); Rousseau, *The Social Contract*; Immanuel Kant, *The Metaphysics of Morals*, trans. Mary Gregor (Cambridge: Cambridge University Press, 1991).

38. Mills, *The Racial Contract*, 18.
39. Mills, *The Racial Contract*, 11.
40. Morgan, *American Slavery, American Freedom*, 381–382.
41. Morgan, *American Slavery, American Freedom*, 381.
42. Mills, *The Racial Contract*, 19–31.
43. Mills, *The Racial Contract*, 21.
44. Piketty, *Capital and Ideology*.
45. Mills, *The Racial Contract*, 34–35.
46. Painter, Nell Irvin. 2011. *The History of White People*; Allen, Theodore W. 1994. *The Invention of the White Race*. Vol. 1. London: Verso Press; Allen, Theodore W. 1997. *The Invention of the White Race*. Vol. 2. London: Verso Press; Ignatiev, Noel. 2008. *How the Irish Became White*. New York, NY: Routledge; Roediger, David R. 1991. *The Wages of Whiteness: Race and the Making of the American Working Class*. London: Verso Press.
47. Although there was some discussion in the activities surrounding the French Revolution about extending rights to those without property, their declaration made clear that property was to be protected as a natural right. There was also discussion about the abolition of slavery in French colonies and an effort to extend the rights of the French Declaration to women, but the advocate for women's rights, Olympe de Gouges, was arrested and executed on the charge that her ideas were counter-revolutionary.
48. Morgan, Edmund, 1975, *American Slavery, American Freedom*, pp. 384-387.
49. Morgan, Edmund, 1975, *American Slavery, American Freedom*, p. 386.
50. Sven Beckert, *Empire of Cotton: A Global History* (New York: Alfred A. Knopf, 2014); Walter Johnson, *River of Dark Dreams: Slavery and Empire in the Cotton Kingdom* (Cambridge, MA: Belknap Press of Harvard University Press, 2013).
51. Beckert, *Empire of Cotton*, xii.
52. Mills, *The Racial Contract*.
53. Davis, *Slavery and Human Progress*.
54. Davis, *Slavery and Human Progress*, xviii.
55. Davis, *Slavery and Human Progress*, xvii.
56. Douglas A. Blackmon, *Slavery by Another Name: The Re-enslavement of Black Americans From the Civil War to World War II* (New York: Anchor Books, 2008).
57. Davis, *Slavery and Human Progress*, 318.
58. Davis, *Slavery and Human Progress*, 319.

15

Inequalities in the Criminal Justice System at the Intersection of Race and Ethnicity

Carlos E. Rojas-Gaona and Arelys Madero-Hernandez

The first half of the year 2020 marked a new chapter in a tense relationship between the citizenry and the criminal justice system in America. Along with a revamped effort by the federal government to bring back zero-tolerance policies, Americans witnessed two tragic incidents involving law enforcement and Black citizens. The deaths of Breonna Taylor[1] and George Floyd[2] at the hands of police officers ignited protests and mobilizations around the country to demand justice and criminal justice reform. These incidents were a wake-up call for some, but for many others were a long-standing confirmation of the stark disparities in how certain groups are treated by the criminal justice system. Race and ethnicity are at the crux of these disparities. This chapter examines the inequalities that stem from the intersection of race/ethnicity and crime and solutions to overcome them.

Crime Differences Across Race/Ethnicity

Criminal involvement across different race/ethnicity groups has been an object of theoretical and empirical inquiry over a long period of time, but the race/ethnicity–crime link is still not well understood. To understand this link, criminologists have traditionally used several sources of crime and victimization data in the United States such as the Federal Bureau of Investigation's (FBI's) Uniform Crime Reports (UCR), the National Incident-Based Reporting System (NIBRS), and the Bureau of Justice Statistics' National Crime and Victimization Survey (NCVS). For example, data from official sources such as the FBI's UCR show that arrest rates for the most serious violent offenses have been historically higher for Blacks compared to Whites, although this gap has declined in recent years.[3] Similarly, nationwide self-report data shows that Blacks tend to offend at higher rates and are somewhat more likely to engage in serious violent offending when compared to Whites, but these differences tend to disappear when analyzing less serious offenses or when factors such as neighborhood

Carlos E. Rojas-Gaona and Arelys Madero-Hernandez, *Inequalities in the Criminal Justice System at the Intersection of Race and Ethnicity* In: *On Inequality and Freedom*. Edited by: Lawrence M. Eppard and Henry A. Giroux, Oxford University Press. © Oxford University Press 2022. DOI: 10.1093/oso/9780197583029.003.0015 conditions, family structure, or peer relations are included in statistical analyses of these samples.[4] That is, if we were to somehow reproduce among Whites the same structural conditions historically experienced by Blacks, the rates of offending would be equivalent across the two groups.[5] The implication of this research is that two young adolescents, one Black and one White, both residing in neighborhoods characterized by the same levels of poverty, receiving poor education, and lacking in parental and community supervision, would have the same probability of getting involved in crime.

To disentangle the race/ethnicity crime link also requires considering Latinos' involvement in criminal behavior. Latinos are a fast-growing population in the United States.[6] An examination of research on this topic reveals that Latinos are more likely to commit serious offenses than Whites, but the correlation disappears after accounting for other factors.[7,8,9] An important caveat of these studies is that, similar to studies of Blacks and Whites, studies of Latinos and Whites also consistently find nonsignificant differences in criminal behaviors across these two groups, net of the effects of variables such as household income, family composition, neighborhood conditions, or parental–community engagement. Interestingly, studies highlight several protective factors among Latinos, such as labor force attachment, generational status, and familism, which work to reduce the probability of involvement in criminal behavior among this group.[10] Researchers also have found within-group differences among Latinos highlighting the role of certain individual-level variables, such as generational status, that might serve as a protective factor for violence. For example, first-generation Latinos (i.e., those who were born outside the United States) are significantly less likely to engage in violence or display violent behaviors throughout the course of their lives, as compared to second- and third-generation Latinos (i.e., those born in the United States). This may be due to the higher levels of social capital they bring as new immigrants, as well as lower levels of acculturation into criminogenic values.[11,12]

Understandably, these facts have ignited debates among criminologists about what explains criminal involvement across race/ethnicity, and whether the observed differences across groups are in fact due to mediating individual- and/or community-level mechanisms. In an effort to better understand the complex mechanisms that explain differences across race/ethnicity on criminal offending, criminologists have relied on a number of theories. Among these theories, anomie/strain,[13] social learning,[14] social control,[15] self-control,[16] social disorganization,[17] collective efficacy,[18] and (sub)cultural theories[19] stand out as the most relevant.

Anomie/strain theory posits that minority groups tend to experience higher levels of economic inequality and discrimination.[20] Experiences such as being denied access to mainstream goals through legitimate means lead minorities to feel higher levels of strain (or negative affective states, e.g., hopelessness, frustration, depression, and anger), which may lead to a host of antisocial behaviors, including delinquency. Empirical research along the lines of anomie/strain theory offers mixed results. For example, researchers find that although Blacks report having higher unemployment rates and lower incomes than Whites, they display higher levels of commitment to economic success.[21] Yet, it appears that experiencing increased exposure to stressors in the form of discrimination is a significant predictor of delinquency, particularly among Blacks.[22,23]

Social disorganization theory is another relevant framework to study why some groups are disproportionately involved in crime. For example, a consistent finding supported by researchers testing social disorganization theory highlight evidence of racial/ethnic differences in crime as the consequence of concentration effects. That is, certain racial/ethnic groups like Blacks would be more likely to engage in crime due to the particular macro-social patterns of disadvantage and deprivation to which they have been historically exposed to. As such, proponents of social disorganization theory argue that compared to Whites, Blacks tend to live in neighborhoods with significant concentrations of disadvantageous conditions such as poverty, single-headed households, limited access to resources, and residential inequality. These conditions produce social isolation from mainstream society and the absence of social buffers in the community that might act as role models to promote law-abiding behaviors. Social disorganization theory explains racial/ethnic differences in crime by adding a cultural component since in socially isolated communities individuals tend to develop their own set of beliefs and modes of interaction that justify deviant behavior as a coping mechanism to structural inequalities.[24,25]

Consistent with this line of reasoning, the code-of-the-street theory proposes another explanation for the race/ethnicity–crime link.[26] The code of the street represents a form of social capital shared by some individuals who reside in economically deprived neighborhoods. In these areas, unlike middle-class neighborhoods, prestige and self-worth are not measured by standards of economic success, but rather by the capacity of individuals to face everyday challenges with violence and demonstrate their ability to engage in it. Arguably, the code of the street emerges as a situational adaptation to contextual constraints (e.g., concentrated disadvantage) where mainstream values are no longer relevant or become useless. The code of the street emerges in predominantly Black neighborhoods that, unlike most White neighborhoods, are characterized by conditions that go above and beyond poverty alone—such as resource deprivation, joblessness, single-headed family households, and welfare dependence. These particular structural conditions promote the enactment of the code, which translates into violence. Interestingly, the code of the street appears to operate among other minority groups as well, particularly Latinos, as they experience similar structural constraints that might pave the way for the emergence of code-related attitudes and delinquency among this group.[27]

Disparities in the Criminal Justice System

Criminal justice responses are enacted in response to observed patterns of crime involvement, but they are similarly informed by prevailing moral narratives and stereotypes. In the United States, race and ethnicity have historically been associated with images of crime; namely, stereotypes often associate people of color with danger and criminal threat.[28] In this racialized context, it is not surprising to observe resulting patterns of disproportional enforcement, disparate sentencing, and uneven incarceration rates that affect people of color in negative ways. As explained previously, the seemingly disproportional involvement of Blacks and Latinos in certain crime categories is not explained by virtue of their race/ethnicity, but rather by disproportional social and economic constraints these minority groups have historically experienced, which in turn increase their likelihood of criminal offending. These factors, along with certain criminal justice policies at the federal level, lie behind the differential treatment of minorities by the criminal justice system. The challenges in accessing opportunities and upward mobility for Blacks have been well documented throughout American history. Redlining policies enacted at the federal, state, and local levels after World War II triggered overt discrimination in housing and engineered the pattern of residential segregation that is too familiar today.[29] That is, Blacks populate middle-class suburbs in few numbers but tend to concentrate in densely populated urban enclaves, a phenomenon also observed among other minority groups, including Asians and Latinos. While the old policies of overt discrimination have been illegal for decades, the vestiges of segregation remain. Recently, the federal government dismantled the 2015 Affirmatively Furthering Fair Housing rule that sought to ensure fair housing practices and reduce racial segregation. As President Trump stated, by rescinding the rule: "There will be no more low-income housing forced into the suburbs. . . . It's been hell for suburbia . . . . Housing prices will go up based on the market, and crime will go down."[30] These policies accentuated the wealth gap between Whites and Blacks, creating geographic pockets of concentrated disadvantage. Meanwhile, the concentration of war on drugs enforcement in these very communities, coupled with mandatory sentences and mass incarceration policies targeted at poor defendants, have resulted in stark inequalities, including how Blacks and Latinos are treated by the criminal justice system relative to their White counterparts.[31] Inequalities are observed at all stages of the criminal justice process, from policing to corrections.

First, studies have long documented disparities in law enforcement outcomes, particularly in traffic stops and use of deadly force. A recent comprehensive study of traffic stops nationwide data spanning over 20 years found that Black drivers were 2.51 times more likely to be searched than White drivers, and Latino drivers were 3.14 more likely to be searched than White drivers.[32] These results are net of confounding factors such as gender, age, out-of-state-license, and certain driving behaviors that may covary with race/ethnicity—such as driving at night, reckless driving, or speeding. Despite mixed results about racial/ethnic disparities in the use of force by law enforcement broadly, there is compelling evidence regarding disparities in the use of *deadly* force more specifically. Until recently, studies found no evidence of racial bias among law enforcement in the use of deadly force.[33] However, these studies lacked measurement validity due to the use of raw frequencies of deadly shootings as an indicator of likelihood of events and failing to standardize shooting events as a fraction of all encounters. After correcting this issue, research showed that the risk of being shot and killed by police was higher among Blacks and Latinos as compared to Whites (2.5 and 1.4 times more likely, respectively).[34]

Second, research on sentencing has consistently shown disparities among minorities compared to Whites. A recent study assessing policy changes across time and the effects of race/ethnicity on sentencing outcomes found that net of relevant legal factors (e.g., criminal history, severity of offense), young Black men tended to receive longer sentences compared to other race/ethnic groups.[35]Among young women, Latinas tended to receive longer sentences compared to other race/ethnic groups.[36] Race/ethnicity appeared to coalesce with other extralegal factors to influence harsher sentencing decisions for minorities. Across levels of criminal history (i.e., no prior crime through extensive priors), Black and Latinos were more likely to receive a prison sentence, as well as receive longer prison sentences, than Whites.[37]

Disparities across race/ethnicity are also observed in longitudinal studies assessing sentencing patterns for violent offenders. Net of crime type and relevant control variables, Blacks were 50% more likely than Whites to receive jail and prison sentences over supervision and more likely to receive longer sentences.[38] Interestingly, these results were conditioned by crime type; namely, compared to Whites, Blacks were more likely to receive prison sentences and more likely to receive longer sentences for violent offenses such as manslaughter, robbery/carjacking, and arson. Disparities in sentencing outcomes are also evident when studying the intersection of race/ethnicity, citizenship, and legal status. In this case, being a non-U.S. citizen, undocumented immigrant, and Latino greatly increased the likelihood of receiving a prison sentence versus alternative placements.[39]

Studies on sentencing across race/ethnicity lend support to two theories. The first is the focal concerns perspective, which proposes the existence of three main concerns among judges that play a role in their decision-making process: offender blameworthiness, community protection, and organizational constraints.[40] The second theory, group threat hypothesis, suggests a process whereby dominant groups use their power to discriminate, criminalize, and punish nondominant groups that are perceived as a threat by virtue of their growing representativeness in the population.[41]

At the concluding stage of the criminal justice process, corrections, disparities by race/ethnicity have also been well documented. Not surprisingly, given the above discussion, there is a gap in incarceration rates among minorities (i.e., particularly Blacks) compared to other groups. Recent trends indicated that among adults sentenced to more than 1 year in federal or state prison, Blacks were the racial group most likely to be incarcerated, followed by Latinos and Whites. In the year 2018, there were 1,501 Black prisoners, 797 Latino prisoners, and 268 White prisoners per 100,000 population, respectively. Although incarceration rates have declined for all three race/ethnicity groups over recent years, minorities still are overrepresented in the prison population. That is, while Blacks represent roughly 12% of the total U.S. adult population, they represent 33% of the total U.S. prison population. Similarly, Latinos represent 16% of the total U.S. population and 23% of the total U.S. prison population. In contrast, 63% of the total U.S. population are Whites, but their representation in the total U.S. prison population is 30%.[42]

Disparities Among Crime Victims

The likelihood of falling victim to a crime is not equal among demographic groups. For decades, the NCVS has provided reliable statistics on the extent and nature of nonlethal victimization in the United States.[43] NCVS reports consistently find that demographic factors such as race, ethnicity, gender, and socioeconomic status are leading correlates of the risk of becoming a victim of violence. Although it is generally the case that most Americans are safer from crime today than they were in the late 1980s, it is also true that certain racial and ethnic groups have been disproportionately at risk.[44]

Racial and ethnic disparities in victimization are most evident for violent crimes (i.e., robbery, aggravated assault, simple assault, and rape).[45] For the most recent decade for which NCVS data are available, the period between 2008 and 2018, the rate of violent victimization was highest for Blacks and those who self-identify as "other race" (25.5 and 22.3 victimizations per 1,000 persons, respectively), followed by Whites (21.6 victimizations per 1,000 persons). Interestingly, rates of victimization were lowest among Hispanics, contrary to what their status as minority suggests, with a rate of 20.3 victimizations per 1,000 persons during this past decade.[46]

Nowhere are disparities in violent victimization more marked than in homicide. In 2017, mortality statistics published by Centers for Disease Control and Prevention indicated that Black Americans were eight times more likely to suffer death by homicide than White Americans (23.2 and 2.9 homicide deaths per 100,000 population, respectively). Hispanics of all races fell between the extremes, at 5.4 homicide deaths per 100,000 population.[47] Such disparities are corroborated by the FBI's Supplementary Homicide Report (SHR). According to the SHR, there were 13,927 homicides in the year 2019. The majority of these incidents (53%) were perpetrated against Blacks. For the same year, 16% of homicides were perpetrated against Hispanics, a much lower incidence as compared to non-Hispanic victims.[48]

A very different picture emerges when examining victimization for property offenses. Estimates of property victimization combine burglary, auto theft, and theft. For the year 2018, the NCVS reported 13,502,837 of these incidents. The vast majority (61%) affected White victims. Hispanic victims accounted for 16% of incidents, followed by Black victims (14%), and people of other races (9%).[49] This pattern of greater risk of property victimization among Whites is paradoxical given the pattern of violent victimization where Whites are generally protected from crime. Two factors are relevant to understand these patterns: neighborhood of residence and household income. The tight connection that exists in American society between race/ethnicity and these two factors allows for making sense of this paradox. Neighborhood of residence matters. Poor communities in America experience the highest levels of violence, whereas more affluent communities have higher rates of property crimes.[50] Poor people, especially people of color, are more likely to reside precisely in the areas where the risk of violence is greatest. Meanwhile, more affluent White households are able to isolate themselves from that context of violence, but their prosperity and possessions make them more attractive targets for theft.

What explains the above-noted disparities in victimization? Criminologists have formulated numerous theories to explain these differentials in the risk of victimization. Some are micro-level explanations that focus on individual characteristics that may lead minorities to suffer violence. Others are macro-level theories that highlight the characteristics of the social contexts where minority groups are embedded, such as neighborhoods. This section reviews these theories and how well they explain victimization disparities by race.

Lifestyle/exposure theory argues that recurrent lifestyles and routines, including vocational activities (e.g., work, school) and leisure activities (e.g., recreation, shopping), expose people to varying degrees of victimization risk.[51]

Participation in these activities stems from role expectations that individuals in society must conform to, as well as structural constraints beyond their control. For example, given schooling demands, youth spend a significant portion of their day at school—a lifestyle that in turn decreases their exposure to street violence. This lifestyle resulting from a role expectation explains why violent victimization of juveniles is lower than their young adult counterparts. Similarly, someone who relies on public transportation to commute to and from work will have a greater chance of meeting strangers every day. This lifestyle that stems from structural constraints will in turn enhance their victimization risk.

As per routine activity theory, criminal opportunities occur when three necessary elements converge in time and space: motivated offenders, suitable targets, and the absence of capable guardians.[52] Four factors that affect the risk of predatory victimization are exposure to risk, guardianship, proximity to motivated offenders, and target attractiveness.[53] The idea is that individuals are the most likely recipients of crime if they (a) are highly exposed in terms of being accessible and visible to offenders in risky situations, (b) lack guardianship, (c) are in closer proximity to potential offenders, and (d) offer greater intrinsic or extrinsic rewards to offenders. Both of these theories suggest that the reason why certain race and ethnicity groups are more likely to be victimized is simply because their routines put them in contact with opportunistic offenders.

In the logic of these theories, the link between race/ethnicity and victimization is to be entirely mediated by personal lifestyles and routines. In other words, the correlation between race/ethnicity and victimization is simply a byproduct of the tight connection between certain lifestyles and routines and race/ethnicity. By implication, it is expected than when individuals change their lifestyles and routines to minimize exposure to risky situations (if they can), disparities by race/ethnicity should disappear. Research has found moderate support for these theories as studies typically find that greater exposure to risky lifestyles and routines leads to greater property and violent victimization.[54,55]

Yet, what these theories have failed to show is support for their expectation that race/ethnicity differences in victimization are to be washed away once the most proximate influences—risky lifestyles and routines—are taken into consideration. This has been the case in studies of victimization where race and ethnicity are included in multivariate models alongside other independent variables that tap into risky lifestyles and routines (e.g., delinquent lifestyles, substance use).[56,57] This enduring power of race and ethnicity as predictors of victimization in the existing research suggests that the way in which a person's profile affects their risk is more complex than what these theories suggests.[58]

Perhaps the roots of victimization disparities can be understood by applying subcultural theories. These theories emphasize how certain groups in society adhere to norms and values different from those in mainstream. Adherence to these subcultural values may influence people's risk of victimization, independently of their routines and lifestyles. One example of these subcultural values is given in *The Code of the Street*.[59] In areas of concentrated disadvantage, people tend to uphold a street code that may condone and/or justify the situational use of violence. The street code seeks to fill the gap left from weak institutions of formal social control (e.g., police, courts) in a context of social dislocation and extreme deprivation. This is the social context of many inner-city communities populated by minorities; the street code becomes the organizing principle of social interactions in these communities. When violence is seen as a legitimate way to handle social interactions, people resort to it at a higher rate, and the risk of victimization rises.[60]

Although it is easy to see how embracing the street code can make one vulnerable to victimization, it is also likely that the code can provide valuable protection by creating a street reputation of toughness and as someone "not to be messed with."[61] Indeed, some studies find that youth adoption of the code promotes safety from violence and reduces victimization, as tough kids are not ideal targets of violence.[62] On the other hand, the street code encourages retaliation from others, thereby increasing the risk of victimization—a hypothesis that has received empirical support as well.[63,64] Considering the reality that minorities are disproportionately concentrated in inner-city areas in America and more likely to adopt attitudes and values supportive of violence,[65] it makes sense to argue that cultural/subcultural issues may be at the root of the persistent racial/ethnic differences in victimization we see.

It is also important to consider the social context where individuals live. In the United States, the neighborhood context differs markedly across racial and ethnic groups, especially with respect to patterns of residential segregation and concentration of poverty. The majority of the Black population resides in urban areas segregated from White neighborhoods.[66,67] Trends of segregation among Hispanics, although not as extreme, closely follow the trends of Blacks.[68] People of color are similarly affected by poverty. Between 2007 and 2011, nearly a quarter of the Black and Hispanic population reported incomes below the poverty line, in comparison with 9.9% of Whites.[69] In 2018, almost a third of Black households and slightly less than a quarter of Hispanic households received Supplemental Nutrition Assistance Program benefits.[70] Even if we examine minorities and Whites within equivalent income brackets, the former are more likely to reside in areas of extreme poverty.[71]

The unique neighborhood context of racial and ethnic minorities affects their chances of victimization, as posited by social disorganization and collective efficacy theories.[72] Collective efficacy refers to a community's level of mutual trust coupled with willingness to intervene to solve common problems. The collective efficacy construct bears significance on victimization, as areas with more of it have lower victimization rates.[73] Considering that one of the factors that inhibits collective efficacy is concentrated poverty, it is not surprising that areas with greater concentrations of racial and ethnic minorities face greater rates of violence as a byproduct of lower collective efficacy.[74] Clearly, inequalities in victimization reflect ecological dissimilarities in contexts of residence. In light of these arguments, if Whites resided in areas with levels of concentrated disadvantage and social isolation similar to those that minorities occupy today, they too would be prone to high rates of violent victimization.

The topic of victimization is multifaceted and still evolving. What is clear is that there are persistent disparities in the risk of suffering violence, disparities where people of color suffer the most risk. Despite the popularity of opportunity theories such as lifestyle/exposure and routine activity, the fact that we continue to see uneven odds of victimization across racial and ethnic groups after accounting for risky lifestyles and routines suggests that there is more to the explanation than what these theories allow for. Other perspectives, including cultural/subcultural models and macro-level theories, face the same problem because they also have failed to explain the totality of these differences. Scholars seeking to disentangle the pervasive race and ethnicity effects on victimization must postulate and test integrated explanations that examine the issue from a multilevel lens.

Breaking Enduring Disparities

For the majority of Americans who in 2020 have come to embrace views of racial justice,[75] the realization that racial inequalities exist has come from grassroot movements, such as Black Lives Matter, and notoriously public cases, like the killing of George Floyd. But for those of us studying crime, victimization, and justice issues, patterns of racial and ethnic disparities are nothing new. While these unique current events highlight a pressing need for criminal justice reform in America, we must take a step back to reflect on the larger forces that brought us to this point, the forces that underlie the persistent disparities in crime and justice outcomes and that are harder to see when one is faced with tragic events.

One cannot understand the persistence of criminal justice disparities without realizing that these events are the manifestations of deeper dynamics of inequality in society, dynamics that cut across cultural norms, structures, and processes. The consensus among scholars is that racial discrimination in crime and justice outcomes stems from more insidious and indirect causal mechanisms that amplify social disadvantages.[76] One of them is neighborhood context.

Neighborhood of residence continues to be a salient factor that determines access to opportunities for upward mobility for Americans. Decades after *Brown v. Board of Education* and other influential policies resulting from the civil rights movement, segregation continues. Most schools are racially segregated because attendance is based on neighborhood of residence, and residential segregation is far from eliminated.[77] Schools in inner-city communities have two things in common: They are predominantly high minority and disproportionally underperforming. Access to quality education is one of the factors that amplifies social disadvantages for minorities.

However, schools are only part of the story. The other is concentration of poverty, joblessness, and single-headed households—a phenomenon known as concentrated disadvantage.[78] A look at American's poorest neighborhoods, defined as areas where the median income is below the federal poverty line, shows that Blacks and Latinos are overrepresented in these areas.[79] This concentration of poverty has devastating consequences for minorities, not only because it translates into greater rates of crime in these communities but also because it correlates with lack of access to services and depleted social capital. In these communities, for example, youth have few working role models to look up to, coupled with overall limited access to extracurricular activities, health, fresh food, libraries, and clean air.[80]

Neighborhood of residence simultaneously impinges on dynamics of application of the law. Police resources target high-crime neighborhoods, and given the concentration of minorities in those areas, people of color are more likely to be stopped and questioned, regardless of their actual level of crime involvement. Beyond the frequency of enforcement, policies tend to be enforced with greater vigor. One example of this is the zero-tolerance policing practices implemented by the New York City Police. Terry Stops, also known as "stop and chat," was a tool in the New York Police Department (NYPD) arsenal that targeted minorities disproportionately since the 1990s. Of the nearly 4.5 million stops conducted by NYPD between 2004 and 2012, over half were stops of Black residents, and a third were of Latinos—despite the two groups making up just above half the population of the city.[81] This model of proactive policing has been credited as precursor of the crime drop. Yet, studies found mixed evidence of crime reductions as a result of Terry Stops specifically.[82] More importantly, while one looks at statistics that show the existence of racial disparities in stops or arrests, it is important to bear in mind that these patterns need not to be the artifact of overt racism or even implicit biases on the part of police officers. In fact, the evidence suggests that arrest decisions are largely determined by legal factors, and that disparities in enforcement outcomes reflect a greater proclivity among certain racial and ethnic groups to engage in criminal activity.[83] This, however, does not deny the operation of selective enforcement processes as well, but the consensus to date is that we do not have conclusive evidence whether the racial and ethnic disparities that are seen on implementation of proactive policing are due to greater involvement of minorities in criminal activity alone or if racial bias also plays a role.[84]

It would be misguided to argue that criminal justice reform will be a short-term agenda. The discussed dynamics are enduring and difficult to change. The challenges we are seeing today are analogous to those that led President Lyndon Johnson to establish the President's Commission on Law Enforcement and Administration of Justice over 50 years ago. In 1967, when the commission issued its report, it laid out seven objectives to guide policy changes; the third objective was "eliminating unfairness."[85] A fair and impartial justice system was seen as a fundamental first step toward gaining the cooperation from citizens that is needed to effectively fight and prevent crime. That goal is still applicable today. Yet, it is naïve to expect that a process of reforming in the system can occur in isolation from reform in the mainstream institutions that lie underneath, most notably the inequalities in the geospatial distribution of resources in America.

Notes

1. Richard A. Oppel, Derrick B. Taylor, and Nicholas Bogel-Burroughs, "Here's What You Need to Know About Breonna Taylor's Death," *New York Times*, October 30, 2020, https://www.nytimes.com/article/breonna-taylor-police.html.
2. Evan Hill et al., "How George Floyd Was Killed in Police Custody," *New York Times*, May 21, 2020, https://www.nytimes.com/2020/05/31/us/george-floyd-investigation.html.
3. "Crime in the United States, 2018," Federal Bureau of Investigations, 2018, https://ucr.fbi.gov/crime-in-the-u.s/2018/crime-in-the-u.s.-2018/topic-pages/tables/table-43.
4. Thomas L. McNulty and Paul E. Bellair, "Explaining Racial and Ethnic Differences in Serious Adolescent Violent Behavior," *Criminology* 41, no. 3 (2003): 709–747.
5. Carlos E. Rojas-Gaona, Jun Sung Hong, and Anthony A. Peguero. "The Significance of Race/Ethnicity in Adolescent Violence: A Decade of Review, 2005–2015," *Journal of Criminal Justice* 46, no. 1 (2016): 137–147.
6. "U.S. Census Bureau Projections Show a Slower Growing, Older, More Diverse Nation Half a Century from Now," U.S. Census Bureau, December 12, 2012, http://www.census.gov/newsroom/releases/archives/population/cb12-243.html.
7. Lorena M. Estrada-Martínez, Cleopatra Howard Caldwell, Amy J. Schulz, Ana V. Diez-Roux, and Silvia Pedraza. "Families, Neighborhood Socio-Demographic Factors, and Violent Behaviors among Latino, White, and Black Adolescents," *Youth & Society* 45, no. 2 (2013): 221–242.
8. Lorena M. Estrada-Martínez et al., "Examining the Influence of Family Environments on Youth Violence: A Comparison of Mexican, Puerto Rican, Cuban, Non-Latino Black, and Non-Latino White Adolescents," *Journal of Youth and Adolescence* 40, no. 8 (2011): 1039–1051.

9. Joanne M. Kaufman, "Explaining the Race/Ethnicity-Violence Relationship: Neighborhood Context and Social Psychological Processes," *Justice Quarterly* 22, no. 2 (2005): 224–251.

10. Rojas-Gaona, Sung Hong, and Peguero, "Significance of Race/Ethnicity."

11. Bianca E. Bersani, Thomas A. Loughran, and Alex R. Piquero, "Comparing Patterns and Predictors of Immigrant Offending Among a Sample of Adjudicated Youth," *Journal of Youth and Adolescence* 43, no. 11 (2014): 1914–1933.

12. Robert J. Sampson, "Rethinking Crime and Immigration," *Contexts* 7, no. 1 (2008): 32.

13. Robert Agnew, "Foundation for a General Strain Theory of Crime and Delinquency," *Criminology* 30, no. 1 (1992): 47–87.

14. Ronald L. Akers, *Social Learning and Social Structure: A General Theory of Crime and Deviance* (Boston: Northeastern University Press, 1998).

15. Travis Hirschi, *Causes of Delinquency* (Berkeley, CA: University of California Press, 1969).

16. Michael R. Gottfredson and Travis Hirschi, *A General Theory of Crime* (Stanford, CA: Stanford University Press, 1990).

17. Clifford R. Shaw, Henry D. McKay, and James F. Short, *Juvenile Delinquency and Urban Areas: A Study of Rates of Delinquency in Relation to Differential Characteristics of Local Communities in American Cities* (Chicago: University of Chicago Press, 1969).

18. Robert J. Sampson, Stephen W. Raudenbush, and Felton J. Earls, "Neighborhoods and Violent Crime: A Multilevel Study of Collective Efficacy." *Science* 277, no. 5328 (1997): 918–924.

19. Elijah Anderson, *Code of the Street: Decency, Violence, and the Moral Life of the Inner City* (New York: W. W Norton, 1999).

20. Agnew, "General Strain Theory."

21. Stephen A. Cernkovich, Peggy C. Giordano, and Jennifer L. Rudolph, "Race, Crime, and the American Dream," *Journal of Research in Crime and Delinquency* 37, no. 2 (2000): 131–170.

22. Sung Joon Jang and Byron R. Johnson, "Strain, Negative Emotions, and Deviant Coping Among African Americans: A Test of General Strain Theory." *Journal of Quantitative Criminology* 19, no.1 (2003): 79–105.

23. Ronald L. Simons, Yi-Fu Chen, and Eric A. Stewart, "Incidents of Discrimination and Risk for Delinquency: A Longitudinal Test of Strain Theory With an African American Sample," *Justice Quarterly* 20, no. 4 (2003): 827–854.

24. Robert J. Sampson and William J. Wilson, "Toward a Theory of Race, Crime, and Urban Inequality," in *Crime and Inequality*, ed. John Hagan and Ruth D. Peterson (Stanford, CA: Stanford University Press, 1995).

25. William J. Wilson, *When Work Disappears: New Implications for Race and Urban Poverty in the Global Economy* (New York: Alfred A. Knopf, 1997).

26. Anderson, *Code of the Street.*

27. Philippe I. Bourgois, *In Search of Respect: Selling Crack in El Barrio* (Cambridge: Cambridge University Press, 2003).

28. Sara Steen, Rodney L. Engen, and Randy, R. Gainey, "Images of Danger and Culpability: Racial Stereotyping, Case Processing, and Criminal Sentencing," *Criminology* 43, no. 2 (2005): 435–468.

29. Richard Rothstein, *The Color of Law: A Forgotten History of How Our Government Segregated America* (New York: Liveright, 2017).
30. Matthew Choi, "Trump Boasts of Pushing Low-Income Housing Out of Suburbs," *Politico*, September 22, 2020, https://www.politico.com/news/2020/07/29/trump-housing-policy-low-income-suburbs-386414.
31. Michelle Alexander, *The New Jim Crow: Mass Incarceration in the Age of Colorblindness* (New York: New Press, 2012).
32. Frank R. Baumgartner, et al., "Racial Disparities in Traffic Stop Outcomes," *Duke Forum for Law and Social Change* 9 (2017): 21–54.
33. David J. Johnson et al., "Officer Characteristics and Racial Disparities in Fatal Officer-Involved Shootings," *Proceedings of the National Academy of Sciences of the United States of America* 116, no. 32 (2019): 15877–15882.
34. Frank Edwards, Hedwig Lee, and Michael Esposito, "Risk of Being Killed by Police Use of Force in the United States by Age, Race–Ethnicity, and Sex," *Proceedings of the National Academy of Sciences of the United States of America* 116, no. 34 (2019): 16793–16798.
35. Jeffrey S. Nowacki, "An Intersectional Approach to Race/Ethnicity, Sex, and Age Disparity in Federal Sentencing Outcomes: An Examination of Policy Across Time Periods," *Criminology and Criminal Justice* 17, no. 1 (2017): 97–116.
36. Nowacki, "An Intersectional Approach."
37. Travis W. Franklin and Tri Keah S. Henry, "Racial Disparities in Federal Sentencing Outcomes: Clarifying the Role of Criminal History," *Crime & Delinquency* 66, no. 1 (2020): 3–32.
38. Peter S. Lehmann, "Race, Ethnicity, Crime Type, and the Sentencing of Violent Felony Offenders," *Crime & Delinquency* 66, no. 6/7 (2020): 770–805.
39. Mercedes Valadez and Xia Wang, "Citizenship, Legal Status, and Federal Sentencing Outcomes: Examining the Moderating Effects of Age, Gender, and Race/Ethnicity," *Sociological Quarterly* 58, no. 4 (2017): 670–700.
40. Darrell Steffensmeier, Jeffery T. Ulmer, and John H. Kramer, "The Interaction of Race, Gender, and Age in Criminal Sentencing: The Punishment Cost of Being Young, Black, and Male," *Criminology*, 36, no. 4 (1998): 763–797.
41. Hubert M. Blalock, *Toward a Theory of Minority-Group Relations* (New York: Capricorn Books, 1967).
42. Ann Carson, *Prisoners in 2018* (NCJ 253516) (Washington, DC: Bureau of Justice Statistics, April 2020), https://www.bjs.gov/content/pub/pdf/p18.pdf.
43. Robert M. Groves and Daniel L. Cork, *Surveying Victims: Options for Conducting the National Crime Victimization Survey* (Washington, DC: National Academies Press, 2008).
44. Jennifer L. Truman, and Lynn Langton, *Criminal Victimization, 2014* (NCJ 248973) (Washington, DC: Bureau of Justice Statistics, August 2015), https://www.bjs.gov/content/pub/pdf/cv14.pdf.
45. Heather Warnken and Janet L. Lauritsen, *Who Experiences Violent Victimization and Who Accesses Services? Findings From the National Crime Victimization Survey for Expanding Our Research* (Washington, DC: Center for Victim Research, 2019).

46. "Violent Victimization by Race or Ethnicity, 2005–2019" (NCJ255578), Bureau of Justice Statistics, October 20, 2020, https://www.bjs.gov/content/pub/pdf/vvre0 519.pdf.

47. Kenneth D. Kochanek et al., *Deaths: Final Data for 2009* (Hyattsville, MD: National Center for Health Statistics, 2012).

48. "Crime in the United States, Table 6," Federal Bureau of Investigations, 2019, https:// ucr.fbi.gov/crime-in-the-u.s/2019/crime-in-the-u.s.-2019/tables/expanded-homic ide-data-table-6.xls.

49. "Percent of Property Victimizations by Race/Hispanic Origin of Head of Household, 2018–2019," Bureau of Justice Statistics NCVS Victimization Analysis Tool, https:// www.bjs.gov.

50. Pamela Wilcox Rountree and Kenneth C. Land, "Burglary Victimization, Perceptions of Crime Risk, and Routine Activities: A Multilevel Analysis Across Seattle Neighborhoods and Census Tracts," *Journal of Research in Crime & Delinquency* 33, no. 2 (1996): 147–180.

51. Michael. J. Hindelang, Michael R. Gottfredson, and James Garofalo, *Victims of Personal Crime: An Empirical Foundation for a Theory of Personal Victimization* (Cambridge, MA: Ballinger, 1978).

52. Lawrence E. Cohen and Marcus Felson, "Social Change and Crime Rate Trends: Routine Activity Approach," *American Sociological Review* 44, no. 4 (1979): 588–608.

53. Lawrence E. Cohen, James R. Kluegel, and Kenneth C. Land, "Social Inequality and Predatory Criminal Victimization: An Exposition and Test of a Formal Theory," *American Sociological Review* 46, no. 5 (1981): 505–524.

54. Terance. D. Miethe and Robert F. Meier, "Opportunity, Choice and Criminal Victimization: A Test of a Theoretical Model," *Journal of Research in Crime & Delinquency* 27, no. 3 (1990): 243–266.

55. Richard Spano and Joshua D. Freilich, "An Assessment of the Empirical Validity and Conceptualization of Individual Level Multivariate Studies of Lifestyle/Routine Activities Theory Published From 1995 to 2005," *Journal of Criminal Justice* 37, no. 3 (2009): 305–314.

56. John D. Burrow and Robert Apel, "Youth Behavior, School Structure, and Student Risk of Victimization," *Justice Quarterly* 25, no. 2 (2008): 349–380.

57. Billy Henson et al., "Gender, Adolescent Lifestyles, and Violent Victimization: Implications for Routine Activity Theory," *Victims & Offenders* 5, no. 4 (2010): 303–328.

58. Arelys Madero-Hernandez and Bonnie S. Fisher, "Race, Ethnicity, Risky Lifestyles, and Violent Victimization: A Test of a Mediation Model," *Race and Justice* 7, no. 4 (2017): 325–349.

59. Anderson, *The Code of the Streets.*

60. Eric A. Stewart, Christopher J. Schreck, and Ronald L. Simons, "'I Ain't Gonna Let No One Disrespect Me': Does the Code of the Street Reduce or Increase Violent Victimization Among African American Adolescents?" *Journal of Research in Crime and Delinquency* 43, no. 4 (2006): 427–458.

61. Chris Melde, Mark T. Berg, and Finn-Aage Esbensen, "'Nerve' and Violent Encounters: An Assessment of Fearlessness in the Face of Danger," *Criminology* 58, no. 2 (2020): 226–254.

62. Mark T. Berg and Rolf Loeber, "Violent Conduct and Victimization Risk in the Urban Illicit Drug Economy: A Prospective Examination," *Justice Quarterly* 32, no. 1 (2015): 32–55.

63. Kevin T. Wolff et al., "Adherence to the Street Code Predicts an Earlier Anticipated Death," *Journal of Research in Crime and Delinquency* 57, no. 2 (2020): 139–181.

64. Susan McNeeley and Yue Yuan, "A Multilevel Examination of the Code of the Street's Relationship With Fear of Crime," *Crime & Delinquency* 63, no. 9 (2017): 1146–1167.

65. Alex R. Piquero et al., "Investigating the Determinants of the Street Code and Its Relation to Offending Among Adults," *American Journal of Criminal Justice* 37, no. 1 (2012): 19–32.

66. Douglas S. Massey and Nancy A. Denton, *American Apartheid: Segregation and the Making of the Underclass* (Cambridge, MA: Harvard University Press, 1993).

67. Ruth D. Peterson and Lauren J. Krivo, *Divergent Social Worlds: Neighborhood Crime and the Racial-Spatial Divide* (New York: Russell Sage Foundation, 2010).

68. Frank D. Bean and Martha Tienda, *The Hispanic Population of the United States* (New York: Russell Sage Foundation, 1987).

69. Suzzane Macartney, Alemayehu Bishaw, and Kayla Fontenot, "Poverty Rates for Selected Detailed Race and Hispanic Groups by State and Place: 2007–2011," U.S. Census Bureau, February 2013, https://www2.census.gov/library/publications/2013/acs/acsbr11-17.pdf.

70. Tracy Loveless, "Supplemental Nutrition Assistance Program (SNAP) Receipt for Households: 2018," U.S. Census Bureau, July 21, 2020, https://www.census.gov/library/publications/2020/demo/acsbr20-01.html.

71. Robert J. Sampson and Lydia Bean, "Cultural Mechanisms and Killing Fields: A Revised Theory of Community-Level Racial Inequality," in *The Many Colors of Crime: Inequalities of Race, Ethnicity and Crime in America*, ed. Ruth D. Peterson, Lauren J. Krivo, and John Hagan (New York: New York University Press, 2006), 8–36.

72. Sampson, Raudenbush, and Earls, "Neighborhoods and Violent Crime."

73. Maria Velez, "The Role of Public Social Control in Urban Neighborhoods: A Multilevel Analysis of Victimization Risk," *Criminology* 39, no 4 (2001): 837–864.

74. Lauren J. Krivo, Ruth D. Peterson, and Danielle C. Kuhl, "Segregation, Racial Structure, and Neighborhood Violent Crime," *American Journal of Sociology* 114, no. 6 (2009): 1765–1802.

75. Steven Long and Justin McCarthy, "Two in Three Americans Support Racial Justice Protests," Gallup, July 28, 2020, https://news.gallup.com/poll/316106/two-three-americans-support-racial-justice-protests.aspx.

76. Robert J. Sampson and Janet L. Lauritsen, "Racial and Ethnic Disparities in Crime and Criminal Justice in the United States," *Crime and Justice* 21 (1997): 311–374.

77. Jessica Trounstine, *Segregation by Design: Local Politics and Inequality in American Cities* (New York: Cambridge University Press, 2018).

78. Sampson and Wilson, *"Toward a Theory of Race."*

79. Patrick Sharkey, *Stuck in Place: Urban Neighborhoods and the End of Progress Toward Racial Equality* (Chicago: University of Chicago Press, 2013).

80. Rothstein, "The Color of Law," 187.

81. Floyd v. City of New York, 959 F. Supp. 2d 540 (2013).

82. National Academies of Sciences, Engineering, and Medicine, *Proactive Policing: Effects on Crime and Communities* (Washington, DC: National Academies Press, 2018).

83. National Academies, *Proactive Policing*, 275.

84. National Academies, *Proactive Policing*, 251.

85. U.S. President's Commission on Law Enforcement and Administration of Justice, *The Challenge of Crime in a Free Society* (Washington, D.C.: U.S. Government Printing, 1967).

16

Let Me Fight Your Battle

Hilarie Burton Morgan

Let's get this out of the way: I am deeply insecure about writing this chapter. To be clear, I have already *lived* this chapter. I have survived it. But writing it down puts it on a silver monogramed platter and then serves it up to complete strangers so that my life may be dissected and analyzed and cross-examined. As a woman, it's an ugly position to be in. There is no upside.

And yet here I sit, drafting the third version of my #MeToo chapter.

The first version was over 5,000 words and still not finished. It was ripe with gory details and the thoughts and fears I'd harbored as a young woman in the entertainment industry. It named names and got into the minutiae of a story that had only been summarized in the press. I'd already encountered the disappointment of sitting for hours and hours of interviews, only to have my experience boiled down to a few spicy sound bites. It feels demoralizing when you confess the endless barrage of microaggressions that chipped away at you, only to have the papers zero in on the one or two perviest experiences you'd had.

I'd read the comments to articles written about me. *That's all? She needs to buck up. She shouldn't have put herself in that position. She wanted it.* Reputable publications can't print anything that isn't corroborated by other witnesses, so it limits what can be reported. I hadn't known that. I thought if I just told the truth that would be enough.

The truth is rarely enough.

So, for the purposes of this book, I droned on and on about the details. I'm sure there are those of you who would maybe prefer that first version, salacious as it is. But I read it back and it didn't actually get to any point. It was just a slow play-by-play of how you take a young woman and groom her to be compliant. I'd initially hoped that by laying myself bare I could add a layer of humanity to the overwhelming #MeToo movement. And if readers understood that I was just a little girl from Virginia who had worked her ass off her entire life for a singular dream only to have that dream perverted by men in power, perhaps the statistics and studies would mean more. Each #MeToo story is a heart broken, a dream that backfired.

But as I said before, I've already lived and survived this story, so I could foresee what would happen. A media outlet would catch wind that I'd contributed to this

Hilarie Burton Morgan, *Let Me Fight Your Battle* In: *On Inequality and Freedom*. Edited by: Lawrence M. Eppard and Henry A. Giroux, Oxford University Press. © Oxford University Press 2022. DOI: 10.1093/oso/9780197583029.003.0016 collection and that I'd divulged never-told-before details. They'd skim the writing until they arrived at the names of the most famous men in my narrative, and then they'd be off to the races, printing headlines about impropriety and painting me as an attention-seeker. The story would never really be about any trauma I'd experienced. Look at any #MeToo narrative and you will see a pattern. Headlines are reserved to drag the most famous men possible. The women are interchangeable and disposable. They are all painted with the same brush. *Ambitious, attractive-enough, insecure girl spends too much time with her superior. She lets too much slide. Now she regrets it.* The handling of these stories becomes a secondary assault, valuing the weight that a famous man brings to the story over the reality of who these women are and what they could have been.

So, I wrote a second version of this chapter. It was vague and dealt more with the psychological aftermath of what a person goes through once they have been swallowed up by the media machine and spit out. But I'm not a psychologist, so my analysis was restricted to my own experience and that of the women in my world. It was a narrow view, and not very helpful.

Helpful. That's the crux of the whole problem, really. Because if you commit to falling on the sword, what you want most of all is to be *helpful*. Veer too far into personal territory and you come off as self-serving. Ride the pendulum in the opposite direction and speak on behalf of the masses and you are pretentious and overstepping. To be helpful to the cause you must confess, but not too much, and defend, but with grace, and speak to the right reporters and not have any incriminating photos and, and, and on and on.

But now as I sit and map out what is my third attempt, I want to explain why I am trying so hard to use this opportunity to be helpful. One of the coeditors of this book, Lawrence Eppard, has been my friend since I was 5 years old. He knows how I worked my ass off, knowing that the only way to get out of Virginia and up to New York City was to overextend myself. He's also seen me walk away from all of it. In the past, I've spoken to kind reporters who ultimately just had to turn my life experience into a sellable headline. When you talk to strangers, it can feel as though you are being set up for something. But I know that is not the case in this volume. I had plenty of self-doubt. Lawrence told me that I should only contribute if I felt comfortable and assured me that my input was valuable should I decide to do so.

For what it's worth, this is what I know.

The biggest lesson I've learned from the #MeToo movement is that you must fight other people's battles. You must.

I was a reluctant participant in the #MeToo movement. In the beginning, no one was naming names. When the Harvey Weinstein story broke, his character was an easy one. He was boorish and rude and to be perfectly frank, ugly. The narrative of this brute as a predator was easy to digest. *Of course*, everyone said. *Why didn't we see it before?*

But there were so many others. Genteel men. Nerdy, unassuming men. No-name, unimportant men. All of whom had cast long shadows on the careers of women I knew and respected.

And then, there was my own personal boogeyman.

Why isn't anyone naming names yet? I railed. *Everyone is being too polite.* Social media was flooded with mentions of nameless men who had derailed the lives of vibrant women. It was all hints and clues, a sea of female voices begging someone to follow the trail of breadcrumbs.

I had a boss once who'd grab my ass. I quit that job. My mentor tortured me psychologically until I gave up my career. I was run out of my office for going to HR. There was a pattern. This polite army of women had collectively quit their passions or had been forced, Chutes-and-Ladders style, back to the beginning of their journey to start anew. I was no different.

It had been decades since I'd been a young actress, making the rounds and taking meetings, praying for the intersection of ambition and opportunity to manifest. My dreams came true, and for 6 years I was simultaneously gifted with the career I had worked for my entire life and psychologically manipulated by the nerd with a God complex who had created my television series. The duality of the situation took years for me to divorce.

So, I did what all of the polite women did. I retreated. I began having children. I put my energy into my husband's career. I found alternative employment. I moved as far away from the industry as I could get—a farm in rural upstate New York. I now had a physical barrier that became my excuse for not working. *I'm so sorry I can't make that audition. I wouldn't be able to do the series anyway. My life is here.*

The idea of signing another long-term contract was crippling to me. From time to time, an old director or producer from my past would call and offer me a fun, juicy guest arc. I'd made a rule only to work with people I already knew. They'd compliment my work ethic, my ease on set, my commitment to the material. My one or two episodes would turn into season-long jobs, and I would feel valued for my work. They'd ask: *Why don't you do another series, Hilarie?* I would feel that flush of affection for working again. The heady buzz of being immersed by a thing you love. But it was always quickly followed by the hangover of shame.

My specific skill set is that of a television actor. It requires stamina and teamwork skills and an ability to commit to a narrative without knowing what the final outcome of the character's journey will be. One must be adaptable. It means having a new director to collaborate with every episode. It means being a public relations machine, simultaneously creating the product and selling the fantasy that the production is unproblematic. And it means a minimum of a 6-year contract. I would never commit to that again.

The news of Weinstein broke on October 5, 2017, in a *New York Times* story that detailed his aggressions against notable actresses Ashley Judd and Rose McGowan. I was pregnant with my daughter and had lived in obscurity for years, only joining social media four and a half months before—at the suggestion of my manager—to keep fake "Hilarie Burton" profiles at bay. My posts were impersonal, vague pictures of flowers and animals here at the farm; another post urging others to support public libraries; things I'd baked. I followed a minuscule circle that included my husband and close friends and coworkers.

The *Times* article alarmed me. I'd never met Judd or McGowan, but I'd heard through the Hollywood grapevine that they were difficult, troubled. I'd not known about their abuse, but the anger I sensed from them felt painfully familiar. An instantaneous alarm went off. If the root of their reputations was based in abuse, and they were not in fact difficult or troubled, but defensive and resentful? Did I have the same reputation?

I was most certainly defensive. I was most certainly resentful. Had that been portrayed as *difficult* behind my back? More than once, my old boss had called producers I was working with or executives I was pitching to. *Got a call from Mark*, they'd say. *Never met him before, but he just wanted to tell me how great you were.* Bullshit. He wanted me to know that with the ease of dialing a phone number, he could connect with any potential boss I would ever have. He wanted me to know they would take his calls. It was reported back to me when the calls were positive. But what if those calls were defamatory? How would I ever know about them? He'd bragged to me years before about how our cast was quarantined in our location of Wilmington, North Carolina, and that gave him the power to go back to Los Angeles and destroy the reputation of one of my colleagues. I'd been naïve to think I was exempt from that malice.

I had two or three trusted friends in common with Rose McGowan and began following her. I watched as she maintained her truth, opening the door for other women to come forward—women who a month before wouldn't have given her a second thought. I watched as her consistent fury began to gain traction in the media. In the beginning, she was met with skepticism. *A washed-up actress with a bone to pick.* And then, as more and more victims of Weinstein's predatory habits came forward, the press began to pivot. Rose the soothsayer. Rose the brave. Rose the maverick.

But then a famous man, who had been Weinstein's golden boy, spoke up on the subject. A former costar of McGowan's, he feigned ignorance and vowed to be a beacon of protection for all women. It was a massive slap in the face to this woman who was risking her entire career and life to expose a monster.

The only problem was that this famous man had groped me on camera during an interview when I was 19 years old. He'd been drunk, or that was the excuse that had been offered up. Even in interviews back in 2002 I called him out. He'd float in and out of rehab, win a few awards, get in trouble, go back to rehab, and emerge as squeaky clean as ever. It was a gross parade to watch, knowing full well that minorities and women are never afforded that many second and third chances.

The media picked up on that old footage of the famous man and me. What happened next was that secondary assault I mentioned earlier. My phone rang off the hook. Reporters who I'd maybe spoken to in the past dug up my number and email and sent endless inquiries. My manager had to turn off the phone. The famous man's publicist really wanted to connect and make amends. I was sent death threats by his fans and more poop emojis from the adolescent and teen boys that idolized him than I could count. The famous man made a vague public apology to me, which really wasn't necessary. I didn't need his apology. But Rose McGowan did.

He discredited her by pretending to be in the dark about Weinstein's indiscretions.

As much as the media machine rocked my world, it felt important to bear all of it because another woman needed the support.

Ten years before, when I'd left the series that was supposed to have been my dream job, I was the woman that needed support. I told anyone and everyone about what I'd experienced on that job. I told those stories through laughter. *Isn't that crazy?* I'd ask, waiting and hoping for someone to really hear what I was saying. Finally, a group of writers on a subsequent job stopped me. *That's not right, Hilarie. That's not how it's supposed to be.* I'd felt that in my gut all along, but to have professionals I respected validate my anger was a turning point for me. It solidified the chip on my shoulder.

A month after the Weinstein story broke, the barrage of the initial media circus regarding the famous man had subsided for me. But with his public lashing came freedom for scores of other women to finally name names. Every morning became a game show of revealing the new abuser of the day. *Let's see who's behind door number 3!* I was glad the spotlight was off of me and my growing family. But with my first daughter on the way, it still nagged at me that the real abuser of my career hadn't been called out yet. All this fuss had been made about a man I'd encountered for maybe 1 hour of my entire life, and nothing for the man who I knew has assaulted or tormented dozens of us for years.

Privately, former castmates and I contemplated saying something. But here's the screwed up thing: We all felt like we couldn't because we were all embroiled in *other* sexual harassment situations. To find a woman who has only experienced one instance of abuse of power is rare. But if she dares make a list of multiple men, then clearly the problem is her. She's the common denominator. She's a whore. She's flirty. She's unprofessional. I'd already been dragged for the famous man. I couldn't be the one to bring up my old boss. He was malicious and vindictive. And my time in the hot seat didn't just affect me. My husband was in the midst of filming and doing a press tour for the premiere of his show. He didn't need microphones thrown in his face about my past.

But just as it happened before with Rose McGowan, another woman bravely spoke up. A writer that came onto my show after I left had posted a long thread on Twitter about the repulsive misogyny and rampant sexual harassment that had occurred in the writers' room of our show. She never named the production, but a fan alerted me to the thread. Before I'd even checked her credits, I knew exactly who she was referring to. It never dawned on me that my old boss's predatory habits extended past the circle of actresses. The fact that he was assaulting and harassing writers was infuriating.

It is so much easier to defend someone else than it is to defend yourself. So we actresses flocked around this writer and sent her public messages of support and validated all of her experiences because we had also experienced them. *Burn it down, sis*, I told her. It became a hashtag rallying cry. We assembled a couple dozen women from our show who had all been affected by the toxicity of that production. We knew what was happening to the reputations of any women who were coming forward with #MeToo stories. So we collectively decided to write an open letter to the press from all of us. We wanted it to be polite, but assertive. We didn't want to go into details and make it tabloid fodder. But we needed to firmly assert that our old boss had been a predator and needed to be held accountable.

The letter went public. And nothing happened.

He was the creator of another show filming in the United Kingdom for E! Network. That very network had run the story of my experience with the famous man countless times. But when dozens of women came forward about one of their employees, it was crickets. For the members of our group who had experienced the worst of it, that feeling of being ignored was crippling.

The problem was that our old boss was not a household name. It didn't matter that there were multiple famous *female* victims. The *man* wasn't famous, and therefore it wasn't a good story. And we hadn't divulged the gory details of his abuse, so the letter fell on deaf ears. Days later, the lead actress of his current show released a letter of her own. She too had experienced relentless harassment by this man. And after that, dozens of women from her cast signed a letter similar to our own. At least four dozen women publicly banded together against one man, with even more former cast and crew members reaching out privately. It should have been enough of a landslide to warrant his termination. It was not. He was put on probation while an investigation was conducted. It was a soft move, and there was a great deal of fear that with the daily discoveries of new predators, he would hide out in the purgatory of probation for a bit and return to work as usual once the spotlight had shifted.

We decided among ourselves that if no one would pay attention to our story without the details, then a few of us would bite the bullet and give details. Danneel Ackles and I were married to successful men. Their paychecks cover our mortgages and bills. And as shitty as it is to admit, the success of these men in our lives is what made it safe for us to speak up. If either of us never worked again, our families would be okay. It wasn't our backbones, or morality, or grit that allowed us to come forward. It was our roles as housewives. Our costars were largely the breadwinners of their families, and repercussions were much greater for them. So Danneel and I were interviewed for hours, over multiple days. Sources were checked. We were asked the same questions over and over to make sure we were accurate.

It was the first time I'd ever walked a stranger through the whole ordeal. It wrecked me. Carrying my own daughter, the havoc I relived in retelling my story was painful. And I don't want to dress it up with flowery language. I broke. I couldn't stand the idea that something similar may happen to my daughter one day. I mourned for the young woman I had been, for all the things I would never accomplish because I walked away. I got really angry at the adults who didn't protect us. It was a messy time.

The story ran everywhere and still nothing happened. He remained on probation. Not one single executive or producer or person who wielded any kind of power reached out to any of us. To this day they still have not. The experiences detailed in my account were mild compared to what happened to the women who came after me. Those stories would tumble out on our group text threads and the remorse I felt for not speaking up a decade earlier compounded. The sexual abuse only escalated once I'd gone. I carried that weight.

Days turned into weeks and there was still no action. Finally, after more than a month, it was announced a few days before Christmas that my former boss had been fired from his show. It wasn't a victory. All of the women from that cast who had bravely spoken up would lose their job when the show was cancelled not long after. There is always a cost.

Something had shattered in me. Warner Brothers had been our studio. Where was their public condemnation of this man? Tollin-Robbins had been our production company—not a word from them. Years before, I'd been gently let go from my agency, WME. It didn't make sense for them to represent me, as I'd stopped auditioning. But then I learned they represented my old boss and still had him on as a client, even after all of the letters and articles and firing.

I could not fight any more battles. This was my boogey man, and what I hadn't known before that I understood in that moment was that when you speak up, you are in the throes of trauma. To speak up is to rip off all the bandages and peel off the scabs and let the wounds bleed anew. It's as though the confession is done with your last breaths because afterward comes a kind of paralysis. And you hope with all your might that someone will swoop in and take your words and keep running.

An A-list actress I'd never met did that for me. She fought my battle.

The agency that still represented my former boss created a #MeToo council, an advisory board that addressed abuse within the business and specifically at their company. One of the actresses on this board had heard about our collective experience. Our respective managers were friendly, and hers reached out to mine to see how we were. I don't know the particulars of what happened next, but I do know this stranger went back to that council and insisted they drop him as a client or lose her.

It was never announced in the press. Again, he wasn't famous, so who would have cared? But the news of his dismissal was sent back to me. He won't ever wield power over any other young women.

Sometimes I wonder if I will ever meet Rose McGowan or if I'll ever have coffee with the writer from our show who blew the whistle. I see the A-list actress in commercials and wonder if she knows what it meant to me that she fought my battle. It overwhelms me even still.

But I fight battles constantly now. My social media feed is a far cry from the old vague images of chickens and flowers. It's a tangle of different advocacies. Black Lives Matter, domestic violence cases, children's mental health facilities, Empathy for Educators, fundraisers for a whole mess of the world's problems. I will fight for those I don't know because it was strangers who fought for and beside me. It's a debt that is an honor to repay.

So, fight, dear reader. Fight like hell.

17

Women in the Man-Made City

Carla Corroto

I like cities because I studied architecture and cities have buildings. It is interesting to see the contrasting urban fabric created when neoclassical styles, with their elegant detail, are juxtaposed against spartan modern architecture. My interest extends beyond the aesthetic merits of buildings to include the spaces architecture creates—the courtyards, plazas, and streetscapes. I like cities because I studied sociology, as well, and cities have people. Curious about the way we understand and experience architecture and those urban spaces, I note how ethnic enclaves create neighborhoods with a diversity of styles and traditions. It is essential to consider the entire urban context, including the multiple ways in which the physical setting for life in cities is established, built on, reinvented, and occasionally abandoned. The built environment reflects the dominant cultures that create it and is an agent that propagates their values. Urban design is a multidisciplinary process with numerous components, including town planning, zoning, architectural engagements, parks, and places. Practitioners describe urban design as "creating the theater of public life."[1]

As an actor in this urban theater, I am aware of how the city is designed for a specific demographic. For example, office workers can commute to their daytime jobs with mass transit and traffic priority. Able-bodied people can find a building's door or stairwell without looking for an oft-unreliable wheelchair ramp or elevator. Middle-class people can afford to park their cars in garages with hourly fees. White people can claim the sidewalk with little fear of "stop and frisk" or "looking suspicious." The upper social classes can find, then afford, safe, quality housing in cities with a high cost of living. Most men can walk about unselfconsciously without having to circumvent catcalls or street harassment. American cities have largely been imagined, designed, and maintained to fit a single actor—a White, middle and upper class, cisgendered, able-bodied man who has no child care or household responsibilities. This is their theater of public life, and they are both the directors and stars of the show; the rest of us are supporting actors, extras, ushers, and stagehands.

We are literally living in a man-made world. With this chapter, I investigate women in relation to the American city's manifest and latent functions—how our freedoms are constrained or enhanced, fought for or taken for granted,

Carla Corroto, *Women in the Man-Made City* In: *On Inequality and Freedom*. Edited by: Lawrence M. Eppard and Henry A. Giroux, Oxford University Press. © Oxford University Press 2022. DOI: 10.1093/oso/9780197583029.003.0017 policed or liberated. Considering urban design decisions as scripts written for the theater of public life offers a framework for understanding who among us can flourish in the city and who is oppressed when navigating the built urban environment. To date, men in dominant positions have been the authors of architectural and urban design schemes and policies. From their vantage points, our cities mostly make sense.

Urbanization, Backstage

Until the mid-nineteenth and early twentieth centuries, most White people in the United States settled across sparsely populated small towns in rural regions. In the year 1800, only about 6 percent of the population inhabited cities. By the early twentieth century, 40 percent of the population lived in cities, and New York had 1 million people. Most families no longer worked cooperatively on farms as industrial-capitalism separated home from work. Contributing to urban population growth, by the mid-twentieth century the Great Migration occurs with 6 million Black people moving from the rural South to the urban North, Midwest, and West. Today, 81 percent of Americans reside in urban areas, and 10 U.S. cities have over a million people, with New York recording 8.4 million residents. *Urbanization* is the process whereby people move from rural areas and small towns to cities. Urban and architectural design, with all of its corollaries, responded to this migration. Fueled by industrialization and social, economic, and political changes, urbanization was sustained by transportation, communication systems, and architectural arrangements that created industrial workplaces, offices, shops, and housing. Immigrants from other countries joined, as people relocated to U.S. cities in order to find jobs, housing, or cultural features that make an urban lifestyle possible.[2]

Actors' Roles

Early urban sociologists weighed in on the advent of urbanization in the United States forming a consistent view of city life. A narrative pattern developed around the dichotomous tropes that small towns are warm and friendly, while big cities are cold and mean spirited; rural America is provincial and simple, while urban America is cosmopolitan and sophisticated. Most theorists posited that rural life creates interdependence based on shared values, while urban environments are impersonal and foster a kind of selfish individualism. The former was framed as positive relationships in tight-knit communities, and the latter as relations defined by a functional need to exchange services, rather than authentic concern for each other's welfare. Of the city, sociologist Ferdinand Tonnies wrote: "Here everybody is by himself (sic) and isolated, and there exists a condition of tension against all others."[3]

Feminists criticize these sociologists for painting the urban experience with a broad and traditionally masculine brush, thereby creating a partial analysis of urbanization. Might some people find anonymity and shifting norms in the city liberating? Is this so-called tension against all others a false supposition not shared by those who find solidarity in the city? Life in an urban environment is informed by the intersection of one's gender, social class, age, disability status, and sexual, racial, and ethnic identities. What has urbanization meant for women from disparate groups in the United States?

In her review of the literature on urbanization, sociologist Lyn Lofland contended that ignoring women's perspectives creates an incomplete theoretical explanation of cities and of the distinct social realities that women and men confront. She wrote that recognizing as customary to the methodological limitations of urban sociology is the habit of depicting women as "part of the furniture of the setting through which the plot moves . . . continually perceived but rarely perceivers . . . essential to the set but largely irrelevant to the action." Lofland asserted that this pattern of analysis results in little attention paid to a "wide range of acts, settings, actors, and patterns of life organization within the urban world."[4]

If the city is the theater of public life, the script writers and critics do not recognize an ensemble cast, let alone "leading ladies." It went unreported that many women find their lives in the city exhilarating because they are away from the controlling institutions and traditional expectations of femininity—that a woman must marry a man, raise children, and remain subservient. Scholar Elizabeth Wilson reframed early urbanization from a feminist perspective, writing that: "The city is the zone of individual freedom. There, the ties of family and kinship may be loosened and avenues of escape may open up."[5] She posited that cities are also invigorating because they present diverse cultural experiences as objects of exploration, inquiry, and analysis. The art of architecture, museums, theater, diverse cuisine, design, and fashion are some of the enchantments for women in the middle and upper classes. In this view, cities are "settings for voyages of discovery."[6]

Urbanization challenged those with power over their ability to impose social control. "Women have always been seen as a problem for the modern city. During the Industrial Revolution, strict boundaries between classes and a firm etiquette designed to protect the purity of high-status white women were fractured by the increased urban contact between women and men, and between women and the city's great seething masses."[7] Many women found a level of freedom in the city by rejecting courtship norms, resisting familial expectations, and enjoying an increasing level of anonymity that the city provided.

Scripts for Separate Spheres

Examining women's relation to design in the history of cities and urbanization in the United States is challenging, as most architectural and urban historians do not identify gender, women, or sexuality in their analysis.[8] I look to sociologists, who contend that urban spatial arrangements codify and pattern a particular set of social relationships in the built environment and are organized around the middle-class notion of "separate spheres."[9] This patriarchal metaphor posits that men occupy public lives as breadwinners, traversing the city's urban core and public spaces, while women are confined to private lives in residential neighborhoods and suburbs. Urban designers supposed women had responsibility (only) for domestic relations, raising children, shopping, cooking, and cleaning in their sphere of unpaid and undervalued labor. The city and metropolis were designed with the male breadwinner–female homemaker model. Residential suburbs developed as so-called bedroom communities from where men commute to their workplaces in urban centers, while middle-class women tended to the demands of domesticity.

Marion Roberts contended that the single-family detached house in the suburbs is the quintessential example of an "architecture of gender," where traditional expectations for girls and boys, men and women are reproduced.[10] Here, planners, contractors, and architects suppose that all women are mothers and are married to men. Analyzing at the micro-level, designated spaces in the suburban house are also gendered. A "man's space" may be a study or a woodshop for tinkering. In the past few decades, these masculine spaces were glibly labeled "man caves," where hardworking men could finally relax when home to watch sports and perhaps drink. There is even a well-known brand of reclining chair called La-Z-Boy, intended for a man as "a space away from work, a napcentric, personal pod of softness."[11] In suburban-gendered residential architecture a woman does not have a space or a designated chair or time off from work. A "woman's place" in the house is, essentially, the kitchen.

Ignored was the fact that working-class women were always in the paid labor force as cleaners, housekeepers, or factory workers. Today, most middle-class families have dual wage earners largely because they cannot afford a stay-at-home parent.[12] So, when scholars study spatial arrangements, the binaries of separate spheres, domestic and public domains and private and public places, become less distinct and incongruous. Nonetheless, the idea that men and women live and work in entirely separate domains continues to inform architectural and urban design philosophy, perspective, policy, and planning. Obviously, how women consume and experience cities are neither distinctly separate nor spherical. We are in the theater.

Act One—The City as Planned

By looking at the use of spaces and places in the city, feminist scholars offer a complete approach to women's experiences, which demonstrates that we have a more complicated relationship to both the domestic and public realms. First, let's look at how we navigate the city. On a single day, many men simply commute to work and back home again. But, research shows that women "trip-chain," or make a number of interconnected short- and medium-length jaunts. This is because, regardless of hours in the paid labor force, most unpaid care work—the face-to-face caretaking that involves the physical needs of others—is still done by women. So, women's travel throughout the city is more complicated. Consider, as an example, an average weekday pattern. A woman drops her children off at school before heading to work. At lunch, she picks up a prescription at the pharmacy and delivers it to an elderly relative, while checking on that relative's well-being. In the afternoon, she fetches the kids from school and drops each at their soccer practice, dance class, and tutor. Returning to work, she logs another hour before shopping at the market for dinner preparations; then on the way home, picks up the children at their respective activities. This is a trip-chain that urban designers and policymakers did not consider when laying out the city's streets, traffic patterns, and transportation routes.

Second, data gathered in U.S. cities show that between 55 and 65 percent of those using light rail, subways, and buses are adult women. Also, in general, women are more likely than men to walk about the city and use public transportation, often with children in tow. In her influential book *Invisible Women: Data Bias in a World Designed for Men*, Caroline Criado Perez documented how urban designers and civil and traffic engineers consider only mobility related to employment when planning for streets, highways, and public transportation. The conventional term used by transportation professionals is "compulsory mobility," and this explains the focus on commuting for work in the paid labor force. In a disdainful critique of their concept that privileges a capitalist economy where unpaid labor is invisible, Perez wrote, "as if care trips are not compulsory, but merely expendable 'me time' for dilettantes."[13]

Transportation specialists, mimicking the conceptual work of those early sociologists who did not consider women's experiences in the public theater, create a "gender data gap" that affects women's freedom in the city.[14] Urban designers are predisposed to plan for the travel paths and schedules of an unencumbered-with-care-work individual. Traffic lanes are designed for maximum capacity at "typical" compulsory mobility commute times, and public transportation is less frequent when women craft their midday or evening trip-chains. In addition, as Perez documented, cold climate cities prioritize snow removal on major thoroughfares. They begin by plowing the main arteries and highways and end by clearing snow from side streets and pedestrian pathways. A woman pushing a baby stroller to a bus stop after a snowfall or negotiating a wheelchair to the subway in icy conditions has quite a difficult journey. After one city changed the sequence of snow clearing to prioritize pedestrians and public transportation users, fewer people were admitted to the hospital with injuries from falling and other mobility accidents. They surmised, correctly, that it is easier for cars to drive over a few inches of snow than it is to navigate snow-covered, slick sidewalks on foot.[15] Indeed, snow plowing in the context of public transportation and navigation is a gendered public health issue.

Act Two—Drama in the Streets

We recognize now that architecture and urban design decisions are not neutral, and in fact, they literally structure, build, and reify patriarchal assumptions. The theater of public life has at its foundation a material organization whereby men dominate. This is at both the structural and individual levels. Borer reminds us that: "The sociology of urban experiences is intrinsically connected to the lived experiences within, and with, places and spaces."[16] Many women experience street harassment or stranger intrusion when they are alone or with other women in the city. This type of urban provocation is acknowledged as an "everyday" form of violence against women and is generally not taken seriously, even though many women report altering their behavior and travel routes in an attempt to avoid confrontations. "The constant, low-grade threat of violence mixed with daily harassment shapes women's urban lives in countless ways. Just as workplace harassment chases women out of positions of power and erases their contributions to science, politics, art, and culture, the specter of urban violence limits women's choices, power, and economic opportunities," wrote geographer Leslie Kern.[17] Stranger intrusion can be intimidating and is coupled with many women's fear for their safety in cities more generally. We may wonder: How can urban design thwart individual men's bad behavior? Some will contend that it doesn't matter how buildings and cities are arranged, men are still going to harass women. Feminist social movements challenge male sexist and aggressive acts with political, cultural, and social forces, and these forces will be expressed in a renewed urban context. It is important to compare places and spaces that are demonstrably more dangerous for women to those urban situations where women perceive and experience safety.

In her classic book *The Death and Life of Great American Cities,* Jane Jacobs reminded us that urban elements have many purposes. For example, a sidewalk is designated for pedestrian passage, but Jacobs contends that busy sidewalks function to maintain street safety because they foster contact, especially in neighborhoods where people interact routinely. On safe city streets, Jacobs wrote: "There must be eyes upon the street, eyes belonging to those we might call the natural proprietors of the street."[18] Jacobs advocated for porches, front stoops with room for benches, and broad staircases where neighbors may sit and chat and keep a watchful eye on the sidewalk. In many American cities, architects have designed modern high-rise buildings as both public and luxury housing with little acknowledgment of the street or urban context. Via elevators, residents are whisked above to their private entrances, and they may not even know their neighbors, let alone have eyes on the streets. Buildings require a meaningful relationship with the street and an orientation to the sidewalk if residents are to be attentive. Jacobs contended that eyes on the street means activity both on the streets and within the architecture. Whether it is commercial or residential, transparency via windows and doors is critical. From inside, you may see outside and vice versa. Would you hesitate to enter a store or a restaurant in a city if you cannot see what is going on inside, if there were walls rather than windows on the street? Further, Jacobs maintains the street should house a mixture of building purposes. Stores, bars, cafes, and housing are necessary to attract people at night, and during the day. The mixture of commercial workplaces and residences generally ensure that there are always a collective of people keeping the streets safe with their continuous presence.

Citing crime data, some may challenge the claim that the city is unsafe for women. It is true that, statistically, women are in more danger from intimate partners in their homes than from strangers in the city.[19] "Arguably the most commonly repeated 'finding' of fear of crime research is that many people overestimate the possibility of becoming a victim of crime, when set against the 'objective risk' of being offended against."[20] The actuality of crime is, indeed, significant. However, sociologists remind us that what we believe is real, is real in its consequences.[21] If some women are afraid to leave their homes at night, walk down certain streets, or relax in a city park, they will amend behavior, thereby limiting their freedom. How does architecture and urban design play into how we assess our risk of becoming victims of crime? Well-lit streets, brightly lit public transportation stations, and illuminated public spaces with cameras help the actuality and perception of safety. Dark passages, alleys, hidden entries, and parking garages in the city communicate danger.

Access to the theater of public life is important for all citizens. International resistance to limiting women's freedom in the city due to the threat of violence is growing, too, and the United States may want to borrow several strategies. In some cities like Barcelona, Spain, where there are distinct districts known for their bars, entertainment, and wide-ranging party scene, "antimachismo" pavilions staffed by feminist community members are assembled to provide women with advice and consultation. "Stay away from *that* bar full of drunk fraternity brothers. Limit your access to *this* road because the street lamps are out. Watch out for *that* man in the gray ski jacket." Women can also report acts of sexual aggression and misconduct. This is part of a citywide "say no to sleaze" and "designing cities for women" campaign that includes urban design interventions as well.[22] "Superblocks" where automobile traffic is eliminated were introduced in Barcelona, with avenues comprising community gardens, benches and tables, lush vegetation, and playgrounds. Streets were returned to pedestrians and light bicycle use, enabling custodial parents to gather and watch after their children at play while the parents chat—eyes on the streets, indeed.

Another innovation used globally is the smartphone application SafetiPin created by a social organization of the same name. It was developed to help women make walking and driving route decisions by encouraging users to rate streets and areas for safety criteria, such as lighting, visibility, people density, gender diversity, security, and transportation. Collecting these data, local urban designers and city planners are using the information to understand what is considered a safe route and where users perceive problems so that they can make responsive design decisions. The application also enables women to designate someone they trust to track their journey. The app developer reported: "We find a lot of women are able to travel at night using these two features. . . . It gives them confidence to travel around the city. And the more women venture out, the busier—and safer—the streets become."[23] SafetiPin's data are crowdsourced and is supplemented with photographs. They can map the city, noting dark spots where there is sparse lighting and streets that contain few safe spaces. This is a dynamic process that is updated frequently as cities are ever-changing entities.

The city communicates at a representational or symbolic level as well. Picture the following: You are waiting at a bus stop embellished with a sexist advertisement featuring a scantily dressed, life-sized female model as an object of consumption, selling perfume or lingerie or car tires. We do not know her name. Across the street, directly in your line of sight, is a monument to a well-respected and revered historical figure who is a man. A larger-than-life-sized marble statue portrays him with dignity, fully dressed in a military uniform, his name etched in stone. The juxtaposition of these representations illustrates how we measure worth. Men are valued for their accomplishments—no matter how dubious—and women for their appearance. This not a neutral place communicating respect for women, but rather an intimidating environment that inflicts a conscious level of dissonance. Images that objectify women can be found around the city on billboards, department store windows, and driving by on the sides of buses. These symbols reinforce the gender binary, or how we construct femininity and masculinity as opposites: Men are strong actors in the theater of public life, women attractive bits of the scenery.

Act Three—Taking the Show on the Road

Urban experiences and symbols reify the social and institutional constructions of gender. Conflating a fear of the city with norms of femininity, some urban hotels in the United States and abroad equivocally offer women traveling on business "alone" (seemingly without a man) a single-sex floor for their safety (*from* men) and special beauty amenities to become more attractive (*to* men).[24] Initially conceived as a marketing concept, these hotels responded by co-opting for profit women's legitimate fear of violence in the city. They offer women-only floors or "man-free zones" in luxury hotels with a fully female staff—from check-in with bellhops and a concierge, to room service delivery and housekeeping—women guests will be served only by other women. Sex segregation is their method for reassuring women business travelers that they will be safe in the city if they check in to what may be aptly named the "architecture of fear."[25]

This arrangement has social class implications. Thinking about the intersection of identities, how are working-class women who service the business travelers protected when they interact with men across integrated spaces in the hotel? If segregation from men is the key to safety, who is looking after the staff? Revealed as the "Me Too" movement took form, hotel housekeepers are among the most vulnerable to sexual assault and victimization.[26] Also, given that hotel workers are available around the clock, working various shifts, how are working-class women protected when they get off work at night or the wee hours of the morning? At the other end of the economic ladder, the hotels offering women-only floors do so at an additional cost that can be up to 25 percent more than their typical business room rate. Given the stagnant gender wage gap, the surcharge for safety is an additional fee levied against a feminine identity.

In several hotels, the architecture and interior designed precautions to "avoid harm" include a private and "discreet" entry from the street—with its own address—for patrons who are women. Individual hotel room doors are outfitted with lower peep holes that respond to the average woman's eye level, and double door lock hardware is designated as "more secure." There are women-only elevators or special key cards for women's floors and women's fitness centers. One hotel advertises: "Ladies who book a room get glossy mags, fresh flowers, a quiet corner table in each room for those women who'd rather dine-in than go out alone,"[27] discouraging women from exploring the city while assuming we have no colleagues, friends, or acquaintances with whom to share a meal.

Conflating fear of crime with femininity, they added the "feminine touches," or gender-specific amenities that have nothing to do with safety or business travel and everything to do with reifying stereotypical notions of femininity, often stressing appearance. For example, the bathroom vanities are made wider to arrange cosmetics and makeup remover, skin care samples, and a cosmetic mirror are standard features.[28] Women-only room service menus offer "reduced calorie or lite meals," indicating women should pay attention to body weight. Available for a "private consultation and assessment" is a female personal trainer in the hotel health club who understands the exercise needs of women travelers. One hotel reminds women that "whether it be a blow dry or manicure a female stylist will also come to the guest's room to help her prepare for those impor- tant meetings." Another hotel offers shorter bathrobes and bath salts that are pH balanced for women. A hotel in Los Angeles publicizes: "For convenience, [the hotel] guarantees a return of within four hours on laundry and dry-cleaning services required for those last-minute functions and meetings. And an inde- pendent personal shopper can be made available; to deliver a variety of clothing items suitable for all occasions that may arise unexpectedly." Indeed, the message is clear that appearance matters. Further crafting gendered differences, one ho- telier suggests he knows what women want because "he also had female-friendly channels such as Hallmark, Oxygen, TLC, and Lifetime" added to the televisions on the women's floor.[29] Seemingly, only male business travelers want news channels, a printer, USB ports, and strong WiFi.

If employment requires travel and women are repeatedly reminded by dom- inant culture and institutions that we should fear interaction in cities, what are the implications for careers and income? Do some women reject job opportu- nities if travel is involved? The urban patriarchy is reified by the gendered ex- pectation that women are to be protected (from men) in their rooms, applying makeup and eating salad while watching a Lifetime Movie featuring the clichéd woman-in-peril.

Curtain

Patriarchy by design has significant implications for women and urbanity. Experience and research demonstrate that women lead complex lives and must utilize intentionality, more time, and greater caution negotiating cities. Popular culture often casts the city as an object of trepidation, and the inference is that women must determine how to navigate the streets, the architecture, and the public spaces to keep themselves safe and functioning—not that men should alter either their preconceptions when designing or behavior when interacting. It is time to rethink the man-made city.

We know urban life is more varied than early theorists posited. Many of us find meaningful connections in the city when we join organizations and social movements, visit museums and enjoy live music, and obtain worthwhile em- ployment with opportunities for travel. It is time for our architecture and urban design to recognize people find multiple meanings in the built environment, and that these meanings are informed by our gendered identities and affiliations. Anonymously walking the streets and lined boulevards, window shopping and people watching, can be pleasurable and liberating. Many women embrace the city for its diversity of experiences and subcultures. Making the architecture of urban experience fit our lives is crucial for freedom in the American city.

When advocating for the importance and consequence of urban design, many architects and planners frequently deploy the Winston Churchill quotation: "We shape our buildings; thereafter, they shape us." Considering women in the built urban environment, I advocate that the "we" shaping urban design consider all actors in the recognition that architectural arrangements—from the micro, hotel room doors to the macro, city planning—have implications for our freedom in the city.

Notes

1. "Indicators of Good Urban Design," A Dash of Design, October 11, 2020, https://adashofdesign.wordpress.com/2010/10/11/good-urban-design/.
2. Mark Gottdiener, Randolph Hohle, and Colby R. King, *The New Urban Sociology*, 6th ed. (Routledge, 2019).
3. Ferdinand Tonnies, *Community and Society (Gemeinschaft and Gesellschaft)*, trans. Charles P. Loomis (East Lansing: Michigan State University Press, 1887/1975) 65.
4. Lyn H. Lofland, "The 'Thereness' of Women: A Selective Review of Urban Sociology," in *Another Voice: Feminist Perspectives on Social Life and Social Science*, ed. Marcia Millman and Rosabeth Moss Kanter (Garden City, NY: Doubleday Anchor, 1975, 139–166, 144–145.
5. Elizabeth Wilson, *The Sphinx in the City: Urban Life, the Control of Disorder, and Women* (Berkeley: University of California Press, 1991) 16.
6. Wilson, *The Sphinx in the City*, 11.
7. Leslie Kern, "Is It Time to Build Feminist Cities?" *Vox*, June 12, 2020, https://www.vox.com/the-highlight/2020/6/5/21279320/feminist-geography-cities-urbanism-safety-motherhood.
8. Andrea J. Merrett, "From Separate Spheres to Gendered Spaces: The Historiography of Women and Gender in 19th and Early 20th Century America," in *The Proceedings of Spaces of History/Histories of Space: Emerging Approaches to the Study of the Built Environment* (Berkeley: University of California, 2010).
9. Shannon N. Davis and Theodore N. Greenstein. "Gender Ideology: Components, Predictors, and Consequences," *Annual Review of Sociology* 35, (2009): 87–105.
10. Marion Roberts, *Living in a Man-Made World: Gender Assumptions in Modern Housing Design* (London: Routledge, 1991).
11. Tracy E. Robey, "La-Z-Boy and the American Dream: The Once-Mocked Recliner Has Become an Aspirational Brand," *Vox*, January 8, 2020, https://www.vox.com/the-goods/2020/1/8/21028575/la-z-boy-recliner-history.

12. Peter Temin, *The Vanishing Middle Class: Prejudice and Power in a Dual Economy* (Cambridge, MA: MIT Press, 2017).

13. Caroline Criado Perez, *Invisible Women: Data Bias in a World Designed for Men* (New York: Abrams Press, 2019), 33.

14. Perez, *Invisible Women.*

15. Perez, *Invisible Women.*

16. Michael Ian Borer, "Being in the City: The Sociology of Urban Experiences," *Sociology Compass* 7/11 (2013): 965–983, 966.

17. Kern, "Is It Time to Build Feminist Cities?"

18. Jane Jacobs, *The Death and Life of Great American Cities* (New York: Random House, 1961), 35.

19. Bureau of Justice Statistics, https://www.bjs.gov/index.cfm?ty=tp&tid=941

20. Murray Lee and Gabe Mythen, *The Routledge International Handbook on Fear of Crime* (London: Routledge, 2017), 1.

21. Robert K. Merton, "The Self-Fulfilling Prophecy," *Antioch Review* 74, no. 3, 75th Anniversary, Part I (2016): 504–521, https://doi.org/10.7723/antiochrev iew.74.3.0504.

22. Christele Harrouk, "What Can Cities Imagined by Women Look Like? The Case of Barcelona," *ArchDaily,* January 2020, https://www.archdaily.com/927948/how-can-cities-imagined-by-women-look-like-the-case-of-barcelona#.

23. Amy Fleming, "What Would a City That Is Safe for Women Look Like?" *Guardian,* December 13, 2018, https://www.theguardian.com/cities/2018/dec/13/what-would-a-city-that-is-safe-for-women-look-like.

24. Susanne Gargiulo, "Women-Only Hotel Floors Tap Boom in Female Business Travel," *CNN Business,* March 20, 2012, https://www.cnn.com/2012/03/07/business/women-hotels-business-travelers/index.html.

25. Nan Ellin, "Shelter From the Storm or Form Follows Fear and Vice Versa," in *The Architecture of Fear,* ed. Nan Ellin (New York: Princeton Architectural Press, 1997), 13–46.

26. Julia Jacobs, "Hotels See Panic Buttons as a #MeToo Solution for Workers. Guest Bans? Not So Fast," *New York Times,* November 11, 2018, https://www.nytimes.com/2018/11/11/us/panic-buttons-hotel-me-too.html.

27. Kat Lister, "How Hotels Are Capitalizing on Women's Fears of Traveling Alone," *Vice,* March 24, 2016, https://www.vice.com/en_us/article/wnwven/how-hotels-are-capit alizing-on-womens-fears-of-traveling-alone.

28. "No Boys Allowed: Hotels With Women-Only Floors," SmarterTravel, September 4, 2014, https://www.smartertravel.com/no-boys-allowed-hotels-with-women-only-floors/.

29. Alissa Ponchione, "Women-Only Floors Cater to Growing Market," *Hotel News Now,* October 2012, https://www.hotelnewsnow.com/Articles/16839/Women-only-floors-cater-to-growing-market.

18

Grinding the Gears of Ideology

Interpellation and Gender in *Us Weekly* and *The Bell Jar*

Luke Ferretter

Louis Althusser's most influential contribution to cultural theory has been his account of ideology, in particular his account of the "Ideological State Apparatuses" (ISAs) in which it functions. Althusser was a member of the French Communist Party, and he wrote his most important accounts of ideology in 1969, shortly after the events of May 1968 in Paris, which seemed to him just one indication of very many that "the revolution is already on the agenda." Some of the popular struggles to which he refers in beginning his work on ideology include "the liberation movements of the 'Third World' countries, the Vietnamese people's victorious struggles against French and then American imperialism, the struggle of Black Americans, student revolts, and so on."[1] He does not mention the contemporary mass movement for women's liberation, but in this chapter I argue for the significance of his theory of ideology for the struggle not only between economic classes but also between genders. Althusser's account of ideology remains crucial in understanding the complexity, the state of struggle enacted in public discourse, both class and gender discourse, in America today. So, after an account of Althusser's theory of ideology, I provide two examples of gender ideology in the Ideological State Apparatuses of contemporary America, an example of "popular" culture and an example of "literary" culture, and assess the state of inequality and freedom and the state of both the class struggle and the gender struggle at work in these ideologies today.

Interpellation

Althusser's first published account of what he called Ideological State Apparatuses appeared in *La Pensée* in June 1970, a condensation of a much longer and unfinished work called "On the Reproduction of the Apparatuses of Production" as a manuscript that he planned to publish with the title *On the Superstructure*. There are two versions of the manuscript. The first is a 150-page typed text, dated March–April 1969; the second "bears a set of corrections and

Luke Ferretter, *Grinding the Gears of Ideology* In: *On Inequality and Freedom*. Edited by: Lawrence M. Eppard and Henry A. Giroux, Oxford University Press. © Oxford University Press 2022. DOI: 10.1093/oso/9780197583029.003.0018 addenda that increase the length of the first . . . by about one-third." Notably, these corrections, modifications, and rewrites stop in the middle of Chapter 8 in a 12-chapter text, indicating that, as the editor of the text Jacques Bidet said, "Althusser never made all the revisions to the manuscript that he originally intended to." Althusser's article in *La Pensée* (published in English translation in 1971 in the collection of his essays, *Lenin and Philosophy*) "does not incorporate all the modifications made to the second manuscript version, which would thus appear to have been revised after the *Pensée* piece appeared."[2] However, there are also modifications in the essay that do not appear in the manuscript. It seems that the essay represents a first rewriting of the first version of the manuscript, and that the second version represents a second rewriting, which was ultimately unfinished. The second version was published in French in 1995, five years after Althusser's death, as *Sur la reproduction*, and in English translation (as *On the Reproduction of Capitalism*) in 2014.

Althusser argued that an addition needs to be made to the traditional Marxist theory of the state. From Marx to the present, he wrote, the state has above all been conceived by Marxists as the "state apparatus," that is "the police, the courts, and prisons—but also the army, which . . . intervenes directly as the repressive force of the last resort when the police . . . are 'overwhelmed by events.' Presiding over this ensemble are the chief of state, the government, and the administration." This could more accurately be called the "Repressive State Apparatus," Althusser argued, in order to be distinguished from "another 'reality' that must clearly be ranged alongside [it], but *is not conflated with it*," which he proposed to call the Ideological State Apparatuses.[3] The Repressive State Apparatus (or RSA) "functions by violence," at least primarily. The Ideological State Apparatuses, on the other hand, "function by ideology," at least primarily. To be precise, the RSA "functions massively and predominantly *by repression* . . . while functioning secondarily by ideology," and the ISAs "function massively and predominantly *by ideology*, but they also function secondarily by repression."[4]

What is an ISA? In "Ideology and Ideological State Apparatuses," Althusser gave his most detailed list:

- the religious ISA (the system of different churches),
- the educational ISA (the system of different public and private schools),
- the family ISA,
- the legal ISA,
- the political ISA (the political system, including the different Parties),
- the trade union ISA,
- the communications ISA (press, radio, and television),
- the cultural ISA (literature, the Arts, sports, etc.).[5]

In *On the Reproduction of Capitalism*, he gave a similar list, in which he included a "Publishing and Distribution [*Edition-Diffusion*]" ISA. He later noted that there is a medical ISA.[6] Both lists are "provisional," needing to be "examined in detail, tested, corrected, and reorganized."[7] An important point emphasized more strongly in the manuscript than the essay is that "there exist 'institutions' or 'organizations' corresponding ... to each ISA. For the [educational] ISA: the various schools and their various levels, from the primary to the tertiary, the various institutes and so on"; "for each ISA, the various institutions and organizations comprising it form a *system*." The institutions and organizations of a state comprise a complex network of ISAs, which furthermore interrelate with each other in conveying the ideology of the ruling classes, the ruling ideology, of that state to its citizens. The ISAs, and the institutions comprising them, are extremely diverse, but they are all ultimately unified, Althusser argued, by the state ideology:

> An Ideological State Apparatus is a system of defined institutions, organizations, and the corresponding practices. Realized in the institutions, organizations, and practices of this system is all or part (generally speaking, a typical combination of certain elements) of the State Ideology.[8]

We still have to define the concept of ideology, by which the ISAs primarily function. In fact, Althusser came to realize that the concept of ideology itself has been thus far inadequately thought in Marxist tradition, and in order to fill this gap he proposed a "preliminary, very schematic sketch" of "a *theory of ideology in general* that is still lacking in Marxist theory as such." The "central thesis" of this theory is this: "Ideology interpellates individuals as subjects."[9] Althusser's French phrase is *L'idéologie interpelle les individus en sujets*. English-speaking readers have been fortunate to have two excellent translators of Althusser's work, Ben Brewster (who translated "Ideology and Ideological State Apparatuses") and G. M. Goshgarian (who translated *On the Reproduction of Capitalism*). Despite the excellence of these translations, however, there is no easy way to get *L'idéólogie interpelle les indivdus en sujets* accurately and concisely into English. The main issue is the verb *interpeller*, which Goshgarian followed Brewster in translating "hails or interpellates." They sometimes use this compound phrase, and sometimes they use either hails or interpellates according to context. Unlike the archaic English cognate interpellate, the French verb (and its corresponding noun) is a common word in ordinary language. The technical sound that the concept of interpellation has in English does not exist in Althusser's French. Second, its semantic range corresponds to no single word in English. *Interpeller* means first to "call out to" or to "shout at" someone. If I see you at a distance and call out your name to get your attention, then I interpelle you. Second, it means to question, or even to interrogate, in a police context. Althusser spoke of *la plus banale interpellation policière (ou non) de tous le jours*, "the most commonplace everyday police (or other) interpellation,"[10] and he can use the phrase *policière (ou non)* because these are the two main contexts for the very term interpellation in French: police or other. Interpellation is "questioning" by the police. *Proceder à des interpellations* is "to take people in for questioning."

Warren Montag has written an excellent account of the connotations of the term. He pointed out that one of the difficulties with using the English term "hail" (chosen because of the sense of "calling out to" someone that the word has) is that the latter has connotations in English of respect, even reverence. But "to be *interpellé* or interpellated is to be spoken to in a 'brusque manner,' to be insulted or to be the object of a demand." In penal law, Montag pointed out, "to interpellate is to take someone into custody or interrogate someone who is police custody, to arrest, detain or stop (as in a 'traffic stop') an individual. . . . In civil law, it is to issue a legal summons to someone." He concluded that the connotations of the French term, as Althusser used it, are an indication of "the violence of interpellation," which "cannot be easily separated from arrest, detention, and torture, even if its material forms are more subtly coercive."[11] So, to interpellate is to both call out to someone, as I would call out the name of someone across a room or a street in order to get their attention, and to question or interrogate someone, with all the threats of force of the state, and the ruling class of which it is the state, as a police officer would do of someone they suspected of a crime against that state.

In this sense, then, ideology interpellates individuals as subjects. The "subject," Althusser argued (as no Marxist before him has done) is "the constitutive category of all ideology." What all ideology does, in both capitalist society and all other previous class societies, is tell me that I am a subject. It calls out to me, initially in a nonthreatening way but potentially with all the force of the state behind it, that I am a subject. The concept has been known (and still is) by other names, "such as the soul in Plato, God, and so on."[12] It can take the form of Duty, Justice, the Fatherland, the Revolution, and many other forms, depending on the ideology in which it functions.[13] But it is the fundamental category of all ideology for Althusser, who summed up: "All ideology hails or interpellates concrete individuals as concrete subjects." By an individual, Althusser meant a person, considered in his or her material reality within the forces and relations of production that constitute the material reality of his or her society, and that determine every aspect of his or her life. By a subject, he meant first of all a person considered as the origin and agent of his or her thoughts and actions, "a free subjectivity, a center of initiatives, author of and responsible for its actions."[14] Indeed, a subject is a person. Now the fact that, in order to make myself clear, I used the word "person" in defining his concept of an individual, indicates the first thing we need to understand about the concept of the subject. It indicates that the concept is everywhere, all around me (and you), so that it is difficult in the first instance to think outside of it. It is obvious that people are people, that is to say, subjects, the origin and agent of their own thoughts and actions. It is so obvious that when I try to define what Althusser meant by an individual as opposed to a subject, it is difficult to avoid using the term "person," which is precisely the kind of concept he meant to be the very opposite of individual, namely subject. As Althusser said:

> As St Paul admirably puts it, it is in the "Logos," meaning in ideology, that we "live, move, and have our being." It follows that for you and me, the category of the subject is a primary "obviousness." . . . It is clear that you and I are subjects (free, ethical, etc. . . .). Like all obviousnesses . . . the obviousness that you and I are subjects . . . is an ideological effect, the elementary ideological effect.[15]

We are always already within ideology (with its fundamental category of the subject), so to think of ourselves as anything other than subjects is initially difficult and strange.

So ideology interpellates us as subjects. It calls out to us that we are subjects and has already been doing so from before our birth, in which we are expected and constituted as such. Althusser gave as an example of this process of calling out to us or interpellation the Christian religious ideology, which was his own set of beliefs and practices until he converted to communism at the age of 30. He noticed several ways in which Christian ideology calls out to an individual, constituting her as a subject, and he argued that these are typical of ideology in general, of the ways in which all ideologies call out to individuals and constitute them thereby as subjects. First, the calling is done by a "Great Subject" (*Grand Sujet*)— a bigger, better, more powerful, perfect subject, which Althusser proposed to designate with a capital S, Subject, "to distinguish it from ordinary subjects."[16] Indeed, interpellation can only occur, Althusser wrote, on the condition that "il y a *un Autre Sujet*: Unique, Absolu," "there is *an Other Subject*: Unique, Absolute," which in Christian ideology is of course God.[17] This Great Subject calls out to the Christian in the practices and rituals of the church, making her into a subject in his own image (as Althusser pointed out, the Bible, the text taught in the church to be authored by God, teaches Christians that human beings are made "in the image of" God [Gen. 1:27]). The Christian ideology tells an individual who lives in it that she is created by God, unique, in his image, loved, even died for by God's son who is also God, that God wants her love in response to his love. The subjects of this ideology, that is, are the "mirrors," the "reflections" of the Subject, and this is how all ideology works; for Althusser:

> The structure of all ideology, interpellating individuals as subjects in the name of a Unique and Absolute Subject, is *speculary*, in other words, a mirror-structure,

and *doubly speculary.* . . . This means that all ideology is *centered,* that the Absolute Subject occupies the unique place of the Center and interpellates around it the infinity of individuals as subjects in a doubly speculary relation.[18]

Althusser uses the phrase "duplicate mirror-structure" to describe the "doubly specular relation" he sees in ideology. He means that the Subject calls the subjects to be an image of itself, while itself constituting a model for those subjects, forming itself in their image so that they can more easily and effectively conform to its. As he put it, in terms of the Christian ideology: "God needs man; the Great Subject needs subjects."

Crucially, this doubly specular relationship "subjects the subject to the Subject."[19] This is the essence of the concept of the subject as it functions in ideology for Althusser. This is why the subject is the constitutive category of all ideology. Because in interpellating individuals as subjects in a philosophical sense, as origins and agents of their own thoughts and actions, it ensures at the same time that they remain subjects in a political sense, that is subjected beings, as one might speak of a king's people as his subjects. This works in the Christian religious ideology as in all ideologies. Integral to the processes of God calling out to an individual as a subject is the *subjection* of that subject to God, the Great Subject. If I am a Christian, I recognize that I am a unique person created in the image of God the Great Person, and at the same time I recognize that I am his subject, answerable to him who rules over me and demands my obedience. This dual constitution of an individual as a subject (in both senses of the word "subject") is the heart of interpellation, for Althusser. This is ideology's most fundamental process and function. In calling out to me that I am a subject in the first sense (i.e., the origin of my own thoughts and actions), ideology in fact ensures that I remain a subject in the second sense (that is ruled over by the ruling classes in my society). By telling me repeatedly and endlessly that I am free and that I am in charge of my life, ideology successfully makes sure that I am neither.

Althusser emphasized to a much greater extent in *On the Reproduction of Capitalism* than in "Ideology and Ideological State Apparatuses" that it is not only the dominant ideologies, the ideologies of the ruling, exploiting classes in society, that are at work in its ISAs. Capitalist ideology, the ideologies that function to perpetuate the capitalist mode of production and the rule of the bourgeoisie within it, dominates in the ISAs of capitalist society. But the ISAs are sites of class struggle:

Since Ideological State Apparatuses are the realization of the *dominant* ideology . . . , all talk of dominant ideology automatically implies that there also exists something that likewise involves ideology but is *dominated,* and thus involves the *dominated* classes. Hence we suspect that ideology, and therefore the Ideological State Apparatuses in which it exists, brings social classes "on stage" [*"mettent en scène" des classes sociales*]: the dominant class and the dominated class.[20]

The ISAs are a kind of theater, a stage, on which is played out (mis en scène) the class struggle in ideology. The ideologies of the dominant class, "the class of capitalists (and its allies)," and those of the dominated class, "the class of proletarians (and its allies)," clash and fight one another to be heard in the ISAs. Althusser called this process the "grinding of the gears" (*les grincements des engrenages*) of ideology.[21] *Grincer* means to "creak" (like a door), to "screech" (like a badly played violin), or to "squeak" (like chalk on a blackboard). It is used in the phrase to "grind" or "gnash" one's teeth. When Althusser wrote that ideological subformations *fassent parfois "grincer les engrenages"* of the ISAs, Goshgarian translated that they "make the gears grate and grind." We might also hear the word "screech" here, as we think of gears not working smoothly. This is what happens in the ISAs. The ideologies of the dominated classes, or "ideological sub-formations" (*sous-formations idéologiques*), make themselves heard and known, clashing, grinding, or screeching in their contradiction and conflict with the dominant ideologies. Althusser called the ISAs "relatively fragile" in this sense. Because they are multiple, distinct, and relatively autonomous, because "they realize the State Ideology, but piecemeal and in a disorganized way," they are "prone to providing an objective field to contradictions which express . . . the effects of the clashes between the capitalist class struggle and the proletarian class struggle."[22]

Us Weekly

Let us take a look and see how this works in practice. I am going to begin with celebrity gossip as an example of contemporary American ideology, especially insofar as it speaks to gender. Celebrity gossip is all around us, on magazine stands, on our televisions, on our smartphones, on our laptops, perhaps in our homes or workplaces, and often part of a shared conversational background. It is precisely its apparently unimportant, ephemeral, trivial nature that makes it so effective as ideology. We do not in our ordinary lives subject it to critical reason. It is simply "there," part of the ideological air we breathe, in the background of our day-to-day lives and of the principles on which our actions are based. Its messages tend to infiltrate our consciousness and practice subliminally, without our thoughtful and conscious rational acceptance or rejection of them, and so it has that characteristic of "obviousness" that Althusser rightly ascribed to ideology.

Celebrity gossip magazines are marketed primarily to 18- to 34-year-old women.[23] I begin with an analysis of the five issues in March 2020 of the most popular magazine of the genre, *Us Weekly*. The process of interpellation is visible from the cover and what follows. In March 2020, each magazine's cover is brightly colored and prominently features the faces of attractive and recognizable people. On March 30, for example, the largest face is that of Prince Harry of the United Kingdom, with a smaller inset face of his older brother, Prince William. Four movie stars and pop singers also look out at the prospective reader from two boxes on the right side of the cover—one a relatively large picture of a demure, smiling Katie Holmes, the second a picture of the faces of three well-made-up, well-dressed, and well-coiffed women: Carrie Underwood, Jennifer Aniston, and Jennifer Lopez. In the case of all five of these pictures on the cover, the names of these celebrities are printed next to the pictures. Indeed, in the case of Aniston and Lopez, they are given the familiar nicknames "Jen" and "J. Lo."

These faces call to me as the reader, whether on the magazine stand or at home once I have bought the magazine, through a combination of their brightness, their size, their beauty, and the structure of their gaze out at me. These qualities together make these images examples, in this genre, of Althusser's Absolute Subject. Although there is not necessarily this intention on the part of the editors of the magazine, these faces function as models. They call me to be like them. In Althusser's language, the Subject of ideology interpellates me as a subject when I look at them (or better, when they look at me). In simpler language, they call me to be like them. No individual necessarily intends that. The editors of the magazine were concerned with marketing—their goal in the cover was only to persuade me to buy the magazine. But in achieving that, an ethical effect occurs, and these images function for me as models on which to base my identity and the actions that constitute it. There is no reason why they should, but in fact they do, and this is the basis of the process of interpellation that Althusser has analyzed.

The first page of the March 30 issue of *Us Weekly*, as with every issue in March, was a full-page advertisement. In this case, it is a double page advertisement. The brand logo (Uncommon James) appears on the first page, and the facing page is a full picture of a model wearing one of the company's dresses, holding a peach, in front of an out-of-focus background of produce in a barn. It is a summer dress, low cut with straps, in pinks, peaches, purples, and whites. The woman is wearing gold jewelry—rings, bracelets, and necklace—and pink earrings that match the dress. She has long blonde hair and is smiling slightly. The image says, "Be like me." "Look like me," that is, young, attractive, with beautiful clothes that make me look especially attractive and beautiful jewelry that does the same thing. These things are expensive, but they are worth it. You will need makeup, again expensive but worth it; you will need constant hair care and products, but you will be happy, and fulfilled, like me. The image suggests a summer vacation, or even a late spring or early fall one, with its colors and barn full of fruits, and it says not only "Look like me," but also "Live like me." The look is a symbol here of an entire image of life. In that image, to which the reader-viewer is called by the advertisement as forcefully as by Althusser's policeman in the street, she is the kind of person who goes on a spring, summer, or fall vacation; sits glamorously by the barn in the pleasant countryside to which she vacations; looks effortlessly beautiful in an attractive dress, jewelry, well-styled hair; and smiles slightly, knowing that all is well, that she has done all that a person should, indeed is all that a person should be, holding an apple or peach in a better world, a better life than the one the reader-viewer lives, struggling unglamorously to pay her bills in the capitalist economy. The fact that living this kind of life myself as the reader is impossible and self-contradictory, as a moment's reflection makes clear, in no way lessens the power of the interpellation. No ordinary reader-viewer has the time or money to live her entire life, not even a day of it, as if she were a professional model on location. Every such reader-viewer is well aware of that. But still the image calls to her, and it calls powerfully and strongly. This is how to live, it says. This is the good life. You should live this way.

The relationship between subjectivity and subjection is clear in the call of this image. As Althusser argued, the image offers a model of subjectivity, of being a person—indeed a good, happy, complete person—in its likeness. The Absolute Subject calls me as an individual to be a subject like her. It offers me freedom, happiness, self-determination, and a full human life. But precisely in that illusion of full human subjectivity to which it calls me, precisely in the desirability to me of living the way the Subject in the image lives, it ensures my subjection to the capitalist economy and the ruthless, inhuman processes, the misery for the majority of the human race, that that economy involves. It keeps me assuming that if I work in and for the capitalist economy as I am expected to, I can buy the dress, the jewelry, the makeup, the hair care, the training regimen, and the vacation that I need in order to be a subject like the Subject in the image. These things will cost a fortune, and the call of the image is endless. The price of subjectivity on the beautiful and desirable model of the woman in the picture is a lifetime of contributing the majority of my energy to the enrichment and empowerment of the ruling classes of the capitalist economy. It is subjection to that economy. In promising me the freedom of a subject in the first sense, the image ensures that I do not in fact have it in the second. In the illusory promise that I will be a philosophical subject, it ensures that I remain a political one.

Much of the message of this first double-page advertisement in Us Weekly would function independently of the context of the magazine as a whole. Within that context, as the first 2 pages of the 60 in the magazine, it becomes part of a massive array of ideological messages about gender, about what it is to be a woman in American capitalist society and how to behave as such. One of these is the feature "Who Wore it Best?" In the March 30 issue, this has pictures of six female celebrities all wearing the same pair of black-and-white snakeskin pattern leather boots. One hundred people voted "who wore them best," and the percentage of the vote is printed in relatively large numbers on each picture, along with the celebrity's name. All six women are dressed in designer clothes, in a carefully thought-out ensemble. The boots, the feature says, are $290, and many of the rest of the outfits of the women wearing them look similarly expensive. Kate Hudson is wearing a long designer dress and Sofia Carson a full-length fur coat. The interpellation is clear—dress well. Be an attractive object of the gaze of others, with expensive and beautiful designer clothes, hair, makeup, and accessories (all of which the women in the pictures are wearing). You can be a professional, even at the top of your profession, as all six women are; indeed, Kate Hudson appears to be giving a presentation or lecture in her beautiful outfit. But you must dress well. And that means expensively, and that means subjection to the capitalist economy and the interest of its ruling classes. You must also be in good physical shape, especially slim and young, which all six women look. There are sanctions for not doing so. Ruth Wilson, who gets the lowest vote of 10%, looks the least glamorous of the six in terms of her outfit, her hair, and the pose in which she has been pictured. It would probably be quite humiliating for Ms. Wilson herself to see this page, in which she looks slightly less glamorous than the other five women and has the lowest vote on how well she wore the boots, and this potential humiliation is conveyed in the interpellation to the reader-viewer. This is the road to perdition, the feature calls, this is the way not to be, this is who not to be. If you do not follow the call to dress attractively, you risk failing to be a successful, whole, good, or happy subject of American society. The entire feature "Fashion Police" says the same thing at length, indeed featuring insults from the writers about the unattractive outfits (in their acerbic judgment) worn in public by five women and one man that week. If you are a woman, these features indicate, you must dress well. You must be slim, look young, and dress well. If not, you will be humiliated, insulted, and not a successful, good, or happy person.

The ideological messages concerning gender are mixed in *Us Weekly* magazine. On the one hand, in addition to the unquestioned and uncriticized emphasis on an attractive appearance, there is a strong emphasis on relationships, on pregnancy, and on family in the articles and the images. There is also a kind of infantilizing or at least slightly regressive idiom in the text in which the reader is interpellated as someone at the intellectual level of a high school student rather than an adult citizen. On the other hand, there is an equally strong emphasis on professions; success within those professions; relationships with friends and family; women's desire, self-worth, activism, charity work, and even religion. The first of the "Hot Pics!" in the March 23 issue is of the celebrity couple

Emily Blunt and John Krasinski, unusually with the entire page devoted to one picture, especially emphasizing this picture. Blunt is looking into her partner's eyes and smiling; he, too, is smiling. The caption reads: "Emily Blunt and John Krasinski . . . prove you can work with your spouse and still feel those heart-eyes emoji vibes."[24] Despite the regressive idiom in the phrase "heart-eyes emoji vibes," the interpellation is clear. The image calls to the reader-viewer that she can be both a successful professional—indeed at the very top of her profession— and have a successful relationship or marriage at the same time. The size of the picture relative to the others in the magazine makes the ideological effect even more powerful. On the next page, the very next of the "Hot Pics!" features Andie McDowell and her two daughters "celebrating her Women Making History Award." She is quoted in the caption as saying: "If I ever say anything derogatory about myself, [my daughters] will remind me not to say hurtful things like that. I taught them that."[25] The picture as whole is titled "Making Herstory!" Despite the slightly diminutive exclamation point, social achievement by women is cel-ebrated here, with the reader interpellated accordingly, as are self-respect and self-worth in women and girls.

Andrea McDonnell has argued that, despite the negative patriarchal narratives and stereotypes in which celebrity gossip magazines trade, the women who read the magazines in practice "talk back" to those narratives and stereo-types, especially when they do so together, in groups. She called this a "process of contestation and reinterpretation" in which "it is the act of reading, partic-ularly in a group setting, that allows [readers] to break down these normative constructions and, through conversation and consensus-building, articulate their own values and ideals."[26] She gave several examples, based on interviews with a group of 11 readers, all women from 18 to 34. One is schadenfreude, in which, "confronted with an endless parade of exceptionally thin, gorgeous, and wealthy celebs, readers express their frustration with these unrealistic 'norms' by taking pleasure in celebrity failure." Second, McDonnell's readers are "able to identify the codes of femininity with which they disagree and to scoff and ridi-cule these codes as they engage with the magazines." Finally, the "ambiguously truthful" quality of celebrity gossip magazines, their clear reliance on editorial techniques such as opinion, unnamed sources, composite photographs, and the like, "allows readers to push back against and, at times, firmly reject the rigid moral guidelines and the feminine stereotypes that gossip narratives set forth."[27] But although this is the main burden of McDonnell's argument, she neverthe-less constantly found herself forced to admit that the interpellations of celebrity gossip magazines remain powerful and negative despite the relative force of the counterinterpellations enacted by readers talking back to them. At the end of her introductory chapter, she concluded: "Yet despite this twist, it remains un-clear whether celebrity gossip magazines do more to undermine or uphold these limiting versions of femininity." At the end of her final chapter, she again had to admit that:

> It would be naïve to suggest that all readers engage in these types of readings at all times or that the impossible standards produced and promoted by the magazines are negated by these sophisticated readings. They are not. Even those readers who challenge the text in certain contexts accept it at face value in others.

She concluded by describing the experience of reading celebrity gossip magazines as a "double-edged sword," a "two-headed monster," and a "love-hate relationship."[28] The interpellations of *Us Weekly* and its competitor magazines remain as strong, as all pervasive, as constant, and as powerful for all the limited opportunities they afford their readers for counterinterpellation.

So, the ideological messages on gender are mixed and in conflict in *Us Weekly* and its competing celebrity gossip magazines. Gender struggle is at work in the interpellations of the institutions that make up the publishing and the advertising ISAs, along with the related institutions of the communications ISAs, in which American citizens look at, read, practice, and discuss celebrity gossip. But the messages are not mixed at all when it comes to fashion and beauty. Here, the dominant gender ideology, which overlaps with and works together with the dominant class ideology, is unquestioned. You must be beautiful. You must buy expensive clothes, makeup, hair care, fitness and training products, diet products, accessories, and personal care and beauty products, and you must do so for your entire lifetime. To fail to do this is simply to fail to be a woman, a subject, a citizen, and a person. Although we see the ideological struggle of women at work in the publishing ISA, and *Us Weekly* magazine in particular, it is not at work here. You must do the lifetime of work in the capitalist economy it takes to be beautiful according to the interpellations of the fashion and beauty ISAs. Not a single message in the celebrity gossip genre contradicts this.

The Bell Jar

Are women's rights promoted more strongly in other ideological formations than celebrity gossip magazines? I now look at a literary text that deals with both women's lives and the ideological discourses in which those lives are lived, Sylvia Plath's novel, *The Bell Jar*. The novel was published in Britain in 1963, but because of a loophole in copyright law, it was not published in the United States until 1971, where it quickly became an iconic text of the women's movement of the 1960s and 1970s. It articulates a feminist critique of numerous patriarchal institutions in American society, including dating, sex, contraception, marriage, childbirth, motherhood, medicine, psychiatry, and employment. One group of patriarchal institutions it very noticeably does not directly criticize, however, is precisely the one whose ideology we have seen so strongly enforced in *Us Weekly* magazine, that of the fashion and beauty industries.

The Bell Jar begins with its heroine Esther Greenwood working on a fashion magazine for a month in New York, just as Plath herself did as a college student. On the second page of the novel, the reader hears how integral clothes and accessories are to Esther's identity:

> I was supposed to be the envy of thousands of other college girls ... who wanted nothing more than to be tripping about in those same size seven patent leather shoes I'd bought in Bloomingdale's one lunch hour with a black patent leather belt and black patent leather pocket-book to match. And when my picture came out in the magazine ... in a skimpy imitation silver-lamé bodice stuck on to a big fat cloud of white tulle, on some Starlight Roof, in the company of several anonymous young men with all-American bone structures ... everybody would think I must be having a real whirl.[29]

It is striking how little has changed since this photograph (taken in 1953 and described by Plath in 1961) and the advertisement for Uncommon James published in 2020 that we analyzed previously. In both cases, a vision of the good life, of full, complete personhood for the reader-viewer is offered, and she is called by the image, called to be a subject like the Subject in it. In both cases, integral to and indeed the foundation of its vision of the good life, of full subjectivity, are clothes, the expensive products of the fashion industry. In the photograph Plath is describing here (of which there is a copy in the Sylvia Plath Papers in the Smith College Archives), the reader is also called to earn enough to afford nights on starlight roofs in Manhattan as well as to associate with attractive young men, for which she will need fashion and beauty products. Esther is herself an obedient subject of this ideology, as the first sentence quoted above makes clear. Not only is she photographed in an image that is transformed into one of the Subject of the fashion ISA, but also she herself feels the call of such ideological Subjects. She goes, "all by herself" as Althusser put it,[30] to buy fashion accessories during her short leisure time working for the fashion magazine in order to look herself in real life the way the countless Subjects of the fashion ISA look in its magazines, advertisements, and shows and in daily life. Esther accurately describes modeling herself on the image of the Absolute Subject of the fashion ISA as "the envy of thousands of other college girls just like me all across America." This is what young women in American ideology are called to want. As Esther puts it, it looks like she is having "the time of [her] life."[31]

Critical as Esther is able to be of many of the patriarchal institutions of her society, she simply feels the pull, the interpellations, of the fashion and beauty ISAs. Only a few more pages into the novel, the reader meets Doreen, "who came from a society girls' college down South," where fashion is especially important. This is Esther's reaction:

> Her college was so fashion-conscious, [Doreen] said, that all the girls had pocket-book covers made out of the same material as their dresses, so each time they changed their clothes they had a matching pocket-book. This kind of detail impressed me. It suggested a whole life of marvelous, elaborate decadence that attracted me like a magnet.[32]

This is an excellent account of interpellation at work—the image of "a whole lifetime of marvelous, elaborate decadence," which "attracts" Esther "like a magnet." Its call is enormously, indeed mysteriously, powerful. It overrides her reason, and her emotions, too, which reject as strongly as her reason a lifetime of submission to the demands of living up to the ideological images of the fashion and beauty industries simply because she has been born female. To be attracted like a magnet is to be an object of greater forces than oneself, and that is precisely what is happening as Esther is interpellated by the ideological calls of the gigantic fashion and beauty industries.

However, Plath's novel, even though unable directly to criticize the ideology of the fashion and beauty industries, does begin to do so indirectly, in a way that celebrity gossip magazines are unable to even today. The grinding of the gears of ideology in the educational ISA as well as in the publishing and cultural ISAs, in all of which *The Bell Jar* functions, is felt more profoundly and progressively by the reader interpellated by the novel than by the reader-viewer interpellated by *Us Weekly*. Although *The Bell Jar* is unable to rise to direct criticism of the fashion and beauty ISAs, it portrays at the level of Esther's felt and lived experience what it is like to live in them and how intolerable for a person this experience is. In the early passages of the novel we have already discussed, we see how integral fashion and beauty products are to Esther's sense of identity, to her subjectivity, to her being what ideology tells her is a successful, happy woman and citizen. At the very same time, however, Plath also portrays how none of these things in fact lead Esther to feel happy, fulfilled, complete, successful, or even a person. The novel portrays both the call of ideology and the miserable experience Esther has as she feels and responds to that call. As Esther says of her time working at the fashion magazine in New York: "I was supposed to be having the time of my life." But in fact she is not having the time of her life. The Subjects of ideology in the publishing, advertising, and educational ISAs are interpellating her in exactly the way she has in fact responded to them, and Esther has been rewarded with full, indeed unusually effective and powerful, subjectivity for her obedience. She seems to be "steering New York like her own private car," in control of the very center of the American capitalist economy. Not only is this not the case, but also it does not even feel the case to Esther. It should, if ideology is doing its job. But it isn't. The interpellations are beginning to fail. In fact, Esther feels:

> I wasn't steering anything, not even myself. I just bumped from my hotel to work and to parties and from parties to my hotel and back to work like a numb trolley-bus. . . . I couldn't get myself to react. I felt very still and very empty, the way the eye of a tornado must feel, moving dully along in the middle of the surrounding hullabaloo.[33]

Scholars of Althusser's work have often needed to develop and nuance his concept of interpellation as they apply it in practice. For example, Ghassan Hage differentiated between three different kinds of interpellation experienced by racialized minorities—"non-interpellation," where "the racialized feel ignored and non-existent"; "negative interpellation," which "hails [the racialized] with negative attributes, 'lazy, dirty, thief, social problem, etc.'"; and "mis-interpellation," in which "the yet-to-be racialized person . . . answers the call thinking that there is a place for him. . . . Yet no sooner do they answer the call than the symbolic order brutally reminds them that they are not part of everyone."[34] What Plath is portraying in The Bell Jar is the partial success and the partial failure of interpellation as the ISAs of her society call to Esther. She obeys, like an iron needle pulled by a magnet, the interpellations of the fashion and beauty ISAs. But she hates doing so. She feels dead, not herself, and not a person as she does so. Ideology promises exactly the opposite—that you will feel fully alive, fully yourself, and fully a person. Plath's novel shows what it is like for interpellation to fail, at least partly. Esther lives in a world where ideology calls her to conform to a long series of (impossible and self-contradictory) images and ideals, and which does so strongly enough for her to obey. But she hates it, and the whole novel is about her hating it. She hates it so much, in fact, that she prefers to die. The first half of the novel is about her gradual experience of emotional breakdown while working for the fashion magazine in New York, and the second half is about the suicide attempt to which this breakdown leads. The novel is very clear about the fact that her recovery, the fact that she is "all right again" when she tells her story, is thoroughly questionable. As Esther says at the end of the novel: "All I could see were question marks"; "How did I know that someday . . . the bell jar, with its stifling distortions, wouldn't descend again?"[35] The entire structure of the novel makes clear that Esther cannot live in the ideologies that she nevertheless has to live in. It is a portrayal of interpellation at work on a recalcitrant subject, on a young woman who obeys the calls of ideology because of their power and effectiveness, but resists at the same time, both with her reason (as when she openly criticizes institutions like sex, marriage, childbirth, or contraception) and with her emotions (as when she is unable to criticize institutions like fashion and beauty, but responds inarticulately with hatred, with a visceral, nervous reaction to the ideological complex of which they are part).

So far, we have discussed how interpellation works in the fictional world of the novel. Now we need to think about how the experience of reading *The Bell Jar* today interpellates readers, reading it as part of the practices of the publishing ISA, the cultural ISA, the educational ISA, or any combination of these. Let us say first that one of the primary interpellative effects of a novel is that the narrated life of the protagonist interpellates the reader as a model in whose terms to understand and even guide the narrative of his or her own life. Esther's story says to the reader: "The story of my life is a model for the story of yours." *The Bell Jar* interpellates the reader with the call that her life has a story and that it is or can be or should be a story like Esther's. Since Esther is a young woman, this interpellation may be especially powerful to young women readers. It functions, however, although we would need to analyze each individual case carefully, in different ways and to different extents with all readers.

How does this work in practice? First, *The Bell Jar* is perhaps most striking now as it was in 1970s America as a powerful feminist critique of the institutions facing and working against the interests of women like Esther. With respect to today's gender ideologies, the novel's first effect is, in my view, counterinterpellative. That is, it continues to call the reader of the 2020s, as it did the reader of the 1970s, to work against unjustly and irrationally patriarchal institutions. But, as we have seen in our analysis of the text of the novel, the patriarchal institutions of which it offers no explicit critique are the fashion and beauty ISAs. So as a reader reads *The Bell Jar* today, she is interpellated by the text not to criticize the ideological messages that work in the interests of the gigantic financial concerns of the fashion and beauty industries and of those sectors of the ruling corporate classes whose power comes from precisely those concerns. The reader of *The Bell Jar*, as she is encouraged by the practice of reading the novel to think of Esther's life as a potential model for her own, is interpellated in such a way that she knows how it feels to think of fashion and beauty products suggesting "a whole life of marvelous, elaborate decadence that attracted me like a magnet." She also, along with Esther, looks at Doreen, as she has looked at other young women in the past and will look at others in the future, all the more surely for having read the following passage, and thinks:

> Doreen looked terrific. She was wearing a strapless white lace dress zipped up over a snug corset affair that curved her in at the middle and bulged her out

again spectacularly above and below, and her skin had a bronzy polish under the pale dusting powder.[36]

Esther is amazed here by Doreen's look, by her successful purchase and use of high-end fashion and beauty products. She gazes almost open-mouthed in amazement, lost for words, at the sheer power and effect of the way Doreen has made herself look, and this is the sense with which the reader of the novel still, even today, is interpellated. The novel says to you: "Women who look like this are amazing. They get what they want in society. If you look this way, you will, too."

But now comes the grinding of the gears. As we saw in our textual analysis of the novel, Plath deliberately and powerfully portrayed the sense of Esther's unhappiness, of how intolerable it is for her, on a daily basis, to live within the ideologies of fashion and beauty, along with all the other ideologies she is more able to criticize and reject. This sense of the intolerability of Esther's life, dramatically portrayed in her increasing lack of ability to function in society and descent into breakdown and attempted suicide, interpellates the reader of the novel as strongly as the dominant ideological messages. The counterinterpellation is as strong as the interpellation. As I read *The Bell Jar*, I learn at one and the same time that I must be an obedient subject of the ideologies of fashion and beauty and also that it will make me profoundly unhappy and dissatisfied, and that it may even kill me if I do. Esther's confusion, her disorientation, her gradual loss of the sense of her self, her identity, and her ability to function as a person, in the ideological matrix in which she lives, interpellates the reader with a similar sense of confusion, disorientation, and ultimately rejection. Although I do not learn to criticize the ideologies of fashion and beauty as the reader of *The Bell Jar*, I do learn that if I do not, I will cease to be able to function as and feel myself to be a person in contemporary American capitalism, in which these ideologies continue to function as powerfully as they did in 1953 or 1971. The reader of the novel is interpellated as an obedient subject of the ideologies of fashion and beauty. She learns subliminally that it remains as important for her as for Esther to buy high-end fashion and beauty products and to keep doing so for her whole life. She learns indeed that this is a condition of her identity, of her subjectivity. But she is also and at the same time counterinterpellated that she must do something else, that she must learn somehow to criticize and reject the ideologies of fashion and beauty, along with all the other patriarchal ideologies the novel directly calls her to reject, or the price she will pay for her identity as a subject of American capitalism will be too high. The novel calls to her that, unless she thinks differently from Esther about the ideologies of fashion and beauty and acts accordingly, Esther's breakdown and potential death will happen to her, too.

So we see that *The Bell Jar* makes a greater contribution to the freedom of the reader in American society in the 2020s than celebrity gossip magazines like *Us*

Weekly do. The texts and pictures of the magazines ceaselessly, consistently, and without a single break in this ideological message (at least in March 2020) tell their reader-viewers that, to be a good, happy, and successful person, they must buy expensive fashion, beauty, and lifestyle products for their whole lives. This means a life of economic subjection to wage work in the capitalist economy, ensuring that that economy continues, and that those classes that profit most from it continue to do so. *The Bell Jar* does this also, even if you are reading it as part of your university education. But, *The Bell Jar* does something else that the celebrity gossip magazines do not or at least do much less. It also tells you that this cannot go on. It does not tell you how to change your subjection to the ideologies of fashion and beauty, but it does tell you that you must. In 2020, many readers of the novel will be aware that many of Esther's individual critiques of patriarchal institutions were in fact begun in practice by the women's movement of the 1960s and 1970s. The reception history of the novel suggests that a mass movement, that organized feminist protest, may be the way that this feminist concern, like so many of the others directly raised in the novel, needs to be addressed. But although it does not say how, the novel powerfully interpellates the reader that she, like Esther, cannot live, neither a full life as a person and citizen nor even perhaps at all, if the ideological matrix in which she lives, which includes an almost total subjection to the ideologies of fashion and beauty, does not change. *The Bell Jar*, that is, counterinterpellates the reader or interpellates her with the ideology of the exploited as well as with the ideology of the exploiting classes in contemporary American society. It interpellates the reader with Esther's experience of hatred, of disgust, of nausea at the ideological matrix out of which she looks to but cannot completely or successfully break. The reader knows, feels even, at the level of the subliminal effect of interpellation, that she, like Esther, must change her subjection to the dominant ideologies or die.

The most influential critic of Althusser's theory of interpellation in English has been Judith Butler. She has argued that Althusser has overprivileged the example—he called it an example, but in fact it is a "paradigm," in Butler's view—of the Christian religious ideology, and as a result has thought of interpellation as a force of comparable strength to that of the voice of God, that is, essentially irresistible. It is no such thing, Butler argued. She was concerned with the possibilities of resisting, avoiding, or in complex ways talking back to the interpellations of ideology in what she called "bad subjects"[37]:

> Although [Althusser] refers to the possibility of "bad subjects," he does not consider the range of *disobedience* that such an interpellating law might produce. The law might not only be refused, but it might also be ruptured, forced into a rearticulation that calls into question the monotheistic force of its own unilateral operation.[38]

Butler was concerned with the "range of disobedience" with which individuals can respond to normative interpellations, with the numerous kinds of response they can make to the call of the law. Althusser simply did not allow for this range of responses, the only hope of many for freedom, justice, and happiness, Butler argued. As we have seen throughout this chapter, this critique can only be made of Althusser's essay "Ideology and Ideological State Apparatuses." Even then it is somewhat overstated, as Althusser made clear reference there to class struggle in the ISAs.[39] But it cannot be made of the full text of the manuscript from which the essay was extracted, which we have been thinking about in this chapter. *On the Reproduction of Capitalism* is about class struggle from beginning to end, and Althusser dealt much more explicitly and at much greater length there with the conflict between the dominating and dominated ideologies in capitalist society. As we have seen in this chapter, so does women's writing. Celebrity gossip magazines offer mixed ideological messages on gender roles, but they insist that you must spend your life buying fashion and beauty products. *The Bell Jar* is able to criticize dominant gender ideologies more fully and explicitly. Although the fashion and beauty ISAs are not directly criticized, nevertheless an inarticulate emotional criticism of what it is like under their regime, in the capitalist economy of which they are part, is raised, and the reader is interpellated accordingly. Althusser places considerable hope in the counterideologies that ISAs, like the educational system in particular, allow to develop in capitalist society. What this analysis of two kinds of women's writing at work in the ISAs of America in the 2020s has shown is that, cautious as one must be about the lack of change between Althusser's time of writing and our own, there are still some grounds for such hope.

Notes

1. Louis Althusser, *On the Reproduction of Capitalism: Ideology and Ideological State Apparatuses*, trans. G. M. Goshgarian (London: Verso, 2014), 6, 5.
2. Althusser, *Reproduction of Capitalism*, xxix, xxx.
3. Althusser, *Reproduction of Capitalism*, 70, 75.
4. Louis Althusser, *Lenin and Philosophy, and Other Essays*, trans. Ben Brewster (New York: Monthly Review Press, 2001), 97–98.
5. Althusser, *Lenin and Philosophy*, 96.
6. Althusser, *Reproduction of Capitalism*, 75, 160.
7. Althusser, *Lenin and Philosophy*, 75, 96.
8. Althusser, *Reproduction of Capitalism*, 76, 77.
9. Althusser, *Reproduction of Capitalism*, 173, 187, 188.
10. Louis Althusser, *Sur la reproduction* (Paris: Presses Universitaires de France, 1995), 305; Althusser, *Lenin and Philosophy*, 118.

11. Warren Montag, "Althusser's Empty Signifier: What Is the Meaning of the Word 'Interpellation'?", *Meditations* 30, no. 2 (2017): 65, 66, 67.

12. Althusser, *Lenin and Philosophy*, 116.

13. Althusser, *Reproduction of Capitalism*, 198.

14. Althusser, *Lenin and Philosophy*, 123.

15. Althusser, *Lenin and Philosophy*, 116.

16. Althusser, *Sur la reproduction*, 231; Althusser, *Lenin and Philosophy*, 121.

17. Althusser, *Sur la reproduction*, 231.

18. Althusser, *Reproduction of Capitalism*, 196–197.

19. Althusser, *Reproduction of Capitalism*, 196, 197.

20. Althusser, *Reproduction of Capitalism*, 157.

21. Althusser, *Reproduction of Capitalism*, 88–89; Althusser, *Sur la reproduction*, 119–120.

22. Althusser, *Reproduction of Capitalism*, 89, 153, 140.

23. Andrea M. McDonnell, *Reading Celebrity Gossip Magazines* (CambridgeMA: Polity, 2014), 2. "A portion of the genre's readership is male (between 15 and 30 per cent, depending on the magazine and date of issue)," but "the celebrity gossip genre is a feminine area: its readers are presumed to be female and its content is aimed at a female audience" (McDonnell, *Reading Celebrity Gossip*, 19).

24. "Hot Pics!" *Us Weekly*, March 23, 2020, 12.

25. "Hot Pics!" 14.

26. McDonnell, *Reading Celebrity Gossip*, 23.

27. McDonnell, *Reading Celebrity Gossip*, 102, 104, 120.

28. McDonnell, *Reading Celebrity Gossip*, 24, 129, 130.

29. Sylvia Plath, *The Bell Jar* (London: Faber and Faber, 1963), 2.

30. Althusser, *Reproduction of Capitalism*, 197.

31. Plath, *Bell Jar*, 2.

32. Plath, *Bell Jar*, 5.

33. Plath, *Bell Jar*, 2–3.

34. Ghassan Hage, "The Affective Politics of Racial Mis-interpellation," *Theory, Culture and Society* 27, no. 7–8 (2010): 121–122. See James R. Martel, *The Misinterpellated Subject* (Durham, NC: Duke University Press, 2017), for the concept of "misinterpellation." See Jean-Jacques Lecercle, *Interpretation as Pragmatics* (New York: St. Martin's, 1999): 167, 185; "Dispute, Quarrel, Interpellation," *Paragraph* 40, no. 1 (2017), 19–26, for the concept of "counter-interpellation."

35. Plath, *Bell Jar*, 3, 233, 230.

36. Plath, *Bell Jar*, 7.

37. Judith Butler, *The Psychic Life of Power: Theories in Subjection* (Stanford, CA: Stanford University Press, 1997), 110, 109.

38. Judith Butler, *Bodies That Matter: On the Discursive Limits of "Sex"* (London: Routledge, 1993), 122.

39. See especially Althusser, *Lenin and Philosophy*, 99. James Martel emphasized the significance of Althusser's phrases "hardly ever" and "nine times out of ten" in his accounts of interpellation in the essay: "If the act of interpellation, of hailing, 'hardly ever miss[es]' their intended individual, that means that sometimes they

do miss. . . . . If nine out of ten subjects are correctly hailed, then at least one in ten are not" (*Misinterpellated Subject*, 37). See also Pierre Macherey, "Judith Butler and the Althusserian Theory of Subjection," *Décalages* 1, no. 2 (2012): 21–22. For a judicious analysis of Butler's reading of Althusser, see Matthew Lampert, "Resisting Ideology: On Butler's Critique of Althusser," *Diacritics* 43, no. 2 (2015): 124–147. In *Althusser and His Contemporaries: Philosophy's Perpetual War* (Durham, NC: Duke University Press, 2013), 159–160, Warren Montag poses the question of why Althusser excised so much that was fundamental to his argument from the ISAs essay.

19

The Question of Queer and Trans Positive Freedom in the United States

Ecem E. Ece, Robert Baez, and K. L. Broad

The American dream remains a dream of freedom, whose actualization can only be practiced by those whose legitimacy is already recognized. Part of that dream of freedom includes an understanding that the United States of America has a rich tradition of social movements advocating for human rights and freedom. The LGBTQ+ (lesbian, gay, bisexual, transgender, queer/questioning and more) movement in the United States is a prime recent example of such efforts of seeking freedom, especially via law. Indeed, the mainstream LGBTQ+ movement touts many recent "advances," particularly Don't Ask, Don't Tell (DADT), marriage equality, and the quite recent decision in *Bostock v. Clayton* wherein the majority opinion of the Supreme Court held that Title VII of the Civil Rights Act, protecting discrimination in employment based, in part, on sex, can be read to extend protections to LGBTQ individuals. However, as many activists point out, there still exists deep inequality that shortens the life chances of many multiply marginalized LGBTQ+ people. In other words, while some may imagine freedom *from* constraints (negative freedom) has been achieved for LGBTQ+ people, many activist voices point out how such freedom from constraint has not been achieved for all those in the LGBTQ+ community and call for the necessity of striving for positive freedom (freedom *to* act with agency). In the words of Dean Spade,[1] many LGBTQ+ persons remain "impossible people," existing in the margins beyond the scope of these instances of positive freedom and unable to actualize an American dream of any sort.

Our discussion of political and social freedom of LGBTQ+ persons embraces Berlin's interpretation of positive liberty. Centrally, Isaiah Berlin defined "the essence of the notion of liberty . . . is the holding off of something or someone—of others who trespass on my field or assert their authority over me, or of obsessions, fears, neuroses, irrational forces—intruders and despots of one kind or another."[2] For Berlin, there are two distinct forms of freedom, wherein negative freedom, highlighting the restrictions and preventions of individuals by law, refers to "freedom from"[3] control. In a recent article discussing these ideas in relation to mask wearing and COVID-19, Gessen[4] explained that those asserting

Ecem E. Ece, Robert Baez, and K. L. Broad, *The Question of Queer and Trans Positive Freedom in the United States*
In: *On Inequality and Freedom*. Edited by: Lawrence M. Eppard and Henry A. Giroux, Oxford University Press. © Oxford University Press 2022. DOI: 10.1093/oso/9780197583029.003.0019

they should have freedom not to wear a mask are asserting a sense of freedom on negative terms, freedom defined by lack of constraint, much like a teenager who wants no rules. On the other hand, positive freedom corresponds to "freedom to,"[5] reinforcing the sense of one being their own ruler, supporting the participation of individuals in public life while being responsible for their actions with their own motivations and rationales. As Gessen reminded us, positive freedom is measured by the question, "By whom am I ruled?" and is, in many respects, an issue of "social and political freedom."[6] In other words, positive freedom is "being one's own master," as a subject of the choices rather than the object of others' decisions.[7] In the example of masks, wearing one can be seen as an act of positive freedom: the choice of a conscious member of society in social relations with others.[8]

By many accounts, when people consider the position of LGBTQ+ people in the United States today, they often allege a certain "new" freedom—freedom from government constraint for LGBTQ+ persons. These types of assertions point out how those of us who are LGBTQ+ are no longer told what we *cannot* do in regard to many important aspects of our lives. We are no longer told we cannot have sex, cannot get married, and cannot serve our country, for example. LGBTQ+ Americans, according to these terms, seem quite free. So free that our LGBTQ+ freedom is marketed globally as a model (and some argue threat) of liberty based on sexual orientation and gender identity/expression. And yet, a good many queer and trans people disagree with these assertions of negative freedom, and a good deal of current movement activism seeks to point out that such understandings of freedom are incomplete. As we discuss in the first section of this chapter, and elaborate in further sections with in-depth examples, some queer and trans activists and activist-scholars chart a much more complex portrait of LGBTQ+ freedom today and point to profound lack thereof. We argue that current LGBTQ+ political analyses highlight how LGBTQ+ freedom must include aspects of positive freedom in order for freedom based on sexuality and gender to exist. What activists and activist-scholars point out is that LGBTQ+ people and communities do not yet have the agency or freedom to act autonomously and choose what lives we one want to live because there are wide-reaching, and quite consequential, political, cultural, and economic patterns of (neoliberal) inequality denying LGBTQ+ people resources and opportunities to thrive. They point out that these patterns of inequality have, in fact, defined the very efforts to gain freedom (in other words, the mainstream U.S. LGBTQ movement is defined by neoliberal disparities and the reproduction thereof). The point is this: Merely providing the absence of constraint (e.g., removing limits about who you cannot marry) is not enough. The existence of complex interacting regimes of inequality means most LGBTQ+ people do not live in circumstances of positive freedom, conditions where we all can realize our freedom.

Positive Freedom and Queer/Trans Justice

In this chapter, we approach the question of freedom for queer and trans people, LGBTQ+ folks,[9] as one best approached through the lens of activism, critique, and praxis. In other words, we view the work of resistance as a critical lens by which to see complex and multiple visions of freedom. However, for our focus on queer, trans, and LGBTQ+ activism, we deliberately do *not* focus on the U.S. mainstream gay and lesbian rights movement and the story often told of it having succeeded by gaining freedom via U.S. policy change, state recognition, and legal rights. Rather, we start with the central understanding, derived from queer and trans radical liberation groups and critical academic work, that not all activist resistance should be understood in terms of mainstream movement work, which minimizes, erases, and obliterates still quite necessary visions and expressions of freedom. Centrally, we understand the activist field today as existing within all-consuming circumstances of neoliberalism, resulting in exacerbating profound inequality and fostering a mainstream movement stripped of its complexity and reinscribing restrictive understandings of freedom such that social justice– and liberation-oriented activism must be remembered, reclaimed, and in some instances invented anew.[10] Hence, in what follows, we draw on multifaceted notions of freedom articulated via queer and trans social justice and liberation activism.

Before we continue, we want to pause to outline some of the significant social forces impacting and defining lesbian, gay, bisexual, queer, and trans lives in ways that demand forms of resistance beyond U.S. legal reform. Political theory and critique detail how queer and trans activist resistance, and attendant visions of freedom, today operate in a robust and multifaceted system of neoliberal forces—cultural, political, and economic—propelling individualistic and privatizing policies and reducing progressive and social justice forms of collective action.[11] In the words of Wendy Brown,[12] today we operate in a "neoliberal culture of unsocial liberty," maintained, in part, by a relentless assault on social justice.[13] Moreover, in these neoliberal contexts, inequality manifests legally (administrative violence), such that mere legal remedy (via attention to discrimination and rights) is not enough and actually ends up marking some queer and trans folks as "impossible people," incomprehensible to institutional rules and regulations.[14] As well, articulations of queer and trans necropolitics point out how this widespread neoliberal conversion has morphed "into its audaciously murderous phase," working in concert with contemporary regimes of "racism, neo/colonialism, 'war on terror,' incarceration, (and) border enforcement" to decide who, among us queers and trans people, lives and dies and reducing the social existence for many queer/trans populations (especially of color) today to merely being the "living dead."[15] In sum, LGBTQ+ persons today exist in a cultural, economic, and political context defined by systems of social power and violence that demand far-reaching projects of freedom beyond simply the recent efforts of gaining marriage rights, military access, and police protection championed by a liberal-oriented, rights-based mainstream movement (of negative freedom for some) in the United States.

A key characteristic of radical social justice–oriented queer and trans activism, and its attendant visions of more positive freedom, is that it is organized as a reclaiming, reorienting, and some argue an entirely new project distinct from the mainstream U.S. movement. Thus, here we succinctly recognize some examples of how neoliberal patterns have manifested in the U.S. LGBTQ+ mainstream movement, producing patterns of limited freedom that characterize that to which some queer and trans social justice activists are currently responding. At the core, recent activist and academic critique details how the U.S. mainstream "gay rights movement"[16] has become depoliticized, such that "social grievances become private and discrete matters"[17] due to neoliberal political and economic forces. Ferguson,[18] in providing a literature review of the research in this area, described it as a process of moving from multidimensional (intersectional) visions of liberation to one-dimensional objectives—centering on sexuality only, whitewashed, patriarchal, class-blind rights. Other work highlighted a similar portrait of the limitations produced by neoliberal movement mainstreaming. Hanhardt,[19] for example, illustrated how such mainstreaming involved the process of gay (especially urban) community politics narrowing to just a White, cisgender, elite gay men's project of safety politics that embraced the state as protector in ways that ultimately limited the freedom of poor and young queer and trans community members of color.[20] Further, Puar[21] identified dynamics of what she termed "homonationalism," tying liberal politics of the LGBT movement to counterterrorist and nationalist agendas to allow some to become living and productive queer subjects while simultaneously producing others as terrorist populations marked for death. As well, we have work today detailing patterns and impacts of the neoliberal capitalist corporatization of nonprofits in the United States, resulting in the co-optation of movement organizations such that they define their priorities in terms of wealthy donors, fundable notions of diversity, and consequentially homonormative standards (prioritizing the needs of those who are White, elite, and cisgender).[22] As Beam's[23] recent work highlights, the impact is profound, creating a circumstance where LGBTQ+ activist nonprofits end up pursuing such a limited sense of freedom that it doesn't reach the lives of many queer and trans constituents (especially poor young queer and trans people of color). It is this pattern that Beam described when stating that "nonprofits make the LGBT movement straight."[24] These are just a few examples that illustrate how the mainstreaming of freedom and liberty via U.S. mainstream movement work was (and is), in effect, also a reproduction of marginalization and complex inequality, expressly impacting some queer and trans communities.

In an expansive neoliberal context where social justice has been reviled and, in many respects, repressed, the persistent insistence by queer and trans activists on doing social justice activism is a vast undertaking to reestablish a radical vision of freedom attendant to intertwined inequalities based on race, class, gender, sexuality, and more. For example, scholars[25] pointed to the activism of FIERCE (Fabulous Independent Educated Radicals for Community Empowerment)—"a community organizing group in New York City comprising trans and queer youth of color" to illustrate how activist groups center those multiply marginalized and create organizational structures intentionally attentive to relations of power. Additionally, Mananzala and Spade explicitly wrote of how to resist "neoliberalism's co-optation of social justice work" and pointed to the Silvia Rivera Law Project as an example of how to create a "radical social justice organization focused on transgender liberation."[26] They discussed a strategy of working from a foundational value that "social justice trickles up, not down," a philosophy that translates concretely to "prioritizing the needs and concerns of those facing the worst manifestations of gender-based marginalization and exclusion" and deliberately embracing "leadership by trans people of color, trans low-income people, trans immigrants and others facing intersectional oppression."[27] Further, DeFillipis and Anderson-Nathe traced what they asserted is a distinctive current queer liberation movement today. They contend there are queer and trans organizations that "constitute a distinct social movement, separate from the Gay Rights Movement and rooted in substantively different political and theoretical foundations, which center intersectional perspectives, multi-issue organizing, and efforts to work from margin to center . . . to privilege the voices and experiences of the most marginal among queer communities."[28] All of these are examples of how intersectional social justice ideals and strategies centering the "impossible people" characterize radical queer and trans politics of liberation today, with different visions of freedom than simply the negative freedom prioritized by a mainstream movement. Below we offer an additional extended example (about the Reclaim Pride Coalition) that elaborates how such activism is envisioning a multidimensional positive freedom rooted in conceptualizations of intersectional social justice and embracing radical resistance to state and capital. Additionally, we offer another extended example focusing on queer migration activism, highlighting the expansion of queer resistance beyond the definition of nation-state, one-dimensional movements, and international human rights to what might be considered freedom imagined as international human justice.

In sum, we approach the question of positive freedom by looking at queer and trans activism, which recognizes the limits of negative freedom of a U.S. mainstream movement and seeks to move beyond it. In the following sections, we turn to two extended examples of such emerging queer and trans social justice radicalism to illustrate the complex visions of freedom that both ground such work and are articulated through it. Each, we argue, is an example of activism seeking freedom "against a neoliberalism that would swallow it whole."[29]

"No Cops, No Corps, No BS": Reclaiming Pride

Despite the alleged success of the mainstream gay rights movement in the United States, queer people—particularly Black, Indigenous, and people of color—continue to face higher rates of poverty,[30] incarceration,[31] and violence from police.[32] Assimilating to mainstream society has benefited those few LGBTQ+ people already privileged with social and economic capital while simultaneously marginalizing people most vulnerable to harm using reductionist strategies of "inclusion" and "equality." The White gay community went mainstream and pushed queer people of color from the movement,[33] the repeal of DADT allows for LGBTQ+ people to serve in the military for certain rights never fully guaranteed,[34] and hate crime laws ignore the greater structural and systemic problems that put our lives in danger.[35] In other words, the LGBTQ+ mainstream movement has assimilated to the governing power structures of ongoing settler colonialism and White supremacy rather than critically evaluating and seeking liberation from institutions that maintain the status quo.[36]

These effects of neoliberalism on the mainstream LGBT movement are rendered most visible during annual Pride commemorations. Pride and its parades now symbolize "the conformity of gay neighborhoods, bars, and institutions"[37] to the mainstream and contribute to "the phenomenon of police rainbow branding practiced in nominally public spaces."[38] Pride parades have changed to include police and military contingents, floats sponsored by military contractors, and politicians, all operating under the auspices of "equality" grounded in (negative) freedom. But queer and trans activists are mobilizing to reclaim the mainstreaming of the movement and Pride around the world. For example, 50 years after the Stonewall uprising, the Reclaim Pride Coalition (RPC) organized the Queer Liberation March and Rally: a grassroots, community-based project without the inclusion of cops, corporations, or bullshit.[39] This is particularly significant because at the same time across New York City (NYC), the World Pride parade was occurring simultaneously.

To explain the movement work of RPC, we first outline some critiques of mainstream Pride. In 2016, Black Lives Matter (BLM) Toronto disrupted the Pride Toronto parade by holding a sit-in. BLM Toronto understood Toronto Pride as being anti-Black and demanded that Toronto Pride further invest in Black and Indigenous people while simultaneously divesting from Toronto Police, noting these people are disproportionately targeted by police oppression and violence.[40] In early 2017, Pride Toronto voted to remove police contingents from their annual parade, resulting in police no longer marching in the Pride Toronto parade. Later that same year, the Gay Officers Action League (GOAL) New York invited Toronto Police to march with them in the mainstream gay pride parade of New York, Heritage of Pride (HOP). GOAL New York's mission is to "promote a positive relationship between the law enforcement community and the LGBTQ community."[41] Mike McCormack, the Toronto Police Association president said of the event, "I think it's sad Toronto couldn't be that progressive and that inclusive."[42] These entanglements between Pride and police in NYC is representative of a larger discussion involving the mainstream politics of visibility and safety.[43] Emma K. Russell argued that this "new face of gay pride" provides police forces with legitimacy and "complicates the task of exposing power and sexual injustice because the powerful proclaim to be on the side of the weak, whilst maintaining or building a position of dominance."[44] This is especially true considering the historical significance of so-called Pride and its radical roots.

In June 1969, the New York Police Department (NYPD) stormed the Mafia-owned bar Stonewall in NYC, and patrons fought back. An instance of routine state violence turned into riots lasting several nights, what is now known as the Stonewall uprising. These riots have been etched into the historical memory as the "spark" that started the contemporary LGBTQ+ movement.[45] This is because in June 1970—1 year after the Stonewall uprising—was the first organized Christopher Street Liberation Day, when about 2,000 people took to the streets in protest, marching uptown on Sixth Avenue from Greenwich Village to Central Park for the "Gay Be-In." Flashforward to 2019, and what was once a community-based protest is now a police-escorted display of corporate floats in an effort to demobilize radical queer politics. World Pride occurred in June 2019 and took place in NYC—for the first time in the United States—to commemorate 50 years after the Stonewall uprising. In an interview,[46] Zoe Gorringe, march event coordinator for HOP, explained how the 2019 parade would be the largest HOP had ever organized, expecting about 1,800 to 2,000 volunteers. The 2018 HOP parade included 50,000 to 60,000 participants, and they expected 150,000 during World Pride in 2019. In 2018, there were about 90 floats, and the official count for 2019 was about 160 floats. These figures demonstrate how the parade had grown over the decades from its start as the Christopher Street Liberation Day. The 2019 HOP parade for World Pride was the most attended Pride event ever organized. How could an organized commemoration of queers fighting back against state violence therefore include police? Said succinctly, the HOP parade is now the mainstream.

Reclaim Pride Coalition, however, has a different approach to demanding (positive) freedom and exemplifies how queer liberation organizations are repoliticizing the movement and reclaiming Pride. Following failed attempts to hold the HOP parade organizers accountable for their ongoing involvement with violent state and exploitative capitalist institutions, such as the NYPD and multinational corporations, RPC decided to organize the Queer Liberation March and Rally, or "Queer March." In stark contrast to HOP, RPC is made up of organizations and individuals who seek to repoliticize pride. The first iteration of the Queer March was held in June 2019, when an estimated 45,000 people marched from the Stonewall Inn up to the Great Lawn of Central Park for a rally—following the original route of the Christopher Street Liberation Day in 1970. As a way to move beyond the sexuality-only analysis of the mainstream movement, the politics of RPC develop from Black feminist analyses of intersecting systems of oppression.[47] Cathy Cohen wrote: "Queer activists must confront a question that haunts most political organizing: How do we put into politics a broad and inclusive left analysis that can actually engage and mobilize individuals with intersecting identities?"[48] Here, we offer the example of RPC's 2019 Queer Liberation March and Rally to highlight the queer and intersectional coalition work Cohen called for nearly 25 years ago. Barbara Smith, cofounder of the Combahee River Collective, commended the organizing of RPC on *Intersectionality Matters With Kimberlé Crenshaw*, saying: "They are trying to get back to our roots. They're not trying to entertain people. It's not going to be the biggest party extravaganza that anyone has ever seen. It's going to be about issues, it's going to be about community, it's going to be about solidarity."[49] Thus, the 2019 Queer March was a moment of movement work that built solidarity between people from various social locations and rendered a lasting vision of (positive) freedom through anticapitalist and abolitionist perspectives.

In a video released by RPC[50] weeks before the Queer March took place, the following text repeatedly cycled across a bright pink background:

QUEER LIBERATION MARCH
SHERIDAN SQUARE
MARCH TO GREAT LAWN
NO CORPORATIONS
NO COPS
NO BS

As the above text repeats, the sound of people declaring "OFF OF THE SIDEWALKS! INTO THE STREETS!" grows louder through the end of the video. This pithily breaks down the movement work of RPC into issue-oriented, politicized statements and produces demands for what needs to be achieved to make queer liberation a reality. That is, beyond demanding the mainstream movement divest from capitalism and policing in a parade, RPC understands these institutions as needing to be fundamentally dismantled and transformed in order for queer liberation and (positive) freedom to be realized.

Why no cops? Hosting World Pride in NYC provided pathways for what Sarah Schulman[51] called "pinkwashing." The NYPD was able to produce new forms of propaganda to promote their organization as "inclusive" without ever having to make structural changes to the institution. For example, the NYC police commissioner, James O'Neill, apologized for the 1969 raid of the Stonewall Inn, claiming: "The actions taken by the NYPD were wrong—plain and simple."[52] But many activists, including Colin P. Ashley of RPC, saw this as an empty gesture. Ashley said in an interview: "He framed it as Stonewall was this thing the NYPD did 50 years ago and it is something that would never happen today. This isn't just historical, it is continual."[53] One day after the NYPD police commissioner apologized, Layleen Cubilette-Polanco of the House of Xtravaganza was found dead in solitary confinement on Rikers Island after suffering an epileptic seizure. She was held in jail after not being able to afford the $500 bail that was set for her release. This one example is connected to a long history, as Ashley explained, of state violence on Black and queer communities that ground the politics of RPC within abolitionist frameworks. In this case, strategies of survival led to incarceration and premature death by the state. Angela Davis reminded us that "decarceration as our overarching strategy" requires we "envision a continuum of alternatives to imprisonment—demilitarization of schools, revitalization of education at all levels, a health system that provides free physical and mental care to all, and a justice system based on reparation and reconciliation rather than retribution and vengeance."[54] Rather than further infusing police with LGBTQ+ politics, RPC rejects policing as the strategy to safe and vibrant communities, pushing instead for the defunding of the NYPD and investing in Black and low-income communities.[55] There is no "Pride" in policing.

Why no corporations? The reason RPC did not partner with corporations became ever clearer in the months following the Queer March. In August 2019, news broke that Stephen Ross, billionaire real estate developer and SoulCycle investor, was hosting a fundraiser for President Trump in the Hamptons with tickets costing $100,000 or more.[56] Soul Cycle and its related companies had participated in Pride for years, providing a concrete example of corporations capitalizing on their brand and advertising during Pride and then using that revenue to support oppressive politics. In reaction, the RPC released a call to action saying, "#QueerLiberation is also freeing ourselves from companies that use our identities for profit while doing everything they can to undermine our existence,"[57] and encouraged queers to boycott the company and cancel any existing memberships. Some have begun to identify this relationship between Pride, the LGBTQ+ movement more generally, and capitalism as "rainbow capitalism," where the economic system simply co-opts rainbows and related imagery for maximum profits while doing no meaningful work to transform the material realities of low-income queers. In building an analysis of this unequal economic system, RPC, too, upholds an anticapitalist vision. There is no Pride in corporate capitalism.

What brought so many people and wide-reaching organizations together for the Queer March is an expansive, multidimensional analysis of queer liberation or, as we explore within this chapter, of (positive) freedom. This queer praxis sees beyond a single-issue LGBT politic (e.g., "marriage equality") and instead expands a coalitional and intersectional politic. By proclaiming a march without ties to capitalism, White supremacy, and with the edge of queer critique, RPC seeks to reclaim pride in—and on the streets of—NYC. The 2019 Queer Liberation March built solidarity between people and made clear a world that does not yet exist, but one that if we achieve, would transform conditions and provide (positive) freedom for queers to act with agency.

No(w) Trespassing: Queer Migration

Understanding the United States' approach to, and history of, law is significant to understand how societal change has been aimed to be controlled in the democratic system. Laws in the United States are to make people more "free," which is far from reflecting the reality of freedom in actual people's lives. Centuries after the attempts of freedom of the late 1700s, and decades after the foundation of the United Nations (UN) in 1945, and the announcement of the Universal Declaration of Human Rights in 1948, the UN Human Rights Council had the first settlement on human rights on the basis of sexual orientation and gender identity in 2011. After a number of international events organized in 2013, the UN Human Rights Council finally decided to fight against violence and discrimination based on sexual orientation and gender identity. Finally, in 2014 international LGBTI human rights got into the UN agenda.[58] In 2018, the Trump administration withdrew from the United Nations,[59] while encouraging countries to contribute more to NATO (North Atlantic Treaty Organization).[60] To conclude, governments' presences within the unions and organizations and their commitments to human rights contracts can be quite dubious. In the U.S. history of freedoms and rights, laws and conventions have mostly been seen as the embodiments of the nation's governmental institutions' commitment to define human rights and ensure (!) individuals' freedoms within its national imaginary of democracy. However, it would be a misconception to think that the amendments in the law are enough to make people freer, the society more equal, and the United States more antiracist, antisexist, anticolonialist, and anti-imperialist.[61]

As Dean Spade also suggested: "The idea is that when social movements rise up against oppression and harm, the result will be the law will change just enough to preserve the existing status quo. . . . Instead of the law changing to bring justice, it changes just enough to make things look good enough to keep things how they are."[62] Accordingly, one of the examples for the law-based perception of social movements can be seen in mainstream LGBTQ+ rights organizations. Mainstream LGBTQ+ organizations have strong emphases on legal issues when they aim to create a change in society for vulnerable people and mobilize the structure of inequalities. Internships in these organizations, for instance, are mostly directed at law students. Reading LGBTQ+ freedom through the lens of mainstream organizational work contributes to the reproduction of existing power dynamics between so-called victims without opportunities and defenders with money and ignores the fact that they both are the creations of the same settler colonial structure. Understanding freedoms and rights through the organizations fighting for LGBTQ+ human rights, composed of advocates with law degrees focusing on the legal issues and deploying a law-based White-supremacist rhetoric, fails to address the needs of marginalized persons who need services more than laws to directly enhance their living conditions.[63] Hence, some nonmainstream activisms of LGBTQ+ persons and activists have been aiming to reshape this frame of freedoms, and its attendant emphasis on human rights, pointing out how the frame of human rights is an unfinished project, an incomplete vision of freedom if you will.

One way to understand the call to address the unfinished project of human rights is to pay attention to the gaps in research. Research on the issues of sexuality and migration has long been conducted in various fields, including anthropology, history, psychology, literature, and sociology. It has even been fostered by the fact that international migration has created changes in social, economic, cultural, and political dimensions of life at both local and global levels. Accordingly, increasing rates of immigration turned the focus of queer studies and sexuality research into the effects of globalization and transnational relocation of the people. Sexuality scholars started to investigate how migration processes affect and transform the structure, organization, and adaptation of sexual identities, communities, and related politics. Meanwhile, migration scholars, as Luibhéid stated, hold a traditional view that " 'all the immigrants are heterosexual" and "all the queers are citizens."[64] In this regard, the intersectional analysis of sexualities and migration dynamics had been avoided for quite a while, as if being queer was only a citizen thing, whereas heterosexuality of migrants had been taken for granted. In the late 1990s, scholars started to focus more on sexuality, separately from gender, as a "dense transfer point for relations of power," which plays a regulatory role in the international flow of migration.[65] Resulting from the conversation between these fields of sexuality and migration, the topic of queer migration has emerged to challenge the heteronormative approach of traditional migration studies, while embracing the methodological tools of queer theory.[66] Influenced mostly by feminists and queers of color, the issues related to queer migration mainly highlight the intersections of sexuality, race, class, ethnicity, gender with geopolitics, and the processes of nation-making and citizenship considering the global histories of imperialist relationships.[67] By doing so, it provides analysis that does not take the boundaries of nation-states and the understanding of nation-based citizenship for granted. Consequently, recognizing the long histories behind the multiple relations of power, queer migration scholarship aspires to give voice to the persons and shed light on their positionalities, which are ignored, underemphasized, and silenced in both queer and migration communities. What is recognized is that to further this field a more comprehensive perspective on the issues of freedom and international human rights is necessary.

Focusing on the issues related to the queer migrants' human rights lets us achieve a corresponding understanding of human rights of both queer folk and migrants and, it is hoped, the incomplete frame of human rights defined through national agendas. Considering the history since the beginning of the 1950s and including the contemporary discussions on international LGBTQ+ human rights, Mertus defined two eras of human rights activism that LGBTQ+ advocates in the United States. The first one reflects the period before 1995 when LGBTQ+ advocates utilized conventional strategies of human rights activism to convey information related to existing conditions of LGBTQ+ persons to the fundamental human rights nongovernmental organizations within the movement. Accordingly, they refer to specific forms of human rights, such as "the right to privacy in the criminal law context; the right to equality; the right to family; the right to non-discrimination; the right to freedom from torture . . . ; and the right of transsexuals to recognition of their new gender."[68] It is advocacy to point out how LGBTQ+ persons in the United States have limited human rights. The other era of human right activism embraced since 1995 is that done by LGBTQ+ advocates, deviating from the mainstream human rights advocacy and aiming to establish a human rights culture to develop a new international human rights frame centered on "the right to sexuality."[69] However, in both types of human rights work, the focus has been on experiences of those in the United States.[70] As a result, queer migrants are invisible in these LGBTQ+ movement discussions, and we might ask: Who has "a right to sexuality"[71] in the United States? In different words, who has human rights and the freedom of sexuality?

In this regard, Chávez,[72] in their book *Queer Migration Politics"* highlights the fact that political activities concerning immigrants have been increasing in the fields of social justice and human rights activism in the United States. However, the possibility of a coalition between LGBTQ politics and immigration politics remains weak since the political strategies that LGBTQ and immigrant activists employ seem contradictory. Additionally, what is needed is more than a mere expansion of the mainstream movement. Expansion, in this sense, to include queer migrants in the movement necessitates going beyond/breaking/passing the boundaries of a national movement, which has focused on establishing itself as a national movement while "interacting" or "cooperating" at the international level. Consequently, the organization of the U.S. LGBTQ+ movement as a national project results in a politics of sexuality as a politics of citizenship. This organization of the U.S. LGBTQ+ movement as a national movement depends on and reproduces notions of a structurally constructed binary between citizens and noncitizens (or more accurately in legal terms: "aliens") and defines particular frames of human rights—human rights that evade the human rights of some "(LGBTQ+) aliens," such as LGBTQ+ asylum seekers, migrants, and refugees. In this regard, Chávez stressed the importance of "coalitional moments" in queer migration politics in the United States in the early 2000s. She referred to "a queer temporality"[73] that points out the possibilities of "another" future and argued that queer immigrants themselves are coalitional subjects involving a complexity of experiences.

Remembering Berlin's[74] terminology on positive and negative freedom explained in the beginning of this chapter, we should ask the question of where "freedom to" sexuality becomes "freedom from" other opportunities related to education, health, occupation, and assemblage. As scholars, LGBTQ+ persons, and activists, committed to challenge the binaries between the West and the East, and the North and the South, it is also significant to recheck our potentially nation-framed visions while discussing beyond-nation issues such as human rights and freedom. Furthermore, it is equally vital to remember the "impossible people," here those considered to be outsiders (i.e., queer migrants), are the very subjects and can also be the key to our seemingly international but still quite fundamentally national questions (i.e., homonormativity and homonationalism). Can we be forgetting the fact that impossible people are defined and objectified in activism and the law by the very same discourse and practices that reproduce homonations? If so, let's remember! There is a lot of freedom to take back, a number of impossible people speaking up, and a great number of boundaries to trespass.

Throughout this chapter we have been suggesting that activism based on social justice is striving toward necessary forms of positive freedom, and that limited notions of liberal equality through law based on negative freedom is not enough (indeed, Berlin and others reminded us that both negative and positive freedom are needed). We acknowledge that the equation is not as simple as social justice versus liberal equality, so we close with the following final thought.

A Final Thought

We write this chapter as the world was responding to the COVID-19 pandemic and systematic racism, among many other ongoing challenges. As such, we are quite aware that we have focused in this chapter only on certain examples of queer and trans activism and so close by acknowledging that there are additional and emerging (and needed) visions of freedom. One form of resistance particularly important in this era is the work responding to understandings of queer and trans necropolitics detailing how "sovereign power (is) fundamentally concerned with death-making."[75] It is activism that seeks to trouble such "death worlds," one strategy of which is creating projects of radical care. Such resistance recognizes that regimes institute forms of political violence that reduce some people (particularly of color) to living in profoundly precarious positions between life and death. It is work that details how the mainstreaming of the U.S. LGBT movement also fosters such death-making. Bassichis and Spade,[76] for example, pointed out how "rhetorical arguments mobilized by gay and lesbian rights discourse rely on and extend foundational racial narratives justifying black premature death." As such, the call is to resist becoming " 'happy queers' (or indeed, nostalgic queers) whose recruitment for sexual celebration serves to euphemize and accelerate the death of Others—who for some of us indeed include our own."[77] In response, some resistance is centered on creating healthy spaces for queer and trans folks to thrive, a politics "fostering survival."[78] For example, some queer and trans communities seek to create radical care projects of "mutual aid," outlined by Dean Spade on his website (http://bigdoorbrigade.com/what-is-mutual-aid/) as efforts by people taking responsibility for caring for one another, building new social relations and political circumstances that are more survivable. These are projects with governance by those most affected, political education, and centering dignity, self-determination, and care. They are efforts drawing on liberation movement strategies (e.g., from Black Panthers), moving away from capitalist nonprofit structures of service, and creating mechanisms for self-determined thriving and living. These are forms of activism that recognize regimes centered on a politics of human disposability compel particular forms of survival resistance. In this moment, we draw from this work and close by recognizing that notions of positive and negative freedom depend on surviving.

Notes

1. Dean Spade, 2009, cited in Joseph Nicholas DeFilippis, and Ben Anderson-Nathe, "Embodying Margin to Center: Intersectional Activism among Queer Liberation Organizations." in *LGBTQ Politics: A Critical Reader*, ed. Marla Brettschneider, Susan Burgess, and Christine Keating (New York: New York University Press, 2017), 113.

2. Isaac Berlin, *Liberty* (Oxford: Oxford University Press, 2002), 204.

3. Berlin, *Liberty*, 326.

4. Masha Gessen, "Life, Liberty, and the Pursuit of Spitting on Other People," *The New Yorker*, May 26, 2020, https://www.newyorker.com/news/our-columnists/life-liberty-and-the-pursuit-of-spitting-on-other-people?utm_source=facebook&utm_medium=social&utm_campaign=onsite-share&utm_brand=the-new-yorker&utm_social-type=earned.

5. Berlin, *Liberty*.

6. Gessen, "Life, Liberty."

7. Berlin, 178.

8. Gessen, "Life, Liberty."

9. We are including all these terms to recognize the varieties of queer, trans, and LGBTQ+ activism. It is the language of activists and community members today, and we recognize these activisms are historically diverse, and there are important differences in how people use these terms and the degree to which they assume they mean the same thing.

10. Wendy Brown, *In the Ruins of Neoliberalism: The Rise of Anti-Democratic Politics in the West* (New York: Columbia University Press, 2019); Jin Haritaworn, Adi Kuntsman, and Sophia Posocco, *Queer Necropolitics* (New York: Routledge, 2014).

11. Lisa Duggan, *The Twilight of Equality? Neoliberalism, Cultural Politics, and the Attack on Democracy* (Boston: Beacon Press, 2004).

12. Brown, *In the Ruins,* 28.

13. Brown, *In the Ruins*, 45.

14. Dean Spade, *Normal Life: Administrative Violence, Critical Trans Politics, and the Limits of Law* (Durham, NC: Duke University Press, 2015).

15. Haritaworn, Kuntsman, and Posocco, Queer Necropolitics, 1, 6.

16. As some refer to it; DeFilippis and Anderson-Nathe, "Embodying Margin to Center," 110–133.

17. Roderick A. Ferguson, *One-Dimensional Queer* (Medford, MA: Polity Press, 2019), 52.

18. Ferguson, *One-Dimensional Queer*.

19. Christina B. Hanhardt, *Safe Space: Gay Neighborhood History and the Politics of Violence* (Durham, NC: Duke University Press, 2013).

20. Ferguson, *One-Dimensional Queer*.

21. Jasbir Puar, *Terrorist Assemblages: Homonationalism in Queer Times* (Durham, NC: Duke University Press, 2007).

22. Rikke Mananzala and Dean Spade. "The Nonprofit Industrial Complex and Trans Resistance," *Sexuality Research & Social Policy* 5, no. 1 (March 2008), 56.

23. Myrl Beam, *Gay, Inc: The Nonprofitization of Queer Politics* (Minneapolis, MN: University of Minnesota Press, 2018).

24. See Note 22.

25. Hanhardt, Safe Space; Mananzala, Rikke, and Spade, "The Nonprofit Industrial Complex," 62.

26. Mananzala and Spade, "The Nonprofit Industrial Complex," 63.

27. Mananzala and Spade, "The Nonprofit Industrial Complex," 54.

28. DeFilippis and Anderson-Nathe, "Embodying Margin to Center," 112.

29. Emily K. Hobson, *Lavender and Red: Liberation and Solidarity in the Gay and Lesbian Left* (Oakland, CA: University of California Press, 2016), 194.

30. M. V. Lee Badgett, Soon Kyu Choi, and Bianca D. M. Wilson, "LGBT Poverty in the United States: A Study of Differences Between Sexual Orientation and Gender Identity Groups," Williams Institute, October 2019, https://williamsinstitute.law.ucla.edu/wp-content/uploads/National-LGBT-Poverty-Oct-2019.pdf

31. Ilan H. Meyer et al., "Incarceration Rates and Traits of Sexual Minorities in the United States: National Inmate Survey, 2011–2012," *American Journal of Public Health* 107, no. 2 (February 2017), 267–273, https://doi.org/10.2105/AJPH.2016.303576.

32. Naomi G. Goldberg et al., "Police and the Criminalization of LGBT People," in *The Cambridge Handbook of Policing in the United States* (Cambridge Law Handbooks), ed. Tamara Rice Lave and Eric J. Miller (Cambridge: Cambridge University Press, 2019), 374–391.

33. Kenyon Farrow, "Is Gay Marriage Anti-Black???" in *Against Equality: Queer Revolution, Not Mere Inclusion*, ed. Ryan Conrad (Oakland, CA: AK Press, 2014), 33–44.

34. Tamara K. Nopper, "Why I Oppose Repealing DADT & Passage of the DREAM Act," in *Against Equality: Queer Revolution, Not Mere Inclusion*, ed. Ryan Conrad (Oakland, CA: AK Press, 2014), 125–133.

35. Yasmin Nair, "Why Hate Crime Legislation Is Still Not a Solution," in *Against Equality: Queer Revolution, Not Mere Inclusion*, ed. Ryan Conrad (Oakland, CA: AK Press, 2014), 199–204.

36. Scott L. Morgensen, "Settler Homonationalism: Theorizing Settler Colonialism Within Queer Modernities," *GLQ: A Journal of Lesbian and Gay Studies* 16, no.1 (2010), 105–131, https://www.muse.jhu.edu/article/372447.

37. Mattilda Bernstein Sycamore, "Gay Shame: From Queer Autonomous Space to Direct Action Extravaganza," in *That's Revolting! Queer Strategies for Resisting Assimilation*, ed. Mattilda Bernstein Sycamore (Brooklyn, NY: Soft Skull Press, 2004), 238.

38. Emma K. Russell, "Carceral Pride: The Fusion of Police Imagery With LGBTI Rights," *Feminist Legal Studies* 26 (2018), 331, https://doi.org/10.1007/s10691-018-9383-2

39. Reclaim Pride Coalition, "Off the Sidewalks!!! Into the Streets!!!" *YouTube*, (June 18, 2019a), video 0:33, https://www.youtube.com/watch?v=ntU7oyDiIQI.

40. Julia Craven, "Black Lives Matter Toronto Stands by Pride Parade Shutdown." *HuffPost*, July 6, 2016, https://www.huffpost.com/entry/black-lives-matter-toronto-pride_n_577c15aee4b0a629c1ab0ab4.

41. Gay Officers Action League New York, "Mission Statement," http://www.goalny.org/mission-statement.

42. Azzura Lalani, "Toronto Police Invited to March in New York City Pride Parade," *The Star*, May 22, 2017, https://www.thestar.com/news/gta/2017/05/22/toronto-police-invited-to-march-in-new-york-city-pride-parade.html.

43. Reina Gosset, Eric A. Stanley, and Johanna Burton, eds., *Trap Door: Trans Cultural Production and the Politics of Visibility* (Cambridge, MA: MIT Press, 2017).

44. Emma K. Russell, "A 'Fair Cop': Queer Histories, Affect and Police Image Work in Pride March," *Crime, Media, Culture* 13, no. 3 (2017), 290.

45. Elizabeth A. Armstrong and Suzanna M. Crage, "Movements and Memory: The Making of the Stonewall Myth," *American Sociological Review* 71, no. 5 (October 2006), 724–751, https://www.jstor.org/stable/25472425; Roderick A. Ferguson, *One-Dimensional Queer* (Medford, MA: Polity Press, 2019).

46. VICE News, "Reclaim Pride & Overcrowding Migrant Facilities: VICE News Tonight Full Episode (HBO)," *YouTube*, July 13, 2019, video 25:18, https://www.youtube.com/watch?v=I_nkUw2wCRM.

47. Audre Lorde, *Sister Outsider: Essays and Speeches* (Trumansburg, NY: Crossing Press, 1984); Kimberlé Crenshaw, "Mapping the Margins: Identity Politics, Intersectionality, and Violence Against Women," *Stanford Law Review* 43, no. 6 (1991), 1241–1299; Patricia Hill Collins, *Black Feminist Thought: Knowledge, Consciousness, and the Politics of Empowerment* (Routledge, 2002).

48. Cathy J. Cohen, "Punks, Bulldaggers, and Welfare Queens: The Radical Potential of Queer Politics?" *GLQ: A Journal of Lesbian and Gay Studies* 3, no. 4 (1997), 449.

49. Kimberlé Crenshaw, "5. Stonewall 50: Whose Movement Is It Anyway?" in Intersectionality Matters With Kimberlé Crenshaw, prod. and ed. Julia Sharpe Levine, June 28, 2019, podcast, MP3 audio 1:01:26, https://aapf.org/ep-5-stonewall-50.

50. Reclaim Pride Coalition, "Off the Sidewalks!!!"

51. Sarah Schulman, "Israel and 'Pinkwashing.'" *New York Times*, November 22, 2011.

52. Michael Gold and Derek M. Norman, "Stonewall Riot Apology: Police Actions Were 'Wrong,' Commissioner Admits," *New York Times*, June 6, 2019, https://www.nytimes.com/2019/06/06/nyregion/stonewall-riots-nypd.html.

53. See Note l.

54. Angela Davis, *Are Prisons Obsolete?* (New York: Seven Stories Press, 2003), 107.

55. Reclaim Pride Coalition, "Reclaim Pride Coalition Announces Queer Liberation March for Black Lives and Against Police Brutality," June 18, 2020, https://reclaimpridenyc.org.

56. Alex Abad-Santos, "SoulCycle Instructors Are as Mad About Its Investor's Trump Fundraiser as Its Riders Are," *Vox*, updated August 9, 2019, https://www.vox.com/2019/8/9/20791646/soulcycle-trump-fundraiser-backlash.

57. Reclaim Pride Coalition (@queermarch), "#Queerliberation Is Also Freeing Ourselves From Companies That Use Our Identities for Profit While Doing Everything They Can Do Undermine Our Existence. We Reject the Blatant #pinkwashing," Instagram, August 8, 2019, https://www.instagram.com/p/B06FDS2FFrU/.

58. David, Paternotte and Hakan Seckinelgin, "'Lesbian and Gay Rights Are Human Rights': Multiple Globalizations and LGBTI Activism," in *The Ashgate Research Companion to Lesbian and Gay Activism*, ed. David Paternotte and Manon Tremblay (New York: Ashgate, 2016), 209–223.

59. Matthew Lee and Josh Lederman, "Trump Administration Pulls US Out of UN Human Rights Council," *AP News*, June 19, 2018, https://apnews.com/9c5b1005f064474f9a0825ab84a16e91/Trump-administration-pulls-US-out-of-UN-human-rights-council

60. John Fritze and Deirdre Shesgreen, "Pay Freeze at the UN? Trump Administration Owes the United Nations $1 Billion," *USA Today*, October 9, 2019, https://www.usatoday.com/story/news/politics/2019/10/09/donald-trump-dismisses-united-nations-deficits-says-others-should-pay/3917554002/

61. Dean Spade, "What Every Activist Should Know Before Going to Law School," April 24, 2020, video 00:52:18, http://www.deanspade.net/2020/04/24/what-every-activist-should-know-before-going-to-law-school/
62. Spade, "What Every Activist Should Know," 3:54–4:16.
63. See Note 59.
64. Eithne Luibhéid, "Heteronormativity and Immigration Scholarship: A Call for Change," *GLQ: A Journal of Lesbian and Gay Studies*, 10, no. 2 (2004), 233.
65. Foucault, 1978:103, cited in Eithne Luibhéid, "Sexuality, Migration, and the Shifting Line Between Legal and Illegal Status," *GLQ: A Journal of Lesbian and Gay Studies*, 14, no. 2–3 (2008), 169, https://doi.org/10.1215/10642684-2007-034.
66. Rachel A. Lewis and Nancy A. Naples, "Introduction: Queer Migration, Asylum, and Displacement," *Sexualities* 17, no. 8 (October 2014), 911–918.
67. Eithne Luibhéid and Lionel Cantú Jr., eds., *Queer Migrations: Sexuality, US Citizenship, and Border Crossings* (University of Minnesota Press, 2005).
68. Julie Mertus, "The Rejection of Human Rights Framings: The Case of LGBT Advocacy in the US," *Human Rights Quarterly* 29, no. 4 (November 2007), 1038.
69. Mertus, *Rejection of Human Rights Framings*, 1039.
70. Joke Swiebel, "Lesbian, Gay, Bisexual and Transgender Human Rights: The Search for an International Strategy," *Contemporary Politics* 15, no.1 (March 2009), 19–35, https://doi.org/10.1080/13569770802674196.
71. Mertus, *Rejection of Human Rights Framings*, 1042.
72. Karma R. Chávez, *Queer Migration Politics: Activist Rhetoric and Coalitional Possibilities* (University of Illinois Press, 2013).
73. Chávez, Queer Migration Politics, 9.
74. Berlin, Liberty.
75. Haritaworn, Kuntsman, and Posocco, Queer Necropolitics, 6.
76. Morgan Bassichis and Dean Spade, "Queer Politics and Anti-Blackness" in *Queer Necropolitics*, ed. Jin Haritaworn, Adi Kuntsman, and Silvia Posocco (New York: Routledge, 2014), 199.
77. Haritaworn, Kuntsman, and Posocco, *Queer Politics*, 20.
78. Haritaworn, Kuntsman, and Posocco, *Queer Politics*, 19.

20

Truth and Freedom

The Debate Over Unauthorized Immigrants and Crime

Alex Nowrasteh, Andrew C. Forrester, and Michelangelo Landgrave

Well-designed laws and public policies help to establish the conditions that allow Americans to enjoy their freedoms to the fullest possible extent. The effectiveness of these laws and policies depends on whether policymakers use facts and sound judgment during the debate, design, and implementation stages. Unfortunately, facts are often undermined and ignored in the American debate over immigration policy—with disastrous consequences.

Donald J. Trump launched his candidacy for the Republican presidential nomination in June 2015 by comments on unauthorized immigrants and the crime they commit in the United States. "When Mexico sends its people, they're not sending their best. They're not sending you. They're not sending you," he said. "They're sending people that have lots of problems and they're bringing those problems with us. They're bringing drugs, they're bringing crime, they're rapists, and some, I assume, are good people."[1] A few weeks after Trump's announcement, 32-year-old Kate Steinle was shot and killed by an unauthorized immigrant José Inez García Zárate in San Francisco, California. Although Zárate was later acquitted of all murder and manslaughter charges, his shooting of Steinle seemed to support Trump's worry about unauthorized immigrants causing a crime spree and helped win him the election in 2016.

As tragic as the shooting and death of Kate Steinle was, it was one of the 13,455 murders that year in the United States, and it does not tell us how many of those victims were murdered by unauthorized immigrants.[2] The most important measure that matters when judging the crime rates of unauthorized immigrants is how likely they are to be criminals compared to other subpopulations. If unauthorized immigrants are more likely to be criminals, then their presence in the United States would raise crime rates, supporting Trump's assertions. But if unauthorized immigrants are less likely to commit crime, then they would lower the nationwide crime rate.

This debate politically spills over to evaluating whether domestic immigration enforcement policies reduce crime. It's also central to the debate over sanctuary jurisdictions that refuse to turn over many unauthorized immigrants

Alex Nowrasteh, Andrew C. Forrester, and Michelangelo Landgrave, *Truth and Freedom* In: *On Inequality and Freedom*. Edited by: Lawrence M. Eppard and Henry A. Giroux, Oxford University Press. © Oxford University Press 2022. DOI: 10.1093/oso/9780197583029.003.0020 to Immigration and Customs Enforcement (ICE), the effects of a border wall, and whether Border Patrol requires more resources to counter crime along the border. Answering whether unauthorized immigrants are particularly crime prone is essential to addressing these concerns and setting efficient anticrime policies.

As important as this question is, there are few data available about unauthorized immigrant criminality to answer this question. Most state governments do not record the immigration statuses of those who are convicted of crimes, and federal census data on the incarcerated population do not identify unauthorized immigrants. However, the little evidence that does exist shows that unauthorized immigrants have a crime rate far below that of native-born Americans, but higher than legal immigrants. This chapter presents the two most important pieces of evidence. The first compelling set of evidence is the relative conviction and arrest rates in the state of Texas, which keeps arrest and conviction data for the number of unauthorized immigrants by crime. The second is the estimates of the nationwide incarceration rates by immigration status, which are consistent with the Texas conviction rates.

Unauthorized Immigration and Crime in Texas

Texas is the only state that records criminal convictions and arrests by immigration status.[3,4] The Texas Department of Public Safety (DPS) has these data because its law enforcement agencies cooperate with federal immigration enforcement authorities at the Department of Homeland Security (DHS) that check the biometric information of all arrestees in the state and tracks them through to their convictions.[5] Unlike other states, the Texas DPS keeps the results of these DHS checks, and they were acquired through a Public Information Act request.[6]

The Texas DPS data quality is excellent, and, if it errs, it is likely to overcount the convictions and arrests of unauthorized immigrants because it counts more total arrests than the other publicly available DPS source.[7] It's particularly fortuitous that Texas keeps these data because it borders Mexico; it has the second-largest unauthorized immigrant population of any state; it is a politically conservative state governed by Republicans; in 2017 it did not have jurisdictions that limited its cooperation with federal immigration enforcement; and it has a law-and-order reputation for severely and strictly enforcing its criminal laws.[8]

Controlling for the size of the population is essential for comparing relative conviction and arrest rates between subpopulations in the state of Texas. This means that the total number of native-born Americans, legal immigrants, and unauthorized immigrants living in Texas is just as important as the number of convictions in calculating their respective crime rates. However, the government doesn't record immigration status in the American Community Survey (ACS), so social scientists estimate the number of unauthorized and legal immigrants using the residual method. We adopted a residual method proposed by Christian Gunadi, in a paper that he published in *Oxford Economic Papers*.[9]

Gunadi imputed legal immigrant status and identified those left over as unauthorized immigrants, which is different from other residual methods that identify unauthorized immigrants first and then count the leftover people as legal immigrants. Using Gunadi's methods, a person is counted as a legal immigrant if he or she met any of the following criteria as recorded in the 2018 ACS: The immigrant arrived after 1980; is a U.S. citizen; received welfare benefits such as Social Security, Supplemental Security Income, Medicaid, Medicare, or military insurance; served in the Armed Forces; works for the government; resided in public housing or received rental subsidies or was the spouse of someone who resided in public housing or received rental subsidies; or was born in Cuba and has a spouse who is a legal immigrant or U.S. citizen.[10] Gunadi also considered occupational licenses, but the method used here dropped that filter because so many states issue licenses to unauthorized immigrants.[11] The number of legal immigrants estimated from this method included those residing in Texas on temporary nonimmigrant work visas and those who had naturalized and earned American citizenship.

There were 28,701,845 people living in Texas in 2018. According to the results of the Gunadi residual method (minus the questions on occupational licensure), there were 23,767,658 native-born American, 3,077,766 legal immigrants, and 1,856,421 unauthorized immigrants living in Texas. These groups represented 82.8 percent of the population, 10.7 percent, and 6.5 percent, respectively. Likewise, there were 337,996 criminal convictions of native-born Americans in Texas that year, 16,470 convictions of legal immigrants, and 14,526 convictions of unauthorized immigrants.

Figure 20.1 shows that the unauthorized immigrant criminal conviction rate was 782 per 100,000 unauthorized immigrants, 535 per 100,000 legal immigrants, and 1,422 per 100,000 native-born Americans in Texas in 2018. The unauthorized immigrant criminal conviction rate was 45 percent below that of native-born Americans in Texas. However, the legal immigrant criminal conviction rate was 62 percent below that of native-born Americans. Figure 20.1 shows the rates for the number of convictions and not the number of individuals convicted. The conviction rates for individuals are slightly lower for every group, but the ratio is roughly the same, with unauthorized immigrants at 743, legal immigrants at 495, and native-born Americans at 1,304 per 100,000 of their respective subpopulations.

That pattern also holds for other more serious crimes like homicide, the most serious criminal offense. In Texas, there were 867 convictions for homicide in

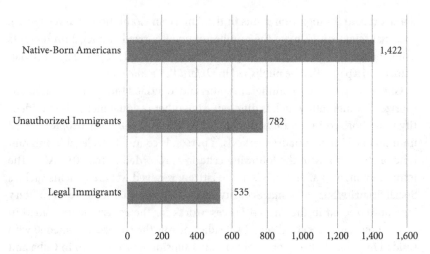

Figure 20.1 Texas conviction rate.

Source: Author's calculations. For data sources, see endnotes.*

*For the data for tables/figures in this chapter, see the following sources: Nowrasteh, "Criminal Immigrants in Texas in 2017," no. 13; Nowrasteh, "Criminal Immigrants in Texas," no. 4.

2018. Of those, native-born Americans were convicted 780 times, unauthorized immigrants 46 times, and legal immigrants 41 times. Figure 20.2 shows that the unauthorized immigrant homicide conviction rate was 2.5 per 100,000 unauthorized immigrants, 1.3 per 100,000 for legal immigrants, and 3.3 per 100,000 for native-born Americans in Texas in 2018. Thus, unauthorized immigrants

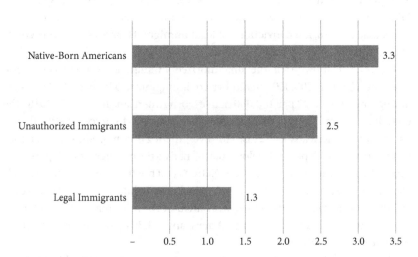

Figure 20.2 Texas homicide conviction rate.

Source: Author's calculations. For data sources, see endnotes.

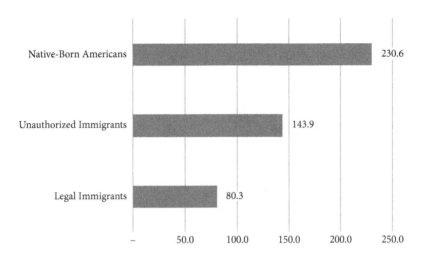

Figure 20.3 Texas violent crime conviction rate.
Source: Author's calculations. For data sources, see endnotes.

had a homicide conviction rate 25 percent below that of native-born Americans in Texas. The legal immigrant homicide conviction rate was 59 percent below that of native-born Americans. Once again, native-born Americans were the most likely to be convicted, followed by unauthorized immigrants, with legal immigrants as the least likely to be convicted of murder.

The unauthorized immigrant conviction rate for all violent crime is about 38 percent below that of native-born Americans, and the legal immigrant conviction rate is about 65 percent below (Figure 20.3). Unauthorized and legal immigrants are substantially less likely to be convicted of property crimes than native-born Americans. Unauthorized immigrants have a convicted rate 74 percent below that of native-born Americans for property crimes, while it is 71 percent below for legal immigrants (Figure 20.4). The low unauthorized immigrant property crime rate can probably be explained by their high rate of employment, especially among men, relative to both legal immigrant and native-born American men.[12] In other words, the opportunity cost for property crimes is higher for unauthorized immigrant men because they are more likely to be gainfully employed.

The sex crime conviction rate, which includes sexual assault and other sexual offenses, is the closest. Figure 20.5 shows that the unauthorized immigrant conviction rate for sex crimes is 24.4 per 100,000 unauthorized immigrants, which is only 0.7 percent below the sex crime conviction rate for native-born Americans at 25.1 per 100,000 natives. Legal immigrants have the lowest sex crime conviction rate at 14.7 per 100,000 legal immigrants, more than 58 percent below that of native-born Americans.

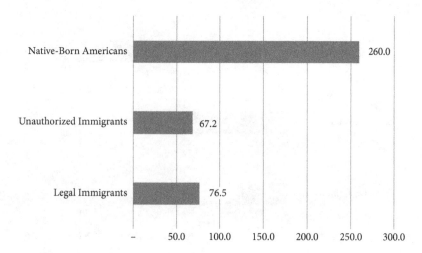

Figure 20.4 Texas property crime conviction rate.
Source: Author's calculations. For data sources, see endnotes.

For arrests, the results are much the same. Texas police made 907,767 criminal arrests in 2018. Legal immigrants accounted for 5.3 percent of all those arrested, and unauthorized immigrants accounted for 4.4 percent, well below their respective 10.7 and 6.5 percent shares of the population, respectively. For all arrests in Texas, there were about 2,142 arrests of unauthorized immigrants for every 100,000 unauthorized immigrants in the state compared to 1,570 for legal immigrants and 3,449 for native-born Americans. By comparison,

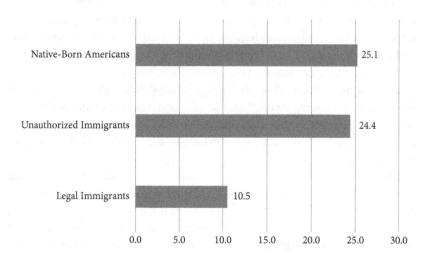

Figure 20.5 Texas sex crime conviction rate.
Source: Author's calculations. For data sources, see endnotes.

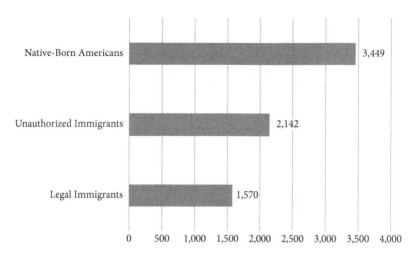

Figure 20.6 Texas arrest rate.
Source: Author's calculations. For data sources, see endnotes.

the unauthorized immigrant arrest rate was 38 percent below that of native-born Americans and the legal immigrant arrest rate was 55 percent below (Figure 20.6).

For every conviction of an unauthorized immigrant, there were 2.7 arrests compared to 2.9 arrests for every conviction of a legal immigrant and 2.4 arrests for every conviction of a native-born American. Looking at the number of individuals arrested relative to the number of individuals convicted reveals a similar pattern of 2.7 unauthorized immigrants arrested for every conviction, 2.8 legal immigrants arrested for every conviction, and 2.3 native-born Americans arrested for every conviction (Figure 20.7). Thus, unauthorized and legal immigrants who are arrested are less likely to be convicted than native-born Americans.

There are several potential explanations for this. First, police could have a bias against legal and unauthorized immigrants, but the rest of the justice system does not and is less likely not to pursue further legal action that would lead to a conviction. Second, immigrants could have better legal representation. Third, many unauthorized immigrants arrested by the police are deported before they can be convicted. However, that doesn't account for the even higher ratio for legal immigrants, who must be convicted in order to be removed. Fourth, immigrants could be more likely to be arrested but also more likely to skip bail and not be convicted. The last possibility is the most serious. After all, about 65 percent of unauthorized immigrants in Texas are from Mexico, so it would be relatively cheap for those released on bail to escape.

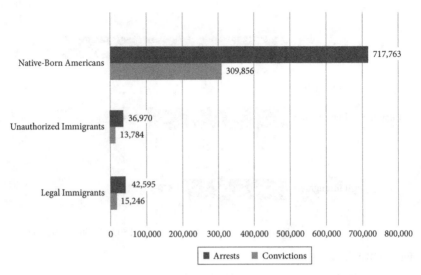

Figure 20.7 Texas individuals convicted and arrested by immigration status.
Source: Author's calculations. For data sources, see endnotes.

However, all Texas police jurisdictions in 2018 cooperated with federal immigration authorities, and they were supposed to turn over arrested or convicted unauthorized immigrants to federal law enforcement for deportation.[13] In 2018, Texas police arrested 36,970 unauthorized immigrants and they turned over 34,949 unauthorized immigrants to ICE for eventual deportation.[14] The small difference between those arrested and those turned over to ICE, the latter of which also includes unauthorized immigrants being released from state prison, does not allow much leakage—there simply cannot be many unauthorized immigrants who are arrested who then escape or who are deported without being convicted.

Arrest rates for specific crimes are closely related to the conviction rates. The unauthorized immigrant homicide arrest rate is 28.8 percent below that of native-born Americans. The legal immigrant homicide arrest rate is 61.2 percent below that of native-born Americans (Figure 20.8). The unauthorized immigrant property and violent crime arrest rates are uniformly below those of native-born Americans (Figure 20.9). The unauthorized immigrant violent crime arrest rate is slightly higher than for legal immigrants, but the unauthorized immigrant property crime arrest rate is lower than it is for legal immigrants. The sex crime arrest rate for unauthorized immigrants is 24 percent below that of native-born Americans and 47 percent below for legal immigrants (Figure 20.10).

The criminal conviction and arrest rates above are not historical aberrations, and the year 2018 was not cherry-picked to show positive results. For every year

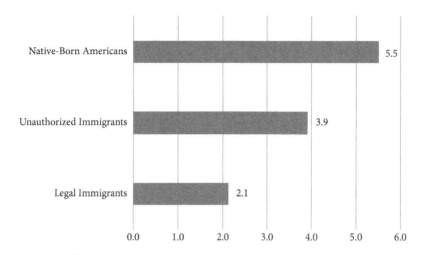

Figure 20.8 Texas homicide arrest rate.
Source: Author's calculations. For data sources, see endnotes.

for which full data are available and there are enough ACS data to use Gunadi's residual method to estimate the number of unauthorized immigrants residing in Texas, they have a lower criminal conviction rate (Figure 20.11). From 2012 through the end of 2018, unauthorized immigrants in Texas had an average criminal conviction rate 42 percent below that of native-born Americans. Legal immigrants had a criminal conviction rate 63 percent below that of native-born Americans during the same period. Arrest rates are also lower for unauthorized

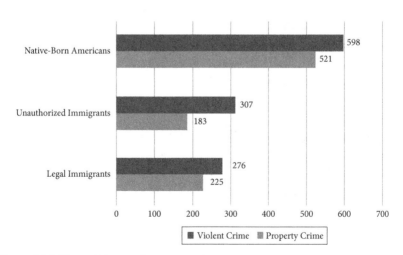

Figure 20.9 Texas violent and property crime arrest rate.
Source: Author's calculations. For data sources, see endnotes.

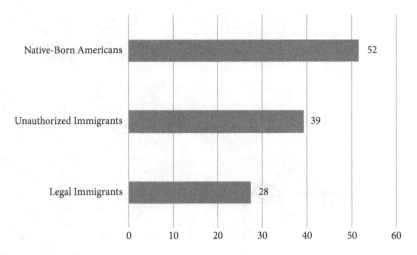

Figure 20.10 Texas sex crime arrest rate.
Source: Author's calculations. For data sources, see endnotes.

immigrants during the entire period, but lowest of all for legal immigrants (Figure 20.12). On average from 2012 through 2018, unauthorized immigrants in Texas were 40 percent less likely to be arrested than native-born Americans, and legal immigrants were 55 percent less likely.

By country of origin, Mexicans comprised the largest group of unauthorized immigrants in Texas in 2018 at 65 percent. According to Texas DPS data on the

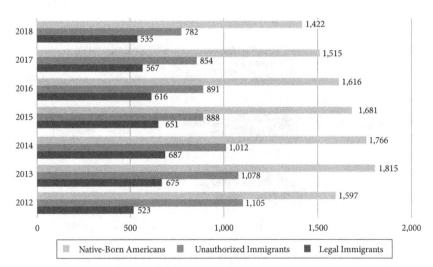

Figure 20.11 Texas conviction rate over time.
Source: Author's calculations. For data sources, see endnotes.

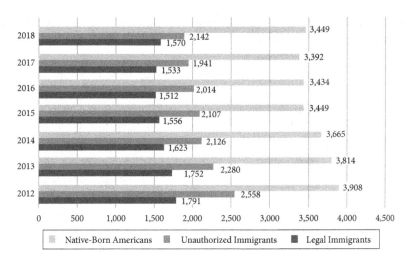

Figure 20.12 Texas arrest rate over time.

Source: Author's calculations. For data sources, see endnotes.

nationality of unauthorized immigrants by country of origin, Mexicans were 65 percent of those convicted of crimes in 2018—exactly proportional to their share of the population. Unfortunately, the Gunadi is not robust enough to identify countries of origin for other unauthorized immigrant populations in Texas as they are too small.

Texas Crime Elasticities by County

Unauthorized immigrant criminal conviction and arrest rates are low throughout the state of Texas, but there could be substantial local variation whereby unauthorized immigrant crime is substantially higher in counties where many unauthorized immigrants reside. Thus, this section examines how a change in the unauthorized immigrant population affected crime on the county level in Texas for the years 2012–2018. The relationship between changes in the unauthorized immigrant population and crime is known as an *elasticity*.

The elasticity between two variables estimates how one variable, the unauthorized immigrant population here, affects another variable, the number of unauthorized immigrant convictions here. For good measure, we also sought to compare the relationship between the unauthorized immigrant population on the county level and overall index crimes as collected by the Texas DPS.[15] We also included a control for the number of law enforcement officers per capita. The results of these regressions are merely correlative and not causal, but it's reasonable to assume a relationship between the number of crimes committed by unauthorized immigrants, crimes overall, and the unauthorized immigrant population for the purposes of these regressions.[16]

We found no statistically significant relationship between an increase in a county's unauthorized immigrant population and the number of unauthorized immigrant convictions *and* the number of overall number of convictions with one exception (Table 20.1). For each regression in Table 20.1, we found statistically insignificant negative point estimates showing that a 10 percent increase in Texas counties' population share of unauthorized immigrant correlated with decreases of 0.07 percent for all convictions and 0.05 percent for convictions of unauthorized immigrants. In each model, the only significant predictor of conviction rates was county population, which suggests that the total population of a county is a more important predictor of criminal convictions than the share of unauthorized immigrant share. Surprise, more people means more crime.

Table 20.1 also breaks down the conviction rates into three subcomponents: murder, all violent crime, and all property crime. The only statistically significant relationship, which is the exception mentioned above, is that a negative association between total violent crime convictions and the unauthorized immigrant share with a point estimate of –0.104 that is significant at the 5 percent level. This exception suggests that a 10 percent increase in the unauthorized immigrants' share of the population was associated with a 1 percent decline in violent crime convictions in our sample of Texas counties.

One of our concerns with the regressions in Table 20.1 is that they are based on the unauthorized immigrant share of the population in just 38 identified Texas counties.[17] We followed the same Gunadi methods mentioned previously in this chapter, including the exception for licensing, to estimate the number of unauthorized immigrants—but the method only works when there is a large population in the counties. Texas has 254 counties, so the 38 for which we could apply Gunadi's methods does give us some pause, but those counties also include most of Texas' population. Because of the small number of counties, we computed wild cluster bootstrap test statistics instead of normal standard errors.[18]

Taken together, these results suggest that higher unauthorized immigrant population shares have little to no relationship with unauthorized immigrant criminal conviction rates or overall index crime rates. The only exception is that unauthorized immigrant shares of the population correlated negatively with violent crime convictions in Texas counties from 2012 to 2018. While these regressions are purely descriptive in nature, they are consistent with the other findings of unauthorized immigrant criminality in Texas.

Even on the margin, for small changes in the unauthorized immigrant population in a local area, there was no statistically significant effect of the unauthorized immigrant population on the rate of criminal convictions, either overall or for unauthorized immigrants specifically.

Nationwide Unauthorized Immigrant Conviction Rates

Texas is the only state that records convictions and arrests by immigration status, but most Americans live in other states. It's tempting to take the results from Texas and apply them to the rest of the country to come to a nationwide conclusion, but one should be cautious in doing that directly. However, there is evidence that the relationship between unauthorized immigration and crime in Texas holds nationwide, and that evidence comes from applying Gunadi's method to another data set in the ACS. The ACS surveys those incarcerated in correctional facilities to such an extent that it is possible to apply Gunadi's residual method to estimate how many nationwide prisoners are unauthorized immigrants. The nationwide number includes those in state and federal prisons, institutions that house very different types of criminals. State prisons housed over 87 percent of all prisoners in the United States in 2016, and they were incarcerated mostly for violent and property offenses.[19] Federal prisoners, on the other hand, account for less than 13 percent of all prisoners and are not representative as federal crimes include immigration offenses and other nonstate crimes.

The ACS inmate responses to questions are reliable as they are ordinarily collected by or under the supervision of correctional institution administrators, so there's no reason to suspect systematic lying on the part of prisoners.[20] Prison staff oversee the interviews, and prisoner information from prison records themselves are the basis for much of the information in the ACS, so the data are trustworthy.

Before applying Gunadi's method to the population incarcerated in adult correctional facilities, the first step is to identify those prisoners in the ACS. This requires isolating the prisoners from the rest of the so-called group quarters population in the ACS as they are all lumped together. Group quarters include all group living arrangements, such as retirement homes, orphanages, student dorms, mental health institutions, and prisons. Narrowing down that population by age through identifying only those in the 18–54 age range is the most important step as people outside of that range are more likely to be in retirement homes or mental health institutions, respectively. Estimating the population incarcerated in correctional facilities adds ambiguity, but the ACS also releases macro demographic snapshots of inmates in correctional facilities, which return total numbers very close to those produced by Gunadi's residual method applied to the population ages 18–54 in adult correctional facilities.[21] Although not perfect, applying Gunadi's method to the 18–54 age groups in the ACS group quarters population is reasonable given the data limitations.

Under this method, there were an estimated 1,933,039 native-born Americans, 83,698 unauthorized immigrants, and 71,472 legal immigrants incarcerated in the United States in 2018. The incarceration rate for native-born Americans was 1,477 per 100,000; 877 per 100,000 for unauthorized immigrants; and 380 per 100,000 for legal immigrants in 2018. Unauthorized immigrants were 41 percent less likely to be incarcerated than native-born Americans. Legal immigrants were 74 percent less likely to be incarcerated than natives. The relative incarceration rates for 2018 were very similar to those since 2012.

Conclusion

Whether one focuses on criminal convictions, arrests, or the number of individuals convicted or arrested, the results are the same: Unauthorized immigrants have a lower crime rate than native-born Americans in Texas. Legal immigrants have the lowest rates of all, except for some measures of property crime, where unauthorized immigrants are even less crime prone. Native-born Americans living in Texas have the highest criminal conviction and arrest rates in all figures above. Even on the margin, there is no statistically significant effect of the unauthorized immigrant population on the rate of criminal convictions, either overall or for unauthorized immigrants specifically.

Crime, at least in the state of Texas, is a domestically produced problem and not an imported one. Texas is one of the states where we would expect higher unauthorized immigrant crime rates if they were an especially crime-inclined subpopulation. The proximity to Mexico, the reputation of its criminal justice system, and the state-level politics all militate toward increasing the unauthorized immigrant crime rate relative to legal immigrants and native-born Americans.

The low unauthorized immigrant conviction and arrest rates in Texas are highly suggestive that they have a lower rate in other states and across the entire country. Nationwide estimates of the unauthorized immigrant incarceration rate are very closely correlated to the Texas unauthorized immigrant criminal conviction rate. Since the nationwide numbers are an estimate and the Texas numbers are based on complete data, the low unauthorized immigrant criminal conviction rate in Texas is more evidence that unauthorized immigrants in every state have a low rate of criminality.

The government is entrusted with an enormous amount of power to protect the lives, liberties, and property of people living in the United States. American residents and citizens are less free when policymakers have poor information about security threats because they react inefficiently. As a result, some threats loom larger than they should, and others don't loom large enough. Better and more accurate information can help policymakers judge threats accurately and respond appropriately. Thus, accurate information can free policymakers from making inefficient choices and liberate taxpayers, citizens, and residents from shouldering the burden of inappropriate government policy. Unauthorized immigration is a serious public policy problem in the United States, but it is not a problem because it increases the crime rate.

Notes

1. Adam B. Lerner, "The 10 Best Lines From Donald Trump's Announcement Speech," *Politico*, June 16, 2015, https://www.politico.com/story/2015/06/donald-trump-2016-announcement-10-best-lines-119066.
2. "Expanded Homicide Data Table 1: Murder Victims by Race, Ethnicity, and Sex, 2015," Uniform Crime Reporting (UCR) Program, Federal Bureau of Investigation, 2015, https://ucr.fbi.gov/crime-in-the-u.s/2015/crime-in-the-u.s.-2015/tables/expanded_homicide_data_table_1_murder_victims_by_race_ethnicity_and_sex_2015.xls.
3. Alex Nowrasteh, "Criminal Immigrants in Texas in 2017: Illegal Immigrant Conviction Rates and Arrest Rates for Homicide, Sex Crimes, Larceny, and Other Crimes" (Immigration Research and Policy Brief, no. 13), Cato Institute, August 27, 2019, 1–2, https://www.cato.org/sites/cato.org/files/pubs/pdf/irpb13_edit.pdf.
4. Much of the research and the methods from this section comes from these briefs: Nowrasteh, "Criminal Immigrants in Texas," no. 13; Alex Nowrasteh, "Criminal Immigrants in Texas: Illegal Immigrant Conviction and Arrest Rates for Homicide, Sex Crimes, Larceny, and Other Crimes" (Immigration Research and Policy Brief, no. 4), Cato Institute, February 26, 2018, https://www.cato.org/sites/cato.org/files/pubs/pdf/irpb-4-updated.pdf.
5. Nowrasteh, "Criminal Immigrants in Texas in 2017," no. 13, 2.
6. "Public Information Act," Texas Department of Public Safety; "Texas Criminal Illegal Alien Data," Texas Department of Public Safety. These data sets are available by email request to Alex Nowrasteh at anowrasteh@cato.org.
7. Nowrasteh, "Criminal Immigrants in Texas in 2017," no. 13.
8. Nowrasteh, "Criminal Immigrants in Texas in 2017," no. 13, 2.
9. Christian Gunadi, "On the Association Between Undocumented Immigration and Crime in the United States," *Oxford Economic Papers* 73, no. 1 (2021): 200–224. Published ahead of Print, September 20, 2019, https://doi.org/10.1093/oep/gpz057.
10. Special thanks to Michelangelo Landgrave for running Gunadi's residual method for me.
11. Michelangelo Landgrave and Alex Nowrasteh, "Illegal Immigrant Incarceration Rates, 2010–2018: Demographics and Policy Implications," *Cato Institute Policy Analysis* (forthcoming), 3.

12. George J. Borjas, "The Labor Supply of Undocumented Immigrants," *Labour Economics* 46 (June 2017), 1–13, https://doi.org/10.1016/j.labeco.2017.02.004.
13. Bryan Griffith and Jessica M. Vaughan, "Map 1: Sanctuary Cities, Countries, and States," Center for Immigration Studies, updated March 23, 2020, https://cis.org/Map-Sanctuary-Cities-Counties-and-States.
14. "Latest Data: Immigration and Customs Enforcement Detainers," TRAC Immigration, Syracuse University, https://trac.syr.edu/phptools/immigration/detain/.
15. Texas Department of Public Safety answer to Nowrasteh's public information act request.
16. To empirically test the correlation between unauthorized immigrant conviction rates and the unauthorized immigrant population, we run the simple regression:

$$\ln(Y_{it}) = ..+ \alpha_i + \lambda_t + \gamma \ln\left(Illegal_{it}\right) + \eta \ln\left(Population_{it}\right) + \beta \ln\left(PoliceRate_{it-1}\right) + \varepsilon_{it},$$

where Y_{it} is the number of convictions in county i in year t. $Illegal_{it}$ represents the estimated unauthorized population, and $Population_{it}$ is the total county population from the ACS. α_i and λ_t denote county and year fixed effects, respectively. In line with the economics and criminology literature, we also control for the number of police officers per 100 population. Our coefficient of interest γ represents the estimated elasticity of the conviction rate with respect to the county population share of unauthorized immigrants. Since we are limited to 38 identified counties in the raw ACS microdata, we compute wild cluster bootstrap test statistics as described in A. Colin Cameron, Jonah B. Gelbach, and Douglas L. Miller, "Bootstrap-Based Improvements for Inference with Clustered Errors," *Review of Economics and Statistics* 90, no. 3 (2008): 414–427, https://doi.org/10.1162/rest.90.3.414.
17. Steven Ruggles et al., "U.S. Census Data for Social, Economic, and Health Research," IPUMS USA, https://doi.org/10.18128/D010.V10.0.
18. Cameron, Gelbach, and Miller, "Bootstrap-Based Improvements."
19. E. Ann Carson and Joseph Mulako-Wangota, "Corrections Statistical Analysis Tool (CSAT)–Prisoners," Bureau of Justice Statistics, https://www.bjs.gov/index.cfm?ty=nps.
20. Michelangelo Landgrave and Alex Nowrasteh, "Illegal Immigrant Incarceration Rates, 2010–2018: Demographics and Policy Implications," *Cato Institute Policy Analysis* (forthcoming), 3.
21. American Community Survey, "Characteristics of the Group Quarters Population by Group Quarters Type (3 Types)," TableID S2602, 2018, ACS 1-Year Estimates, U.S. Census Bureau, https://data.census.gov/cedsci/table?q=S2602&tid=ACSST1Y2018.S2602&vintage=2018&hidePreview=true.

PART IV
FREEDOM IN OTHER DOMAINS

21

Grievance Media

How Two Sets of "News" Hampers Democracy

Alison Dagnes

Technological advancements in the past 50 years have led to a citizenry who walk around with media providers in their pockets, delivering easily accessed and constant content. At first glance, this is a positive development: The gatekeeping function of the press that had been in only a few hands was now open to the world. With so many different platforms available, more voices could be heard, and the control of news and information was diversified. The public was free to hear from a multitude of voices, and much of the content was, in fact, free.

But the media grew so expansively that many people felt overwhelmed by too many choices. It was difficult to decide what to watch, even more challenging to ascertain what was legitimate information. Furthermore, with so many options, the public looked for help to decide whom to trust. All of this happened at the same time the country was growing more ideologically divided, and thus the media exacerbated our partisan divisions as a means to attract a dedicated audience.

The political media today afford the American people the freedom to choose from numerous outlets, but they also provide the freedom to select a variation on the truth that feels comfortable and unchallenging. By encouraging their viewers to simply accept their version of events without question, and by urging viewers to pick a political side, our modern-day partisan media rejects the notions of positive freedoms in favor of a singular fealty toward a specific group. This chapter explains how we got to this point and explores the consequences of having a divided political media system as it addresses the importance of having trusted political information.

The Functions of the American Political Media

Americans are increasingly reliant on their smartphones, tablets, and gadgets that provide news, information, entertainment, and social connections. According to the Pew Research Center, 96 percent of American adults own a cell

Alison Dagnes, *Grievance Media* In: *On Inequality and Freedom.* Edited by: Lawrence M. Eppard and Henry A. Giroux, Oxford University Press. © Oxford University Press 2022. DOI: 10.1093/oso/9780197583029.003.0021 phone or smartphone of some kind, and this number is remarkably consistent along gender, age, racial, and educational lines.[1] In normal times, these devices brought the public content that was both useful and distracting. But when the COVID-19 pandemic hit, technology became a sort of lifeline for many people. Not only did work move online, but also so did socialization, and during this time, many Americans became even more dependent on technology.

One of the primary functions of communication media is to inform the public, and this information takes different forms. It can literally inform us about things we did not already know, it can connect us to like-minded citizens, and it can educate us on issues small and large. This is the greatest benefit of living in the communication age of the twenty-first century: Our ability to connect with one another provides the potential for a great equalizer. The public no longer has to take the word of a few elites who decide what is important. We can hear from a multiplicity of voices and make decisions for ourselves.

Modern America has watched as media platforms developed from broadcast television that required antennae to streaming services that (seemingly) require little more than a screen. Today, media content can be received on our watches, something heretofore only Maxwell Smart could have envisioned. The ability to gather information and communicate quickly is a terrific development for activists, advocates, and an engaged citizenry. But at the same time, media expansion has led to an overflow of information, some of which is less than credible. This inevitably leads to the question: Whom can we trust? As Americans become increasingly tethered to their phones, information providers more and more shape how we think about social problems and react to them.

Shaping the Coverage

The dramatic media expansion led to the trend called "niche programming," where media mavens and content providers could tailor their product for smaller audiences. Instead of broadcasting, which was casting a wide net for the largest audience via the least objectionable programming, this kind of narrowcasting encouraged media outlets to tailor their programming to a smaller number of viewers. As long as they kept this reduced audience devoted, they could stay financially solvent. The trick was to keep the audience adherent.

For many sources of political news this meant bucking the journalistic tradition of impartiality, practiced in the twentieth century, to instead take sides. Producing news to appeal to specific voters has been at one time incredibly lucrative for the content providers, and at the same time terribly damaging for the greater electorate. When political news organizations perform as activists instead of neutral truth tellers, the result is a public with different sets of information, varying collections of facts, and entirely different narratives about our social problems and inequities.

News and content providers have several essential methods with which they shape their coverage. One is gatekeeping, the process by which news organizations choose the stories they will cover. Story coverage is important for a few reasons; stories inform viewers of critical events, and coverage also denotes significance as it cues the reader or viewer to pay attention to something. For example, studies have shown that during the 2020 presidential impeachment hearing in the United States Senate, *Fox News* did not air live coverage of the event, instead maintaining their regular programming.[2] This gave *Fox News* viewers the impression that the impeachment hearings were not as important as the other media outlets who, by airing live coverage, signaled their significance.

Another method by which the media shapes their content is through framing, which is how news outlets construct their storytelling. One story can be framed multiple ways, which also sets up the audience to evaluate the story in a certain way. For example, from the time Black Lives Matter (BLM) was created in 2014 until the present, the press has framed BLM marches and protests differently. One account of early press framing said that a local reporter in Minneapolis framed the protest as "a rude, maybe scary, inconvenience," while more recent protests were framed as peaceful and important.[3] It can be argued that changing the framing of the protests has also helped to change views of race relations in America since news viewers receive their prompts about how to interpret the protests from this more positive framing.

A third technique the media has to influence their coverage is known as agenda setting, which is how the story selection affects the national discussion. When news organizations select stories to cover, they establish topics of conversation and reinforce issue importance. In 2018, Hurricane Maria devastated Puerto Rico, killing almost 3,000 people. This was, by all measures, an important story, but during the same period of time, the television star Roseanne Barr tweeted racist and offensive statements, and her show was cancelled. The story about a racist celebrity was covered 16 times more than the tragedy in Puerto Rico.[4] Choosing to cover the Roseanne story set the agenda for the public, many of whom did not hear about the events in the U.S. territory but who heard instead about the Roseanne kerfuffle.

Put together, gatekeeping, framing, and agenda setting can help shape the ideological spin of news stories. It is important to note that in the past 50 years, conservatives have argued that the mainstream media are liberally biased and use these exact methods to corrupt their coverage. As a result, conservatives looked to these same techniques to right the ship (so to speak) when crafting the right-wing alternative they deemed necessary for fairness. Since the successful launch of *Fox* News in 1996, right-wing political media outlets have grown in number, influence, and support. By providing purposely right-leaning content for their niche audience, outlets within this ecosystem argue that they are simply offering the kind of balance that has been eschewed by the liberal mainstream press. Their mission statements are explicit: They exist to purposely provide a conservative counterpoint to the news.

The Escalation and Devastation of Polarized Political Media

Conservatives hailed the creation of news providers who spoke directly to them, and with some reason. The mainstream press, headquartered in New York, Washington, and Los Angeles, spent the better part of the twentieth century operating inside their own bubble. Because these journalists worked within the self-defined norms of their profession that mandated impartiality, they bristled against the accusations of liberal bias without very much self-reflection. Perhaps a touch more introspection would have provided the mainstream press the understanding that their newsrooms were stacked with East Coast, White, Ivy League educated men, like a pile of polo shirts from Vineyard Vines. As the right-wing charges of bias grew louder, the mainstream media fought back with supercilious disregard, and the battle lines were drawn.

When cable expanded in the 1980s and 1990s and *Fox News* was launched in 1996, many conservatives naturally moved to the cable news channel that reaffirmed their suspicions that the mainstream media were unfair and predisposed toward coverage that made them look bad. The *Fox News* verification that conservative grievances were true was at one time soothing for their right-wing viewership, the formation of a successful template for other right-wing outlets to copy, and extremely profitable for the cable news organization. Accordingly, this kind of antiliberal grievance programming worked like a charm.

Yet despite its success for *Fox News* and the outlets that followed in its footsteps, separating the news by political ideology has been problematic on several fronts, not the least of which was that this process separated the audiences as well. Inflaming the political passions of their supporters might have been good for business, but it has proven to be detrimental for policymaking. Using the aforementioned methods to shape news coverage, the three cable news networks inform their viewers about different events, cover the same events contrarily, and provide their audiences contradictory narratives that sometimes bear no resemblance to reality. For example, a poll conducted by the Pew Research Center in mid-March of 2020 found that 56% of those polled who self-identified as *Fox News* viewers believed the threat of the COVID-19 virus was "greatly exaggerated," while 12% of self-identified *MSNBC* viewers felt the same way.[5]

In other words, sorting the news through a partisan lens affected the information processed by the varying audiences. This is especially troubling given the fact that the allegations of bias, which had a toe in reality, were way overblown. For one thing, the impartiality creed by which journalists abide did mandate overall fairness. Another issue was that objective news was the reigning standard for the previous half-decade, which meant that legacy news organizations competed against each other using these metrics. And finally, academic study after academic study showed that the accusations of liberal bias in the news media were, for the most part, false.

Dave D'Alessio, associate professor of communications at the University of Connecticut, has studied media bias going back to 1948 and conducted an analysis of studies examining bias in campaigns from 1948 through 1997. Professor D'Alessio found: "Neither the overall analysis, nor any of the differences between proportions of coverage, statement, or gatekeeping bias favoring Democrats or Republicans, was statistically significant."[6]

These findings buck against conventional wisdom, especially for those on the right. It is in the best interest of any political candidate or party to call "bias" against the institutions that investigate them. By getting their team united against a perceived foe, the party or candidate can do two things at once: ramp up the grievance politicking and shoo away reports of wrongdoing by members of their team. There is a name for this: the "hostile media effect." Political actors yell, "The media is against me!" and the supporters follow suit, regardless of evidence.

No one has banged the drum of perceived grievance louder than former President Trump, whose frequent accusations of "fake news" are so commonplace now as to feel old. Layering on top of these calls are his recurrent shouts about the media as the "enemy of the people" and the name-calling against specific outlets. Asked about this on a Poynter piece from 2016, D'Alessio stated that the claims of media bias today are nothing really new:

> It's more vociferous, but accusations of media bias have existed for decades. . . . There are quotations of various presidents throughout time that indicate that Jefferson hated the newspapers. Lincoln shut them down. Teddy Roosevelt wasn't really fond of the press. Woodrow Wilson shut down a couple of newspapers. . . . As I said before, the media bias in a sense is a perception. If the media are not telling things the way they should be told, then they're wrong. And when you're the president, that's how you feel about stuff. You want everyone on the same page and on your side, and it's frustrating beyond all heck when that's not the case.[7]

The problem, of course, is that skepticism is healthy, but rampant media distrust, unsubstantiated yet sworn to be true, is far more common and extraordinarily pernicious. All of the media options should allow an interested public the ability to fact-check and discover valid sources of information, but few people actually take the time to do this. They opt instead to return to the news that tilts information in the direction they want, a phenomenon known as "confirmation bias." Additionally, beyond accepting news only from outlets with which they disagree, many Americans accept the calls of "liberal bias" without question or proof. Those who are inclined to believe in bias cannot be swayed, despite the peer-reviewed and replicated studies that show, time and again, that: "Despite the overwhelming liberal composition of the media, there is no evidence of liberal media bias in the news that political journalists choose to cover."[8] It does not help that the loudest voices charging bias come from the most important political positions in the country.

How This Is Harmful for Democracy

The mass media are vital in a democracy for a number of reasons, not the least of which is that journalists hold politicians accountable and provide valuable information and investigation in the public service. We are now at a time where dependable and trustworthy information is essential, and there are too many information sources that view their mission as one of activism instead of reporting.

Further attacks on the media only sow more doubt and distrust, with not only the press but also the institutions they cover. Former Breitbart executive chairman Steve Bannon addressed this in 2018, according to Joshua Green, who wrote a book about him. According to Green, Bannon voiced this strategy when discussing the 2018 midterm elections: "The Democrats don't matter. The real opposition is the media. And the way to deal with them is to flood the zone with shit."[9] The objective of this flood is to make sure that people become disaffected by those in power; when that happens, the powerful have the leeway to do as they please because there are no standards worth meeting. Worse, when journalism as an institution is in doubt, then the reports of political corruption are far more easily shrugged off and excused.

Russian Chess master Garry Kasparov tweeted in 2017: "As with most disinformation, the goal is to create doubt and deniability, to cast evidence as personal or partisan, a post-truth world." He followed this up in an interview with Vox that the zone flooding was purposeful and effective:

> By constant bombardment, your senses become overwhelmed. You start to doubt, to shrug your shoulders, to tune out, and that makes you vulnerable. Instead of pushing one lie, one fake, they can push a dozen, or a hundred, and

that's pretty good odds against one lonely truth. They win when you say: "Who can be sure what really happened?"[10]

The attacks on a free press and the purposeful production of confusion do immense harm to American democracy. We need valid and credible information with which we can make important decisions. We also need facts with which we can judge significant situations and assess them accurately. We also need to gain knowledge that will bring a diverse populace together for the good of the whole. Divisions may make for immediate political victories, but they are not conducive toward productive policymaking for the sake of the public interest.

Along these lines, the American public needs to trust that the press will inform them of the issues that are most affecting and vital and educate constituencies about those running for office. When the press slides into the role of partisan advocate, they negate their primary function, which is to inform. When they put their finger on the scale for one candidate over another, they deny their duty to hold our politicians accountable for their actions. And finally, when the political media allow politicians and political actors to "flood the zone with shit," they discourage an active and participatory democracy. So much confusion, doubt, and distrust are corrosive for a republican democracy and disheartening for the public.

Social media algorithms are designed to perpetuate our anger and thus entice us to return for another hit of emotion. Guests are booked on cable news who "bring the heat" and make us yell at our TV sets. Instead of sustaining the current polarized and angry political media system we have today, Americans would be better off to disavow it entirely. Denying these outlets their financial reward would starve the system of the air it needs to endure, and at the same time the public would benefit greatly from unvarnished truth and honest journalism. This, of course, would demand work on the part of the public and necessitate a movement away from the shiny objects that entertain and amuse.

The financial imperatives of the mass media are too immense to hope that they will modulate their own actions. Instead, the public has to hold them accountable and demand more. This means that the public must also demand more from ourselves and step up to the challenge of strengthening our own democracy. During the founding, a woman named Elizabeth Willing Powel was the hostess for many political salons where the most important men of the time (and their wives) gathered to discuss and debate the most important issues of the day. These became, as we know now, the most important issues of our nation. And men of different opinions spent time together, at work and at rest, to hammer out their differences and craft the blueprint of our country.[11]

It was Mrs. Powel who asked Benjamin Franklin if the framers of the Constitution had adopted a monarchy or a republic. Franklin famously answered: "A republic, if you can keep it." Our hopes of keeping our republic rest in the idea that we can gather together and agree to disagree, compromise, and work out the differences between us. The current polarized political media gain from the divisions they propagate. The country would gain more if we reject this instead.

Notes

1. Pew Research Center, "Mobile Fact Sheet," June 12, 2019, https://www.pewresearch.org/internet/fact-sheet/mobile/.
2. Darcy, Oliver. 2020. "Instead of Airing the Impeachment Trial, Fox News Fed Viewers Pro-Trump Opinion in Prime Time," *CNN Business*, January 24, 2020. https://www.cnn.com/2020/01/23/media/fox-news-impeachment-coverage/index.html.
3. "Have Americans' Views On Race Relations And Police Brutality Changed Since Ferguson?" *FiveThirtyEight* (chat), June 2, 2020, https://fivethirtyeight.com/features/have-americans-views-on-race-relations-and-police-brutality-changed-since-ferguson/.
4. Alison Dagnes, *Super Mad at Everything All the Time* (New York: Palgrave Macmillan, 2019).
5. Mark Jurkowitz and Amy Mitchell, "Cable TV and COVID-19: How Americans Perceive the Outbreak and View Media Coverage Differ by Main News Source," Pew Research Center, April 1, 2020, https://www.journalism.org/2020/04/01/cable-tv-and-covid-19-how-americans-perceive-the-outbreak-and-view-media-coverage-differ-by-main-news-source/.
6. Melody Kramer, "Is Media Bias Really Rampant? Ask the Man Who Studies It for a Living," Poynter, October 24, 2016, https://www.poynter.org/ethics-trust/2016/is-media-bias-really-rampant-ask-the-man-who-studies-it-for-a-living/.
7. Kramer, "Is Media Bias Really Rampant?"
8. Hans J. G. Hassell John B. Holbein, and Matthew R. Miles, "There Is No Liberal Media Bias in Which News Stories Political Journalists Choose to Cover," *Science Advances* 6, no. 14 (2020): eaay9344.
9. Sean Illing, "'Flood the Zone With Shit': How Misinformation Overwhelmed Our Democracy," *Vox*, February 6, 2020, https://www.vox.com/policy-and-politics/2020/1/16/20991816/impeachment-trial-trump-bannon-misinformation.
10. Alexander Bisley, "A Top Putin Critic on How to Oppose Trump: 'Making Him Look Like a Loser Is Crucial,'" *Vox*, February 11, 2017, https://www.vox.com/conversations/2017/2/11/14577834/garry-kasparov-putin-trump.
11. Zara Anishanslin, "What We Get Wrong About Ben Franklin's 'a Republic, If You Can Keep It,'" *Washington Post*, October 29, 2019, https://www.washingtonpost.com/outlook/2019/10/29/what-we-get-wrong-about-ben-franklins-republic-if-you-can-keep-it/.

22

Social Media and the Collapse
of American Public Life[*]

Yevgeny Simkin

Let's take a short walk down memory lane. It's 1995. A man stands on a busy street corner yelling vaguely incoherent things at the passersby. He's holding a placard that says: "THE END IS NIGH. REPENT." You come on this guy while out getting the paper. How do you feel about him? You might feel some flavor of annoyance. Most people would also feel compassion for him as he is clearly suffering from something. No reasonable person would think of convincing this man that his point of view is incorrect. This isn't an opportunity for an engaging debate. This guy doesn't kill at parties. This guy doesn't *go* to parties. He's only out here because he's not violent and there's no room for him at Bellevue.

Now fast forward to 2020.

In terms of who this guy is and who you are absolutely nothing has changed. And yet here you are—arguing with him on Twitter or Facebook. And you, yourself, are being brought to the brink of insanity. But you can't seem to stop. You *have* to respond or read the comments of the other people responding, and your cortisol and adrenaline levels are spiking and your blood pressure is rising and you're suddenly at risk of a heart attack.

And the ugly truth is that you've become addicted to arguing with the End Is Nigh sandwich board guy (let's call him the EIN guy from this point). The guy you used to quietly skirt, you now seek him out and you bring your friends and for some idiotic reason you think that if you just post a little bit more you're going to get him to see reason, or put him in his place, or maybe you don't even know why you're doing it. But you can't stop, won't stop.

Back in 2011, Chamath Palihapitiya left Facebook and said of his former company: "It literally is a point now where I think we have created tools that are ripping apart the social fabric of how society works." Keep in mind that was *2011*, which we now think of as a lost Golden Age.

---

[*] This piece originally appeared in *The Bulwark* on July 31, 2020. It has been reprinted here with permission. To see the original piece, please visit their website: https://thebulwark.com/social-media-is-the-problem/

Yevgeny Simkin, *Social Media and the Collapse of American Public Life* In: *On Inequality and Freedom*. Edited by: Lawrence M. Eppard and Henry A. Giroux, Oxford University Press. © Oxford University Press 2022. DOI: 10.1093/oso/9780197583029.003.0022

I'm here to make the case that all modern social, political, and sociological ills can be traced to social media. It is single-handedly responsible for the tearing apart of our social fabric that Palihapitiya so presciently predicted. It's not "part of" the problem. It *is* the problem: an insidious malware slowly corrupting our society in ways that are extremely difficult to quantify, but the effects of which are evident all around us.

Antivaxxers, antimaskers, QAnon, cancel culture, Alex Jones, flat Earthers, racists, antiracists, anti-antiracists, and of course the Twitter stylings of our Dear Leader. All this nonsense is here for your endless irritation, consternation, bewilderment, and ultimately outrage. And it's all brought to you exclusively and specifically by social media. It is exacerbated by two things:

1. The fact that your phone in your pocket guarantees that you can get your fix at every minute of every day.
2. The unfortunate reality that media organizations are so starved for content that every time something outrageous garners a small buzz on social media, they immediately project and amplify it out to the masses.

However, if we compare this with the Four Horsemen of the Apocalypse, social media is Death. The other horsemen are playing supporting roles, but without Death their effects would not be particularly detrimental.

Before the Internet, people socialized in relatively small, geographically constrained groups. They had friends and colleagues and relatives, and they communicated with these people largely in person or via the phone using the rules of engagement that have been evolving for generations. These include facial movements and vocal intonation or more global cues, such as: "Does this person look and smell like they haven't showered for a week?" These are tried and true and essential components to a healthy social "network."

In such an environment the only place for the EIN guy to get an audience is on the street corner. He wouldn't have been allowed to do this at work during his smoke break. He probably didn't have friends who would grant him an audience at birthday parties. He was insane, and his insanity was relegated to the corner on which he stood. And we ignored him.

But along came the Internet, and the EIN guy became an anonymous Internet denizen who could insert himself into conversations across the globe. First he did this on listservs and chat rooms and message boards. Then he did it in the comments sections. And with the advent of social media, he did it right in your face, courtesy of "The Algorithm" (peace be upon it).

But you know how it is: On the internet, as Peter Steiner observed, nobody knows you're a dog. And so now the EIN guy isn't a dude wearing a sandwich board on a street corner. He's in your feed and basically looks like everyone else.

He uses the same fonts as you. His icon can be just as cute as your icon. His rants are laundered by the mediation of the Internet so that you can't see his deranged glare, vocal tone, and the fact that he hasn't showered in 2 weeks. EIN guy is now just part of the crowd. And what's worse, while every town has one EIN guy, the Internet has allowed all of the EIN guys to find each other so that now they think they're just as normal as everyone else.

And what are you supposed to make of their little brigade? Now you're doubting yourself, too, because it's one thing to ignore one crazy guy, but a crazy movement? No—you can't ignore that—it's your duty as a responsible citizen to quash it before it gets out of control and you don't even realize that instead of quashing it, you're now part of it.

Because what EIN guy always wanted—more than anything—was for the normies to stop walking past him. He wanted them to notice him and argue with him because that would be a sign that what he had to say was important and legitimate. And here you are. Standing on the corner. Arguing with the crazy guy wearing the sandwich board saying that the End Is Nigh, which, actually, kind of makes you look like a crazy, too.

Social media has made it possible for deranged people to break through what I think of as the holistic herd immunity of sanity that geography has traditionally conferred. And once they broke through, thanks to social media, the traditional media decided to start elevating them.

Perhaps you have noticed that journalistic outlets now rush to broadcast anything weird enough to draw an audience, which, practically speaking, means taking people from social media and holding them up for all to see. This is a form of validation, even if the media disagrees with them. Because otherwise, why would they even bother presenting it as a debate?

Maybe the Earth is flat?! Maybe QAnon is right?! Maybe vaccines are superdangerous?! Of course, these are patently insane ideas that don't deserve consideration. But there you are considering them. And it annoys you and you turn to your spouse and say: "What the heck are these people talking about? Who could believe this nonsense? Why the hell are these people being quoted on TV?" And all the time your cortisol levels are going up, up, up.

Have you heard of "incels"? If you haven't, I'm genuinely sorry to bespoil you of your ignorance. The incels were a big deal a couple years ago. They are (were?) a cohort of college-age men who are celibate and that celibacy is involuntary, and they were *pissed* that women aren't having sex with them. So they posted really ugly diatribes that explained how the women who rejected them were just angry self-righteous "bitches" out to wield power. Their language was substantially more acerbic, as I'm sure you can imagine.

And right on cue, the world's media swooped in to see what the fuss was all about and rebroadcast their concerns to the world. And before you knew it, the incels were a movement. Social media *made* those people, full stop. No social media, no incels. I'm not here to outrage you about the incels; they're so 2018. My point is that the incel phenomenon is just one molecule of lead in our water, and we're all drinking from the heavily leaded well of social media.

So, what's the answer? It's shockingly simple. Leave all social media. Try it for 1 month—just 30 days! Depending on how addicted you are, it might be hard. You can't peek. Uninstall it. Add a blocker to your browser so that it won't let you see TwitterDOTcom.

But you should do it because the incels and the QAnon imbeciles and the people who think the Earth is flat—*they* aren't going away. Those genies are out of the bottle, and we're not putting them back. There may (or may not) be a way to quell their cacophony eventually, but there's nothing you can do about them right now, and listening to them or arguing with them is definitely *not* the answer.

There are very real actions that social media companies can take to help move things back toward sanity. People like Tristan Harris and Jaron Lanier and Roger McNamee have been discussing this for years. But social media companies aren't going to do anything helpful as long as the incentive structure is what it is today.

Like most evil things that are bad for you, social media has enough attractive, useful, and even beneficial components to give you the false impression that it's actually a good thing—or at least harmless. I mean, smoking helps you control your appetite and focus your attention. This does not mean that smoking is, net-net, good for you. In the future, we may be able to defang and declaw it, and everyone can have it as a pet. But that's somewhere down the road when Mark Zuckerberg isn't the most powerful man in the world. We'll get there.

But for now, go uninstall it, and take a walk with a friend you haven't seen since the plague began. You'll thank me.

23

Disability, Ableism, and the Production of Inequality*

Allison C. Carey

By many measures, people with disabilities are a disadvantaged group in America. Statistics from the 2018 American Community Survey offer several indicators of inequality for people with disabilities, including far lower rates of employment, lower earnings for full-time workers, lower rates of high school graduation, and higher rates of poverty.[1]

Not only are people with disabilities far less likely to be employed and more likely to be in poverty, but also they experience higher levels of material hardship than people without disabilities. Material hardship measures the inability to meet one's needs. It considers not only income but also necessary costs. Forms of material hardship include food hardship (hunger or insufficient food); bill-paying hardship (difficulties paying for utilities, rent, or mortgage); health hardship (unmet medical and dental care needs); and housing hardship (living in substandard housing). A 2015 study by Julia Drew found that focusing on poverty alone underestimates the hardship experienced by people with disabilities because they tend to have higher expenses.[2] She found that, across all groups of people with disabilities, even full-time workers and college graduates, between 40 percent and 70 percent of people with disabilities experienced at least one form of material hardship.

The inequality experienced by people with disabilities has been relatively resistant to social change as well. Activists and policymakers designed the Americans With Disabilities Act of 1990 (ADA) to address economic inequality by removing physical barriers and prohibiting discrimination in the workplace. Despite optimism after its passage, evidence is clear that for people with and people without disabilities, the gap in employment rates, earnings, and poverty has not decreased over time.[3] In fact, the gap seems to have widened.

Why do we see chronic inequality between people with and without disabilities despite legislative efforts like the ADA? Many people *naturalize* the

* Acknowledgement: This material draws closely on a chapter in Allison C. Carey, *Disability and the Sociological Imagination* (under contract with Sage Press)

Allison C. Carey, *Disability, Ableism, and the Production of Inequality* In: *On Inequality and Freedom.* Edited by: Lawrence M. Eppard and Henry A. Giroux, Oxford University Press. © Oxford University Press 2022.
DOI: 10.1093/oso/9780197583029.003.0023

inequality of people with disabilities; in other words, they assume that the poverty and social marginalization of people with disabilities is best explained by the biological limitations that hinder success. While biology might be part of the story, sociological research indicates that social factors, including attitudes and policy, play a large role. Developing a *minority model of disability*, sociologists have asserted that people with disabilities are a minority group who experience social disadvantage enforced via prejudice, discrimination, and structural inequalities.[4] Their disadvantaged position limits their opportunities and ultimately their freedom. This chapter explains several of the key social processes creating and perpetuating disability inequality, including the role of ableism, inaccessibility, segregation, and cultural discourse.

Ableism—Prejudice, Discrimination, and Structural Inequality

Most people are acquainted with the ideas of racism and sexism; however, many have not heard of the parallel idea for disability: ableism. Ableism is a worldview that assumes the superiority of able bodies and minds and the inferiority of those who do not fit in within the normative expectations. In an ableist worldview, the disabled body is viewed as "less than," and people with disabilities are expected to either strive toward cure/rehabilitation or accept relegation to an inferior status.[5]

Ableist attitudes manifest in everyday interactions in many ways. One might

- Overgeneralize the implications of a trait, such as assuming that people who are deaf lack intelligence or can't enjoy music;
- Demand a particular way to do something without considering or offering flexible ways to accomplish a goal, such as underestimating a student's knowledge because they underperform on a single testing strategy like multiple-choice exams;
- Assume that people with disabilities have a tragic or unfortunate life, such as believing people who use a wheelchair would be better off dead or feeling pity for people who have disabilities; or
- Exclude people with disabilities, such as refusing to hire a qualified person with disabilities due to stereotypes of unreliability.

Ableism is extremely common in American society. In fact, due to the dominance of medical perspectives regarding disability, people are taught to associate disability with tragedy, to believe that people with disabilities should want to be "fixed," and to approach people with disabilities as objects of pity.[6] Pity is not always a negative sentiment, but it can be denigrating to people with disabilities when their lives are automatically assumed to be pitiable and defined by suffering. Also, pity too often ignores that social factors like discrimination and inaccessibility really undergird the challenges people with disabilities face in life.

Ableism is deeply intertwined with racism, sexism, and other forms of oppression. Talila Lewis argued that ableism is

> a system that places value on people's bodies and minds based on societally constructed ideas of normalcy, intelligence, excellence and productivity. These constructed ideas are deeply rooted in anti-Blackness, eugenics, colonialism and capitalism. This form of systemic oppression leads to people and society determining who is valuable and worthy based on a person's appearance and/or their ability to satisfactorily [re]produce, excel and "behave."[7]

Lewis and other scholars argued that racism *relies on* ableism to define people of color as biologically unfit and to deny rights and access on the basis of that presumed biological unfitness.[8] Sexism and homophobia similarly define particular bodies as inadequate and deny rights on this basis. Indeed, historian Doug Baynton showed that the concepts of ability/disability have been central to movements both to deny and to gain civil rights, as those who seek to deny particular populations rights portray them as biologically and mentally unfit/ inferior to exercise rights and those seeking rights present themselves as "able" (e.g., competent, rational, and productive).[9] Through all of these debates lies an underlying assumption that it is acceptable to deny rights, exclude and segregate due to disability and an evaluation of biological inferiority.

Ableism plays out on many levels, including prejudice (beliefs), discrimination (behavior), and institutional ableism (structural inequality).

Prejudice

Prejudice is a set of negative attitudes and beliefs about a social group. It is intimately tied to stereotypes—generalizations that are often false, simplified, and/ or negative about a group, which may be used to judge individual people. People with disabilities encounter significant prejudice in their daily lives.

Stereotypes about disability are both impairment specific and cross disability.[10] *Impairment-specific stereotypes* assign a distinct trait or judgment to people with a specific disability. For example, stereotypes of people who are blind include that they are helpless and/or gifted with mystical wisdom.[11] People with autism are often described as being in a world of their own and/or as brilliant savants.[12] People with psychiatric disabilities increasingly are portrayed in the media as violent, although in reality they are far more likely to be a victim of violence than to perpetuate it.[13] Each of these stereotypes (even "positive" stereotypes) simplifies the impairment and the person, leads to a narrow set of expectations, and ultimately discounts the humanity of people with disabilities.

Stereotypes also may be applied to the broad range of people with disabilities. In other words, people with diverse disabilities are often seen as more similar to each other than different. In particular, people with disabilities are often stereotyped as dependent, tragic, and (the flip side of this coin) heroic. A 2010 study by Michelle Nario-Redmond examined stereotypes by disability and gender.[14] She asked respondents to list traits considered by society to be stereotypical of each group. Dependence was the most common stereotype for disability; 91% of respondents mentioned dependence. Seven of the top 10 stereotypes for disabled men and disabled women were the same: dependent, incompetent, asexual, unattractive, weak, passive, and heroic. Nondisabled men and women, in contrast, shared far fewer stereotypes. Only 3 of the top 10 traits overlapped for nondisabled men and women: ambitious, independent, and domineering. None of these three traits was among those shared by disabled men and women. Thus, men and women with disabilities were seen as far more similar to each other than to men and women without disabilities.

Moreover, Nario-Redmond also analyzed the stereotypes that most exclusively defined each group (in other words, stereotypes that were common for one group and rarely used for the others). Nondisabled men were described as *employed* and nondisabled women as *nurturing*—results that fit well with expected gender stereotypes in America. However, disabled men were described as *angry* and disabled women as *vulnerable*, suggesting the perceived consequences of not meeting the expectations of one's gender in society.

People with disabilities tend to experience a mix of positive and negative stereotypes. They are seen as heroic and innocent (positive stereotypes) as well as dependent, tragic, and incompetent (negative stereotypes).[15] Keep in mind that even positive stereotypes can be harmful. The view of people with disabilities as heroic is often rooted in the belief that disability is a tragedy and in very low expectations. If society believes that disability is a fate worse than death, then just surviving can be portrayed as heroic; if society expects nothing from you, then any typical accomplishment (e.g., high school graduation, marriage, getting a job) can be heralded as heroic.

This blend of positive and negative stereotypes falls in line with predictions from the stereotype content model.[16] The stereotype content model argues that two types of traits are particularly important in determining the content of stereotypes: warmth and competence. Warmth refers to a group's motives and moral qualities, such as likability, honesty, and friendliness. Competence refers to whether a group has the ability and resources, such as intelligence and power, to carry out its agenda. People with disabilities, like children and the elderly, tend to fall in the high-warmth, low-competence group.[17] In other words, they are generally considered friendly and compliant (warm), as well as dependent and incapable (incompetent). As such, they are seen as unthreatening. The typical response to unthreatening groups is paternalism (treating people like children) and pity. In contrast, for groups that are warm and competent, one might show deference. For groups that are cold and incompetent, one might objectify, segregate, and denigrate them.

Although this model predicts that people with disabilities will experience pity, not objectification or segregation, people with disabilities have certainly been subjected to objectification and segregation. At different times in history and in contemporary society for a variety of reasons, people with disabilities are seen as threatening, leading to harsh reactions. When eugenics was at its height in the early twentieth century, for example, eugenicists believed disability to be the root cause of crime, poverty and social dysfunction.[18] This led to mass institutionalization and compulsory sterilization. In modern America, people with mental illness, in particular, face accusations of being violent and dangerous, leading to their segregation and incarceration.[19] As people with disabilities have gained rights to accommodations and benefits, they increasingly face accusations of getting "unfair" privileges and of sucking resources from society, which also leads to harsh reactions.[20]

In fact, research suggests that our implicit biases regarding disability may be much more negative than explicit reporting suggests. Implicit bias refers to the unconscious attitudes and stereotypes that shape our behaviors. Tests for disability implicit bias reveal a very pervasive negative bias against people with disabilities.[21] In one study, 76 percent of respondents showed a stronger preference for people without disabilities than for people with disabilities, one of the strongest effects across social groups, including gender, race, sexuality, and political orientation.[22]

Studies of social distance also indicate that people believe that they should have a positive regard for people with disabilities yet hold an implicit bias against people with disabilities. A classic 1980 study by Melvin Snyder and his colleagues offers a vivid example.[23] Undergraduates were asked to watch a movie in a dorm common room setting. In the first scenario, there were two seating areas, one with a wheelchair user present and one with a nondisabled person present. The same film was being shown in both seating areas. In the second scenario, there were again two seating areas, one with a wheelchair user present and one with a nondisabled person present, but the areas were showing different films. For both scenarios, Snyder recorded with whom the undergraduate sat. When there was no choice of movie, 58% of subjects sat with the person with the disability. When there was a choice of movies, only 17% of subjects sat with the person with the disability. Given the random assignment of movies, it seems that, when subjects could justify avoiding the disabled person by claiming to prefer a different movie, they tended to do so. When they had no justification (they couldn't say they preferred a particular movie), a majority sat with the person with a disability to avoid being *seen as* biased. This suggests that the inclusion of people with disabilities may be heavily dependent on societal pressure.

Discrimination and the Consequences of Stereotypes

Our beliefs, and even our implicit biases, often shape our behavior. Strong negative beliefs about disability, particularly beliefs regarding the incompetence, dependence, and tragic nature of people with disabilities, lead to discrimination in many areas of life.

Healthcare and treatment. Labeling theory argues that a label can become a master status, so that people respond to one's label rather than to one's actual behavior. In the classic 1973 labeling study *Sane in Insane Places,* David Rosenhan sent eight people, including himself, to mental hospitals.[24] They were instructed to each say that they briefly heard voices (words such as "empty" and "hollow"), and then they were instructed to act as they normally would. All were admitted, received diagnoses, and stayed as a patient in the hospital for between 7 and 52 days. While in the hospital, the label of schizophrenic shaped perceptions of the patients' behavior. For example, when patients paced out of boredom, it was interpreted as a symptom of mental illness; when they took notes for the study, nurses labeled the notetaking as a compulsive behavior. Once the label was applied, the actual behavior of the patient no longer mattered; their behavior was interpreted in terms of the label of schizophrenia. The patients reported feeling dehumanized, objectified, and ignored.

In today's world, negative stereotyping of people with disabilities sharply decreases their opportunities. Although it may be surprising, access to healthcare is still negatively impacted by both stereotypes and discrimination.[25] Healthcare providers have been socialized into a culture of curing and fixing, and they tend to have negative attitudes toward living with a chronic disability.[26] Indeed, doctors' attitudes about the quality of life of people with disabilities tend to be just as negative, or more negative, than the public's[27] and far more negative than the opinion of people with disabilities themselves.[28] For example, "in a survey study of attitudes of 153 emergency care providers, only 18% of physicians, nurses, and technicians imagined they would be glad to be alive with a severe spinal cord injury. In contrast, 92% of a comparison group of 128 persons with high-level spinal cord injuries said they were glad to be alive."[29]

Negative stereotypes affect access to and the quality of medical care. For example, people with disabilities are widely believed to be asexual, and doctors too often assume or even assert that women with disabilities should not need access to contraceptives, family planning, and testing for sexually transmitted diseases (STDs).[30] Women with disabilities wait longer for a diagnosis and receive less care for STDs. Stereotypes of incompetence also affect physicians. New mothers with disabilities are far more likely than new mothers without disabilities to be defined by doctors as "high risk" and to have social services called in, even when the observed challenges, like difficulties with breastfeeding, are common for both sets of women.[31]

Education. Students with disabilities have lower rates of high school and college graduation than students without disabilities, and studies showed part of the educational achievement gap is due to ableism. Negative stereotypes can lead to the very outcome expected based on the stereotype—or, in other words, to a self-fulfilling prophecy. Sociologist Dara Shifrer used a national data set of 10th graders to examine the extent to which the educational achievement gap between disabled and nondisabled students was due to the disability itself (e.g., difficulty reading, IQ), factors like socioeconomic background and educational motivation or the negative impact of the disability label.[32] Due to the large data set, Shifrer was able to compare students who were alike in terms of many factors (e.g., grades, motivation level in school, behavioral record, socioeconomic status) but differed on whether or not they had a label of learning disability (LD) or not. Among *otherwise similar students,* teachers were 82% less likely to expect students with LD labels to receive a bachelor of arts (BA) or higher compared to students without the LD label. Parents were 48% less likely to expect their children with LD labels to achieve a BA or higher than parents of children without a label. Elissa Molloy and Michelle Nario-Redmond similarly found that college faculty held lower expectations of students with learning disabilities—including expecting that students with disabilities were more likely to drop out and they might perform better in less rigorous majors.[33] They held lower expectations *even when told that the students with disabilities had high grades.* Low expectations held by teachers may have a grave impact on the opportunities and careers that students are channeled toward and the way students come to see their own potential.

These negative effects may be especially harmful to students of color and students from low socioeconomic backgrounds who are overidentified as disabled and for whom labels are less likely to lead to helpful resources and more likely to lead to segregated educational tracks with low expectations. The disproportionate labeling of poor and minority children creates the illusion that poor academic performance is due to their own individual biology/deficits rather than systemic inequities in educational treatment and access.[34] Research by Beth Ferri and David Connor (2006) and Colin Ong-Dean (2009) argued that the intertwining of race, class, and disability inequalities are part of a long history of naturalizing inequality for racial minorities and using disability as a means to justify segregation.[35]

The workplace. Dependence and incompetence are two of the primary stereotypes associated with disability, and these stereotypes hinder success in employment. Employer attitudes specifically contribute to the low rate of employment among people with disabilities. A review of scholarship on employer attitudes and disability conducted in 2015 by Robert Gould and his colleagues reported that: "Stigmatized perceptions of disability impact a variety of employment decisions, including hiring, advancement, and providing reasonable accommodations." Employers express concerns about lower productivity, higher costs (e.g., accommodations, absenteeism), and the fear of litigation.[36] Interestingly, employers with experience hiring people with disabilities are more likely to hire someone with a disability again. Thus, the actual experience of employing someone with a disability dispels many of the negative stereotypes.[37]

Employees with disabilities, in comparison to employees without disabilities, report lower pay, less job security, and more negative treatment by their employers.[38] Studies show that people with disabilities who perceive high levels of stigma are less likely to disclose their disability in the workplace or request workplace accommodations.[39] Therefore, although the ADA is supposed to ensure access to accommodations, many people do not feel comfortable asking for them.

Institutional Ableism

Institutional discrimination, and for our purposes, institutional ableism, occurs when broad institutional patterns such as policies, procedures, and funding systems disadvantage or harm people with disabilities more than other groups. These effects may be intentional or not, but regardless of intent, they create and maintain systemic inequality. This inequality is not reliant on prejudiced individuals; in fact, individuals may express positive attitudes regarding people with disabilities, yet the systems in place ensure the perpetuation of inequality. There are many possible examples of institutional ableism. For our purposes here, two examples are highlighted that document how institutional ableism works to perpetuate inequality.

The institutional bias. In the sociology of disability, the term *institutional* may take on two different meanings. The first refers to the patterns found in society's social structures (e.g., education, healthcare). For instance, the idea of "institutional discrimination" calls attention to the patterns of inequality as embedded in and manifest through policies and laws. The second meaning of institutional refers to the warehousing of people with disabilities in large-scale, segregated settings called institutions. For instance, institutional care is the care provided in large-scale, segregated settings. The institutional bias refers to both—the ways in which the channeling of people with disabilities into large-scale, segregated settings (institutions) rather than community settings is encouraged by and embedded in (institutionalized through) our national laws and policies.

Care in institutional settings is deeply problematic because it deprives people of freedom and individual choice. As Erving Goffman discussed in his classic 1961 book *Asylums*, institutions operate around a central authority and enforce standardized rules, demanding conformity and erasing individual difference.[40] In institutional settings, people have limited choices; they do not choose their roommates, staff, daily activities, daily schedules, or even when or if to take a shower. They cannot come and go based on their own preferences. Their lives are *administered*, shaped by institutional needs like staffing schedule and cost efficiencies. Because citizens should have a right to freedom, long-term institutional care should be avoided except in the most dire of circumstances, when essential for the safety of the person with a disability or others. Most services administered in institutional settings can be provided, often more effectively and more cheaply, in community settings while retaining individual liberty.

The legal rights to liberty and access to the community have been inscribed in law in the ADA and in Supreme Court decisions (*Olmstead v. L. C. 1999*). However, America still heavily relies on institutional care. For example, a 2011 court case determined that North Carolina "fails to provide services to individuals with mental illness in the most integrated setting appropriate to their needs in violation of the ADA. The State plans, structures, and administers its mental health service system to deliver services to thousands of persons with mental illness in large, segregated adult care homes, and to allocate funding to service individuals in adult care homes rather than in integrated settings."[41] We see a similar heavy reliance on segregation in the provision of housing, day programs, and vocational opportunities for people with developmental disabilities. And, many older Americans who would prefer to live in their homes with in-home assistance are pushed into nursing homes.

Why do we still rely so heavily on institutional care despite the ADA's community mandate? This occurs because of the ways in which federal policy pays for long-term care. In 1965, legislation mandated that the federal government use Medicaid and Medicare to financially support long-term care in nursing homes and institutional settings for those who met financial eligibility requirements. The law did not similarly mandate federal financial support for community services or individualized personal assistance.[42] This means that individuals who need care and support can more easily access public funding to meet their needs if they are placed in a nursing home or institutional setting rather than if they stay at home with individualized services. Policies created in the 1960s continue to channel people with disabilities into institutional settings, depriving them of liberty if they need support.[43] Thus, the institutional bias perpetuates segregation and limits freedom, even if individual attitudes seem accepting of the inclusion of people with disabilities in the community.

Employment disincentives and occupational structures. As noted, economic inequality has also been persistent despite the passage of the ADA. Sociologists Michelle Maroto and David Pettinicchio argued that the ADA has not remedied persistent attitudinal and structural inequalities due to employer attitudes (which we've already discussed) and broader, systemic issues of occupational structure (e.g., patterns of work inequality).[44]

These occupational structures include the concentration of people with disabilities in low-wage and part-time jobs, the reliance on entrepreneurship and nonstandard work arrangements to better fit particular disability-related needs, and work/benefits policy.[45] Workers with disabilities are highly concentrated in low-wage, service-sector jobs; according to Schur, Kruse, and Blanck, 58% of the employed people with disabilities work in occupations with low or very low wages. Moreover, because the "standard" work environment demands 35 hours of work or more a week and offers little flexibility, many people with disabilities are channeled into part-time work and entrepreneurship. Entrepreneurship may provide more flexibility but usually yields little pay or benefits.[46] Furthermore, because employment can threaten one's eligibility for public benefits, including access to Medicaid/Medicare, people with disabilities may be discouraged from working unless they can maintain full-time employment that will confer pay and benefits comparable to or better than Social Security payments and Medicaid.[47] Therefore, even if employers' attitudes change, the structure of work and the distribution of pay and benefits for work remain in place and disadvantage people with disabilities in the workplace.

Inaccessibility

Ableism and inaccessibility are deeply intertwined. Access refers to the power and opportunity to enter into, use, participate in, and have a sense of belonging or control over a social space or interaction.[48] Access may be physical, shaped by factors such as landscape, architecture, and technology. More broadly, access is social, shaped by factors such as interpersonal relationships, money, communication systems, and policy. Disability activist and scholar Jacobus tenBroek argued in 1966—soon after the passage of the Civil Rights Act—that people with disabilities must have the "right to be in the world" and to be free from unnecessary confinement, thereby situating access as a cornerstone of disability rights.[49] Access enables (and inaccessibility disables) many of our basic civil rights, such as the rights to assemble, to vote, to move freely through the nation, to enjoy public spaces and services, and ultimately to freedom and the pursuit of happiness. Ableism is the ideological underpinning on inaccessibility—the imagination that people with disabilities don't need or shouldn't have access.

Inaccessibility potentially hinders people with disabilities in all areas of life: housing, work, religion, leisure, education, technology, health, and more. To develop a few examples, healthcare is shockingly inaccessible. One study found that 65% of alcohol and drug abuse treatment programs that were approached by a person with a significant physical disability for services denied them services based on inaccessibility.[50] Sociologists Heather Dillaway and Catherine Lysack found inaccessibility to be a major barrier for women with physical disabilities seeking gynecological healthcare.[51] The inaccessibility of doctors' equipment, like their examination tables, makes it impossible for some people to get a proper exam. Doctors also lack knowledge about safely assisting people in transferring from wheelchairs to tables and conducting safe exams. Thus, even though people with disabilities on average need more medical care, they have difficulty accessing it.

For housing, few homes and only 1% of the rental housing market are accessible, and accessible housing tends to cost more.[52] In his 2008 study of minority men with spinal cord injury, Noam Ostrander showed that, after rehabilitation, most men returned to inaccessible housing and communities.[53] They relied on family and friends to assist them, at times carry them, in and out of their homes/apartment buildings on a regular basis. Inaccessibility limited their movement, threatened their safety (e.g., they could not safely leave in case of emergency), and damaged their sense of masculinity.

As a third example, religious organizations are exempt from the ADA, and their access issues are often grave: steps leading into churches and/or into social spaces, pews with no room for people in wheelchairs except blocking aisle traffic, cavernous rooms without adequate systems for people with hearing impairments or who used American Sign Language, liturgical rituals that demand specific forms of participation (e.g., silence, kneeling, repeating prayers), and paternalistic attitudes that portray people with disabilities only as objects of charity.[54] Thus, although people with disabilities hold religious views at the same rate as those without disabilities, they are less likely to participate in religious services.

Inaccessibility is not just a product of happenstance or ignorance. Sociologists argue that the organization of social spaces, and the distribution of people and goods through these spaces, are processes shaped by power. Accessibility and inaccessibility emerge from decisions about who *should* be included, who has value, and who belongs. Through these processes, we define boundaries, create inclusions/exclusions, structure actions and opportunities, and provoke a wide range of social effects.[55] Studying higher education, sociologist Tanya Titchkosky showed the many ways that administrators continue to justify the inaccessibility of higher education, simultaneously claiming that they value students with disabilities while offering many justifications (e.g., cost, tradition, inefficiency) to excuse unequal educational access.[56] Titchkosky's work pointed out that the exclusion of people with disabilities is too often easily excused, assumed to be acceptable and even necessary for the best interests of people with disabilities and/ or of society. This logic leads to exclusion, segregation, invisibility, and, too often, violence.

Segregation, Invisibility, and Violence

The segregation of people with disabilities is widespread and often unquestioned. Nicki Pombier Berger first questioned this pervasive segregation when her son was unexpectedly born with Down syndrome. She said: "My beginning [with disability] was as (inter)personal as it gets; I never had a meaningful encounter with a person with intellectual disability until I gave birth to one. As I began to process this fact in those early days, I saw that this was by design: the world, written by and for an idea of "normal," has kept us apart."[57]

Often, people believe that segregation is the best "solution" for the "special needs" of people with disabilities. Challenging this widespread myth, disability rights activists have demanded the rights to inclusion and empowerment. Drawing on lessons from the civil rights movement, they declare that separate is not equal. This does not mean that there are never ways that people with disabilities may benefit from specialized services or enjoy participating in groups specifically for people with disabilities. It does mean that the imposition of segregated environments on people with disabilities, especially over long periods of time and/or across multiple systems, systematically denies the "right to be in the world."

Although segregation is often explained as in the best interest of the person with the disability, when we explore this rationale more deeply we often find that segregation has more to do with cost efficiency, bureaucratic ease, and preserving the "normal" routines and practices for people without disabilities by diverting people with disabilities into separate settings. For example, despite evidence of the positive impacts of inclusive educational practices, school districts defend their continued high reliance on segregated education based on costs, insufficient professional training, inaccessible buildings, and the negative impact of program disruptions.

Al Herzog's work on religious ministry offers an illuminating discussion of segregation versus inclusion.[58] In an attempt to meet the religious needs of people with disabilities, many churches have, with good intentions, created "special" religious programs and services for people with disabilities. The problem with special services, however, is that they position people with disabilities as marginal to the religious community. Special services imagine a world, typically designed and led by people without disabilities, for a group of people whose needs seemingly can't be met alongside others. In contrast, Herzog encouraged the creation of *inclusive* services open to all. Inclusive services are held in an accessible environment, minimize complicated language, and allow flexibility in practice and movement (e.g., people can move about and stim, people who use augmented communication devices can sing in the choir). Inclusion imagines many ways for diverse people to participate. Not all people would love this service; other services may embrace other styles, too. But many people—disabled and nondisabled—might love it, including parents with small children, young adults looking for more active ways to participate, and older people who benefit from the accessibility features.

Segregation, although historically heralded by medical experts and policymakers as optimal for people with disabilities, reinforces the devaluation of people with disabilities, denies liberty, and makes people with disabilities largely invisible—out of sight, out of mind. Once invisible, people with disabilities become highly vulnerable to neglect and violence. The rate of violence against people with disabilities is shocking. According to the Bureau of Justice Statistics, between 2009 and 2015 individuals with disabilities were at least twice as likely to be victims of violence as individuals without disabilities, with people with mental and intellectual disabilities at highest risk.[59] Both men and women with disabilities had higher rates of sexual victimization than men and women without disabilities.[60] The vast majority of victims of violence know the perpetrators, and 20 percent believe that they were targeted because of their disability.[61] Despite the mythical positive benefits of segregation, studies showed that segregated settings yield higher rates of violence. Violence is an act of power often wielded against those who have little ability to resist. Segregation reduces the avenues for reporting abuse while simultaneously delegitimizing the victims' credibility. In contrast, inclusion and a strong network of relationships with people in the community better serve to protect people from abuse.[62]

When we discuss violence against people with disabilities, we often discuss instances of interpersonal violence. But people with disabilities have also experienced mass, systemic violence committed by the state and professional systems. Large-scale institutional hospitals for people with disabilities quickly became warehouses with little treatment and mass dehumanization, neglect, and abuse.[63] Under compulsory sterilization laws, more than 60,000 people labeled as disabled were sterilized in America without their consent. People with disabilities have been the victims of medical experimentation and violent medical "treatments," including electric shocks, social isolation, and confinement to cages.[64] Through war, colonialization, mass incarceration, and forced displacement, the state also creates disability.[65] Indeed, although we often imagine disability as a product of nature, state violence is strongly related to the creation of disability.

Cultural Discourses Legitimating Inequality

Systems of inequality are justified through ableist language and discourses. Negative words for diverse bodies (often rooted in prior or current medical terminology)—such as crazy, lame, retarded, defective, and moron—abound. The language of disability often demeans, while imposing a master status. As an example, when doctors use the language of birth "defect," they subsume an entire, complex being under a singular negative label. When a person becomes "a schizophrenic," their identity is similarly reduced to one trait. Moreover, the trait is assumed to be wholly and simply negative. Birth defects and schizophrenia may entail many challenges, but they also may provoke creativity, resiliency, alternative perspectives, and entry to new communities.[66]

Negative words connect to broader discourses that justify inequality. Two of the most powerful related to disability are social Darwinism/eugenics and meritocracy. Social Darwinism centers on the maxim of the survival of the fittest. This maxim suggests that the human race and society both evolve toward perfection when we allow for open, unhindered competition where the strong rise to the top and the weak fall to the bottom. The strong will be more likely to marry and breed, passing their superior traits to the next generation, whereas the weak will face destitution, have few children, and die earlier, and therefore their genetic lines will end. Social Darwinists argued that helping the poor and disabled undercuts the positive influence of "natural selection."

Eugenicists took this sentiment even further. Eugenicists believed that creating a better population should not just be left to nature. Rather, that state could improve population quality through encouraging selective breeding. Eugenicists argued that the state had a responsibility to protect society from public health threats, including disease, disability, and degeneracy. Therefore, they advocated institutionalization, compulsory sterilization, and immigration restrictions, among other policies, to ensure that those they deemed "unfit" could not move freely around in America or procreate.[67]

Social Darwinism and eugenics still influence thinking about disability. People with disabilities face stereotypes that they cannot and should not parent. Fetuses identified with birth defects are aborted at high rates; 90–94 percent of fetuses identified with Down syndrome are aborted.[68] People often assume that the world would be better if disability, and people with disabilities, were eradicated.[69] Addressing current initiatives to identify and eradicate Down syndrome based on the premise that Down syndrome is a devastating defect, self-advocate Frank Stephens advised: "See me as a human being, not a birth defect, not a syndrome. I don't need to be eradicated."[70]

A second, closely related, narrative that justifies the inequality of people with disabilities is meritocracy. Meritocracy asserts that people succeed and fail based on their own merits. Meritocracy is closely connected to a belief in individualism. People who believe that America is a meritocracy and embrace individualism show less support for social welfare programs and for antidiscrimination efforts.[71] Considering disability, ideals of meritocracy justify the denial of social supports and even accessibility measures since each person is expected to compete for their own success (much like in social Darwinism). Moreover, meritocracy glosses over the structural inequalities that shape outcomes and presents the wealthy and successful as if they earned their position and the poor as if they failed to work hard enough. Meritocracy ignores the role of individual and structural discrimination and segregation.

Once ideology effectively naturalizes inequality by erasing the impact of discrimination and inaccessibility, people with disabilities come to be seen as "naturally" incapable and deficient.[72] Paternalism then is offered as the dominant response.[73] Paternalism asserts that some set of people with expertise and authority *should* limit the rights and participation of those defined as incapable/deficient because social control is in fact in the "deficient's" best interests. Paternalism allows systems of segregation, social control, and violence to appear benevolent and to go largely unquestioned.

Part of the power of these ideologies is that they perpetuate inequality, even without appearing antidisability. Eduardo Bonilla-Silva's 2003 book *Racism Without Racists* argued that ideologies rooted in liberal political philosophy and meritocracy are used to prevent interventions designed to achieve equality, erase institutional disadvantages, and uphold the status quo.[74] These ideologies perpetuate racial inequality, even in an era when fewer Whites espouse explicitly racist views. Whites do not need to be racist to benefit from race privilege; they need only ensure the status quo, which they can do through embracing individualism and meritocracy. Similarly, with long-standing systems of segregation and marginalization already established, explicit antidisability sentiment is not necessary to ensure inequality. If one simply does not challenge ableism, the inequalities remain.

Conclusion

Ableism is common. In fact, it's widely accepted to perceive people with disabilities as tragic, to assume that they suffer, and to treat them as objects of pity. Many Americans believe that the poverty of people with disabilities is a natural result of biological limitations, with little consideration of the impact of discrimination and policy. Yet, ableism, and the varied ways it manifests—attitudes, discrimination, inaccessibility, segregation, violence, and ideology—is central to creating and perpetuating the inequality of people with disabilities. Each element of ableism must therefore be addressed to ensure the freedom and equal participation of people with disabilities in society.

Notes

1. A. Houtenville and S. Boege, *Annual Report on People With Disabilities in America: 2018* (Durham, NH: University of New Hampshire, Institute on Disability, 2019), https://disabilitycompendium.org/sites/default/files/user-uploads/2019%20 Annual%20Report%20---%20FINAL%20ALL.pdf.
2. Julia A. Rivera Drew, "Disability, Poverty, and Material Hardship since the Passage of the ADA," *Disability Studies Quarterly* 35, no. 3 (2015), https://dsq-sds.org/article/ view/4947/4026.
3. Michelle Maroto and David Pettinicchio, "Twenty-Five Years After the ADA: Situating Disability in America's System of Stratification," *Disability Studies Quarterly* 35, no. 3 (2015), https://dsq-sds.org/article/view/4927/4024.
4. Sharon N. Barnartt and Katherine D. Seelman, "A Comparison of Federal Laws Toward Disabled and Racial/ Ethnic Groups in the USA. Disability," *Handicap & Society*, 3, no. 1 (1988): 37–47; Richard K. Scotch, *From Good Will to Civil Rights* (Philadelphia: Temple University Press, 1984).
5. Fiona Kumari Campbell, *Contours of Ableism: The Production of Disability and Abledness* (New York: Palgrave Macmillan, 2009); Vera Chouinard, "E & P Search Results: Making Space for Disabling Differences: Challenging Ableist Geographies," *Environment and Planning D: Society and Space* 15, no. 4 (1997): 379–387.
6. Eli Clare, *Brilliant Imperfection: Grappling With Cure.* (Raleigh, NC: Duke University Press, 2017); Mike Oliver, *The Politics of Disablement* (London: Macmillan Education, 1990).
7. Talila A. Lewis, "Ableism 2020: An Updated Definition," Talila A. Lewis (website/ blog), 2020, https://www.talilalewis.com/blog/ableism-2020-an-updated-definition.
8. Isabella Kres-Nash, "Racism and Ableism," American Association of People with Disabilities (AAPD) (website), 2016, https://www.aapd.com/racism-and-ableism/.
9. Douglas C. Baynton, "Disability and the Justification of Inequality in American History," in *The New Disability History: American Perspectives,* ed. Paul K. Longmore and Lauri Umansky (New York: New York University Press, 2001), 33–57; see also Kim E. Nielsen, *A Disability History of the United States* (Boston: Beacon Press, 2012).
10. Michelle R. Nario-Redmond, *Ableism: The Causes and Consequences of Disability Prejudice* (Hoboken, NJ: Wiley, 2020).
11. Paul K. Longmore, "Screening Stereotypes: Images of Disabled People in Television and Motion Pictures," in *Why I Burned My Book and Other Essays,* ed. Paul Longmore (Philadelphia: Temple University Press, 2003), 131–146.

12. Douglas Bilken, *Autism and the Myth of the Person Alone* (New York: New York University Press, 2015).

13. Jonathon Metzl, *The Protest Psychosis* (Boston: Beacon Press, 2010); Jonathon Metzl, "Let's Talk About Guns, But Stop Stereotyping the Mentally Ill," in *Beginning With Disability: A Primer*, ed. Lennard Davis (New York: Routledge, 2018), 165–169; Jo C. Phelan et al., "Public Conceptions of Mental Illness in 1950 and 1996: What Is Mental Illness and Is It to be Feared?" *Journal of Health and Social Behavior* 4, no. 2 (200): 188–207.

14. Michelle R. Nario-Redmond, "Cultural Stereotypes of Disabled and Non-Disabled Men and Women: Consensus for Global Category Representations and Diagnostic Domains," *British Journal of Social Psychology* 49, no. 3 (2010): 471–488.

15. Nario-Redmond, *Ableism*.

16. Peter Glick and Susan T. Fiske, "An Ambivalent Alliance: Hostile and Benevolent Sexism as Complimentary Justifications for Gender Equality," *American Psychologist* 56, no. 2 (2001): 109–118; Susan T. Fiske et al., "A Model of (Often Mixed) Stereotype Content: Competence and Warmth Respectively Follow From Perceived Status and Competence," *Journal of Personality and Social Psychology* 82, no. 6 (2002): 878–902.

17. Glick and Fiske, "An Ambivalent Alliance."

18. Sharon L. Snyder and David T. Mitchell, "Eugenics and the Racial Genome: Politics at the Molecular Level," *Patterns of Prejudice* 40, no. 4–5 (2006): 399–412; Sharon L. Snyder and David T. Mitchell, *Cultural Locations of Disability* (Chicago: University of Chicago Press, 2005); James W. Trent Jr., *Inventing the Feeble Mind: A History of Mental Retardation in the United States.* (Berkeley: University of California Press, 1994).

19. Metzl, "Let's Talk About Guns."

20. Doron Dorfman, "[Un]Usual Suspects: Deservingness, Scarcity and Disability Rights," *UC Irvine Law Review* 10, no. 2 (2020): 557–618.

21. Steven R. Pruett and Fong Chan, "The Development and Psychometric Validation of the Disability Attitude Association Test," *Rehabilitation Psychology* 51, no. 3 (2006): 202–213; Odile Rohmer and Eva Louvet, "Implicit Stereotyping Against People With Disability," *Group Processes & Intergroup Relations* 21, no. 1 (2018): 127–140.

22. Brian A. Nosek et al., *"Pervasiveness and Correlates of Implicit Attitudes and Stereotype,"* *European Review of Social Psychology* 18 (2007): 36–88.

23. Melvin Snyder et al., "Avoidance of the Handicapped: An Attributional Ambiguity Analysis," *Journal of Personality and Social Psychology* 37, no. 12 (1980): 2297–2306.

24. David L. Rosenhan, "On Being Sane in Insane Places," *Science* 179, no. 4070 (1973): 250–258.

25. Kenneth L. Robey, Linda Beckley, and Matthew Kirschner, "Implicit Infantalizing Attitudes About Disability," *Journal of Developmental and Physical Disabilities* 18, no. 4 (2006): 441–453.

26. Joan Cassell, *Life and Death in the Intensive Care* (Baltimore: Johns Hopkins University Press, 2005).

27. Elizabeth Pendo, "Disability, Equipment Barriers, and Women's Health: Using the ADA to Provide Meaningful Access," *Saint Louis University Journal of Health Law & Policy* 2 (2008): 15–56.

28. Carol J. Gill, "Health Professionals, Disability, and Assisted Suicide: An Examination of Relevant Empirical Evidence and Reply to Batavia," *Psychology, Public Policy, and Law* 6, no. 2 (2000): 526–545.

29. Gill, "Health Professionals," 530, citing the following study: K. A. Gerhart et al., "Quality of Life Following Spinal Cord Injury: Knowledge and Attitudes of Emergency Care Providers," *Annals of Emergency Medicine*, 23 (1994): 807–812.

30. Heather E. Dillaway and Catherine Lysack, "'Most of Them Are Amateurs': Women With Spinal Cord Injury Experience the Lack of Education and Training Among Among Medical Providers While Seeking Gynecological Care," *Disability Studies Quarterly* 35, no. 3 (2015), https://dsq-sds.org/article/view/4934; National Council on Disability, *The Current State of Health Care for People with Disabilities* (Washington DC: NCD, 2009), https://www.ncd.gov/rawmedia_repository/0d7c848f_3d97_43b3_bea5_36e1d97f973d.pdf

31. Angela Frederick, "Risky Mothers and the Normalcy Project: Women With Disabilities Negotiate Scientific Motherhood," *Gender and Society* 31, no. 1 (2017): 74–95.

32. Dara Shifrer, "Stigma of a Label: Educational Expectations for High School Students With Learning Disabilities," *Journal of Health and Social Behavior* 54, no. 4 (2013): 462–480.

33. Elissa Molloy and Michelle R. Nario-Redmond. "College Faculty Perceptions of Learning Disabled Students: Stereotypes, Group Identity and Bias," in *Disabled Faculty and Staff in a Disabling Society: Multiple Identities in Higher Education*, ed. Mary Lee Vance (Huntersville, NC: Association on Higher Education and Disability, 2007).

34. Dara Shifrer, C. Muller, and R. Callahan, "Disproportionality and Learning Disabilities: Parsing Apart Race, Socioeconomic Status, and Language," *Journal of Learning Disabilities* 44, no. 3 (2011): 246–257.

35. Beth A. Ferri and David J. Connor, "Tools of Exclusion: Race, Disability, and (Re)segregated Education," *Teachers College Record* 107, no. 3 (2005): 453–474; Beth A. Ferri and David J. Connor, *Reading Resistance: Discourses of Exclusion in Desegregation and Inclusion Debates* (New York: Peter Lang, 2006); Colin Ong-Dean, *Distinguishing Disability: Parents, Privilege and Special Education.* (Chicago: University of Chicago Press, 2009).

36. Robert Gould et al., "Beyond the Law: A Review of Knowledge, Attitudes, and Perceptions in ADA Employment Research," *Disability Studies Quarterly* 35, no. 3 (2015), https://dsq-sds.org/article/view/4935/4095; H. Stephen Kaye, Lita H. Jans, and Erica C Jones, "Why Don't Employers Hire and Retain Workers With Disabilities?" *Journal of Occupational Rehabilitation* 21, no. 4 (2011): 526–536.

37. Brigida Hernandez, Christopher B. Keys, and Fabricio E. Balcazar, "Disability Rights: Attitudes of Private and Public Sector Representatives," *Journal of Rehabilitation* 70, no. 1 (2004): 28–37.

38. Lisa Schur, Douglas Kruse, and Peter Blanck, *People With Disabilities: Sidelined and Mainstreamed?* (Cambridge: Cambridge University Press, 2013).

39. David M. Engel and Frank W. Munger, *Rights of Inclusion: Law and Identity in the Life Stories of Americans With Disabilities* (Chicago: University of Chicago Press, 2003); Susan G. Goldberg, Mary B. Killeen, and Bonnie O'Day, "The Disclosure Conundrum: How People With Psychiatric Disabilities Navigate Employment," *Psychology Public Policy and Law* 3 (2005): 463–500.

40. Erving Goffman, *Asylums: Essays on the Social Situation of Mental Patients and Other Inmates* (New York: First Anchor Books, 1961).

41. Vicki Smith, "North Carolina's Institutional Bias: Enforcing the ADA's Integration Mandate," *North Carolina Medical Journal* 73, no. 3 (2012): 219–221.

42. Center for an Accessible Society, "The 'Institutional Bias' in Long-Term Care Policy," n.d., http://www.accessiblesociety.org/topics/persasst/instbias.htm.

43. "The Institutional Bias Is Costly and Morally Wrong for People With Disabilities," *NY Examiner*, April 25, 2010, comop.org/the-institutional-bias-is-wrong-for-people-with-disabilities.

44. Maroto and Pettinicchio, "Twenty-Five Years After the ADA."

45. Maroto and Pettinicchio, "Twenty-Five Years After the ADA."; see also Schur, Krause, and Blanck, *People With Disabilities*; Lisa Schur, "Barriers or Opportunities? The Causes of Contingent and Part-time Work Among People With Disabilities," *Industrial Relations* 42, no. 4 (2003): 589–622.

46. Shur, Kruse and Blanck, *People With Disabilities*.

47. Paul K. Longmore, *Why I Burned My Book and Other Essays* (Philadelphia: Temple University Press, 2003).

48. Tanya Titchkosky, *The Question of Access: Disability, Space, Meaning* (Toronto: University of Toronto Press, 2011); Bess Williamson, "Access," in *Keywords for Disability Studies,* ed. Rachel Adams, Benjamin Reiss, and David Serlin (New York: New York University Press, 2015), 14–16.

49. Jacobus tenBroek, "The Right to Live in the World: The Disabled in the Law of Torts," *California Law Review* 54, no. 2 (1966): 841–919.

50. Steven L. West, Carolyn W. Graham, and David X Cifu, "Rates of Alcohol/Other Drug Treatment Denials to Persons With Physical Disabilities: Accessibility Concerns," *Alcohol Treatment Quarterly* 27, no. 3 (2009): 305–316.

51. Dillaway and Lysack, "Most of Them Are Amateurs."

52. J. Dalton Stevens, "Stuck in Transition With You: Variable Pathways to In(ter) Dependence for Emerging Adult Med With Mobility Impairments," in *New Narratives of Disability: Constructions, Clashes, and Controversies*, ed. Sara E. Green and Donileen R. Loseeke (Bingley, U.K.: Emerald, 2020), 169–184.

53. R. Noam Ostrander, "When Identities Collide: Masculinity, Disability, and Race," *Disability and Society* 23, no. 6 (2008): 585–597.

54. Al A. Herzog Jr., *The Social Contexts of Disability Ministry: A Primer for Pastors, Seminarians, and Lay Leaders* (Eugene, OR: Cascade Books, 2017).

55. Martina Löw, *The Sociology of Space: Materiality, Social Space, and Action* (New York: Palgrave Macmillan, 2016).

56. Titchkosky, *The Question of Access*.

57. Nicki Pombier Berger, phone interview conducted by author, September 2018.

58. Herzog, *The Social Contexts of Disability Ministry*.

59. Office of Victims of Crime, "Crimes Against People With Disabilities," 2018, https://ovc.ncjrs.gov/ncvrw2018/info_flyers/fact_sheets/2018NCVRW_VictimsWithDisabilities_508_QC.pdf.

60. Kathleen C. Basile, Matthew J. Breiding, and Sharon G. Smith, "Disability and the Risk of Sexual Violence in the United States," *American Journal of Public Health* 1–6, no. 5 (2016): 928–933.

61. For more information on hate crimes, see Mark Sherry, *Disability Hate Crimes: Does Anyone Really Hate Disabled People?* (New York: Palgrave Macmillan, 2016).

62. Al Condeluci, *The Essence of Interdependence* (Pittsburgh, PA: Lash Associates, 2009).

63. Madeline C. Burghardt, *Broken: Institutions, Families, and the Construction of Intellectual Disability* (Montreal: McGill-Queen University Press, 2018); Allison C. Carey, *On the Margins of Citizenship: Intellectual Disability and Civil Rights in Twentieth Century America* (Philadelphia: Temple University Press, 2009); David J. Rothman and Sheila M. Rothman, *The Willowbrook Wars* (New York: Harper and Row, 1984).

64. Eunjung Kim, *Curative Violence: Rehabilitating Disability, Gender, and Sexuality in Modern Korea* (Raleigh, NC: Duke University Press, 2017).

65. James I. Charlton, *Nothing About Us Without Us: Disability Oppression and Empowerment* (Berkeley: University of California Press, 2000); Nirmala Erevelles, *Disability and Difference in Global Contexts: Enabling a Transformative Body Politic* (New York: Palgrave Macmillan, 2011).

66. Clare, *Brilliant Imperfection*.

67. Snyder and Mitchell, *Cultural Locations of Disability*.

68. Ronald Berger, *Introducing Disability Studies* (Boulder, CO: Lynn Reinner, 2013).

69. George Estreich, *Fables and Futures: Biotechnology, Disability, and the Stories We Tell Ourselves* (Cambridge, MA: MIT Press, 2019); Alison Kafer, *Feminist, Queer, Crip* (Bloomington: Indiana University Press, 2013).

70. Frank Stephens, "I Am a Man With Down Syndrome and My Life Is Worth Living" speech at United Nations, Geneva, Switzerland, 2018, https://www.youtube.com/watch?v=1d8ocuPrlT8.

71. Lawrence M. Eppard, Mark R. Rank, and Heather E. Bullock, *Rugged Individualism and the Misunderstanding of American Inequality* (Lehigh, PA: Lehigh University Press, 2020).

72. Snyder and Mitchell, *Cultural Locations of Disability*.

73. Charlton, *Nothing About Us Without Us*.

74. Eduardo Bonilla-Silva, *Racism Without Racists: Color-Blind Racism and the Persistence of Racial Inequality in the United States* (Lanham, MD: Rowan & Littlefield, 2003).

24

The Obsolescence of Freedom?

Inequality, Symbolic Violence, and the Ongoing Dilemma of American Education

Dan Schubert and Elizabeth C. Lewis

Freedom has for a long time served as the ideology of inequality in the United States. Even in an era of increasing economic inequality and a heightened awareness that class, racial, and gender inequalities persist, Americans at least know that they are free. They have the freedom to get a high school diploma, the freedom to work and to work hard even as wealth and income inequalities continue to rise, the freedom to get and to change jobs, and the freedom to grow increasingly politically polarized. That inequalities persist amid all this freedom is a consequence of individual actions rather than structural barriers.—or so it seems in the land of freedom. Our point of departure in this chapter is that freedom is an ideology that has protected and perpetuated unequal social relations and served as the basis of symbolic violence that results from practices informed by this ideology.[1] In fact, symbolic violence is a consequence of these practices that ends up making the ideology of freedom all but unnecessary. And, given the increasing encroachment on individual rights that we currently see in the United States, as well as the fact that this encroachment is stratified by issues of class, race, gender, and ability, this is an increasingly important point. Once people realize that their world is natural and that their place in it is normal and a result of their own inherent abilities, they don't even entertain the thought that it should or even could be changed. The violence is thus done, and the ideology of freedom has become obsolete. We are not claiming that freedom as an ideology has disappeared or that it will. Instead, we are suggesting that its importance as a legitimizing force that protects the interests of dominant groups is waning. It is an increasingly contentless and vapid signifier, but that doesn't matter because symbolic violence is alive and well and working at least as well.[2]

Symbolic violence is a concept brought into the sociological and anthropological mainstream by French sociologist Pierre Bourdieu in the last quarter of the twentieth century. Bourdieu used it in his analyses of Algerian colonization, French educational systems, and patterns of consumption. In his analysis of the expansion and democratization of French schooling after the Second World War,

Dan Schubert and Elizabeth C. Lewis, *The Obsolescence of Freedom?* In: *On Inequality and Freedom*. Edited by: Lawrence M. Eppard and Henry A. Giroux, Oxford University Press. © Oxford University Press 2022.
DOI: 10.1093/oso/9780197583029.003.0024

for example, Bourdieu and Passeron identified the ways in which students of the lower and working classes were disproportionately *un*successful in the completion of their education, and students from the middle and upper classes were disproportionately successful in the completion of theirs.[3] Of particular relevance here is the fact that those who failed blamed their plight not on the state, as they had when they had been excluded prior to the expansion of education, but on themselves, just as those who were successful attributed that success to their own seemingly inherent abilities, as if they had somehow *inherited* those traits. Neither group looked at structural reasons for the outcomes they experienced. According to Bourdieu, students from the poor and working classes were essentially condemned to failure, and the misrecognition of this social cause and effect, as well as the tendency to then blame the self for failings built into social structures, is a form of symbolic violence.[4] It isn't that students from poor- and working-class homes were stupid or lazy, or at least any more stupid or lazy than other students, it was that they did not have the kinds of cultural and linguistic capital that were necessary for success in educational systems that credentialed the kinds of capital found in middle- and upper-class homes as *the* legitimate forms of culture and language in schools and other privileged French institutions.[5] And, as Bourdieu pointed out, schools credentialed this capital as such because it is exactly from the privileged classes that they took it in the first place. Schools took the ways that members of the privileged classes spoke, worked, and thought; in teaching them to all children, universalized them as *the* ways to speak, work, and think. In universalizing, the schools elided their class, race, gender, heteronormative, and ability origins.[6]

In this chapter we examine the ways in which symbolic violence works to maintain inequalities in the United States, focusing on K–12 schools that function largely as places where inequalities are reproduced across generations. While this is certainly a depressing thing to think about, at least for those wanting a more just and equitable society, we close on something of a hopeful note and remind the reader that Bourdieu's intent went far beyond a mere description of the ways in which inequalities are reproduced. As Grenfell has argued, he was a kind of *agent provocateur*, not describing social laws of reproduction but rather identifying sites where social and political change could occur.[7] Bourdieu believed that "scientific explanation, which gives us the means to understand and even to exonerate, is also what may allow us to make changes."[8] The scientific argument in this case is accurate, so we close this essay by turning to some of the sites where that social and political change is happening. We describe ways in which certain pedagogical approaches *are* legitimizing the cultural and linguistic practices of disadvantaged and marginalized youth, rather than imposing one way of knowing on all populations. Specifically, we present an exploration of culturally responsive teaching (CRT) in order to illustrate how school settings can be transformational spaces where agency is recognized, nurtured, and credentialed. Of course, this may be *too* hopeful of a note. That this and similar approaches are currently available to relatively small numbers of students may in fact itself be contributing to the reproduction of inequality, even if it is one that sanctions a slightly wider range of cultures. It is, after all, "through the school system that the monopoly of the legitimate violence of the state is exercised."[9] Max Weber, from whom Bourdieu drew in developing the notion of cultural capital, explained some of the consequences of this violence:

> Today, educational credentials are what proof of ancestry was in the past: a pre-condition for equality of birth, a prerequisite for access to royal endowments... The possession of an educational certificate supports its holder's claim to marriage into circles of notables . . . and, most of all, to a monopolization of the socially and economically advantageous positions.[10]

So what if a few more students avoid this symbolic violence and gain access to academic credentials? That only serves to prove that anyone can make it and that anyone who doesn't is to blame. What is ultimately needed is an expansion of CRT and similar forms of education so that singular ways of knowing that have been themselves created and lauded exactly by marginalizing and silencing other ways of being and knowing (other *native tongues*, as Anzaldúa described them) can be destroyed.[11] Future attention needs to be focused at least as much on schooling as an institution as it is on the students that pass through particular schools. What is needed is educational and symbolic revolution.[12] To better understand just why such a revolution is needed, we must first understand symbolic violence and its prevalence in contemporary societies.

Symbolic Violence

When most people think of violence, they think of physical violence. An interesting thing about that is that *physical* violence isn't in most cases an end in itself. It is designed to stamp out opposition and critique and is thus a means to a symbolic end. This is true at the micro level, as when two people fight over ownership of an object or when one (usually) man lashes out at another after being dissed, and at the macro level, as when nation-states direct violence at their own or other people, often killing them.[13] Physical violence is designed to impose a symbolic order that legitimizes economic, gender, racial, and ability orders. For the most part, however, social order in Western societies is maintained symbolically rather than through physical violence.[14] It isn't armies on the streets that maintain domestic order, but social institutions such as schools, courthouses, and the culture industry. That doesn't mean, however, that violence has disappeared. Today, those kinds of orders are established with seemingly gentler methods, but gentle in this instance doesn't mean nonviolent. A turn to Bourdieu helps us realize how violent those methods can be.

Symbolic *power* is, for Bourdieu, the power of world making and is in this sense consistent with the Foucauldian notion that power is constitutive rather than repressive. It is an imposition of ways of seeing the world and being in the world, an ability to "impose the legitimate vision of divisions, to impose the right perspective on, and view of, the social world."[15] This means that much of the recent work done in the philosophy of language misses an important sociological concern with the position of the speaker in social space. For example, anyone in a courtroom can utter "court is adjourned," but the phrase is only illocutionary when spoken by the judge. Similarly, anyone in a public school classroom can say "I pass this class," or "I graduate from this school," but a student only passes or graduates when a state-certified teacher says so. When people who are not judges or teachers say these kinds of things, they expose themselves as illegitimate speakers, as illegitimate arbiters of what is real. In part, Bourdieu's sociology is intended to identify who is "perceived as authorized" to make such illocutionary statements and to analyze how that legitimacy is maintained.[16] He wants to examine "every power which manages to impose meanings and to impose them as legitimate by concealing the power relations that are the basis of its force."[17]

If symbolic *power* is the power of world making, then symbolic *violence* is what results when this power is exerted and is misrecognized as such. We use the term "misrecognize" here out of deference to Bourdieu and Richard Nice, his translator.[18] What he is saying is that our ways of knowing are structured and that those ways of knowing align with things, or structures, that can be known. In his words, they are homologous.[19] So, we actually do accurately recognize things as they are constituted, but we misrecognize that the categories with and in which that constitution takes place are social in origin and that they serve social purposes of classification and hierarchization. Violence occurs when people don't understand that there are social origins to ways of being and ways of classifying the world, and thus they (usually) unknowingly participate in their own domination by willingly being the very subjects that have been constituted through processes of social obfuscation.[20] The violence is in the individualization and internalization of powers that are social, so that if I don't *know* something or *recognize* something or *do* something in the right way, it is my fault. If I don't know how to read a particular kind of text in school, if I don't recognize a particular kind of art on a wall in a museum as legitimate, or if I don't hold the right kind of fork in a particular restaurant, it is my fault. Knowing, recognizing, and doing are social things that are socially organized, valued, and sanctioned.

Such violence can lead those who experience it to self-censor—to drop out of school, to stay out of art museums, and to avoid interacting with those who frequent fancy restaurants—and to "feelings of demoralization and demobilization."[21] They do this of their own accord and are thus no threat to social order. They feel unworthy and (sometimes) lousy, and their absence from particular kinds of social settings seemingly makes the settings they avoid all the smarter, more beautiful, and classy, thereby lending credence to those who do frequent such establishments and who maintain that they are naturally smarter, more aesthetically aware, and higher class. These are the people who maintain that they belong because *they* deserve to belong. Goffman (emphasis added) called this a process of "*social sanitation* enjoining torn and tattered persons to keep themselves packaged up."[22] Their self-packaging sanitizes social situations for those who have the kind of cultural capital that is considered legitimate and matches the field in which they find themselves. It keeps those places "clean," a term that is defined by the absence of things that don't fit. Unpackaged others aren't around to make things messy because they seemingly don't deserve to be there in the first place. Physical violence isn't necessary to maintain social order, and neither is freedom as an ideology.

Symbolic Violence and American Education

While Bourdieu's account of symbolic violence in education focused on the expansion of French schooling after the Second World War, we use it as a tool to understand what happens—and what is not happening—in classrooms in the United States today. Our point of departure is the same as his: the evidence. In the United States, all children have access to a K–12 education or its equivalent. However, students from the poor and working classes, students of color, students with disabilities, and students from families new to the United States disproportionately do worse than their peers in school. One indicator of this performance is school dropout rates. As Bustamante pointed out, while the overall status dropout rate for students aged 16–24 in 2017 declined to 5.4%, high school dropout rates for Hispanics (6.5%) and Blacks (5.5%) were significantly higher than Whites (3.9%), and low socioeconomic students are 2.4 times more likely than middle SES families, and 10 times more likely than high SES students to drop out of school.[23] Perhaps most jarring of all the data that Bustamante presented is the fact that 36% of students with disabilities dropped out of high school in 2017. We may like to applaud ourselves for the improvements that have been made since the ADA was amended in 2008, but we have a long way to go. If, as Weber suggested in the quote provided previously, receipt of a degree is an important credential for access to jobs and colleges, as well as entry into particular social circles, we can pretty easily figure out which people will be excluded from those privileged positions.

We join the many researchers who attribute these differences at least in part to inequalities in educational funding, but we add to that explanation a focus on the symbolic violence that occurs in schools throughout the country and begin our exploration of this violence with the insight of Kozol and others that students themselves are aware of such dramatic differences in funding.[24] They visit other schools for extracurricular events, they see other schools in traditional and social media, and they talk to students from other schools. So, the divide between economic inequalities and symbolic violence is somewhat arbitrary here and is best thought of as an analytical separation. Economic violence then, like physical violence, itself signifies and is symbolic of the ways in which we value children differently, and students in poor districts know that they are getting the short end of the stick. As the saying goes, *money talks*, and they know that they are seen as less valuable than students in richer districts.[25]

The terms *education* and *school/schooling* are often used interchangeably. We want to stress that education is a lifelong process by which one "gains greater understanding . . . [of] one's world."[26] We all are, and should be, lifelong learners. Schooling, on the other hand, is a more formalized process centered on routinized procedures intended to ensure that students follow rigid schedules, meet academic standards, and adhere to strict rules for behavior and learning deemed appropriate in school settings. So, while education happens both inside and outside of schools, it is on the inside that learners are necessarily evaluated and credentialed. Perspectives on the purpose of school in relation to the U.S. educational system often include the aim of students achieving specific economic, moral, and social goals for the good of society. However, given the pluralistic nature of the country, the curricula implemented for students' attainment of such goals can at best be described as varied and at worst, as we believe it is for many students, disenfranchising. This is, in fact, evident from the infancy of the country. In 1790, George Washington proposed a national university, the purpose of which was to train students—young, White men—to be political leaders for the new republic, students who most certainly would come from the wealthiest U.S. families since only those from the upper class could afford to send their sons to institutions of higher education.[27] Even as Thomas Jefferson attempted to thwart the elitism inherent in Washington's plan, his own included 3 years of free education only for "all nonslave children . . . the most talented [of whom] were to be chosen for further education."[28] Thus, schooling in the United States has from its origins played a role in the establishment and maintenance of inequalities across social classes, races, and genders. And remember, of course, following Weber, that this was a new country in which ancestry and blood lines weren't supposed to matter.

That said, there have been periods in which schools have attempted to mitigate these effects. For example, in the early nineteenth century, Horace Mann, often referred to as the "father of public schools" in the United States, suggested that education could be the great equalizer across social classes.[29] He warned of the dangers of one social class possessing all wealth and education at the expense of others, who would be left "poor and ignorant" despite the fact that in this same time period slavery existed and Indigenous Americans were denied citizenship.[30] A more contemporary example of U.S. schools purportedly addressing social inequalities is school choice. Advocates posit that the freedom to choose the site and source of a child's education in and of itself defines equality, despite the fact that economic and cultural capital, not to mention free time, impact the ways in which parents consider academic options and make schooling decisions. Indeed, the consequences of initiatives like school choice have included the reification of class-based, hierarchical power structures, institutional racism, and re/ segregation. And if the parent didn't get their child into a better school then, well, that is their own fault.

Curricula in U.S. K–12 schools are nearly identical, regardless of geographic or social location. Inasmuch as the curricula in U.S. schools comprise specialized knowledge that originates from a particular position is a system of inequality, its seemingly apolitical presentation across these locations replicates the processes Bourdieu identified in French schools. That this is a form of symbolic violence is nowhere more obvious than in the institution of standardized testing. To evaluate the degree to which students have effectively learned standardized content, they are required to take standardized assessments. In some apolitical version of theory, *standardized* here implies objective and neutral. Thus, if all students are taught the same information, they all have the same opportunity to acquire the same content knowledge, at the same rate, and to the same degree and depth. However, differences in students' cultural backgrounds and experiences—their *cultural capital*—as well as disparities in school resources and funding render this impossible. When institutional resources and funding are adequate (or, just imagine, abundant) this provides a circumstance that all but guarantees students' academic and social success, or at least the success of those students whose cultural capital mirrors that sanctioned by schools. Inadequate school resources and funding exacerbate the rates of student failure and school inequality. As we have noted already, these equations of student success and failure are often punctuated by attributes of class, race and ethnicity, and ability. Furthermore, students whose cultural capital is reflected in the curricula they learn at school often come from families that have the economic capital to all but solidify their academic success, and thus they can go to band or soccer camps, learn to play the piano, and/or travel globally. In addition, their families have the means to afford private tutoring or classes designed to enhance knowledge and skills necessary to score well on standard-ized exams such as the SATs (Scholastic Aptitude Tests) and Graduate Record Examinations (GREs). In contrast, when a student's cultural background and experiences are *not* reflected in the curriculum they learn in schools, and hence do not mirror the capital of dominant groups, students are more likely to either fail outright or perform poorly and thus not be able to move on to univer-sity and the employment and economic and social capital that higher educa-tion promises. Symbolic violence remains a cornerstone of the U.S. education system. It always has been. Armies on some streets, and ideologies of freedom, remain present, but they are increasingly unimportant. After all, if I don't do well in school, it is my fault, my parents' fault, my community's fault, or—in a phrase that is ever so easy for folks familiar with the testing mechanisms of schools at all levels to recite—some combination of all of the above.

Culturally Responsive Pedagogy as a Means to Replace Symbolic Violence With Education

That symbolic violence has always informed the practices found in schools in the United States does not mean that it always must, and so in the fine tradition of American positivity, and because while ideology may be obsolete, it certainly is not dead, we end this chapter on a hopeful note. Against centuries of systematic, structural, and interpersonal racism, classism, patriarchy, ableism, and hetero-normativity we turn to the individuals who, often against staggering odds, are doing their best to help all students, including those who have been marginalized by traditional educational methods. We recognize the brave and often profes-sionally dangerous efforts of teachers.

Consistent with Bourdieu and Passeron's assertion that educational institutions are sites in which particular kinds of knowledge and privileged forms of culture are transmitted and sanctioned, we contend that they are ideal for pedagogical approaches that interrupt, challenge, and transform the status quo. Culturally responsive pedagogy is one such challenge. It is a means of transforming teaching and learning from passive processes that help reproduce hierarchical power structures to dynamic ones that cultivate critical conscious-ness and social action.[31]

Bourdieu and Passeron considered pedagogical action essential to how sym-bolic violence gets perpetuated in institutional settings and provides an effective framework for illustrating how culturally responsive pedagogy can provide an opportunity for transformative teaching and learning to take place in schools. To best illustrate this, we first define *pedagogical action* and its elements. Second, we explain the theory of *culturally responsive pedagogy*. Third, and finally, we describe how culturally responsive pedagogy can inform the educational and symbolic revolution called for by Bourdieu.[32]

Pedagogical action consists of teaching *content* and *context*.[33] Content includes the curricula taught in schools and the ways in which they are implemented. Content is inextricably tied to *context*, the historical and social situation in which curricula are developed. In this way, content reflects the social origins of the specialized knowledge offered by schools, but under the façade of subject-specific neutrality. As Kupfer pointed out, by accepting this seeming neutrality, the dominated "internalize the legitimacy of their exclusion."[34] Furthermore, the degree of influence that pedagogical action has on students corresponds with the degree to which their cultural capital mirrors that of their teachers and the content being taught.

Culturally responsive pedagogy includes teaching with the intentionality that students will develop critical consciousness and the ability to challenge—and attempt to eradicate—social inequities. This instructional practice relates to what is also known as culturally *relevant* pedagogy, a theoretical approach so named by Ladson-Billings, who defined it as a "pedagogy of opposition."[35] Culturally responsive pedagogy comprises three key components: the institution, including school setting and policy; the person (e.g., administration, teachers); and instruction, such as teaching methods and materials.[36] Foundational to integrating culturally responsive pedagogy into one's instruction is the belief that acquiring knowledge is a socially constructed and structured process and, as such, is influenced by individuals' cultural backgrounds and experiences.[37] When culturally responsive educators engage in reflexive work, which includes critiquing the curricula they are more often than not *required* to teach, they expose the symbolic violence maintained in their institutional settings through pedagogical practices.

The reflexive work culturally responsive teachers engage in includes taking deliberate measures to learn about the backgrounds and experiences of their students, a practice that in and of itself interrupts preservation of hierarchical power structures. This means they gain a deep understanding of their students' cultural capital. This understanding informs the approaches they take to revise—and *reenvision*—the curricula they teach. As such, their students do not learn narrow, sinisterly simplistic versions of subject area content. Instead of imparting seemingly neutral information to students as passive vessels, culturally responsive educators emphasize the teaching of perspectives that have been historically and deliberately excluded from curricula. Such perspectives often align with and center students' own experiences, specifically those gained living and learning in marginalized social spaces.

One example of culturally responsive curricula is the range of social justice–oriented materials organizations such as *Rethinking Schools* and *Teaching for*

Change provide for K–12 educators' use. In fact, these two organizations jointly fund the Zinn Education Project, which offers a framework for teaching U.S. history as emphasized by Howard Zinn in *A People's History of the United States*.[38] As described on its website, instructional resources, including lesson plans and articles, foreground the project's central focus on "the role of working people, women, people of color, and organized social movements in shaping history" and are designed for teachers to "equip students . . . with the analytical tools to make sense of and improve the world today."[39] Pedagogical approaches and materials such as those offered by the Zinn Education Project ensure that stories and histories of the dominated so frequently omitted from traditional curricula are instead centered in the content and context of what is taught.

Concurrent with teaching curricula designed to empower students through their cultural capital, culturally responsive teachers also provide students with myriad opportunities to develop the skills and knowledge they need to challenge the status quo. In part, employing culturally relevant pedagogy in this way fosters within students an awareness of how they are themselves situated in marginalized social spaces. Students recognize nothing is "by chance," or neutral, and that their positionality is in many ways reproduced in the very schools at which they learn. Thus, they also recognize their own role in this perpetuation. Engaging in learning facilitated by culturally relevant instruction means students cultivate and hone critical consciousness as well as locate the agency with which to act on and eradicate social injustices.

In sum, culturally responsive educators work on the premise that learning is a social process that is rooted in existing social conditions. It is itself a part of the process of social construction. Built on this is the aim of culturally responsive pedagogy to foster within students the recognition that social inequalities exist, and that the school itself is one of the structures by which inequalities have been reproduced over time. They can be eradicated when both teachers and students understand they can be agents of change for justice and equality. This is the transformative aim of culturally responsive pedagogy; teachers who implement culturally responsive instructional methods do so by infusing curricula with opportunities for students to develop the skills to analyze the social, political, and historical contexts in which they are situated.

The work of culturally responsive teachers is critical and can be part of a revolutionary change in the ways in which we think, teach, and learn. It is exemplary in combatting the symbolic violence that takes place in U.S. schools. We worry, however, that culturally responsive pedagogy as a practice is but a small pebble splashing in the giant lake of the symbolic violence that occurs in schools. And while schools are the primary place where this plays out, symbolic violence is found in countless other settings. In fact, symbolic violence so permeates contemporary U.S. culture that it has largely replaced the ideology of freedom as a means of maintaining and reproducing social hierarchies. As Bourdieu and Passeron have said:

> The more directly a pedagogic agency reproduces, in the arbitrary content that it inculcates, the cultural arbitrary of the group or class which delegates to it its *pedagogic authority*, the less need it has to affirm and justify its own legitimacy.[40]

Notes

1. To be more specific, we draw on the fifth and sixth definitions of ideology offered by Eagleton, to say that it "signifies ideas and beliefs which help to legitimate the interests of a ruling group," and that those ideas permeate the "material structure of society as a whole." Terry Eagleton, *Ideology: An Introduction* (London: Verso) 30. For Pierre Bourdieu (167), around whose ideas this chapter is organized: "Ideologies serve particular interests which they tend to present as universal interests, shared by . . . groups as a whole." Pierre Bourdieu, *Language and Symbolic Power*, trans. Gino Raymond and Matthew Adamson (Cambridge, MA: Harvard University Press, 1991), 167. As will be apparent, our take on Bourdieu's account differs from authors such as Swartz, who conflate ideology and symbolic power in Bourdieu's work. David Swartz, *Culture and Power: The Sociology of Pierre Bourdieu* (Chicago: University of Chicago Press, 1997) 89.
2. The vapidity of freedom in the United States has never been clearer than it has become in the era of the coronavirus. Freedom in this time amounts to the freedom not to wear a mask during a global pandemic in which at-risk populations are dying and the freedom to carry an assault rifle to display the extent to which we will go to protect that freedom. In Wuthnow's words, freedom is now little more than "moral outrage." See Robert Wuthnow, *The Left Behind*, 2nd ed. (Princeton, NJ: Princeton University Press, 2019), 110.
3. See Pierre Bourdieu and Jean-Claude Passeron, *Reproduction in Education, Society, and Culture*, trans. Richard Nice (London: Sage,1977); and Pierre Bourdieu and Jean-Claude Passeron, *The Inheritors: French Students and Their Relation to Culture*, trans. Richard Nice (Chicago: University of Chicago Press, 1979).
4. In the exact words of Bourdieu and Passeron, "for the most disadvantaged classes," school is "purely and simply a matter of *elimination*" (Bourdieu and Passeron, *Inheritors*, 2). As we show further in this chapter, in the United States these most disadvantaged classes consist disproportionately of the poor and people of color.
5. If anything, many of these students are probably *less* lazy than their more privileged counterparts. As Orenstein and others have suggested, disadvantaged students are more likely to have responsibilities in the home that require their attention, thus taking time that might otherwise be dedicated to studying and/or other pursuits recognized by schools as legitimate forms of cultural capital. Peggy Orenstein. *School*

Girls: Young Women, Self-Esteem, and the Confidence Gap (New York: Anchor). In addition, Accardo argued that the "moral burden placed on the child's shoulders" when less privileged families are either depending on him/her/them to improve the family's plight or blaming him/her/them for wanting to somehow be better than everyone else in the family can be immense. Alain Accardo, "Academic Destiny," in *The Weight of the World: Social Suffering in Contemporary Society,* ed. Pierre Bourdieu et al., trans. Priscilla Parkhurst Ferguson (Stanford, CA: Stanford University Press), 514. See also Melissa Moreland, "'You Think You're Better Than Me?' Symbolic Violence and Upward Mobility: Working-Class Students at Dickinson College Go Back Home" (BA honors thesis, Dickinson College, 2009).

6. Ability always seems to get left out of these kinds of conversations, as if "united we *stand*" and "we *look up* to our leaders and *look down* on our enemies" are not somehow rooted in ableist languages and perceptions of reality.

7. Michael Grenfell, *Pierre Bourdieu: Agent Provocateur* (London: Continuum).

8. Pierre Bourdieu, *Homo Academicus*, trans. Peter Collier (Stanford, CA: Stanford University Press, 1988), 4. Thus, while Bourdieu's work is obviously important to discussions about schools and their relationships to social stratification, this wasn't really his primary focus. He saw them as contributing to the reproduction of social inequalities, but his primary concern was not with schools per se. It was with schools as institutions of symbolic violence.

9. Pierre. Bourdieu, *Classification Struggles,* trans. Peter Collier (Cambridge, U.K.: Polity Press), 126.

10. Max Weber, "Bureaucratic Authority," In *Max Weber: Sociological Writings*, ed. Wolf Heydebrand (New York: Continuum, 1994), 105.

11. Gloria Anzaldúa, "How to Tame a Wild Tongue," in *The Routledge Critical and Cultural Theory Reader*, ed. Neil Badmington and Julia Thomas (London: Routledge, 2008).

12. Pierre Bourdieu and Loïc Wacquant. *An Invitation to Reflexive Sociology* (Chicago: University of Chicago Press., 1992), 95.

13. On the gendered component of all this violence, see James Gilligan, *Violence: Reflections on a National Epidemic* (New York: Vintage, 1997).

14. We say for the most part because we recognize that large swaths of people in the United States *do* live under conditions that resemble a police state. The United States has seen armies, or at least police forces dressed as armies and using the weaponry of armies, on *some* of its streets in recent years. While not our focus in this chapter, this is not unrelated to the issues of education, symbolic (and physical) violence, and the reproduction of inequality that we do address. And it is certainly not unrelated to the issue of freedom. Mass incarceration in the United States damages mainly poor communities and/or communities of color. Education plays its part in this. Both the school-to-prison and the school-to-college pipelines are alive and well. On the former, see Michelle Alexander, *The New Jim Crow: Mass Incarceration in the Age of Colorblindness* (New York: The New Press, 2012); Nancy Heitzeg, *The School to Prison Pipeline: Education, Discipline, and Racialized Double Standards* (Westport, CT: Praeger, 2016); and Monique Morris, *Pushout: The Criminalization of Black Girls in Schools* (New York: New Press, 2018). On the latter, see Shamus Rahman

Kahn, *Privilege: The Making of an Adolescent Elite at St. Paul's School* (Princeton, NJ: Princeton University Press, 2012); and Julie A. Edmunds et al., "Expanding the Start of the College Pipeline: Ninth-Grade Findings From an Experimental Study of the Impact of the Early College High School Model," *Journal of Research on Educational Effectiveness* 5, no. 2 (2012): 136–159, https://doi.org/10.1080/19345 747.2012.656182.

15. Bourdieu, *Classification*, 88.

16. Bourdieu, *Classification*, 89.

17. Bourdieu and Passeron, *Inheritors*, xv.

18. Bourdieu and Passeron, *Inheritors*, xxvi.

19. Bourdieu, *Language*, 214.

20. Thus, Judith Butler goes to great length to explain that she is uncomfortable saying that she *is* a lesbian. She may perform lesbian, but conversations about what she *is* are really just juridical accounts that say more about the discourse of domination than they do about the people being dominated. See Judith Butler, "Imitation and Gender Insubordination" In *The Routledge Critical and Cultural Theory Reader*, ed. Neil Badmington and Julia Thomas (London: Routledge, 2008), 366. Similarly, Foucault told us not to ask him who he is and not to ask him to remain the same: "Leave it to our police and our bureaucrats to see that our papers are in order." See Michel Foucault, *The Archaeology of Knowledge & The Discourse on Language* (New York: Vintage), 28.

21. Pierre Bourdieu and Hans Haacke, *Free Exchange* (Stanford, CA: Stanford University Press, 1995), 82.

22. Erving Goffman, "On Cooling the Mark Out," in *The Goffman Reader*, ed. Charles Lemert and Amy Branaman (Oxford, U.K.: Blackwell, 1997), 16.

23. Jaleesa Bustamante, "High School Dropout Rate," Education Data Initiative, https://educationdata.org/high-school-dropout-rate/.

24. Jonathan Kozol, *Savage Inequalities: Children in America's Schools* (New York: Harper Perennial, 1992). On the vast national inequalities in school funding, as well on the abilities and variations across states in willingness to address these differences, see Bruce D. Baker, Matthew Di Carlo, and Mark Weber, "The Adequacy and Fairness of School Finance System," Annual Report, Albert Shanker Institute, Rutgers Graduate School of Education, http://schoolfinancedata.org/wp-content/uploads/2020/02/SFID_AnnualReport_2020.pdf. In Pennsylvania, the state where Dickinson College is located, the richest 20% of school districts spent in excess of $3,700 per pupil more than the poorest 20% in 2016–2017. See Dale Mezzacappa, "Spending Gaps Are Wider, School Conditions Worse, Petitioners in School Funding Lawsuit Say," Philadelphia Public School—The Notebook, https://thenotebook.org/articles/2018/07/06/spending-gaps-are-wider-school-conditions-worse-petitioners-in-school-funding-lawsuit-say/. We are grateful to Mark Price for help identifying the sources used in this section.

25. John Ogbu offered a more contextualized understanding of this, suggesting that the long periods of subordination that some racial and ethnic groups in the United States have experienced has resulted in a general feeling of distrust among members of those groups toward social institutions, including schools. Cited in Joel Spring,

American Education, 19th ed. (New York: Routledge, 2020). Spring, *American*, 2020. For Ogbu, this serves as a basis for resistance to those institutions. John Ogbu, "Class Stratification, Racial Stratification, and Schooling," in *Class, Race, and Gender in American Education*, ed. Lois Weis (Albany: State University of New York Press, 1988). Perhaps, then, higher dropout rates among students of color should be seen as a form of resistance rather than internalized failure. This is a good point, and the relationship between symbolic violence and resistance is underdeveloped in Bourdieu's work and is worthy of continued thought. See Swartz, *Culture and Power*, 1997. Prudence Carter spoke to the ways in which academically successful students of color "straddle" cultural divides, resisting dominant cultures while adopting those parts that are deemed necessary for future success. Prudence L. Carter, *Keepin' It Real: School Success Beyond Black and White* (New York: Oxford, 2005).

26. Kevin Ryan and James M. Cooper, *Those Who Can, Teach*, 10th ed. (Boston: Houghton Mifflin, 2003), 4.

27. Spring, American Education, 9.

28. Spring, *American Education*, 9.

29. Importantly for discussions of race, Du Bois made a somewhat similar but until recently overlooked case for the importance of education for African Americans. In *The Souls of Black Folk*, he claimed that it is *only* through a particular kind of education, and for Du Bois this meant a higher education that resembles what is found in many liberal arts colleges today, that a talented 10% of African Americans can receive an education with which they can return to their communities to help others rise from the depths of American slavery to realize the full potential of African American communities. For Du Bois, who originally published this work in 1903, it was obvious that White America would not do that job because southern Whites didn't want racial equality and northern Whites thought equality had been accomplished with the abolition of slavery. And so it goes. W. E. B. Du Bois, *The Souls of Black Folk* (New York: Dover, 1994).

30. Spring, *American Education*, 31.

31. Geneva Gay, *Culturally Responsive Teaching: Theory, Research, and Practice*, 2nd ed. (New York: Teachers College Press, 2010).

32. Bourdieu and Waquant, *Invitation*, 95.

33. Bourdieu and Passeron, *Inheritors*.

34. Antonia Kupfer, "Symbolic Violence: Education as Concealed Power," in *Power and Education: Contexts of Oppression and Opportunity*, ed. Antonia Kupfer (New York: Palgrave MacMillan, 2015), 32.

35. Gloria Ladson-Billings, "But That's Just Good Teaching! The Case for Culturally Relevant Pedagogy," *Theory Into Practice* 34, no. 3 (1995): 160.

36. Heraldo V. Richards, Ayanna F. Brown, and Timothy B. Forde, "Addressing Diversity in Schools: Culturally Responsive Pedagogy," *Teaching Exceptional Children* 39, no. 3 (2007): 64–69.

37. Jacqueline Jordan Irvine, "Relevant: Beyond the Basics," *Teaching Tolerance*, no. 36 (2009), 41–44.

38. Howard Zinn, *A People's History of the United States*, reissue ed. (New York: Harper Perennial Modern Classics2015).
39. Zinn Education Project, Home page, https://www.zinnedproject.org/.
40. Bourdieu and Passeron, *Inheritors*, 29.

25

Constituting, Empowering, and Stratifying Individuals

Education as an Institution in Modern World Culture

David B. Monaghan

Are schools primarily loci of empowerment or stratification? Modern social science appears quite undecided. Education often appears to be the very essence of empowerment through the inculcation of general skills deployable across domains (as in human capital theory), the cultivation of the mind to contemplate and query the universal (the liberal arts paradigm), or the development of the capacity to critique structures of power (critical theory). However, many mainstream researchers discuss schools as first and foremost "sorting machines," and more critical voices portray them as arenas of domination, particularly for working-class and minoritized students.[1] What accounts for such fraught contradictions?

Some clarity can be achieved by realizing that no one involved in this debate actually positions themselves as antieducation. Mainstream critics, largely guided by human capital theory, take for granted that education is of great value to its recipients and to society as a whole; the issue they raise is the unequal distribution of access to it. Critical theorists dissociate the cherished ideal of *education* from its fallen earthly incarnation, *schooling*, permitting continued and even excessive devotion to the former while condemning nearly all practical manifestations thereof.[2]

In fact, though aspects of school systems frequently give rise to controversy, education itself tends to be regarded with near-universal reverence in modern societies. It is held to be good for both individuals and societies, improving not only productivity but also health, civic engagement, tolerance for diversity, and even parenting skill. The educated are by default considered more capable, responsible, persevering, open-minded, and trustworthy. Education is thus multidimensionally "good": desirable, admirable, and righteous. The breadth and depth of positive regard for education is truly astounding; perhaps only "the family" is today so universally and automatically valued.[3] Indeed, it may be that schooling is so contentious precisely because we expect so much from it.

David B. Monaghan, *Constituting, Empowering, and Stratifying Individuals* In: *On Inequality and Freedom.*
Edited by: Lawrence M. Eppard and Henry A. Giroux, Oxford University Press. © Oxford University Press 2022.
DOI: 10.1093/oso/9780197583029.003.0025

In what follows, I consider how education relates to empowerment and stratification through the analytical lens of institutional theory, which places the cultural dimensions of modern schooling front and center. Ultimately, institutionalists argue that schooling—as both liberating and stratifying—is much more deeply and centrally embedded in the moral and ontological architecture of modernity than either mainstream or critical scholars tend to appreciate.

What Is Institutional Theory?

Institutional theory, originally dubbed "the new institutionalism" or neoinstitutionalism, arose in sociology in the late 1970s as a cultural approach to the study of organizations and education.[4] The approach revolutionized organizational theory, but failed to make a comparable mark in the study of education. Initially developed by John W. Meyer, it developed into a school of contributors developing various fields of investigation. In the spectrum of social theories, institutionalism is both constructionist (rather than realist) and structuralist (rather than methodologically individualist),[5] applying a phenomenological approach to largest scales of human activity.

The centerpiece of institutional theory is, naturally, the institution. Institutions are defined as "frameworks of programs or rules establishing identities and activity scripts for such identities" that take on an automatic, rule-like quality.[6] As such they are experienced by actors as objective and external social realities. Institutions can be as simple as the handshake or as complex as a police force, human rights, or the World Bank. The world is thick with them, and they channel action through shaping expectations, interpretations, goals, and desires.

Institutional theory is thus radically culturalist. Mainstream social theory reserves the term *culture* for the idiosyncratic residuals filling interstices between social structures. But for institutionalists, culture "includes the institutional models of society itself"; it "defines and integrates the framework of society, as well as the actors that have legitimate status and the patterns of activity leading to collective goods."[7] Meanwhile "social structure" is "a collective social codification of what is going on in a given activity domain . . . a cultural depiction or account of actors, action and relationships."[8] And the central "actors" of society—states, organizations, and individuals—are not naturally existing entities but are embedded in and constituted internally through the wider cultural-institutional environment. This theory of culture puts institutional theory at odds with currently reigning Marxo-Weberian conflict models of culture (e.g., Bourdieu) and closer to Durkheim, Geertz, and Douglas.[9]

Whereas much "cultural analysis" consists of reading through the surface of hegemonic discourse to reveal its (ostensibly truer) latent structures, institutionalists take the manifest content of hegemonic ideology seriously. But in contrast to realist social theory, they bracket it as cultural and trace its structuring effects, seeking to "denaturalize features of social life that appear natural and inevitable."[10] Finally, in contrast to Marxian approaches, institutionalists do not see "myths" or "ideologies" as distortions of a knowable objective reality; instead, they view a society without constitutive myths and ideologies as an impossibility.

Modern World Culture

Institutional theorists claim that the current cultural environment is worldwide in scale. Particular models of social reality initially germinated in the West and subsequently diffused to every corner of the globe, particularly since the end of World War II. Diffusion led institutions everywhere to develop along similar lines—to become "isomorphic"—despite the absence of a coordinating world-scale political entity; the modern world is a culturally unified "polity." World culture foregrounds the individual, is legitimated around notions of progress and justice, and operates according to myths of rationalization and scientization.[11]

The origins of hegemonic world culture lie in medieval Latin Christendom. Like the modern interstate system of which it is a forerunner, medieval Europe was politically decentralized but culturally unified through the church.[12] Christianity laid the ground for the myths of modern science by projecting a "distinctively simplified and abstracted" underlying ontology, with a unitary high god who became "increasingly universalistic, abstracted, and separated from human activity" over time.[13] This generated a "radically dualistic" cosmos, with human society simultaneously embedded within but distinct from parallel physical–natural and transcendental–moral universes, both of which were also lawful and universalistic. As the high God became increasingly "non-invasive in nature and society" and nature was "purged of animist and spiritual forces," charisma and actorhood devolved largely onto individuals.[14] The modern individual was also presaged by the Christian formal equality of human souls, each of which, regardless of social station, had a direct connection to divine authority, granting it sacred status and moral standing. Finally, the medieval conception of the human soul as improvable through spiritual work bequeathed the modern person as capable of rational development.[15]

Knowledge and the Cosmos

The broad features of the Christian cosmos were "secularized" into the ontological structure of modern science. In modern world culture, the cosmos—and its natural, social, and moral domains—is unified and lawful and as such accessible to human comprehension and intervention. Elements are endlessly decomposable into component parts with lawful relations, and both elements and relations have universal reach. "Knowledge" is the mapping and articulation of universally transposable laws and principles governing abstracted entities and their relations. All particulars are to be understood as instances of general abstractions; the local is a "microcosm of the global and universal."[16]

Modern culture is thoroughly "scientized," with scientific authority expanding over an ever-expanding domain and an ever-growing number of people certified to generate and act on scientific accounts. Scientific theories and models are the legitimate frames through which the world is to be understood, problems identified, and solutions defined. Institutionalists hold that scientization has permeated thoroughly into everyday life in the modern world polity. Through the perpetual activity of science, the modern world is highly "theorized"; an avalanche of rationalized (largely causally functionalist) theories continually constructs all aspects of its operation. The abstract and universal quality of these theories facilitates the rapid diffusion of cultural models and practices.[17]

The Individual

Embedded within this lawlike universe is the individual. For institutionalists, the individual is an "institutionalized myth," highly scripted by elaborate cultural rules. People, in this perspective, do not act so much as *enact* the cultural model of individual actorhood. Because this model has expanded worldwide, the individual is increasingly isomorphic across widely varying societies and social locations.

On one hand, the individual is understood to be, and understands themself to be, a cognitively capable and autonomous rational actor capable of both grasping the lawlike character of the universe and acting on it through means–ends rationality—the "institutionalized theory of rational behavior."[18] Thus, individuals are "endowed with enormously expanded competencies and powers as protagonist" in society.[19] This aspect of the individual is elaborated through rationalized theories of action that proliferate in modern culture (e.g., rational choice theories in economics and political science). These theories often decree the individual to be the *sole entity* capable of "action," the source of all value and indeed of all social reality—which is in turn understood to be the aggregate of individual actions. Because agency is "highly standardized and enacted," the individual-as-actor is "an abstract, relatively contentless, entity in social space."[20] Thus, individuals-as-actors are constructed as formally equal, isomorphic, bounded, purposive, and rational.

The individual-as-actor is the agent for the other aspect of the institutional-ized individual: the self as a repository of legitimate interests, preferences, tastes, and rights. The self is distinctive and subjective, the carrier of authentic unique-ness that can be sought and discovered. But selves are also carriers of givenness; they are nonagentic. The tension between the authentic self and scripted rational actorhood is highly theorized in therapeutic discourse: techniques for authentic self-expression as well as those for self-development. This tension is "the central dialectic in Western history," generating conflicts between equality and achieve-ment, self and society, human experience and technical development. But both actor and self "are institutions and both are institutions of individualism."[21]

Following Durkheim, institutionalists hold modern culture to be a "cult of the individual." The individual is presumed to be ontologically primary, the foun-dational unit of human society.[22] Models of the economy, the state, culture, and even modern religious reality are elaborated around (and constitute) the indi-vidual. Individuals are linked directly to the state through citizenship and to the economy as consumers and producers legitimated to conduct exchanges. The in-dividual possesses vastly expanded, and continually expanding, rights and cap-acities, and is the only legitimate beneficiary of economic or political goods. In short, the individual is deeply *sacralized* in modern world society.

Individualism is increasingly universalist. As states have receded as primor-dial entities and sources of sacredness, the individual is increasingly legitimated directly through the world polity. Human rights ideology, "the cult of the indi-vidual for a global society,"[23] has proliferated since World War II. Accordingly, states increasingly incorporate into citizenship wave after wave of previously marginalized peoples—women, homosexuals, ethnic minorities. Incorporation occurs (in part) through social movements, which themselves enact widely dispersed actorhood and leverage institutionalized logics of human rights and inclusionary justice. The "profusion" of identities in the modern world is the po-litical legitimation of *new classes of individuals* rather than properly corporate groups.[24]

Society and the State

In institutional theory, individual states are neither autonomous nor autoch-thonous. Instead, the world polity is organized into an *interstate system*, and individual states are embedded in, penetrated by, and constituted through the broader world cultural environment. In many ways, states are constructed as individuals writ large. World culture constitutes states as well as individuals as formally equal despite vast differences in effective resources. Because world cul-ture produces legitimated models to which individual nation-states must comply, states (like individuals) tend toward isomorphism. Like individuals, states are held to be, and must present themselves to internal and external constituencies as, bounded, purposive, rational, and responsible actors. And like individuals, states enact the myth of rational actorhood as much as they can be conceived to "act."[25]

The state has distinct relationships to other legitimated entities—society, the nation, citizen, and economy. In the modern world polity, society is reconceptualized as a rational project for the realization of progress and justice. In the nineteenth century, proper societies were held to be primordial "nations" composed of an aggregation of individuals occupying a given territory to which they were linked by an origin myth. The state was the sole proper "defender of the nation," legitimated to use force within the national territory. These myths remain, but in attenuated form. Territorial boundaries of the state are coterminous with those of a national economy to which the state has an intimate moral connection: to facilitate and regulate it in the interests of collective national progress while safeguarding the rights of their individual citizen-members. Thus, far from being in conflict, the nation-state and individual are symbiotic institutions, and both expand at the expense of corporate groups (e.g., tribes, clans, extended families).[26]

Since the 1800s, the nation-state form has diffused worldwide. Not only the form but also the aims of states are derived from the cultural environment. Like the societies on whose behalf they are they are legitimated to act, states must be rationally oriented to advancing progress and justice. Progress is institutionally defined as economic development measured through standardized metrics like gross domestic product per capita, and justice reduces to formal equality among citizen-members. Models of how these goals ought to be achieved diffuse rapidly through networks of scientists and other professionals, intergovernmental and international nongovernmental organizations, and globally linked social movements.[27]

Education in the World Polity

Education has a tripartite relationship with world culture in institutional theory. First, mass education is culturally embedded in the central myths of the modern world polity. This culture accounts for why mass schooling arises, disseminates around the world, takes similar forms around the world, and attains massive and largely taken-for-granted importance. Second, now highly institutionalized, education is central to the regenerating, further disseminating, and deepening this culture. Educational systems, and the university in particular, become beacons of hegemonic scientific-universalist world culture.

Third, education remakes this culture in its own image, further underscoring and strengthening its own institutional centrality. Modern society is increasingly "schooled."

Cultural Sources of Education's Power

Celebrating the Individual

Institutionalists view mass education as a secular ritual extolling the autonomous individual as the constitutive unit of society. Worldwide practices of schooling systems pay homage to both poles of modern personhood—the rights-bearing self and the rational actor. Education ritualizes the universal equality of individuals-as-selves through universal inclusion and considerable standardization. On the other hand, schools "celebrate the reality of individual choice and responsibility" through emphasis on individual performance and achievement.[28]

Schools also become the primary locus for realizing the latent capacities of individuals. Modern individuals are institutionalized as possessing greatly expanded potential capacities requiring rational development. Cognitive abilities have come to be universally privileged as the master human asset, the key to individual autonomy and empowerment. Though variance in cognitive potential is acknowledged, individuals are universally held to be capable of, as well as entitled to, cognitive enhancement. Since modern culture makes it axiomatic that cognitive development occurs predominantly through schools, individuals are held to be universally educable, and schooling becomes a basic human right on par with housing, food, and physical security.[29]

Linking the Individual to Society and State

Schools link society as a progressive project organized by a rational state to the formally equal, autonomous, rational individuals that compose it. This occurs first through the institution of citizenship, which binds the individual to the state through rights and duties. Modern individuals have both the right and the duty to become educated. Indeed, institutionalists interpret education as "chartering" individuals to be fully incorporated actor-members of a modern society, and the extension of education has been a central means of incorporating previously excluded classes of individuals into citizenship.[30]

Schools also link individuals to society as institutional theories of socialization. Early modernity in Europe witnessed the "discovery of childhood" as a separate stage of life that was quickly legally demarcated and socially segregated. Simultaneously, Europeans elaborated various "theories of socialization," constructing individuals as morally and otherwise cultivatable through carefully controlled experiences. Childhood was established as a stage of particular malleability, and proper individual development was held to be contingent on proper childhood experiences. Across much of Europe and North America, by the late 1800s schools had been institutionally chartered to carry out the proper socialization of children as citizens of the integrating state.[31]

Myths of socialization thus sketch (state-directed) society and its individual components as analogous units, both capable of development and progress. Mass education comes into being because of the vastly different conception of society that leads states and individuals, as rationalized institutions, to expand in concert. Education is an institutionalized myth that charters the properly agentic members—citizens, producers, consumers, and selves—of the progressive, rational society led by the state. Schools initiate the individual directly into a collective that is itself seen as progressing.[32]

Thus, the modern state, held to be responsible for progress of the national collective, establishes mass education systems as part of its central mission. Mass education systems aspiring to universal participation and expanding university sectors are now obligatory for modern states, even quite poor ones.[33] The educational revolution reaches worldwide, with striking isomorphism across national school systems (including universities), practices, and curricula.

Linking the Individual and State to the Cosmos

In modern culture, persons are universally "entitled and obligated to have a direct and equal relation to the wider natural and moral cosmos."[34] Schools institutionally initiate individuals into the mysteries of the lawful cosmos and celebrate the unity and validity of scientific knowledge. This is why modern education is, worldwide, strongly generalist rather than functionally differentiated, theoretical rather than applied. Schools depict a universe explicable through general principles, for which all particulars are instances of universals.

Schools ritualize the bestowal of universal knowledge and the development of cognitive capacity required to grasp this knowledge. This is particularly true of the university, which "exists to design and assemble . . . an expanded map of a universalistic cosmos"[35] through continuously expanding human knowledge and inquiry into previously inaccessible or forbidden realms and rationalizing them. In the college-for-all era, individual persons are reconceived as universally possessing the expanded powers of understanding necessary for grasping the basic structure of the cosmos.

Universities and the scientific discourses they produce also link states as rationalized actors to the lawful cosmos. Universities produce cultural materials constructing the world as knowable and models of legitimate state action to address "problems." They generate classes of personnel authorized to generate and act on authorized scientific models who staff expanding state agencies. Finally, universities and university-educated professionals are empowered to identify and produce a proliferating set of problems requiring state management. Thus, they underscore rational state legitimacy, making it "reasonable to suppose that our world can be held together by expanded and competent persons schooled in the common objective culture of science and rationality."[36]

Schooled Realities

Once institutionalized, schools further transform taken-for-granted reality. First, schools not only celebrate the individual but also are powerfully *individualizing* institutions, further entrenching the individual's taken-for-granted primordiality and ontological primacy. Educational systems extract persons from natal corporate group membership (e.g., in families or tribes) and rewrite them as individual members of a national society. Schools then progressively differentiate these individuals according to universal criteria through standardized evaluations of cognitive performance, and results are interpreted as reflecting developing ability and character with astounding worldwide uniformity. Education thus forges a rationalized bridge linking ascribed familial location to achieved occupational career through a system of legitimated, "earned" credentials. Indeed, it is largely through compulsory education that the standardized individual life course (childhood, schooling, career, retirement) crystalized and institutionalized in the twentieth century.[37] Education provides the foundation of the "résumé" that differentiates individuals in standard ways as they progress through this standardized life course.

Second, schools become the sole legitimate credentialing agency for modern societies. Formal education is socially chartered to produce a highly standardized, stable, and legitimated system of social classifications for its products— nongraduates and graduates of various levels and specialties. Each classification is a distillation of scripted assumptions about competence and productive virtue that properly socialized members of modern cultures are bound to recognize. As such, schools are functionalist theories of personnel allocation and therefore of legitimate social stratification. Education is increasingly the sole legitimate determinant of life chances because only school-based attainment is consistent with the basic ontological and ethical architecture of modernity. A society of equal, enhanced actor-individuals in which cognitive skill is the key to progress, and happiness takes for granted that achievement in schools—temples to human knowledge that generate cognitive enhancement—is the only legitimate criteria for differentiating among individuals.[38]

Third, schools not only certify individuals as legitimate aspirants to existing positions, but also continually generate new competencies along with both the occupational positions that these imply and the legitimate certifications for entry. Schools create new professional specializations and new differentiations within professionalizing fields. Thus, if you will, schools expand and render increasingly complex a society-wide organization chart. New competencies, once generated and legitimated, must be taken into account by competent and responsible organizational actors. Formerly amateur domains become the province of schooled specialists, and new domains with their schooled practitioners become institutionalized aspects of organizations. Increasingly, then, competence becomes schooled competence.[39]

Fourth, schools are central to the reproduction and alteration of taken-for-granted collective reality within which, increasingly, all of humanity now lives. They not only transmit (legitimate) knowledge, but also distinguish between the valid and invalid knowledge-claims and frames. Mass schooling produces universal literacy, inculcates broad definitions of citizenship and human rights, and institutionalizes a shared natural reality through science and a shared logic through mathematics. Universities are chartered to generate new knowledge, impose definitive classification on knowledge, and expand this classification system itself by generating new knowledge categories. Schooled, scientized models of reality are binding on states as well as individuals. States are compelled to staff agencies with highly educated professionals, to legitimate policies using scientific models and rhetoric, and to engage with the models of appropriate governance, economic development, human rights, and civil society continually produced by universities, the scientific and professional associations that are largely their creations, and the international organizations staffed by their graduates.[40]

An Intensifying Centrality

Globally, it is taken for granted that schools educate and that education happens nearly exclusively through the schools. "Schools" are organizations inhabited by "teachers" with given credentialing, "students" arranged into classes and classifications, standardized curricula varying by grade level, and standardized accounting and evaluation practices. School systems involve a standardized series of linked organizational stages and standardized credentials for those who progress properly through the system. Schools gain resources and insulation from inspection by conforming to institutionalized expectations regarding formal structure. In the postwar period, this model diffused globally, generating strikingly isomorphic systems of education in which the world's entire population spends more and more time.[41]

Institutionalists argue that global diffusion occurred because universal education had become incorporated into the taken-for-granted definition of what a legitimate nation-state ought to do. Global diffusion of educational models continues to intensify. Today, states are assessed in terms of globally standardized educational metrics, and a poor showing can be profoundly delegitimating vis-à-vis both internal and external constituencies. Educational difficulties can be framed as national crises, as in the influential reports *A Nation at Risk* or *A Test of Leadership*. These phenomena reflect the institutionalized myth of national progress through citizen cognitive development formalized in human capital theories. These theories hold the solution for economic woes, including inequality, to be ever more education distributed ever more widely.[42]

Indeed, because modern culture holds moral as well as economic progress to be primarily realizable through individual development, schools are often by default how states attempt to solve a vast array of "social problems," whether or not they are intuitively connected to schooling.[43] In the United States alone, a partial list of what schools have been drafted to combat includes teenage pregnancy, the spread of HIV, racial prejudice, financial illiteracy, drug addiction, poverty, crime, inequality, food insecurity, ecological damage, and civic apathy. Schools, as true believers in the near-omnipotence of education, have generally enthusiastically answered these calls. Ironically, the educationalizing of social problems continually problematizes schools as they inevitably fail to solve many or most social problems routed through them. But equally ironically, the perpetual failure of schools to solve social problems has little impact on the practice of using schools as comprehensive tools for social engineering. For instance, the educationalization of antipoverty policy results in a perennial legitimacy crisis for schools serving the socially marginalized. But the solution continually proposed is more, or different, or better schools.

Finally, it seems that schools have qualitatively changed the development of human capacities in a manner that underscores schools' own importance. In the 1980s, political scientist James Flynn reported (and subsequent studies confirmed) that nonnormed population IQ scores had increased by about 15 IQ points (about a standard deviation) in each successive generation over the course of the twentieth century. This does not mean that that people today are more intelligent than their ancestors; instead, it seems the greater time spent by each successive generation in schools has progressively shifted cognitive skill in a direction compatible with what is measured in IQ tests. Most of the gains are in "fluid IQ," or "domain-general intelligence": executive functioning, working memory, spatial reasoning, and attention-shifting. Because schools prioritize these capacities, whole populations devote more time and energy to their development—and by implication, allow others to atrophy. These "high-level cognitive abilities" also turn out to be the capacities most valorized in modern culture.[44]

Conclusions

In this chapter, my framing has rested on a convenient analytic falsehood. I have discussed schooling as distinct from institutionalized models of reality, as generated from a cultural matrix that they then impact. But for institutionalists, schools are inseparable from and central to the evolving cultural matrix of modernity. Indeed, schooling is itself continually reconstructed by the deepening individualization, universalism, and scientism of world culture. Pedagogical practices become increasingly flexible, individualized, and student oriented. Disciplines emphasizing the relational and dynamic eclipse those emphasizing passive categorization. Globally, curricula increasingly validate previously excluded peoples, expand conceptions of human rights, and construct a unified humanity in which the heritage of any is the heritage of all. And calls for the use of "evidence-based" education policies have risen worldwide.[45]

Institutionalist theories strongly suggest that presently influential reproductionist and credentialist theories of educational stratification dramatically underestimate the centrality of schooling to modern culture. These theories consider schools to be passively directed by powerful external actors and hold the role of education in stratifying processes to be essentially arbitrary— resulting from series of historical accidents. But universal schooling is both extraordinarily expensive and amazingly imprecise as a mechanism of status transmission or resource hoarding. Additionally, these theories cannot account for the worldwide reach and global isomorphism of mass schooling. The institutional approach, by contrast, explains the centrality of education to legitimate allocation as rooted in deeply institutionalized models of reality in which schools are the proper means of producing rational individual member-components of rationalized, progressive societies—and as thus neither arbitrary nor easily replaceable. All evidence—such as continually staggering increases in global postsecondary enrollments or the increasingly commonsense characterization of the contemporary world as a "knowledge society"—suggests that the institutional importance of education is only increasing.[46]

Particularly relevant at the present moment is the tight cultural linkage between schools, science, and cosmopolitan universalism. As discussed above, schools are deeply tied to a rationalist and universalist individualism. Educational models are worldwide in scope and intimately bound up with science, the cosmopolitan and universalist ideology par excellence. Worldwide, schools increasingly claim to serve humanity rather than individual nation-states, advance universal human rights, and initiate students into an individualist global citizenship.[47]Education as a worldwide institution is a potent counterforce to the nationalisms and gender—and racial essentialisms presently resurgent worldwide. This is not to minimize, for instance, schools' historical complicity in scientific racism or their role in intergenerational status transmission. But it helps explain why conservatives increasingly conceive of universities as hostile territory, why academics are overwhelmingly liberal, why campuses are particularly fertile grounds for movements advancing universalist claims, and why education is strongly positively correlated with racial and sexual tolerance.[48] It also sheds light on why women and historically oppressed racialized groups make *greater* use of the education system (net of family income), and appear more dedicated to it, than do males or the racially privileged, ceteris paribus.[49]

My goal in this chapter has been to rethink how education is linked with both empowerment and stratification. Institutionalist theory helps us to appreciate how mass education and the concept of positive freedom have common roots in modern culture's foundational models of reality.

Both are informed by the institution of individual actorhood, in which formally equal individuals possessing expanded rights and capabilities are the constitutive units of society, the sources of all value, and the sole legitimate beneficiaries of social progress. Collective progress is contingent on the rational transformation of individuals, and progress consists of the expansion of individual rights and capabilities. Schools are the means through which properly developed citizen-agents are chartered to inhabit rationalized society. As near-perfect enactments of the myth of meritocracy, they are also (increasingly) the sole legitimate locus of social stratification. Worldwide, they are the hegemonic myths of both collective progress and individual allocation, as detailed in various functionalist and human capital theories. Whether these myths are "true" is largely beside the point. For as Meyer argued: "If education is a myth it is a powerful one. The effects of myths inhere, not in the fact that individuals believe them, but in the fact that they 'know' everyone else does, and thus that 'for all practical purposes' the myths are true."[50]

Notes

1. Thurston Domina, Andrew Penner, and Emily Penner, "Categorical Inequality: Schools as Sorting Machines," *Annual Review of Sociology* 43 (2017): 311–330; Ann Arnett Ferguson, *Bad Boys: Public Schools in the Making of Black Masculinity*

(Ann Arbor, MI: University of Michigan Press, 2010); Michael W. Apple, *Education and Power* (New York: Routledge, 2013).

2. Stanley Aronowitz, *Against Schooling: For an Education That Matters* (New York: Routledge, 2015); Michael Hout, "Social and Economic Returns to College Education in the United States," *Annual Review of Sociology* 38 (2012): 379–400.

3. Paul Attewell et al., *Passing the Torch: Does Higher Education for the Disadvantaged Pay Off Across the Generations?* (New York: Russell Sage Foundation, 2007); Walter W. McMahon, *Higher Learning, Greater Good: The Private and Social Benefits of Higher Education* (Baltimore, MD: Johns Hopkins University Press, 2009); David B. Monaghan, "Moral Education: The Cultural Significance of Higher Education in the Discourse of Non-Traditional Undergraduates," *American Journal of Cultural Sociology* in press (2020).

4. I concentrate on the strain of institutionalism developed by Meyer and colleagues, which has been called phenomenological institutionalism, radical neoinstitutionalism, world polity theory, and the Stanford School.

5. John W. Meyer, "Reflections on Institutional Theories of Organizations," in *The Sage Handbook of Organizational Institutionalism*, ed. Royston Greenwood et al. (New York: Sage, 2008), 790–811; Ronald Jepperson and John W. Meyer, "Multiple Levels of Analysis and the Limitations of Methodological Individualisms," *Sociological Theory* 29, no. 1 (2011): 54–73.

6. Ronald Jepperson, "Institutions, Institutional effects, and Institutionalism," in *The New Institutionalism in Organizational Analysis*, ed. Walter W. Powell and Paul J. Dimaggio (Chicago: Chicago University Press, 1991), 147.

7. John W. Meyer, John Boli, and George M. Thomas, "Ontology and Rationalization in the Western Cultural Account," in *Institutional Environments and Organizations: Structural Complexity and Individualism*, ed. W. Richard Scott and John W. Meyer (London: Sage, 1994), 17.

8. John W. Meyer, "Conclusion: Institutionalization and the Rationality of Formal Organizational Structure," in *Organizational Environments: Ritual and Rationality*, ed. John W. Meyer and W. Richard Scott (London: Sage, 1983), 263.

9. More precisely, institutionalism uses the social phenomenology of Alfred Schutz, Thomas Luckman, and Peter Berger to reimagine Weberian rationalization as a cultural process.

10. Martha Finnemore, "Norms, Culture, and World Politics: Insights From Sociology's Institutionalism," *International Organization* 50, no. 2 (1996): 329–330.

11. Meyer, "Reflections"; A. Benavot, "Institutional Approach to the Study of Education" in *International Encyclopedia of the Sociology of Education*, ed. Lawrence Saha (Oxford, UK: Elsevier, 1997), 340–345; Ronald L. Jepperson, "The Development and Application of Sociological Neoinstitutionalism," in *New Directions in Contemporary Sociological Theory*, ed. Joseph Berger and Morris Zeldich Jr. (New York: Rowman and Littlefield, 2002), 229–266; Francisco O. Ramirez, "The World Society Perspective: Concepts, Assumptions, and Strategies," *Comparative Education* 48, no. 4 (2012): 423–439.

12. John W. Meyer, "Conceptions of Christendom: Notes on the Distinctiveness of the West," in *Cross-National Research in Sociology*, ed. Melvin Kohn (New York: Sage, 1989), 395–413.
13. Meyer, Boli, and Thomas, "Ontology," 25.
14. John W. Meyer and Ronald L. Jepperson, "The 'Actors' of Modern Society: The Cultural Construction of Social Agency," *Sociological Theory* 18, no. 1 (2000): 103.
15. Meyer, "Conceptions of Christendom."
16. David John Frank and John W. Meyer, "University Expansion and the Knowledge Society," *Theory and Society* 36, no. 4 (2007): 288.
17. Gili S. Drori and John W. Meyer, "Scientization: Making a World Safe for Organizing," in *Transnational Governance: Institutional Dynamics of Regulation*, ed. Marie-Laure Djelic and Kerstin Sahlin-Andersson (Cambridge: Cambridge University Press, 2006), 31–52; David Strang and John W. Meyer, "Institutional Conditions for Diffusion," in *Institutional Environments and Organizations: Structural Complexity and Individualism*, ed. W. Richard Scott and John W. Meyer (London: Sage, 1994), 100–112.
18. Meyer, Boli, and Thomas, "Ontology," 21.
19. John W. Meyer, "World Society, Institutional Theories, and the Actor," *Annual Review of Sociology* 36 (2010): 9.
20. Meyer and Jepperson, "The 'Actors' of Modern Society," 110.
21. John W. Meyer, "The Self and the Life Course: Institutionalization and its Effects," in *Institutional Structure: Constituting State, Society and the Individual*, ed. George M. Thomas et al. (Newbury Park, CA: Sage, 1987), 244.
22. Emile Durkheim, "Individualism and the Intellectuals," in *Emile Durkheim on Morality and Society: Selected Writings*, ed. Robert Bellah (Chicago: University of Chicago Press, 1973), 43–57; David John Frank and John W. Meyer, "The Profusion of Individual Roles and Identities in the Postwar Period," *Sociological Theory* 20, no. 1 (2002): 86–105.
23. Michael A. Elliott, "Human Rights and the Triumph of the Individual in World Culture," *Cultural Sociology* 1, no. 3 (2007): 353.
24. John Boli, and Michael A. Elliott, "Façade Diversity: The Individualization of Cultural Difference," *International Sociology* 23, no. 4 (2008): 540–560; Frank and Meyer, "Profusion of Individual Roles"; David John Frank and Elizabeth H. McEneaney, "The Individualization of Society and the Liberalization of State Policies on Same-Sex Sexual Relations, 1984–1995," *Social Forces* 77, no. 3 (1999): 911–943; David John Frank, Tara Hardinge, and Kassia Wosick-Correa, "The Global Dimensions of Rape-Law Reform: A Cross-National Study of Policy Outcomes," *American Sociological Review* 74, no. 2 (2009): 272–290; David John Frank, Bayliss J. Camp, and Steven A. Boutcher, "Worldwide Trends in the Criminal Regulation of Sex, 1945 to 2005," *American Sociological Review* 75, no. 6 (2010): 867–893.
25. John W. Meyer, "The World Polity and the Authority of the Nation-State," in *Institutional Structure: Constituting State, Society and the Individual*, ed. George M. Thomas et al. (Newbury Park, CA: Sage, 1987), 109–137; John W. Meyer et al., "World Society and the Nation-State," *American Journal of Sociology* 103, no. 1 (1997): 144–181.

26. Meyer, "World Polity"; Francisco O. Ramirez and John Boli, "The Political Construction of Mass Schooling: European Origins and Worldwide Institutionalization," *Sociology of Education* 60 (1987): 2–17; George M. Thomas and John W. Meyer, "The Expansion of the State," *Annual Review of Sociology* 10, no. 1 (1984): 461–482.

27. John Boli and George M. Thomas, *Constructing World Culture: International Nongovernmental Organizations Since 1875* (Stanford, CA: Stanford University Press, 1999); John W. Meyer, "The Changing Cultural Content of the Nation-State: A World Society Perspective," in *State/Culture: State-Formation After the Cultural Turn*, ed. George Steinmetz (Ithaca, NY: Cornell University Press, 1999), 123–143; Robert Fiala and Audri Gordon Lanford, "Educational Ideology and the World Educational Revolution, 1950-1970." *Comparative Education Review* 31, no. 3 (1987): 315–332; John W. Meyer, "Globalization: Theory and Trends," *International Journal of Comparative Sociology* 48, no. 4 (2007): 261–273.

28. John Boli, Francisco O. Ramirez, and John W. Meyer, "Explaining the Origins and Expansion of Mass Education," *Comparative Education Review* 29, no. 2 (1985): 149.

29. David P. Baker, *The Schooled Society: The Educational Transformation of Global Culture* (Stanford, CA: Stanford University Press, 2014); Meyer and Jepperson, "The 'Actors' of Modern Society."

30. Ramirez and Boli, "Political Construction"; Francisco O. Ramirez and Jane Weiss, "The Political Incorporation of Women," *National Development and the World System*, ed. John W. Meyer and Michael T. Hannan (Chicago: University of Chicago Press, 1979), 238–249.

31. John Boli-Bennett and John W. Meyer, "The Ideology of Childhood and the State: Rules Distinguishing Children in National Constitutions, 1870–1970," *American Sociological Review* 43 (1978): 797–812; Boli, Ramirez, and Meyer, "Explaining the Origins"; John W. Meyer et al., "Public Education as Nation-Building in America: Enrollments and Bureaucratization in the American States, 1870–1930," *American Journal of Sociology* 85, no. 3 (1979): 591–613; Yasemin Nuhoglu Soysal and David Strang, "Construction of the First Mass Education Systems in Nineteenth-Century Europe," *Sociology of Education* 62, no. 4 (1989): 277–288.

32. John Boli and Francisco O. Ramirez, "Compulsory Schooling in the Western Cultural Context," in *Emergent Issues in Education: Comparative Perspectives*, ed. Robert F. Arnove, Phillip G. Altbach, and Gail P. Kelly (Albany, NY: SUNY Press, 1992), 25–38; Boli, Ramirez, and Meyer, "Explaining the Origins"; Ramirez and Boli, "Political Construction" .

33. Ramirez and Boli, "Political Construction"; Evan Schofer and John W. Meyer, "The Worldwide Expansion of Higher Education in the Twentieth Century," *American Sociological Review* 70, no. 6 (2005): 898–920.

34. Meyer, "Reflections," 212.

35. Frank and Meyer, "University Expansion," 296.

36. John W. Meyer et al., "Higher Education as an Institution," in *Sociology of Higher Education: Contributions and Their Contexts*, ed. Patricia J. Gumport (Baltimore, MD: Johns Hopkins University Press, 2007), 25–26.

37. Margaret Frye, "Bright Futures in Malawi's New Dawn: Educational Aspirations as Assertions of Identity," *American Journal of Sociology* 117, no. 6 (2012): 1565–1624; Meyer, "The Self and the Life Course"; Ramirez and Boli, "Political Construction."

38. David P. Baker, "Forward and Backward, Horizontal and Vertical: Transformation of Occupational Credentialing in the Schooled Society," *Research in Social Stratification and Mobility* 29, no. 1 (2011): 5–29; John W. Meyer, "The Effects of Education as an Institution," *American Journal of Sociology* 83, no. 1 (1977): 55–77; John W. Meyer and Brian Rowan, "The Structure of Educational Organizations," in *Organizational Environments: Ritual and Rationality*, ed. John W. Meyer and W. Richard Scott (London: Sage, 1983), 71–98.

39. Baker, 2009; Emily Rauscher, "Educational Expansion and Occupational Change: US Compulsory Schooling Laws and the Occupational Structure 1850–1930," *Social Forces* 93, no. 4 (2015): 1397–1422.

40. Baker, "Schooled Society"; Frank and Meyer, "University Expansion"; Meyer, "Effects of Education"; Joel Spring, *How Educational Ideologies Are Shaping Global Society: Intergovernmental Organizations, NGOs, and the Decline of the Nation-State* (New York: Routledge, 2014).

41. John W. Meyer et al., "The World Educational Revolution, 1950–1970," *Sociology of Education* 50 (1977): 242–258; Meyer and Rowan, "Structure of Educational Organizations."

42. Boli, Ramirez, and Meyer, "Explaining the Origins"; David Pierpont, *A Nation at Risk: The Imperative for Educational Reform: A Report to the Nation and the Secretary of Education* (Washington, DC: U.S. Department of Education, 1983); Claudia Dale Goldin and Lawrence F. Katz, *The Race Between Education and Technology* (Cambridge, MA: Harvard University Press, 2009); Francisco O. Ramirez, John W. Meyer, and Julia Lerch, "World Society and the Globalization of Educational Policy," in *The Handbook of Global Education Policy*, ed. Karen Mundy et al. (New York: Wiley, 2016), 43–63; Margaret Spellings, *A Test of Leadership: Charting the Future of US Higher Education* (Washington, DC: US Department of Education, 2006); Alexander W. Wiseman, "Policy Responses to PISA in Comparative Perspective," in *PISA, Power, and Policy: The Emergence of Global Educational Governance*, ed. Heinz-Dieter Meyer and Aaron Benevot (Oxford, U.K.: Symposium Books, 2013), 303–322.

43. David F. Labaree, "The Winning Ways of a Losing Strategy: Educationalizing Social Problems in the United States," *Educational Theory* 58, no. 4 (2008): 447–460.

44. Baker, "Schooled Society"; David P. Baker, "Minds, Politics, and Gods in the Schooled Society: Consequences of the Education Revolution," *Comparative Education Review* 58, no. 1 (2014): 6–23; David P. et al., "The Cognitive Impact of the Education Revolution: A Possible Cause of the Flynn Effect on Population IQ," *Intelligence* 49 (2015): 144–158; James R. Flynn, *What Is Intelligence? Beyond the Flynn Effect* (Cambridge: Cambridge University Press, 2007).

45. Patricia Bromley, John W. Meyer, and Francisco O. Ramirez, "Student-Centeredness in Social Science Textbooks, 1970–2008: A Cross-National Study," *Social Forces* 90, no. 2 (2011): 547–570; Steven Brint, *Two Cheers for Higher Education: Why American*

Universities Are Stronger Than Ever—And How to Meet the Challenges They Face (Princeton, NJ: Princeton University Press, 2019); Jay Gabler and David John Frank, "The Natural Sciences in the University: Change and Variation Over the 20th century," *Sociology of Education* 78, no. 3 (2005): 183–206; Alexander W. Wiseman, "The Uses of Evidence for Educational Policymaking: Global Contexts and International Trends," *Review of Research in Education* 34, no. 1 (2010): 1–24.

46. Baker, "Schooled Society"; Pierre Bourdieu, and Jean-Claude Passeron, *Reproduction in Education, Society and Culture* (Beverly Hills, CA: Sage, 1972); David K. Brown, *Degrees of Control: A Sociology of Educational Expansion and Occupational Credentialism* (New York: Teachers College Press, 1995); Randall Collins, *The Credential Society: An Historical Sociology of Education and Stratification* (New York: Academic Press, 1979); Schofer and Meyer, "Worldwide Expansion"; Frank and Meyer, "University Expansion"; Angel J. Calderon, *Massification of Higher Education Revisited* (Melbourne, Australia: RMIT University, 2018).

47. Patricia Bromley, "Cosmopolitanism in Civic Education: Exploring Cross-National Trends, 1970–2008," *Current Issues in Comparative Education* 12, no. 1 (2009): 33–44; John W. Meyer, Patricia Bromley, and Francisco O. Ramirez, "Human Rights in Social Science Textbooks: Cross-National Analyses, 1970–2008," *Sociology of Education* 83, no. 2 (2010): 111–134; Francisco O. Ramirez, Patricia Bromley, and Susan Garnett Russell, "The Valorization of Humanity and Diversity," *Multicultural Education Review* 1, no. 1 (2009): 29–54.

48. Amy J. Binder and Kate Wood, *Becoming Right: How Campuses Shape Young Conservatives* (Princeton, NJ: Princeton University Press, 2014); Neil Gross and Ethan Fosse, "Why Are Professors Liberal?" *Theory and Society* 41, no. 2 (2012): 127–168; Suzanne Mettler, *Degrees of Inequality: How the Politics of Higher Education Sabotaged the American Dream* (New York: Basic Books, 2014); Julianne Ohlander, Jeanne Batalova, and Judith Treas, "Explaining Educational Influences on Attitudes Toward Homosexual Relations," *Social Science Research* 34, no. 4 (2005): 781–799.

49. Claudia Buchmann and Thomas A. DiPrete, "The Growing Female Advantage in College Completion: The Role of Family Background and Academic Achievement," *American Sociological Review* 71, no. 4 (2006): 515–541; Christina Ciocca Eller and Thomas A. DiPrete, "The Paradox of Persistence: Explaining the Black-White Gap in Bachelor's Degree Completion," *American Sociological Review* 83, no. 6 (2018): 1171–1214.

50. Meyer, "Effects of Education," 75.

26

Environmental Justice

The Struggle Continues

Robert Cavazos

The fight for environmental justice (EJ) has a long history in the United States. According to the Environmental Protection Agency, EJ is "the fair treatment and meaningful involvement of all people regardless of race, color, national origin, or income with respect to the development, implementation, and enforcement of environmental laws, regulations, and policies."[1] Robert Bullard defined EJ as "all people and communities [being] entitled to equal protection of environmental and public health laws and regulation."[2] The EJ movement seeks to understand why certain groups (in particular, certain races and classes) bear more environmental risk than others.

The landmark study that paved the way for the EJ movement was *Toxic Waste and Race in the United States*, in which an African American community in Warren County, North Carolina, suffered from the dumping of toxic waste.[3] The case presented insights into environmental racism[4] experienced by African Americans in the United States.[5] Since then, numerous studies have documented that people of color and the poor are particularly vulnerable to environment impacts, exposures, and risks; in contrast, middle- to upper-class White communities are shielded from environmental hazards.[6] Bullard's classic *Dumping in Dixie* was the first study that connected environmental racism to hazardous waste.[7] He found that communities of color were being deliberately targeted. Bullard's work inspired a series of scholarly works that would examine racial and economic disparities in the distribution of environmental hazards. This would then lead to the first national EJ policy in the United States: Executive Order 12898 required agencies to adopt and practice EJ in their decision-making.[8]

People of color and of low socioeconomic status still are forced to live and work next to locally unwanted land uses (LULUs)[9] across America. These groups are routinely targeted because policies allow this injustice. Related, zoning targets communities of color, creating environmental racism.[10] Low-income communities, which are often communities of color, experience higher levels of injustice because they lack the economic power needed to fight off corporate elites. As Pellow and Park noted: "Power, privilege, and wealth are relational which often

Robert Cavazos, *Environmental Justice* In: *On Inequality and Freedom*. Edited by: Lawrence M. Eppard and Henry A. Giroux, Oxford University Press. © Oxford University Press 2022. DOI: 10.1093/oso/9780197583029.003.0026 means that one's person's riches and leisure time are derived from another's impoverishment and hard labor; one socioeconomic or racial/ethnic group's access to safe, high salary jobs and clean neighborhoods is frequently linked to another's groups relegation to dangerous, low wage occupations and environmentally contaminated communities."[11] Poor communities and communities of color lack economic resources and are not represented in the environmental policymaking process; as a result, they are prime targets for LULUs, while affluent White communities are able to avoid such outcomes. White communities are able to say, "Not in my backyard" (NIMBY) and "Place in Blacks' backyard" (PIBBY) because they have greater influence in the environmental policymaking process,[12] which scholars believe explains modern-day racism.[13] Demographics determine where the environmental hazards—which impact environment, health, and longevity—will occur. Poor minority communities experience a majority of "environmental bads,"[14] while affluent White communities are able to avoid them.[15] Research demonstrated that people of color and of low economic status continue to have their civil liberties and other freedoms taken away.

The struggle of people of color and poor people is why the EJ movement is so important. EJ "is a political response to the deterioration of the conditions of everyday life as society reinforces existing social inequalities."[16] The driving force of the EJ movement is advocacy of social justice. As societies continue to advance, social inequalities continue to widen, which is why the EJ and human rights movements are coming together to effect social change.[17] The EJ movement started in the 1980s and is at the forefront of the movement to oppose social inequality in the United States.[18] The field of EJ has documented social inequalities across race and class, which (along with environmental degradation) continue to increase.[19] These trends sparked a social movement that has infused the "discourse of public health, civil and human rights, antiracism, social justice, and ecological sustainability with tactics such as civil disobedience, public protest, and legal action to prevent the construction or expansion of unwanted and controversial facilities and developments."[20] These tactics bring attention to the discourse on social justice, equity, and rights for people of color and of low economic status.

The lack of civil liberties and the environmental degradation that people of color and of low economic status face is appalling, which heightens the need to understand why these issues still exist in the twenty-first century. Why do such people not enjoy the right "to be free from ecological destruction; to be from any form of discrimination or bias, the right to clean air, land, water, and food; the right political, economic, cultural and environmental self-determination of all peoples; and the right to a safe and healthy work environment"?[21] The EJ movement must continue to bring attention to the social injustice that people of color and of low economic status endure in order to extend to them the freedoms that a majority of Americans take for granted.

Notes

1. U.S. Environmental Protection Agency. Environmental Justice home page. https://www.epa.gov/environmentaljustice.
2. R. D. Bullard, "Environmental Justice: It's More Than Waste Facility Siting," *Social Science Quarterly* 77, no. 3 (1996): 493.
3. B. F. Chavis and C. Lee, *United Church of Christ Commission on Facial Justice, Toxic Waste and Race in the United States: A National Report on the Facial and Socio-Economic Characteristics of Communities With Hazardous Waste Sites* (New York: United Church of Christ, 1987).
4. This includes racial discrimination in environmental policymaking and enforcement of regulations and laws, deliberate targeting of communities of color in the placement of toxic waste facilities, official sanctioning of life-threatening poisons and pollutants in communities of color, and excluding people of color from leadership in the environmental movement. See R. Holifield, "Defining Environmental Justice and Environmental Racism," *Urban Geography* 22, no. 1 (2001): 78–90.
5. D. N. Pellow and R. J. Brulle, "Power, Justice, and the Environment: Toward Critical Environmental Justice Studies," in *Power, Justice, and the Environment: A Critical Appraisal of the Environmental Justice Movement*, ed. (2005), 1–19.
6. Chavis and Lee, *United Church of Christ Commission*; T. Maher, "Environmental Oppression: Who Is Targeted for Toxic Exposure?" *Journal of Black Studies* 28, no. 3 (1998): 357–367; R. W. Williams, "Environmental Injustice in America and Its Politics of Scale," *Political Geography* 18, no. 1 (1999): 49–73; R. Bullard, "Environmental Justice in the 21st Century," in *People of Color Environmental Groups. Directory* (2000), 1–21; L. W. Cole and S. R. Foster, *From the Ground Up: Environmental Racism and the Rise of the Environmental Justice Movement*, vol. 34 (New York: New York University Press, 2001); L. S. H. Park and D. N. Pellow, *The Slums of Aspen: Immigrants vs. the Environment in America's Eden*, vol. 2 (New York: New York University Press, 2013).
7. R. D. Bullard, *Dumping in Dixie: Race, Class, and Environmental Quality* (Westview Press, 1990).
8. The order directed all federal agencies to make achieving environmental justice part of their mission by identifying and addressing disproportionate adverse health or environmental effects of their programs, policies, and activities on minority populations and low-income populations. See P. Mohai, D. Pellow, and J. T. Roberts, "Environmental Justice," *Annual Review of Environment and Resources* 34 (2009): 405–430.
9. The LULUs are landfills, incinerators, sewer treatment plants, lead smelters, refineries, and other noxious facilities that are disproportionately placed in minority communities. See Bullard, "Environmental Justice in the 21st Century."
10. J. Sze, *Noxious New York* (Cambridge, MA: MIT Press, 2006).
11. Pellow and Brulle, "Power, Justice, and the Environment," 3.
12. Bullard, "Environmental Justice in the 21st Century."
13. Mohai, Pellow, and Roberts, "Environmental Justice."

14. Environmental bads are clusters of toxic industrial facilities sited in working class neighborhoods. See K. Hobson, "Environmental Justice: An Anthropocentric Social Justice Critique of How, Where and Why Environmental Goods and Bads Are Distributed," *Environmental Politics* 13, no. 2 (2004): 474–481.
15. J. Agyeman, R. D. Bullard, and B. Evans, "Exploring the Nexus: Bringing Together Sustainability, Environmental Justice and Equity," *Space and Polity* 6, no. 1 (2002): 77–90.
16. Pellow and Brulle, "Power, Justice, and the Environment," 3.
17. Mohai, Pellow, and Roberts, "Environmental Justice."
18. D. Schlosberg, "Theorising Environmental Justice: The Expanding Sphere of a Discourse," *Environmental Politics* 22, no. 1 (2013): 37–55.
19. Pellow and Brulle, "Power, Justice, and the Environment."
20. D. N. Pellow, *What Is Critical Environmental Justice?* (Polity Press, 2018), 4.
21. Mohai, Pellow, and Roberts, "Environmental Justice."

PART V
PARTING THOUGHTS

27

Social Welfare, Democratic Citizenship, and Freedom

Deondra Rose

The coronavirus pandemic has raised major questions about freedom in the United States, pushing us to consider which circumstances warrant restrictions on personal liberty. These discussions have centered on what has been described as "negative freedom"—a conceptualization of liberty that centers on the absence of barriers or external interference limiting individual agency. It is this conceptualization of freedom that has driven vocal objections to policymakers' efforts to restrict the spread of the virus by shutting down states, closing businesses, and requiring that people wear face masks. In April 2020, for example, when Michigan's governor enacted a stay-at-home order that closed schools and most businesses, critics objected to the state lockdown on the grounds that it interfered with their freedom, going so far as to stage an armed protest in the Michigan State capitol.[1]

While an emphasis on negative freedom has characterized much of the popular discourse surrounding COVID-19, the concept of "positive freedom" is at least as relevant when considering the impact that government efforts related to the pandemic have on freedom.[2] This conceptualization of freedom recognizes that having access to resources and socioeconomic stability that make it possible to engage in self-determination is also necessary for freedom. By intervening with programs providing Americans with emergency support, including direct checks for taxpayers and their dependents, expanded unemployment benefits, government-funded coronavirus testing, and student loan forbearance, the government has played a central role in addressing challenges to social welfare during the pandemic.[3] This support has been especially crucial for traditionally marginalized populations, such as racial and ethnic minorities, low-income citizens who are especially vulnerable to the challenges of economic volatility, and women who face poverty and socioeconomic insecurity at higher rates than men.[4]

The coronavirus pandemic has placed a bright light on the extent to which inequality can limit individual agency and prevent certain populations from exerting control over their own lives. For example, Black, Latinx, and Native

Deondra Rose, *Social Welfare, Democratic Citizenship, and Freedom* In: *On Inequality and Freedom.* Edited by: Lawrence M. Eppard and Henry A. Giroux, Oxford University Press. © Oxford University Press 2022. DOI: 10.1093/oso/9780197583029.003.0027

American populations are significantly more likely to be diagnosed with coronavirus and to die as a result of it.[5] This reflects a number of factors, including higher rates of susceptibility to coronavirus and a greater likelihood of suffering from particularly severe illness. It also reflects persistent inequalities in health insurance coverage, unequal access to quality healthcare, and vast income and wealth disparities that not only limit people's ability to access the resources necessary to get or stay well but also may make these populations more likely to be exposed to the virus. The pandemic has pointed to the critical role that the state plays in marshaling collective resources to promote positive freedom by combating inequality.

In what follows, I use the examples of income support policies, education policy, and policies shaping democratic participation to make the case that the government has played a central role in shaping positive freedom in the United States. In its capacity to promote social welfare and to determine who can participate in democratic governance, the state has served as an important source of liberation. While the government has played a central role in expanding positive freedom in the United States, the nature of contemporary inequality suggests that there is still work to be done to secure the promise of freedom for all Americans. As discussed here, other countries offer valuable lessons for how the United States might develop additional policies that promote freedom.

Social Welfare, Democratic Citizenship, and Freedom

To exercise true self-determination, people must possess the resources necessary to be in full control of their own destinies and—in a democracy—to take part in the democratic process. In the United States, inequality has long limited the freedom of historically marginalized groups like racial and ethnic minorities, women, and low-income individuals. The legacy of state-sanctioned oppression and inequality that emanated from institutions like slavery, the exclusion of marginalized groups from full citizenship under the Constitution, and legally sanctioned discrimination in schools, housing, and other public accommodations have made it difficult for some groups to gain access to the resources necessary to fully participate in social, economic, and political life.

For many Americans, poverty acts as a powerful barrier that limits their choices and the scope of possibilities that they can consider in the first place. Since the 1970s, economic inequality has grown precipitously as the gap between low-income Americans and those in the highest income brackets has approached a level not seen since the Great Depression.[6] In 2018 in the United States, 11.8 percent of people lived in poverty. This trend has had a particular impact on racial and ethnic minorities, women, children, and the disabled, who are disproportionately represented among those living in poverty. Economic inequality and the increasing distance between the "haves" and the "have-nots" in the United States is layered on top of long-standing racial and gender inequalities.[7] For example, women earn 80 cents for every dollar that men earn, and jobs that are typically held by men—such as chief executive officer, computer software engineer, and airline pilot—tend to be better paid than jobs that are typically held by women, like nurse, secretary, and preschool teacher.[8]

In addition to the barriers that come with socioeconomic disparity, unequal participation in the democratic process serves to limit freedom. An imperative of democratic governance is that power ultimately rests with the people. Citizens use the democratic process to select representatives to promote their interests in governing institutions and in the production of public policy. To participate in the political process, citizens must possess voting rights. Since the eighteenth century, access to voting rights in the United States have expanded to include previously excluded populations like women and racial and ethnic minorities. These expansions significantly increased the probability that their interests will be represented in the halls of power. As we will see in the following sections, the state has played a central role in promoting social welfare and extending access to democratic citizenship. In doing so, it has helped to extend the reach of freedom.

Income Support

The early development of the U.S. welfare state was rooted in the government's efforts to shield military veterans and widowed mothers and their children from poverty.[9] Prior to the American Civil War, relief for the poor was largely a private enterprise. Those who could not participate in productive labor—or who had no access to a husband, father, or other male breadwinner—looked to charities, churches, and relatives for financial support. Poorhouses constituted a limited avenue of public support on a predominantly local level.[10] In the wake of the Civil War, the government began providing pensions to war veterans and widowed mothers.[11] This system remained steady until the Great Depression of the 1930s, which ushered in the first of two significant expansions of the American welfare state.

The federal government's role in supporting social welfare expanded significantly with President Franklin D. Roosevelt's New Deal initiative. The New Deal created unprecedented support for the poor and unemployed through programs like the Social Security Act, which provided old age insurance for citizens over the age of 65 and established Aid to Families With Dependent Children (now known as Temporary Assistance to Needy Families), a financial assistance program that is most commonly associated with the term "welfare." It also created unemployment insurance for workers who were unable to find employment;

the Works Progress Administration, through which the federal government hired millions of workers to execute public works projects; and the Fair Labor Standards Act, which protected workers by establishing maximum work hours and minimum wages. The federal government played a critical role in helping the nation emerge from the economic depression of the 1930s and has since continued to play a central role in providing access to economic security that is part and parcel of freedom. During the 1960s, the second major expansion of the welfare estate occurred under President Lyndon B. Johnson's Great Society policy initiative, which created programs like Medicare and Medicaid that offered unprecedented healthcare assistance for seniors and low-income citizens and further involved the state in the welfare of its citizens.

These policies have helped to expand freedom in the United States by lifting millions of Americans out of poverty. Yet, shortcomings in policy design and discrimination in program administration have meant that their full potential for extending positive freedom has gone unrealized. For example, the 1935 Social Security Act excluded agricultural laborers and domestic service workers—a large proportion of whom were African American—from its benefits.[12] Thus, the program's policy design that overwhelmingly excluded this segment of the population reinforced existing racial disparities that contributed to high rates of Black poverty. In addition to policy designs that treat some groups differently than others, funding cuts and failing to index social programs to inflation limit their capacity to meet citizens' needs.

Discrimination in program implementation can also limit a social program's ability to promote freedom. As the front-line administrators who engage most closely with public assistance beneficiaries, government bureaucrats often make consequential decisions that shape the nature of program beneficiaries' interactions with income support programs like Temporary Assistance to Needy Families (and its predecessor, Aid to Families With Dependent Children) and can even exercise discretion over whether beneficiaries will receive any benefits at all.[13] Research has shown, for example, that Black program participants report lower levels of support from White bureaucrats and are more likely to face sanctions than their White counterparts.[14] To effectively combat poverty and to help marginalized populations attain the resources necessary for self-determination, income support programs must be fully funded and implemented in ways that ensure equitable treatment for all groups.

Education

Education is widely regarded as one of the most reliable mechanisms for addressing inequality, combating poverty, and promoting positive freedom.

Those who have higher levels of educational attainment tend to earn more money and work in jobs that provide benefits like health insurance and retirement plans. Americans with college degrees are also more likely to have access to social networks that yield valuable personal and professional opportunities. Moreover, those with more education are significantly more likely to participate in political activities like voting—which I discuss at greater length in the following section—contacting elected officials, volunteering for political causes, and contributing to political campaigns.[15] They are also more likely to be mobilized for political participation by candidates and political parties.[16] The state has used higher education programs to expand access to resources like knowledge, skills, and credentials that are associated with higher socioeconomic status and greater freedom.

The history of U.S. higher education policy offers powerful examples of state efforts to combat inequality by promoting equal opportunity. Lawmakers have used higher education programming to help expand the freedom of marginalized communities in two important ways. First, they have significantly expanded access to college degrees through need-based financial aid programs like the federal Pell Grant Program, Perkins Loans, and work study. The Servicemen's Readjustment Act of 1944 (the "GI Bill"), for example, offered a combination of benefits that helped give virtually an entire generation of White low-income men access to the middle class.[17] The program offered generous financial support for World War II veterans who wanted to pursue college degrees or vocational training, low-interest home mortgages and small business loans, and employment services. However, discrimination in program administration combined with discrimination in related areas, such as mortgage lending and college admissions, meant that non-White and women GIs were largely excluded from the GI Bill's generous benefits and the freedom they promoted. After the GI Bill, lawmakers passed the National Defense Education Act of 1958 and the Higher Education Act of 1965, which provided student financial aid on the basis of need, thereby expanding college access for groups like women, racial and ethnic minorities, and low-income people who had long struggled with financial need as a barrier precluding college attendance.[18]

Second, lawmakers have used measures like the landmark 1954 Supreme Court decision in *Brown v. Board of Education* and regulatory programs like the 1964 Civil Rights Act and Title IX of the 1972 Education Amendments to expand equal opportunity in education by preventing institutional discrimination against marginalized groups.[19] Such policies were necessary because, even after government support for education had helped to provide public K–12 education and to make college affordable, school segregation and discriminatory admissions policies at the postsecondary level prevented equal educational opportunity. For example, colleges and universities routinely used exclusionary policies and quotas to limit the number of women and racial and ethnic minorities that they would admit or to exclude them entirely. The fact that these marginalized groups only had access to a limited number of seats in higher educational institutions meant that the competition for these seats was fierce, and women and racial minority applicants knew that they generally needed to meet higher admissions standards than their White and male counterparts. Policy interventions have helped to expand access to education and the freedom that often comes with it. In *Brown v. Board of Education*, the U.S. Supreme Court ruled that state laws permitting racial segregation in public schools was unconstitutional and ordered schools to desegregate (though the ruling failed to offer more specific guidance for how this was to be achieved). The Civil Rights Act of 1964 outlawed race-based discrimination in college admissions, and Title IX of the 1972 Education Amendments prohibited sex-based discrimination in college admissions.

The history of higher education policy development demonstrates the trend by which policymakers have strategically used social policies in the form of "carrots" and "sticks" to ensure that public resources intended to expand access to equal opportunity are matched with fair treatment by institutions that, left to their own devices, cannot always be trusted to treat all groups impartially. By carrots I mean social benefits like funding for public K–12 schools, federal financial aid for college students, and direct funding to colleges and universities that supports infrastructure, programming, and research. Sticks, on the other hand, are requirements—such as regulatory programs that ensure that institutions behave in a nondiscriminatory manner so that public resources are made broadly accessible. By combining redistributive policies with government regulations, U.S. lawmakers have leveraged the power of the state to expand educational access and, thus, to promote positive freedom. Moreover, it is worth noting that state efforts to promote individual freedom through education have involved efforts to restrict the freedom of institutions to discriminate.

Voting Rights

Voting represents a central part of democratic governance. Through this basic right of citizenship, members of the polity elect representatives who will advocate for their interests in governing institutions. Lawmakers are particularly attentive to segments of the population that vote at high rates and respond to their preferences when crafting public policy. For example, senior citizens in the United States vote at high rates. Not surprisingly, lawmakers often respond to their preferences and tread carefully around programs that are targeted toward this group, such as Social Security and Medicare. As this example illustrates, voting and enjoying the right to vote represent an important part of democratic citizenship.

The United States has a history of unequal voting rights. Today, all native-born or naturalized citizens over the age of age of 18 are eligible to vote, with the exception of convicted felons in most states. During the nineteenth century, however, suffrage was limited to White males over the age of 21, and some states included additional requirements for voting, like property ownership and a certain level of tax contributions. In the wake of the Civil War, the 15th Amendment to the U.S. Constitution extended suffrage to African Americans in 1870, though noncompliance in southern states would prevent many Black citizens from exercising their right to vote until after the passage of the Voting Rights Act of 1965. The 19th Amendment to the Constitution extended suffrage to White women, and the next major expansion in voting rights occurred in 1971 when the 26th Amendment to the Constitution gave 18-year-olds the right to vote.

Since the 1970s, public policies have continued to shape voting rights. For example, state policies denying voting rights to convicted felons who have completed their prison sentences currently disenfranchise millions of Americans. This is partially due to the precipitous growth in incarceration in the United States since the 1970s, which disproportionately affects young Black men and high school dropouts. For these populations, positive freedom is limited by the inability to participate in democratic citizenship. While two states—Maine and Vermont—do not restrict the voting rights of those convicted with a felony and even allow prisoners to vote, others like Ohio, Illinois, and Nevada restore voting rights to those who have completed their prison sentences. States like Alaska, Mississippi, and Washington restore voting rights once convicted felons complete their prison terms as well as parole and probation.[20] States also invoke a variety of other policies that influence voter participation, such as voter identification laws, same-day registration, and early voting. State variation means that democratic inclusion looks different depending on where a citizen lives. Given the significance of voting to citizens' capacity to participate in the political process that ultimately shapes how they are governed, the right to vote is an imperative for positive freedom.

Learning From Others: How Other Countries Promote Positive Freedom

The charge that American government is "too big" and its corollary—that it "lags" behind other advanced democracies in providing aid to needy citizens— effectively characterize the contentious debate over the appropriate reach of state intervention into the lives of American citizens. The aforementioned income support programs, education policies, and frameworks shaping democratic participation are central to the expansion of positive freedom in the United States. Yet, many social and civic needs go unmet as social programs and policies shaping democratic participation fall short of addressing chronic inequalities.

Without a comprehensive set of social insurance programs that targets support across all age groups, and due to the federalized system of social welfare provision that gives states a large measure of discretion over how they implement social programs, the United States relies on an uneven system of income support to address poverty. Social Security has effectively shielded most elderly citizens in the United States from poverty, but children have not been as lucky. The nation's system of educational support is similarly uneven. While federal, state, and local governments support primary and secondary education, the dominant system whereby schools are funded through local property taxes results in substantial resource inequalities across districts. At the postsecondary level, although the government offers financial aid programs that help to make college more affordable, many struggle to earn postsecondary degrees in the face of high tuition costs and the burden of staggering student loan debt. In terms of democratic participation, the United States falls behind many of its peers when it comes to voter participation. While the state has played a central role in expanding access to freedom, persisting inequalities signal that many have yet to achieve true freedom. What lessons can the United States learn from other countries?

Although many members of the global community share similar material needs, such as childcare for dual-earner families, affordable healthcare, and higher education for young adults, there is striking variation in the levels at which similarly suited countries provide public support for citizens. While public benefits are primarily targeted toward the youngest and oldest citizens in the United States, the Canadian and Western European governments tend to provide public benefits across age groups.[21] In Canada, social programs include financial assistance for low-income citizens, Old Age Security for seniors, unemployment support, and publicly funded universal healthcare. In Britain and Germany, political elites have enacted broad-reaching public policies that provide a range of benefits, such as public child care, paid parental leave, and regulations making it illegal for employers to impose mandatory overtime demands on workers.[22] Nordic countries generally offer a comprehensive set of social safety net programs that include universal healthcare and public pension plans. Swedish lawmakers, for example, have created programs like universal day care and parental leave policies that offer critical support enabling women and men to remain in the labor force after having children.[23]

Western European comfort with extensive government intervention into the lives of citizens is rooted, at least in part, in the nineteenth century policy decisions made by German Chancellor Otto von Bismarck.[24] Policies like old age insurance and health insurance that were enacted during his tenure set the tone—through direct policy experience and policy diffusion throughout the region—for what subsequent political elites viewed as viable policy options. In the United States, on the other hand, widespread mistrust of government intervention and excessive government power have driven the development of a more austere welfare state. Policymakers in the United States have been slow to press for social provisions that mirror those adopted by their counterparts in Canada and Western Europe, but such programs provide a powerful model for those interested in combating inequality and expanding positive freedom.

In the United States, students have access to publicly funded primary and secondary education, but the nation lags behind many of its peers when it comes to providing additional resources to support the development of future workers and citizens through education. While the U.S. government has yet to expand publicly supported education to include universal prekindergarten programming, the Canadian provinces provide preprimary education for children under the age of 5 years old.[25] Norway also offers preprimary education for students under the age of 5, framing it as a universal right that is woven into the national education system.[26] At the level of primary and secondary education, the U.S. system of highly localized education allows states and communities to have a great deal of control over what students learn; however, this approach also results in considerable variation in the content and quality of the education that students receive. The Canadian system again offers valuable lessons for addressing this problem. At the elementary and secondary levels, Canadian education is governed primarily by the provinces and territories. There is sufficient coordination to yield equitable spending and similar curricula across the country, which helps to promote greater equality in student outcomes.

Moreover, when compared to their counterparts in the United States, Canadian teachers are better paid, receive better benefits, and are required to complete more rigorous training requirements.[27] The global community offers additional examples for how the United States can help to expand educational opportunity for its citizens. Countries like Brazil, France, Germany, Kenya, and Sweden offer free or nearly free college.[28] By providing publicly funded college in the United States, the government would significantly expand higher educational opportunity to low-income and middle-class families that have struggled to meet the increasing cost of tuition. Moreover, this struggle has been exacerbated by the fact that government aid that once offered a combination of loans and grants to help citizens meet the cost of college has become increasingly dominated by loan programs. As tuition increases, millions of people are left with staggering student loan debt.

In addition to the lessons that the global community provides for providing effective income and educational support, the United States could also learn from a number of its democratic peers when it comes to expanding voter participation.[29] Important features of the U.S. electoral system contribute to this trend. For example, the United States has weekday elections, which means that work schedules, parenting duties, and other responsibilities may make it difficult for people to make it to the polls. One solution for this dilemma is to hold elections on weekends, as other countries—including Australia, Chile, Finland, France, Germany, Japan, Mexico, New Zealand, Sweden, and Switzerland—do. Alternately, the United States could follow Israel's and South Korea's lead in making election day a national holiday.[30]

In addition to policy reforms that could enhance citizens' capacity to participate on election day, lawmakers could use comprehensive early voting programs to extend the period of time that people can cast votes while also ensuring that an inability to make it to the polls on election day does not preclude voter participation. Some U.S. states do offer early voting options, but there is considerable variation across the nation.[31] Other countries offer more comprehensive approaches. For example, Canada's system of advance polling provides for early voting in federal and provincial elections, as well as many municipal elections.[32] In addition to electoral reforms that can alter the logistics of voter participation in ways that facilitate participation in the democratic process, lawmakers can also increase voter eligibility. Felon disenfranchisement represents an important limit on electoral participation in the United States, as many states prevent those who have felony convictions from casting votes, even after they have completed prison, parole, and probationary sentences.[33] Rather than revoking voting rights, countries like Germany, Denmark, Spain, and Switzerland permit citizens to vote even when they have been convicted of a criminal offense. Moreover, some countries even permit voting among incarcerated inmates serving prison terms.[34]

Even when citizens exercise their right to vote in the United States, there are serious questions about how well the electoral system ensures that their voices will be heard and that their political interests will be represented in the halls of power. The U.S. first-past-the-post electoral system permits voters to select only one candidate for an office, and the candidate who wins a plurality of votes wins the race. This system has resulted in two-party dominance that offers fewer opportunities for minor party participation in governing institutions. The U.S. electoral system is also susceptible to gerrymandering—the practice of drawing political boundaries with the purpose of giving advantage to one group over another. This results in a system where lawmakers increasingly select their electors, rather than the other way around. The United States could reform its electoral system in ways that offer better representation. For example, it could adopt the multimember district system that some European countries use. Such a reform could provide an opportunity for minor parties to gain greater representation in governing institutions.[35] By introducing reforms that enhance democratic participation and effective representation, lawmakers can play a pivotal role in expanding freedom in the United States.

Conclusion: The State as Liberator

Freedom is more than having the right to act absent restraint or interference. It also means having access to resources necessary to engage in self-determination. For marginalized populations in the United States, the match between the nation's vaunted values and the lived experiences of its most vulnerable populations has always been imperfect. Racial and ethnic minorities, women, and low-income people, for example, have faced disproportionate challenges when it comes to achieving social inclusion, economic opportunity, and political influence. In a nation that advocates democracy and values like freedom, justice, and equal opportunity abroad, a long history of discrimination and the force of rising inequality belie those values at home.

One of the most consequential results of inequality is that marginalized populations do not enjoy the same freedom as their more privileged counterparts. We have the capacity to address this inequality by engaging in collective coordination using social policy. Indeed, some would argue that the government bears responsibility for helping to address inequality, given the role that past policies have played in shaping its contours. While the state has been complicit in perpetuating chronic inequalities and restricting the freedom of marginalized communities, the government has nevertheless been the source of important efforts to increase positive freedom. U.S. policymakers have a history of using social policies to promote the general welfare, such as programs offering income support and access to food, education, and healthcare. They have also used public policy to enhance citizens' capacity to take part in the democratic process. Through such programs, the government has played a central role in providing citizens with the resources necessary to exert autonomy over their own lives. The government has also expanded access to the democratic process in ways that have enabled previously marginalized groups to help shape the contours of political power and the dynamics of policymaking.

Assessments of the U.S. government's effectiveness in protecting freedom often center on whether it shields citizens from interference that limits their capacity to act freely. However, these assessments must also consider whether the government is facilitating access to the resources necessary for self-determination. Chronic socioeconomic and political inequalities serve as a barrier to freedom, and additional policy reforms are necessary to extend freedom to marginalized groups. As we have seen, U.S. social policies have helped to promote positive freedom. Building on these programs and drawing on lessons from other countries, policymakers can use government programs to enhance freedom, expanding the social and economic opportunity and access to the democratic process that promote it.

Notes

1. Abigail Censky, "At Michigan Capitol to Decry Stay-At-Home Order," *NPR*, May 14, 2020, https://www.npr.org/2020/05/14/855918852/heavily-armed-protesters-gather-again-at-michigans-capitol-denouncing-home-order
2. Isaiah Berlin, "Two Concepts of Liberty," in *Four Essays on Liberty* (New York: Oxford University Press, 1969), 118–172.
3. Tara Siegel Bernard and Ron Lieber, "F.A.Q. on Stimulus Checks, Unemployment and the Coronavirus Plan," *New York Times*, June 25, 2020, https://www.nytimes.com/article/coronavirus-stimulus-package-questions-answers.html.
4. Michael B. Sauter, "Faces of Poverty: What Racial, Social Groups Are More Likely to Experience It?" *USA Today*, October 10, 2018, https://www.usatoday.com/story/money/economy/2018/10/10/faces-poverty-social-racial-factors/37977173/.
5. "COVID-19 in Racial and Ethnic Minority Groups," Centers for Disease Control and Prevention, 2020, https://www.cdc.gov/coronavirus/2019-ncov/need-extra-precauti ons/racial-ethnic-minorities.html.
6. Christopher Jencks, "Does Inequality Matter?" *Daedalus* 131, no. 1 (Winter 2007), 49–65; Joseph E. Stiglitz, *The Price of Inequality: How Today's Divided Society Endangers Our Future* (New York: W. W. Norton, 2012); Lawrence R. Jacobs and Theda Skocpol, "American Democracy in an Era of Rising Inequality," in *Inequality and American Democracy: What We Know and What We Need to Learn* (New York: W. W. Norton, 2012).
7. Jessica Semega et al., "Income and Poverty in the United States: 2018," United States Census Bureau, September 10, 2019, https://www.census.gov/library/publications/2019/demo/p60-266.html#:~:text=Poverty%3A,14.8%20percent%20to%2011.8%20percent; Sauter, "Faces of Poverty."
8. Elise Gould, Jessica Schieder, and Kathleen Geier, "What Is the Gender Pay Gap and Is It Real? The Complete Guide to How Women are Paid Less Than Men and Why It Can't Be Explained Away," Economic Policy Institute October 20, 2016, https://www.epi.org/publication/what-is-the-gender-pay-gap-and-is-it-real/.
9. Theda Skocpol, *Protecting Soldiers and Mothers: The Political Origins of Social Policy in the United States* (Cambridge, MA: Harvard University Press, 1995).
10. Michael B. Katz, "Poorhouses and the Origins of the Public Old Age Home," *Health and Society* 62, no. 1 (1984), 110–140.
11. Skocpol, *Protecting Soldiers and Mothers.*
12. Ira Katznelson, *When Affirmative Action Was White: An Untold History of Racial Inequality in Twentieth-Century America* (New York: W. W. Norton, 2006).
13. Joe Soss, "Lessons of Welfare: Policy Design, Political Learning, and Political Action." *American Political Science Review* 93, no. 2 (1999): 363–380.

14. Lael R. Keiser, Peter R. Mueser, and Seung-Whan Choi, "Race Bureaucratic Discretion, and the Implementation of Welfare Reform," *American Journal of Political Science* 48, no. 2 (2004), 314–327.

15. Nancy Burns, Kay Lehman Schlozman, and Sidney Verba, *The Private Roots of Public Action: Gender, Equality, and Political Participation* (Cambridge, MA: Harvard University Press, 2001); Suzanne Mettler, *Soldiers to Citizens: The G.I. Bill and the Making of the Greatest Generation* (New York: Oxford University Press, 2005); Deondra Rose, *Citizens by Degree: Higher Education Policy and the Changing Gender Dynamics of American Citizenship* (New York: Oxford University Press, 2018).

16. Steven J. Rosenstone and John Mark Hansen, *Mobilization, Participation, and Democracy in America* (New York: Macmillan, 1993).

17. Katznelson, *When Affirmative Action Was White*; Mettler, *Soldiers to Citizens.*

18. Rose, *Citizens by Degree.*

19. Rose, *Citizens by Degree.*

20. Jean Chung, "Felony Disenfranchisement: A Primer," Sentencing Project, 2019, https://www.sentencingproject.org/publications/felony-disenfranchisement-a-primer/.

21. Jacob S. Hacker, "The Historical Logic of National Health Insurance: Structure and Sequence in the Development of British, Canadian, and U.S. Medical Policy," *Studies in American Political Development* 12 (1998), 82; Anthony King, "Ideas, Institutions and the Policies of Government: A Comparative Analysis: Parts I and II," *British Journal of Political Science* 3 (1973) 291–313;; Janet C. Gornick and Marcia K. Meyers, *Families that Work: Policies for Reconciling Parenthood and Employment* (New York: Russell Sage Foundation, 2003), 39–42; Suzanne Mettler, "The Transformed Welfare State," in *The Transformation of American Politics: Activist Government and the Rise of Conservatism,* ed. Theda Skocpol and Paul Pierson (Princeton, NJ: Princeton University Press, 2007). Theda Skocpol, "Targeting Within Universalism: Politically Viable Policies to Combat Poverty in the United States," in *The Urban Underclass,* ed. Christopher Jencks and Paul E. Peterson (Washington, D.C.: Brookings Institution, 1991), 418–419, 425–427. It is important to note that this support is skewed in favor of the last, as public support for senior citizens comprises the preponderance of social provision in the United States. While Social Security's retirement funds are available to all citizens over the age of 65 who have satisfied criteria related to personal (or spousal) labor force participation, public support for children is generally granted on the basis of means testing.

22. Gornick and Meyers, Families That Work.

23. Kimberly J. Morgan. *Working Mothers and the Welfare State: Religion and the Politics of Work-Family Policies in Western Europe and the United States* (Stanford, CA: Stanford University Press, 2006), 1–7.

24. King, "Ideas, Institutions" ; Margaret Weir, Ann Shola Orloff, and Theda Skocpol, "Introduction: Understanding American Social Politics," in *The Politics of Social Policy in the United States,* ed. Margaret Weir, Ann Shola Orloff, and Theda Skocpol (Princeton, NJ: Princeton University Press, 1988), 10–13.

25. Martha Friendly et al., *Early Childhood Education and Care in Canada, 2016* (Childcare Resource and Research Unit, April 2018), https://www.childcarecanada.org/sites/default/files/ECEC-in-Canada-2016.pdf.

26. Kristin Holte Haug and Jan Storø, "Kindergarten—A Universal Right for Children in Norway," *International Journal of Child Care and Education Policy* 7 (2013): 1–13.

27. "Education Policy Outlook: Canada," Organization for Economic Cooperation and Development, 2015, http://www.oecd.org/education/EDUCATION%20POLICY%20OUTLOOK%20CANADA.pdf.

28. "Countries With Free College 2020," World Population Review, 2020, https://worldpopulationreview.com/country-rankings/countries-with-free-college.

29. Drew DeSilver, "U.S. Trails Most Developed Countries in Voter Turnout," Pew Research Center, May 21, 2018, https://www.pewresearch.org/fact-tank/2018/05/21/u-s-voter-turnout-trails-most-developed-countries/.

30. Drew DeSilver, "Weekday Elections Set the U.S. Apart From Many Other Advanced Democracies," Pew Research Center, November 6, 2018, https://www.pewresearch.org/fact-tank/2018/11/06/weekday-elections-set-the-u-s-apart-from-many-other-advanced-democracies/.

31. "State Laws Governing Early Voting," National Conference of State Legislatures, August 2, 2019, https://www.ncsl.org/research/elections-and-campaigns/early-voting-in-state-elections.aspx.

32. John Paul Tasker, "Roughly 4.7M Ballots Cast in Advance Polls, Elections Canada Says," *CBC News*, October 15, 2019, https://www.cbc.ca/news/politics/advance-poll-turnout-surges-1.5321915.

33. Chung, "Felony Disenfranchisement: A Primer."

34. James A. Gardner and Guy-Uriel Charles, *Election Law in the American Political System* (New York: Wolters Kluwer, 2018), 177.

35. "Electoral Systems Around the World," Project Fair Vote, 2020, https://www.fairvote.org/research_electoralsystems_world.

28

On Government, Agency, and the Violence of Inaction*

Lawrence M. Eppard with Noam Chomsky

Freedom from the government telling you what you can and cannot do is of course an important aspect of liberty. But an equally important aspect is the freedom to live the life that you wish to lead—and government is vital in helping to enable this aspect of freedom.

True freedom requires agency, or the ability to freely choose the life that you want to lead and to be able to think and act autonomously in pursuit of that desired life. To do this, one needs to (a) have their abilities developed and (b) have access to important resources and opportunity pathways. Government is crucial to ensuring that the conditions exist that allow all Americans to possess true agency.

Good Government Works

Americans have every right to criticize their government for failing to do more to enable true freedom for all citizens. But the solution is not the absence of government, but government administered in the most democratic, equitable, and effective fashion possible. And there is good cross-national evidence to suggest that, when well designed and effectively implemented, government social policies help to *enable* freedom for millions. As Richard Wilkinson argued: "If Americans went to countries like Sweden and Norway they would feel more rather than less free."[1] This is hard to disagree with, given the lower levels of poverty and income inequality in each country compared to the United States.

---

* This chapter is adapted from a 2020 article from the *Journal of Working-Class Studies* with the permission of the journal's editors. For the original article, please visit their website: https://workingclassstudiesjournal.files.wordpress.com/2020/07/jwcs-vol-5-issue-1-june-2020-eppard-chomsky.pdf

Lawrence M. Eppard with Noam Chomsky, *On Government, Agency, and the Violence of Inaction* In: *On Inequality and Freedom.* Edited by: Lawrence M. Eppard and Henry A. Giroux, Oxford University Press. © Oxford University Press 2022. DOI: 10.1093/oso/9780197583029.003.0028

If you refer to Chapter 1, these data make it clear that the countries that are most committed to equality are able to achieve significant reductions in income inequality and poverty, while less-committed countries fail to do so.[2]

Despite lagging behind most Organization for Economic Cooperation and Development countries on a number of measures of government effectiveness, there is much about American government that works well. Take Social Security as an example. In a recent analysis, it was estimated that Social Security helped bring the elderly poverty rate down from close to 40 percent to below 10 percent.[3] This program is successful in helping to alleviate the burdens placed on the elderly by forces beyond their control, allowing them to lead longer, healthier, and happier lives.[4] There are many groups in the United States—such as children, as but one important example—who could have their freedoms expanded in a similar fashion by better social policies.

If government social policies, when properly designed and funded, actually work quite well,[5] why isn't the United States doing more to reduce economic insecurity? Why are measures of poverty and economic inequality in the United States at the top end among wealthy countries? Why isn't the U.S. government attempting to enable true freedom for all its citizens?

Political and Cultural Dysfunctions

A variety of political and cultural factors are important to consider when determining the source of the American welfare state's more minimalist approach compared to many other wealthy countries. A few important factors that we want to focus on are dysfunctional features of the American political system, as well as widespread ideologies of racism and individualism. As Alberto Alesina and his colleagues have demonstrated:

> Americans redistribute less than Europeans because (1) the majority believes that redistribution favors racial minorities, (2) Americans believe that they live in an open and fair society and that if someone is poor it is their own fault, and (3) the political system is geared towards preventing redistribution.[6]

There are a number of features of the American political system that help to ensure that Americans' social democratic tendencies are underrepresented in social policy. These include the influence of money in American politics, the structure of the electoral system, aspects of the political system that encourage plurality rule,[7] low voter turnout among the poor and working class, a low level of unionization, weak leftist politics, numerous checks and balances, the decentralized nature of American government, and the disproportionately low percentage of elected government officials who are female, non-White, and/or marginalized in some other manner.

Beyond political dysfunctions that limit the American welfare state, there are important cultural factors as well, including racism and individualism. Much like a doctor cannot prescribe the proper treatment plan without knowing what afflicts their patient, Americans cannot solve social problems if they cannot first properly identify their causes. Widespread ideologies of racism and individualism cause Americans to misrecognize the causes of many social problems. As a result, such ideologies help to ensure that politicians in the United States do not face the same degree of pressure as their European counterparts to develop and/ or maintain robust and structurally oriented social policies. In the absence of racism and individualism, American politicians might face such pressure, given the many social democratic tendencies of the general population.

Racism in America is a major influence on Americans' individualism and skepticism of government. Widespread racist notions of poverty as a "Black problem," combined with racist assumptions about the supposed immorality and laziness of African Americans, reinforce individualism and government skepticism among White Americans.

Welfare is a prime example. Welfare has been demonized, especially by Ronald Reagan with his tales of Black welfare queens supposedly driving around in their limousines to steal Americans' hard-earned money at the welfare office. Now most of the poor are not Black and most Black Americans are not poor, and neither a majority of the poor nor African Americans are immoral or lazy. But if these racist and individualistic (and sexist, in the case of welfare queens) notions are activated, regardless of their veracity, support for social policies can be effectively undermined.

Perhaps the classic statement on this phenomenon was the book *Why Americans Hate Welfare* by Martin Gilens. If you take a look at Table 28.1, based on his work, you will see how influential racism is in Americans' thinking about poverty and welfare. When Americans think most welfare recipients are White (a supposedly more "moral," "hard-working," and "deserving" group in their minds), they are much less critical of recipients' morality, work ethic, and deservingness. When they believe most recipients are Black (supposedly more "immoral," "lazy," and "undeserving"), however, they are much more critical.

A second cultural factor limiting social policies, American individualism, has also been well documented. In a recent cross-national survey of 44 countries, for instance, the United States was much more individualistic than most other countries concerning the role that forces outside of one's control play in determining their success in life.[8] And a number of studies suggested that the more one

Table 28.1 Race and Americans' Perceptions of Welfare Recipients

	Think Most Welfare Recipients Are Black	Think Most Welfare Recipients Are White
In your opinion, what is more to blame when people are on welfare?		
Lack of effort on their own part	63%	40%
Circumstances beyond their control	26%	50%
Do most people on welfare want to work?		
Yes	31%	55%
No	69%	45%
Do most people on welfare really need it?		
Yes	36%	50%
No	64%	50%

Source: Martin Gilens, *Why Americans Hate Welfare: Race, Media, and the Politics of Antipoverty Policy* (Chicago, IL: The University of Chicago Press, 1999), p. 140. Reprinted with permission of The University of Chicago Press.

supports individualistic beliefs, the less likely they are to support many government programs.[9]

We recently conducted a survey with 353 American college students enrolled in introductory sociology courses at universities in Pennsylvania, Virginia, and West Virginia.[10] Table 28.2 demonstrates the manner in which racial prejudice and individualism are associated with government support among our sample. Our prejudice and individualism variables were strongly correlated with each other, as well as strongly correlated with our government support variable. We also ran a regression model with prejudice and individualism as our independent variables—along with race/ethnicity, social class, gender, religiosity, and political orientation—and government support as our dependent variable. Prejudice, individualism, and Republican political orientation were each associated with less government support, while none of the other variables were statistically significant.

As our survey and a number of other studies demonstrated, racism and individualism both play major roles in Americans' "skeptical altruism"[11] toward disadvantaged groups. What is meant by this term is that many Americans are indeed bothered by many aspects of inequality, are morally committed to helping the poor, and have many social democratic tendencies. But they are also

Table 28.2 Association Between Racial Prejudice/
Individualism and Government Support

Government/Social Policy Belief	% Agreement
SNAP should be expanded	
High-prejudice individuals	27%
Low-prejudice individuals	80%
Strongly individualistic individuals	35%
Weakly individualistic individuals	89%
Government assistance has a mostly positive impact on society	
High-prejudice individuals	57%
Low-prejudice individuals	81%
Strongly individualistic individuals	62%
Weakly individualistic individuals	89%
Government is responsible for reducing income inequality	
High-prejudice individuals	25%
Low-prejudice individuals	62%
Strongly individualistic individuals	26%
Weakly individualistic individuals	83%
Adults need to pass drug tests to receive food stamps/ SNAP for themselves and their families	
High-prejudice individuals	90%
Low-prejudice individuals	45%

Continued

Table 28.2 *Continued*

Government/Social Policy Belief	% Agreement
Strongly individualistic individuals	82%
Weakly individualistic individuals	28%
Adults need to work in the paid workforce to receive food stamps/SNAP for themselves and their families	
High-prejudice individuals	81%
Low-prejudice individuals	42%
Strongly individualistic individuals	73%
Weakly individualistic individuals	39%
High-income Americans should pay higher taxes than middle- and low-income Americans	
High-prejudice individuals	51%
Low-prejudice individuals	88%
Strongly individualistic individuals	50%
Weakly individualistic individuals	100%
United States should adopt a government single-payer healthcare system	
High-prejudice individuals	29%
Low-prejudice individuals	77%
Strongly individualistic individuals	33%
Weakly individualistic individuals	100%

Note: All group differences reported here are statistically significant below .05.

Source: Lawrence M. Eppard, Troy Nazarenus, Lucas Everidge, and Debbie Matesun, "Effects of Anti-Black Prejudice and Individualism on Government Support Among U.S. College Students," *The New York Sociologist* 8 (August 2020): 19.

suspicious of the morality, work ethic, and deservingness of many recipients of government assistance (especially Black recipients), believe Americans possess a high degree of agency regardless of background, are skeptical of government, and prefer individualistically—rather than structurally oriented—social policies. Because of this, they are overly concerned with whether a social program rewards a truly deserving recipient who is worthy of aid (a person who works hard, makes smart choices, has responsible fertility, etc.), or whether it rewards an undeserving recipient who does not merit aid.

Support for or opposition to a given social policy often hinges not on whether Americans agree with the structuralist and/or social democratic principles that inform the particular policy, but whether policy opponents can successfully frame the policy in racist and/or individualistic terms. In the absence of the activation of prejudice and individualism in political and popular discourse, a policy that aligns with Americans' social democratic tendencies might expect support. But if a program can be sufficiently linked to racist and/or individualistic fears, it can be defeated.

As an example, a recent Kaiser Family Foundation survey revealed that a slight majority of Americans supported a national government healthcare plan that covered all Americans. When the question was worded differently, however, responses changed. While 63 percent expressed a positive reaction to "Medicare-for-All," only 46 percent reacted positively to "socialized medicine." Likewise, 71 percent of respondents supported a Medicare-for-All plan that would guarantee health insurance coverage as a right for all Americans, but only 37 percent if it led to an increase in taxes.[12] These changes in support seemed to be driven less by opposition to government-run healthcare generally, but whether such a program violated critical beliefs concerning government and individualism.

The same type of relationship exists between race and social policies: When a program is framed in a manner that conjures images of African Americans, the policy in question typically receives less support than it would otherwise. Fifty-eight percent of Americans believe government spends too much on "welfare," compared to 15 percent who say too little. But only 16 percent believe government spends too much on "assistance to the poor," compared to 56 percent who say too little.[13] The wording of these questions makes a big difference in whether racist and individualistic fears are triggered in respondents' minds. When such fears are not activated, their social democratic preferences are more likely to inform their answers. As Ashley Jardina noted, antipoverty policies can be made popular by "avoiding racialized terms, like welfare. . . . Otherwise popular policies may be dragged down." She explained further:

> Despite the fact that white Americans benefit more from government assistance than people of color, means-tested aid is primarily associated with black people

and other people of color—particularly when the term welfare is used. For many Americans, the word welfare conjures up a host of disparaging stereotypes so strongly linked to stigmatized beliefs about racial groups that—along with crime—it is arguably one of the most racialized terms in the country....

... Part of why Social Security is so relatively popular compared to welfare is because of how both policies are racialized. Social Security... has been framed as a policy that is both universal—that is, it benefits all groups—and as one that has been contrasted with welfare as an earned reward for hard work (stereotypes associated with white people), rather than a handout for the lazy and dependent (stereotypes associated with black people).[14]

The Violence of Inaction

In the sport of American football, there is a drill that many coaches use in practice called a "gauntlet drill." The objective of the drill is to help players become better at staying on their feet and maintaining possession of the football amid the chaos and physical contact of the game. Figure 28.1 demonstrates how this drill works. One player starts with the football and must run between two rows of players and make it to the other side. They must accomplish this without falling down or losing the ball. As the ball carrier passes through this gauntlet, the opposing players attempt to swipe the ball away and/or knock the ball carrier down.

The American stratification system works in a similar fashion. We are each born with different (either more or less challenging) gauntlet configurations based on our starting social position (our race/class/gender, family, neighborhood and community, region, country, historical period, etc.). In Figure 28.1, Player B faces far more opposing players than Player A, not unlike the likelihood that somebody born at the bottom of the socioeconomic hierarchy will face more obstacles to success than somebody born at the top. Does this guarantee that Player B will fail and Player A will succeed? No, but the risk of failure is much higher for Player B, and neither player is truly responsible for the different configurations that they face. Furthermore, if this is truly a metaphor for society, the *abilities* of these players to confront these challenges would likely be unequal and heavily influenced by forces beyond their control.

Neither the challenges (both in number and severity) they face nor the abilities and resources they possess to overcome them are primarily the result of choices they have made for themselves. As Raoul Martinez argued:

We do not choose to exist. We do not choose the environment we will grow up in. We do not choose to be born Hindu, Christian or Muslim, into a war-zone or peaceful middle-class suburb, into starvation or luxury. We do not choose our

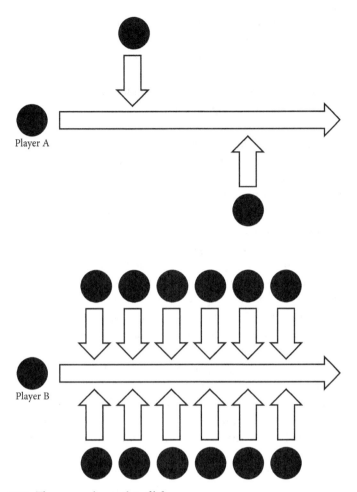

Figure 28.1 The unequal gauntlet of life.

parents, nor whether they'll be happy or miserable, knowledgeable or ignorant, healthy or sickly, attentive or neglectful. The knowledge we possess, the beliefs we hold, the tastes we develop, the traditions we adopt, the opportunities we enjoy, the work we do—the very lives we lead.... This is the lottery of birth."[15]

These unequal gauntlets that we face are a form of "structural violence," or the

avoidable limitations society places on groups of people that constrain them from achieving the quality of life that would have otherwise been possible.... Because of its embedding within social structures, people tend to overlook them as ordinary difficulties that they encounter in the course of life. . . . Unlike the more visible forms of violence where one person perpetrates physical harm on another, structural violence occurs through economically, politically, or culturally driven processes working together to limit subjects from achieving full quality of life. . . . Structural violence directly illustrates a power system wherein social structures or institutions cause harm to people in a way that results in maldevelopment or deprivation.[16]

Government policies can help to mitigate or even eliminate structural violence. Unfortunately, the dysfunctional U.S. political system hinders the development of more generous and effective social policies, making government inaction itself a form of structural violence.

Ideologies infused with racism, individualism, and government skepticism can cause, exacerbate, and/or help to perpetuate structural violence, constituting a second form of violence: symbolic violence. Symbolic violence refers to "power which manages to impose meanings and to impose them as legitimate by concealing the power relations which are the basis of its force."[17] When dominant culture ignores or misrecognizes structural violence, it reinforces it and helps to perpetuate it. As Johan Galtung noted: "The object of personal violence perceives the violence, usually, and may complain—the object of structural violence may be persuaded not to perceive this at all."[18]

Luckily, Americans have many social democratic tendencies. To allow them their full impact, we need to continue to fight against ideologies of racism and individualism. We need to build on the momentum of Black Lives Matter, #MeToo, Occupy, the activism of countless young people and teachers, and the efforts of many others, all of which have helped Americans develop a more structural and critical vocabulary of inequality. We need to highlight the importance and effectiveness of good government. We need to give power to all Americans, regardless of race, social class, gender, sexual orientation, religion, or any other social categorization unnecessarily undermining our solidarity. And we desperately need to strengthen our democracy—get money out of politics, reform our political system, get out the vote, bolster the power of unions, and just generally make our elected representatives more responsive to the preferences and interests of the majority of the population.

These are all tall tasks, and yet it seems that a generation of young people has emerged that is not only committed to achieving these things, but also has already realized many successes. Let us commit ourselves to ensuring that they achieve many more.

Notes

1. Lawrence M. Eppard, Arlie Hochschild, and Richard Wilkinson, "'A Little Crow in the Tree': Growing Inequality and White Working-Class Politics in the U.S.," *Journal of Working-Class Studies*, 3, no. 1 (2018): 143. Wilkinson similarly goes on to state that: "I suspect a great many people think about freedom as if it is about freedom from government regulation. But things like health inequalities deprive large swathes of the population of more than ten percent of life expectancy. The effects of poverty and inequality are forms of structural violence and limitations on true freedom. These things affect the quality of life very deeply."

2. This is a result of both taxation (which brings income groups closer together) and social spending (which increases household resources, particularly at the bottom of the income hierarchy).

3. Kathleen Romig, "Social Security Lifts More Americans Above Poverty than Any Other Program," Center on Budget and Policy Priorities, February 20, 2020, https://www.cbpp.org/research/social-security/social-security-lifts-more-americans-above-poverty-than-any-other-program.

4. Social Security is popular and effective, and there is no reason why it should not be sustainable. The problem is not whether we have solutions, but whether our politicians are up to the task of implementing them. One very easy change, for instance, is simply removing the payroll cap on taxable earnings. For more, see https://www.pbs.org/newshour/economy/what-impact-would-eliminating.

5. As David Brady's empirical work demonstrates: "Across all varieties and types of welfare states, there is a strong linear negative relationship between welfare generosity and poverty. The welfare state's influence is unmatched by any other cause. The effects of welfare generosity are always significantly negative regardless of what one controls for. . . . The generosity of the welfare state is the dominant cause of how much poverty exists in affluent Western democracies." See David Brady, *Rich Democracies, Poor People: How Politics Explain Poverty* (New York: Oxford University Press, 2009), p. 166.

6. A. Alesina, E. Glaeser, and B. Sacerdote, "Why Doesn't the U.S. Have a European-Style Welfare State?" discussion paper, Harvard Institute of Economic Research, 1933, 2001, 39.

7. In 2016, for instance, Republicans gained control of the presidency, the House, and the Senate, despite failing to win a majority of the votes for any of the three. As Simon Barnicle pointed out: "Democrats can routinely win the majority of votes cast in federal elections but fail to translate those votes into power because their voters are in the wrong places. For example, in the 2018 midterms, Democratic Senate candidates collectively beat Republican candidates by nearly twenty percentage points. But because of where those votes were cast, Republicans didn't just hold on to their majority in the Senate, they actually *increased* it, picking up two seats. . . . By 2040, it is estimated that 40 percent of Americans will live in just five states. Half the population will be represented by 18 Senators, the other half by 82." See Simon Barnicle, "The 53-State Solution" *The Atlantic*, February 11, 2020.

8. George Gao, "How Do Americans Stand Out From the Rest of the World?" Pew Research Center, https://www.pewresearch.org/fact-tank/2015/03/12/how-do-americans-stand-out-from-the-rest-of-the-world/.

9. Matthew Hunt and Heather Bullock noted that individualistic beliefs generally decrease support for redistributive policies, while nonindividualistic beliefs generally increase support for such initiatives. See M. O. Hunt and H. E. Bullock, "Ideologies and Beliefs About Poverty," in D. Brady & L.M. Burton, eds., *The Oxford Handbook of the Social Science of Poverty* (New York: Oxford University Press, 2016), 93–116. For more on studies demonstrating this relationship, see Lawrence M. Eppard, Mark Robert Rank, and Heather E. Bullock, *Rugged Individualism and the Misunderstanding of American Inequality* (Bethlehem, PA: Lehigh University Press, 2020).

10. Lawrence M. Eppard et al., "Effects of Anti-Black Prejudice and Individualism on Government Support Among U.S. College Students," *New York Sociologist* 8 (August 2020): 1–41.

11. See Eppard et al., *Rugged Individualism.*

12. Kaiser Family Foundation, "Public Opinion on Single-Payer, National Health Plans, and Expanding Access to Medicare Coverage," October 16, 2020, https://www.kff.org/slideshow/public-opinion-on-single-payer-national-health-plans-and-expanding-access-to-medicare-coverage/.

13. A. Jardina, "Why People Love 'Assistance to the Poor' but Hate 'Welfare,'" Talk Poverty, January 29, 2019, https://talkpoverty.org/2018/01/29/people-love-assistance-poor-hate-welfare/.

14. Jardina, "Why People Love."

15. R. Martinez, *Creating Freedom: The Lottery of Birth, the Illusion of Consent, and the Fight for Our Future* (New York: Pantheon Books, 2016), 3.

16. B. X. Lee, "Causes and Cures VII: Structural Violence," *Aggression and Violent Behavior* 28 (2016), 110.

17. P. Bourdieu and J. C. Passeron, *Reproduction in Education, Society and Culture*, 2nd ed. (Thousand Oaks, CA: Sage, 1990), 4.

18. J. Galtung, "Violence, Peace, and Peace Research," *Journal of Peace Research*, 6, no. 3 (1969): 173.

Index

For the benefit of digital users, indexed terms that span two pages (e.g., 52–53) may, on occasion, appear on only one of those pages.

Tables and figures are indicated by *t* and *f* following the page number.